Women and Higher Education in Africa
Reconceptualizing Gender-Based Human Capabilities and Upgrading Human Rights to Knowledge

Women and Higher Education in Africa
Reconceptualizing Gender-Based Human Capabilities and Upgrading Human Rights to Knowledge

Edited by

N'Dri T. Assié-Lumumba

CEPARRED

To Diane,
With best wishes.
Ithaca, New York; November 6, 2008
N'Dri Assié-Lumumba

Women and Higher Education in Africa:
Reconceptualizing Gender-Based Human Capabilities and Upgrading Human Rights to Knowledge

First published in 2007 by CEPARRED

Copyright © CEPARRED

CEPARRED is the PanAfrican Studies and Research Center in International Relations and Education for Development/*Centre Panafricain d'Etudes et de Recherches en Relations Internationales et en Éducation pour le Développement* headquartered in Côte d'Ivoire. It is a non-sectarian, non-profit, and non-governmental international Pan-African institution. Its main objectives are: 1) to conduct and facilitate basic/theoretical and applied research; 2) to promote publications including a professional journal, books, monographs, and practical guides; 3) to set up a library and data unit; 4) to create a Masters Program and to organize practical trainings; and 5) to develop a gender unit as a forum for theoretical/scholarly and policy debates and research, and which, while open to discourses on gender globally and in the different regions of the world, provides a space for African perspectives in particular.

The address for CEPARRED is:
**22 B. P. 559 Abidjan 22, Côte d'Ivoire <board@ceparred.org> or
C/O N'Dri T. Assié-Lumumba, Africana Studies and Research Center,
Cornell University, Ithaca New York, 14850, USA, <na12@cornell.edu>**

ISBN 0-9749723-0-4

Cover design by Jeanne Butler and N'Dri T. Assié-Lumumba
Typeset by N'Dri T. Assié-Lumumba

Printed in the United States of America by BookMasters, Mansfield, Ohio

CEPARRED would like to express its deepest gratitude to the Cornell University program on Poverty, Inequality, and Development (PID), the Ford Foundation, the Partnership for Higher Education in Africa (Carnegie Corporation of New York, Ford Foundation, John D. and Catherine T. MacArthur Foundation, Rockefeller Foundation, William and Flora Hewlett Foundation, Andrew W. Mellon Foundation, and Kresge Foundation), UNIFEM (United Nations Fund for Women) Regional Office for West and Central Africa in Dakar (Senegal), and AWOMI (African Women's Millennium Initiative on Poverty and Human Rights) also in Dakar (Senegal) for their generous financial support for this publication. It also acknowledges with appreciation the constructive critiques of the external reviewers.

LINGUISTIC GROUP IN WEST AFRICA (Ghana : Côte d'Ivoire)

• 15th to 19th century dominated gold mining : gold trade in the region

• Akan most dominant : present culture in Ghana today

About the Kente, Gold Weight, and Adinkra symbols on the cover:

The Akan have developed a complex system of communication and ideographs (graphic) including the talking drum, representations on metal work such as the Gold Weight, and fabric designs of which the most known are the Kente and Baoulé cloth and Adinkra symbols.

Besides the utilitarian use of the cloth for personal adornment and aesthetic expression and the practical function of the Gold Weight to measure the value of gold dust, both the cloth design and Gold Weight represent ideograms and a sophisticated medium of communication. They are scripts that constitute conceptual representations of the Akan and broader African ethos and knowledge systems.

The Kente (cloth), Gold Weight, and Adinkra symbols on the cover convey a message of strength in unity and commitment for collective well-being, wisdom in learning from the shortcomings and achievements of the past to build a world of freedom and justice and responsibility in sustaining societies where gender is consistently a ground for promoting empowering and positive complementarity and equality of opportunity, aspiration, expectation and attainment.

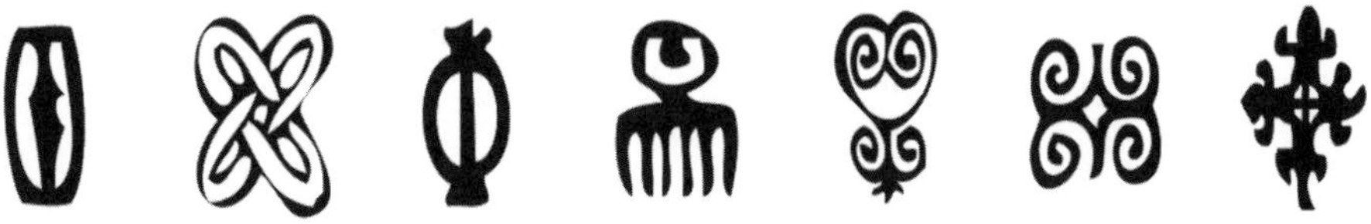

ADWO: peace, calmness under pressure.

KRAMOBONE: one bad makes all look bad.

WAWA ABA: overcoming barriers, movement and progression.

DUAFE: feminine virtue, everlasting love.

SANKOFA: mistakes can be rectified, look to the past for solutions.

OSRANE NE NSORAMA: wisdom, learning, humility.

FUNTUNFUNAFU: need for unity, working together.

*To the African women
in appreciation of their contribution to the struggle
for building an inclusive and human-centered society
to promote collective well-being and
sustainable social progress*

Table of Contents

List of Abbreviations

ARSTM	The regional Academy of Maritime Sciences and Technology
AU	African Union
AVU	African Virtual University
BECE	Basic Education Certificate Examinations
BEPC	Brevet d'Études du Premier Cycle
BTS	Diploma for Higher Technicians
CAFOP	Centers of Guidance and Teacher training
CBCG	Center of Office Automation, Communication and Management
CEDAW	Convention on Elimination of Discrimination Against Women
CELIA	Center of Electronics and Applied Data Processing
CEPARRED	Centre Panafricain d'Études et de Recherches en Relations Internationales et en Éducation pour le Développement/Panafrican
CICE	Center for the Study of International Cooperation in Education
CIIFAD	Cornell International Program of Food, Agriculture, and Development
CIRT	Ivorian Center for Technology Research
CME	Center of Electrical Trades
COBET	Complementary Opportunity for Basic Education in Tanzania
COPE	Complementary Opportunity for Primary Education
CRAU	Centre de Recherches Architecturales et Urbaines
CRE	Center for Environmental Research
CRO	Center for Oceanologic Research
ECG	Management and Commercial School
EFA	Education for all
EFCPC	School for Continuing Education and Training of high Officers
EMSPA	Higher Multinational School of Postal Services of Abidjan
ENA	National School of Administration
ENP	National Police Force School
ENS	Standard Higher School
ENSA	The Higher National School of Agronomy
ENSEA	Higher National School of Statistics and Applied Economics
ENSTP	The Higher National School of Public works
ESA	Higher School of Agronomy

ESAR	Eastern and Southern Africa Region
ESCAE	Higher School of Trade and Administration of Enterprises
ESEA	East and South East Asia
ESI	Higher School of Industry
ESIE	Inter-African Higher School of Electricity
ESMG	Higher School of Mines and Geology
ESTP	Higher School for Public Works
FAWE	Forum for African Women Educationalists
FCUBE	Free Compulsory Universal Basic Education
FDI	Foreign direct investment
FLACSO	Facultad Latinoamericana de Ciencias Sociales
FTAA	Free Trade Agreement of the Americas
GATS	General Agreement on Trade and Services
GDP	Gross Domestic Product
GEAR	Growth, Employment and Redistribution
GEM	Girls Education Movement
GER	Gross Enrolment Ratio
GERME	Study Groups and Research in Electron Microscopy
GES	Ghana Education Service
GGC	Gender and Global Change
GNP	Gross National Product
GWSAfrica	Gender and Women's Studies for Africa's Transformation
HAIs	Historically Advantaged Institutions
IAB	Agricultural Institute of Bouaké
IDEFOR	Forests Institute
IDESSA	Savannah Institute
IIEP	International Institute for Educational Planning
IMF	International Monetary Fund
INFAS	National Institute of Education of Health Agents
INFS	National Institute of Social Education
INJS	National Institute of Youth and Sports
INP-HB	Félix HOUPHOUËT-BOIGNY National Polytechnic Institute
INSAAC	Higher National Institute of Arts and Culture
INSET	The Higher National Institute of Technical Teaching
INS	National Institute of Statistics
INSP	National Institute for Public Health
IPCI	Pasteur Institute of Côte d'Ivoire
IPNETP	National Pedagogical Institute for Technical and Vocational Education

IREN	Institute for Research on Renewable Energy
IRMA	Research Institute for Applied Mathematics
ISAPT	African Higher Institute of the Post and Telecommunications
ISCU	International Council for Science
ISTC	Institute of Communication Sciences and Technology
I_2T	Ivorian Society of Tropical Technology
JEDIRAF	Journal of Comparative Education and International Relations in Africa
JSS	Junior secondary schools
KNUST	Kwame Nkrumah University of Science and Technology
MDGs	Millennium Development Goals
MESRIT	Ministry of Higher Education, Research and Technological Innovation
NAB	National Accreditation Board
NEPAD	New Partnership for African Development
NETRIGHT	Network for Women's Rights in Ghana
NGOs	Non-Governmental Organizations
NICRO	National Institute for Crime Prevention and the Rehabilitation of Offenders
NICs	Newly industrializing countries
PESC	Physical education sports and culture
PID	Poverty, Inequality, and Development
PNDEF	National Development Plan of the Educational /Training Sector
PRC	People's Republic of China
PREP	Primary Education Programme
PRSPs	Poverty reduction strategy papers
RDP	Reconstruction and Development Plan
SADC	Southern African Development Community
SAPES	Southern Africa Political Economy Series
SAPs	Structural Adjustment Programs
SARDC	Southern African Research and Documentation Centre
SARDC	Southern African Research and Documentation Center
SCI	Sara Communication Initiative
SEPHIS	South-South Exchange Programme for Research on the History of Development
SGL LAMTO	Station of Ecology and Geophysics of Lamto
SSA	Sub-Saharan Africa
SSS	Senior secondary schools
SSSCE	Senior Secondary School Certificate Examination

STME	Science, Technology and Mathematics Education
TGNP	Tanzania Gender Networking Programme
TTC	Teacher training colleges
TVET	Technical and vocational education and training
UAA	University of Abobo-Adjamé
UBKE	University de Bouaké
UDS	University of Development Studies
UFR	Units of Education and Research
UFR	Unité de Formation et de Recherche
UNAM	Universidad Nacional Autónoma de México
UN	United Nations
UNC	University de Cocody
UNDP	United Nations Development Program
UNESCO	United Nations Educational, Scientific and Cultural Organization
UNIFEM	United Nations Fund for Women
URES	Regional Units of Higher Education
USAID	United States Agency for International Development
WDR	World Development Report
WID/GAD	Women in development/Gender and development

Foreword

The topic of gender and higher education in African contexts is being increasingly explored by scholars and feminist scholar-activists both on the continent and elsewhere committed to the quest for gender equality. As N'Dri Assié-Lumumba notes in her Introduction, access to education, which has been denied the majority of Africa's women and girls, is an economic and political issue. No country on the continent has achieved the goals of universal primary education, much less the goal of ensuring access to higher education for women.

A body of writing is emerging focused on women's access and participation in higher education systems in particular country settings. This highlights the gains made versus the chasms yet to be bridged in overcoming disciplinary barriers in the sciences and technology, the generally hostile institutional environments in which women study and work, and their under-representation in educational leadership. In particular, the community of feminist scholars working in the Gender and Women's Studies for Africa's Transformation (GWSAfrica) organized under the aegis of the African Gender Institute, University of Cape Town, have called attention to the sites and politics of knowledge production in African Higher Education that have proved resistant to transformational impulses and the inclusion of women as equal partners in the production of scholarship and as learners. Yet the challenge of taking women seriously as students, researchers, faculty members and educational leaders cannot be gainsaid if Africa is to develop the wealth of professional talent, skill, creativity and innovation it requires to secure the inclusive knowledge needed to break out of its developmental predicaments. This underlines the current attention to theorising gender and education in Africa that this volume continues.

The volume, *Women and Higher Education in Africa: Reconceptualizing Gender-Based Human Capabilities and Upgrading Human Rights to Knowledge,* issued in English and French, brings together an impressive array of Africanist scholars and their collaborators who bridge theoretical and conceptual preoccupations to present country and institutional case studies as well as comparative analyses of Africa with South-East Asia and Latin America. These authors are well known as scholars or activists involved in promoting gender equality and more inclusive knowledge in African higher education and knowledge production systems and demonstrate a commitment to, and engagement with, Africa's future. They locate their studies within the current context of globalization and the neo-liberal economic frameworks and policies that are promoted by international donor agencies and implemented by African states that have affected policy directions and choices in the critical areas of education, health, social welfare and local government. However, as more than one author notes, this context has not paid sufficient attention to gender issues, and the implications of globalization and the restructuring in education and the labor market on gendered women and men.

The role of higher education in particular in combating the HIV/AIDS pandemic through strengthening its linkages with basic education and foregrounding issues around gender and sexuality in the curriculum is highlighted. And in contrast to the exclusionary practices in current higher education, science and technology, some authors urge the transformation of the cultural and intellectual foundations of science to include other knowledge categories such as indigenous knowledge systems, in order to rebuild Africa's scientific and technological capacity.

An unusual feature in the coverage of the volume is its ability to bridge the Anglophone/Francophone divides in Africa as well as in providing other south-south perspectives to enhance our understanding of trends, convergences, divergences and strategies in the area of gender and higher education in different regions of the global south. It is my hope that the volume will find a welcome reception among scholars, activists and policy makers and contribute to closing the gaps in our knowledge, and extending the scope for action.

Takyiwaa Manuh
University of Ghana
Legon, Ghana

Preface and Acknowledgments

The contributions in this book are in great part drawn from a conference initiated by CEPARRED (Centre Panafricain d'Études et de Recherches en Relations Internationales et en Éducation pour le Développement/Panafrican Studies and Research Center in International Relations and Education for Development) and jointly organized with the Cornell University Program on Poverty, Inequality and Development (PID) in March 2002 at Cornell University in Ithaca, New York. The topic was "Women and Higher Education in Africa: Engendering Human Capital and Upgrading Human Rights to Schooling."

This Cornell University conference was initially designed as the second part of a two-part meeting for the third biennial conference of CEPARRED. The first part of the seminar that was planned for December 2001, in Abidjan (Côte d'Ivoire), was rescheduled and then postponed *sine die*. The first two CEPARRED biennial conferences were held in Abidjan, on "Economic Reform and Investment in Education in Africa: Assessment of the Current State and Strategies for an Effective Response to the Challenges of the 21st Century" in December 1996 and on "Reforms and Innovations in African Higher Education" in February 1999.

At the Cornell conference, major papers concerning gender inequality, particularly its effects on women in higher education in Africa, were presented by some noted scholars in social sciences and education policymakers. The final papers were to be reviewed for possible publication according to the established criteria of selection by the members of the Editorial Committee of the journal published by CEPARRED, JEDIRAF (Journal of Comparative Education and International Relations in Africa). The papers recommended and satisfactorily revised would have been published in a special issue of JEDIRAF.

However, in view of the number of potentially publishable papers presented, it would have been difficult to publish all of them in one issue of the journal. Thus, for reasons of efficiency, it was decided to include all of the selected papers in one book rather than two or three issues of the journal. To better capture the substance of the ideas of the conference and the papers, the title of the conference was changed to *Women and Higher Education in Africa:*

Reconceptualizing Gender-Based Human Capabilities and Upgrading Human Rights to Knowledge.

Most of the chapters of this book are revised versions of papers that were presented at the conference while the papers with inadequate revisions are not included. To expand the aspects of the topic to be covered in the book, a few papers were solicited afterward and constitute some of the chapters. Each of the contributions is briefly presented in the introduction. CEPARRED envisioned various forms of publications, in addition to its already established referred journal. Therefore, the conference papers presented a great opportunity to start its book publication series.

Following the attrition in the process of the revision of the papers initially considered this volume is composed of sixteen chapters out of which fourteen were originally written in English and two in French. To ensure that a wider audience would be reached, it was deemed preferable to translate all the accepted papers in order to publish two volumes, one in English and the other in French.

Therefore, in spite of the fact that the translation would delay the publication process, a decision was made to translate the accepted papers. Thus, this publication is the volume in English. It should be noted that the contributions are written either in American or British English, depending on the original choices of the respective authors. The publication of the volume in French is scheduled for early 2008.

Within the broad activities of its gender unit and concretely through this conference and the subsequent publication, CEPARRED intended to continue to be involved in the critical examination and debates of the theories, epistemology, and knowledge production with regard to women and gender from an African perspective. This perspective is key to a proper understanding of historical and contemporary factors with paradigmatic implications as well as pragmatic policy formulation, design and implementation for social progress in Africa.

Social progress can be achieved only through social inclusion of all members of society, especially the female population that constitutes a substantive half or more of the population. CEPARRED's gender unit was conceived to make sure that the philosophical foundation and the outcomes of the Center's activities consistently reflect and highlight the gender dimensions in all its programs and activities and also to organize specific activities that focus on gender as a priority such as the 2002 conference and this book.

Several academic units at Cornell University and neighboring institutions provided financial contributions that made it possible to organize the conference. CEPARRED wishes to acknowledge and express its gratitude for the contributions of the following Cornell academic units: the Center for the Study of Inequality; the Vice Provost for Diversity and Faculty Development; the Africana Studies and Research Center; Office of the Dean of the College of Architecture, Art, and Planning; the Mario Einaudi Center for International Studies; the Department of Education; the Program on Gender and Global Change (GGC); the Cornell International Program of Food, Agriculture, and Development (CIIFAD); the International Students and Scholars Office; the Cornell Institute of Public Affairs; the Institute of European Studies; the Institute for African Development; and the South East Asian Program. The Office of the Dean of Wells College made a major contribution.

The bulk of the funding was provided by the Cornell University Program on Poverty, Inequality, and Development (PID), whose Director, Professor Ravi Kanbur, enthusiastically endorsed the initial proposal and committed funding that was decisive in organizing the conference held at Cornell and the coverage of the cost of some of the post-conference activities, especially the publications.

Following the postponement of the Abidjan conference, part of the initial funding pledged by the Director of the Regional Office for West and Central Africa in Dakar of the United Nations Fund for Women (UNIFEM), Ms. Yassine Fall, has been allocated to the publication project. CEPARRED wishes to express a deep appreciation for UNIFEM's support, which helped make this specific publication possible.

CEAPRRED would like to acknowledge and express its profound gratitude to the African Women's Millennium Initiative on Poverty and Human Rights (AWOMI) for its generous contribution in support of the publication.

The publication project received a grant from the Ford Foundation and the Partnership for Higher Education in Africa (Carnegie Corporation of New York, Ford Foundation, John D. and Catherine T. MacArthur Foundation, Rockefeller Foundation, William and Flora Hewlett Foundation, Andrew W. Mellon Foundation, and Kresge Foundation). CEPARRED would like to express its sincere appreciation for this generous support that was significant in making it possible to publish this volume in English and to prepare the forthcoming volume in French.

The conference participants came from various countries and

institutions in Africa, India, Brazil, France, as well as many institutions in the United States. Despite extraordinary efforts, many more participants from various countries, including Canada, Ghana, Kenya, Tanzania, Uganda, and Senegal could not attend due to visa delays, flight cancellations or missed flights, among other reasons. Among those who made it, and even among those who traveled inside the United States, some had to go through odysseys to arrive in Ithaca, New York. In addition to financial support, a considerable number of Cornell University faculty members also provided solid intellectual contributions by agreeing to present papers while some served as chairs and discussants. Faculty members from other institutions in the area, namely, Wells College, Ithaca College, Syracuse University, and Colgate University, made vital intellectual contributions as well.

Given the perspective of the conference, the role and voices of the youth were vital, and male and female students from the African continent and the Diaspora also brought a much-needed critical and engaged message for the future. Besides faculty and staff members and students, people from the wider community attended the conference.

A list of the participants who were on the panels is in the appendix. Although it is not possible to name all the active participants from Cornell, other institutions, and the Ithaca and surrounding community, we want to acknowledge their contributions to the success of the conference.

Administrative and technical assistance was provided by several staff members and students. Among them, it is worth noting that Joyce Knuutila who is Administrative Assistant in the Cornell Department of Applied Economics and Management, and Maeve (Kristen) Powlick, a Wells College student assistant to Professor Tukumbi Lumumba-Kasongo, provided assistance with enthusiasm and diligence throughout the process. This conference and earlier activities of the CEPARRED were supported by students and administrative staff members of the Africana Studies and Research Center. Their inputs range from the consistent encouragement and advice from the beloved late Daisy Halstead-Rowe and the genuine interest expressed by Patricia Dean to the more recent assistance from Cynthia Telage. I would like to also thank Gerald Fils, Sylvia Nyana, Sandra Lwanga, Zandile Mbuya, and Sam Fanfan who provided much needed assistance toward the preparation of the manuscript.

The CEPARRED, and specifically its Director, its Associate Director in charge of its gender unit, and its Board of Directors wish to express their sincere and deep appreciation to Cornell University for hosting the conference and to faculty members in the Africana Studies and Research, other academic units and all the participants for the support that they provided, which made the conference an intellectually stimulating and productive gathering.

Many people outside Cornell University have made a range of contributions to CEPARRED at different stages of its development, from the encouragement and guidance by Douglas Windham, Samir Amin, Nelly Stromquist, Yassine Fall, Remi Clignet, the late Paul Ricœur, and Haklilu Habte, to the full commitment and financial contribution by Hakell Ward, and the unfailing presence of Moses G. Nkondo. Suzanne Grant Lewis is also among the persons that I would like to acknowledge specifically for her continuous support over the years. Additionally it is important to recognize many scholars, policymakers and government officers in Côte d'Ivoire for their support to CEPARRED. It is worth mentioning specifically the decisive and energetic support of Saliou Touré, Christophe Wondji, Francis Wodié, Denise Houphouët-Boigny, Jean-Claude Brou, Kouamé N'Guessan, Adèle N'Dioré, Jean Kouadio, and Jacques Adom. I want to make a general statement of appreciation to many more committed persons.

I want to also express my most profound gratitude to my family, starting with my first colleague and daily companion Tukumbi for his critical role in the pursuit of the development of CEPARRED and our children Disashi, Enongo, and Lushima for their unfailing support and for always enthusiastically volunteering for CEPARRED in the realization of its various activities, including the 2002 conference and the preparation of this book.

The process of producing this book was long and it entailed a high level of commitment. The work involved was both intellectually engaging and at times tedious. As indicated above, some of the papers were prepared for presentation in the 2002 CEPARRED Conference while others were written for other purposes and, thus, were not yet ready for publication immediately after the Conference. Therefore, while a few of the chapters herein needed only minor inputs from the editor, for several of them, the work required was considerable, both in terms of intellectual contributions and communications with the contributors.

Indeed, even the papers that were presented in the 2002 Conference required some adjustments to fit the conceptual framework of human capabilities as opposed to human capital. The contributors needed the relevant feedback in order to make the required adjustments. Despite the intensive work involved, the process was exciting and the final product was very fulfilling, given the anticipation that this volume will help fill a theoretical gap and provoke needed debates geared toward fostering new policies of gender equity in educational systems that can ensure the production of relevant knowledge for social progress in Africa.

Finally, despite considerable work done by the editor to finalize the process of publishing this book, it is needless to insist that the substantive positions of the contributors and the outcome of the work are shared common intellectual responsibilities.

N'Dri T. Assié-Lumumba

Abidjan, Côte d'Ivoire

June 2007

Introduction: General Issues and Specific Perspectives

N'Dri T. Assié-Lumumba

The main objective of this book is to contribute to the discourse on education, gender equality and social development in the African context. This discourse in turn has implications for reflection and policy formulation in a social justice and progress perspective. African educational systems have been characterized by highly ingrained structural inequality with regard to region, rural or urban residence, religion, ethnicity, and social class. More than any of these socially significant factors, gender has been, and remains, the most widespread and persistent facet of inequality, especially at the higher education level. Denial of access to advanced learning has implications for those who are deprived of the opportunity, in terms of their right to optimal self-realization. Lost learning opportunities, especially in today's globalized world and what is also referred to as knowledge-based society, constitute a loss of full participation in the development of families, communities, countries, sub-regions, the continent as a whole and global Africa.

Compared to the colonial period and the situation inherited at independence, considerable advances have been made in increasing general and female school attendance. Still, many countries have not yet achieved even universal primary school attendance. Gender inequality is most severe in contexts where general enrollment is lower. Furthermore, several countries had a severe setback in the early 1980s, as their enrollment rates were either stagnant or declining. The persistent economic crisis meant that the previous targets of universal primary enrollment in 1980 and then 2000 could not be met. Since the Dakar Conference of 2000, the new target for universal primary enrollment is 2015, just ten years away.

Basic or primary education is not conceptualized as the terminal step, but rather as the entryway to the pyramid of learning and knowledge acquisition and legitimization. There is an assumption that a higher level, or greater quantity, of education is better. We also assume that knowledge in the formal educational system is organized in a stratified framework. Thus, those who have access to the highest level are considered to have learned more and acquired more knowledge. This learning and knowledge confer agency onto those who acquire it. Those who do not have access to or have limited exposure to formal education lack the power and the legitimacy that knowledge provides. Thus, through formal learning or lack of it, self-realization and participation in social processes can be either enhanced or hindered. While not all learning takes place in the context of schooling, the acquisition of socially sanctioned knowledge is organized within the context of formal educational systems and those learning institutions called schools.

Educational statistics in African countries in general reveal consistent patterns of female under-representation in the distribution of education. Despite some policy reforms and political efforts in the past four decades in most countries, repetition, dropout, and forced-out rates are still high (significantly and consistently higher for females than for males). As a result of lower enrollment rates and higher attrition rates among females, the gap between males and females increases considerably from the primary to the tertiary levels.

Furthermore, at the tertiary level, especially at the university, there is an even smaller proportion of female students registered in fields such as science in comparison to the humanities and social sciences, creating an asymmetrical gender representation in the labor market and in the occupational structure. This would not constitute a problem if the social prestige and economic value carried by these fields, especially in the new globalization process, were not significantly different. Southern African countries have a different pattern, as female enrollment is equal to or even higher than male enrollment in that region, particularly at the lower level of the system. In a few cases this pattern persists at the higher educational level. Nevertheless, even in these cases, the apparent edge in access is not clearly reflected in the location of women and men on the occupational ladder and in the job market.

The fact is that, in the Western/received model of education, the learning process and knowledge are highly fragmented. Beyond primary/basic education, students have to choose, or are assigned to, tracks that become more and more compartmentalized from the lower to higher levels of education. In *Education in a Globalized World: The Connectivity of Economic Power, Technology, and Knowledge*, Nelly Stromquist (2002: xiii) remarks that with the "new globalization era" in which education constitutes one of the "promises" with highly prized "advanced skills and sophisticated knowledge", this knowledge is "heavily weighted in favor of science and technology." If, as Stromquist adds: "There appears to be a consensus that the twenty-first century will continue to devote unabated attention to science and technology carrying on the accelerated pace of development begun in the 1970s" (Stromquist 2002: 63), it can be then asked: "What consequences has globalization brought on the social construction of gender" (Stromquist 2002: 133) especially as mediated through education as an agent of social reproduction, and in higher education where new paradigms are formulated for the entire society and where legitimization for access to the highest steps of the occupational and social ladder takes place?

In contemporary African societies, education systems have been heavily influenced by a Western tradition that bears the mark of patriarchal rules that excluded the female population from most of the formal educational process. Even where enrollment ceased to be an issue decades ago, the boundaries between social groups have been moving, not disappearing, and the grounds for inequality have been mutating or shifting in terms of emphasis. For instance, the issue of unequal opportunity has moved from access to basic education to post-secondary education, the type of higher education institution attended, and the disciplinary specialization that is characterized by the concentration of female students in humanities and social sciences and some specific sub-fields within the scientific disciplines.

CEPARRED on the whole, and especially its gender unit, has been concerned with rethinking gender inequalities in Africa within the framework of the current political changes, the rise of liberal democracy, the accelerated process of globalization and liberalization of the economy and their corollaries: the deepening of poverty (especially in peripheral states) contradicting the promises of the global green pasture, the crisis of education, major health challenges, the shortage of food production, and gaps in global communication and access to technology.

Following the UNESCO universal declaration of human rights in 1948, education is defined as a human right in all contemporary societies. This right has been implicitly associated with access to basic education. This is why compulsory attendance laws have applied to elementary or lower secondary levels, or to age groups associated with these levels. Limiting compulsory attendance, as a right, to these levels is neither a natural phenomenon nor a popularly endorsed policy, nor a socially desirable choice equitably offered to all members of society. Yet, following these recent traditions, when issues about women's access to education are raised in terms of human rights, there is a tendency to lean toward adult non-formal education, literacy programs, and training whereby there is a pattern of acquisition of technical skills for income-generating activities separate from reflective education. In this book, the argument is that there is no philosophical and social justification, besides past practices that reproduce social inequality, for associating human rights to education with mainly basic and technical education and functional literacy. Even technical skills are not provided in a neutral space, outside of development paradigms.

Access to education is an economic and political issue. It is also a major source of the development of human capabilities and potential with consequences for socio-economic development. Adults, youth, and children of both genders as citizens of their nation-states seek to have access to education as an instrument for self-realization and for the socio-political and socio-economic development of their societies. In general, states and governments also consider education as an investment. Yet policies of African states have increasingly led to extreme social cleavages. Despite major achievements in the increase of enrollment at all levels in the post-colonial states, very few African countries have even achieved and sustained universal enrollment at the primary level. Thus every year more out-of-school youth move on to add to the numbers of adults classified as functionally illiterate.

For the female population, the economic crises and the direct policy decisions made by international institutions such as the World Bank (Subbarao, Raney, Dunbar, and Haworth 1994) or prescribed to the African countries in the context SAPs (Assié-Lumumba 2000) have had a negative impact on women's access to higher education.

Being illiterate in the official languages, which in nearly all countries are European/colonial languages, does not mean that one is illiterate in understanding social realities. However, in the overwhelming majority of African educational systems, European languages are used especially at the higher education level. Until there is a comprehensive change in language policy, serious limitations will remain in the way one can function with confidence and effectiveness in social processes and in utilizing the resources and information available to advance one's well-being within a given community. The wider the gap between the actual level of education and the highest possible level, the greater the challenge, and the more limited the effectiveness individuals and groups can have in contributing to the social/national agendas and family and individual efforts for progress. Given their lower representation in the higher levels of the educational systems, women in Africa confront these challenges to the greatest extent.

Under such prolonged conditions of under-representation, dating back decades to the inception of European education in Africa, if rigorous analysis and relevant policies are not consistently considered and implemented, inequalities may reach a level at which future generations of Africans may consider them as societal norms or natural social phenomena.

Scholars and institutions have identified gender inequality in all sectors of education in Africa as one of the most important internal factors that continue to contribute to the underdevelopment of Africa. Women have played a considerable positive role in the processes of decolonization, state formation, household economy, and the African economy generally. Historically, pre-colonial/endogenous systems of education were organized on the foundation of separation by gender within the philosophy of different but equal, that empowered both male and female members of society as producers and transmitters of knowledge with equal rights and an equal duty to be educated. The vital contribution of women as actors in the contemporary, least-westernized sectors of the post-colonial context, amidst considerable odds, in the so-called informal economic sectors and social systems, in sustaining the lives of African families and states, is evident throughout the continent. This is an eloquent indicator of women's capabilities in the former and current indigenous contexts and also of their potential.

The structural economic and political problems related to the nature of the African states have had a devastating impact on the distribution of resources and sharing of power across the continent. Thus, women and girls have been marginalized in most African societies, as they have had less access to resources on the continent. African women are to the African societies what African states are to the global system; they are key contributors to the vitality of economic and social production, but make little or no contribution to major decisions. They have the least return and are generally marginalized with deliberate efforts to reduce them to voiceless, passive contributors.

These inequalities, which have been exacerbated by the dynamics of economic programs adopted by most African states since the early 1980s, have been promoted and supported by global institutions within the framework of free market dogma and liberal economic principles.

Within the current discourse on social, economic and political reforms, the discussion on gender inequality has not been systematically, consistently and seriously undertaken. As indicated earlier, women's access to education has concentrated in most cases on access to basic education instead of on a holistic education. CEPARRED's vision is that access to education for any marginalized group, especially women, who cut across the entire society, should not focus on a single level. Indeed, all levels are connected. There cannot be any good system of education based on just one level. The philosophical foundation for the conceptualization and the policy formulation and design for access of the female population to education must entail a holistic education system in which all levels are interconnected and considered and treated as equally important.

Indeed, without girls' access to primary/basic education, women's access to higher education via the secondary level will not be possible. There is a practical justification for focusing on basic/literacy education for women, considering the consequences of past policies. Indeed, the large proportion of out-of-school girls and women among the illiterate population segments justifies the emphasis on basic education. Gender parity in education must, however, consider all levels. Furthermore, women's rights to knowledge must be articulated at all levels simultaneously, highlighting the greater needs in higher education considering the accumulated gap. Women's limited presence in higher education is an infringement on women's rights and has implications in terms of their limited contribution in knowledge production at all levels, the absence of their vision in policy formulation, and their negatively skewed distribution in the labor force with consequences for income distribution.

Gender inequality is a central issue in economic development, state building, and social progress paradigms. It is also the most important characteristic of the African economy and its underdevelopment. Understanding its causes and their manifestations is the key to exploring policy options that take into account common factors and national as well as local specificities. It helps in dealing with policy options more systematically and comprehensively. No policy recommendations will sustain a long-term positive impact until there is a good understanding of the nature of gender inequality and of how women should be fully considered as agents of social change in pragmatic ways.

There is in fact a vicious cycle that has been entrenched in society and that requires bold and creative policies to break. The 2002 conference and this book aim to make a contribution to the reflection and actions undertaken in this context.

The main objectives of CEPARRED in organizing the conference that led to this book on the issue of gender inequality in higher education were:

1. to identify and examine the historical configurations that were the concrete causes of inequality, especially within the framework of current reforms and national policies adopted since the 1980s;

2. to explore strategies for designing longitudinal studies of indicators and manifestations of inequality in students' access, performance, retention, and attrition at African institutions of higher learning including universities and professional and technical institutions;

3. to study the impact of gender inequality on women's collective efforts and on development policies, and the way this impact retards social progress; and

4. to propose and recommend new intellectual and policy guidelines for dealing more effectively with inequality.

This book addresses both theoretical aspects of gender inequality at the tertiary level of education and its practical policy dimensions. It provides analytical insight into the dynamic relationship between higher education and the other levels of the educational system and between education and other social institutions.

Many public and private institutions, international organizations and NGOs have been involved in the design and implementation of projects and programs that aim to contribute to closing the gender gap in access to education. There are also academic units that contribute to the analysis of gender inequality. However, few are involved in both scholarly analysis and policy design as dynamically and dialectically interconnected areas. In its activities, CEPARRED has created a space for theoretical articulation, reflection, discourse and also for policy analysis and design among researchers and policymakers. The chapters in the book reflect this comprehensive philosophy.

CEPARRED's gender unit is conceived as a forum for theoretical/scholarly debates, research, publications and practical policy/training programs that, while open to discourse in the different regions of the world using a comparative approach, at the same time provide space for an African perspective.

The most important questions in dealing with the discourse on development remain: Which kind of education is best for African societies at large and which kind of higher education for what kind of society? Higher education is one of the most important sectors of human resource formation, especially in a developing world. It is an area where philosophers, technicians, scientists, and humanists are formed and produced. In principle, with their specialized and general knowledge, skills, research and innovative capacities, these actors can be considered as the primary agents or engines of social, political, and economic progress in any given society, especially in the context of a globalized economy. That is not to dismiss the knowledge and actual contribution to social production and reproduction by members of society who do not have access to higher education. In fact, one of the key issues is the rigid barriers that prevent fruitful cross-fertilization of endogenous knowledge and knowledge acquired in the space where Westernized vertical knowledge lines reign. How then do we rethink and redefine which knowledge ought to be in the space of what is considered legitimate and relevant knowledge for Africa's progress? Who will do this rethinking, and how can Africans take a leading role in redefining this space to make it more inclusive for all members of society? The chapters in this book address different aspects of these questions as fundamental issues.

The structure of the book is guided by the foci of the contributions. As indicated earlier, the title of the conference included the term "human capital," which has been replaced in the book title by "human capabilities." These two terms have different conceptual meanings and different theoretical positions. To explain their respective linkages to the discourse and practical situation of women and higher education in general and particularly in Africa, Chapter 1 provides some definitions and conceptual clarifications. Chapters 1, 2, 9, and 16 are more theoretical while chapters 5, 10, 12, and 13 are oriented toward policy. Chapter 5 illustrates the active engagement and leadership of African women in combating gender inequality in education and promoting gender justice in society at large. A few contributions, especially chapters 3, 4 and 5, are general and apply to the global international or continental African contexts. Several other contributions, specifically chapters 6, 7, 8, 10, 11 and 12 are case studies focusing on either a single country or sets of countries. The common theme of chapters 9, 10, 11 and 12 is science and technology. Chapter 13 addresses the challenge of HIV/AIDS and the role of the education sector as a whole in producing practical knowledge and using the appropriate approach to sensitize various population segments and disseminate relevant information aimed at helping learners transform their respective behaviors with respect to gender. Chapters 14 and 15 provide comparative analyses of the situation in Africa and in two other world regions, namely East and South-East Asia and Latin America.

The first chapter, "Human Capital, Human Capabilities, and Gender Equality: Harnessing the Development of Human Potential as a Human Right and the Foundation for Social Progress," by the editor, is an addition to the papers presented at the conference and aims at introducing the conceptualization and articulation of the differences between human capital and human capabilities. The historical evolution of the concept of human capital and the more recent articulation of human capabilities and their respective limitations and general critiques, especially with regard to their articulation of gender are discussed.

In "Mis-measuring Gender Disparities in the Educational Establishments" Remi Clignet sets the stage for questioning positivism and the assumed sanctity of, and uncritical approach to, data collection. He addresses fundamental epistemological and methodological issues in the study of unequal educational opportunity by gender. With a conceptual articulation and some illustrations, he analyzes what he considers to be the scientific and political shortcomings in the measurements of gender disparities. He critically examines data collection and interpretation. As he cautions, these measurements are marked by unavoidable biases and fallacies of logical and political origin; instead of serving to address the gender gap effectively, the existing measurements are ineffective and tend to contribute to the perpetuation of the status quo. The chapter offers a cautionary note that applies to some of the contributions to this volume that rely on data as accurate indicators of the actual magnitude and nature of gender inequality.

The chapter by Teboho Moja, "Politics of Exclusion in Higher Education: The Inadequacy of Gender Issues in the Globalization Debates," analyzes globalization as a phenomenon of worldwide magnitude. She argues that it hinders progress toward gender equality as it is characterized by the significant absence of gender issues in the discourse. Yet, globalization and restructuring in education and in the policies and practices of the labor market have significant implications for the reproduction of gender inequality. She stresses the necessity for creating the forum for women's involvement in the discourse and in all policies of globalization.

Presenting the general picture, and also based on specific national and institutional cases as illustrations, in "Women's Participation in Higher Levels of Learning in Africa," Ruth Meena analyzes the general pattern of gender gap in African educational systems with a focus on sub-Saharan countries.[1] She critically examines specific issues that are related to typically sharp increases in the gender gap from primary education to the tertiary level, especially in the university. The general arguments are substantiated with data, which, although they may not represent a sample of the various national contexts, still constitute indicators of persistent inequality, even when keeping in mind the cautionary note from chapter 2.

"The Significance of Higher Education in Gender and Educational Reforms in Africa: The FAWE Experience" is an examination by Penina Mlama of the works and lessons drawn from the experiences of the Forum for African Women Educationalists (FAWE), a pan-African non-governmental organization founded in 1992. FAWE is dedicated to promoting female education in sub-Saharan Africa, using the power, authority, and clout of its members, who include female ministers of education and vice-chancellors as well as male ministers of education as associate members in partnership with national chapter-level membership of educational practitioners and researchers and gender activists that operate in 32 African countries. In this chapter, Mlama addresses the challenge of dealing effectively with dependence on external funding and the quest for ownership that is necessary for relevant educational development plans and reforms.

In "Current Status of, and Legislation to Redress, Gender Inequalities in South Africa," Philip Higgs critically examines the post-Apartheid South African effort for transformation from a racial and patriarchal structure through a fundamental reconstruction, striving for a non-racist and non-sexist society. He analyzes the record and the question of the relationship between constitutional rights and social change aimed at achieving gender equality by eliminating the ideologies that constitute the foundation of patriarchal domination. He calls for radical restructuring in the sexual division of labor, as well as a concomitant change in the consciousness, discourse, and behavior of

---

[1] The first version of this paper was presented at the 10th General Conference of the Association of African Universities (AAU) on "African Universities and the Challenge of Knowledge Creation and Application in the New Century" that was held at Kenyatta University, Nairobi, Kenya. CEPARRED expresses its gratitude to AAU for granting the permission to include the revised version of the paper in this book.

men and women where gender roles are concerned. The challenge suggested by this chapter is to see how the plethora of laws, no matter how important and relevant, can lead to transformative actions.

"Asymmetric Relations and Other Gender Issues in Ghanaian Higher Education" is an analysis by Cyril K. Daddieh of Ghana's educational system, its past achievements, and some of its persistent challenges. He focuses on the ever-pressing question of gender disparity in participation and achievement at the tertiary level, and more specifically on issues of gender participation, equity, gender-sensitive classroom environments, and gendered performance in higher education. This is a concrete case study that sheds light on the key issues and shows how limited the substantive and also quantitative changes that have taken place over the decades have been, despite officially proclaimed concerns and commitment.

Rudo B. Gaidzanwa's article, "Academic Women at the University of Zimbabwe: Institutional and Individual Issues in Reforming Higher Education in a Stressed Economy," is an empirical study using real life stories of academic women at the University of Zimbabwe to engage issues pertaining to gender and to women's experiences as academics in the learning space of the University. She analyzes the interactions among various aspects of the lives of academic women, including work, family life, and achievement.

In "Philosophical and Institutional Challenges in Integrating Women in Science and Technology in Africa," Catherine A. Odora Hoppers critically addresses the question of the need for transformation of the cultural and intellectual foundations of science to accommodate both men and women and to ensure inclusion of other knowledge categories like indigenous knowledge systems as a *sine qua non* for building scientific and technological capacity in Africa that would work for sustainable peace and poverty eradication. She argues that integration strategies for women in science and technology are a necessity in the context of Africa's rebirth that requires revisiting the principles underlying science, gender, and society.

The study of "Ivorian Women: Education and Integration in the Economic Development of Côte d'Ivoire" by Rose Eholié analyzes the unequal quantitative representation of Ivorian women in higher education. She focuses on the female students' participation in the various scientific fields and subfields. From the perspective of education as an investment in human potential, the author analyzes the subsequent distribution of women science graduates in the occupational structure, which is characterized by gendered inequality. She further examines women's roles in the national development process, assessing the hindering and facilitating factors that explain the persistent gender gap. She also makes recommendations for improvement in educational access and output for social progress.

In "'In A Nutshell, Science and Technology Must Be for the Welfare of the People:' African Women Scientists and the Production of Knowledge," Josephine Beoku-Betts analyzes cases based on a qualitative study she conducted that includes fifteen African women scientists representing various disciplines and countries mainly from English-speaking West Africa. The author examines the factors that motivate women and girls to strive for achievement in scientific disciplines, the way particular educational and employment contexts impact their lives and ability to accomplish their academic and career goals, and the way the experience of marginalization in local and global contexts, including the global scientific community, shapes their perspectives and understandings and situates them in the opportunity structure in scientific disciplines.

"Women and Scientific Education: The Case of Higher Education in Côte d'Ivoire," by Denise Houphouët-Boigny and Frederica Koblavi Mansilla is a critical examination of the location of the young Ivorian women in the fields of science in Ivorian higher education, including universities as well as Grandes Écoles, which are elite and selective professional schools in the fields of science, and other tertiary institutions. As these authors indicate, their study is, although not longitudinal, a late twentieth–century follow up to an earlier study by Rose Eholié, who analyzed the unequal quantitative participation of female students in the various scientific fields and subfields and the subsequent unequal representation of women science graduates in the occupational structure. Using some of the data from Eholié's study along with new data, Houphouët-Boigny and Mansilla argue that despite considerable progress in the proportion of female students in higher education in general, the earlier patterns of female under-representation and the tendency of gender-based clusters in Eholié's findings are confirmed, indicating that despite some progress, the system still remains essentially characterized by gender inequality.

In "Linking Basic Education to Higher Education by Addressing Gender, Sexuality and HIV/AIDS in Education: The Case of Eastern and Southern Africa," Changu Mannathoko articulates the vital importance of strengthening the linkages between higher education and basic education in order to effectively address gender, sexuality and HIV/AIDS in education as a means to curb the HIV/AIDS pandemic in Eastern and Southern Africa and by the same token to foster policies of poverty eradication. She also argues that education is a complex system embedded in political, cultural and economic contexts. A gender perspective in the analysis of HIV/AIDS makes it necessary to identify the interfaces with political choices made by the state in the critical areas of health, nutrition, economic exploitation, finance, social welfare and local government and to promote gender-sensitive learning environments, life-skills education and research and development.

In "Women's Employment and Well-Being in East and South East Asia: Lessons for Africa," Amiya Kumar Bagchi analyzes the period since the inception and growth of capitalist production relations, a period that has been characterized by a triple process of marginalization and devaluation of women and their labor in East and South East Asia as women lost many of their traditional occupations and were more rigidly confined to their homes. In this process their labor became more narrowly confined to niche occupations, decreasing the value of the earnings for those who were compelled to sell their labor on the market. Finally those women who took up "men's" occupations were consistently offered lower pay for the same work until laws against gender discrimination corrected this in some countries. The author compares experiences of the treatment of women and girls in specific countries in Asia and Sub-Saharan Africa and addresses the question of any lessons that African countries and societies might learn from the Asian region.

At the March 2002 conference Asma Barlas served as discussant for Bagchi's paper. Rather than revising his paper to take into account the critique that was made by Barlas, Bagchi decided to submit separately for publication, along with his paper, his response to Barlas' response. In order to enable the readers to fully understand Bagchi's response, it became necessary to include Barlas' response as discussant. Thus, Chapter 14 has three components: Bagchi's paper, Barlas's response to Bagchi's paper and Bagchi's response to Barlas.

In "Higher Education in Africa and Latin America: Comparative Insights from Globalization and Gender Perspectives," Nelly P. Stromquist analyzes developments in higher education and addresses interrelated questions dealing with whether the globalization forces affecting African and Latin American universities are similar and thus trigger trends toward convergence rather than divergence. She explores the forms and manifestations of gender policies in higher education in Africa and Latin America, and the space for social critique in the increasingly globalized universities in the two regions.

"A Theoretical Perspective on Capitalism and Welfare States and their Responses to Inequality with a Focus on Gender: What Lessons for Africa?" by Tukumbi Lumumba-Kasongo discusses the paradigms of and contradictions derived from both capitalism and liberalism in their political and philosophical contexts, shedding light on the nature of their impact in Africa at large and their universalistic assumptions about development. He then critically examines the questions of gender relations as reflected in the gender-based division of labor and unequal distribution of resources, positing that gender relations are essentially power relations. The author provides particular insight into the current structures of the state and political economic relations within the broader social and historical context, comparing the capitalist world and welfare states and drawing implications for effective approaches to the question of gender equality.

The conclusion synthesizes the central arguments made in the individual contributions, arguments that highlight the main goal of this book, namely, the rethinking and reconceptualizing of African education based on a philosophy of inclusiveness. It is argued that social progress is a global, integrated and comprehensive process of continuously improving the well being of all members of society, making positive use of all available resources, including human resources, that is, the capabilities of the male and female population. Social progress is a cumulative process that makes use of past experiences, learning from past mistakes and limitations, but also building on achievements, ideas, science and technical know-how from a human-centered ethos. This ethos requires involvement of all members of society in economic and cultural production and in political participation and decision-making processes at various levels of society for the wellbeing of all.

CHAPTER 1

Human Capital, Human Capabilities, and Gender Equality: Harnessing the Development of Human Potential as a Human Right and the Foundation for Social Progress [1]

N'Dri T. Assié-Lumumba

Introduction

This introductory chapter first briefly recalls the history, main arguments, and the critique of the concepts of human capital and of human capabilities. The issues and the relevance of these concepts for gender and women's access to education in Africa are articulated.

Human capital is a concept that is perhaps as old as the earliest systematic educational activities that were organized by humans with the objective of providing the individuals in a given community with particular conceptual and technical skills for use as productive members of the community. There has been a debate as to whether the individuals or the society engages in education for consumption only or for a deliberate investment in the future.

---

[1] The section on human capital draws from earlier works, especially the following article: N'Dri T. Assié-Lumumba, "Gender, Race, and Human Capital Theory: Research Trends in the United States from the 1950s to the 1990s," *Journal of Comparative Education and International Relations in Africa* 4 (1-2, 2001):1-25. I would like to thank Gerald Fils who, while he was a Cornell University graduate student, served as my research assistant. I want to acknowledge his considerable contribution to the review of the literature on human capabilities.

In Western literature, the concept of human capital that became the object of a major theoretical framework with direct policy application for states and families/individuals was systematically elaborated by Adam Smith in his 1776 book, *An Inquiry into the Nature and Causes of the Wealth of Nations*. He referred to "the savage nations of hunters and fishers," where all members of society work to satisfy their needs through, for instance, hunting and gathering and are "miserably poor" (Smith: 2). In contrast, he stated:

> Among civilized and thriving nations, on the contrary, though a great number of people do not labour at all, many of whom consume the produce of ten times, frequently of a hundred times more labour than the greater part of those who work; yet the produce of the whole labour of the society is so great, that all are often abundantly supplied, and a workman [sic] even of the lowest and poorest order, if he is frugal and industrious, may enjoy a greater share of the necessaries and conveniences of life than it is possible for any savage [sic] to acquire. (Smith: 2)

Marx would have argued that the workers are treated with the crumbs falling off the table, whereas the owners of the means of production, who do not work, control the fruit of the workers' labor. Those who work are urged to work harder if they want to increase their share of the crumbs. Here, interestingly Adam Smith refers to frugality, even if those who do not work have levels of consumption that suffer from no restrictions.

Education and Human Capital Theory

Education as an investment in developing people's productive capacity is considered the key to the accumulation of production of the aforementioned wealth. A major assumption of the statement above is that it may not be necessary for all members of society to work in order to have high productivity and secure provision for all the members. However, the statement does not address the question of agency for those who have neither the choice not to work nor the power to decide what part of the fruit of their labor they would like to have. It does not address the question of the desired level of consumption, satisfied according to social origin, relation to the production process, and power to participate in the decision to dispose of the fruit of the labor of those who work. Thus there is a question of power that must be addressed.

The concept of human capital enjoyed a renewal throughout the twentieth century and peaked in popularity after World War II. It was at this time that the unexpectedly fast recovery of European countries was attributed to the human capital that these countries had and that helped put to effective use the financial assistance that came under the Marshall Plan, which was set up by the United States government to reconstruct Western Europe.

According to Schultz (1972) human capital "is the source of future earnings, or of future satisfactions, or of both of them. It is human because it is an integral part of man" [sic] (Schultz: 5). For the individual, this implies that the higher the number of years of schooling, the more productive a person becomes. It is thus assumed that the individual will benefit from the investment and therefore has a vested interest in acquiring an education, even if, in the context of capitalist system, he/she may not have decision-making power over the fruit of his/her labor and is indirectly advised to be "frugal" even if those who do not participate in the production process but control the means of production may not have any ceiling placed on what they can have.

At the macro level of nations, the theory articulates that the higher the aggregate level of education of the population of that country, the higher the volume of production and the growth rate. It is the high individual productivity made possible by education that leads to higher income and greater national economic output and growth.

Since the early stage of its articulation, especially following seminal work of Adam Smith, this concept encountered strong criticism, initially formulated on philosophical and moral grounds. Thus for Stuart Mill, for instance, as cited and criticized by Schultz, it is morally unacceptable to consider human beings as capital, by equating them with financial and other material commodities that produce wealth for the satisfaction of the needs of human beings that cannot, paradoxically, be reduced to the same category as material means that can be legitimately referred to as capital.

There are many other grounds on which human capital theory has been criticized, including fallacious assumptions. In "Economic Theory and the Fate of the Poor," Bluestone (1977), for instance, considers unrealistic the likelihood that a potential employee may be actually hired and the level of his/her wage determined by his/her human capital. In "Education and Economic Equality,"

HC — stock of skills & knowledge embodied in the ability to perform LABOR so as to produce economic VALUE

obs / info gained through observation, experience or experiment

Thurow (1977) argues that the statistical evidence does not support the major claim of human capital theory that people may increase their income as a result of their increased levels of education, as evidenced by the fact that, in the United States, for instance, the diminished gap in educational attainment of Blacks and Whites is not matched by proportional decrease in the discrepancies in income distribution.

Human capital theory and its attendant empirical research provide a seemingly scientific explanation for the higher earnings of the privileged by claiming to prove that those who earn more do so because they are more productive, and they are more productive because they have greater human capital. However, for those who criticize the theory and its research base, it merely legitimizes the privileges of the dominant class or the elite.

Among the various grounds for criticism of the theory, the absence of gender in decades of research is of importance in this chapter, which aims to clarify the concepts of human capital and human capabilities and their relevance for the articulation of gender as an analytical concept. In an earlier work referred to above (Assié-Lumumba 2001), it was argued that in addition to all the other criticisms, it is of particular importance to ask why the target populations in the studies from the 1950s to the 1970s in the United States, for instance, were consistently composed of "males," almost all the time "white males." The question of the interface between gender and race and other social factors in this theory and its associated scholarship was not addressed by scholars, including most of its early critics, for decades.

Only a few among the scholars who formulated a criticism of the theory took gender and related factors into account. As Carnoy (1977), argues, the assumptions of "other things being equal" and of potential workers who have a higher level of education being more likely to secure a job in the competition and also more likely to have a higher salary—are false, since non-modifiable characteristics such as gender, race, ethnic origin, and age are key determining factors for employers.

Human capital theory was considered the appropriate and potentially the most effective framework for designing not only the domestic policy for combating entrenched poverty, but also for the United States' foreign policy, especially for assistance to developing countries and the policies of international financial institutions. As Schultz states:

The new capital available to these countries from [industrial countries] as a rule goes into the formation of structures, equipment and sometimes also into inventories. But it is generally not available for additional investment in man [sic]. Consequently, human capabilities do not stay abreast of physical capital, and they do become limiting factors in economic growth (Schultz 1977: 317).

Convinced of the causal relation between education and economic growth, Schultz recommended that education be considered appropriate "assistance to underdeveloped countries to help them achieve economic growth," as "it simply is not possible to have the fruits of a modern agriculture and the abundance of modern industry without making large investments in human beings" (Schultz 1977: 317).

In this optimistic view of the power of human capital, however, the emphasis was on "man" not as the generic for humankind, but as an expression of the need to focus exclusively on the male as the one whose education constitutes an investment. Cultural and historical gender biases in industrial countries inevitably had an immediate and long-term impact on the foreign assistance projects and programs of these industrial countries and international institutions in their relations with developing countries.

Schultz (1972) later recognized the main conceptual and practical limitations deriving from the theory's inattention to gender when he stated:

One of the major omissions in the studies on human capital is the investment in the education of women. One might conclude that human capital is the unique property of the male population! If so, we would do well to drop the term "human capital' and replace it with "male capital.' It would serve notice that human capital is sex-specific! Despite all of the schooling of females and other expenses on them, they appear to be of no account in the accounting of human capital. If females are capital-free, in view of all that is spent on them, we are in real trouble analytically, unless we can show that it is purely for current consumption. But if there is little to show for it, how do we patch up the economic behavioral assumption underlying the investment in education? (Schultz 1972: 38)

Increasing the potential of women by providing them with the possibilities of developing their productive capacities has been one of the main arguments for advocating increased access to education, within the framework of human capital theory. Beyond the major limitations related to the omission of the gender component and other grounds for the earlier criticism of human capital theory, there has been criticism of the theory formulated in a human capabilities framework. For the purpose of this book and this chapter in particular, the focus is on the thoughts of the scholars who have more directly engaged the concept of human capabilities.

[handwritten margin notes: KANT — ①DUTY vs. rather than emotions, around some principle, rationality ② Act only from moral rules ③ Act so that you always treat others on an end and not a means to the end.]

Human Capabilities

Sen has been, —arguably, the leading scholar in the conceptualization of human capabilities. While some of his case studies and examples apply to specific Asian contexts, the theoretical arguments and even his analysis of concrete aspects have relevance for African contexts.

Sen uses Kantian and Aristotelian concepts of humanity, common good and social good to explain the universal rights that all humans should be entitled to enjoy regardless of economic status, race, gender, nationality, religion, or creed. He articulates the capabilities and entitlements approach as analytic frameworks that provide discursive methods for critical examination of issues such as social justice, poverty, famine, and gender inequality. He criticizes the methodologies used by classical and neo-liberal economists, who discuss human needs in terms of statistical indicators. The major thesis of his work proposes that people's well being throughout the world should be measured through a conceptualization of their human capabilities and entitlements.

In *Hunger and Public Action*, Drèze and Sen (1989) define entitlements as follows: "The set of alternative bundles of commodities over which a person can establish such command will be referred to as this person's 'entitlements.'" (Drèze and Sen: 9). Entitlements can be understood as the set of legal rights of ownership and socially sanctioned rights of individuals. For instance, a legal right may be an individual's right to her/his land so that she/he can farm and sell the proceeds. Socially, sanctioned rights, on the other hand, may include the "right" for a man to physically abuse his spouse without retribution or rebuke from the state. Therefore, the man's physical abuse of his spouse is sanctioned by the societal attitude that nothing should be done to assist the abused women. Drèze and Sen refer to these socially sanctioned forms of entitlement as extended entitlements. As they state, "Extended entitlements is the concept of entitlements extended to include the results of more informal types of rights sanctioned by accepted notions of legitimacy" (Drèze and Sen: 11).

Sen would perhaps argue that the extended entitlements of the husband in this instance impinged upon the wife's capabilities through her husband's abuse and through society sanctioning her being abused by not enforcing laws that would condemn such abuse. Indeed, "[w]hile the *entitlement* of a person is a set of alternative *commodity* bundles, the *capability* of a person is a set of alternative *functioning* bundles" (Drèze and Sen: 13).

It can be argued that the state itself, with particular leadership, can adopt actions that are detrimental to particular groups, in this case women, without any possibilities or fear of being rebuked. In the case of African countries, policies that constituted a hindrance to the efforts to achieve gender parity in education, for instance, were adopted in the 1980s, thus reversing earlier post-independence commitment to socially progressive public policies.

Furthermore, the state can even be induced to adopt harmful policies by higher agencies. This is the case when powerful and undemocratic international financial institutions using neo-liberal frameworks shape domestic policies that further deprive marginalized groups of their basic rights, for instance, public policies within the structural adjustment programs and imposed fees for access to primary health care, basic education, and across-the-board tuition for higher education. The lack of investment in the health and education infrastructures directly reduce access by the most vulnerable groups, especially women, affecting their immediate well-being related to health care needs and limiting their chances for improvement in the future owing to lack of access to education.

In *The Quality of Life*, Nussbaum and Sen (1993) define human capability by arguing that the "capability of a person corresponds to the freedom that a person has to lead one kind of life or another" (Nussbaum and Sen 1993: 3). Drèze and Sen continue to argue that "[f]ormally, a person's capability is a set of functioning bundles, representing the various alternative "beings and doings' [functioning] that a person can achieve with his or her economic, social, and personal characteristics" (Drèze and Sen 1989: 12).

In order to comprehend fully what is meant by capabilities, functioning must be defined. In *Commodities and Capabilities*, Sen (1985) states: "A functioning is an achievement of a person: what he or she manages to do or to be" (Sen 985:10). Therefore, capability has to do with what a person has already accomplished and achieved and who they are in society, i.e., his or her entitlements. It also has to do with a person's ability and potentiality. In addition, capability involves factors that are external to the individual's power and entitlements. Thus, the ability to avoid undernourishment may depend on a person's access to health care, medical facilities, clean drinking water, and the like (Drèze and Sen 1989). Nussbaum as viewed by Sen explains these items as combined or external capabilities.

In *Sex and Social Justice*, Nussbaum (1999) points to three types of capabilities: basic, internal, and combined (external). Basic capabilities are the natural tools of individuals that are necessary to develop more advanced capabilities (Nussbaum 1999). Internal capabilities provide the sufficient conditions for applying abilities in real world activities. For the purpose of this book and this introductory chapter, it is worth pointing out that an example of internal capabilities would be education (Nussbaum 1999). Combined capabilities are defined as internal capabilities in addition to the external conditions that make the application of a function a possibility (Nussbaum 1999). For example, providing clean water for individuals may make it possible for these individuals to have a more nutritious and safe diet and therefore live a healthier life. Such initiatives are usually the actions of public policy and therefore external to individual capabilities and entitlements.

Nussbaum (2000) also examines real lives in their material and social settings, focusing on women's lives. She argues that the central capabilities are instrumental to further pursuits, for they hold value in themselves in making the life that includes them fully human. She proposes a new perspective on women that is genuinely international and argues for an ethical underpinning to all thought about development planning and public policy; she moves beyond the abstractions of economists and philosophers to embed thought about justice in the concrete reality of the struggles of poor women. She further argues that international political and economic thought must be sensitive to gender difference as a problem of justice, and that feminist thought must begin to focus on the problems of women in the developing countries. Taking as her point of departure the predicament of poor women, she shows how philosophy should be the foundation for basic constitutional principles that should be respected and implemented by all governments, and used as a comparative measure of quality of life across nations.

Nussbaum and Sen are concerned with the capabilities of individuals as a mode of analysis that will enable policymakers to understand the manner in which individual freedom can be enhanced through combined capabilities. In *Development as Freedom*, Sen (1999) develops the notion of freedom as a facilitator of development. He provides three key ways to conceive freedom: 1) negative freedom, 2) substantive (or positive) freedom, and 3) well-being (or happiness). Negative freedom is defined as freedom from coercion or tyranny. Substantial freedom is freedom that provides individuals with opportunities (education, access to health care, ability to pay for needs, and the like). Substantial freedom has to do with "enhancing the lives we lead and the freedoms we enjoy" (Sen 1999: 14). Substantial freedom allows individuals to become "fuller social persons, exercising our own volitions and interacting with—and influencing—the world in which we live" (Sen (1999: 15). Well-being (or happiness) is defined as being satiated and having no wants or needs. For Sen, it is the role of public action to provide the means by which humans pursue what is desirable. Therefore, through public policy, the capabilities of an individual are combined with the state to grant negative and substantial freedom. The individual acquires well being (happiness) with the assistance of public policy. Thus the adoption of policies that objectively diminish assistance leads to de facto reduction in well-being among those who are subjected to such policies.

Sen makes it clear that well-being cannot be equated with availability of resources and income. It is worth recalling that human capital focuses on income, and education is supposed to be a factor that leads to increased productivity, which is assumed to be the explanation and justification for income distribution. Instead, wellbeing has to do with "spaces of functionings" (Drèze and Sen 1989: 12) or the ability to achieve various sources of well-being and happiness. An important contribution of human capabilities scholars, such as Sen, is the desire to transform the way policymakers view traditional indicators of human well-being. For instance, in *Commodities and Capabilities*, Sen contends that "formal economics is not interested in a person's states and interests" (Sen (1985: 2), as it largely deals with indicators that do not take into account the capabilities and entitlements of individuals.

Consequently, Drèze and Sen's notion of capability goes beyond the conception of standard of living or poverty line (Drèze and Sen: 12). They consider that such discussions limit analysis to income and resource availability. According to them, "[i]ncome is a rather dubious indicator of the opportunity of being well nourished and having nutrition-related capabilities" (Drèze and Sen: 179). For them, people may not be able to fulfill their capabilities even with incomes that are above the technically designated poverty line or with access to some resources.

They also see a need for entitlement analysis dealing with policy to be broadened, as they argue: "The focus on entitlements, which is concerned with the command over commodities, has to be seen as only instrumentally important, and the concentration has to be, ultimately, on basic human capabilities" (Drèze and Sen: 13). Whereas they view starvation as entitlement failure, they view poverty as "failure of basic capabilities" (Drèze and Sen: 15). The notion of human capabilities rests on the power and freedom to achieve. In the state of poverty, an individual's ability to achieve is denied through various avenues. For instance, if a wage laborer loses his/her job and he/she is not able to fulfill his/her basic needs such as food and shelter he/she is said to be impoverished. Drèze and Sen suggest that poverty line analyses do not come to grips with the reality that even if an individual is above the poverty line, she/he may not be able to fulfill her/his basic capabilities.

For instance, an individual who lives above the poverty line may still be undernourished if he/she has responsibilities that are not taken into account within an aggregate analysis. It is commonly the case for women who are clustered in the lowest-paying jobs but have to fulfill family obligations. In the context of economic crisis and the structural adjustment programs and other economic reforms in Africa, there have been many losses of jobs in the formal sector by dismissal or forced early retirement. When male members of households lose their formal-sector jobs (they are more likely than women to have such jobs) many African women manage to meet the needs of their respective households with their precarious resources raised from the informal sector. Poverty is the deprivation of human capabilities. It may lead to premature mortality, undernourishment, persistent morbidity and widespread illiteracy (Sen 1999: 87). Poverty does not necessarily occur because of an individual's low income. For Drèze and Sen (1989), it happens because of a breakdown in human capabilities.

Drèze and Sen (1989) criticize policymakers and scholars who fail to view such issues from a human capabilities standpoint and instead approach issues from a formal economic perspective. They view an indicator such as GNP (Gross National Product) as problematic because it does not explain the capabilities of individuals in relation to GNP. GNP cannot be related to individual lives and efforts. For instance, they state:

First, the GNP gives a measure of the aggregate opulence of the economy, and the translation of this into the pattern of individual prosperity would depend also on the distribution of income over the population. Second, as we have seen, the capabilities enjoyed by people depend on many factors other than the command over commodities which can be purchased in the market. (Drèze and Sen 1989: 180).

They also suggest that there is dissonance between GNP per capita and the ability for individuals to live long lives. They argue that GNP cannot provide a substantial view of the human capabilities of individuals in order to achieve development. In *Development as Freedom*, Sen argues that support-led processes or public action do not wait for increases in GNP but work to alleviate social problems while focusing on freedom provides greater access to understanding and accomplishing development goals than formal economic indicators do. He contends:

Development can be seen, as argued here, as a process of expanding the real freedoms that people enjoy. Focusing on human freedoms contrasts with narrower views of development, such as identifying development with growth of gross national product, or with the rise in personal incomes, or with industrialization, or with technological advance, or with social modernization (Sen 1999: 3).

For Sen, development is part of the process of establishing negative freedom, (substantial freedom) and well-being. For him, this process should not be driven by a concern for increasing economic growth. Instead, development should be guided by a concern for achieving basic human capabilities that in turn will produce development. He continues to argue: "Viewing development in terms of expanding substantive freedoms directs attention to the ends that make development important, rather than merely to some of the means that, 'inter alia,' play a prominent part in the process" (Sen 1999: 3)

This argument, albeit circular, is guided by the belief that economic development cannot occur where people do not possess political freedoms, economic wellbeing, and access to health care and education. For Sen, freedom involves the actual processes that allow for freedom of action and the actual opportunities people have (Sen 1999: 17). Again, he contends: "Development requires the removal of major sources of unfreedom: poverty as well as tyranny, poor economic opportunities as well as systematic social deprivation, neglect of public facilities as well as intolerance or overactivity or repressive states" (Sen 1999: 3). Sen indicates that education, good health, political liberties, economic opportunities and social power are part of freedom (ibid.). Such items are integral to economic progress whereas GNP is simply an indicator which may or may not provide for such understandings (Sen 1999: 3).

Sen argues that freedom is central to the development process for two reasons, one having to do with evaluation—Are the freedoms people possess enhanced?—and the other with effectiveness—Do people achieve free agency through development? (Sen 1999: 4) Sen does not fully disregard the potential of economic growth to provide development. As he remarks: "The contribution of the market mechanism to economic growth is, of course, important, but this comes only after the direct significance of the freedom to interchange 'words, goods, gifts' has been acknowledged" (Sen 1999: 6). While he suggests that his theory is a break from traditional economic thought on development, he admits that part of his understanding of flourishing emerges from Aristotelian thinking, which looks at wealth and income as integrally tied to freedom.

For Sen, economic growth should be guided by ethical reasoning. Economic growth should take the moral stance according to which hunger throughout the world is intolerable. As they argue:

> The enormous expansion of productive power that has taken place over the last few centuries has made it, perhaps for the first time, possible to guarantee food for all, and it is in this context that the persistence of chronic hunger and the recurrence of virulent famines must be seen as being morally outrageous and politically unacceptable (Drèze and Sen 1989: 3-4).

Given the gender roles in economic production and women's critical contribution as an actual or potential productive force, it is important to address the gender ramification of human capabilities.

The Gender Factor in Human Capabilities

Sen expands the Lockeian notion of the social contract to include an international dimension involving states and local communities. This moralistic view of the responsibilities of states and international communities is also taken up in Nussbaum's human capabilities discussion.

Nussbaum uses John Rawls' conception of justice as the focus of her argumentation. In *Sex and Social Justice* Nussbaum (1999) argues a theory "that lies at the heart of Rawls' project . . . the idea of the citizen as a free and dignified human being" (Nussbaum: 46). She explains the principle of freedom and equality of personal and political freedom as well as equal opportunity within a system that benefits all members of society without regard to social location. Nussbaum adds an international approach, as indicated above. She contends that "the moral equality of persons gives them a fair claim to certain types of treatment at the hands of society and politics . . . [this treatment] must respect and promote the liberty of choice, and it must respect and promote the equal worth of persons as choosers" (Nussbaum: 57). Nussbaum also embraces Sen's concept of substantial freedoms or capabilities and continues:

> At the heart of this tradition [of liberal political thought] is a twofold intuition about human beings: namely, that all, just by being human, are of equal dignity and worth, no matter where they are situated in society, and that the primary source of this worth is a power of moral choice within them, a power that consists in the ability to plan a life in accordance with one's own evaluation of ends (Nussbaum: 57).

Nussbaum takes the capabilities approach and focuses on individual rights within the world. She argues that individuals should have access to real opportunities and that citizens as well as governments should commit to this right for all people.

Nussbaum and Sen make it clear that these rights are not gender exclusive: they are ontological and thus they should include women. Sen (1999) characterizes women "as active agents of change: the dynamic promoters of social transformations that can alter the lives of both women and men" (Sen, 1999: 189). Therefore, he proposes that women should act as vital partners within the process of development and within world affairs. He further argues that the limited role of women in the workplace and education negatively affects the lives of all people (Sen 1999: 191). He suggests that women throughout the world and especially in the Third World are not allowed to fulfill their human capabilities.

In the introduction to *Women, Culture and Development* (Nussbaum and Glover 1995), Nussbaum (corroborates Sen's views when she argues: "Women, a majority of the world's population, receive only a small proportion of its opportunities and benefits" (Nussbaum and Glover: 2). She indicates that women are less likely to be literate and traditions are partly to blame for women's unequal state: "Customs, in short, are important causes of women's misery and death" (Nussbaum and Glover: 3). She attempts to buttress her claim by advocating that women's issues be looked at from a broader perspective.

In the same text, Nussbaum urges that we "[b]egin with the human being: with the capacities and needs that join all humans, across barriers of gender and class and race and nation. To a person concerned with the equality and dignity of women, this advice should appear in one way promising." (Nussbaum and Glover: 61). She suggests that scholars focus on what is common to all humans instead of on what is different. She indicates that what makes humans the same are their mortality, their body (its extensions and limitations, hunger, thirst, shelter, sexual desire, mobility), and the ability to feel pleasure and pain, cognitive capability, and so forth. She advocates such a generalist approach to gender in order to demonstrate the viability of equality arguments for women.

Along with other scholars of human capabilities, Nussbaum argues that inequalities in treatment of women are a mirror of the moral defects of the world. Denying women access to education, independent income, literacy, ownership rights, and decision-making power acts to stifle the human capabilities of women.

Sen and Nussbaum argue that equal and mandated access to such rights not only enhances women's standing in society and in the household, it also enhances society as a whole. They contend that women's acquisition of their full human capabilities provides for development. Providing greater decision-making power also increases society's freedom as a whole. Women's education and literacy tend to reduce child mortality rates, and women's empowerment also tends to reduce gender bias, particularly against young women and girls (Sen 1999: 195). Sen contends in addition that women's ability to make decisions reduces fertility rates (Sen: 198).

Annas (1993) discusses in "Woman and the Quality of Life," the human capabilities approach and how it provides a different way to view women's issues. She argues that gender shapes men's and women's lives differently. In "Justice, Gender, and International Boundaries," O'Neill (1993) makes the point that justice is homogenized and does not take gender into account as a significant variable. She holds that such theories of justice create abstract individuals and neglect to look at relationships of independence and interdependence.

Chen (1995) observes in "A Matter of Survival: Women's Right to Employment in India and Bangladesh," that caste standards often confine widowed women to households. In Bangladesh, women were traditionally confined to their homesteads. Women leaving their homes and looking for work were breaking with tradition (Chen: 37). Women were initially denied work, and were paid less than men. Chen posits that women who sought work after the Bangladesh famine paved the way for others because they made the plight of women visible in Bangladesh. In relation to the human capabilities analysis, work in and of itself is not enough to allow women to develop their capabilities. Work must be under just terms and lead to just and reasonable ways of living for women in general (Chen: 44).

Li (1995) in "Gender Inequality in China and Cultural Relativism," makes claims similar to Chen's, by arguing that women in China are said to have equal access to work but many have to take lower paying and less challenging positions. Li also suggests that the education system has not given priority to women, as evidenced by the large number of school dropouts and illiterates, who are mainly women. Li's major points are against relativists who believe that women's wellbeing should be defined at the local level (Li 1995: 409). Li also contends that the tradition of Confucianism is patriarchal as evidenced by the Confucian maxims according to which "women are burdensome" (Li: 412-413) and the goodness of a man is judged by how well he plays his social roles as a father, son, and husband; a woman's goodness is judged by her performance as a daughter, wife, and mother (Li: 412). In her role as wife, the woman is meant to be obedient to her husband, while the husband is meant to protect his wife; hence Li argues that women's roles are domestic and inferior. These roles have implications for access to education. Li contends that the communist revolution did not effectively address the structural and cultural gender inequality and suggests that women are entitled to universal principles that trump local cultural traditions because of the basic humanness of women, and society must create conditions in which all human capabilities are possible across gender. Li finally argues that a society is not a good society if it does not provide for people's human capabilities to flourish.

Valdes (1995) also advocates, in "Inequality in Capabilities between

Men and Women in Mexico," for a gender approach to human capabilities for Mexico. She suggests that there are no laws that openly advocate for gender inequality in Mexico. In Latin America in general, she further argues that women are not legally denied access or resources. She argues that society should not only give or grant rights, it should also provide freedom to have functions in society. Women in Mexico suffer from inequality and injustice and are deprived of their capabilities (Valdes 1995: 427). Valdes states that only 29% of women are economically active and those who are active are paid less than men (Valdes 1995: 427). In Mexico, 15% of women are illiterate, 38% finish high school, 10% of women have never attended school, and only 57% have finished primary school (Valdes 1995: 427). She argues that "women [in Mexico] are not functioning in many characteristically human ways because of local patriarchal social structures and because of the ancestral history of subjection" (Valdes 1995: 428). Valdes holds that Third World women need to change the way they are perceived by others and by themselves because women often accept their lesser roles. She further suggests that there is no reasonable basis for denying women of their capabilities (Valdes 1995: 428).

Nzegwu (1995) in "Recovering Igbo Traditions: A Case for Indigenous Women's Organizations in Development," like other African scholars, especially women, critiques the generalist development approach and she argues that colonization silenced the voice of women and led to the denial of education for women, employment, decision-making powers, and access to resources (Nzegwu: 445). Furthermore, she posits that the pre-colonial political culture of the Igbos, for instance, was dual sexed. Women's organizations allowed women to maintain and share economic and political connections (Nzegwu: 447); this presupposes equal access to knowledge, which women did not enjoy in the colonial and post-colonial eras (Assié-Lumumba 1998, 2000).

Through a historical analysis of the Igbo in Nigeria, for instance, (Nzegwu: 447) argues that in pre-colonial context, women had recourse when men wronged them. For instance, the practice of "sitting on a man" or forcing a man to apologize when he offended or abused a woman (Nzegwu: 448) was a social practice that guaranteed protection of women against abuse by men. She discusses the use of women as council members who resolve conflicts in villages. She also points to the 1929 Women's War against the British colonial administration over the taxation of women as an act of agency in which women sought to regain some of their pre-colonial powers. She also advocates for traditional women's organizations as means to facilitating development and fulfilling women's human capabilities (Nzegwu: 459).

With reference to African women specifically, Sen concurs as he contends that, even in the contemporary world, Sub-Saharan Africa substantively demonstrates less gender discrimination than the rest of the world. Drèze and Sen (1989: 54) argue:

> Anti-female discrimination in health and nutrition is endemic in South Asia, but much less noticeable (perhaps even absent) in the case of sub-Saharan Africa . . . . There is indeed a good deal of anthropological and statistical evidence on the greater autonomy of African women (in terms of land rights, access to gainful employment, control over property, freedom of movement, etc.) in comparison with the general position of South Asian women. ... particularly in relation to the role of 'gainful' employment.

However, he still suggests that gender inequities exist within Sub-Saharan Africa. Sen's analysis would have been stronger if he had adopted a historical approach in which, without claiming any close-to-perfect gender philosophy, African culture had a gender foundation that, despite the assaults since the implementation of the colonial policies, appeared to have a resilience that is manifested in some of the realities that are analyzed and conceived as less detrimental to women in Africa compared to other regions.

The human capabilities analytic framework is also utilized to examine other aspects of human life. For instance, in "Equality of What? On Welfare, Goods, and Capabilities," Cohen [1993] discusses that traditional concerns such as incomes, utilities, resources and primary goods may be inadequate measures of people's lives. However he questions whether the capabilities approach is the answer. In addition, in "Descriptions of Inequality: The Swedish Approach to Welfare Research" Erikson (1993) discusses strategies for measuring quality of life that have been used by Scandinavian social scientists. He contends that the capabilities approach provides some support for the Scandinavian analysis. The Swedish Central Statistical Office and other Scandinavian research organizations focus on needs that are concerned with need satisfaction. In "Quality of Life Measures in Health Care and Medical Ethics," Brock (1993) discusses quality of life in health care and medical ethics.

There are also critics of the human capabilities approach. In *Explaining the Expansion of Human Capabilities in Developing Countries*, Calfat (1997) analyzes Sen's conception of entitlements and capabilities and argues that Sen's concept of entitlements is sometimes problematic, and that the determinants of entitlements are typically numerous and complex (Calfat: 6). Calfat contends that critics of Sen consider it difficult to operationalize and place value on the potential or capabilities of human beings. A major criticism is that it is far easier to measure the end than it is to measure the input or the means to the end. Calfat suggests that "[f]inally GDP per capita and other resource/ income based measures continue to play a crucial role to facilitate the development of basic capabilities" (Calfat: 1).

Many of the contributors to *Social Capability and Long-Term Economic Growth* (Perkins and Koo 1995) counter the human capabilities arguments in that they view economic growth as the means for development. In their introduction, Perkins and Koo argue that social capability can be regarded as the human potential for economic growth (Koo and Perkins: 3). They posit that, "[i]n essence, social capability includes a wide variety of institutions and human resources that make it possible for some nations to develop more rapidly than others." (Koo and Perkins: 3). They hold the position that what allows for the disparate growth capabilities is technology (ibid.). While they concede that the Harrod-Domar and Solow models of growth are outdated, they conclude that these models need revision. In addition, Dahlman and Nelson (1995) in "Social Absorption Capability, National Innovation Systems," suggest that technological change can be seen as technological capability. For them, technological capability is embodied in human beings and not machines (Dahlman and Nelson: 82); technological capacity is required of human capital and people working together. In "Why Growth Rates Differ: The Political Economy of Social Capability in 21 Developing Countries," Lal (1995) argues that there is no significant correlation between human capital and growth. Lal views the level and efficiency of investment as the "proximate causes of the difference in growth performance" (Lal: 290).

Conclusion

Under the human capital theory and social capability approach, scholars tend to place weight on economic growth and performance as indicators of development, whereas the human capabilities approach suggests that levels of human capabilities are the true markers of development. In addition, the human capabilities approach posits that expansion of human capabilities provides an avenue for development. Women play a vital role in the human capabilities analysis in that development very much hinges on their treatment as equal members of the human family. The human capabilities approach is about providing an equal playing field for all humans in terms of political and personal liberties and economic opportunities.

Women's access to and use of their education at all levels is the key to enjoying their human rights and developing their capabilities as social agents. African societies will initiate a process of social progress when they conceptualize, design, implement and evaluate policies that are grounded in a philosophy aimed at systematically maximizing human capabilities and upgrading human rights to learning and knowledge production without regard to gender.

References

Annas, J., 1993. "Woman and the Quality of Life: Two Norms or One." In *The Quality of Life,* ed., M. Nussbaum and A. Sen, 279-96. New York: Oxford University Press.

Assié-Lumumba, N. T., 2004. "Sustaining Home-Grown Innovations in Higher Education in Sub-Saharan Africa: A Critical Reflection." *Journal of International Cooperation in Education* 7 (1).

Assié-Lumumba, N. T. 2003. African Gender Institute, University of Cape Town, <*http://www.gwsafrica.org/knowledge/ndri.html*>, first published by AAWORD in *Visions of Gender Theories and Social Development in Africa: Harnessing Knowledge for Social Justice and Equality.* Dakar: Association of African Women for Research and Development, AAWORD Book Series pp. 95-113.

Assié-Lumumba, N. T. 2001. "Gender, Race, and Human Capital Theory: Research Trends in the United States from the 1950s to the 1990s." *Journal of Comparative Education and International Relations in Africa* 4 (1-2).

Assié-Lumumba, N. T. 2000. "Educational and Economic Reforms, Gender Equity, and Access to Schooling in Africa." *International Journal of Comparative Sociology* 41 (1): 89-120.

Assié-Lumumba, N. T. 1998. "Women in West Africa: Dynamics of Issues in Education, Economy, Culture, Health and Politics." In *Women in the Third World: An Encyclopedia of Contemporary Issues,* ed. N. Stromquist. New York: Garland Publishing.

Assié-Lumumba, N. T. 1997. "Educating Africa's Girls and Women: A Conceptual and Historical Analysis of Gender Inequality." In *Engendering African Social Sciences*, ed. A. Imam, A. Mama, and F. Sow. Dakar: Council for Development of Social Science Research in Africa (CODESRIA).

Assié-Lumumba, N. T. 1996. "The Future Role and Mission of African Higher Education." *South African Journal of Higher Education* 10 (2).

Assié-Lumumba, N. T. 1994. "Rural Students in Urban Settings in Africa: The Experiences of Female Students in Secondary Schools." In *Education in the Urban Areas: Cross-National Dimensions*, ed., N. Stromquist. Westport, CT: Praeger.

Assié-Lumumba, N. T. 1994. "History of Women's Education in Francophone Africa." *International Encyclopedia of Education*. 2nd ed. Oxford: Pergamon Press.

Assié-Lumumba, N. T. 1994. "Les politiques d'éducation des filles en Afrique: Instrument de promotion ou processus de marginalisation des femmes." In *L''egalité devant soi: Sexes, rapports sociaux et développement international*, ed. M.-F. Labrecque. Ottawa: International Development and Research Center.

Becker, G. S., 1964. *Human Capital*. New York: National Bureau of Economic Research.

Blaug, M., 1972. "The Correlation Between Education and Earnings: What Does It Signify?" *Higher Education* 1: 53-77.

Boserup, E., 1970. *Women's Role in Economic Development*. London: George Allen and Unwin Ltd.

Bowles, S., and Gintis, H., 1975. "The Problem With Human Capital: A Marxian Critique." *American Economic Review* 6: 74-82.

Brock, D., 1993. "Quality of Life Measures in Health Care and Medical Ethics." In *The Quality of Life*, ed. M. Nussbaum and A. Sen, 95-132. New York: Oxford University Press.

Calfat, G. G., 1997. *Explaining the Expansion of Human Capabilities in Developing Countries: The Role of Economic Growth and Deprivation*, Antwerp: University of Antwerp, Centre for Development Studies.

Carter, M., and Carnoy, M., 1974. "Theories of Labor Markets and Worker Productivity." Discussion paper. Palo Alto, Calif.: Center for Economic Studies.

Chen, M., 1995. "A Matter of Survival: Women's Right to Employment in India and Bangladesh." In *Women, Culture and Development: A Study of Human Capabilities*, ed. M. Nussbaum and J. Glover, 37-60. New York: Oxford University Press.

Cohen, G. A., 1993. "Equality of What? On Welfare, Goods, and Capabilities." In *The Quality of Life*, ed. M. Nussbaum and A. Sen. New York: Oxford University Press.

Dahlman, C., and Nelson, R., 1995, "Social Absorption Capability, National Innovation Systems," In *Social Capability and Long-Term Economic Growth*, ed., B. H. Koo and D. H. Perkins, 82-122. New York: St. Martin's Press.

Denison, E. F., 1962. "The Sources of Economic Growth in the United States and the Alternatives Before Us." Supplementary Paper Number 13. New York: Committee for Economic Development.

Dixon-Mueller, R., and Anker, R., 1988. "Assessing Women's Economic Contributions to Development." *Training in Population, Human Resources and Development Planning* 6. Geneva: International Labour Office.

Drèze, J., and Sen, A., 1989. *Hunger and Public Action*. New York: Oxford University Press.

England, P., 1993. "The Separate Self: Androcentric Bias in Neoclassical Assumptions." In *Beyond Economic Man*, ed. M. A. Ferber and J. A. Nelson. Chicago: The University of Chicago Press.

Erikson, R., 1993. "Descriptions of Inequality: The Swedish Approach to Welfare Research." In *The Quality of Life*, ed. M. Nussbaum and A. Sen, 67-83. New York: Oxford University Press.

Fagerlind, I., 1989. *Education and Development*. New York: Pergamon Press.

Gintis, H., 1971. "Education and the Characteristics of Worker Productivity." *American Economic Review* 61: 266-79.

Karabel, J., and Halsey, A. H., eds., 1977. *Power and Ideology in Education*. New York: Oxford University Press.

Koo, B. H., and Perkins, D. H., eds., 1995. *Social Capability and Long-Term Economic Growth*. New York: St. Martin's Press.

Lal, D., 1995. "Why Growth Rates Differ: The Political Economy of Social Capability in 21 Developing Countries." In *Social Capability and Long-Term Economic Growth*, ed. B. H. Koo and D. H. Perkins, 288-309. New York: St. Martin's Press.

Li, X., 1995. "Gender Inequality in China and Cultural Relativism." In *Women, Culture and Development: A Study of Human Capabilitie*, ed. M. Nussbaum and J. Glover, 407-26. New York: Oxford University Press.

Lloyd, C. B., and Neimi, B. T., 1979. *The Economics of Sex Differentials*. New York: Columbia University Press.

Nussbaum, M. 1995. "Human Capabilities, Female Human Beings." In *Women, Culture and Development: A Study of Human Capabilities*, ed. M. Nussbaum and J. Glover, 61-104. New York: Oxford University Press.

Nussbaum, M. 1995. Introduction to *Women, Culture and Development: A Study of Human Capabilities*, ed., M. Nussbaum and J. Glover, 1-36. New York: Oxford University Press.

Nussbaum, M. 1999. *Sex and Social Justice*. New York: Oxford University Press.

Nussbaum, M. 2000. *Women and Human Development: The Capabilities Approach*. New York: Cambridge University Press.

Nussbaum, M., and Glover, J., eds. 1995. *Women, Culture and Development: A Study of Human Capabilities*. New York: Oxford University Press.

Nussbaum, M., and Sen, A., eds. 1993. *The Quality of Life*. New York: Oxford University Press.

Nzegwu, N. 1995. "Recovering Igbo Traditions: A Case for Indigenous Women's Organizations in Development." In *Women, Culture and Development: A Study of Human Capabilities*, ed. M. Nussbaum and J. Glover, 444-67. New York: Oxford University Press.

O'Neill, O. 1993. "Justice, Gender, and International Boundaries." In *The Quality of Life*, ed. M. Nussbaum and A. Sen, 303-23. New York: Oxford University Press.

Schultz, T. W. 1977. "Investment in Human Capital." In *Power and Ideology in Education*, ed. J. Karabel and A. H. Halsey, 313-24. New York: Oxford University Press.

Schultz, T. W. 1972. *Human Capital: Policy Issues and Research Opportunities*. Human Resources Colloquium, Atlanta University. New York: National Bureau of Economic Research; distributed by Columbia University Press.

Sen, A. 1993. "Capability and Well-Being." In *The Quality of Life*, ed. M. Nussbaum and A. Sen, 30-53. New York: Oxford University Press.

Sen, A. 1985. *Commodities and Capabilities*. New York: Elsevier Science Publishing Company Inc.

Sen, A. 1999. *Development as Freedom*. New York: Alfred A. Knopf, Inc.

Thurow, L. C. 1977. "Education and Economic Equality," In *Power and Ideology in Education*, ed. J. Karabel and A. H. Halsey, 325-335. New York: Oxford University Press.Valdes, M., 1995. "Inequality in Capabilities between Men and Women in Mexico." In *Women, Culture and Development: A Study of Human Capabilities,* ed. M. Nussbaum and J. Glover, 426-32. New York: Oxford University Press.

Windham, D. M. 1976. "Social Benefits and Subsidization of Higher Education: A Critique." *Higher Education* 5: 237-52.

CHAPTER 2

MIS-MEASURING GENDER DISPARITIES IN THE EDUCATIONAL ESTABLISHMENTS

Remi Clignet

Introduction

The purpose of this chapter is to highlight the scientific and political weakness of the measurements of gender disparities currently used by international as well as national agencies. While the function of such measurements should be to identify the socio-cultural profile of the relevant inequalities in order to eradicate—or at least to reduce—them, these measurements are at best inoperative and at worst they facilitate the perpetuation of the *status quo*.

This author's critical remarks are twofold. On the one hand, the measurements are marred by a number of biases difficult to avoid. On the other hand, a more specific point is to show how they mirror a particular fallacy, which has both a logical and political origin. Indeed, they do not address the difficulties of choosing an appropriate unit of analysis. This is owing to the fact that social scientists unduly endow the individual with a decision-making capacity that he or she does not have. Strangely enough, the solution that will be suggested should serve both scientific and political purposes.

This study will start from the observation that, for reasons of convenience, officials define "attendance rates" as the number of individuals attending school divided by the number of individuals eligible to attend school. The numerator, that is, the number of individuals attending school, is collected by school officials, and this is what makes it so attractive. The denominator is tricky as it corresponds to the number of boys and girls that belong to the age group expected formally or informally to attend school. At first glance, apart from the ecological fallacy referred to below, mixing the two independent data bases—in other words, educational statistics and census materials—is problematic for at least four reasons.

First, the logic underlying the definition of age differs, since it is normative in the case of decisions concerning educational trajectories, but descriptive in the case of census taking[1]. On the one hand, school administrators identify the age at which it is proper for children to attend a primary, secondary or postsecondary educational institution for the first time, whereas there are no evident strings attached to the ages reported by the people interviewed by census takers. On the other hand, at least in the case of countries where children are allowed or obliged to repeat grades, the age groups used by educational administrators, by clients of the schools, and by demographers do not coincide. Thus, parents will hide the real age of a failing child they intend to enroll in another institution. As a result, two similarly high enrollment rates may reflect two distinct phenomena. One of these rates may mean that a high number of school-aged children pass quickly through the local educational system. The second may indicate that a high proportion of those attending school repeat their grades, and move so slowly across the successive classes that form a primary (ages 6-14), secondary (15-21), or postsecondary (16-21+) sector that they are older than the denominator supposes them to be.[2]

Second, the validity of the rates depends on the time difference between the dates on which educational statistics and census materials were collected. The greater the difference between the two dates, the more likely it is that the denominator underestimates the significance of migrations and of the mortality affecting the younger age groups. Correspondingly, two similarly high enrollment rates may point to two distinct phenomena. The first may mean that a high number of school-aged children attend school, and the second that the denominator underestimates the number of children expected to attend school in view of their age.

Third, the threats faced by the validity of these rates differ between the two genders. On the one hand, boys and girls are not exposed to the same mortality rates during 1) the earliest stages of their life cycle, 2) before attending school, and 3) during the ages at which they are supposed to attend primary school. In the same way, boys and girls are rarely involved in the migrations of their familial groups. On the other hand, boys and girls do face obstacles, not necessarily comparable to the same extent, to attending school or to moving across grades both within and between

---

[1] Census criteria for grouping may involve a normative definition of age as the number of individuals older than a critical threshold may be counted for tax purposes.

[2] Repetition of a grade is considered a "waste." Economically speaking, this is biased. Moreover, enrollment may or may not depend on the student's home residence. For example, the enrollment figures may include private and public schools.

educational sectors[3]. Absenteeism, drop-out, and failure rates differ between the two genders at various points on the educational ladder.

Fourth and last, the increased emphasis placed on the formal education of girls induces officials in a growing number of developing countries to provide families with a variety of incentives to increase female school enrollments. The end result may be to render enrollment rates more sensitive to seasonal variations. Correspondingly, gender disparities may change in direction as well as in magnitude, as the academic year unfolds and incentives disappear.

To conclude, the measurements of gender disparities used by public authorities do not have one single meaning. As such, they are neither valid nor reliable and hence, they cannot be used for comparative purposes or *a fortiori* as foundations on which governments might rely in order to change the distribution of educational amenities.

Educational Mismeasurements and the Problem of the Ecological Fallacy

The term coined by Robinson in 1950 has more than one manifestation. Initially, Robinson's purpose was to criticize Durkheim, who sought to explain variations in the suicide rates of French counties in terms of the relative numbers of local Protestants. While Durkheim observed that the higher the proportion of Protestants in an area, the higher the suicide rates, he imputed the corresponding correlation to the fact that Protestantism enhances the sense of guilt to such an extent that the individual is overwhelmed when he faces major crises in life. In contrast, he argued that Catholics are less tempted to commit suicide since the special type of interaction embedded in confession allows them to get relief from failures and crises. Yet Robinson showed that, however convincing Durkheim's data might appear, they do not address the issues he raised, since counties defined as spatial or administrative units have no psychological properties whatsoever. In general terms, then, "the ecological fallacy" consists in endowing a specific unit of observation with features it does not and cannot have.

As they are currently computed, enrollment rates offer a case in point. Indeed, the way these rates are calculated presupposes implicitly that school-aged children have no siblings or that the decisions taken with regard to the formal education of these siblings are irrelevant as far as their own educational trajectories are concerned. Yet, these presuppositions are invalid on a number of counts. First, they unduly privilege the social

---

[3] Indeed, in 1992, for example, more girls attended secondary schools than boys. In one group of 36 students 6 to 15 years old, 21 were girls and 15 boys.

autonomy of young children, and this mirrors the triumph of individualist ideologies prevailing among many of the social scientists operating in Western societies. Regardless of these ideologies, the fact is that the educational aspirations and expectations of these children are formed, informed and controlled by adults. To be sure, in the world of developing nations, the identity of these adults is highly problematic, since the notion of fostering is increasingly complex and contingent on culturally specific factors.[4] Second, the normative definition of autonomy and its implications on educational choices and trajectories depend on the economic environment. The higher the educational costs, for instance, the higher the tuition fees demanded by schools or universities, the more dependent the individual becomes on the assistance of adult actors, those willing and able to contribute[5].

To summarize this particular argument, the current computation of enrollment rates takes place as if the behavior of school-aged individuals was comparable to atoms independent of the behavior both of the molecules in which they are embedded and of the adjacent atoms. Scientifically, this posture corresponds to a reification which is no longer considered tenable by chemists. In the case of the social sciences, this posture highlights the importance of the distinction made by Lévi-Strauss (1958) between conscious and unconscious models. The first of these models evokes the set of culturally specific norms and preferences that individual actors use to justify their choices and rationalize their behaviors. The second model suggests the systemic regularities identified and hence constructed by social analysts to explain the interaction between the various conscious models used in one single culture or between conscious models comparable across cultures. The pertinent questions raised by this distinction are whether the selection of the unit of observation is and should be a byproduct of either one of these two models and whether there is a legitimate sequential order in their use.

In positing that educational trajectories depend more on the characteristics of the familial groups concerned than on the individual's own set of abilities and motivations, this author runs the risk of being charged with the sin of paternalism and of imposing his own conservative

---

[4] Goody (1982) began theorizing about fostering in Ghana. However, economic and demographic and educational dynamics have helped increase the complexity of the phenomenon. This complexity is further increased as a result of potential discrepancies in the vocabulary used in local and European languages to describe the phenomenon.

[5] . Constant increases in the tuition fees charged by American institutions of higher learning have reduced proportionately the likelihood that candidates for admission might finance their studies with odd jobs such as delivering newspapers or working as cashiers at local supermarkets.

bias on the data. Thus, in the case of non-Western countries and in the case of the underprivileged segments of industrialized societies, the actors themselves define the challenges raised by formal schooling in terms of the sacrifices and the benefits it represents for the domestic group of the individual concerned rather than for themselves (Leclerc 1979). In other words, to consider such a domestic group as the significant unit of analysis is to adopt the conscious model of the relevant actors as the cornerstone of the analysis. In this sense, this chapter is faithful to the logic of Lévi-Strauss who argues that the analysis must start from conscious models. Further, this author contests the criticism of most social scientists in charging that they unduly project their own individualistic ideologies on a social landscape on which they have no bearing and within which their own ideologies are irrelevant.

The Implications of Choosing Domestic Groups as the Units of Analysis in Studying Educational Trajectories

To retain domestic groups as units of analyses is to highlight the importance of giving as much weight to *intra* as to *inter* family variations in assessing gender disparities in the educational realm. *Intra* family variations in gender disparities imply that in specific circumstances, heads of household are unable and/or unwilling to provide all their children with the same amount of formal education; thus they are obliged to make a selection. In Madagascar for example, during the academic year 1996-1997, only seventeen per cent of the households with *two children between 6 and 14 years of age* sent one of them to school. In comparison, for households with three children in the same age group, the proportion selecting one or two children to receive a formal education climbed to one-third. The proportion of households with four children in the same group reached 35 per cent. As the number of families with more than two children of the same age group is negligible, it is clear that intra family competition is a significant statistical problem. It is similarly clear that its components and its implications should be analyzed. Indeed, the competition that opposes children of the same family to one another in this regard takes a variety of forms.

Immediate Competition

The larger the number of children present in the same age group expected to attend school, the more severe the competition is among them for being and remaining enrolled in any institution. This is so for two complementary reasons. On the one hand, the ensuing educational expenses increase accordingly, and they have to be covered simultaneously.

On the other hand, the presence of a large number of children in the same age group represents an indicator of traditional family orientations most likely to be at odds with the educational values and aspirations underlying formal schooling.

Yet competition among children differs with their residential status. Foster children seem to be uniformly less often educated than the offspring of household heads. Further, relevant contrasts between the two types of children are more marked for girls than for boys. This is because the former are most likely to be used as household servants and to perform tasks that are usually performed by the daughters of the household head. Thus, in the case of Benin, diachronic studies show that fostered girls tend to be the ones who first bear the brunt of the economic difficulties that the families sheltering them face as a result of the structural adjustment policies (Charmes 1993).

As far as the children of the household head are concerned, competition does not take on the same intensity in families having children of the same gender as it does in families having both sons and daughters. Thus, whether in Togo or in Madagascar, the enrollment rates of boys having brothers exclusively or of girls having sisters exclusively show very little sensitivity to family size. In fact, their variations are slightly curvilinear and they tend to decline only in the case of households with three or more children. In other words, immediate competition among siblings in families having only sons or only daughters has no negative effect on the school attendance of each child. Commitment to equity overrides other considerations.

At the same time, while the enrollment rates of boys and girls originating from families with both sons and daughters tend to decline with the numbers of their siblings, male and female educational trajectories depend on the relative numerical importance of each gender. In Togo, male enrollment rates for the age group between 6 and 14 years of age tend to be uniformly indifferent to the number of sons relative to the number of daughters and indeed to the overall number of children (Table 1).

Conversely, the percentage of girls attending schools is uniformly greater among households where daughters are at least as numerous as sons. Further and most important, gender disparities are more limited in the case of smaller families where daughters are in the majority. Thus, the educational expectations or aspirations those parents entertain toward the formal schooling of their sons and their daughters are not indifferent to the distribution of their offspring by sex. As a matter of fact, everyday language acknowledges this phenomenon, as exemplified by the French expression *garçon manqué*. Girls with masculine aspirations and/or treated in educational terms as sons by frustrated parents are certainly not distributed randomly within and among families. In addition, their treatment is unquestionably affected by specific cultural norms. Of course, the same holds true in the case of *"garçons efféminés"* whose educational aspirations and trajectories are at odds with the dominant values held by their familial groups (Solloway 1975).

Table 1: Togolese male and female enrollment rates by children of each sex expected to attend school (6-14 years old) present in the household (a one tenth sample for the 1981 census)

	Two children	Three children		Four children		
		B maj	Gmaj	Bmaj	Equal	Gmaj
Boys	73.5	73.7	76.4	79.9	78.5	76.5
Girls	55.3	49.1	57.4	44.0	55.5	58.0
N Boys	407	452	203	273	256	81
N girls	407	226	406	91	256	243

	Five children		Six children			Seven children		Eight children		
	Boys maj	Girls maj	Bmaj	Equal	Gmaj	Bmaj	Gmaj	Bmaj	Equal	Gmaj
Boys	75.9	81.5	70.7	57.9	70.5	52.1	61.5	81.9	60.0	52.3
Girls	5.3	12.3	7.1	23.1	0,0	3.8	2.1	-	-	-
N boys	332	119	123	57	30	92	26	94	40	21
N girls	164	226	45	57	62	47	44	36	40	36

Finally, for this author to suggest that educational competition among the sons and daughters of the same households depends on their respective number triggers the question of whether gender disparities are alike for firstborn sons and daughters on the one hand, and the subsequent sons and daughters on the other. This in turn suggests that whereas firstborn sons are more frequently encouraged to achieve academically than all the remaining children, firstborn daughters are more often treated as substitute mothers who must sacrifice themselves and enter the labor market as early as possible to finance the formal education of at least one of their younger male siblings (Greenhalg 1985). In the case of Madagascar, the obstacles to school attendance faced by girls as a result of immediate competition and the presence of younger siblings are less marked for those who are not firstborn than for those who are firstborn. However, firstborn girls are likely to achieve more and enter a secondary institution earlier than their younger siblings, and this particular contrast is even more marked for the subsequent age group (15-24).

Distant Competition

While enrolling and remaining in school depend on the *intra* and *inter* gender competition opposing sons and daughters within the same age group, it also depends on the presence of younger siblings. Not only does this presence weigh unevenly on older brothers and sisters since the division of domestic labor by gender is not balanced, but there are also differences in the tasks assigned to firstborn children as a result of the presence of younger children. First-born sons are more likely to be asked to enter the labor market earlier in order to alleviate the financial burden of the domestic group as a whole. Firstborn daughters are more likely to be asked to act as servants and nannies so as to relieve their mothers of some of their usual chores.

Indeed, in the case of Madagascar, it is obvious that the weight of distant competition varies both with the gender and the birth order of the children included in the 6-14 age group (Table 2)

Table 2: Male and female enrollment rates in function of birth order and of the number of children 0 to 14 years of age in Madagascar (1997)

Birth order and Gender	One sibling	Two siblings	Three siblings	Four siblings	Five & more siblings
Firstborn boys	0.71	0.62	0.63	0.63	0.54
Other boys	0.85	0.68	0.60	0.64	0.53
Firstborn daughters	0.60	0.66	0.73	0.68	0.42
Other daughters	0.78	0.90	0.61	0.59	0.51

To be a firstborn daughter lowers the chances of attending school in the case of both the smallest and largest families, but this is not the case for households in between. In contrast, to be a firstborn son has a similar effect only in the case of the households with a limited number of children. As a result, gender disparities within domestic groups are not evenly distributed. They differ not only between firstborn and later-born children but also between small, medium and large-sized domestic groups.

Characteristics of Households

Of course, *intra* household competition among children for gaining access to school depends on the economic and cultural capital acquired by the household head. This author would like to provide two examples of the ensuing theoretical dilemmas[6]. The first one concerns the gender of the person heading the household. Indeed, the effects of intra-gender solidarity should combine with those of the economic marginality of matrifocal families. While enrollment rates should be uniformly lower for families headed by women, the corresponding decline should be more significant for sons than daughters. This theoretical reasoning turns out to be wrong. This is because the origin of matrifocal families is increasingly diverse, some of the female heads having a sufficient level of educational and occupational attainment to get rid of a systematic male presence while other female heads have been abandoned and rendered marginalized by their partners (Pilon 1996). Correspondingly, in such families, gender disparities in formal schooling vary to a large extent, the enrollments of sons being more frequent than those of daughters in the case of the households headed by women who are the most marginal in economic terms. The more hard pressed these women are, the more they are obliged to play the labor market as it is in order to increase the chances of the survival of the domestic group and the more they give priority to the formal schooling of their sons.

The second theoretical dilemma concerns the impact of the educational level attained by the adults present in the household. Empirical literature highlights the significance of the formal schooling acquired by women in this regard. It shows that the contrasts between the enrollments of children whose mothers have been in school for a maximal and a minimal amount of time are greater than contrasts between the enrollments of children whose fathers have the same maximal and minimal educational characteristics.

Yet this style of analysis may be somewhat misleading for a variety of reasons. First, the contrast observed between the two partners in this regard does not necessarily have the same meaning for developed as for developing societies. In the second case, the scarcity of educated mothers means that one cannot be sure whether their behaviors as socializing agents result from values acquired at school or from those acquired at home. Furthermore, in either case, one cannot be sure which part of the overt or hidden curriculum should be held responsible for the educational investments chosen by the individuals concerned.

Finally, in the most general terms, the consequences of the human capital accumulated by fathers and by mothers are not independent of one another. As it turns out in developing countries, educated females are scarcer than educated males, and the former are more likely to marry an educated partner than the latter. Correspondingly, the variable that is the

---

[6] First, more children are attending school in polygamous than in monogamous households. Second, mothers and fathers are identified by their children's schooling.

most powerful negative predictor of gender disparities is positive educational "homogamy", that is the fact that both husbands and wives have graduated at least from the primary cycle of studies.

Table 3: Enrollment rates of Antananarivo children (15-24) by maternal and paternal level of education, considered independently and jointly (1997)

Level of schooling	Boys	Girls
Father minimal level	29.0	35.9
Father maximal level	73.4	68.9
Mother minimal level	30.0	21.3
Mother maximal level	66.6	74.9
Both parents minimal level	24.8	25.5
Father maximal, mother minimal	35.8	27.1
Mother maximal, father minimal	45.1	54.4
Both parents maximal	77.6	79.1

Thus, in the case of Antananarivo, children in the age group of 15 to 24 years are more likely to be still at school when their mothers rather than their fathers have attended school beyond the primary grades. However, the fact remains not only that in families where both parents have a similarly high level of schooling children in this age group are still most frequently enrolled in school, but also that girls receive the most favorable educational treatment.

Time, Educational Competition and Gender Disparities

By now, school enrollment is almost exclusively a by-product of educational demand.[7] As a result, the corresponding gender disparities reflect the diverging attitudes of parents or of children themselves toward the costs and benefits of educational investments. The situation changes as soon as one defines gender disparities in schooling in terms of educational trajectories and hence of the duration of the studies undertaken by boys and girls. In this case, disparities reflect a distinct pattern of interaction between the behavior of school administrators and teachers, on the one hand, and male and female students as well as their parents, on the other. Thus, it is misleading to define the analysis exclusively in terms of comparing male and female attendance rates, as this approach leads to treating gender disparities as timeless entities (Carpentier et Clignet 1998).

---

[7] . Gender disparities were previously a by-product, and hence a source of supply, of specific policies whenever educational institutions were along these lines. Yet, the effect of this type of segregation may be to reduce disparities (Linarés 1967).

The fact is that as girls encounter more difficulties entering a school system than boys, they also tend to survive better the academic obstacles that both are expected to overcome throughout a particular cycle of studies. While girls are regularly in the minority, less numerous than boys at the beginning of a cycle, they become the majority as they advance in their studies. This confirms the validity of Blau and Duncan's observation (1967) regarding divergences in the academic and occupational trajectories of young Black and White Americans. The more severe the initial selection, the more likely it is that those who are initially at a disadvantage will fare better than the others later on. Thus, as noted earlier, Malagazy female students enter secondary schools earlier and in larger numbers than their male counterparts. Similarly, the firstborn female students of the Malagazy capital city have more chances to pursue their studies beyond primary school than their younger sisters. This suggests that it is more fruitful to make a threefold distinction among individuals who are still attending school at a certain age or date, those who have dropped out of the system earlier, and those who have never joined any educational institution, rather than limit the analysis to the dichotomy between those who are in school and those who are not.

Yet differences in individual academic trajectories are not exclusively the effect of a homogeneous life cycle (Ryder 1965). First, this is because identical ideological and structural forces do not govern male and female academic experiences. To the extent that female formal schooling continues to be influenced by traditional, and for instance, religious values, it evolves primarily within the long term that the historian Braudel termed *temps long*. In contrast, as the formal schooling of boys is more contingent on the vagaries of the labor market, male enrollments should vary more over time. Indeed zero order correlation between the female enrollments observed in Madagascar for 1992 and 1997 is 0.83 while in the case of males, it is only 0.66. In other words, familial strategies toward the education of their daughters are more invariant than the same familial strategies toward the education of their sons.

In the second place, it is also because, as has been suggested, gender disparities in education are related to gender disparities in the labor market. As the labor market evolves both for structural reasons and as a result of the economic cycle, the hiring decisions of employers change as well, and so do the occupational strategies of students and their parents. As a result, as shown by Duru et al. (2001), the direction and the magnitude of educational gender disparities do change over time. This is because these disparities are the byproduct of historical constructs. The underlying changes do not stem exclusively from changes in the relevant attitudes and cognitive skills of male and female students, but they also mirror changes in the curricula and in the hierarchical rank order assigned to various disciplines. This makes it even more necessary to introduce measurements of the changes in gender disparities by birth cohorts and to ask specific questions about the time necessary for facilitating significant increases in the number of women enrolling in, and graduating from, specific streams of secondary or postsecondary studies. More explicitly, it is not sufficient to assess the way contrasts in the number and profile of male and female students change as they move from the beginning to the end of a particular cycle of studies. Indeed, it is just as necessary to evaluate the way these contrasts increase or decrease across birth cohorts.

Conclusions

This chapter points to three major scientific and political recommendations. The starting point of these recommendations is that while educational institutions process individuals, these individuals belong to households committed to reconciling legitimacy and rationality through the application of norms of equity. To acknowledge this fact of life is to insist that the data necessary for evaluating *intra* and *inter* family gender disparities in education should not be collected by educational actors because of the costs and the technical difficulties involved. Since the relevant data are already collected by demographers in the context of the census, medical surveys, or other population studies, the solution consists in making these data available to the public sector as a whole.

While the development of modern bureaucracies leads to specialization and increased competition among agencies with a concomitant misuse and inefficient use of existing resources, it seems urgent to identify at least one specific incentive to promoting cooperation among the actors of local educational systems and the statisticians that have developed significant skills in data gathering and analyses. Incidentally, such a plea in favor of an interagency cooperation underlines Merton's recommendation (1973) concerning the norm of communalism. Scientific development requires interdisciplinary work and, as a first step in that direction, the sharing of data collected for distinct purposes.

One of the possible objections to this stance is that there are discrepancies in the agenda and the timetable of educational and other institutions. The response may be that educational behaviors evolve slowly, whether individual or collective. To the extent that one is obliged to accept the postulate that gender disparities result from attitudes and behaviors embedded in tradition, the first task should be to use the body of existing data to ascertain the pace at which their respective components do change.

But, to plead in favor of changes in the politics of the measurements used in this regard, amounts to pleading in favor of the postulates on which these politics are built. To rely on the existing rates is to postulate the absence of any significant layer between individuals and schools. It is implicitly to postulate the feasibility of one single description and prescription and hence to affirm the postulate of the preeminence of a macroscopic solution.

Yet, everybody knows that the marketing of a specific product or of a particular service requires the adoption of differentiated strategies and the recognition that markets are segmented. This line of thought suggests that Fanon (1960) was not acting only as a wise political strategist in castigating the abstract universalism attached to the concept of Negritude and in underlining the fact that the forms and the extent of oppression differ for example between African-Americans who are citizens of the United States, Brazilian citizens of African origin, people from Africa living in the West Indies, citizens of African countries who have been subjected to distinct forms of colonialism and finally, Africans who have migrated to Europe. *Mutatis mutandis*, an analogous argument should be developed about women and the hurdles they face in their effort to achieve the same educational opportunities as their male counterparts.

Thus Fanon's stance is not exclusively political. By suggesting that modes of action, and hence explanations, are partial and relative, he asserts that analyses are valid to the extent that their authors are consciously and willfully grounding them in the notion of contingency. In the social sciences as in ethics, humility stands as a prerequisite. It is about time for international experts to understand that universalism might be more subtle than they imagine.

References

Blau, P., and R. Duncan, 1967. *The American Occupational Structure.* New York: Wiley and Sons.

Carpentier, R., and R. Clignet, 1998. *Du temps pour les sciences sociales.,* Paris: L'Harmattan.

Charmes, J., 1993. *Suivi des caractéristiques et comportements des ménages et des groupes vulnérables en situation d'ajustement structurel 1990-1992 (ELAM2).* Projet BEN/87/023: Cotonou.

Duru, B., M. A. Kieffer and C. Marry, 2001. "Dynamique des Scolarités." *Revue Française de Sociologie* 42 (2): 251-80.

Fanon, F., 1960. *Les Damnés de la terre.* Paris: Maspero

Goody, E., 1982. *Parenthood and Social Reproduction: Fostering and Occupational Roles in West Africa.* Cambridge: Cambridge University Press.

Greenhalg, S., 1985. "Sexual Stratification: The Other Side of Growth with Equity." *Population and Development Review* 11: 265-314.

Lévi-Strauss, C., 1958. *Anthropologie structurale.* Paris: Plon.

Leclerc, G., 1979. *L'observation de l'homme.* Paris: Le Seuil.

Linares, A., 1967. "Évolution de l'école et des idéologies scolaires en Espagne." In *Éducation développement et démocratie,* ed. R. Castel and J.-C. Passeron, 151-80. Paris: Mouton.

Merton, R., 1973. *Sociology of Science.* Chicago: University of Chicago Press.

Pilon, M., 1996. "Les femmes chefs de ménage en Afrique: État des connaissances." In *Femmes du sud, chefs de famille,* ed. J. Bisilliat, 235-56. Paris: Karthala.

Robinson, W., 1950. "Ecological correlations and the behavior of American Individuals." *American Sociological Review* 15: 145-64.

Ryder, N., 1965. "The Concept of Cohort in the Study of Social Change." *American Sociological Review* 30: 840-61.

Solloway, S., 1996. *Born to Rebel.* New York: Vintage.

CHAPTER 3

POLITICS OF EXCLUSION IN HIGHER EDUCATION: THE INADEQUACY OF GENDER ISSUES IN THE GLOBALIZATION DEBATES

Teboho Moja

Introduction

A forum addressing gender issues in higher education faces new challenges that require the same questions to be raised, but they must be put in a different form. The significant absence of gender issues in the debates on globalization and the restructuring that is taking place in education and in the workplace is quite noteworthy. It must be remembered constantly that exclusion is not always open but that there are subtle discriminatory practices even in circumstances in which there are policies in place governing appointment and promotional practices, peer reviews and publications. It is not a surprise that a joint World Bank and UNESCO report on higher education reform in developing countries—aimed at helping countries reform their higher education systems to be responsive to the demands of the global knowledge-based economy—only refers to women as part of the disadvantaged groups and does not specifically address gender issues in a document targeting policy makers and implementers (World Bank 2000).

Issues that need to be raised include the impact of globalization on women in higher education. Globalizing economies have raised the price tag for higher education, as rates of return for higher education have increased[1]. The shifts in the role seen for higher education in the new global economy make higher education institutions more knowledge intensive. Institutions that

---

[1] Note that the rate of return analysis for higher education has been abandoned by the World Bank to be replaced by World Bank acknowledgement of the centrality of quality higher education for development with a focus on science and technology as well as the inclusion of women in science and technology education.

recognize these changes in focus attract new types of learners especially in the field of knowledge management to help foster national development appropriate to this new technology and information era. It is safe to assume, even without data, that these new types of learners mainly consist of males, not females. The assumption is based on the historical exclusion and/or under-representation of women especially in fields such as science and technology and in the corporate world.

There is a sense of urgency for reforms in higher education and some scholars attribute this to the global changes in the socio-economic and political environment. "Globalization" has become a catchall term for the trend, and many are still struggling to understand its meaning and definition. Unquestionably, it has had tremendous impact on all sectors of society including education and higher education in particular. Its impact on society requires that all human potential be unleashed by investing in human capital. While this discussion does not focus on the debate about globalization, the changes referred to in higher education include: the increased use of technology in teaching, research, and administration; the restructuring and re-prioritization of programs, the changes in hiring practices, the changing student population and their needs, and the alternative sources of funding available to institutions.

Restructuring Higher Education and Emerging Gender Issues

Globalization has projected higher education to center stage because of the role that higher education must play in social and economic development. The global economy is knowledge intensive and requires laborers with high-level skills. Higher education is under pressure to produce high-level skilled labor as well as skills in accessing, producing and using knowledge. There is pressure on higher education to produce skilled human resources. In some instances, the changes taking place in response to this pressure have had a negative impact on women in their roles as faculty, staff and students.

New patterns of employment mobility and major workplace changes are emerging in those nations which are part of the globalized economic, social, and political environment. The registration of students at multiple sites or institutions and the fact that faculty are taking positions with multiple employers raises new issues as to who takes advantage of those opportunities as well as who gets exploited in those arrangements. Globalization has also had an effect on the workloads of academics. A case study in South Africa indicates that Blacks and women are opting out of academic careers (Saunders 2001). The reconstruction of the workplace has led to more outsourcing of jobs, and that has had negative implications for workers at the lower levels of employment where there is often a concentration of women with low-level skills. This is an emerging form of exclusion as a result of the impact of global changes on higher education. Higher education reforms need to address the issue of discarded labor, which mainly involves women, and how women can acquire new skills where priorities are skewed more to high-level skills. There is obviously a growing need to address the effects of the market on staffing and student profiles in higher education institutions as well as on conditions of service owing to the changes taking place globally.

Many new global knowledge partnerships and research networks continue to be male-dominated in areas that are historically gender biased such as research and consulting. For example, research in South Africa remains controlled by white males, as indicated by figures that show that men produced 83% of the scientific output between 1990 and 1998 (Cloete 2002). Women have not featured prominently in knowledge production through mode 1 and there is concern over their under-representation in the new knowledge networks that are being formed or what is referred to as mode 2 of knowledge production, to keep up with the need for the output of knowledge: Gibbons (1998) addresses these new modes of knowledge production.

Governments are expanding their higher education systems as a strategy for attracting foreign capital. Carnoy (2000) argues that the pressure for expansion of higher education systems could work in favor of women because there is more demand for access to higher education by women and other marginalized groups. The implications are that women will access higher education programs that are becoming less marketable and will fill places that have been vacated as their male counterparts move on to programs that provide highly marketable skills. Slaughter and Leslie have termed this trend "academic capitalism"; it is created by globalization, because new structures, incentives and rewards are created for some aspects of academic careers (Morrow and Torres 2000). These new forms of exclusion are subtler than the discriminatory practices that were more overt in their exclusion in the rates of women's participation in higher education. It must be acknowledged that there is growth—though not enough—in the rates of women's participation in higher education. The challenge is to make sure that opportunities are created for participation in the new emerging fields of the knowledge economy.

Higher education institutions in this modern age of knowledge produce information and disseminate it for the development of the knowledge economy. They play a role in the social and scientific development of nation-states including those in Africa. Higher education has always contributed significantly to development, but the impact of globalization has contributed to putting the role of higher education programs under scrutiny. As a result, there is more demand for accountability on the part of higher education institutions, but accountability has been narrowly defined mainly to refer to demands for quality education without any call for ensuring that there is equal participation from men and women in all programs and activities.

Globalization has led to the emergence of new challenges for higher education, and as these matters are addressed, gender issues are not part of the discussions. In addition, traditional higher education providers face new competition from distance education and for-profit providers, and higher education's role as the sole producer of knowledge is contested by other agencies that have claimed a stake in knowledge production. The private sector has targeted instruction in some areas as a profitable market worth billions of dollars. In many developing countries the private sector is competing with public institutions for students. The World Trade Organization (WTO) is currently discussing and negotiating to make the provision of higher education services part of the General Agreements on Trade in Service (GATS). The implications are complex and unknown, and gender issues need to be made part of the agenda in these debates.

Higher education is expected to contribute to economic development for the benefit of society at large. Higher education institutions particularly in developing countries have largely remained elite institutions that have failed to focus adequately on the science and technology requirements of the information revolution that require increased female participation rates and better gender representation. Most of these systems continue sexist practices that foster gender inequality and remain bastions of privileged groups and classes.

The politics of exclusion are both complex and subtle. It would be hard to identify overt proponents of exclusionist politics for women in higher education, but, overall women, remain under-represented. Agencies operating across borders have called for broadening access and improving participation of women at all levels of education.[2] National policies address these issues; international agencies have organized conferences leading to the adoption of world declarations on gender equality in education at all levels, and inclusion of women in all fields of study. Nonetheless the inequalities remain. In the last

---

[2] See for example the Convention Against Discrimination in Education adopted by UNESCO in 1960, and the Convention on the Rights of a Child adopted by the U.N. in 1989. UNESCO General Conferences and many other international bodies have issued related statements.

two decades, the sector has experienced unprecedented growth, but women remain under-represented. Despite international, regional, and national declarations, policies, and the good intentions of many activists, the problems persist.

The importance of women in development is almost universally acknowledged. It is therefore crucial to understand factors that hamper women's contribution to national progress. It is in this context that this paper focuses on some of the problem areas that need attention if women are to take their place in society and make a contribution toward national development. The aim here is to show the extent to which inequities still exist in education at both the lower and higher education levels. The injustice in higher education has its roots in the school sector. Fewer girls than boys have access to school, and they have higher dropout rates than boys. Girls tend to be also sexually abused in schools, with great detriment to their academic performance. These are some of the factors that influence female participation and impact the supply pipeline for higher education.

Gender Inequalities in Schools – Where Are the Girls?

It can well be argued that the exclusion of women in the globalization debates has its roots in the entire education system in Africa. Gender inequality remains a problem in all sectors of education, in certain disciplines and programs. In 47 out of the 52 countries identified as having a gender gap of 5% or more at the primary school level, girls are identified as the disadvantaged group (UNESCO 2002). Gender under-representation in higher education has its roots in the school sector and remains a concern of organizations such as the United Nations and its agencies. Table I indicates the scale of the problem with figures of girls' net enrollment ratios (NER) that are 85% or below for the age cohort in African countries. More than 50% of the countries identified are in Africa. The bottom range for a net enrollment ratio for girls is 7% in a country like Somalia.

Concern over the under-representation of women in education by supranational agencies such as UNESCO, other UN agencies, policy makers, and national education organizations are based on the need for equity, justice, and democracy in society. There is also concern with issues of development, i.e. women's personal growth as well as their contribution to societal progress. There is evidence that higher education qualifications, particularly lead to a better quality of life, and that women are clearly disadvantaged by not being educated or by stopping their education at the lower levels.

There is minimal change in the figures recorded in the five-year period between 1995 and 1999 despite UNESCO efforts to have access to education for all, through a declaration to achieve "Education for All by the Year 2000" (EFA 2000). The declaration was adopted at the World Conference on Education held in 1990 in Jomtien, Thailand. Table II indicates that the regional averages for girls' net enrollment ratios for their age cohort have gone up in all regions and are higher than the ratios for boys despite the number of girls that are still out of school. An issue of concern is that as the inclusion of girls in education is promoted, care should also be taken to make sure that there is gender representation and not just girls' representation in education.

Table I: List of African Countries with N.E.R. below 85%

Version 21/12/01

Countries with N.E.R. of Girls 85% or Less	Year	Net Primary Education Ratio			Number out of School (000s)	
		Girls	Boys	Gender Gap	Girls	Total
Angola*	1996	48	52	4	416	800
Benin	1997	50	75	25	278	413
Burkina Faso	1997	28	40	12	732	1,348
Burundi	1998	37	38	1	363	725
Cameroon	1989	71	82	11	360	373
Central African Republic	1997	27	51	24	223	351
Chad	1997	39	65	26	411	645
Congo, Dem. Rep. of	1997	51	66	15	2,252	3,815
Côte d'Ivoire	1996	47	63	16	686	1,168
Djibouti	1997	28	39	11	37	70
Eritrea	1998	35	40	5	163	315
Ethiopia	1997	28	43	15	3,708	6,607
Gabon	1998	83	82	0	16	32
Gambia	1998	55	64	9	43	77
Ghana*	1998	74	74	0	395	791
Guinea	1997	30	49	19	441	776
Guinea-Bissau	1987	32	58	26	63	102
Lesotho	1997	65	55	-10	63	144
Liberia	1999	31	43	12	137	266
Mali	1997	33	47	14	618	1,107
Mauritania	1995	53	61	8	102	187
Morocco	1998	64	77	13	720	1,204
Mozambique	1999	40	47	7	875	1,636
Niger	1996	19	30	11	737	1,407
Nigeria	1996	33	38	5	6,398	12,484
Rwanda	1997	68	67	-1	230	469
Senegal	1997	55	65	10	346	620
Sierra Leone*	2000	40	42	2	253	491
Somalia	1985	7	13	6	893	1,734
Sudan	1998	37	43	6	1,916	3,715
Tanzania	1998	57	56	-1	1,439	2,939
Togo	1997	61	85	24	148	206
Uganda	1997	83	92	9	408	611

*Instead of Net primary enrolment ratio the net primary attendance ratio has been indicated

Source: UNESCO Education News, 01/24/02.
www.unesco.org/education/news_en/210101_background.shtml

Teboho Moja

Table II: Regional Summaries of NERs as an Average from 1995 to 1999

Regional Summaries (from 1995 to 1999 data)				Out of School (000s)	
				Girls	Total
Sub-Saharan Africa	57.6	49.7	8	27,031	50,003
Middle East and North Africa	84.9	75.8	9	6,009	9,711
South Asia	78.7	65.6	13	26,332	43,397
East Asia and Pacific	97.4	96.0	1	3,459	5,995
Latin America and Caribbean	91.2	91.4	0	3,167	5,937
CEE/CIS and Baltic States	93.1	89.6	4	1,590	2,690
Industrialized Countries	95.4	95.8	0	1,239	2,547
Developing Countries	83.4	76.3	7	67,718	112,926
Least Developed Countries	64.3	55.2	9	23,840	43,277
World	84.7	78.4	6	70,072	118,016

Source: UNESCO Education News, 01/24/02.
www.unesco.org/education/news_en/210101_background.shtml

In April 2000, a U.N. meeting held in Dakar to assess progress made toward education for all mandated UNICEF to lead programs in support of the U.N. Girls' Education Initiative (UNGEI). The main goals of the initiative are to encourage girls' participation in education especially in the 61 countries identified as having enrollment figures below 85%. The expressed aim was to achieve gender parity in attendance at primary and secondary levels by 2005.

Under-representation of girls in primary and secondary schools has implications for girls' representation at higher educational levels. The supply is reduced through under-representation, low pass rates in school, and inadequate opportunities to study subjects prerequisite to pursuing certain careers, especially in the natural sciences and technology.

Gender Inequalities in Higher Education: Where Are the Women?

The second half of the last century saw a historically unprecedented expansion in higher education all over the world. Participation rates increased from 13 million in 1960 to 82 million in 1995 (UNESCO 1998). Despite growth in this sector, women remain under-represented as students as well as faculty, researchers, and senior administrators.

There is a lack of representation in decision-making structures in higher education institutions. Human development statistics indicate that only 33% of women are in higher education in Sub-Saharan Africa in comparison to men. Figures indicating under-representation in graduate studies in science, engineering, technology (SET), and senior management positions are even more striking. A pyramid best illustrates women's representation in higher education. In society, women often make up over half of the population and as they enter school they are still fairly represented, but then the figure tapers to the tip especially at levels such as university presidents. The South African higher education system has had major reforms, especially in its governance structures and management. In the last decade, black male university presidents have replaced the majority of white male presidents. But in 1999, only 4 of the 36 higher education institution presidents were women and in 2002 only 3 were women. Two of the women presidents moved on to take international jobs in the US and the UK. There is a significant increase in the number of women occupying second and third tier positions in South African universities.

South Africa is one of the few countries that have managed to increase women's enrollment figures within a short period of time. Female enrollment figures there went up from 43% in 1993 to 52% in 1999 (Cloete and Bunting 2000: 17). However, the 1998 data indicate that professional and senior positions in higher education remained dominated by white males. Most of the data available in South Africa tend to focus on race and less on gender in higher education institutions. Women remain in the majority in low-level administration positions and non-professional categories. Overall, the number of women in faculty positions rose from 30% in 1992 to 35% in 1998. The increase was much more pronounced in historically disadvantaged institutions (HDIs), i.e. black institutions where vacancies were created by the departure of male faculty for positions in government and the private sector soon after the first democratic elections.

Globalization has been characterized by inequities within countries and between countries as well as by new forms of inclusion and exclusion. Higher education is one of the sub-sectors in education that has been directly impacted by changes in the global economy. There are scholars who point out the positive effects of globalization pressures on higher education institutions as an increased opportunity to open up access for women and other marginalized groups. They argue that the information and communications technology has had tremendous impact on education by increasing opportunities for more women to access higher education through distance education, and that women can therefore be reached through nontraditional methods of teaching at higher education levels. There are other issues to be raised regarding nontraditional access to higher education that will not be covered in this paper. The globalized economy needs to be supported by more highly skilled human power. In order to provide the economy with the necessary females in the work force, the opportunities for women to enter higher education need to be increased. Access to education needs to entail high-quality programs and real possibilities of success.

Increased Access: Different Forms of Exclusions

Historically, the last two decades have been characterized by unprecedented expansion in higher education. However, increased access has not translated into increased opportunities for women in higher education institutions. There is a need to study enrollment patterns in a variety of programs, particularly those that are historically male dominated such as science, technology, and engineering. It is also important to study the success rates of female students in higher education in general. Table III, below, indicates that for the world at large and for developed countries the gender gap has decreased as enrollments have increased, but for Africa and for developing countries in general the gender gap has increased despite an expansion in the sector.

Table III: Gross Enrollment Ratios in Higher Education

World	Males	Females	Difference
1970	11.2	7.1	4.1
1997	18.1	16.2	1.9
Africa	Males	Females	Difference
1970	2.4	0.7	1.4
1997	8.6	5.2	3.4
Developing Countries	Males	Females	Difference
1970	1.6	0.3	1.3
1997	4.6	1.7	3.9
Developed Countries	Males	Females	Difference
1970	31.8	20.3	11.5
1997	47.7	55.7	-8.0

Source: UNESCO Institute for Statistics,II.S.5

It is most significant that there are instances where women students are starting to outnumber males in higher education institutions but are concentrated in programs that do not offer highly marketable skills for the new economy. The new economy requires information-literate workers who know how to access, evaluate, and use knowledge in a responsible way, and also how to manage knowledge.

Women also remain under-represented in the teaching profession in higher education institutions. However, in South Africa the current reforms have increased the number of women in academia and in administrative positions. Table IV indicates that representation ranges between 9.5% in Ghana, which is the lowest amongst the Commonwealth universities to 28% in Swaziland, which is higher than the average for the Commonwealth of just below 24%.

Table IV: Full–time Academic Staff in Commonwealth African Universities – 1997/98

Country	Women	%	Men	%	Unspecified	%	Total
Ghana	78	9.5	735	89.6	7	0.9	820
Kenya	72	13.0	445	80.2	38	6.8	555
Lesotho	58	23.9	182	74.9	3	1.2	243
Nigeria	893	13.6	5508	83.6	188	2.8	6589
Sierra Leone*	13	15.3	71	83.5	1	1.2	85
South Africa	1277	26.1	3468	70.8	150	3.1	4895
Swaziland	60	28.0	148	69.2	6	2.8	214
Tanzania	89	11.0	710	88.0	8	1.0	807
Uganda	26	19.3	107	79.3	2	1.4	135
Zambia	71	10.9	550	84.5	30	4.6	651
Zimbabwe	9	9.7	81	87.1	3	3.2	93

* The numbers are for Njala College only. The same applies for Table V.

Source: Adapted from Helen Lund – A Single Sex Profession, Commonwealth Higher Education   Management Services (CHEMS), September 1998.

The impact of globalization on higher education institutions can be observed through the increased level of professionalism in the management of institutions. Unfortunately, women remain under-represented in these high-level professional jobs and are also less represented in senior academic positions within institutions. At the bottom or entry level, the percentages of women in institutions are generally closer to those of male colleagues. For example, amongst the Commonwealth universities in Africa, only South Africa has a high record of about 45% at this level and the next is Swaziland at 35.7%. The lowest on record is about 10% in countries such as Ghana, Tanzania, Zambia, and Zimbabwe. Representation figures drop drastically at higher levels of employment such as at the professorial level and in institutional chief

Teboho Moja

executive positions. The figures at the professorial level (equivalent to senior professor in the US system) range from zero% in countries such as Kenya, Lesotho, Sierra Leone, and Swaziland to 16.7% in Uganda, i.e., 2 professors out of a total of 12 (see Table V).

Table V: Professors in Commonwealth African Universities – 1997/98

Country	Women	%	Men	%	Total
Ghana	1	10.0	9	90.0	10
Kenya	0	0	9	100	9
Lesotho	0	0	10	100	10
Nigeria	40	5.0	762	95.0	802
Sierra Leone	0	0	3	100	3
South Africa	73	8.0	844	92.0	917
Swaziland	0	0	8	100	8
Tanzania	5	8.6	53	91.4	58
Uganda	2	16.7	10	83.3	12
Zambia	2	8.3	22	91.7	24
Zimbabwe	0	0	4	100	4

Source: Adapted from Helen Lund, "A Single Sex Profession," Commonwealth Higher Education Management Services (CHEMS), September 1998.

Women scholars, women's studies departments, and organizations concerned with issues of gender equity in higher education have produced research that indicates the barriers to success in higher education for faculty and for students. There is also research that indicates barriers to graduate studies as well as studies in science, technology and engineering (Margolis and Fischer, 2002). The list seems to get longer and more overwhelming each time research is produced on women's status in higher education. The next section focuses on three areas from the long list of issues that are considered crucial for addressing gender concerns in the education sector, viz., the need for gender-specific data, the problem of organizational culture, and the lack of commitment to change on the part of those responsible for progress at political levels as well as in institutions.

Organizational Culture
Are Institutions of Learning Safe and Inclusive?

Exclusion from education is not always obvious, but women have suffered from various forms of such injustice. In this section it will be useful to focus on factors that are not always openly discussed because they are deemed to be too sensitive. In advancing an argument for increasing women's participation in higher education, it is most important to ask the question as to whether the institutions provide a safe and friendly environment for women to participate in learning or to advance their careers there. Organizational culture is one of the reasons often cited as an impediment or obstacle for women to succeed in higher education as students, and their lack of upward mobility as faculty. There is general consensus on the need to create a woman-friendly environment in higher education institutions.

The culture in higher education institutions mirrors the culture of the society within which they are located. It can be persuasively argued that society reinforces acceptance of practices that often blight the lives of those who eventually seek careers in higher education or enter advanced education as students. For example, sexual abuse and harassment is prevalent in some societies and such practices are not adequately addressed as unacceptable. In primary and secondary schools, these practices may lead to girls dropping out of school or under-performing. As a result, the supply of female students to participate in higher education diminishes. The following is extracted from a report by Human Rights Watch (2001).

> A thirteen-year-old girl dropped out of school after being gang-raped by classmates. A fifteen-year-old dropped out after being sexually assaulted by a teacher. A fourteen-year-old under-performs because of harassment in school that is ignored by teachers. A mother of a nine-year-old feels that her daughter is not safe at school after she was gang raped by older classmates."

One would wish that such statements were not true, but one knows they are, and also that such practices extend to the higher education sector. To address the problem it is important to study it throughout the entire education sector rather than in a single sub-sector. In addressing the issue of equal access to education, most of the literature focuses on factors that are obstacles to accessing education and less on obstacles within the educational system itself. Documented impediments within the school include gender insensitive curricula and teachers' attitudes toward girls. This is true particularly in science, mathematics or technology-related courses.   Less information is available on abuse and sexual harassment as obstacles to achievement within schools.

A report by Human Rights Watch (an organization based in the U.S.) titled "Sexual Violence against Girls in South African Schools" is one of the few reports that actually address the issue at the school level (Human Rights Watch 2001). Sexual violence in education continues to be a major obstacle for women to access education and to contribute effectively to national development in many countries.   The South African Human Rights Commission has recently prioritized investigation of sexual violence and human rights abuses in schools after realizing that on average 500 cases of child abuse by teachers are reported every month to the Medical Research Council.[3]   The figures are not a surprise when one looks at the rape levels within the broader society in South Africa, especially the surge in rape cases of infants fueled by the myth that having sex with a virgin cures AIDS. Sexual abuse by fellow students and by teachers has been a dominant news item in the South African media.   The government recently issued a statement that a multiparty meeting would be convened to discuss the problem. One of the major campaigns in South Africa on restoring the "Culture of Learning, Teaching, and Service" (COLTS) has emphasized the need to make schools safe and to create a safe environment for effective learning.

Sexual violence, abuse, and crime at the primary and secondary levels of schooling are one of the reasons fewer women gain access to higher education. There is evidence that abuse at school could lead girls to drop out of school or fail to perform well at school. These factors contribute to lower numbers of students seeking access to higher education institutions. Those who pursue higher education after being sexually abused in school are likely to have contacted sexually transmitted diseases, including the AIDS virus. Reports indicate that high numbers of students in higher education institutions especially in Sub-Saharan Africa have the deadly virus. A study by Kelly (2001) on the AIDS situation at six universities in Africa revealed that even in the absence of records on the cause of death, there were increased mortality rates amongst students, staff, and faculty and that the numbers were rising.

Sexual harassment in higher education is reported to be serious and many institutions have not developed policies and strategies to address the issue. To date there seem to be two types of institutional approaches that have

---

[3] Child abuse here includes corporal punishment and sexual harassment; see Medical Research Council report, www.news24.co.za, 01/27/02. 2:56

emerged in dealing with issues relating to sexual aggression within higher education institutions. The approaches are not mutually exclusive. The first approach involves developing sexual harassment policies for the institution as well as the establishment of mechanisms and structures for dealing with specific cases. The second approach entails mainstreaming gender issues in the curriculum to sensitize the entire institutional community to issues of gender relations.

Some of the initiatives that address gender inequities in higher education are programs similar to the ones being implemented at Makerere University and Dar-Es-Salaam. These universities have adopted a two-pronged strategy with financial support from the Carnegie Corporation. They have received grants to design and implement an undergraduate women's scholarship alongside their other strategies for increasing women's participation in higher education. The universities are also implementing programs to mainstream gender activities into the university strategic plans.

Other strategies have been adopted at national and international levels. For example the Forum for African Women Educationalists (FAWE) has targeted national Action Plans for implementing UNESCO's declaration for "Education for All 2000." FAWE is currently working with teams developing National Action plans for Kenya, Malawi, Zambia, Ethiopia, Tanzania, Uganda, Mali, Senegal, and Guinea on strategies for mainstreaming gender issues. FAWE has also hosted a General Assembly on "Dealing with Sexual Harassment in Tertiary Institutions in Africa" (Mlama 2001). In most cases, sexual harassment policies are in place, but there is an absence of appropriate procedures that make women feel comfortable reporting individual cases.

Gender Disaggregated Data as a Strategy for Becoming Inclusive

The issue of the importance of gender-disaggregated data has been raised on numerous occasions. This need should be underscored, and it could well be argued that there is a need for institutions to generate gender-specific data that will enable policy makers to respond to the new demands of globalization. Over the years, there has been a dearth of gender-specific information on higher education in the form of data from institutions and from government sources. The issue was also raised as a major concern by FAWE at the "General Assembly of the Association of African Universities" (AAU) in February 2001, and again at a policy forum on "Innovations in African Higher Education" sponsored by the Ford Foundation in October 2001. It is argued that gender-disaggregated data in higher education would highlight problem areas that are detrimental to women's participation in higher education as students, administrators, and faculty. There is a need not only to argue for the generation of these specific data but also to seek further data that will indicate whether higher education is developing the human capital among women that is needed for the new global economy.

Gender-specific data should provide information that will help in addressing new challenges posed by globalization to the higher education sector. The data collected at the institutional level should relate to the real world outside of institutions. For example, there is a need for data on women's employment, remuneration, and upward mobility after graduation. There is also a need for qualitative data on a new cadre of women who are breaking the glass ceiling to be appointed to chief executive officer positions in higher education institutions as well as in the private sector. Such data would contribute to an understanding of the factors that make it possible for women to succeed in higher education institutions and in the private sector. Preliminary data on their backgrounds indicate that the majority of them come from elite families and that their advantaged positions within society and family have contributed indirectly to their success. Similar data and research would signal factors that contribute to success in higher education and assist in the development of policies and strategies that would ensure women's upward mobility as well as their contribution to decision making and development.

At an institutional level, some progress has been made in the last decade to generate gender-disaggregated data that helps institutions identify problem areas in need of attention. FAWE has developed an instrument for collecting qualitative gender-sensitive data that it has shared with members of the AAU. Similar data need to be generated at the level of national systems in order to address the problem holistically. The Gender Advisory Board of UNESCO has also developed a toolkit on gender indicators in engineering, science, and technology. In South Africa, data on race most often takes precedence over gender-specific data. Yet data on both of these socially significant variables are needed. It is hard to access gender-specific data on employment patterns in higher education, research publication, work loads, student admissions in different programs, and success rates.

At an international level, the problem is that the data that are generated are often inconsistent owing to gaps left by the reporting countries and missing data on some of the years. This problem makes it difficult to track emerging patterns in the participation rates of women students and the mobility of staff and faculty to senior positions. Data available from the UNESCO Institute for Statistics on researchers and technicians are gender-disaggregated but the years of reporting are inconsistent so it is difficult to determine whether there has been an increase in women participating in research or serving as technicians.

Organizations concerned with gender issues do attempt to generate data on women in higher education, but their scope is often limited. There is insufficient data covering higher education as defined to include all studies beyond schooling at the lower levels, and there is no data on higher education participation in private institutions, especially the for-profit institutions that often do not have to report their data to education departments. FAWE commissioned a study that presented a statistical overview of women's participation in four African universities: Kenyatta University, University of Dar-Es-Salaam, Abdou Moumouni University, and Makerere University. For students, the study focused on admissions, program distribution, graduation rates, graduate studies, and residence allocations. For faculty and staff, the study focused on ranks in appointments. Similar studies are needed for all institutions of higher education in Africa.

The Commonwealth Higher Education Management Service (CHEMS) produced statistics that were limited to faculty and staff at Commonwealth universities. The CHEMS report concluded that women are still under-represented, especially in academic and senior administrative positions in the Commonwealth universities. In South Africa, a new cadre of senior women administrators has recently been appointed and it is hoped that they will move up the ranks to occupy the most senior positions of the institutions and influence policies that would ensure the representation of women in education.

Excellent Policies: What about Political Will?

International organizations and nation-states have developed policies and strategies to address the issue of women's representation in higher education, but change is coming about very slowly. Numerous declarations and strategic plans on gender parity exist at the school level, along with declarations on increasing women's participation in higher education, and on equity in science, engineering, and technology. There is an initiative to reach gender parity in primary and secondary education by 2005. The goals are articulated in "Millennium Development Goals," the Dakar "Framework for Action," and "Gender Equality and Education For All by 2015."

At the national level, the "South African National Plan for Higher Education" by the Department of Education (2001) is one example of a systemic attempt to address the inequities in higher education programs. The plan states that "the spread of women students across different program areas is uneven with female students clustered in the humanities and under-represented in science, engineering, technology, business and commerce, and in post-graduate programs." The Department has also developed a "Strategy for Mathematics, Science, and Technology" specifying that there will be quotas, special incentives for girls, special schools for girls, and other special incentives as a way of ensuring that girls have access to science-related education. School safety has also been targeted as a project of the Department of Education in conjunction with other ministries. These are just a few examples of well-articulated policies addressing gender issues in education at the national level.

The question remains as to why in the presence of such good policies very marginal changes are made. But, it is well known that policies are only as good as their enforcement. Developing and proclaiming policies seems much easier than implementing them. In most cases, policies are not developed into implementation plans with targets and dates to ensure that intended changes take place. Policy statements seem to temporarily satisfy political needs and silence advocates of women's issues. There seems to be no political will to drive change by developing specific programs to ensure that policies are enforced or incentives are developed to encourage implementation of policies.

Another problem in implementing policy seems to be a lack of resources, both human and non-human, to implement these policies. Personal experience suggests that there is more interest on the part of funding agencies in providing the necessary resources for policy formulation processes than in providing resources for policy implementation. Given the lack of political will and the shortage of resources, it is clear that unless serious interventions are made there are not going to be any significant changes in the participation of women in higher education.

Conclusion

Exclusion from higher education subsequently means lack of participation in key processes in society, for example, participation in decision-making structures that impact development. If African countries are serious about addressing development then they need to increase women's participation in education and particularly in higher education. If women acquire the high-level skills required for economic development, then this will increase their productivity levels in their respective countries. There is a correlation between participation rates in higher education and economic development. Overall participation rates in higher education in Africa are very low and need to be increased to levels that would make a difference. Exclusion from participating in higher education impacts negatively on development efforts of African countries. In making efforts to raise participation rates, planners could formulate strategies that would ensure that women are given the opportunity to contribute to development.

There is a need to address the absence of mechanisms for providing training and for filling the skills gap alongside mechanisms to address equity problems. Strategies need to be developed to ensure that women are not excluded once more as the world moves toward a global economy. There is a need for increased access in general, and even more need in some of the key areas that contribute to development.

There are tried and tested innovative strategies at different levels that have been used to increase women's access to higher education in other countries; these could be adapted by all higher education institutions in African countries. For example, changing a hostile environment can improve opportunities for women to participate in science programs. Changing the environment has proved to encourage women to pursue careers that are historically dominated by males (Read 2002)

Sweden's experience provides evidence that if there is political will and institutions and government work co-operatively on addressing the issue of under-representation of women faculty in higher education, then the situation can be turned around within a short period of time. The Swedish strategy set specific targets, created affirmative action positions for faculty and for graduate studies, and mainstreamed gender issues while promoting gender research

(Olsson 1998). There are numerous examples of success in addressing the issue at the institutional level as well. For example, a recently released book on a case study of the department of computer science at the University of California at Los Angeles indicates success in raising women's participation to 40% within a short period of time (Read 2002).

Some progress has been made in addressing gender issues in education, but this is not sufficient if there is to be a serious commitment to making sure that women contribute effectively to development. There is a need to continue to raise gender issues in education so that changes in education will be made in such a way as to reflect the real changes taking place in society owing to the globalization of the world's economies.

References

Brock, R., 2002. "Two Professors Offer Advice on Making Computer Science More Open to Women." *Chronicle of Higher Education,* January 25. *http://chronicle.com/free/2002/01/2002012501.htm*   (Accessed 01/20/2002)

Carnoy, M., 2000. "Globalization and Higher Education." *Perspectives in Education* 18 (3).

Cloete, N., et al., eds., 2002. *Transformation in Higher Education: Global Pressures and Local Realities in South Africa.* Cape Town, South Africa: Juta & Co.

Department of Education, 2001. "National Plan For Higher Education in South Africa." Department of Education, Government of South Africa, February. http://education.pwv.gov.za/DoE_Sites/Higher_Education/HE_Plan/national_plan_for_higher_educati.htm (Accessed 02/20/2001)

___, 2001. "National Strategy for Mathematics, Science and Technical Education in General and Further Education and Training." Department of Education: Government of South Africa, November. *http://education.pwv.gov.za/DoE_Sites/Maths%20and%20Science/Final-doc.pdf* (Accessed 01/20/2002)

Gibbons, M., 1998. *Higher Education in the 21st Century.* Washington: World Bank.

Human Rights Watch Report, 2001. *Scared at School: Sexual Violence against Girls in South African Schools.*

Karega, R. G. M., 2001. Statistical Overview on Girls' Education at the University Level. Paper commissioned by the Forum for African Women Educationalists (FAWE).

Kelly, M. J., 2001. "Challenging the Challenger: Understanding and Expanding the Response of Universities in Africa to HIV/AIDS. Report commissioned by the ADEA Working Group on Higher Education, March.

Mlama, P., 2001. "Gender Equity Programming in Higher Education." Paper presented at the Ford Foundation Policy Forum, Nairobi, October.

Margolis, J., and A. Fischer, 2002. *Unlocking the Clubhouse: Women in Computing.* Cambridge, Mass.: M.I.T. Press.

Masanja, V., et al., 2001 (February). "Female Participation in African Universities: Issues of Concern and Possible Action. Paper presented at the General Assembly of the African Association of Universities, Nairobi.

Morrow, R. A., and C. A. Torres, 2000. In *Globalization and Education: Critical Perspectives*, ed. N. C. Burbules and C. A. Torres. New York: Routledge.

Olsson, B. 1998. "How to Make Universities Gender Aware: The Swedish Experience." Paper presented at the World Conference on Higher Education. Thematic Debate on Women and Higher Education: Issues and Perspectives, Paris, October.

Saunders, S., 2001. Case study. Paper presented at a conference titled "Globalisation and Higher Education: Views from the South," Cape Town, March 27-29.

World Bank, 2000. "Higher Education in Developing Countries: Peril or Promise." Washington, D. C.: World Bank Task Force on Higher Education and Society

CHAPTER 4

WOMEN'S PARTICIPATION IN HIGHER LEVELS OF LEARNING IN AFRICA

Ruth Meena

Introduction

Africa's educational system is pyramidal, with a broad base at the primary level tapering precipitously through the secondary level to a narrow apex at the tertiary level. The gender gap in Sub-Saharan Africa increases in severity with each higher level of education. Most African countries have made some significant progress in bridging a gender gap at the primary and secondary levels, but the gender gap at the tertiary level, including university education, remains large. At the tertiary level, females are grossly under-represented, with a gross tertiary enrolment gender ratio of 0.22%, and proportionately fewer females than males are enrolled in science curricula. Females make up 34%, 22% and 12% of primary, secondary, and tertiary level students (UNDP 2000).

This study focuses on female participation in tertiary and higher levels of education in Africa. Africa is so full of diversities that one cannot claim to do full justice in generalizing about factors that affect levels of female participation in the educational process. While attempts have been made to select a few cases, it will be necessary to make some generalizations based on the data that have been obtained from different countries for the purposes of this paper. The first part of this study will focus on policy environment that promotes gender equality generally and gender equality in the field of education in particular. This will be followed by an analysis of the gender gaps in the tertiary sector. The final section will provide some recommendations as a way forward.

The majority of African states have made some commitments to redressing gender imbalances at all levels of the economy. In this section it will be argued that, a good number of countries have made both international and national commitments to redress gender inequalities in social sectors including education in general and the tertiary level in particular. Few countries, however, have managed to have coherent operational strategies that translate these policies into actions. It is recommended that African states move beyond the rhetoric of "official" commitments into concrete proposals and plans which must define achievable targets, and that resources be allocated to this effect. The section that follows examines briefly the commitments that African states have made for redressing gender inequalities.

Given the space available and the number of countries, educational traditions and institutions on the African continent, it is not possible to analyze all the cases here. Thus, different countries and institutions and their respective policies and applications are used as illustrations in different parts of the article.

International/Regional Commitments

At the regional and international level, African states have made some commitment to redressing the gender gap at all levels of education. Most of these states are party to various international human rights instruments that commit states to prohibit discrimination either morally or legally, and that call for concrete actions to correct historical gender imbalances. Additionally, at the regional level, African states have made several declarations that reinforce international commitments to redress gender imbalances in the field of education. Such regional commitments are further reinforced at the sub-regional level and finally translated into constitutional commitments, policy guidelines, and operational plans and programmes.

Following is a summary of some of the major commitments that have been made by most of the African states toward promoting gender parity in the field of education. International commitments by African governments to redress gender gaps in education include the following:

I. Article 10 of the Convention on Elimination of Discrimination Against Women (1979) states that "State parties shall take appropriate measures to eliminate discrimination against women in order to ensure to them equal rights with men in the field of education and in particular on a basis of equality of men and women." Among other things, state parties are to ensure equal access to the same curriculum, same examinations, same teaching staff with the same standards of qualification, the elimination of stereotyped concepts about sex roles, the same opportunities for scholarships and grants, and access to same programmes of continuing education (CEDAW: 1979: U.N. publication)

ii. Article 2 of the Universal Declaration of Human Rights (1948) forbids any kind of discrimination, be it based on race, colour, sex, language, religion, political or other opinion, that would prevent the enjoyment of basic freedoms. Articles 22-27 stress education for all.

iii. The World Plan of Action, prepared for the occasion of the International Women's Year (1975) and the United Nations Decade for Women (1975-85), identifies national areas of intervention in favour of women, including political participation, education and training, health and nutrition.

iv. Paragraph 191 of the Nairobi Forward Looking Strategy states that women should be viewed as users and agents of change in science and technology. Their technological and scientific skills should be improved in order to enhance their participation in industrial production, design innovations, and product adaptation techniques. It also stresses the need to promote equal access of girls to education and particularly in fields that are traditionally controlled by men/boys.

v. Additionally, the United Nations Conference on the Environment and Development (1992) stresses the role of women in the management of environment, and hence recommends promotion of women in environmental education.

vi. The International Conference on Population and Development (1994) recognises that education is one of the instruments that will facilitate greater participation of women in the development process and as a result, recommends special attention to girls' and women's education as a way of bridging the gender gaps in education and training.

vii. The World Summit For Children (1990) calls upon countries of the world to facilitate the promotion of girls' and women's education so as to bridge the gender gap between girls and boys, men and women.

viii. In its Declaration on Education For All (1990), the World Conference for Education for All recommends that "the most urgent priority be granted to ensure equality of access and improvement in the quality of women's education, to removing all barriers that might be a handicap to their participation, and to eliminating any gender related stereotyping in the field of education.

ix. The Fourth Conference on Women (1995) stresses concrete measures to be taken with the aim of sensitising educators to the disparity between genders, and sensitising parents to the necessity to educate their daughters and increase girls' school attendance, which has been lower compared to boys'.

x. In addition to promoting equal access for all, the Ouagadougou Declaration and Action Framework recommended special measures to ensure that in all schools the staff is composed of 50% female teachers.

xi. The Kampala Declaration (1996) calls upon governments to implement affirmative actions to ensure equal access of girls and women to vocational and technical training.

xii. The Nairobi Action Plan for Technical Vocational Education in Africa: recommends the elimination of stereotypes that discourage women from participating in technical and scientific fields.

xiii. The UNESCO Project +2000 aims at promoting scientific and technology literacy for both women and men, girls and boys.

xiv: Article H. V. of the SADC Gender Declaration recommends enhancing access to quality education for women and men and removing gender stereotyping in the curriculum, career choices and professions.

International commitments are made either in the form of declarations that bind states morally or in the forms of conventions that bind them legally to adhere to the various commitments, in full or in part if a given state has some reservations. As indicated above, African states are presumably committed to eradication of gender gaps in education, as indicated by the number of agreements signed by most of them. Signing such agreements has some value. Recognition of the problem of gender inequality in education at the global and regional level is a step toward finding solutions to the problem. Such commitments are also significantly important to women in general and more specifically to feminist and social movements that have been demanding transformations that will enhance gender equality. These movements form an anchor for activism around the problem.

These commitments are further translated into commitments at the national level through constitutional provisions banning discrimination on grounds of sex as well as providing ground for affirmative action in favour of historically disadvantaged groups, and including women and girls. In the following section a quick perusal of several constitutions will establish the existence of such provisions.

Constitutional Provisions and Gender Equality in Education

In this section it is argued that most of the African states have either banned discrimination on grounds of sex, or provided comprehensive clauses that spell out women's rights including accessing education at all levels. This chapter questions, however, the extent to which such constitutional provisions have impacted women's participation in education, and particularly accessing the tertiary levels of education. Reference will be made to a few country constitutions.

In their respective constitutions, South Africa, Malawi, and Uganda, for instance, have listed specific rights that women ought to enjoy. Article 21 of Uganda's current constitution spells out that:

> All persons are equal before the law and under the law in all spheres of political, economic, social and cultural life and in every other respect and shall enjoy equal protection of the law. Without prejudice to clause (I) of this article, a person shall not be discriminated against on the grounds of sex, race, colour, ethnic origin, tribe, birth, creed or religion or social economic standing, political opinion or disability. For the purpose of this article, "discrimination" means to give different treatment to different persons attributable only or mainly to their respective descriptions by sex, race, colour, ethnic origin, tribe, birth, creed, or religion, or social economic standing, political opinion or disability.

Article 33 of the same constitution further states that:

- Women shall be accorded full and equal dignity of the person with men.
- The State shall provide the facilities and opportunities necessary to enhance the welfare of women to enable them to realise their full potential and advancement.
- The State shall protect women and their rights, taking into account their unique status, and natural maternal function in society.
- Women shall have the right to equal treatment with men and that right shall include equal opportunities in political, economic and social activities.
- Without prejudice to article 32 of this constitution, women shall have the right to affirmative action for the purpose of redressing the imbalances created by history, tradition or custom.

- Laws, cultures, customs or traditions which are against the dignity, welfare or interest of women or which undermine their status, are prohibited by this constitution.

Using these constitutional provisions, women in Uganda can put pressure on their government to pursue affirmative actions that will make it possible for an increased proportion of women to have access to the tertiary sector, including university education and related technical fields from which they suffer historical exclusion.

The South African constitution pledges that the new South Africa is going to be based on non-racist and non-sexist principles and that affirmative actions were going to be implemented to redress the historical imbalances including gender imbalances. Additionally, a Women's Charter stated that:

> Our struggle for equality involves the recognition of the disadvantages that women suffer in all spheres of our lives. As a result similar treatment of women and men may not result in true equality. Therefore, the promotion of true equality will sometimes require distinctions to be made. No distinction, however, should be made that will disadvantage women. Within this context programmes of affirmative action may be a means of achieving equality. (CA: Republic of South Africa, 1996: see Women's Charter, article 1, paragraph 1)

Similarly, the Malawi current constitution is based on equality principles, which recognises the historical discrimination which women have suffered. The Malawi constitution categorically states that, the national policies will be guided by a gender equity principle through:

- Full participation of women in all spheres of Malawian society on the basis of equality with men;
- The implementation of the principles of non-discrimination and such other measures as may be required; and
- The implementation of policies to address social issues such as domestic violence, security of the person, lack of maternity benefits, economic exploitation and rights to property.

Chapter Four of the Malawi Constitution provides a specific clause protecting women's rights. Article 20 of Chapter Four states:

20. (1) Discrimination of persons in any form is prohibited
and all persons are, under any law, guaranteed equal and effective protection
against discrimination on grounds of race, colour, sex, language, religion,
political or other opinion, nationality, ethnic or social origin, disability,
property, birth or other status.

The impact of these commitments on gender equality in the field of
education has yet to stand the test of time in Malawi.

To a similar tune, the Mozambican constitution guarantees equality
between the sexes in all aspects of political, economic, social and cultural life.
The preamble of Namibia's Constitution guarantees all Namibians, a right to
life, liberty and pursuit of happiness regardless of race, religion, colour and
sex. Article 10 of this constitution provides for equality and freedom from
discrimination, while Article 20 provides that all people shall have a right to an
education; primary education is made compulsory. Article 23 provides for
affirmative action against apartheid only. However, this provision makes it
possible for other disadvantaged groups to demand affirmative action in their
favour.

Affirmations of the principles of equality and affirmative action as well
as comprehensive clauses for women's rights in constitutions are significant
steps toward improving the conditions of women. A country's constitution is
the primary law of the land, which normally provides policy makers, planners
and programme persons with a legal mandate for their activities. In the
following section, the policy environment in selected countries will be
examined in order to assess the extent to which policy guidelines, plans and
programmes, reflect on the one hand, the constitutional provisions of
promotion of gender equality in the field of education and particularly on the
tertiary level, and, on the other hand, how such policy frames guide planners
and programme directors in charting out strategies and actions to redress
gender inequality in the field of education generally and in the tertiary sector
particularly.

The Policy Environment for Promoting Gender Equality in
Tertiary Education in Some African Countries

In a study conducted for the Forum for African Women Educationalists
(FAWE) early in 2000, there were some inconsistencies and one noteworthy
discrepancy between the policy commitments on the one hand and the plans
and strategies for redressing gender imbalance in the field of education on the

other.[1] It was particularly observed that in some few countries where policies of redressing gender inequality were clearly articulated in National Gender Policy, this was not followed up in education policies. In still other instances where there were educational policies that clearly articulated the desire to redress gender inequality in the sector; this was not reflected in plans or programmes (FAWE 2000). It is argued that such discrepancies result from either lack of commitment on the part of policy planners or lack of knowledge about how to mainstream gender issues in policies, programmes and strategies, or a combination of the two. It is argued that some governments adopt gender policies as a symbolic gesture in order to appease activists and particularly feminists, and that others do this as a symbolic demonstration of their commitment to the international agreements they have made without any intention of transforming the gender imbalance; still others do the same thing with an intention to transform gender relations but lack the skill and capacity to mainstream gender in the core country programme processes.

Although the Namibian First National Plan (1995-2000) considers gender inequalities in accessing education as a problem, and even though it provides for affirmative action to redress such imbalances, it falls short of setting gender-disaggregated targets for redressing such imbalances. Of the strategies mentioned in the plan, only one focuses on girl's access, by encouraging girls to pursue technical subjects. We have argued elsewhere (FAWE 2000) that this provision is as vague as it is non-committal. It is a redundant strategy in that it does not commit the government to act, except by encouraging girls to participate.

While the plan considers access and equality as constituting what it constructs as "core value" and whereas due consideration is given to regional and gender disparities in admission for candidates and review of curriculum, at programme level, gender equality is not addressed at all. Of the 13 programme objectives, not a single one addresses gender equality. No programme objective addresses improving access and equality at all levels. This implies that there will be no budgetary allocation for this core value. What is considered as a core value ends up as rhetoric: it does not constitute part of the programme objective and hence one would not anticipate a budget at the

---

[1] In this section, extensive reference will be made to earlier work done for the Forum for African Women Educationalists which contains a review of policy documents from several countries. I wish to thank FAWE for allowing me to make use of this earlier work.

operational level. This is probably the context within which
the National Gender Policy came into being.

Namibia's Gender Policy launched in 1997, identifies priority needs
for women in the following areas: rural development, housing, education and
training, reproductive health, violence against women, political empowerment,
among others. The objectives of the policy are to "ensure equal opportunities
between men and women, to empower women by recognizing, accepting and
valuing their contribution to the general good of society and remove obstacles
which hamper their development or deny them their entitlements" (NM,
SARDC 1997: 18). In this context, education is considered as a tool for
liberating the Namibian women from historical imbalances resulting from
colonialism and the apartheid system of rule. Some of the strategies identified
for bringing gender equality in education include:

- Develop new legislation through amending and reviewing old laws which were discriminative.
- Ensure access and maintain female participation in primary, secondary and tertiary education, in particular for the most disadvantaged groups.
- Eliminate gender disparities in access to all areas of secondary and tertiary education by ensuring that, from the early years of schooling on, both girls and boys, men and women have access to career counselling, training, bursaries, and by adopting purposeful positive action in favour of girls and women.
- Improve and enhance access and retention of women in science, mathematics and technical related fields through motivation and directed affirmative action.
- Support research and documentation.
- Increase access of disadvantaged children to education (SARDC 2000: 250).

These strategies were expected to lead to enhanced progressive laws,
gender-sensitive policies and guidelines in education, and gender-sensitive
curricula and educational materials. In the field of education, gender equality
principles are guided by yet another policy document which is a White Paper
on higher education entitled: "Investing in People, Developing a Country:
Higher Education in Namibia"

This document assigns higher education four major functions. First,
higher education is considered as an investment in national development. The
second function is a contribution to human resource development. Thirdly,

higher education is supposed to be serving as a crucible for cultural renewal and revitalisation. Finally, higher education is expected to provide a basis for unblocking the potential and actual talents of the men and women of Namibia to enable them to use their talents for their personal and collective development.

Depending on how one translates these functions, they can lead to redressing gender equality or they can just lead to reinforcing existing gender hierarchies. Development, for instance, is not a gender-neutral process. If there are no gender-sensitive programmes and plans, development may lead to increased patterns of gender hierarchy. Similarly, a human resource development process that is not gender-sensitive can result in increased patterns of gender hierarchies. Cultural renewal may also lead to renewing those patriarchal elements that were undermined by the colonial state, and this will not necessarily lead to a redefined culture based on principles of gender equality.

Alternatively, if one uses the lenses of gender, development can be holistic only if it is based on a true assessment of both the practical and the strategic needs and interests of women and men, young and old, of a given society. People-oriented development has to be gender sensitive. Similarly, human resource development from a gendered perspective has to include development of all the talents of women and men in a given society. Discriminatory human resource development policies will not lead to the "unblocking" of the talents of women and men which are being referred to in this document.

While Namibia has made a commitment to redress gender imbalances as a matter of constitutional principle and as a policy guide, at the operational level, issues of equality and access, and particularly gender equality, have faded away. Despite this, women and feminists in Namibia have been able to use the constitution and the gender policy to demand affirmative action in favour of disadvantaged groups generally and particularly women. This is what accounts for higher levels of women's participation in the tertiary sector compared to other countries, as will be illustrated in this chapter.

The main policy challenge for South Africa is how to address both race and gender equity in its higher education framework. Formal abolition of apartheid has not necessarily led to automatic transformation of structures that sustained apartheid. In the field of education, however, affirmative action has made it possible for Blacks and women to access education and particularly institutions of higher learning. South Africa has bridged the gender gap at both

the primary and secondary levels as well as at the tertiary
level, except in a few disciplines, as will be elaborated later in this chapter.

Mozambique's National Education Policy and Strategies for
Implementation defines the overall goal of education as that of promoting
"peace, stability and national unity." These are heavily loaded concepts that
can be subjected to a variety of interpretations, depending on what lenses are
worn. If peace is taken in its broad sense to include both the private and the
public contexts and also to include the processes of building and maintaining
peace, issues of gender equality will naturally be encompassed in efforts of
promoting peace. Similarly when stability is conceived to include family
dimension, then issues of gender relations will be considered, as they constitute
a primary area in which emerging personal conflicts emerge potentially, and
lead to local and even national-level conflicts which may threaten the social
fabric of society and hence create instabilities. Finally, national unity is not
gender-neutral. National unity assumes some levels of consensus among
individuals within the national boundaries.

Building national consensus has to result from lower-level processes in
which individuals are socialised in consensus-building through family, schools,
religious structures; to develop a national ideology that is not based on gender
discrimination, a culture that does not condone the authoritarianism and
intolerance inherent in current patriarchal societies.

Adherence to these broad principles is supposed to facilitate
elimination of absolute poverty and to improve the life of the people, with
particular concern for education, health, rural development and employment. It
further underscores the need for the creative, free and democratic participation
of each individual and of the society at large as a basic precondition for re-
establishing political stability. In dealing with inequalities that are construed to
have resulted from centuries of accumulation, the government claims that it
will have to start a dialogue with the various social actors. These social actors
must be women and men. It is in the light of this context that educational goals
and objectives are defined.

In this perspective, education in Mozambique is considered as a
fundamental right of each citizen and a key instrument for improving living
conditions and for upgrading the technical and scientific levels of the workers
(presumably men and women alike). In this context, the aims of educational
policies are to provide massive access to education as well as to improve
service delivery at all levels. The overall objectives are:

- To eradicate illiteracy,

- To guarantee basic education to all, and
- To guarantee equal access to professional training (on access and equity, the policy aims at increasing access and accessibility by removing barriers that hinder girls and women from participating).

The policy document provides for affirmative actions that will promote girls' participation, retention, and promotion to all levels. This should include waiving fees as necessary, supporting poor families, and sensitising society to the need for girls' participation in education.

While the goal of reducing the gender gap may be clearly articulated, the implementation strategies are not equally clear in articulating specific actions that will reduce that gap. Beyond efforts to increase enrolments, other factors such as issues of quality and relevancy, physical facilities, and training of teachers are not linked to gender inequalities and gender responsiveness. Just increasing classroom space without taking the practical needs of girls and women into account might not solve the drop-out problem for girls at lower levels or the problems of women's access to higher levels of education and training.

Similarly, issues of quality and relevancy have to address the gender-stereotyped curriculum, the classroom interactions, and the hidden messages which are conveyed on a day-to-day basis that discourage girls from enjoying the learning process. In the same way, the training and re-training of teachers has to include pedagogic issues which take into consideration gender stereotyping in the school environment, and act to discourage girls' retention, and improve performance. These shortcomings in the education policy may have affected the development of the Education Sector Strategic Plan to which we turn in the next section.

Mozambique's Education Sector Strategic Plan for 1999-2003 identifies several key problems, which include limited access, with girls being particularly affected at the secondary, tertiary, and technical levels, the quality of education and training, and resource constraints. The articulation of the problem is clearly gender-responsive.

The plan claims to have affirmed priorities that were identified in the education policy statement with particular emphasis on making basic education accessible to all Mozambican children. Education for all could mean for both girls and boys, and this can be used as an official commitment to gender parity in basic education.

In terms of strategy, the document assigns both expansion and improved quality a high priority in implementation. Again, at the

implementation level, the only gender concern is the increased
access of schooling for girls. Issues of quality are not directly linked to
concerns of gender inequalities. Such issues are addressed in a separate
document titled "Mainstreaming Gender in Education and Education for Girls
in Mozambique."

In this document, low participation of women in education and
particularly at the higher levels of learning is a major issue of concern. Gender
disparities in rural/urban and district variations are also viewed as significant
issues of concern. The contributing factors summarised in the document
include the social/cultural norms and values that assign women and girls lower
social status, the domestic workload, poverty, the lack of female role models
among female teachers and school administrators, violation of professional
ethics, the distance from homes to schools, and the tension between formal and
religious education.

Some of the strategies recommended include mainstreaming gender in
planning. This calls for mainstreaming gender concerns in the core plan. Part
of this plan involves promoting gender-sensitive school environments by
improving physical facilities in a gender-sensitive way, changing the way
learning is organised, mainstreaming gender concerns in teacher education, and
developing gender-sensitive educational curricula. Finally, the plan includes
advocacy for girls' education as part of their basic rights. This will entail
sensitising the community on the need for girls' education, identifying
community needs for girls' and women's education, and offering material
support to girls as an incentive, particularly to those from poor families. The
main challenge for education in Mozambique is how to mainstream these
proposals in the core plans.

Sierra Leone's National Education Action recognises the problem of
gender inequality and aims at redressing the imbalances. But at the operational
level, its strategies are narrowed down to improving the physical infrastructure
only. In enhancing physical facilities for instance, two main concerns are
providing separate toilets for girls and building boarding facilities for girls.
The activity, directed at providing support for teaching/learning materials and
textbooks, does not address issues of stereotyping in curricula and textbooks.

The problem of pupil performance and examinations does not touch on
poor performance of girls and boys in different subjects. The plan for
enhancement of non-formal and adult education makes reference to reducing
the illiteracy rate of women by 50% and that of men by 40% without
necessarily addressing issues of the relevancy and content of the curriculum

from a gendered perspective. No strategies are mentioned for reducing this gap.

Similarly, stating the need to restructure management does not touch on the aspect of management skills that would make the school environment gender-friendly.

Additionally, the discussion of reforming financial systems does not address the need to have additional resources for gender mainstreaming, nor does it take into account the need to have technical skills to have school budgets that are gender responsive. In a nutshell it can be said that the plan mentions gender concerns in an ad hoc manner and makes no attempts to mainstream the core problem issues that were addressed in the separate section in the policy document, as mentioned above. The plan, and particularly the education section, was supposed to have been guided by the 1995 New Education Policy, to which attention is now turned.

The New Education Policy for Sierra Leone spells out the aim of education as to enhance integral development of the individual for the building of a cohesive, healthy and strong nation with a sustainable and dynamic economy, a free, just, and peace-loving society, a democratic and harmonious society and a moral and disciplined society. These are overloaded concepts that have to be interrogated in gender terms. A cohesive, strong, and healthy nation with a dynamic economy does not necessarily mean a nation that respects the rights of women and men. Gender-sensitive people are needed, however, to translate these principles, so that peace is not only considered as absence of war, but encompasses everything that threatens the security of women and men, boys and girls, from the household level on.

Translated into specific objectives, useful education is supposed to increase access to basic education, improve its quality and relevancy, expand and upgrade technical/vocational education, provide equity in education, and develop appropriate attitudes, skills and values in children. Again these are given in a very general language and gender-sensitive persons are needed to interpret them at the operational level.

The document does mention the need to define measures that will increase access and retention of women and girls in education at every level. In defining the major objectives of education, the document does mention the objective of providing equity in education by enforcing the policy of non-discrimination in all schools and also by monitoring the standards and quality of education. The issue of gender equality, however, fades away the moment one moves to the specific sub- sector objectives.

For instance on the proposed new structure for primary school there is no mention of gender concern other than expansion of the physical space. Discussions of quality, involvement of the private sector, continuous assessment, and counsellor/teacher guidance do not mention the need to mainstream gender concerns. Similarly the discussion of junior secondary schools does not mention issues of gender equality, gender responsive curriculum, or improvement of teaching materials from a gendered perspective. Regarding the senior level as well as the tertiary, and university levels, the text is also silent on gender concerns.

There is, however, a separate section that deals with the need to promote girl's and women's participation in the education sector. Some of the issues raised in this section have little to do with the priorities of the planned core activities, such as gradual revision of laws. This latter item is not included in any of the sub-sector aims or the general goals. The re-admission of mother-child is also not included in any of the sub-sector aims, nor is increased participation of girls in mathematics, and provision of child-care centres. The problem of separating women's needs from the general and sub-sector aims and concerns is that they may end up being nobody's business. The ability to mainstream these aspects into the core activities remains the main challenge for the educational activists in Sierra Leone. The extent to which these discrepancies are affecting the realisation of gender equality at higher levels of learning, particularly the tertiary level, is a subject of discussion in the subsequent sections of this study.

From the few cases cited, it can be observed that a significant number of countries have incorporated gender equality principles in their constitutions, and also a good number do have WID/GA policies that acknowledge the problem of gender inequality in education. The majority of the cases cited have problems in translating the commitments into operational plans, strategies, and programmes. This might explain why the gender gap in education and particularly in higher and tertiary education is still so large in the majority of the countries in Sub-Saharan Africa. The following section reviews the state of women's participation in tertiary education in a few African countries.

Participation of Women and Girls in Tertiary Institution in Africa

The Gender Gap in Education

Significant progress has been made in many Sub-Saharan African countries in expanding basic education to the majority of the people. Yet illiteracy rates among adults are still high in Africa and more so among women. The Human Development Report (1999) reveals that the literacy rate for Sub-Saharan Africa was 49.6% for females and 65.9% for males (UNDP 1999). This was lower than the average for all developing countries, which was 62.9% female and 80.0% male. The 2000 UNDP report, however, indicates a slight increase of female literacy rates for Sub-Saharan Africa, from 49.6% in 1997 to 51% in 1998 for the 15+ years old. This was 76% of the male rate. During the same period, the female primary age group enrolment as a percentage of all school age girls was 51.8%, which represented 85% of the male ratio. At the secondary school level, the female secondary age group enrolment as a percentage of all secondary school girls during the same period was just 35.8% (UNDP 2000).

It is being argued in this chapter that literacy levels and particularly women's literacy rates have an impact on the nature and level of women's participation in all levels of education generally and particularly in tertiary education. Literate parents will be more likely than illiterate parents to have the will and means to support a girl child's education to the highest levels.

The combined first, second, and third levels of gross enrolment for Sub-Sahara Africa is 39% female and 49% male; this is lower than the average for all developing countries which is 55% and 64% for females and males respectively. While combined gross enrolment ratios for some countries such as Djibouti is as low as 17% for females and 24% for males, the United Republic of Tanzania has 32% female enrolments and 33% male; Mozambique has 20% and 20% for females and males respectively. A few countries have a high literacy rate and a low gender gap (UNDP 1999: 141).

Access to tertiary education is highly competitive for both men and women, owing to limited space. Sub-Saharan Africa is for instance considered to have the lowest Gross Enrolment Ratio (GER) in the world. The GER for Sub-Saharan Africa is 5% compared to the world average of approximately 16% (1996 data). Out of all qualified male and female applicants, only 25% are admitted to university (African Virtual University 2001). Women applicants compete from a disadvantaged position in most of the fields but are worst off in natural sciences and engineering.

In Togo for instance, women in tertiary sector are just 13% of the total females in this sector; in the United Republic of Tanzania, they are 16% of total student population; in Central African Republic they are only 11%, while in Namibia they constitute up to 61%. The gender gap at this level is high for the majority of the countries, and trends indicate little progress. Figure 1 illustrates typical cases in the Sub-Saharan African countries.

Figure 1: Admission by Gender 1999/00 in Three Selected Universities in East Africa

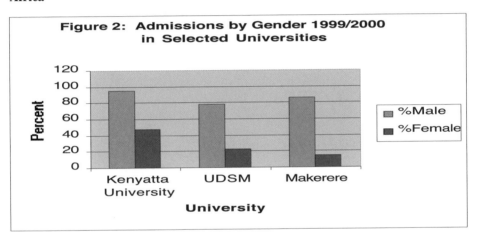

Source: FAWE 2001

In the natural sciences, women are under-represented with country variations. In Central African Republic, Togo, Tanzania and Burkina Faso, they constitute less than 10% of the total students in this field (FAWE 2001). This means that women will be excluded from certain fields that have science subject combinations as prerequisites. This is further illustrated in Table 1

As also illustrated in Table 1, with the exception of a few countries such as Namibia, Lesotho, and Botswana, women's participation in tertiary education as a percentage of the total tertiary enrolment is still very low. And in some countries like Tanzania, Togo, Central African Republic and Benin, that percentage is lower than 20%. UNDP records show that from 1994 to 1997, for every 100,000 women in the following countries, very small numbers of women were enrolled in tertiary education: Zambia 135, Côte d'Ivoire 263, Senegal 120, United Republic of Tanzania 22, Benin 96, Uganda 118, Eritrea

24 Gambia 106, Guinea 24, Malawi 34 (UNESCO 1998: 258). During the same period, the proportion of female tertiary students in relation to males was as follows for the following countries: Zambia 39%, Côte d'Ivoire 31%, Senegal 32%, United Republic of Tanzania 24%, Benin 23%, Uganda 49%, Eritrea 15%, Chad 16%, and Mozambique 14% (UNESCO 1998: 258).

Table 1: Percentage of Female Students in Tertiary Education by Field in Selected Countries in Sub-Saharan Africa

Country	All Fields	Educa-tion	Huma-nities	Law & Social Sciences	Natural Sciences & Engin & Agr	Medical Sciences	Gender Segre gation Index (%)
Algeria	43	27	62	45	35	52	8
Benin	18	20	1.	20	11	23	3
Botswana	50	61	53	59	26	-	11
Burkina Faso	22	14	32	22	8	24	7
Central African Republic.	11	7	13	11	3	8	3
Côte d'Ivoire	23	10	29	31	10	23	8
Djibouti	47	61	_	41	-	-	8
Ethiopia	20	22	25	28	11	17	7
Lesotho	55	68	52	67	21	-	17
Madagascar	35	36	66	25	31	46	12
Malawi	31	38	40	18	15	79	11
Morocco	41	31	51	42	28	49	7
Mozambique	26	35	33	22	21	55	7
Namibia	61	55	56	40	31	85	12
South Africa	49	64	61	46	29	61	10
Swaziland	45	51	67	52	16	43	13
Togo	13	10	16	13	5	18	3
Tunisia	44	46	58	42	28	54	9
Uganda	32	29	28	40	17	29	7
UR Tanzania	16	18	-	20	9	28	6
Zimbabwe	35	41	33	44	14	35	10

Source: UNESCO World Education Report (1998): 152-536.

A study conducted by FAWE in ten African countries illustrates that women have less than half as much access to universities as men do. In addition to low levels of participation, women are concentrated in the few fields which are stereotyped as female disciplines. Data collected by the Human Sciences Research Council for South Africa at the end of 1995, for instance, indicated that women constituted just 25% of those who were registered in economics, management, commerce and administration, and just 37% of those registered in engineering, agriculture and architecture. In the medical fields, however, women constituted more than 50% of postgraduates and 57% of all postgraduates (SARDC 2000). A further gender analysis at universities in South Africa indicated that 52.2% of all enrolments were males and 47.8% were females, while at technical colleges 71% were male and 29% were female.

In terms of the field of study, males constituted 100% in industrial arts, 93.2 in engineering, and 83% in architecture, while women constituted 99% of the enrolments in home economics (SARDC 2000). In technical colleges, most of the students in architecture, agriculture, building science, computer sciences and engineering were males while females were concentrated in the secretarial courses (SARDC 2000: 242). From 1994 to1997, female tertiary science enrolment as a percentage of the total females in the tertiary sector was as follows for the respective countries: Tunisia 32.4%, South Africa 36.8%, Zimbabwe 14%, Chad 6.5%, United Republic of Tanzania 9.1%, Benin 12.6%, and Uganda 16.7% (NDP 2000: 258).

In Tanzania, the percentage of women in tertiary institutions is not only very low but in some fields it has been declining. Enrolment at the University of Dar es Salaam in all fields for instance stagnated at 17% from 1989/90 to 1994/95. In commerce it decreased from 18% in 1989/90 to 17% in 1993/94 and increased slightly to 18% in 1994/95. Similarly in engineering, it decreased from 5% during the same period to 3% in the two consecutive years, that is, 1993/94 and 1994/95. In computer sciences it decreased from 15% in 1991/92 to 3% in 1994/95. Similar trends are observed in certain fields at the Sokoine University of Agriculture. Although total enrolments for females increased from 15% to 23% between 1990/91 and 1994/95, in veterinary medicine it declined from 8% to 3% during the mentioned period, while in agricultural engineering, women have never enrolled in this field (SARDC/TGNP: 1997:44). In technical colleges, enrolment of females declined from a total of 13.1% to 6.1% during the mentioned period.

Meena

As a result of the low participation of women in the tertiary sector, the number of staff being recruited from this pool is equally low. Figures from the University of Dar es Salaam illustrate this in the following table:

Table 2a: Academic Members of Staff by Gender: University of Dar es Salaam

Year	Prof		As/ Prof		S/lec		Lec.		As/ Lec.		Tuto rials	
	F	M	F	M	F	M	F	M	F	M	F	M
2000/01	4	53	8	90	23	215	39	224	21	138	95	720
01/02	5	53	10	101	27	228	47	193	29	106	118	681
02/03	5	63	9	99	34	220	53	192	32	116	113	690
03/04	6	71	9	100	38	221	60	190	33	108	146	690
04/05	7	69	10	102	39	227	64	192	37	102	157	692
%F 03/04	9%		9%		15 %		25 %		27 %		18%	

Source: Directorate of Planning and Development: Facts and Figures 2004/05

Table 2b: University Academic Staff by Gender in Niger (1999/ 2000)

Faculty	Males	Females	% Females
Science	60	5	7.7%
Agriculture	24	1	4.0%
Humanities and Arts	61	8	11.6%
Medicine	31	4	11.4%
Education	25	4	13.8%
Law and Economics	30	2	6.3%
Mathematics Teaching Research Institute	2	0	0%
Humanities Research Institute	9	2	18.2%
Radio-isotopes Institute	8	1	11.1%
Total	250	27	9.7%

Source: FAWE 2001

The above discussion suggests that one of the deep-rooted aspects of inequality in education in Sub-Saharan Africa is the inequality between sexes. The section that follows explores some of the causes of the existing gender gap in education and its effect on the economy.

Causes of the Gender Gap in Education

Existing literature has identified major factors which have been limiting the progress of the education for girls and women. Poverty has been singled out as the most pervasive factor, one that is affecting and frustrating any effort to enhance gender equality in education in Africa. Secondly, socio-cultural norms, values, and practices that relegate women to a subordinate position in the society but assign women more roles in the reproductive sphere constitute yet another factor constraining women's access to education and particularly to the tertiary levels. Related to this is the schooling environment that tends to repel females owing to stereotyping and a female-unfriendly context. Finally and not least is the ideology of social exclusion, which perpetuates the subordinate position of women as African states fail to carry out a social transformation that will dismantle power hierarchies based on gender relations.

Increased Levels of Poverty

The SADC Gender and Development report (1999) defines poverty from a human development perspective as "denial of choices and opportunities, which are most basic to human development." The report further maintains that poverty covers a wide range of deprivations affecting people, including deprivation in health, survival, knowledge, and opportunities for a creative and productive life, for freedom as well as income. In this context, human poverty is viewed as a denial of human development (UNDP/SAPES 1999).

It is estimated that about 42% of the population in Sub-Saharan Africa is living on less than US $1 per day, and 40% are living in abject poverty. Data from the UNDP Human Development Report (2000) indicate that from 1990 to 1998, out of 43 countries in Sub-Saharan Africa, only one had a GNP growth rate of 4%, three had between 3-4%, twenty had between 0-3% and nineteen had a negative growth rate.

The same report further pointed out that, while income and human poverty have declined in other developing countries, in Sub-Saharan Africa, it is either increasing, or stagnating. Where there was slight decline in percentages, the numbers were still high relative to other regions. In the context of poverty, resources for education are, generally, shrinking, which makes it even more difficult to argue for the additional resources required for mainstreaming gender in educational programmes.

Despite these levels of poverty, a good number of countries in Sub-Saharan Africa have been struggling to allocate a higher percentage of their national budget to education. This amount increased from 4.8% in 1990 to 6% between 1995 and 1997 (UNDP: 2000). There are country variations,: Nigeria's expenditure declined from 1.0% in 1990 to 0.7% between 1995 and 1997, Zambia's from 2.6% to 2.2%, Senegal's from 4.1% to 3.7%, and Niger's from 3.2% to 2.3% during the same period.

Increased percentages, however, do not tell us the full story of the total amounts allocated relative to the needs. In this period of structural adjustment programmes when government budgets have been cut back to very limited amounts, an increased budget might barely be sufficient to maintain a government bureaucracy. In such an environment, gender equality programmes might not be considered by policy makers and planners as a practical priority even for the well-meaning governments. In the context of increased poverty neither African states nor peoples are able to translate into actions some of the commitments that need additional resources for operationalisation. This calls for international support for women's and girls' education as part of the effort to fight against poverty and to enhance human rights with a gender perspective.

Bridging the gender gap in education will inevitably require additional resources in terms of expanding facilities and improving educational quality through training and retraining teachers as well as re-writing textbooks and audio-visual materials in order to remove stereotyped materials. Resource allocation will have to be complemented by commitments to redress the gender gap, and willingness to allocate resources for this purpose. It will require an understanding that Africa is wasting a lot of its human resource through discriminatory practices that are denying the majority of the African people a right to develop their intellectual capabilities to the maximum of their ability.

Socio-Cultural Factors

The existing sexual division of labour, which assigns most of the social reproductive tasks to women, is a constraint for girl's education. As part of socialisation, younger girls are forced to assume domestic responsibilities at an earlier age than boys. As a result, in some cases, they may not enrol at all, or if they enrol, they may not be able to perform as well as boys; hence will not be able to transit to higher levels. When the workload is too stressful, they may decide to drop out before they even complete the first level. This implies that there may be fewer females accessing the second tier of learning and fewer still accessing the third tier or tertiary level.

School/College Gender-Unfriendly Learning Environment

Related to the socio-cultural factors, and resulting from socio-cultural norms and values that position women in low social status, is a school environment that tends to discourage female pupils. The school curriculum, both written and hidden, is stereotyped. When the University of Dar es Salaam in Tanzania opened an Engineering Faculty, for instance, there were no toilet facilities for female students. It was assumed that the Faculty was "naturally" for male students. The "oversight" did not stop here, as it was followed by very hostile treatment of females who dared to cross the boundary of a male-dominated discipline. Some female students had to suffer "academic sanction" if they excelled more than expected.[2] Reports of such incidents repel potential candidates from wanting to go through such ordeals during a learning process.

The school and the college environment do not only repel female pupils and students, but also repel female teachers, tutors, and professors. Most of the African learning institutions are male dominated. Sub-Saharan Africa except Sudan, Somali and Djibouti has the lowest rates of female staff at all levels of schooling, with an average of 36% and 29% for primary and secondary respectively (ibid.). Chad has the lowest level of female teachers at both primary and secondary (4.1% and 3.4 %,) followed by Mauritania and Guinea, where less than 20% of the primary teachers and about 8% of the secondary teachers are females.

Lesotho, Botswana and Swaziland have the highest rates, between 75% and 80% at the primary level and from 37.1% to 51,1% at the secondary level, making them higher than the Latin America's rates. In the Seychelles, more than 80% of primary school teachers are women, the highest in the region, and more than twice the rate of Sub-Saharan Africa as a whole. However, at the secondary level their percentage drops to 37.4% (ibid.). The condition at tertiary levels is even worse. At the University of Dar es Salaam during the academic year 1994/95, for instance, the Faculty of Arts and Social Sciences had only two full female professors against 11 male full professors, 4 female associate professors against 15 male associate professors, 2 female assistant

---

[2] Stories narrated to the author during a research on "gender relations" at the University of D.S.M., 1998

lecturers against 33 males. In total the faculty had 16 female academic members of staff against 164 male members of staff.

The Faculty of Commerce during the same period had 6 female members of staff against 35, law had 3 female members of staff against 34, and engineering had one against 109 male members. The Computer Sciences did not have any female member of staff. The entire University of Dar es Salaam during this time had only 66 female academic staff against 573 males (Education Statistics: relevant years: Government Printer).

The low participation of women in the tertiary sector affects their level and form of participation in their respective economies. The following section summarises the effect of women's low participation in tertiary education in Africa.

Effects of Women's Low Participation in Tertiary Education

The above trends in education have affected trends in accessing the labour market as well as the participation of women in political and decision-making bodies. Compared to other regions, women's participation in the labour force in Sub-Saharan Africa is low and declining. From the 1970s to the 1990s, female labour force participation declined in Sub-Saharan Africa, dropping from 57% in 1970 to 53% in 1990 and to 37.8% in 1998 (World Women 1995 and UNDP 2000). Participation in political processes, including legislative processes, and access to ministerial positions have been increasing, but at a very low rate. Very few countries have reached, or are about to reach, the target of 30% that was set by heads of state in Beijing in 1995. In Southern Africa for instance, except for the exceptional earlier case of Lesotho, only Mozambique has reached the 30% target, with a few other countries such as South Africa and Namibia nearing that goal. This implies that women are not effectively participating in decisions that affect their day-to-day lives, including resource mobilisation and allocation. This trend affects, in turn, progress in improving the legal and regulatory environment for promoting gender equality in Africa, since very few women are influencing the legislative processes.

Interventions to Redress the Gender Imbalances

There are some initiatives under way in the Sub-Saharan region to redress the gender imbalances discussed in the previous sections of this chapter. As already mentioned, many governments do recognise that the gender gap is a problem; most of them have made commitments to redress such imbalances, and a few of them have translated these commitments into educational policies and plans. A majority have yet to allocate resources to implement plans of action. There are a few cases where affirmative programmes have worked with some recognisable achievements. The University of Dar es Salaam in Tanzania, for instance, has been pursuing two strategies. One is to admit females with lower cut-off points. This is controversial as it raises issues of quality and merit. The other strategy has been to offer a pre-entry course administered by the science faculty. These strategies have led to increased admission from 15% to 27%, as illustrated in Table 3 below.

Table 3: Impact of Equal Opportunity Policy at the University of Dar es Salaam (2000/01)

Programme	Total Admitted	Total Female	Female Same Criteria	Female Affirmative Action	% Female Same criteria	% Female after affirmative Action
BA	494	242	74	168	23%	49%
B.COM	273	45	45	Not used	16%	16%
B.A.Edu	144	35	20	14	15	24
B.Ed.Com	14	0	0	Not used	%	0%
Engineering	405	23	11	12	3%	6%
Law	197	101	61	40	39	51%
Architecture & Land	212	25	17	8	8%	12%
Medicine	132	33	22	11	18	25%
Dentistry	14	0	0	Not used	0%	0%
Pharmacy	26	12	12	Not used	46%	46%
Physical Edu and science	25	13	13	3	12	8%
Nursing	23	13	3	10	23	57
Sciences	382	87	44	43	13	23
Total	2341	628	310	318	15%Average	27%

Source: Masanja V.G. (FAWE 2001).

As illustrated in Table 3, affirmative action impacted girls/women's access to University in the 2000/2001 admissions by faculties at the University of Dar es Salaam (UDSM). It is observed that the average female admission percentage without affirmative action is 15% while the admission with affirmative action is 27%. Although affirmative action has almost doubled female admissions, it is also clear that the admission rate for women at UDSM is still far from attaining gender parity.

On the other hand, some faculties have easily attained gender parity in admissions by instituting affirmative action, notably physical education, sports and culture (PESC), while admissions to arts, law, nursing, and the pharmacy faculty are near parity without affirmative action. Within the faculties, some programmes have attained parity as a result of affirmative action, for example chemistry and the biological sciences (zoology and botany). The main challenge has been to demonstrate that this will not lower the "standards." Masanja's study for the University of Dar es Salaam indicates that such affirmative actions have yielded positive results in some of the disciplines. In the academic year 1999/00, for instance, in the departments of chemistry, biology and B.Sc. (Education), among the 20 top best performers in final examinations, 13 were women, and this is more than half of the total who sat for the examinations in these departments. In other disciplines such as mathematics and physics, the performance was quite low, as 50% of those who were admitted under the programme have been discontinued and the rest are said to be performing "marginally" (Masanja 2001).

The two contradictory impact results suggest that, whereas in some fields cut-off points work, in others, a pre-entry course is needed. In still others, the pre-entry course might need to be backed up with other programmes to help women perform better. At the end of the day, the main problem may be the quality of the education girls and women are receiving prior to entering the university. This is an area in which universities might wish to intervene.

There are also some initiatives to improve the learning environment through instituting policies that prohibit sexual harassment and promote equal opportunities. The Universities of Natal and Cape Town in South Africa have instituted sexual harassment policies that have helped discourage acts of sexual harassment against female students and staff.

Conclusions and Recommendations

Education as a Human Right

Invariably all countries seem to agree that education is a fundamental human right and that girls and boys, women and men, have equal rights to access education at all levels. Countries have made commitments at the international, regional and national levels to redress gender inequalities. A few countries have formulated policies that provide guidelines on how to redress such imbalances. The main challenge remains how to implement these policies as strategies with targets and time frames, in order to redress imbalances at the tertiary levels.

At the primary level, gender parity in enrolment ratios seems to have been achieved, or almost, by the majority of states through the strategy of making primary education universal and compulsory. Mechanisms to retain girls, to facilitate the completion of their studies and their transition to higher levels have not been defined. Hence, even though more or less equal numbers of girls as boys enrol in primary education, more girls tend to drop out, fewer of them perform well, and fewer of them transit to higher levels of learning, particularly the tertiary level.

Few African countries seem to consider the content of education and the overall curriculum as problems in terms of stereotyping females and males into traditional disciplines, practices that continue to locate women in lower social positions. As a result, education, including tertiary education, continues to reinforce gender relations, stereotyping women and men in disciplines that reinforce gender hierarchies in the public sector, and relegating women into less well-paid jobs and keeping them in areas where they cannot influence decision-making processes.

Education for Empowerment/Social Transformation

Education is not empowering African citizens, particularly women and poor men, to challenge the power structures, including patriarchal structures that perpetuate ideologies of social exclusion. This can be attributed to two related factors. First, the low participation of women in the tertiary sector leads to their exclusion in decision-making processes, hence to denial of opportunities to challenge the power structures and corresponding ideologies that continue to relegate women to a low social status. Additionally, the stereotyped curriculum in all levels continues to reproduce submissive citizens and particularly women who are socialised into accepting subordinate social positions. The need to revisit the curriculum, both written and hidden, the overall pedagogy and its gendered nature are being underscored in this study. Accessing education is necessary, but the type of education being offered also has to be interrogated, so that it not only enhances human rights awareness levels but also empowers girls and boys, men and women, to develop their human potential and their creative abilities.

Quality and Relevancy

Most countries do agree that the quality of education has been deteriorating and that internal inefficiencies exist. The link between quality of education and gender inequality has not been established and there is no consensus. Educational stereotyping is not conceived as a quality problem; thus strategies to revise curricula and educational materials are ad hoc and have not been given the attention they deserve.

Related to the issue of quality is the aspect of relevancy. Tertiary education in Africa does not seem to be offering knowledge and skills that are directed toward the solution of African problems, particularly the problem of poverty and technological backwardness. African technical education has failed to liberate African women from being beasts of burden as they continue to till the land with hand hoes, use their heads as the principal means of transporting goods from the farm and market to their homes, and they carry babies on their backs. The need to redefine the role of tertiary education in the light of growing poverty and its feminine character is being underscored in this study.

Shrinking Resources

Most countries have experienced resource constraints owing to increased levels of poverty. The amount of resources available to revamp education, improve its quality and reduce inequalities is constrained by increased levels of impoverishment. The link between resource constraints and the gender gap in education has not been clearly articulated except in a few cases.[3] Hence appropriate budget strategies have not been developed. This is despite the fact that many countries have agreed to allocate 20% of their resources to social services, including education, through the 20/20 initiatives. The strategy here is to mobilize resources from various sources including the private sector and international agencies, tapping both multilateral and bilateral sources. Massive resources are required to improve education services generally, and particularly to make them accessible to the majority of African citizens, that is, women.

---

[3] Countries such as Tanzania, South Africa and Uganda, which have conducted gender budget analyses of their core budgets, have demonstrated how shrinking budgets affect universal primary education policies and adult literacy campaigns, and how this in turn leads to lower enrollment rates for girls and women.

Low Female Transition Rates

Female access to the tertiary sector is low, and most countries acknowledge that this is a problem. There is no agreement on strategies for improving transition rates to the higher level. The links between transition rates and improved human resources have not been established. This is an area where affirmative action has to be done with caution. Uganda, Zimbabwe and South Africa have attempted to introduce affirmative action to promote women's access to the tertiary level, and Tanzania provides a pre-entry science course for potential science candidates. These initiatives have to be carefully supported and studied so that they do not contribute to further eroding women's self-confidence and esteem at this level.

Given these Observations, What has Been and What Ought to be Done to Address the Gender Gap in Tertiary Education in Africa?

As we have seen, most the African states admit that the gender gap at all levels of education, and particularly in higher and tertiary education, is a development problem and an issue of human rights concern. Most of the African states have made some commitments at international, regional, sub-regional and national levels in redressing the gender gap in education. However, very few countries have managed to translate these commitments into operational project activities and programmes. A few national, regional, and sub-regional non-Governmental organisations have also lobbied to influence governments to pursue progressive educational policies and programmes that will address the gender gap. In the following section, reference will be made to several cases from the SADC region known to this author.

Malawi has made secondary education free for girls in its effort to bridge the gender gap. This is an important step in improving women's access to higher education because in order to access the tertiary sector one has to go through basic and second education. This initiative will be successful only, however, if there are other back-up services that may enable girls to perform well and hence transit to tertiary education (SARDC 1999).

Similarly, the Angolan government has made education free in all government schools. This will open doors to poor families who are unable to send their girls to school owing to poverty and low resources. Again, if this measure is supported by other initiatives that enable girls to perform well, it will open doors for more girls to access the tertiary and higher levels of learning. In addition to making education free, the government of Angola has also undertaken a special project that is enabling women and girls to access vocational training. This has increased the number of female tutors and teachers in traditionally male-dominated disciplines such as mechanics, carpentry, electronics, and metallurgy. The problem with this project, however, is lack of sufficient resources (SARDC 1999).

Mauritius has declared education free for all from grade one to the college and university level. This has resulted in enrolment ratios favouring girls. Records for 1995 for instance show that for every 100 girls who sat for high school certificate examination, 72 passed whereas only 64 boys out of 100 passed the same examination (SARDC 1999).

The University of Dar es Salaam has introduced an affirmative action program to support female access to various faculties and particularly in natural sciences including medical school. A pre-entry science course has been introduced to enable potential female candidates to prepare for entry to the university. These initiatives are constrained, however, by a lack of sufficient resources.

In addition to government initiatives, organisations such as FAWE have conducted a series of programmes to sensitise government officials to the need to take appropriate measures to support women's and girls' education generally, including access to higher education. FAWE continues to lobby various funding agencies to provide scholarship grants to support women's access to higher education. Though resources for such scholarships seem to be shrinking, some agencies such as the Ford Foundation and Fulbright continue to provide a few scholarship grants to women for higher education. As a beneficiary of such grants during her graduate studies, this writer appreciates the difference small amounts of support can make for individuals and society at large, since such individuals may serve society, for example by taking on activist roles in supporting women's movements for self-advancement.

This author is aware of a number of initiatives that governments, donor agencies, individuals and NGOs have undertaken to improve women's access to tertiary and higher education. Most of these initiatives have been ad hoc, and temporary. Each initiative that has affected the life of an African woman has made a big impact on her life and the life of her community. What is needed is more systematic programming that will holistically address the issue of discrimination against women in education generally and in tertiary and higher education particularly. Given the above observations, the following recommendations are made:

African Governments Must Accept the Primary Responsibility for Redressing the Gender Gap

Africa, and particularly Sub-Saharan Africa, is the only continent which entered the 21st Century with increased human and income poverty. Africa cannot break from the poverty cycle with more than half of its citizens constrained from accessing education generally and higher education in particular. African countries have to bring forth concrete proposals on how to redress this gender gap. These will have to entail multiple strategies and multiple actors. The first responsibility lies with the African governments which must ensure that their international, regional and national commitments are translated into policies and programmes, that strategies for implementation are clearly defined, that resources are mobilised and targets with time frames are realistically set. In those countries where the legal and regulatory environment is still a barrier, measures have to be taken immediately to reform existing laws and to institute progressive laws that will facilitate the implementation of equality principles. Programmes to support women's access to tertiary education should be holistic and should start during the very early years, for example with pre-school programmes.

African Universities Must Be More Proactive in Redressing the Gender Gap

The African universities, both private and public, have a major responsibility that consists in redefining their role with gender sensitivity, re-visiting their programmes, and reorganising the way knowledge has been produced, disseminated and controlled in order to enable women and girls to be part of the critical mass that produces and consumes knowledge. Universities must ensure that the learning environment does not repel either female students or female faculty. In this respect, affirmative action policies governing hiring, promotion, and recruitment have to be implemented with some caution so that they do not contribute to undermining the self-esteem of the targeted females and other disadvantaged groups. Universities should proactively solicit funds in order to establish special scholarships to support women who fail to access University due to lack of funding.

Funding Agencies Including the Private Sector Must Provide More Resources

The international community, particularly multilateral and bilateral agencies as well as transnational companies, need to support African states, and African women in particular, in the struggle to increase access to higher education. A need to establish a special fund for women's education at the national, regional, or sub-regional levels is being underscored. In this respect, organisations such as FAWE could be entrusted to be custodians of such a fund. Similar funds could be established at the national level.

African Women and Progressive Men Must Lobby for Girls' and Women's Education

Last but not least, African women–particularly those who have had an opportunity for higher education--and progressive African men should not let governments rest until true equality is achieved. NGOs in particular have to continue to offer with programmes aimed at sensitising men and women to the importance of promoting girls' education generally and higher education in particular.

References

African Development Bank, 1996. "Africa in the World Economy: Towards Policies for Long term Growth and Development in Africa: Economic and Social Statistics on Africa." African Development Report.

African Gender Institute (AGI), 2000. Newsletter 6 (May). Cape Town: University of Cape Town.

DAC, 1999. "DAC Scoping Study of Donor Poverty Reduction Policies and Practices: A Synthesis Report. DAC, 1999. DAC Informal Network on Poverty, March.

Diane, H., and C. Taspcott, 1991. "Affirmative Action and Equal Opportunity for Women in Namibia." ILO, Technical Background Paper.

Economic Commission for Africa (ECA), United Nations, 1994a. "African Platform for Action Dakar, Senegal.

Economic Commission for Africa (ECA), United Nations, 1994b, Fifth African Conference on Women, Nov 16. Dakar, Senegal.

Economic Commission for Africa (ECA), United Nations, 1994c. "Women, Environment and Sustainable Development. Fifth African Conference

on Women, Conference Papers on Priority Issues: Part
V. vol. 2, Nov. 16. Dakar, Senegal.

Economic Commission for Africa (ECA), United Nations, 1994d. "Critical Issues of Equity and Sustainable Development with Examples from Africa." Fifth Regional Conference on Women, Women's Rights, vol.2, part 11A.

Economic Commission for Africa (ECA), United Nations, 1999. "The Status of Women: Liberia, Zimbabwe, Burkina Faso. Congo, Swaziland, Somalia. Sierra Leone, Egypt, Zambia, Sudan, Botswana, South Africa Seychelles, Lesotho, Eritrea, Ethiopia and Nigeria."

Emang Basadi Women's Association, 1999. *The Women's Manifesto: A Summary of Botswana Women's Issues and Demands.* Gabarone

Kasente, D., 2001, *Popularising Gender: A Case Study of Makerere University.* FAWE publication.

Karega, R. M., 2001. *Statistical Overiew on Girls Education at the University Level.* FAWE publication.

Leah, N.W., 1997. *Beyond Beijing. Fourth Conference on Women: A Summary of the Global Platform and Africa Regional Platforms for Action with a Focus on Education.,* FAWE publication.

Masanja, V. G., 2001. *Structural Changes and Equal Opportunities for All: A Case Study of the University of Dar es Salaam Tanzania.* FAWE publication.

Meena, R., 2000. *Gender Frameworks for FAWE Country Chapters.* FAWE publication.

Meena, R., ed., 1992. *Gender in Southern Africa: Conceptual and Theoretical Issues.* SAPES publication.

Mukholi, D., 1995. *A Complete Guide to Uganda's Fourth Constitution: History, Politics, and the Law.* Kampala, Uganda: Fountain Publishers.

Schultz, P., 1992, *Investment in the Schooling and Health of Women and Men: Quantities and* Returns. World Bank publication.

Republic of Namibia, 1997. National Gender Policy". Office of President: Department of Women's Affairs.

SADC, 1999. Gender and Development: A Declaration by the Heads of State or Government of the Southern African Development Community."

SARDC, 1997a. "Beyond Inequalities: Women in South Africa. University of Western Cape.

SARDC, 1997b, "Beyond Inequalities: Women in Namibia. University of Namibia.

SARDC, 1997c. "Beyond Inequalities: Women in South Africa. Southern Africa Research and Documentation Centre."

SARDC, 1999. "SADC Gender Monitor: SARDC in Collaboration with Women in Development." Southern Africa Awareness Project 1 (Feb.).

SARDC, 2000. "Beyond Inequalities: Women in Southern Africa.

Schultz, P. T., 1991. "Differences between Returns and Investments in the Education of Women and Men." Seminar paper, Institute of Policy Reform.

United Nations, 1989. "Statistics Indicators on Women in Africa, Department of International Economics and Social Affairs."

United Nations Development Program (UNDP), 1995. *Human Development Report*. New York: Oxford University Press.

United Nations Development Program (UNDP), 1999. "Human Development Report." UNDP publication.

United Nations Development Program (UNDP), 2000. *Human Development Report: Human Rights and Human Development*. New York: Oxford University Press.

UNDP/SAPES, 1998. "Governance and Human Development in Southern Africa." SADC Regional Human Development Report. SAPES publication.

United Nations Educational Scientific and Cultural Organization (UNESCO), 1999., *Statistical Yearbook*. Paris: UNESCO Publishing & Bernan Press

United Nations, 1995. *The World's Women*. New York: United Nations.

World Bank, 1988. *Education in Sub-Saharan Africa: Policies for Adjustment, Revitalization, and Expansion*. Washington, D.C.: The World Bank.

CHAPTER 5

THE SIGNIFICANCE OF HIGHER EDUCATION IN GENDER AND EDUCATIONAL REFORMS IN AFRICA: THE FAWE EXPERIENCE

Penina Mlama

Introduction

The last two decades have witnessed great attention to the status of education in the world, with particular emphasis on the developing countries. At the 1990 Jomtien Conference on Education for All, focus was directed at the world's failure to provide education for the children, especially those of the developing countries. The 1990 Jomtien Declaration on Education for All was, therefore, a commitment by governments to make sure that all children have access to education by the year 2000.

In 2000, governments and educators from 180 countries gathered again in Dakar, Senegal, to assess the achievements of the ten years after Jomtien. Although some gains had been recorded, especially with regard to increase in enrolment at the first grade level, the situation had not changed much and the numbers of children out of school were still phenomenal. In 2000, girls still constituted about one third of the over 113 million out of school. One third of the 800 million illiterates were women.

Sub-Saharan Africa recorded the worst level of achievement. About 42 million children were out of school; only 66% of the children who entered grade one reached grade five and most of them were girls. Even though a significant increase in enrolment for girls had been recorded in the ten years after Jomtien, Africa was the only continent where the gender gap had actually increased, though marginally.

The major causes for this situation were the intensification of poverty and the failing economies of most of the countries in Africa. The increase in armed conflict with over ten countries either in armed conflict or post-conflict situations contributed to this situation. The devastating HIV/AIDS scourge also dealt a severe blow to all aspects of human development on the continent including the education systems. In addition, bad governance and mismanagement of resources had negative effects on the quality of education provided. Dakar, therefore, constituted a re-commitment by governments, civil society, and the donor community to the provision of education for all. The Dakar Framework for Action pays special attention to gender and one of its goals is stated as follows:

> Eliminating gender disparities in primary and secondary education by the year 2005, and achieving gender equality by 2015, with a focus on ensuring girls' full and equal access to and achievement in basic education of good quality. (Goal no 5, Dakar framework for Action)

It was also at the Dakar Conference that the United Nations' Secretary General Kofi Anan launched the United Nations Girls' Education Initiative, which was directed at achieving gender equality in education.

The 2000 Millennium Development Goals adopted the Dakar Gender Goal as its goal number three, and its goal number two stated that by 2015, all African countries will "achieve universal primary education—ensure that all boys and girls complete a full course of primary schooling." (United Nations 2000)

Educational Reforms in Sub-Saharan Africa

After Dakar, African countries have seriously stepped up their efforts towards the provision of education for all. Serious analysis has gone into identifying the problems, formulating policies, charting out implementation strategies and mobilising funding for far-reaching education reforms to ensure quality education, access, retention, and performance for all children.

At this Dakar meeting in 2000, it was agreed that every country should come up with a country EFA Action Plan charting out how and when the EFA goals will be attained. The EFA Country Action Plans are supposed to have been drawn by the end of 2002. A commitment was made in Dakar that the donor community would not deny resources to any country that came up with a credible plan.

Governments have followed different processes in effecting educational reforms. Some countries have adopted a sector-wide approach whereby educational reform is incorporated in an overall reform of a country's social economic development policies and plans. In other countries, educational reform is linked to the Poverty Reduction Strategies. On the whole, all countries are engaged in some form of educational reforms in the realisation that no development would be forthcoming without an investment in education.

However, educational reforms in sub-Saharan Africa are complicated by a number of factors. It is pertinent to mention here that most of the educational reforms in Africa are donor driven. At both bilateral and multilateral levels, governments in Africa deal with a large number of donors, each with their own interests and conditionalities. In many cases, the scenario is quite confusing as to which direction the countries' education policies and plans are going and whether the governments themselves are in control,

For example, there is a bit of confusion and indeed, tension in some countries between the EFA Plans, education sector plans, sector-wide investment plans, poverty reduction strategies, and other such development plans often conceived and designed externally. Governments, which hardly own the processes of educational reforms, are often pulled in different directions to please the different donors. Dependency on donors for resources makes most governments powerless to challenge the donor partners' directions and demands. The point to be made here, though, is that educational reforms in Africa are taking place under very difficult conditions and it is no wonder that the goals for the provision of education for all still seem so remote and very difficult to attain.

Educational reforms are also seriously impacted by the high levels of poverty, which show little sign of improvement. Both governments and parents find it difficult to meet the cost of good quality education. As a result, governments are forced to be too dependent on external donors, leading to a loss of ownership of the processes of educational reforms. Poor parents withdraw their children from school because of a lack of ability to meet school expenses. Girls become the worst victims in the process, owing to the lesser value accorded to girls' education by many communities.

The HIV/AIDS pandemic ravaging Africa has caused untold havoc to all spheres of life including education. Not only are teachers dying in large numbers, but also hundreds of orphans of HIV/AIDS are without support to undergo schooling. Girls are also dropping out of school to look after their sick parents or to take care of their siblings after the death of their parents. A major concern relates to the disturbing fact that young girls are more vulnerable to infection than their male counterparts. Many girls are infected with HIV/AIDS through rape and coerced sex.

The African continent is also unfortunate enough to be home to a large number of armed conflicts or post-conflict situations. It goes without saying that the loss of life, destruction of infrastructure, displacement of large numbers of people, trauma, sexual violence, and rape that come with war are not good backgrounds for the provision of any type of education.

The persistence of negative cultural attitudes continue to militate against education, especially that of the girl child. Many communities still believe in marrying off their girls at a school-going age; genital mutilation not only violates the rights of the girls but also takes them away from schooling, sometimes for a long period; and the unfavourableunfavorable division of labourlabor puts a heavy burden of domestic chores on the girl child, thus impinging on her ability to study.

Some of the problems and failures of Africa's education systems can also be attributed to bad governance. It is no secret that corruption, inefficiency, and poor management contribute to many of the problems of poor quality education in Africa.

The above-mentioned factors have contributed significantly to the inability of the educational reforms to achieve quick or significant results in the provision of education for all, and to reach the targets set at Dakar. Even though some significant progress has been achieved, especially in increasing enrolment at the first grade level, the UNESCO global monitoring report, 2003/4, observes that 60% of the 128 countries for which data was available are likely to miss reaching gender parity at the primary and secondary levels by 2005. It is significant that 40% of these countries are at risk of not achieving gender parity either at the primary [9] or the secondary level [33] even by 2015, the target year according to the Dakar Education for All Framework for Action as well as the Millennium Development Goals (UNESCO 2003/4).

Gender and Educational Reforms: FAWE's Experience

Any discussion of gender and education at any level in Africa needs to take cognisance of the above background relating to educational reform processes. Before discussing gender and higher education, a look at the overall situation of gender and education in Africa is pertinent. Lessons are drawn from the experiences emerging from the work of the Forum for African Women Educationalists (FAWE).

FAWE is a pan-African non-governmental organisation engaged in the promotion of girls' education in Sub-Saharan Africa. Founded in 1992, FAWE's membership consists of female ministers of education and vice-chancellors. Male ministers of education have associate membership status. In addition, FAWE has a national chapter-level membership of educational practitioners and researchers and gender activists in 32 African countries.

Although full membership has been open to former and current female cabinet members and high-level academic officers only, with some associate members such as male ministers of education, FAWE works with various groups outside its membership. For instance, academics are called upon to make contributions through research with results and findings expected to be used for the formulation of policy that aimed at promoting change with educational implementation in the future. FAWE insists on the necessity of linking academic research and efforts to promote change. FAWE takes the lead in pushing for policy initiatives; its members work closely with scholars. What FAWE requests from scholars includes academic inquiry that (even in the case of basic/theoretical research) can lead to concrete recommendations that can be made to contribute to designing new policies for change and enlightening the old ones.

Many FAWE members are also academics who, given their cabinet and administrative positions and the mission of FAWE, are well positioned to navigate productively between theory and praxis.

The FAWE work programme is centred on the following four strategic objectives:

- To influence policy formulation, planning and implementation in favourfavor of increasing access, improving retention, and strengthening the performance of girls.
- To build public awareness and consensus on the social and economic advantage of girls' education through advocacy.
- To demonstrate, through practical demonstrative interventions on the ground, how to achieve increased access, improved retention, and better performance and achievement by girls.
- To influence replication and mainstreaming of the best practices from the demonstrative interventions into broader national policy and practice.

Through its national chapters FAWE undertakes various activities all over Sub-Saharan Africa aimed at achieving gender equality in terms of access, retention, and performance at all levels of education. More information about FAWE activities is available in the FAWE annual reports and publications as well as on the FAWE website: www.fawe.org

The starting point for this brief review of gender and educational reforms should be recognition of the fact that studies have exposed gender disparity and inequality in education at all levels. Attention has been repeatedly drawn to the unfavourable low enrolment rates, the numerous constraints to girls' education in the area of access, retention, performance, and quality. Poverty, negative cultural attitudes, and practices such as early marriage, female genital mutilation, unfriendly school environments, gender violence, the impact of HIV/AIDS, poor quality of education, distance from school, safety and security in and outside school, and numerous other factors have been extensively analysed and suggestions to solutions widely disseminated. It is not the purpose of this paper to repeat what is already known.

These factors are largely responsible for the fact that female enrolment at the tertiary level and especially in universities is still very low. The UNESCO EFA Global Monitoring Report notes that "no countries in Sub Saharan Africa with the exception of South Africa, have GERs girls' enrolment rates higher than 15%; indeed all countries of Sub Saharan Africa, with the exception of Mauritius, Namibia and South Africa have the equivalent of fewer than 5% of the age group enrolled." (UNESCO 2003/4).

It is obvious that unless enrolment, retention, and performance of girls at the basic education level are significantly improved, there is little hope of increasing the female enrolment at the tertiary level.

As mentioned above, most African countries are implementing educational reforms geared at providing access to quality education for all children. The educational reform plans are long term, often spanning periods of ten years or more; the targets for the EFA framework of action and the Millennium Development Goals are set for 2015. It is expected, therefore, that the educational reforms will pay serious attention to all factors critical to the attainment of education for all, including the gender inequality that characterises the education systems and communities at large.

It is sad to note, however, that this is not the case in relation to gender equality. Despite the commendable efforts by gender activists over the last three decades at raising gender awareness, most of the policy makers and planners responsible for designing the educational reforms are still not gender responsive, as a result of which education policies and plans do not address the gender inequalities in education adequately.

FAWE's experience shows that there is a serious gap in addressing gender equality in the ongoing educational reforms in Africa. In 2000, FAWE undertook a review of educational policies and plans for gender responsiveness in 32 countries where FAWE is operational. The findings were disappointing in that most of the documents reviewed were lacking in gender analysis or responsiveness. Most of the documents state in general terms the problem of gender inequality in education and make vague statements of intent to address the gender imbalances. The analysis of the factors behind the gender inequality is often inadequate, leading to a serious lack of strategies and non-allocation of resources for rectifying the situation (FAWE 2000). Concerted efforts are required, therefore, to make the educational reforms gender responsive. Intensive advocacy targeted at education policy makers, planners and practitioners at all levels is required.

In 2003, FAWE undertook another exercise to review the Education for All Country Action Plans of eighteen countries in Sub-Saharan Africa. With the exception of Guinea, Namibia, Zambia, and Senegal, most of the plans did not give serious attention to gender responsiveness despite the fact that the Dakar Framework for Action to which the plans are responding has specific goals on gender to be attained (FAWE 2003). A review of poverty reduction strategies, sector-wide plans and other such development plans that have implications for education revealed the same results in relation to the lack of sufficient gender responsiveness. In response to this gap, FAWE undertook to work closely with ministries of education to try to influence the education policy and planning processes for gender mainstreaming. Some improvements are visible, although much remains to be done to make the policies and plans comprehensively gender responsive.

Advocacy is also required at the grassroots level where deeply rooted cultural attitudes and practices continue to militate against girls' access, retention, and achievement. Parents, community leaders, teachers, and community members in general still harbour attitudes that work against the girl child and that lead to early marriage, reluctance by parents to meet school costs for girls, excessive domestic labour, sexual abuse and trafficking, and female genital mutilation, to cite just a few impediments.

Serious advocacy is required to change the attitudes and values of people who see girls and women as merely sexual objects for the pleasure of men. It is this attitude to life that makes the fight against HIV/aids infection very difficult. Africa is still suffering too many incidences of rape and other forms of sexual harassment which demean the dignity of women and lead to many forms of torture, including death through HIV/AIDS infection.

Not enough attention is paid to advocacy for peace so that the political leadership does not resort to armed conflict to stay in power. Over twenty countries in Africa are either in armed conflict or post-conflict situations, and many others are constantly threatened by various types of conflicts. The impact of such conflict on development, including education is far-reaching. The girls and women who are treated as loot suffer untold miseries including rape, forced marriage to soldiers, widowhood and death. Africa needs to undertake much more serious advocacy for peace than is presently the case.

Advocacy is also necessary for girls and women themselves to empower them to overcome the results of their gender-biased socialisation. They need to conquer the internalisation of the assumed docility and subservience of women, to build up their confidence and their ability to assume public roles, and bring out their ability to perform well in the various spheres of life, including the academic sphere.

Various explanations are advanced for the lack of adequate gender responsiveness within ministries of education. One points to the negative attitudes towards gender equality among the policy makers, most of whom are men and have been socialised to see women as inferior to themselves. With such attitudes, they continue to ignore the gender dimension not only of education policies and plans but also of development processes as a whole.

Blame is also apportioned to the gender units within ministries of education for their ineffectiveness in influencing the mainstreaming of gender. Many ministries of education have gender units or gender focal points. It is argued, however, that many of the officers in charge of the gender departments do not seem to understand their basic responsibilities. Even where the units have people with the right skills, they are either under-resourced or run by junior officers with no power to influence the decision-making processes. Others pointed out that gender issues were largely considered to be part of the donors' agenda so unless pushed by donors, ministries paid minimal attention to gender.

FAWE's experience, however, shows that while the above points have merit and indeed affect the mainstreaming of gender, one major factor for lack of effective action is inadequate capacity and skills for gender policy analysis and gender mainstreaming. There are many gender specialists in Africa who in the past three decades have contributed significantly towards raising the gender awareness of people at all levels. Hundreds of workshops for gender awareness have been conducted and numerous research reports produced. Indeed, Africa is more knowledgeable on gender today, thanks to the unfailing efforts of gender activists, researchers, and consultants.

However, policy analysis for gender responsiveness and the process of mainstreaming gender require more skills than raising gender awareness does.

Skills are required to analyse education policies for gender responsiveness. Such skills are particularly critical in a situation where, as is often the case in Africa, policy formulation is not widely participatory. Education policies in Africa are normally formulated within the ministries of education and then passed by parliaments. It is a common scenario to see gender activists running around trying to make a policy gender responsive just when it is about to be passed by parliament because they did not go about it in time to have input. More often than not, by the time it is realised that something is seriously wrong with the policy, it is too late.

This calls for the ability to read and understand quickly the policy document, identify the gender gaps, and chart suggestions for changes to be incorporated into a revised document within short time limits. For such fast-track processes to bear fruit, it is necessary that the gender experts have sound knowledge not only of gender issues but also of the subject under discussion, backed by statistics.

Experience has shown that policy analysis and gender mainstreaming require high levels of education because they go beyond mere gender activism to the ability to understand the forces behind development processes, to understand policy formulation and planning processes, to interpret the gender implications of the policies and to incorporate alternatives in policies and plans. The already complex processes of policy formulation and planning are made more complex by the external agenda of the external donors who, as indicated earlier, are often in the driver's seat. Skills in gender mainstreaming have to include some understanding of the dynamics of development aid.

Educational reforms do not end with policies and plans. The major challenge is in the translation of the policies and plans into action that can bring change on the ground. There are many examples of good policies and plans recorded in relation to gender that remain on the shelves. Whereas gender awareness has increased to a commendable level compared to ten years ago, this awareness is not translating into action on the ground.

FAWE's experience has shown that even where ministries of education are aware of gender disparities and say so in their education plans, there is not enough evidence of how to make the education implementation plans gender responsive in practical terms. For example, even though education officials know that in certain areas girls are withdrawn from school and married off at an early age, there are no strategies on how the education system can stop parents from forcefully marrying off their children. And indeed, on FAWE's visits to schools the head teachers sometimes report cases of girls dropping out of school due to forced marriage. However, the school heads often do not have any plan for dealing with the parents of the victims or stopping similar future events. In fact the teachers do not consider that as part of their mandate in running the school.

To confront such a problem in practical terms, therefore, calls for more than gender awareness. An understanding of the cultural set-up of the community; and advocacy skills to change the attitudes of parents and raise their awareness of the value of girls' education become necessary tools to change the situation. Curriculum and teacher training colleges must incorporate knowledge and skills on these sensitive cultural factors. Legal skills are also required where legislation is necessary to keep the girls in school. Many times the head teachers claim that they have no legal powers over the parents to stop them from marrying off their daughters as they wish. Even where legislation exists to prevent early marriage, neither teachers nor the Ministry of Education officials are equipped with the information or the skills to take legal action on behalf of the aggrieved girls. The same community-based approach is required to confront the cultural attitudes and values towards sex that tolerate practices that make girls and women vulnerable to HIV/AIDS infection. To effect change on the ground, therefore, gender and educational reforms require multiple skills. At the moment, most gender training does not equip the experts with such skills.

Many small-scale interventions have been undertaken by various organisations, including FAWE, to improve access, retention, performance, and quality of education from a gender perspective. Non-governmental organisations and civil society in particular have done commendable work to provide access to disadvantaged children such as girls who have dropped out of school and also orphans. Gender sensitisation of parents, community leaders, teachers and students on the importance of girls' education, gender-responsive teaching methodologies, bursary schemes for disadvantaged girls, re-entry into education systems for teenage mothers, gender-responsive teaching and learning materials are some examples of areas where cases of good practice exist.

The challenge, however, is in learning how to replicate, scale up, and mainstream these good practices into the wider education systems. For replication, scaling up, or mainstreaming to take place, it is necessary for the good practices to be identified, documented, and marketed to the major education providers and practitioners. Skills are also lacking in this area as well. The majority of researchers in Africa are trained to identify and analyse problems and not success stories. Very little expertise exists on how to replicate, scale up, or mainstream what has been proved to work. It is common for experts to ignore the lessons from the rich practical experiences of the people out in society and instead keep to churning out new development theories and plans. More generally, it is worth indicating that the pattern has been to focus on negative African cultural factors that hinder progress. Such a selective perspective may not be constructive. Indeed, identifying and finding ways to use positive African cultural factors can make significant contributions to achieving the goals of equity and empowerment.

Insofar as education and gender are concerned, there is a need to document the good practices and use them to guide the ministries of education on what works in improving gender equality. The same goes for skills in programme implementation, especially in the area of monitoring and evaluation. The education sector in Africa is still struggling with how to monitor and measure the impact of education policies and programmes. The need is felt more in measuring gender-related change. For example, how does one measure impact in raising gender awareness among policy makers, parents, or teachers and its impact on performance for girls? It is often disappointing to see policy documents that are not gender-responsive, especially where the officials who have produced them have been expressing gender awareness in meetings or gender-sensitisation workshops.

What are the indicators for the empowerment of girls, and at what point is one sure that they have gained sufficient confidence to overcome the different types of gender constraints in their education? Indeed, there is sufficient evidence for the need for specific tools for monitoring and evaluation of impact in gender responsiveness with specific reference to gender equality in education.

Higher Education, Gender and Educational Reforms

Considering the observations and gaps discussed above in relation to gender and education reforms, the question is: what role can higher education play in addressing this situation? Before an attempt is made to answer this question, it is important to review briefly gender and higher education.

Historically, higher education in Sub-Saharan Africa has made a significant contribution to gender studies in a number of ways. One is in the area of research whereby beginning in the1960s research on gender brought out the gender inequalities in all aspects of life, including education. This research, which has continued to be carried out by universities, contributes significantly to insightful analysis and provides facts and figures to gender activism and political campaigns for the elimination of gender discrimination.

Secondly, a number of universities have established gender studies or women's studies departments which have strived to put gender studies on a par with other academic disciplines as well as producing graduates with an understanding of the gender perspective in development. Such training has contributed to the current improvements in gender mainstreaming in government development policies and plans.

Thirdly, universities have produced many gender experts who serve in various capacities nationally and internationally, in pushing for the incorporation of the gender dimension in the development processes.

When it comes to gender and educational reforms, however, it is unfortunate that higher education institutions have not offered leadership in a number of areas. First of all, higher education institutions have not taken enough measures to reform their institutions to be gender responsive. Recent studies for gender responsiveness indicate that universities in Sub-Saharan Africa are still characterised by stark gender inequalities with regard to enrolment, academic performance, staff recruitment, staff development, and student and staff welfare, as well as university policies and plans (Bunyi 2003, Gomile-Chidyaonga 2003, and Houphouët-Boigny 2003).

Ironically, while universities have produced professionals who have become gender experts championing the gender cause nationally and internationally, they have not done very well in instituting significant gender reforms in their own institutions.

Many universities in Sub-Saharan Africa still do not have gender responsive policies and plans to address the various forms of gender inequalities still rampant in these institutions. Only a few universities, such as the University of Dar es –Salaam in Tanzania and Eduardo Mondlane in Mozambique address gender inequality in their strategic plans and come up with specific strategies to reduce the gender gap in student enrolment, staff recruitment, staff development, and social welfare.

University curricula have remained generally non responsive to gender, thus producing experts in the form of economists, engineers, teachers, planners, scientists, doctors, and others who then go to lead professional development sectors without the necessary skills to mainstream gender in the development processes. Faculties of education, for example, could go a long way in making the entire education system gender responsive by including in their curricula modules on gender responsiveness in relation to school management, environment, pedagogy, and general teaching methodologies.

It is also a matter of concern that universities have not played a very active role in the processes of Education for All of the last two decades. For example, owing to donors' decisions that efforts to bring about education for all will focus on basic education, universities have tended to ignore the processes of policy formulation, planning, and implementation of Education for All, even though the educational reforms that have arisen out of the Education for All processes have a lot of implications for the universities.   For example, in relation to gender, there is a significant increase in enrolment of girls because of the gender goals of Education for All.   There is also increased awareness of gender equality among the primary school children owing to the educational reforms that have introduced gender into the curricula. Universities need to prepare themselves for this cohort in terms of catering to increased numbers of enrolment of girls as well as handling a gender-responsive student body.

Considering that many countries in Sub-Saharan Africa have few universities, they tend to be residential so as to cater to students who come from all over the country. Any increase in enrolment means an increase in residential facilities. Experience has also shown that this is especially important for girls who are more vulnerable to abuse if they reside in off-campus facilities. Lack of campus facilities can easily deter girls from joining universities.   Thus universities need to start expanding their facilities to prepare to meet the needs of future students as a result of the expanding enrolment in primary grades and of the educational reforms at that level.

At the same time, though, universities must also address the quality of life on their campuses whether residential or not. Many universities in Africa are lacking in measures to address gender responsiveness especially in the area of sexual harassment which is rampant. It is gratifying to see that some universities, such as Cape Town University in South Africa and the University of Dar es Salaam in Tanzania have now introduced anti-sexual-harassment policies. However, much more work is required in this area, especially considering the high rates of HIV/AIDS infection recorded in these universities. It is also encouraging to note that more attention is currently paid to addressing HIV/AIDS at the institutions of higher learning. A study and tool kit produced by the Association of African Universities in Accra, Ghana, is a good example of such efforts. However, a lot remains to be done. Similarly, long-term expansion programmes are required with respect to academic programmes, with teaching and learning facilities to support the achievements of the educational reforms at the lower levels.

In view of the poor performance of higher education institutions with regard to gender, as indicated above, one might hesitate to suggest that the same institutions could contribute significantly towards improving gender equality in educational reforms. It is legitimate to state that higher education institutions should seek to put their own house in order first with regard to institutionalising gender equality. Indeed, universities, for example, must as a matter of urgency pay serious attention to the need to have gender-responsive policies and plans, and must also take action to eliminate gender inequalities in terms of enrolment, staff recruitment, promotion, governance structures, curricula, staff and student welfare, and all other aspects of university undertakings. As institutions of higher learning, they must be the role models for the lower levels of education and for society as a whole.

However, as they pursue justice and equality at home, the institutions of higher learning can at the same time play a key role in addressing the gender needs of educational reforms at the other levels. It is encouraging to note that some universities in Africa are already undertaking reforms to make their institutions gender responsive. One good example is the University of Dar es Salaam in Tanzania, which through the UDSM 2000 Transformation Programme initiated in 1993, has mainstreamed gender responsiveness into its policies and strategic plans. Through this programme the university has attained commendable progress in reducing the gender gap in enrolment, with the average female enrolment now standing at 37% compared to 19.5% in 1998, while some faculties such as Law, Medicine, and the Humanities have surpassed 45%.

This was achieved through specific strategic objectives that expected faculties to reach targets towards gender parity, and affirmative admission in favour of female students as well as the establishment of a sponsorship programme for needy female students. For example, the pre-entry course for science and engineering subjects designed to improve entry qualifications for girls that was introduced in 1997 had by 2000 provided admission to 214 female students. Other interventions have included preferential allocation of on-campus accommodation for female students, establishment of a gender management unit, gender sensitisation programmes for both staff and students, and general advocacy for gender equality (University of Dar-Es-Salaam 2003). Other universities in the region that have instituted similar programmes include Makerere University in Uganda, which has an affirmative admission and scholarship programme and a women's studies department.

In general, various universities have instituted one gender intervention or another to improve gender equality including affirmative admission (Kenya and Zimbabwe), women/gender studies programmes (Eduardo Mondlane in Mozambique, Ibadan in Nigeria, Western Cape in South Africa), legislation to combat sexual harassment (Cape Town, Durban, Natal- South Africa), and gender sensitisation (Chancellor College in Malawi) (Bunyi 2003).

As the above information suggests, there is no doubt that some efforts are being directed towards gender reforms in institutions of higher education themselves. It is also true; however, that these efforts are a far cry from what needs to be done. Higher education needs to do much more if there is to be any hope of creating gender-responsive conditions in these institutions.

While such efforts are continuing, however, higher education can at the same time play a critical role in influencing educational reforms at the lower levels of the education systems. Because of the role of higher education in providing intellectual leadership and professional expertise to society, it can assist these educational reforms and infuse them with gender responsiveness down the ladder in various ways.

The discussion above shows a demand for skills in policy analysis for gender responsiveness, gender mainstreaming, advocacy, translating policy and plans into action on the ground, replicating and mainstreaming good practices and monitoring and evaluation. It is clear that such skills are largely not available among the gender experts in Sub-Saharan Africa. Gender training in universities for example, still produces researchers, gender analysts, and experts for awareness creation. Higher education institutions could, therefore, take up the challenge to train a critical mass of people with adequate skills for gender mainstreaming who can then effectively change education policies and plans in favour of gender equality.- Mainstreaming gender into the higher education curricula can also play a critical role in producing economists, development planners, policy analysts, education planners, curriculum developers, and teachers who can then positively influence educational reforms in favour of gender equality.

Since societies often look upon higher education institutions as role models, making universities gender responsive could in itself send positive messages on behalf of gender equity to the rest of the society. Because of this, the need to increase the enrolment of women in higher education cannot be overemphasised. The current low levels of female enrolment in higher education in Africa are unacceptable. Even though women graduates may not necessarily be gender responsive, experience has shown that women tend to be more conscious of gender inequalities because they are the victims. As a result, they tend to be more pro-active in addressing gender concerns. If the number of women graduates increases, there will be more chances for improving the gender responsiveness of educational reforms at all levels.

There is also enough evidence to show that participation of girls in education improves with the presence of female teachers especially in the rural areas. (UNESCO 2003/2004)   Having more women university graduates provides role models for many girls, encouraging them to go to school, and thus contributes towards reducing the gender gap. Higher education must, therefore, continue to give priority to increasing the number of female university graduates in Africa.

In addition, gender training for both men and women should be given more priority than is currently the case in African universities. Many universities still treat gender studies as an option specifically for women. Experience has shown that gender permeates all spheres of development and unless serious attention is accorded to the gender dimension, Africa's development will be elusive for a long time. As indicated above, gender expertise is critical in policy analysis, policy formulation, and implementation. Both men and women need gender training for educational reforms and for development processes in general.

As stressed earlier, gender training in Africa needs to go beyond creating gender awareness: it needs to provide the tools for gender policy analysis, gender responsive policy formulation, advocacy, gender responsive programme planning, implementation, monitoring and evaluation. Without this wide range of gender expertise, it will be difficult to effect any meaningful change in the current unfavourable gender construct which is deeply entrenched in Africa today and which threatens to undermine not only educational reform but the development of the continent as a whole. Higher education institutions, therefore, need to revisit their curricula and reposition themselves to play a more meaningful role in making educational reforms at all levels gender responsive.

Conclusion

There is no doubt that the African institutions of higher learning, which have spearheaded the gender struggles of the past four decades, are capable of standing up to the challenges of gender and educational reform in Africa today. The question of funding is crucial. However, political will is even more important in defining a first stage for the articulation of the vision and practical planning for any real change. It should be emphasized however, that owing to the complexity of the challenges discussed above, the higher education sector has to reposition itself decisively if it is to be counted as having much relevance in effecting meaningful education reforms in Africa.

Formulation and implementation of educational reform offer opportunities for FAWE to have an impact on the nature and extent of changes leading toward the closing of the gender gap. Many FAWE members are also academics who, given their cabinet and administrative positions and the mission of FAWE, are well positioned to navigate productively between theory and action.

References

Bunyi, G., 2003. *Interventions that Increase Enrolment of Women in Tertiary Institutions.* World Bank Regional Training Conference on Improving Tertiary Education in Sub Sahara Africa. Accra.

Houphouët-Boigny, D., 2003. *Improving Women's Participation in Tertiary Education: The Case of the University de Cocody.* World Bank Regional Training Conference on Improving Tertiary Education in Sub-Sahara Africa. Accra.

FAWE, 2002- 2006. "Strategic Plan." Nairobi.

FAWE 1994, 1995, 1996, 1997, 1998, 1999, 2000, 2001, 2002, 2003. Annual Reports. Nairobi: FAWE.

FAWE, 2001a, "Statistical Overview on Girls' Education at the University Level." Nairobi: FAWE.

FAWE, 2001b. " Promoting Girls' Education through Community Participation." FAWE Best Practices, Paper No 1.

FAWE, 2001c. "Promoting Female Access to University Education through Affirmative Action: A Case Study in Tanzania." FAWE Best Practices, Paper no 2.

FAWE, 2001d. "In Search of an Ideal School for Girls." FAWE Centers of Excellence. Nairobi: FAWE.

FAWE, 2003. "Mainstreaming Gender into Education for All National Action Plans." Nairobi: FAWE.

Kasente, B., 2001. "Popularizing Gender; A Case Study of Makerere University." Paper commissioned by Forum for African Women Educationalists (FAWE) and presented at the 10th General Conference of the African Universities Association. Nairobi: FAWE.

Masanja, V., 2001. "Structural Changes and Equal Opportunities for All: A Case Study of the University of Dar es Salaam." Paper commissioned by FAWE and presented at the 10th General Conference of the Association of African Universities. Nairobi: FAWE.

Mlama, P., 2001. "Gender Equity Programming in Higher Education." Higher Education Policy Forum. Nairobi.

Musisi, B. N., 2001. "A Reflection On and Taking Stock of Innovations at Makerere University." Higher Education Reform. Nairobi.

World Bank, 2001. "Africa Development Indicators." Washington, D.C.: World Bank.

UNESCO, 1998. "Higher Education in Africa; Achievements, Challenges and Prospects" Dakar.

UNESCO, 2000a. "Dakar Framework for Action." World Education Forum. Paris and Dakar: UNESCO.

UNESCO, 2000b. "Statistical Document." World Education Forum. Paris and Dakar: UNESCO.

UNESCO, 2003/4. "EFA Global Monitoring Report, Gender and Equality for All; The Leap to Equality.," Paris: UNESCO.

CHAPTER 6

CURRENT STATUS OF, AND LEGISLATION TO REDRESS, GENDER INEQUALITIES IN SOUTH AFRICA

Philip Higgs

Introduction

The movement for the transformation of gender relations and the achievement of gender equality in South Africa is associated with what can be referred to as the women's movement in Africa, or also, African feminism. As a women's movement, African feminism can be described as a political, pragmatic, reflexive and group-oriented form of feminism, also referred to as the "sisterhood of Africa." This form of a peculiarly African feminism focuses on the struggles of African women to create a space of independence and dignity out of a triple layer of oppression, namely, the oppressive regimes created by colonial, western patriarchal and African patriarchal cultures. Furthermore, it criticises Western and European feminists for trying to speak for African women, thereby denying them the ability to voice their own thoughts. African feminism argues that African liberation depends on the development of an independent feminist voice that will perpetuate the tradition of female involvement in African societal affairs. This critical response is directed at those attempts to interpret feminism as a Western cultural phenomenon, attempts that are seen to ignore alternative perspectives on feminism that emphasise the historical conditions under which women's movements, and particularly those in Africa, challenge patriarchal cultures.

African feminism also focuses on the politics of gender, that is, the power relations between men and women, which are structured around opposing notions of masculinity and femininity. In a fundamentally patriarchal social space, a division is drawn between the public sphere (the outside workplace for males), where power is located, and the private sphere (the inside home for females), where there is no power. Contrary to this division, African feminism sees the role of women as based on male-female complementarity in overcoming discrimination by means of more equitable gender relations and changes in the sexual division of labour.

In what follows, an attempt will be made to contextualise these issues by directing attention to the current status of, and legislation to address, gender inequalities in South Africa.

Profile of South African Women

According to Tshoaedi (1998), Flood (1998), and Kethusegile (2000), South African society was, and still is, extremely patriarchal. The common perception is that it is the responsibility of a woman to take care of her family and children while the man is out establishing a career. The issue in this instance is not simply that woman and men perform different jobs but rather, that the duties they perform are valued and rewarded differently and unequally, with one not rewarded at all. This is notwithstanding a change in direction for women's politics in South Africa which took place when the *Joint Standing Committee on Justice* met on 9 August 1993 to consider legislation aimed at the promotion of equality between women and men and the prevention of family violence. This equality clause, according to Milazi (1993) became a terrain of struggle for women who wished to challenge issues of socio-economic rights, parental rights, customary rights, and so on. The challenge facing women since 1993 has been one of bringing these constitutional rights into line with the way women currently live in South Africa, knowing full well that the position of black South African women is dismal, to say the least.

Black South African women constitute the poorest socio-economic sector of the population (May 2000). While most of the economically active white, Indian and coloured women are found in the clerical, sales, supervisory, technical, professional and manufacturing sectors, the majority of black South African women who are employed, are concentrated in service and agricultural work, work that was until recently excluded from protective legislation. The small percentage of black South African women in the professional sector is found mostly in the teaching and nursing professions.

According to Wilhelm (1998), the majority of black South African women are unemployed and are tucked away in impoverished rural areas, while 82% Coloured, 92% White and 96% Indian women live in urban areas. Of all households in the rural areas, women head 59 percent.

Kadalie (1995) estimated that three million adult black South African women were functionally illiterate. The low status of black South African women is further compounded by the extreme forms of violence they have been subjected to over the past decades. Huge refugee populations, consisting mainly of women, children and the elderly, have been left homeless in areas where political violence has been most severe. Equally epidemic is the occurrence of domestic and sexual violence against women. Up until 1993, NICRO (National Institute for Crime Prevention and the Rehabilitation of Offenders) estimated that one rape occurs every 83 seconds, a thousand rapes a day.

Flaherty (1995: 12) also points out that gender inequity in the socio-legal system affects women in various ways. While the majority of black South African women are, in fact, breadwinners, the state, employers, and the church have until recently regarded men as the breadwinners, in order to justify low wages for women. While a variety of family forms exist in reality (owing to relocation, resettlement, influx control, migrant labour, and the high rates of divorce), the state and the employers, nevertheless regard the nuclear family with a male head, dependent wife and children as the norm, and accordingly treat men, women and children as though they exist within this unit throughout their entire lives. However, as Flaherty notes (1995: 20), anthropological studies supported by empirical evidence suggests that black South African women are increasingly eschewing marriage because of patriarchal domination and abuse, so that it is commonplace for women as single parents, including the widowed, the divorced and the deserted, to head families. These "anomalies" were not, until recently, taken into account by welfare regulations where the nuclear family was regarded as the norm. Consider, for example, the following clause:

A parent's grant shall . . . not be paid to a women if she cohabits with
a man with whom she is not married and is in such circumstances as,
in the opinion of the Director General, are not conducive to the
welfare of the children. (Children's Act 1960, as amended)

A woman seeking a grant for her children had to prove that the father of her children could not provide maintenance, and she had to demonstrate that she had undertaken legal proceedings in order to obtain such maintenance. In effect, a family, according to welfare regulations, could be constituted by a father, mother and children, or father and children, but could never be headed by a mother alone.

The subordination of black South African women was further compounded by several marital regimes that could apply in South Africa. In civil marriages contracted by Whites, Coloureds and Indians before 2 December 1988, wives were considered legal minors. Marital power has now been abolished, effectively making both partners equal. And yet these amendments do not affect the law relating to the position of husband as head of the family, or the law relating to domicile or guardianship. For example, many customary marriages place the control of the family in the hands of the male. It is evident, therefore, as Moll (1998) notes, that there were many pitfalls inherent in equality legislation for women. For this reason, women carefully drafted their demands in terms of the diversity of family arrangements, marital regimes, and religious, cultural and ethnic practices that exist in various forms across the country.

With the drawing up of the Interim Constitution, a significant victory was won when women overturned the recommendations of traditional leaders that customary law be exempt from the effects of a Bill of Rights. At the same time, however, in order to woo the support and loyalty of the traditional chiefs, the Negotiating Council inserted a clause in the Constitution ensuring that: "The institution, status and role of traditional leadership, according to indigenous law, shall be recognised and protected in the Constitution" (Schedule W, Article XIII).

This placed an added burden on black South African women who had to argue for equality against constitutional clauses, which entrenched patriarchal power in the political, social and cultural spheres.

Then also, unequal access to labour in the various employment sectors has created, over the years, a differentiated labour market in which class, race, ethnicity and gender have operated historically at specific moments in time, and as allocation mechanisms in the economy, to keep women subordinate to men, and more specifically to keep black South African women subordinate to other women and to men in general. Black South African women, unlike white women and to a lesser extent Coloured and Indian women, have been subject to the harshest statutory controls for the greater part of their lives. But it is time to pay attention in more detail to the whole issue of labour and gender inequality in South Africa.

Labour and Gender Inequality

Women in South Africa have historically been confined to careers with limited promotional prospects and lower salaries than men. This situation has, however, gradually changed with the promotion of equity in the Constitution, the Labour Relations Act, and the Employment and Occupational Equity Act. Job applicants are now protected, and discrimination against pregnant women can be challenged under both the Labour Relations Act and the Constitution. Equality and anti-discrimination are primary principles underpinning the new democracy in South Africa. This is upheld in the interim Constitution and reaffirmed in the final Constitution. However, the arduous task of redressing the structural gender and race inequality that pervades workplaces in South Africa is still being addressed. Bhoola (1996) maintains that affirmative action, or employment equity is a powerful mechanism for redressing structural and systematic discrimination which is often hidden in workplace practices.

In considering affirmative action or employment equity measures, it must be borne in mind that women in South Africa are a diverse, heterogeneous group with different race and class interests. This implies that the interests of black and white women, and working-class and middle- class women, do not always coincide. In selecting the appropriate applicant for a job, an employer will often have to distinguish between a white woman from a middle-class background who has not been disadvantaged, and a black working-class woman who has succeeded despite apartheid and Bantu education. However, it is in the interests of all women in the labour market to see discrimination eliminated and measures taken to improve their position at work.

In the adoption of such measures, it is important to clarify what is meant by "affirmative action" and "employment equity." These terms refer to initiatives to redress employment disadvantage suffered by members of specific groups as a result of discrimination. "Affirmative action" policies range from quotas—the most controversial, requiring that a certain number of jobs be reserved for disadvantaged groups—to giving disadvantaged groups preference in employment. "Employment equity" refers to removing barriers to make recruitment, hiring, promotion and benefits more equitable, while seeking to ensure that employees are given the opportunities for which they are qualified.

Affirmative action and employment equity, therefore, encompass the removal of barriers and the provision of fair opportunities, on the understanding that merit is not undermined. Barrier removal measures might include:

- Offering child-care services and flexible work schedules for women employees.
- Modifying the workplace to accommodate workers who are physically disabled.
- Providing equal promotion and training opportunities.
- Generally utilising measures aimed at breaking down sexual, ethnic or racial ghettos within an organization.

Affirmative action and employment equity thus include institutional and societal mechanisms to transform the workplace, making it more diverse and responsive to the needs of disadvantaged groups. These important transformational measures are safeguarded in the South African Constitution of 1996, especially as regards employment equity. In clause 9, the Constitution guarantees the right to equality before the law and equal protection and benefit of the law. It provides further that:

> Equality includes the full and equal enjoyment of all rights and freedoms. To promote the achievement of equality, legislative and other measures designed to protect or advance persons, or categories of persons, disadvantaged by unfair discrimination may be taken.

This is the constitutional safeguard for employment equity. It emphasises that employment equity is not an exception, but rather a necessary means to achieve equality. The equality clause prohibits unfair discrimination, directly or indirectly, on a number of grounds including: race, gender, sex, pregnancy, marital status, ethnic or social origin, colour, sexual orientation, age, disability, religion, conscience, belief, culture, language and birth.

These provisions apply to everyone, and are, therefore, applicable to employers and can be enforced against them. The Constitution also provides that legislation must be enacted to prevent or prohibit unfair discrimination.

The constitutional safeguard of equality and employment equity has been translated by the Labour Relations Act No. 66 of 1995 into specific protection for employees in the workplace. The unfair labour practice definition in the Labour Relations Act prohibits discrimination in terms very similar to those found in the Constitution. In addition to the grounds listed in the Constitution, it also prohibits discrimination on the basis of political opinion and family responsibility.

One of the significant advances of the Labour Relations Act is that applicants for jobs are also protected from discrimination. Victims of discrimination can lodge a complaint with the Council for Labour Disputes, the body established under the Labour Relations Act to conciliate workplace disputes. The Labour Relations Act and the Constitution, therefore, provide the impetus for employers to immediately begin redressing inequality through appropriate measures.

One of the concepts in the anti-discrimination provision in the Labour Relations Act and the Constitution is direct and indirect discrimination. Discrimination generally refers to the failure to treat people as individuals, and to assign them group stereotypes, for example, representing all women as unreliable workers. Such assumptions related to unreliability are often based on sociological facts. For instance, the fact that women are caregivers in the family forces them to miss work whenever a member of the family, especially a child, is sick. The question that should then be asked is: how are these sociological facts dealt with legally and practically to combat such perceptions of unreliability?

Direct discrimination refers to the unfavourable treatment of an employee on the basis of a prohibited ground, such as gender. It is manifested, for example, in job advertisements that say "Male technician required." Often there is an intention on the part of the employer to exclude women. Indirect discrimination refers to neutral practices, which have a more severe impact on members of a certain group, because of their position in society. It occurs in requirements that applicants, say for police jobs, have to be of a certain height or weight. It has a more detrimental effect on women because fewer women than men can comply with the job requirement. The employer's intention is irrelevant because the requirement discriminates against women by denying them access to those jobs. This type of requirement would be discriminatory unless the employer can justify the need for a female nurse for an obstetrics ward, for example, or a Catholic teacher for a Catholic school. In the United States this is referred to as justification on the grounds of "business necessity," and is not discriminatory.

Thus if the practice is justified irrespective of the person to whom it is applied, it is not discriminatory (see Griggs v Duke Power Co 401 US 424 [1971] and Dothard v Rawlinsony 433 US 321 [1977]). The new Labour Relations Act incorporates a similar defense by providing that where something is an inherent requirement of the job, it is not unfair discrimination.

Merely prohibiting discrimination is, however, unlikely to improve the status of women substantially. Positive measures are required in the form of employment equity, and can take various forms. These range from legislation obliging employers to employ a specific number of women in specific jobs to fixed quotas and preferential treatment.

Employment equity legislation, on the other hand, requires employers to identify barriers to the employment of women in certain occupational categories and to remove them. It emphasises flexible goals for the employment and promotion of women and targets for meeting those goals.

Employment equity legislation defines different disadvantaged or target groups and requires employers to review their workforce composition, and to draw up plans for the achievement of employment equity. It does not mean merely employing a few women in top positions, irrespective of their qualifications or experience, as most corporations are inclined to do.

A critical mass of women must be created in occupations in which they are under-represented, but women must also be advanced through accelerated training, developing career-paths or mentoring in order that they function effectively in those positions. Placing unqualified women in top positions merely to enhance a corporation's profile is retrogressive. It results in a greater stereotyping of women as it reinforces the notion that women cannot succeed. Relevant training and support must be given, but the employer must also create an environment that is conducive to women's advancement.

Sexual harassment and abuse of women must be dealt with effectively through disciplinary measures to create a supportive environment for women employees. Developing sexual harassment codes is another mechanism for highlighting and dealing with behaviour that undermines women's equality.

The Canadian Supreme Court has held, for instance, in the context of a quota for women on the Canadian National Railways, that "to combat systemic discrimination, it is essential to create a climate in which both legislative practices and negative attitudes can be challenged and discouraged" (Action Travail des femmes v Canadian National Railway Co 40 DLR (4th) 193 SCC at 210).

Ensuring equality for women in the workplace ultimately means recruiting women into the fullest range of employment opportunities; equal pay for work of equal value; fair consideration for promotions; participation in corporate policy and decision making; paid parental leave; and equal pensions and benefits. There is also a need for changed attitudes towards women so that they are taken seriously as workers, rather than being marginalized, and improved access to education and training to permit women to compete for the widest possible range of options, are essential. Areas for the implementation of such measures include:

Recruitment

Changes in recruitment practices are imperative. The Supreme Court of Canada has affirmed that a quota for employing women in jobs previously reserved for males in the Canadian National Railways was consistent with equality because it sought to redress systemic discrimination suffered by women. In workplaces where there is an under-representation of women generally or in senior positions, attempts should be made to promote women already in the workplace and to train them where necessary. External recruitment should be embarked upon only when the internal pool of qualified applicants has been exhausted. Where the under-representation of women is serious, employers may have to give preference to women over men. Therefore, implementing equity for women would involve re-evaluating recruitment practices and eliminating those that foster discrimination. This might mean reconsidering the newspapers and magazines in which jobs are advertised, the placement of advertisements in the Vacancies-Male column, interview questions that reflect gender discrimination such as "Do you plan to have children?" and questions about marital status.

Training and Removing Barriers

This does not mean training women *en masse* for the same jobs, but developing individual career paths in consultation with the employees concerned. Employers are often reluctant to invest in women through training because they feel the value is wasted when women leave to have or take care of children. These attitudes have to change.

Employers have to analyse and remove all workplace practices or policies that could prevent the employment and advancement of women. Examples of such practices include the requirement that all employees be regarded as full time, and that no flex-time is permitted. Discrimination is a significant barrier, and manifests itself in for instance, the unequal provision of benefits. A company's pension and provident fund scheme may, for example: provide that women pay higher contributions because they are expected to live longer; have different retirement ages for men and women; not allow women time off to attend to child care responsibilities or care for sick children, which could be discrimination on the grounds of family responsibility. Employers' attitudes constitute significant barriers and until employers re-evaluate the work women do, and are capable of doing, women will still be restricted to underpaid jobs with limited prospects. Eliminating discrimination means destroying one of the most significant barriers to women's advancement.

Equal Pay for Equal Work

Because women's work is often undervalued, they earn less than men do for comparable jobs. Equal pay policy does not mean all employees doing the same work should get the same pay. Instead, there should be no discrimination on illegitimate grounds, such as race or sex. Also, the jobs women are often confined to - clerical, secretarial and administrative—must be revalued and paid accordingly.

Pregnancy

This is one of the major areas of discrimination. In the United Kingdom, the House of Lords has confirmed that to dismiss or refuse to employ a women owing to possible pregnancy is unlawful discrimination (see Webb v Emo Air Cargo [1992] 2 AER 43 (CA)). Also, to select a woman for retrenchment because she is pregnant and would in any event require maternity leave constitutes discrimination against women. Employers have been made aware that any disadvantageous treatment of women on account of pregnancy is discrimination under both the Labour Relations Act and the Constitution. In particular, dismissal on the grounds of pregnancy or intended pregnancy is automatically unfair under the Labour Relations Act. The concerns of women employees in this regard must be addressed and plans developed around leaves that accommodate pregnant women. In some northern European countries, there are maternity and paternity leave arrangements assuming that fathers and mothers are granted leave associated with childbirth, thus making this kind of leave less a phenomenon associated solely with women.

Employment Equity Plan

An employment equity programme should aim to remove systemic barriers which impede the full employment of women. Also, to ensure equitable representation of women, remedial measures to benefit women for a specific period of time should be undertaken. These could include providing accelerated training for women, especially those in dead-end jobs; recruiting women specifically; and support measures to assist women. Support measures could include child-care, flexible working hours, transport and counselling. The employer should set goals for the recruitment, training, promotion of women and the timetables for achieving these goals. Whatever employment equity policy is implemented, however, this must not be done in isolation from a general human resource development plan. The policy should not mean that women who are not suitably qualified are employed or promoted, which would mean lowering standards. It is a temporary measure to facilitate equal opportunity through equal educational opportunity, eradicate race and sex discrimination, and realise the potential of all participants in the workforce.

The above measures for implementation become increasingly urgent because the South African labour market has been, and is still, characterised by occupational inequality. In the case of women, this is reflected in their distribution across job categories and up and down the job hierarchy. While most women of working age are now in the labour force, they are confined to a narrow range of careers with limited prospects for promotion, and their average still lags far behind their male counterparts. For example, women are concentrated in the service and administrative sectors and are under-represented in the managerial and technical sectors. Reasons for this include complex social factors like discrimination by employers who fail to hire, promote or train women because of stereotypes about women being unable to succeed in "a man's world." However, there are underlying factors linked to the unequal division of labour in the home. This makes women primarily responsible for the home and child-care, which reduces their employment opportunities.

Anti-discrimination legislation which attempts to change employer behaviour, is not, therefore, enough to change women's subordinate status in society. Remedial initiatives have to go beyond prohibiting discrimination to actually address the social pattern of disadvantage and discrimination which combine to render women subordinate in the workplace.

All in all, labour discrimination against women in the South African society is inextricably linked to the status of women in that society. And in this regard, attention will now be directed at recent legislation affecting the status of women in South Africa.

Recent Legislation Affecting the Status of Women in South Africa

In the continuing quest to address those problems which detract from the status of women in the South African society, numerous legislative measures have been passed since 1994 with the onset of a new democratic dispensation. South Africa ratified the United Nation's Convention on the Elimination of All Forms of Discrimination Against Women without any reservations in December 1995. Through ratification of the Convention, South Africa condemned discrimination against women and agreed to pursue by all means and without delay a policy of eliminating all forms of discrimination against women in South Africa. The Constitution of the Republic of South Africa (1966) recognises and protects the right to equality, including gender equality. The founding provisions of the Constitution, which are contained in Chapter 1 of the Constitution, state that the Republic is founded on the values of *inter alia* the achievement of equality, non-racism and non-sexism. Section 9, contained in the Act of Rights, states that "everyone is equal before the law and has the right to equal protection and benefit of the law." Furthermore, this section does not allow the state or any person to discriminate unfairly, directly or indirectly, against any person based on among other things: gender, sex, pregnancy or marital status. Section 9(4) also provides for the enactment of national legislation to prevent or prohibit unfair discrimination. Equality is thus viewed as a core value underlying the democratic society envisaged by the 1996 Constitution. The founding provisions of the

Constitution furthermore state that the Republic of South Africa is one sovereign democratic state founded on, *inter alia*, the achievement of equality and non-racism and non-sexism. The Bill of Rights itself affirms that it is "the cornerstone of democracy in South Africa" and that it "enshrines the rights of all people in our country and affirms the democratic values of human dignity, equality and freedom."

Furthermore, de Koker (1999) notes that during the past few years a number of new statutes have been passed and existing Acts amended that directly or indirectly affect the position of women in South Africa. Among the three specific Acts that relate to the position of women in the private sphere are the Maintenance Act 99 of 1998, the Domestic Violence Act 116 of 1998, and The Recognition of Customary Marriages Act 120 of 1998.

The Maintenance Act 99 of 1998

The Maintenance Act 99 of 1998 came into being in an effort to address the administrative and practical problems encountered in the application of the Maintenance Act 23 of 1963. The Act improves on the 1963 Act in that it provides for the following:

- The appointment of maintenance investigators and the determination of the powers and functions of these investigators.
- The setting of core guidelines regarding the duty of parents to support their children.
- The payment of maintenance from money owed or accruing to persons against whom maintenance orders had been made.
- The making of maintenance orders in the absence of persons who have a duty of support in appropriate cases [orders by default].
- The civil execution of arrears in terms of a maintenance order.

The Domestic Violence Act 116 of 1998

The Domestic Violence Act primarily aims at replacing and improving the provisions of the Prevention of Family Violence Act which was promulgated in 1993 in an effort to improve the position of women and to combat and prevent domestic violence. The Prevention of Family Violence Act was, however, very limited in scope and proved to be ineffective in practice. The Domestic Violence Act recognises that domestic violence is a serious crime against society and that women constitute the majority of victims of domestic violence. The Act furthermore recognises that domestic violence is an obstacle to achieving gender equality.

This Act entails a substantial broadening of the limited scope of its predecessor, the Prevention of Family Violence Act. The most important improvements are the following:

> The concept of "domestic violence" was redefined to mean any controlling or abusive behaviour that harms the health, safety or well-being of the applicant or any child in the care of the applicant. The definition includes but it is not limited to the following actions: Physical abuse or a threat of physical abuse; sexual abuse or a threat of sexual abuse; emotional, verbal and psychological abuse; economic abuse; intimidation; harassment; stalking; damage to or destruction of property; or entry into the applicant's residence without consent, where the parties do not share the same residence.

Many relationships in which abuse often occurs did not fall within the ambit of the Prevention of Family Violence Act. The Domestic Violence Act remedied this situation. In terms of the new Act a "victim" can be any person who is a partner in a domestic relationship with her/his abuser. The Act, *inter alia*, recognises the following persons as partners in domestic relationships:

- Married or divorced couples; including marriages according to any law, custom or religion.
- Couples of the same or the opposite sex who live or lived together in a relationship in the nature of marriage, although they are not, or were not, married to each other, or are not able to be married to each other.
- Parents of a child or people who had parental responsibilities for a child.
- Persons who are engaged or dating.
- Persons in a customary relationship.
- Persons who share or shared the same household or residence.

The new Act recognises that victims of domestic violence are disempowered persons. An application for a protection order may therefore be brought on   behalf of the applicant by any other person (including a member of the South African Police Service) who has a material interest in the well-being of the applicant.

The Recognition of Customary Marriages Act 120 of 1998

The main object of this Act is to extend full legal recognition to marriages entered into in accordance with customary law or traditional rites. The Act also improves the position of women and children within these marriages by introducing measures that bring customary law into line with the provisions of the Constitution and South Africa's international obligations.

The Act lays the foundation for a uniform code of marriage law that will be applicable to all South Africans. It provides a structure that allows for the future recognition of religious and other forms of marriages. The Act removes elements of discrimination against the customary legal tradition and gives expression to the right to systems of family law based on any tradition or religion, and the cultural pluralism guaranteed by the Constitution. The Act furthermore strives to reconcile the preservation of culture and tradition with the competing claims posed by the constitutional requirement to establish norms of equal treatment and non-discrimination.

The Act is important to women, particularly African women in South Africa, for the following reasons:

- It recognises monogamous and polygamous African customary marriages as valid marriages, affording women married in terms of African customary law the same status and protection as women married in terms of the Marriage Act.
- It provides for the equal status and capacity of spouses in a customary marriage, doing away with the Customary Law principle that women are minors and always under the guardianship and marital power of her husband or father.
- It regulates the proprietary consequences of customary marriages entered into after the commencement of the Act.
- The proprietary rights of women and children in existing customary marriages are protected in cases where the husband enters into further customary marriages. A husband intending to marry another wife must present a court with a property settlement agreed to by all parties involved.
- Spouses in existing customary marriages can change the property system in their marriage, under the supervision of a court of law.
- It provides for automatic community of property in the case of de facto monogamous, "new" marriages.

In terms of African customary law, African customary marriages can be dissolved by the spouses' families outside the court system. This situation puts women and children at risk. The Act, therefore, stipulates that any subsisting customary marriage may be terminated only by a decree of the court. Only one ground of divorce is recognised: irretrievable breakdown of the marriage. Courts granting divorces are given the powers they already exercise in respect of marriages contracted under the Marriage Act 25 of 1961. The courts should take any customary principles, such as maintenance already paid under customary law, determination of where a child's best interests happen to lie, into account when granting divorce orders.

Finally, the Act repeals a number of laws that discriminated against women living under African customary law:

- Section 11 (3) of the Black Administration Act of 1927 is repealed to remove South Africa's most notorious reason for the "perpetual minority" of African women.
- Sections 22 and 27(3) of the 1985 KwaZulu Act on the Code of Zulu Law and section 27(3) of the 1987 Natal Code of Zulu Law are repealed as they entrench the notion of a man as head of the family, and the marital power.
- Sections 3, 29, 37, 38 and 39 of the 1978 Transkei Marriage Act, are repealed because they are incompatible with the Act in diverse areas such as minimum age, marital power, and consequences of and procedures for divorce.

At present a serious debate is taking place as to the actual and assumed content of customary law. The question that is under consideration is: how much of the assumed content of customary law is actually authentic customary law as opposed to an interpretation and creation of pseudo-customary law, which is sometimes the result of distorted or misinterpreted indigenous practices mainstreamed in the new dominant paradigms?

The Promotion of Equality and Prevention of Unfair Discrimination Draft Bill of 2000

This Bill was approved by the South African Cabinet in 2000, and outlaws discrimination on nineteen counts, including race, gender, marital status, ethnic or social origin, sexual orientation, age and disability. In structure, the Bill has elaborate provisions defining its purposes and guiding principles. It emphasises the grounds of race and gender and then covers employment, education, health- care, accommodation, property and land, insurance, pensions, goods, services and facilities, associations and partnerships, clubs and sports, and the media. The Bill focuses on a few fundamental points. These include the requirement of positive measures by the state and private persons to promote substantive equality and punitive measures against unfair discrimination. This is felt to be critical because inequalities cannot be eliminated or substantially reduced by merely preventing unfair discrimination. At the same time, practices that perpetuate unfair discrimination and incidents of harmful discrimination are to be dealt with more severely than has been the case before. The other important innovation is its provision for special equality courts. To avoid the proliferation of new institutions that the nation cannot afford financially, and in terms of human resources, special training for magistrates and judges of existing courts will be a precondition. The courts of these magistrates or judges will be designated equality courts and will be empowered to enforce the new law. Those who seek remedy under this new legislation will not be burdened or discouraged by prohibitive legal costs charged by private legal practitioners. The law is for the people and not for lawyers.

However, despite these innovations in legislation, recent research has shown that the social pattern of disadvantage and discrimination against women is also revealed in another social arena, namely, the law.

The Law and Gender Inequality

The first comprehensive research to identify inequality and discrimination against women that exists in the law was undertaken in 1999 as an Audit of Legislation that Discriminates on the Basis of Sex and Gender. The aim of the audit was to identify laws that discriminate on the basis of sex and gender and to highlight areas for law reform. The audit, prepared by the Gender Research Project of the Centre for applied Legal Studies at the University of the Witwatersrand, was launched by the Commission on Gender Equality.

It found that legislative discrimination still exists and occurs both directly and indirectly. However, according to Dr Cathi Albertans, head of the Gender Research Project and a part-time gender commissioner, "South Africa has made progress in the elimination of direct discrimination in the law." Some areas of concern relate to the customary laws of succession and inheritance, the exclusion of domestic workers from the benefits of the Unemployment Insurance Fund and Compensation for Occupational Injuries and Diseases Act, and the lack of legal protection for women and gay couples in cohabiting relationships. But with the introduction of the Recognition of Customary Law Marriages act in 1998, some of the most profound forms of direct discrimination against women were removed from the statute books.

Despite this progress, the audit indicated that "most of the inequality and discrimination experienced by women lies not in the letter of the law but in its impact." This hidden or systemic discrimination, which occurs when an apparently neutral law has a disproportionate effect on women or where laws are implemented in a discriminatory manner, continues to impact on women's lives. It is also clear that often inequality and discrimination lie in the existence of gender-biased or gender-neutral policies and programmes.

The audit also highlighted the discrimination faced by working women. The traditional marginalization of women in the workplace has led to wage discrimination, sexual harassment and a lack of opportunities for promotion and training. Pay equity continues to be a serious problem, despite the prohibition of discrimination under the Labour Relations Act and Wage Act.

The audit also identified a more persistent inequality relating to pay equity, which is the manner in which "different types of jobs are valued and rewarded. . . based upon gendered assumptions about his and her jobs. Thus, professions and occupations traditionally filled by women are undervalued and badly paid." It remains to be seen whether the Employment Equity Act will alleviate these problems.

Of specific concern to the Commission was the issue of women's access to justice. The Commission received numerous complaints from women who cannot afford the services of lawyers and who are consequently not represented in court. The Legal Aid Board favours the provision of legal aid in criminal cases, in which men predominate, yet it does not provide funds at all in cases related to maintenance and domestic violence. Women are therefore not able to "freely obtain the legal assistance needed to protect themselves. . . and do lose out on the division and distribution of the marital property on divorce."

Finally, the audit found inequalities and discrimination within the political process. South Africa signed the Convention on the Political Rights of Women in 1993, but has yet to ratify it. Although South Africa presently has one of the highest proportions of female representatives in the world in Parliament, this is not the case for provincial and local governments. Research on the representation of women has indicated that much depends on the type of electoral system chosen. Despite submissions by the Commission and other non-governmental organisations to the Ministry for Provincial Affairs and Constitutional Development indicating that a system of proportional representation would address the participation of women effectively, the recently released White Paper did not introduce a legislation quota, but rather left it to the discretion of political parties.

The findings of the audit show that, in the words of Nelson Mandela, "the long walk is not over." Despite some significant legislative victories for women in the recent past, for example, the Customary Marriages Act, the Domestic Violence Act, and the Maintenance Act, many women, particularly those who live on the periphery of society, have yet to taste the fruits of South Africa's new democracy. In order to address this unsatisfactory situation, the Commission on Gender Equality was called into being in 2000.

The Commission on Gender Equality

The Commission on Gender Equality is one of six state institutions set up in terms of the Constitution to promote democracy and a culture of human rights in South Africa. The Commission's role is to advance gender equality in all spheres of society and make recommendations on any legislation affecting the status of women. The Commission aims to transform South African society by exposing gender discrimination in laws, policies and practices; advocating changes in sexist attitudes and gender stereotypes; and instilling respect for women's rights as human rights. Although the Commission acts in the interests of women generally, it pays particular attention to disadvantaged women, those living in rural and peri-urban areas, on farms, and those in domestic work.

The Commission's functions are to monitor all organs of society to ensure that gender equality is safeguarded and promoted; assess all legislation from a gender perspective; commission research and make recommendations to Parliament and other authorities; educate and inform the public with regard to gender issues; investigate complaints on gender-related issues; and monitor South Africa's progress towards gender equality in relation to international norms.

Conclusion

South Africa has been regarded historically as a society in which patriarchy is deeply embedded and women are oppressed by the country's social structure. However, since the dismantling of apartheid, South Africa has been engaged in a process of fundamental reconstruction, striving for a non-racist and non-sexist society with the African feminist movement contributing to the process. Such a contribution was initially taken up with the launching of the Women's National Coalition in 1992. Its main objective was to identify women's needs and aspirations and ensure that these were codified. These needs and aspirations were not assumed but were formulated after a two-year long consultation process that culminated in the adoption of the Women's Charter in 1994.

This was accompanied by the liberation of South Africa and its peoples from centuries of racially discriminatory colonial rule and domination, and the establishment of a constitutional democracy on 27 April 1994. The Constitution that emerged in 1996 from this historical experience enshrines the founding values of human dignity: it commits to the achievement of equality, non-racism and non-sexism as well as to a Bill of Rights that entrenches rights that can be justly ensured; and it guarantees freedoms in the areas of human dignity, equality, education, culture, religion, languages, research, artistic creativity, environment and property, among others. Thus the election of a new government in 1994 set South Africa on a path of renewal and transformation that had, and still has, a direct bearing on the question of gender equality.

It is fair to ask how effective the new laws, bills, and commissions really are in achieving their aims. In this regard, it should be noted that, over the last decade, the debates about gender equality amongst women in South Africa have alerted women to the realisation that formal equality in a constitution does not automatically secure equal treatment. There is not an automatic relationship between legislation and social change, that is, constitutional rights do not necessarily guarantee full equality for women. In the light of this, it has been realised that, substantive equality needs to be sought by women, by way of addressing the different realities of their lives and questioning the ideologies underlying patriarchal domination. What has become clear during the debates over this contested issue is that, unless there is a radical restructuring in the sexual division of labour as well as a concomitant change in the consciousness, discourse and behaviour of men and women about gender roles, women will remain trapped as wives, mothers and lovers instead of being accorded citizenship in their own right.

References

Basson, A. C., 1999. "The Regulation of Unfair Discrimination by the Employment Equity Act 55 of 1998." *South African Mercantile Law Journal* 11 (2).

Bhoola, U., 1996. "Working Women: Equity and Affirmative Action." *Indicator South Africa* 13 (4).

Bhorat, H., 2001. "Wage Differences." *South African Labour Bulletin* 25 (1).

De Koker, J Y., 1999. "Recent Legislation affecting the Status of Women in South Africa." *The Bluestocking*.

De vos, P., 2000. "Equality for All: A Critical Analysis of the Equality Jurisprudence of the Constitutional Court." *Tydskrif vir Hedendaagse Romeins-Hollandse Reg* 63 (1).

Flaherty, D., 1995. *Regional Inequalities in South Africa: Issues, Measurement and Policy Implications*. Halfway House: Development Bank of Southern Africa. 12, 20.

Flood, T., 1998. *Beyond Inequalities: Women in South Africa*. Oxford: African Books Collective, 27.

Gernholtz, L., 1999. "Gender Bias in Law." *The Sowetan* (16 March).

Kadalie, R., 1995. "Women in South Africa." *Publico* 15 (4): 25.

Kethusegile, B. M., 2000. *Beyond Inequalities: Women in Southern Africa*. Bellville: UWC, 15.

May, J. ed., 2000. *Poverty and Inequality in South Africa: Meeting the Challenge*. New York: Zed Books, 32.

Milazi, D., 1993. *African Women in Decision-Making Positions: Vanguard for Gender Equality?* Pretoria: Centre for Development Analysis. 4.

Moll, P., 1998. *Discrimination Is Declining in South Africa but Inequality Is Not*. Cape Town: South African Network for Economic Research, 5.

Tshoaedi, M., 2000. "In the Union . . . Women Union Officials Speak Out." *South African Labour Bulletin* 22 (2): 55.

Van Reenen, T P., 1997. "Equality, Discrimination and Affirmative Action: An Analysis of Section 9 of the Constitution of the Republic of South Africa. *South African Public Law* 12 (1).

Wilhelm. 1998. "Rural Unemployment in South Africa." *Social Forum*, 40.

CHAPTER 7

ASYMMETRIC RELATIONS AND OTHER GENDER ISSUES IN THE GHANAIAN HIGHER EDUCATION

Cyril K. Daddieh

Cross-country studies show large social returns to investing in women's education and health. Improved education for women results in reduced fertility and mortality rates. Women who are healthier and more educated will be more productive members of the economy. Furthermore, improving the health and education of women produces long-term benefits by improving the health and productivity of their children.

> The World Bank, "Ghana: Women's Role" (1999)

In general, women in developing countries with seven or more years of education (and presumably from the better-off classes?) marry approximately four years later than those without education, have higher rates of contraceptive use, and enjoy lower maternal and child mortality rates—so both they and their offspring have better chances in life.

> Paul Kennedy, *Preparing for the Twenty-first Century*, quoted in Robert Isaak, *Managing World Economic Change* (1995)[1]

---

[1] The two opening citations echo the insights of the eminent Ghanaian educator, Dr. James Kwegyir Aggrey, who remarked early in the 20th century that "[i]f you educate a boy, you simply educate an individual, but if you educate a girl, you educate a family and a nation."

Introduction

Education has been the royal jewel in the Ghanaian development crown. Not even a decade into political independence after 1957, Ghana had already established itself as the bellwether African country with a vastly increased stock of educational facilities and expanding access to schooling. Concerted government effort, complemented by private (for profit) and church-based (non-profit) initiatives, resulted in a proliferation of educational institutions, including primary and secondary schools, commercial and technical schools and universities, which allowed a growing number of Ghanaian youth to be educated. Even more impressively, the education that those institutions provided was of uniformly high quality. As a result, Ghanaian higher education gained worldwide acclaim for the academic excellence of its graduates, many of whom distinguished themselves in international civil service and professional careers all over the world. Unfortunately, because the educational system was heavily subsidized and higher education in particular was primarily dependent on government funding, when Ghana began to experience a prolonged economic crisis from the mid-1970s, it dragged education down with the rest. The gains the country had made in education began to suffer serious erosion.

The worst affected was higher education. As the former Minister of Education confessed to me in an interview, the universities were plagued by lack of equipment and essential instructional materials, low morale among staff, and falling academic standards owing to inadequate funding. That was why it was deemed necessary to implement comprehensive reforms of the entire educational system from basic to higher education, during the 1980s (Chambas 2000). However, even with these reforms, when the issues of gender participation, equity, gender-sensitive classroom environments, gendered performance in higher education, and so on, are placed under the microscope the jewel loses much of its luster. This chapter examines Ghana's record of educational achievement, highlights some of the unresolved challenges facing the education sector, including the continuing gender disparities in participation and achievement at the tertiary level, and reviews some of the remedies that have been proposed or tried.

Evidence of Achievement

Compared to most African and other Third World countries, Ghana has, indeed, made remarkable progress toward providing quality education to an increasing number of students at all levels of its educational system (Najafizadeh and Mennerick 1992: 242-48). As the official statistics for 2001/02 reveal in Table 1 (in the Annex), there were roughly 15,285 primary schools, 7,582 junior secondary schools (JSS), 510 senior secondary schools (SSS), 23 technical and vocational education and training (TVET), 42 teacher training colleges (TTC), and 24 special education institutions. In addition, there are currently 10 polytechnics, and 5 public universities in the country. Over 2 and a half million children are attending primary schools. In gross enrollment terms, this represents an 80 percent ratio. While these figures are impressive for a developing country, especially because they reveal a relatively broad access to primary education, gross enrollment ratios were actually only 64 percent at the JSS level and 18 percent at the SSS level in 2001/02. There is a dramatic decline in enrollment ratios as one climbs up the education ladder. Overall, only a modest 40 percent of JSS leavers gain admission into SSS. The remaining 60 percent have limited opportunities for further development and advancement (Republic of Ghana 2002, 5 :10-12).

In 1993, as part of the ongoing education reforms, the government elevated the polytechnics to tertiary status and doubled their number to 8. Enrollment rose from 1,689 in 1993 to 9,942 in 1997/98, an increase of 489%. By 2001/02 polytechnic enrollment had nearly doubled to 18,459 students (see Table 1). Meanwhile, universities, the key component of tertiary education, have been increased to six with the addition of two relatively new ones, the University of Development Studies (UDS) in the north and the University College of Education at Winneba (Daniel 1998)[2] and the recently-minted University of Mines and Technology. Total university enrollment rose significantly by 125%, from 11,857 in 1991/92 to 26,684 students in 1997/98. Again, as Table 1 reveals, by 2001/02, these 5 universities were bursting at the seams with 40,673 students. However, even with these increases, the government understates the case when it acknowledges that "there is still a large pool of deserving students unable to gain admission into tertiary

---

[2] The former Diploma Awarding Colleges, namely, the Specialist Training College, the Music Academy, the Advanced Teacher Training College, the Ashanti-Mampong Agricultural Teachers' College, Ajumako School of Ghana Languages, the Kumasi Technical Teachers' College, and the Akwapim-Mampong School for the Blind have been transformed into a multi-campus University College of Education at Winneba (UCEW). For an overview of the development of universities in Ghana, see the review article by the Registrar of the University of Ghana, G. F. Daniel, "The Universities in Ghana," *The Commonwealth Universities Year Book 1997-98*, Vol. 1 (1998), pp. 649-656.

institutions" (Republic of Ghana 1999: 25). The current reality is that the universities are able to absorb only about 10 percent of any batch of SSS students. The overall participation rate of the 18-21 age-group in tertiary institutions in the country is a paltry 2.5 percent, compared to 30-40 percent for the corresponding age-group in developed countries (Republic of Ghana 2002: 17).

This growing mismatch between qualification and admission accounts for the apparent national acceptance of the advent of private universities. Indeed, private universities are growing like mushrooms in the rainy season. Through the National Accreditation Board (NAB), the government has accredited 15 private tertiary institutions at different stages of development, most of them church-affiliated, with more in the pipeline. All but one of the 15 are designated as "university colleges."[3] In a proactive move, the 1992 Constitution gave legal backing to the development of private universities by stipulating in Article 25 (2) that "Every person shall have the right, at his [sic] own expense, to establish and maintain a private school or schools at all levels and of such categories and in accordance with such conditions as may be provided by law" (Republic of Ghana 1992: 37).

The Genesis: Popular Demand and National Commitment

Ghana's record of educational achievement and the forward-thinking about education that is reflected in the relevant provisions of the 1992 Constitution is the result of the interplay of three mutually reinforcing factors: unwavering government commitment, unrelenting popular demand, and ongoing financial exigencies. Government commitment to education began in the waning years of colonialism following World War II and was driven largely by new political realities – the nationalist challenge to colonial rule and the need to mitigate it by initiating long overdue social investments in the colony.

From the very beginning, Kwame Nkrumah captured the popular imagination as well as raising popular expectations, which, in turn, translated into mass support. Nkrumah and the CPP attracted a mass following partly by presenting an expansively populist social agenda, including the right to education.   Indeed, when the colonial government came to the belated realization that nationalist promises were seriously undermining its ability to govern the colony, it initiated its own plan of educational expansion in a futile

---

[3] Valley View University which is affiliated to the Seventh-Day Adventists (SDA) has been granted a Presidential Charter as a full-fledged university.

last ditch effort to counter the increasing nationalist political awakening and Nkrumah's growing popularity.

Nkrumah and the CPP wasted no time in delivering on their promises when Nkrumah became Leader of Government Business in 1951 after winning the first of three post-war elections that year, a prelude to independence in 1957. Political calculations aside, nationalist leaders also needed to produce skilled manpower within a relatively short time to run a modern government and economy and to endow the emerging postcolonial state with administrative competence and policy efficacy, as well as to foster national unity (Daddieh 1995: 23-55). This felt need was further reinforced by an unflinching faith, buttressed by modernization theory, in the positive developmental impact of education (Haddad et al. 1990).

Furthermore, from the onset, the Ghanaian public displayed an insatiable appetite for education because of its perceived power to produce spectacular results: security of employment, affluence, prestige, "big man" status, and other benefits (Price 1974; McKown and Finlay 1974). In short, beyond the political calculations, Ghanaian families kept up the pressure and displayed a penchant for increased educational investments because of the popular association between schooling and upward social mobility for individuals, their extended families and even their hometowns. African leaders almost universally declared education a priority area of national development. Luckily for Ghana, the nationalist government of Kwame Nkrumah translated the commitment into action. In addition to initiating extensive educational infrastructure development, the government instituted fee-free, compulsory primary education. It awarded generous scholarships to deserving students to study at home and abroad; it pampered this "fortunate few" with book and living allowances, well-stocked school canteens, three sit-down meals per day, 4 o'clock tea and biscuits to boot, as well as room cleaning services.[4] It also instituted affirmative action admission and scholarships for underprivileged students from northern Ghana.

While subsequent post-independence governments have generally professed a similar posture of commitment to education, they have simply failed to match and/or sustain over the long haul the kind of indulgence seen in the early years of independence. The "good old days" were a time when educational financing was not a major concern. The national coffers were far

---

[4] This has been confirmed in interviews with several alumni who enjoyed those privileges and speak nostalgically about those "good old days." One such interview was conducted with Dr. Kofi Blay, a sociologist at Delaware State University, May 1990.

from depleted and even though the pressure for education was increasing, the demand was still manageable. Those days have been long gone. Indeed, since the mid-1970s Ghanaian governments have struggled to meet the financial obligations imposed by the very large increases in educational enrollments at all levels.

One unfortunate consequence of the new realities is that since the early 1980s Ghanaian students have clashed repeatedly with governments over funding, the overall direction of and rationale for education, and over whether university education in particular is "a right" or "a privilege."[5] Confrontations between students and school administrators entrusted with the daunting task of running educational institutions with burgeoning enrollments and vastly diminished financial resources have also multiplied (Salia 1992: 27). Such clashes often resulted in the destruction of already inadequate physical assets and material, followed by school closures and, in some cases, the cancellation of the entire academic year. Again, these difficulties have contributed to the erosion of the quantitative and qualitative gains Ghana had made in roughly the first two decades after independence.

It is remarkable that despite persistent and growing financial difficulties, the national commitment to education remains apparently undiminished. Witness how, in spite of the unrelenting fiscal crisis confronting the Ghanaian state, the framers of the 1992 Constitution enumerated certain educational rights for all citizens and imposed related legal obligations on Ghanaian governments. Article 25 (1) of the Constitution stipulates that:

> *All persons shall have the right to equal educational opportunities and facilities and with a view to achieving the full realization of that right*—(a) basic education shall be free, compulsory and available to all; (b) secondary education in its different forms, including technical and vocational education, *shall be made generally available and accessible to all by every appropriate means*, and in particular, *by the progressive introduction of free education*; (c) higher education shall be made equally accessible to all, on the basis of capacity, by every appropriate means, and in particular, by progressive introduction of free education; ...(e) *the development of a system of schools with*

---

[5] In a recent survey conducted·by the author, over 98% of faculty felt that the government has a responsibility to increase funding to higher education and nearly 86% felt that the government has not given tertiary education the high priority in deserves. For one such row over tuition, see Albert K. Salia, ". . . But SRC Rejects Any Such Moves," *Daily Graphic.* Accessed on 10/31/2001 at http://www.graphic.com.gh/dgraphic/topstories/a23.htlm

adequate facilities at all levels shall be actively pursued (Republic of
Ghana 1992: 27; emphasis added).

It must be noted that although Article 25 (1) is at first glance
empowering because it offers the possibility for Ghanaian students seeking
educational access to challenge legally a nonperforming or nonconforming
government, the implementation clauses of the constitution appear to mitigate
the legal obligations of the state. On close inspection, what appears to be a
constitutional mandate turns out to be more hortatory. The apparent
equivocation provides ample wriggle room for Ghanaian governments to
minimize their obligations. A critical reading of "The Directive Principles of
State Policy" (Chapter Six, Article 38) reveals that the Ghanaian state has only
to provide educational facilities and access and implement free, compulsory
and universal basic education "*to the greatest extent feasible*" and only "*subject
to the availability of resources*" (Republic of Ghana 1992: 40; emphasis added).

Although the foregoing constitutional provisions are flexible enough to
shield governments from potential lawsuits, governments of the Fourth
Republic, like their predecessors, have officially embraced a commitment to
education. Both the former NDC and the current NPP governments unveiled
plans to promote education. The NDC blueprint, christened *Ghana Vision
2020*, sought to achieve functional literacy of all Ghanaians regardless of
gender or social status. The education system was assigned the primary
responsibility for promoting the skills necessary for functioning effectively in
an increasingly competitive global economy. The Ministry of Education was
tasked to pursue a number of strategic objectives, including improved access,
participation and equity at all levels, with emphasis on science, technology
education and training and decentralized management and efficiency gains. The
Vision 2020 blueprint highlighted two priority areas: the need to make higher
education responsive to the developmental needs of the nation and to sustain
funding by exploring alternative sources, including cost-sharing. The
document signaled the government's intent to curtail financing in non-academic
areas such as residential accommodation as well as to make universities more
financially self-reliant and less dependent on government subventions
(Republic of Ghana: 3-6).

When the New Patriotic Party (NPP) assumed office in January 2001 it
was quick to register its own commitment to education. This was unfurled in
the form of a banner headline, "C173b Released to 5 state varsities," in the
state-owned newspaper, *Daily Graphic*. The newspaper revealed that an
additional amount of C6.3 billion had been earmarked for expansion and

rehabilitation of senior secondary schools throughout the country. Moreover, it reported that the Minister of Education had indicated that his government placed a high priority on the educational sector "since it is the bedrock of national development." The government was therefore determined *"to make education a right, not a privilege"* (Asamoah 2001). The Minister reiterated his government's directive to second-cycle and tertiary institutions to hold the line on fees for the 2001/2002 at the previous year's level. He insisted that the government had honored its obligation by making available to both second-cycle and tertiary institutions a total of C85 billion to meet their needs. He also acknowledged the contributions of religious bodies and Parent-Teacher Associations (PTAs) towards raising the standards of education in the country (Asamoah 2001).

Apparently dissatisfied with the state of education in the country when he assumed office in January 2001, President John Agyekum Kufuor inaugurated a 30-member committee in January 2002 and gave it 4 months to undertake a thorough review of the education system with a view to making it more responsive to current challenges. This task was apparently so onerous that it took the committee 10 months to present its report. While the committee report raised the issue of gender equity, it failed to address it in any direct or profound way (Republic of Ghana 2002: 24). However, it made general recommendations, including a significant restructuring of the current system. Properly implemented, some of these recommendations are bound to have a positive impact on female enrollment and retention rates.

The State of Gender Participation

The foregoing overviews underscore a broad national commitment to education and, in response to popular demand and their own search for popular support and legitimacy, government interest in providing improved access to all Ghanaian citizens. The evidence also suggests significant progress in this national educational endeavor. However, there are persistent gender problems as well as regional disparities in educational availability and access. While the base of the Ghanaian educational system is sufficiently broad to permit expanded access to a majority of school-age children, access is considerably narrowed at higher levels of the educational ladder, with serious implications for female participation in particular. Indeed, despite earlier achievements and progress following independence, the growing gender gap in enrollment and retention in recent years remains one of the more vexing issues facing the Ghanaian educational system. While the differential ratio of girls to boys at the primary levels is important but not huge, fewer girls remain long enough in school to reach the level of higher education.

The data provided in Table 1 for 2001/02 are illustrative of the general pattern. Whereas 47 percent of all students enrolled in primary 1-6 were female, the figure falls to roughly 45 percent of all students in JSS 1-3 and then tumbles to roughly 41 percent in SSS 1-3. It is interesting to note that the level of attendance from primary to JSS stayed a consistent 49 percent in the private sector. In other words, from a position of relative parity in primary school, female enrollment declines to roughly four in ten in SSS. As might be expected, by far the greatest disparities between male and female enrollments occur not just at the tertiary level where roughly three in ten (30%) and slightly more than two in ten (22%) students in the public universities and polytechnics respectively were women but also in TVET (13%), and TTC (27%) (see Table 1). The President's committee summed up the lack of gender equity this way:

> The average male/female enrollment for the past five academic years 1996/97-2000/2001 was in the ratios of 73:27 for universities and 79:21 for the polytechnics as against the national norm of 50:50. The major factor accounting for this has been the low female enrollment rates at the pre-tertiary level. For example, in the 1999/2000 academic year, the gross enrollment rate for girls was 49.4% at the pre-school, 47.2% at primary and 45.4% at the JSS (Republic of Ghana 2002, 24).

Although data for female participation in the fledgling private universities are not available, the picture there is not likely to be much different or better especially given the much greater financial costs and logistics involved in getting access.

Gender Streaming

Once women have access, how do female experiences compare with those of men in terms of choice of course of study, campus and classroom environmental challenges, and financial burdens? It is important to interrogate gendered experiences because there is evidence to suggest that they may have a greater impact on differential rates of gender participation and achievement than is generally acknowledged. One common experience faced by women from the polytechnics to the universities is the pervasiveness of gender segregation by academic discipline. In virtually all areas of study in the Polytechnics, men outnumber women by wide margins. Moreover, in a number of important areas such as refrigeration and plumbing, women are either completely absent or have only a token representation. This is true of automobile, electrical, electronic, agricultural and mechanical engineering; building construction technology; general, chemical, and metallurgical engineering; carpentry and joinery; welding and fabrication; furniture design and wood processing. It is equally revealing that the only areas of study in the Polytechnics in which women outnumber men are the traditional female professions of fashion, design and modeling; cooking; secretarial and management studies; hotel, catering and institutional management.

Similar patterns of "gender streaming can be observed at the universities." It is true that there is a heavy concentration of both male and female students in the arts, humanities, and social sciences in all the universities. The case of the University of Ghana-Legon is indicative of the general pattern. More than six in ten (5,205 out of a total of 8,606) students at Legon in 1997/98 were in the faculties of Arts, Social Studies and Law. Fewer than two in ten (14%) were enrolled in the Natural Sciences. Less than 19% (225 out of 1,205) of students in the Natural Sciences were women. By contrast, nearly eight in ten (80% or 82 of the 103) students enrolled in Home Science were women. Similarly, for the same year, the data from the Kwame Nkrumah University of Science and Technology (KNUST) in Kumasi show that only 8% (92 out of 1,144) of the Engineering students were women. While female participation remained unchanged from the preceding year, male enrollment actually went up by slightly more than 15% (140 students). Similarly, in the sciences, females accounted for roughly 15% (218) of the 1,414 students. This figure actually represented a modest increase of about 12%, but it still lagged behind the male enrollment increase, which was twice as high.

It is intriguing that male students were also over-represented in the faculties of Agriculture, Environmental and Development Studies, and Renewable Natural Resources. These are areas where one would have expected female students to make a much stronger showing because of socio-historical factors coupled with the traditional conception of women as custodians of land and forests. The data from the University of Cape Coast tell an almost identical story. For the academic year 1997/98 roughly 16% of the students enrolled in the natural sciences were women (138 of the 876 students). Women accounted for roughly 16% of students pursuing agriculture (66 of the 511) but represented nearly 44% (898 out of 2,041) of students pursuing degrees in education.

Despite the apparent gender disparities, the Ghanaian case offers a picture of a glass that can be more aptly described as half full. The evidence clearly points to long term improvements in female student participation in higher education. However, female participation rates still lag a considerable distance behind male participation. In addition to the participation gap, there is significant gender segregation by discipline from senior secondary schools and above. Female participation in the sciences, mathematics and technology in both the Polytechnics and the Universities is considerably lower. Roughly five times more men than women are enrolled in undergraduate programs in science. The gender gap is even more pronounced at the postgraduate level where female enrollment is negligible. In contrast to their under-representation or very low participation in mathematics, natural sciences, technical subjects and agriculture, Ghanaian female students tend to dominate disciplines such as home economics, social science, and business studies, all of which prepare them for traditional female professions such as catering, secretarial work, teaching, and social work, with important implications for postgraduate income disparities and social status (Someah-Addae 1988).

Explaining Differential Rates of Gender Participation

The persistence of gender inequality in participation, the apparent female aversion to scientific and technical subjects or disciplines, the over-concentration in subjects and programs traditionally considered female, all constitute pressing problems requiring focused attention in Ghanaian higher education. To gain an enhanced understanding of these enduring problems, it is necessary to concentrate our collective minds on a number of antecedent conditions and practices and to interrogate how they have impinged on the realities at the tertiary level. First, there is a strong link between pre-tertiary and tertiary gender disparities in both enrollment and subject choice.   The President's committee took cognizance of this fact when it noted that the ultimate solution to the gender equity problem has to be found at the primary and secondary level where the transition rate is lowest (Republic of Ghana 2002: 24). Second, the vastly different experiences of male and female students in the Ghanaian education system merit greater scrutiny.   Third, the motivational bases of decision making at the household level which ultimately determine who receives sustained financial sponsorship to attend school and who is left behind must be acknowledged.   Finally, we must interrogate developments at the tertiary level itself. Hence the rest of this chapter turns to a mixture of attitudinal, socio-cultural, economic, and logistical factors as key contributors to these differential outcomes.

Societal/Parental Attitudes and Cultural Forces

Female participation in formal education across the board faces a host of entrenched cultural practices and attitudes, including stereotypic notions about the proper role and place of women in society, the perceived threat posed by education to such a role or the perceived corrupting influences of education on proper gender relations, as well as the persistence of the "male-as-breadwinner" ideology. In rural and low-income urban communities in particular, negative parental attitudes and cultural practices have tended to devalue female educational achievements and thereby undermined their educational participation. Such communities generally place a much higher premium on the reproductive and traditional roles of women and pay less attention to nurturing their educational and career aspirations. Female education is considered a waste of money, a commodity already in very short supply, especially in rural communities.

These cultural forces, attitudes and orientations have had profound negative impacts on female enrollment and retention. A useful synthesis of available evidence from focus group discussions organized by the Federation of African Women Educationalists (FAWE) in seven districts in northern Ghana, the region with the lowest enrollment and retention rates for girls, already exists (Amua-Sekyi 1998: 1-9). One pervasive set of attitudinal orientations identified by Amua-Sekyi includes the following:

> The woman is expected to be provided for by her husband. Since education is a gateway to highly paid jobs in the formal sector, it is more important for boys to have formal education. If a woman has a career, it is only to support her husband and her family. A woman must be submissive to her husband. ... [T]he more educated the woman is, the less submissive, arrogant, sophisticated and discontented she will be with her lot in life. A woman with high educational and career aspirations, who actively pursues it, is considered aggressive and unlikely to find a husband (Amua-Sekyi: 3).

Ironically, oftentimes both fathers and mothers share stereotypic notions about gender roles and the irrelevance of education for women. In one case, a father is adamant that "[t]he boy is the bread winner, therefore he must be given the best opportunities right from the beginning, including the best education. This will enable him to perform his manly [sic] duties properly in future" (Quaisie 1988: 3). A mother echoes his sentiments when she insists that it is futile to educate a girl because "No matter how much education you give a girl, she will one day end up in someone's kitchen and all her needs will be catered for" (Quaisie: 3).[6] As Amua-Sekyi has argued:

> These attitudes negatively affect aspirations of both parents and girls. Parents tend to have low aspirations for their daughters. Female students tend to incline towards traditionally female dominated areas of specialization, for example nursing, catering, home economics, hairdressing, teaching, etc. In conformity with societal expectations and probably as a survival strategy, some women appear happy at the bottom of the ladder and appear to be happy to serve (Amua-Sekyi 1988: 3).

In certain traditional homes, formal education is considered bad for girls because it is presumed to have corrosive effects on traditional values. In some Muslim communities, western education is considered satanic presumably because it teaches western culture, which is perceived to turn children or young people on to drug abuse, illicit sexual practices, and teenage pregnancy (Atakpa 1996). As Amua-Sekyi contends, "[a] parent who believes that secular education teaches vices, is not likely to send his/her daughter to school where the teachers are predominantly male" (Amua-Sekyi 1988: 3). Ironically, these same attitudes may be shared by local teachers, thus ensuring that they will devote much less attention or give less encouragement to girls in their classrooms.

Factors Affecting Household Decision Making

Although governments can improve female participation by increasing the number of available educational facilities in the country, providing increased funding to education and establishing merit-based scholarships and loans for indigent students, especially during periods of relative economic prosperity, decisions regarding which members can benefit from existing educational opportunities generally occur at the extended household level. In the Ghanaian context, such decisions often hinge on sources and levels of household income or level of poverty, household expenditures, the gender

---

[6] Since studies show that educated mothers will usually opt for education for their daughters, we have to presume that the view that the woman's place is in the kitchen is held by a woman who was herself deprived of education.

sensitivity of the decision maker, and the perceived opportunity costs associated with schooling.

High Cost of Female Education

The costs associated with education often exceed the capacity of most poor households to finance. Even where education is relatively free, as in Ghana, parents have to pay a variety of fees: registration, school uniforms, sports apparel, textbooks, school supplies, and transportation. The gender dimension of educational costs becomes an important consideration insofar as the costs associated with schooling are generally higher for girls than for boys. Uniforms for girls generally cost more and girls are less likely to go to school in tattered clothes. Moreover, for safety reasons, transport arrangements have to be made for girls, which add to cost.

The high cost of female education means that girls are often the first to be sacrificed when households are faced with financial difficulties and have to make painful choices. Not surprisingly, many more girls than boys drop out of school especially in rural communities. Moreover, the poverty of households often makes girls vulnerable to the advances of so-called "sugar daddies" and even male teachers. The resultant pregnancies tend to exacerbate the rate of female dropouts in so far as girls are almost invariably expelled from school but not the real culprits -- the boys who got them pregnant in the first place (Tembe 2002).[7] From the vantage point of households already struggling to make ends meet, pregnancies not only impose additional burdens but are also a visible manifestation of wasted investments. Thus, pregnancies provide the perfect pretext and real justification for some households to prefer sending boys rather than girls to school.

School versus Farm and Market Conundrum

In addition, for most rural households, the opportunity cost of school attendance is the labor service that is foregone in the form of field work,

---

[7] Even when older men or "sugar daddies," including teachers, are responsible for the pregnancy, they invariably go unpunished. A recent case in Mozambique where six girls, aged 14-17 years, were expelled from school for having babies caused such an outrage that the country's Prime Minister was compelled to intervene. School administrators said they had expelled them "to set an example to other girls and avoid more teenage pregnancies." The expulsion order was subsequently rescinded and the girls went back to school. One girl asked pointedly "why schoolboys who become fathers are never punished." See Jose Tembe, "Mozambique's Mothers Back in School," *BBC News*, Tuesday 19 March 2002.

household chores, marketplace activities, and so on. For families living on the margins, control of or access to child labor is often a critical component of their survival or suffer-manage strategies (Chazan 1983; Pellow and Chazan 1986). Such households, especially female-headed ones, require greater inducements to send their children, their girl-child in particular, to school. But even where a girl-child is fortunate enough to be enrolled, her repeated withdrawal from school to perform some needed household task that cannot wait or long absences from class for one household reason or another may discourage completion of studies or passing competitive national examinations. Here is the real crux of the matter:

> Child labor at home is indispensable to the survival of some households. Though boys perform a larger share of family labor, for example herding cattle and plowing fields, girls do more home and market place work than boys. Girls cook, clean, and may stay out of school to look after siblings. After a series of such absences from school, the girl has difficulty catching up with the rest of the class and in due course, gives up school completely[8] (Amua-Sekyi 1988: 3).

Girls whose mothers or guardians are engaged in petty commodity trading may fare no better than girls from farming or rural communities. A mother who feels she is succeeding at commerce is less likely to encourage her girl-child to pursue formal education. She might prefer to get her started in the business earlier rather than later because she could presumably earn a better living than the income that education could provide. Again, as Amua-Sekyi (1988: 4) contends:

> A parent who cannot afford school uniforms, who feels she needs her daughter to take care of younger siblings or who feels the child will learn how to make more money than she would probably make after years of formal education, would withdraw her at the earliest opportunity. To those parents, sending a girl to school represents an opportunity cost. It is quite clear that parents' negative perception of the value of education is a strong reason for the low enrollment and retention of girls in schools in the rural areas.

---

[8] A similar experience has been reported for Tanzania where "girls attend school on a less regular basis than boys due to heavy household workloads, traditional practices biased against girls' education, and environments in schools that are unfriendly to girls' participation" (Liganga 2002:27).

To summarize, for poor households, the opportunity cost of attending school is higher for girls than for boys because girls perform more household chores than boys and also engage in farming, food vending, and marketing. Hence, the apparent lack of legislation and/or effective enforcement mechanism for ensuring parental compliance with compulsory education legislation means parents can keep their children out of school as and when they want with impunity. Almost invariably it is the girl-child who is short-changed. The problem is exacerbated by the limited availability of facilities geared to those who might want to pursue their studies on a part-time basis. The overall rigidities or inflexibility of educational systems in Ghana and elsewhere in Africa make it virtually impossible for those who drop out to re-enter the system. It may be concluded that "[g]irls' access to education is hindered by the high overall costs of education and parents' common perception that education for girls is not as important as education for boys. Other obstacles are girls' outside time constraints, which are difficult to overcome because of rigid school schedules and schools that are far away" (The World Bank 1999: 4).

Educational Delivery and Infrastructure

In addition to the aforementioned factors, both the delivery system and the school environment act as powerful inhibiters to admission and retention of Ghanaian school children in general and to girls' education in particular. The documented experiences of two schools—Experimental School and Forster International—are symptomatic of broader processes at work. They are both located in Accra New Town, a densely populated, low-income suburb of Accra. Experimental School was opened as a public primary school in 1952 with only 113 pupils. It has grown tremendously and now operates a shift system for 2,400 students. The school is plagued by overcrowding, shortage of textbooks and other instructional materials. Available resources are so stretched that only the theoretical aspects of courses designed to provide practical training such as "cookery" are taught. The school has neither the time nor the resources to enable the students to engage in practical or experiential learning. A new classroom block has been under construction for more than ten years. When completed, it is expected to have room for a science lab and perhaps even a computer lab. Understandably, Mrs. Nyarko, the headmistress, is not too sanguine about its completion let alone such luxuries as labs.

> In the meantime the classrooms bulge with pupils. The government recommends no more than 30 pupils per teacher. But at Experimental most

classes have between 48 and 55 pupils. . . . Many here cannot afford to send their children to private schools, meaning there are often more pupils than Experimental can take. The final limit comes when the last line of the register has been filled – each register can carry a maximum of 58 names (Simpson 2003).

By contrast, Forster International, a nearby private school, faces a different order of problems. Class sizes are within government guidelines and so there has been no need to institute a shift-system. The combined primary and JSS population of the school is about 500, a more manageable situation compared to Experimental. Forster's major problem is that, as a private institution, it is not entitled to government-supplied textbooks. Parents must therefore be willing to buy them. They have not been too keen to add that burden to their already mounting education costs. Most of the parents are traders with limited disposable income. They pay substantially more to educate their children at Forster compared to Experimental, anywhere from C130,000 per child per term for nursery school to C230,000 per term for JSS students. Based on three terms in the school year, they pay C690,000 or the equivalent of US$80 for a JSS level student per annum (Simpson 2003: 18). Their inability to invest in textbooks means that most students do not have access to the basic tools of education. This makes both teaching and learning challenging, to say the least. It certainly does not foster enthusiasm for learning. There is a proliferation of private, for-profit international or preparatory schools throughout the country. Regrettably, most of them are in the same boat as Forster. They present the illusion of educational excellence without the record of achievement.

In any case, the dearth of textbooks and other instructional materials is not the only deprivation that impoverishes the educational experience and creates disincentives for all but the most highly motivated parents and children to sustain an appetite for education. The unwillingness of trained teachers to report to work in rural areas or low-income urban communities and their tendency to abandon their posts even in midstream contributes to the widening gap in participation and performance between rural and urban areas, between poor and affluent neighborhood schools, between public and private schools where this problem is minimized, and between boys and girls. Moreover, the dearth of appropriately trained teachers prevents children from mastering basic literacy skills and scientific knowledge. For girls, this problem is exacerbated by the general disinterest shown by most of their male teachers in encouraging their pursuit of science or the pervasiveness of a culture of lack of nurturing of science aptitude in girls enrolled in co-educational schools.

The approach to teaching science subjects is not user-friendly. Naturally, most students and most especially girls are turned off by these subjects. There is the preconception that science is for boys and the humanities for girls. Any aptitude shown by girls in the sciences is either not encouraged or is belittled. Science is conceived in terms of inventing things and female intelligence is considered limited in this regard. There is also a glaring absence of strong female role models in science-related professions and activities (Amua-Sekyi 1988: 6).

It must be emphasized that primary and secondary schools are not the only institutions plagued by overcrowding, lack of adequate physical facilities, including classrooms, dormitories or hostels, laboratories, acute shortage of instructional materials such as textbooks, laboratory equipment and supplies and shortage of qualified and committed instructors. The polytechnics and universities suffer from similar deprivations. As the former Vice Chancellor of the University of Ghana, indicated at his inauguration in 1996, the University of Ghana-Legon's physical infrastructure, which was built 30 to 50 years ago, had become overwhelmed and woefully inadequate to meet the demands of the rapidly growing number of school leavers who qualify each year to enter the University. The existing five Halls of Residence and their corresponding annexes were inadequate to accommodate all qualified students. Classroom and laboratory space is similarly limited. In most departments, with no room to sit, many students are forced to stand during lectures. (Ivan Addae-Mensah 1996).

The deterioration of existing building stocks as well as the lack of new infrastructural development or capital investments are symptomatic of the serious erosion in the level of government funding of tertiary institutions brought on by the ongoing economic crisis and in the face of increased demand for higher education. At the institutional level, the strategy adopted to cope with the infrastructural challenges was a ritual annual raising of the entrance bar to keep out about 40 percent of students who are otherwise qualified to receive University education. As Vice-Chancellor Addae-Mensah lamented, "A situation where applicants for the humanities can only be sure of gaining admission if they have aggregate 7 or better, or aggregate 10 or better for science, should be considered by all stakeholders as a serious crisis in our human resource development" (Addae-Mensah 1996). He opined that "parents and potential applicants to the University are under a lot of psychological stress because of the uncertainties about getting admission into Legon in spite of their excellent qualifications" (ibid.).

Competitive National Examinations

The refreshingly blunt remarks by Vice-Chancellor Addae-Mensah revealed another major barrier to women's access to higher education in Ghana. The admission process continues to be based primarily on grades earned in highly competitive national examinations. Under-achievement in such examinations has been a major barrier to adequate female representation at secondary and post-secondary levels of education, particularly in the areas of science, technology, and mathematics. In Ghana female students perform far below their male counterparts in national examinations at the JSS and SSS levels. The result is that only a limited number of girls obtain qualifying grades to allow them to pursue higher education. It has been suggested that "as many as 70% to 80% of girls fail to get an aggregate of six at the Basic Education Certificate Examinations (BECE) or a pass mark of E at the Senior Secondary School Certificate Examination (SSSCE) respectively" (Amua-Sekyi 1988: 5).

Furthermore, the prerequisite of a passing grade in mathematics in order to gain admission to teacher training colleges and science-related programs in the polytechnics and the universities accounts for the paucity of female participation in Ghanaian higher education. Given the lackluster performance of Ghanaian girls in science, mathematics and technology-related subjects in national examinations, the math requirement effectively bars the door to female admission. When the relative gap in academic performance between boys and girls is combined with the already reduced participation of girls in JSS and SSS—again, the most important way stations on the academic cross—it becomes self-evident why the enrollment and retention rates in Ghanaian higher education are so skewed in favor of male students. Amua-Sekyi's insightful assessment is that "The low level of female participation in tertiary education can be traced to low levels of female participation on the academic ladder, low transition rate from one level to the next, poor examination results, a preference for part-time study and the aversion to mathematics, which means many do not make the credit in mathematics required for entry into most institutions of higher learning" (Amua-Sekyi: 5-6).[9] The culprit is not genetics but rather social engineering, as suggested earlier.

Low Staff and Student Morale

As if the above problems are not vexing enough, Ghanaian universities had been plagued by an epidemic of strikes, demonstrations, work stoppages,

---

[9] Ibid, pp. 5-6. It is intriguing that once girls are admitted, their performance in tertiary institutions is apparently comparable to that of boys even in science courses.

and, sometimes, violent clashes. At different times students, faculty or workers have been pitted against the university administration and, by extension, against the government. These conflicts and the resultant disruptions have sometimes resulted in school closures and even cancellation of entire academic years. Although there is no data to substantiate this, my hunch is that the attrition for female students is much higher any time the academic year is disrupted. It apparently also induces very low morale among students as well as faculty. Many students become disillusioned because of the uncertainties that surround their future; the senior faculty, apparently also give up. Faced with such a situation, many young academics are turning to the more lucrative private market or migrating to greener pastures elsewhere or are simply not going into teaching. As the President's committee noted, the attraction and retention of qualified staff is a major challenge facing tertiary institutions. The polytechnics, in particular, cannot compete with industry in attracting and retaining qualified faculty. About 40% of the faculty positions in the universities and 60% of those in the polytechnics are vacant. Meanwhile, more than 34% of the teaching staff in the universities are above 50 years old (Republic of Ghana 2002: 18). Quite clearly, such a situation does not augur well for the quality of the products the university is turning out into the world of work.

The dearth of both teachers and physical facilities, including university accommodation, poses serious challenges to women. It is clearly implicated in the strategy of limiting enrollments, which usually works to the disadvantage of women. Female students who are not assigned on-campus housing are particularly handicapped. They generally find it much more difficult to resort to "perching" or to become "refugees,"[10] a widespread survival strategy which male students have turned into a virtual rite of passage at Ghanaian universities. Ironically, perching puts pressure on existing facilities which become even more degraded over time.

Furthermore, overcrowded classrooms and lecture halls and the daily struggle for food have produced a rather retrogressive sexual division of labor in which many female students skip classes in order to prepare meals to be exchanged for lecture notes or information (known on campus as the "*apor*") prepared by their male counterparts who act in effect as their surrogates at these lectures. In other words, while boys may queue long hours to get a seat or just

---

[10] These are some of the more evocative campus names given to the hundreds of non-residential students who, instead of residing outside the campus as expected, are illegally sharing cramped quarters with friends in campus housing.

to stand in crowded lecture halls, girls struggle in the "kitchen" to cook for their men. Whatever its merits, it is hard to conceive of this relationship as balanced. Indeed, it smacks of "unequal exchange." Furthermore, regarding faculty morale, it is unlikely that a faculty that has "given up" will devote much energy to nurturing female students in particular without asking to be unofficially compensated in cash or in kind.

Sexual Harassment and HIV/AIDS on University Campuses

This brings us to the important but neglected issues of sexual harassment and HIV/AIDS which are likely to have serious implications for rates of female participation and retention. Newspapers across the continent are replete with accounts of sexual harassment on campuses. A scathing indictment appeared in the *Ghanaian Chronicle* of February 7, 2001. The newspaper reported an upsurge in sexual harassment "in our offices/working establishments, first and second cycle and also tertiary institutions" (*Ghanaian Chronicle*, February 7, 2001).[11] It lamented that "Some tutors/lecturers in our second cycle and tertiary institutions promise students with mouth-watering high marks, as to woo them sexually" (*Ghanaian Chronicle*, February 7, 2001). It went on to opine that:

> Those students who give in especially in the second cycle, forget that their SSCE papers will not be marked by these shameful tutors. With our ladies in the tertiary set-up who also give in, they graduate, as half-baked bread not braced up for the challenges ahead when they are employed. *And for those*

---

[11] See "Bottom Tree: Sexual Harassment In Our Schools: Action Needed," *Ghanaian Chronicle* (Accra), February 7, 2001. The Kenyan experience has been recounted in "Why Violence And Rape Thrive In Schools," *The Nation* (Nairobi), May 1, 2000. The paper points out that "[s]exual coercion does not just affect adults. As Mariam, Veronica and many others will testify, sexual harassment and violence towards girl students is well established at universities and even earlier – in primary schools." In its April 24, 2000 edition, *The Nation* (Nairobi) noted that "[s]tudents have to cope in an already hostile economic environment and increasingly institutions are making them pay for services that were once heavily subsidized by the State. Many girls find that they must compromise their morals and integrity by latching onto 'sugar daddies' to take care of some of their living expenses." The paper also revealed that girls can sometimes be perpetrators and not just victims. "University male students also feel pressurized by their female peers to take on the burden of feeding, clothing and entertaining them. This breeds attitudes of contempt of one sex towards the other, especially if one party feels justified in demanding sexual favours in exchange for material support."

resilient ladies who flatly refuse the sexual demands of tutors/lecturers, some are greatly pressured or pursued till their resilience [sic] wears off, but those who remain 'die-hards' and rebuff these advances are rewarded with scorn, given an environment eluded [sic] of peace necessary for academic work, treated with scorn, given low "cooked" marks and grades to show them where power lies (Ibid.; emphasis added).

The newspaper posits correctly that there is a link between sexual harassment and the possibility of HIV/AIDS transmission. Although Ghana appears to be quite a long way from that point, as the disease spreads it will put a strain on education budgets, which are likely to suffer further contraction as governments are forced to allocate the lion's share of national budgets to the health sector to cope with the pandemic. As the southern African experience suggests, teaching staffs and health care workers may become heavily infected, resulting in high attrition and impaired performance. Loss of teachers and administrators would affect adversely the quality of planning, training and support. These consequences would erode or reverse recent gains in basic education. More importantly, such losses would place girls in an even greater caretaking role which, in turn, would make their enrollment and retention more precarious.

With respect to universities, recent "findings" by the World Bank suggest that the disease is already exacting a heavy price in terms of high operating costs, productivity losses (especially through high absenteeism), diversion of resources and income losses. The "findings" have revealed that the university in Africa is a high-risk institution for the transmission of HIV. "Sugar-daddy practices, sexual experimentation, prostitution on campus, unprotected sex, gender violence, multiple partners, and similar high-risk activities are all manifested to a greater or lesser degree" (The World Bank 2001).

Female students in particular and others in subordinate positions (secretaries, junior staff, other female workers) are highly vulnerable because of their inability to negotiate for either no sex or for safer sexual practices on account of their subordinate status and associated lack of empowerment. They experience "consensual rape" because of their lack of empowerment. "The female partner consents (under duress) to intercourse in order to preserve a relationship, avoid a beating, ensure financial support, or repay favors. The prevailing climate on university campuses may encourage such violence and thereby facilitate the spread of HIV/AIDS" (The World Bank 2001: 2).

It has been suggested that HIV/AIDS now exists in all regions of Ghana. The estimated national infection rate of 4.8 percent is relatively low compared to that of many African countries, but it is approaching the critical threshold of 5.0 percent, the level at which infection tends to expand rapidly and exponentially. Tertiary education communities are particularly vulnerable to HIV/AIDS "due to their age group (which constitutes the peak period for HIV infection), close physical proximity, relative autonomy from adult or community supervision, and inclination towards sexual networking" (The World Bank 2001). It has been suggested that "[t]his vulnerability introduces a sizeable risk to the expected returns on investments made by families and government in the education of tertiary students. In spite of this risk, tertiary institutions have not yet established institutional policies or programs for the management and prevention of HIV/AIDS" (The World Bank 2001: 5).[12]

Some Policy Interventions

Having addressed some of the major issues in Ghanaian education in general and in higher education in particular, we turn to a few of the significant initiatives or policy interventions attempted by the government to increase women's access and participation at all levels of the education system and in all academic disciplines, but especially the sciences. Space does not permit an exhaustive analysis. Suffice it to say that at a general level, the government had introduced Free Compulsory Universal Basic Education (FCUBE) in the hope of ensuring that all children receive at least the equivalent of Junior High School education. Meanwhile, the government has been exhorting District Assemblies to devote a portion of the District Assemblies' Common Fund to establish scholarship schemes to assist needy parents to send their children to school (Amua-Sekyi 1988: 6). Even if successful, however, such general interventions are rather blunt instruments that can at best improve the situation of girls only marginally, especially given the array of factors that constrain their access and participation.

Girl-Child Participation and Retention in Science, Technology, and Mathematics

---

[12] *Ibid,* p.5. To understand better the challenges posed by the disease to tertiary institutions, and to identify potential risk-reducing interventions, IDA has reportedly joined with the National Council for Tertiary Education to commission an assessment of the current situation (HIV/AIDS in Tertiary Institutions in Ghana). I am not aware that the report has been issued.

Fortunately, there is an appreciable awareness of the need for specific or targeted interventions. This is reflected in the move by the Ghana Education Service (GES) to initiate a program known as the Science, Technology and Mathematics Education (STME) Clinics for girls in 1987. This program was intended to increase and sustain girls' participation in science, technology and mathematics. Initially the program brought together about 200 girls from all over the country for a two-week period during which they engaged in hands-on or experiential learning under the watchful eyes of female scientists who served as role models. Since then, this annual STME program has catered to about 2000 girls at the SSS level. The STME activities run the gamut from scientific talks, hands-on activities, group discussions, career guidance sessions and video shows (Amua-Sekyi 1988:6; Republic of Ghana 1999: 20).

In 1997, the program was further refined and decentralized to regional and district levels. It was expanded to cover the entire basic and junior secondary education system. For instance, in August 1999, 2172 girls participated in the clinics in all ten regions of the country. It is hoped that the discussions and interactions with women scientists and technologists would dispel the notion that scientific professions are not appropriate for women. An interesting feature of the program is that participants in the clinics become agents of diffusion to other JSS and SSS girls in their respective districts (Amua-Sekyi 1988: 6).

The Girls' Education Unit (GEU) and District Girls' Education Officers

In an effort to strengthen girl-child education, a girls' education unit was established in 1997 under the auspices of the Ghana Education Service to advocate policy and special programs for enhancing the participation of girls. This unit compiles research and makes recommendations on girls' education in Ghana and works with the Forum for African Women Educationalists (FAWE, Ghana Chapter), a non governmental organization that supports girls and women to acquire education for development.

Furthermore all district and regional education offices are expected to institute district and regional girls' education officers. The task of the DGEOs is to promote and foster an awareness of girls' education at the district level through advocacy, networking, community participation, basic PLA (Participatory Learning and Action) methodologies, and the collection of gender-segregated data. The DGEOs are expected to work in cooperation with the Science, Technology, Mathematics Education Organizers (STMEOs) and report to the RGEOs. Training of DGEOs and STMEOs is conducted by the

Girls' Education Unit through workshops. At the national level, in October 1999 the GEU conducted a workshop on gender issues in education for senior officials of the Ministry of Education (MOE) and GES. The aim of the workshop was to strengthen the capacity of MOE/GES officials for making and implementing gender sensitive policies and decisions. The GEU also publishes a newsletter aptly called *Gender Matters* that highlights the activities of the Unit. Three issues of the newsletter had been produced and disseminated nationwide as of 2006.

Other Responses

The GEU has also established a Female Education Scholarship Scheme for girls whose families cannot afford the direct and opportunity costs of education. The scholarship will provide needy girls with enrollment fees, uniforms, footwear, stationery and a stipend. A pilot program designed to increase enrollment and retention of girls was also initiated in 1991 under the Primary Education Programme (PREP) with funding from USAID. This program provided scholarships for girls from poorer families in areas with low female enrollment (Republic of Ghana 1999: 20).

The quality of teaching of SMT subjects is also being addressed through training workshops targeted at JSS teachers of SMT subjects. Workshops designed to develop training manuals for JSS teachers in innovative science, and science-related teaching methods have been conducted by the GEU with the involvement of JSS teachers, MOE/GES staff, university lecturers and school principals. A nation-wide exercise designed to train the trainers for JSS teachers from all districts was unveiled in the second half of 1999.

Conclusions

Since independence in 1957, Ghana has placed a very high premium on education. Successive governments have devoted a disproportionate share of the national budget to education. Within the last decade alone, educational spending has consumed between 28 percent and 40 percent of the annual budget. However, after a period of rising enrollments and qualitative gains in cognitive achievements, the education system began to experience a deepening malaise. Today, there is a general recognition that Ghanaian education has entered a period of profound crisis. Indeed, the shifting structure of the Ghanaian education system reflects a groping for answers to arrest the downward spiral through comprehensive reforms. Girl-child education is, arguably, the greatest casualty of the ongoing crisis.

Overall, despite significant gains and some innovative policy interventions, gender inequality, especially at the tertiary level, remains a nettlesome problem for the Ghanaian education system. The gap in enrollment, retention and academic achievement between boys and girls in polytechnics and universities remains largely unaltered. It may even have widened. Gender streaming of girls into traditional rather than scientific and technical subjects continues unabated. Parental, teacher, societal attitudes and cultural practices, including those that were inherited from the colonial/missionary education package, as well as oppressive school and classroom environments, have compromised women's access to and participation in primary education (Daddieh 1997).

With the foundation for female participation in tertiary education weakened, it is not surprising that women are under-represented in polytechnics and universities or concentrated in disciplines that lead to careers that can be more easily reconciled with their domestic roles later in life. This Ghanaian case study demonstrates that with a national political will or commitment, buttressed by significant expenditure outlays and rational reforms, a country can make inroads into gender inequality in access, retention, and academic performance. The degree to which progress can be sustained on all these fronts, however, depends upon robust national economies and adequate funding by governments and parents. Finally, unless the looming menace of HIV/AIDS is confronted openly and creatively, its impact on the student population, especially the females, will be catastrophic. It is absolutely essential that policy interventions intended to redress gender inequalities and other problems facing higher education be carefully targeted or gender-specific rather than general or diffuse if they are to produce the desired benefits for girls and women.

Ultimately, successful mediation of the asymmetries in gender relations and other gender inequities in higher education in Ghana as elsewhere in Africa requires not only healthy and dynamic national political economies but also a genuine commitment to rights-protective legislation for students in general and female students in particular coupled with vigorous prosecution of violations of those rights..

References

Addae-Mensah, I., 1996. "Vice-Chancellor's Address at His Induction," University of Ghana-Legon, October 9, 2. Accessed on 2/3/99 at *http://www.ug.edu.gh/vcspeech.htm.*

Amua-Sekyi, E. T., 1988. "Ghana: Education for Girls." Paper presented at the Women's Center at Eastern Washington University, May, 1-9.

Atakpa, S. K., 1996, *Factors Affecting Female Participation in Education in Relation to the Northern Scholarship Scheme.* Accra: Ministry of Education, cited in Amua-Sekyi 1988, 3.

Blay, K., 1990. Interview conducted at Delaware State University, May 1990.

Boahene A., 2001. "C173b Released to 5 State Varsities," *Daily Graphic.* Accessed on 10/31/2001 at *http://www.graphic.com.gh/dgraphic/news/ g26.htlm.*

Chambas, M. I., 2000. Interview conducted in Accra, August 31.

Chazan, N., 1983. *Anatomy of Ghanaian Politics: Managing Political Recession, 1969-1982.,* Boulder, Colo.: Westview Press.

Daddieh, C. K., 1995. "Education Adjustment Under Severe Recessionary Pressures: The Case of Ghana." In Kidane Mengisteab and Ikubolajeh Logan, ed., *Beyond Economic Liberalism in Africa: Structural Adjustment and the Alternatives,* London: Zed Books Ltd., 23-55.

Daddieh, C. K., 1997. *Education and Democracy in Africa: Preliminary Thoughts on a Neglected Linkage.* Accra, Ghana: Institute of Economic Affairs, Occasional Papers Number 10.

Daniel, G. F., 1997-98. "The Universities in Ghana." *The Commonwealth Universities Year Book,* vol. 1, 649-56.

"Education Policies," n.d. p. 2. Accessed on 3/27/2002 at http://www.ghana. edu.gh/present/policies.html.

Ghanaian Chronicle, 2001. "Bottom Tree: Sexual Harassment in Our Schools: Action Needed." Accra, February 7.

Haddad, W. D., et al., eds., 1990. *Education and Development: Evidence for New Priorities,* Washington, D.C.: World Bank Discussion Papers, 95.

Liganga, Lucas., 2002. "Equal enrolment is just a start," *Africa Recovery,* Reprint Edition (May).

Mckown, R. E., and D.J. Finlay 1974. "Ghana's Status Systems: Reflections on University and Society." *Journal of Asian and African Studies* 11 (July-October): 166-79.

Najafizadeh, M., and L. A. Mennerick, 1992. "Professionals and Third World Public Well-Being: Social Change, Education, and Democratization."

In *Development and Democratization in the Third World: Myths, Hopes and Realities,* ed., Kenneth E. Bauzon. Washington: Crane Russack, 242-48.

Nation, The, 2000. "Why Violence And Rape Thrive In Schools." Nairobi: May 1.

Pellow, D. and N. Chazan, 1986. *Ghana: Coping with Uncertainty.* Boulder, Colo.: Westview Press.

Price, R., 1974. "Politics and Culture in Contemporary Ghana: The Big Man Small Boy Syndrome." *Journal of Modern African Studies* 1 (2, Summer): 173-204.

Republic of Ghana, 1999. *A Decade of Educational Reforms: Preparation for the Challenges of a New Millennium.* Background paper prepared for the Ministry of Education by the Forum Technical Committee. Accra: November.

Republic of Ghana, 1992. *Constitution of the Republic of Ghana.* Accra: Government Printer, Assembly Press.

Salia, A. K., n.d. "But SRC Rejects Any Such Mover, *Daily Graphic:* Accessed on 10/31/2001 at *http://www.graphic.com.gh/dgraphic /topstories/a23.htlm.*

Samoff, J., J. Metzler, and T. Salie, 1992. "Education and Development: Deconstructing a Myth to Construct Reality" In *Twenty-First Century Africa: Towards a New Vision of Self-Sustainable Development,* ed., Ann Seidman and Frederick Anang. Trenton, N.J.: Africa World Press, 101-147.

Someah-Addae, K., 1988. "The Educational System in Ghana as a Source of Gender Inequality in Vocational and Technical Education. Thesis presented to the Department of Vocational and Technical Education, Faculty of Education, University of Cape Coast in partial fulfillment of the requirements for the Master of Philosophy Degree (Vocational and Technical Education).

Tembe, J., 2002. "Mozambique's Mothers Back in School." *BBC News:* Tuesday, March 19.

Whitaker, J. S., 1988. *How Can Africa Survive?* New York: Council on Foreign Relations Press (see especially chapter 6).

World Bank, 1988. *Education in Sub-Saharan Africa: Policies for Adjustment, Revitalization, and Expansion.* Washington, D.C.: The World Bank.

World Bank, 1999. "Ghana: Women's Role in Improved Economic Performance." *Findings* 145 (October). Washington, D.C.: The World Bank.

World Bank, 2001. "Sub-Saharan Africa: HIV/AIDS on University Campuses." *Findings* 188 (August). Washington, D.C.: The World Bank.

World Bank, n.d. Document related to "Education Adjustment" under the project "Ghana-Education Sector Development," accessed on 10/21/2002, at *http://www.worldbank.org/pics/pid/gh50620.txt.*

Cyril Daddieh

Appendix

TABLE 1: Enrolment by level and types of institutions: Selected Statistics for Education (2001/2002)

	No. of Institutions	No. of Students	% female	GER %	No. of teaching staff	PTR	% of total education spending
Kindergarten/ Pre-School	9,634	702,304	49	46.2	27,882	25	
Public	6,321	457,597	50		19,043	24	7.4
Private	3,313	244,707	49		8,839	28	
Primary	15,285	2,586,434	47	80	80,552	32	
Public	12,335	2,113,749	47		64,197	33	34.0
Private	2,950	472,685	49		16,355	29	
Junior Secondary	7,582	865,636	45	64	47,445	19	
Public	6,414	741,895	45		40,011	19	22.7
Private	1,168	123,741	49		7,434	17	
Senior Secondary	510						
Public	474	249,992	41	18	10,791	21	15.2
Private	36						

TVET							
Public	23	17934	13	N/A	1150	16	1.2
Teacher Training (TTC)	42	19686	27	N/A	n/a	n/a	
Public	38	18766	31		1209	16	4.5
Private	4	920	n/a		n/a	n/a	
Tertiary				N/A		N/A	
Public					1480		11.5
University	5	40673	30		951		
Polytechnics	10	18459	22		80		
Other (IPS, GIL)	5	n/a	n/a		n/a		
Private	21[1]	n/a	n/a		n/a		
Non-Formal	8000	196170	62%	N/A	8000	25	0.5
Special Education	24	3807	N/A	40	264	14	0.5
Management	N/A	N/A	N/A	N/A	N/A	N/A	0.3
Subvented bodies	N/A	N/A	N/A	N/A	N/A	N/A	2.2

[Based on various data from MoE, GES and current reports (2002)]

Notes: N/A Not Appropriate; N/A Not Available
[1] Six of them are degree awarding: a further 60 awaiting accreditation
Source: Government of Ghana, Education Strategic Plan 2003 to 2015, Volume 1: Policies, Targets and Strategies (Accra: Ministry of Education, May 2003), p. 6.

CHAPTER 8

ACADEMIC WOMEN AT THE UNIVERSITY OF ZIMBABWE: INSTITUTIONAL AND INDIVIDUAL ISSUES IN REFORMING HIGHER EDUCATION IN A STRESSED ECONOMY

Rudo B. Gaidzanwa

"Why do you have a double-barreled (sur) name?"
"You want to bring Beijing to this university?"
"This women's activism is unacademic and misconceived."
"What political party do you support?"

Introduction

The thrust of this chapter is to analyze higher education, especially the university as a social space that plays a key role in the reproduction of gendered educational inequality. It focuses on the case of the University of Zimbabwe, using real life stories that illustrate process within a concrete sociological context. The aim of the paper is not to restate the problems that academic women experience in Zimbabwe but also to illuminate the internal lives, choices and circumstances that academic women operate in.

While it may be useful to describe the structures of institutionalized gender discrimination, it is also useful to understand the operation of the processes of discrimination and struggles against it from the vantage points of the gender that is discriminated against.

How does gender discrimination "work" in the lives of women of different ages and with different ethnic, racial and marital characteristics? It is necessary to understand the choices the women make because these choices may reinforce, complicate or reduce the negative consequences of gender discrimination for the women in question. Linking women's individual maneuvers in their quest to build fulfilling academic careers helps to illuminate the possible areas for intervention. The paper also indicates some of the possibilities for instituting change in the context of economic crisis and dwindling institutional financial and human resources.

The issue of women and their struggles for justice in the academy has been discussed, debated and documented by researchers from different institutions worldwide. Osborne (1995) on Canada, Assié-Lumumba (2002) and Sall on Africa (2000), Barrow on Black Afro-Caribbean women in higher education in the UK, Morley and Walsh (1996) on Europe, Bacchi (1993) on Australia, have all described and discussed the struggles of academic women with violence, injustice and discrimination against them in academic settings. According to Osborne, the 'chilly' academic climate that women endure in the academy needs to be problematised and transformed to make it more supportive to women and to create freedom to learn, experiment and teach.

The context

Many readers would conclude that each of the statements cited at the beginning of this chapter was most likely made in a casual setting such as a bar, a staff common or tearoom, a sheltered environment where friends could joke around and pull each other's legs. They would all be wrong. All these statements were made before academic appointments boards where candidates applying for lecturers' jobs at the University of Zimbabwe are interviewed. A vice chancellor or a pro-vice chancellor chairs these interviews. Only in exceptional circumstances would a faculty dean preside over an academic appointments board.

These statements were made to four different women who went through interviews necessary for appointments to the lecturing staff. The women were all taken aback and could not believe that what these senior men had said to them was deemed acceptable in the institution in which they intended to work. They reported these statements to their friends, colleagues, and to the Affirmative Action Project of the University of Zimbabwe, which the author runs. Needless to say, they were aghast. The female whose double-barreled surname had raised the ire of a senior man at the Academic Appointments Board thought that the Labour Relations Act did not allow any potential employer to raise an issue with an interviewee on the basis of their name, sex, colour, creed, etc. She wanted to understand why her name would raise eyebrows in an institution dedicated to pursuing knowledge, truth and enlightenment in an atmosphere of tolerance, observance of different people's rights and respect for all.

The second woman wanted to know what it is that could be construed as "bringing Beijing to this university" in an appointments interview. The third woman was at a loss to understand why activism would be considered incompatible with academic and scholarly pursuits. The fourth woman, it turned out, had been one of three or four interviewees for an academic position and at least one other interviewee who was asked about their political affiliation was a man. "Welcome to the University of Zimbabwe" a cynical woman told them in the course of the discussion. One woman who was privy to the discussion on these Academic Appointments Boards suggested that these statements could have been flippant, perhaps misplaced jokes, meant to lighten the atmosphere in a formal context. Three of the women disagreed, citing the definite air of hostility surrounding the utterance of the questions and statements. One of the women interviewees pointed out that her interview had lasted nearly three times as long as those of the other candidates because of her responses to the gibe about women's activism and scholarship. She was so angry and agitated after the interview that she was unable to sit for thirty minutes, playing back the whole interview.

The consensus that emerged from this discussion was that there was definite hostility to female candidates for lectureships if these female candidates were assertive, unapologetic and not as deferential as the key male panelists expected them to be. Needless to say, the majority of Academic Appointment Boards are male-dominated except for the presence of administrative staff, who might be females and who take the minutes, and the occasional department chair who might be standing in for a male chair on leave or rarely, might be department chair in her own right. This reality puts a great burden on women to manage their politics, public demeanour and appearances in a male-dominated environment where they do not constitute a critical mass that can insulate the assertive woman from male hostility. At the University of Zimbabwe, women academics always constituted between 17% and 21% of the academic staff from 1979 to 2001. With the economic crisis in Zimbabwe and an exodus of academic staff, the proportions of male and female staff are constantly in flux as academics move out in search of better opportunities.

The Gender Spread in Academic Hiring

In 2001, the last year for which reliable statistics on academic staff were available, there were 959 male lecturers and 207 female lecturers, 65 male professors and 5 female professors and one dean of faculty. Of the ten deans of faculties, only one woman was a dean of the commerce faculty until another female was appointed dean of education late in 2001. There has always been a huge disparity in the proportions of men and women on the academic staff of the University of Zimbabwe despite the increase in enrolment of female students from 20% to about 30% at the highest points of the Affirmative Action Programme (See Chivaura 2001). Thus, while women constituted 17.7% (207) of the academic staff in 2001, they accounted for only 7.6% (5) of the professorial grades. In comparison, male lecturers constituted 82.2%, (959) of the academic staff and 92.8% of the professorial grades, indicating that there are problems of upward mobility for women within the university system. Within the sexual divisions, only 2.4% of the women were in professorial grades in comparison with 6.7% of the men. Thus, while women may secure academic employment in the university, their upward mobility is much slower than men's.

This disparity is attributable to many factors, some of which lie outside the university. These factors include the low numbers of women who qualify to enter "A" level studies as indicated by Kajawu (2001) and the bunching of women in the arts, social sciences and education, areas in which there is a lot of competition among men too. Those women who qualify for post-graduate study are disadvantaged because of the problems of mentoring, selection and encouragement to persist with post-graduate studies in a male-dominated institution.

As was indicated in a study by Gaidzanwa et al. (1989), the age of post-graduate study coincides with the age of marriage for women in Zimbabwe. Many women attending universities in Zimbabwe graduate between the ages of 22 and 23 and get married between 23 and 28. Thus, post-graduate study competes with marriage in graduate women's lives while the gender politics of the University of Zimbabwe disadvantage women in their competition with men for post-graduate grants and studies and in hiring for academic posts. The women's experiences with academic appointments boards mentioned earlier illustrate the gender-specific hoops that women have to jump through in the process of getting hired.

However, this is not to say that there are no problems endemic in the university that affect women's choices to leave or to persist in the pursuit of academic careers. As shown by the anecdotes of the academic women, there are many problems in the university, problems that affect women's teaching and learning environment negatively. Some of these issues were raised in Bernard's work on academic women in the United States of America as early as 1964. The discussion below picks up various issues and themes raised by twelve academic women who were interviewed for this study. These issues include parental influence, choice of marriage and marriage models and partners, decision to have children and the numbers of children, commitment to an academic career and the time at which this commitment is made in a woman's life. This chapter also draws on the experiences of the Affirmative Action Programme at the University of Zimbabwe. This programme was developed in 1995 as a result of the realisation that the university had a lopsided gender profile in student enrolment, staff hiring, and in the general ethos of the institution.

Entry into Academia

Of the twelve women whose stories were volunteered or told to the researchers for this chapter, the majority did not plan to become academics. Only three of the women, two lecturers and one associate professor, had planned to teach at the university level. The rest wandered into or ended up in academia, having tried other careers and occupations. In particular, the interviews with five women who traveled circuitous routes into academia will be used as examples. Two women, both in the lecturer grade, went through the teaching route, experiencing stops and starts to their careers. One of the women chose to accommodate her husband's job, which took him around Zimbabwe before she embarked on post-graduate study. The second woman got married in colonial Zimbabwe, effectively truncating her career and benefits in the education sector. Her marriage to a foreign man introduced another dimension to her career, uprooting her from Zimbabwe after she had already gained teaching experience and seniority in colonial Zimbabwe. By the time she returned to Zimbabwe, she had "lost" career time and advancement in Zimbabwe although, later, as a divorced woman, she was able to devote more time and effort to her career and secure significant seniority in the teaching service.

Significantly, it is the women who entered academia at relatively early stages in their careers who have achieved recognition in the terms of the university's status structure as presently defined. Two women in particular managed to achieve professorial rank at the university in the early nineties, ahead of most women and many men, one at the age of 35 and the other at the age of 41. The one who became a professor at 41 has a career closely resembling that of academic men, in that she went into post-graduate study up to the doctoral level without a break. She has no children and is not married, factors that facilitated her commitment to academia and an uninterrupted participation in institutional activities. The woman who became a professor at

35, the first black woman to reach professorial grade, is not married and was able to enter the university straight from school, gaining knowledge of the academic system, securing a mentor very early on in her career and entering an emerging field of academic endeavour, women's studies. Significantly, both professorial women are single and like almost all the women who contributed stories and were interviewed for this study, they are children of schoolteachers. The careers of the parents of most of these women most likely facilitated the entry of their children into education and their commitment to it.

The first black woman to chair a department at 25 and the first black woman to become a dean of faculty at 40 chose the administrative track within academia early on in her career and performed very well in that track. She also had very significant support for her career from her spouse and from her mentors.

Two women in the lecturer grades in commerce and the social sciences started off in different career tracks, one in administration and the other as a broadcaster/presenter. Both women had children before they settled into their initial careers. The first woman, a lecturer in commerce, had to make a conscious effort to change careers while the second one, a demographer, pursued her degrees studies while raising children, holding a job, a marriage and had a home to mind. The demographer's career is particularly remarkable because she has managed to achieve so much coming from so far behind the other women who are her peers and colleagues. She too, is the child of a schoolteacher.

Thus, the stories of these women indicate many possibilities about academia, women's career choices and achievement. They indicate the significance of personal choice in a woman's career trajectory. Personal choices may include choice of career specialisation, time for specialising throughout one's lifespan, choice of marriage, spouse and model of marriage, the decision to have children and the level of achievement desired by a woman in a specific career. It is important to discuss the issue of marriage since it influences men and women's careers differently in academia.

Marriage and Academic Careers

From the interviews and stories of the different women in this study, marriages are transacted in a variety of ways, all of which have different implications for the careers of the women involved in them. The story of the demographer indicates that marriage may not necessarily preclude participation in academia. Another woman, a lecturer in education, indicated that developing her academic career collided with her spouse's idea of marriage, effectively terminating the marriage. The third woman in the professorial grade, a lawyer, indicated that marriage did not interfere with her academic career. If anything, her spouse supported her academic career by taking on some nurturing work. The lecturer in commerce indicated that her career switch into academia was not impeded by marriage because her husband was supportive and respected her choices. Two women, the dean of commerce and a lecturer in linguistics, indicated that their marriages have not hampered their academic careers.

Thus, from these stories, it is evident that marriages can make or break careers in academia depending on the characters of the partners, the contents and premises of the marriages. The professorial woman in the law faculty postponed her career when she married because she wanted to put most of her effort into nurturing her partner and children early in her marriage. Six of the women in the study did not postpone their careers but have been in wage employment since they left school or university. Two of the academic women, who are divorced, chose not to remarry, while two of the three professorial women have chosen to remain single.

During the workshop held by the Project with academic women in 2000 and during focus group discussions held in 2001, academic women indicated that marriage has significant impact on academic women in Zimbabwe. As argued by Bernard (1964), marriage looks very different from the woman and the man's vantage points. Marriage is also constructed to mean different things to men and women. For women in Zimbabwe, marriage is a standard by which their social conformity and achievements are measured. In Zimbabwe in particular, women are supposed to "make the home" as reflected in the Shona saying: "Musha mukadzi" (a home is made by the woman).

This saying refers to a home constituted by a husband and a wife who, in some circumstances, may be parted by death. It was not supposed to refer to women's homes, which they currently set up on their own outside marriage. In Shona and Ndebele 19th to mid-20th century cultures, single women did not set up homes on their own outside parental control and outside marriage. Therefore, women are supposed to "make homes" as part of their self-definition and as a social requirement, inside marriage. Married academic women, like other women, also have to "make homes." Academic men in Zimbabwe do not have to "make homes" in the same manner since they are not expected to cook, clean, feed spouses and children, nurture them and tend to their bodily and social needs on a daily basis. Academic men, like other men, are expected to work outside the home and to be breadwinners who fend for their families. The dilemma for academic women arises because like other women in wage-paying employment in Zimbabwe, they have to work a double shift. Women worldwide handle the double shift in different ways. In Zimbabwe, wage-earning women handle the double shift through the hiring of resident and non-resident domestic labour.

From the Affirmative Action Project's workshops and focus group discussions with academic women, one sees the dilemma for academic women: their work is not structured around the nine-to-five routines that are common in the rest of the economy. Academic work, like housework, is never done. It is always present, is reproduced continuously through new publications that need to be read and written, research crying out to be undertaken, student work that needs assessment, and consultations with past, present, and future students. The public also demands information, commentary and explanation on various issues continually. Conferences and seminars need attending and colleagues and contacts need to be cultivated formally and intellectually throughout the world. Fundraising for research is critical in an economy such as Zimbabwe where state provision is not adequate. When does academic work end? It never does!

The academic work described above is premised on specific assumptions, namely, that academics have undivided time and no other commitments to impede the search for knowledge. As indicated by Sciama (1984) on Cambridge wives, Oxford and Cambridge universities in Britain have monastic traditions, which scholars have had to struggle against. Women used to be denied degrees at Oxford, and the struggle for women's education is mirrored in the histories of the universities derived from the British institutions. These traditions remain embedded in the processes of generating and pursuing knowledge. These processes demand considerable time, to the exclusion of most other social duties, the availability of funding for research and publications, contact with other scholars outside the home, serenity and undivided time within the home. These demands are not compatible with family life. These demands are particularly incompatible with the social expectations placed on women in general and married women in Zimbabwe in particular.

Part of the marriage expectation in Zimbabwe is that every woman will understand, without being told, that the truest and most fulfilling sphere for a woman is the home. It is also expected that a wife will perform personal services for a spouse. Personal services may include cooking, cleaning a husband's clothes, making the marital bed and entertaining the husband after he returns from work. As was indicated by Hansen (1986) in her work on domestic work in Zambia, for a wife to delegate such personal work indicates her lack of commitment to her husband and to her marriage. Academic women, like other women in paid work, have to fulfill these expectations, in various ways, at home and still perform as well as or better than their male colleagues at work. These expectations place great stress on women in academia. As was indicated in Gaidzanwa et al. (1989) and by Dyanda's research on academic women and publishing at the university in 2000, at the University of Zimbabwe, women academics, proportionally to men, earn fewer doctoral degrees, publish less frequently and occupy the lowest rungs of academia as temporary staff, teaching assistants, tutors, demonstrators, technicians, and the most junior lecturers, on the academic totem pole. Busari (2000) also found that younger women academics in sciences suffer more frequently from burnout and stress related to their work than other academics.

Freedom from marriage and child-rearing responsibilities in the earlier stages of their careers is a very important variable in accelerating the achievements of valued institutional academic statuses. This is the case, as indicated earlier, in the stories and interviews with two women in the professorial grade, whose career trajectories most resemble those of male academics in the same cohort.

Thus different women make different choices with respect to marriage. However, marriage tends to be accompanied by the production of children, in most parts of the world. In Zimbabwe, even those women like one of the women lecturers in this study, who might not have produced children who are biologically theirs, have experienced the joys and trials of motherhood and the impacts of children on academic careers. All the women who contributed their life stories, except one professor, have, (and some are still mothering) children who may or may not have been biologically produced by them. Childrearing introduces another dimension to the factors affecting academic women's careers.

Childrearing and Academia

Academia demands that academics be physically and socially mobile as a means of networking and building up career contacts. It also necessitates travel to seminars, conferences, field trips and workshops. The story of the demographer best illustrates the conflicts and choices that academic women may be called upon to make in their personal and academic lives. The woman mentioned, with anguish, the choice that she had to make in taking her child off the breast to attend an important professional meeting in Indonesia. A linguistics lecturer's story, best illustrates the contradictions and complexities of combining careers with motherhood. Despite the fact that she had no biological children, she mothered two children and was not able to pursue some career-advancing activities because she had nobody else to take care of the children in her custody. If anything, single parenting may be especially difficult for women because of the absence of a spouse who could take on child-rearing responsibilities occasionally.

When women are offered the option of bringing their children along to meetings and formal academic events, the benefits for the child and the mother/academic woman tend to be mixed. Some of the women in this study have exercised the option of taking their children along to formal academic meetings and events. However, most have mixed feelings about this option. Their dilemma centres on the need for a caravan of people and equipment that is characteristic of people travelling with children. From personal experience, shared by many women, travelling with a baby-minder, small tub, kettle for heating food and water, toy basket, clothes and accessories for a child can take the ease out of travel, whether local or regional. International travel with a child who has to be baby-sat by strangers in a hotel or confined surroundings conjures images of abuse, exhaustion, and constant anxiety for both child and mother. The prospect of taking a child to a country with a language foreign to the child for a month or three is daunting, to say the least.

Perhaps the worst experience related to the Affirmative Action Project was that of an academic woman who, steeped in the notions of equal opportunities for men and women to partake in academic interaction, took her child to a country where there was a simmering civil war. The academic woman stayed in a hotel with the child and on the second day, the child's stomach started running. By dawn, the child had lost a third of her weight. Attempts to secure the services of a hotel doctor failed, perhaps owing to language problems and perhaps because no such person existed. Needless to say, the mother was in tears and decided to use her common sense and approach the army of Zimbabwe which was involved in defending the regime of that country from rebels. The Zimbabwe National Army took the child into their camp, hooked the child to a drip and began treatment. The mother never attended the rest of the conference and the child and mother moved into the army camp from whence they boarded their plane when the child was able to travel. As the mother/academic remarked to me months later, amidst lots of laughter and relief: "Rudo, I will salute the Zimbabwe National Army whenever they request me to do so. My child will now stay at home and I willingly forfeit my right to take the child to conferences."

However, not all academic women experience life-threatening problems with children during their work. One academic woman in the social science faculty routinely took her baby son with her during her research on squatter settlements in Harare in the 1970s and early 1980s. She argues that this experience was very positive for her son because it encouraged him to value what his parents provided for him, namely, food, clothing, a home, education, and parental care. Her son was able to see how little other children had, materially and otherwise, in comparison to himself.

Unlike responsibilities to husbands, childrearing can be delegated more easily, and two of the academic women were able to leave Zimbabwe to further their studies and have their husbands look after their children in the interim. Another lecturer in business was able to pursue her education and work because her parents performed the child-caring work for her and her husband. Thus, children can be left with other people, including husbands while wives study, attend meetings, and undertake fieldwork. Of course, many of the women agonise around these choices because they realise that they are judged harshly by their society for pursuing careers at all and for leaving their children with husbands. Furthermore, not all husbands would support these specific choices, putting the onus on each academic woman to negotiate with her spouse whatever arrangement is workable for them as a couple.

In the study by Gaidzanwa et al. (1989) and in the focus group discussions with academic women held in 2001, many women mentioned that the flexible schedule of an academic woman facilitated the loading of many women with childcare work that other career women escape. It is ironic that academic women find themselves bound more tightly into mothering and nurturing because of their schedules, while similar schedules emancipate other members of their households from childcare. Given the absence of a care facility or school for small children at the university, academic women have childcare activities intensified by their schedules, eroding the time that is potentially available to them for their research, teaching and publishing. Unless an individual academic can negotiate an equitable childcare role for herself, she is likely to find her time taken up increasingly by childcare and other domestic work. In the context of the economic crisis, the erosion of discretionary time has been intensified by the need to procure extra work for enhancing household incomes.

While child-minders can take care of children, there are aspects of domestic work and childcare that cannot be delegated. For example, taking children to doctors and dentists, school consultations, sports galas, and other activities, is usually considered a parent's, particularly a female parent's, work.

Certainly, in this author's experience, other parents look down upon parents who delegate this work to maids, drivers, and other employees. In any event, as the story of one of the lecturers in linguistics shows, women can negotiate childcare work and when they have sacrificed their careers for their children and spouses, they have a better bargaining position when they decide to spend more time studying, researching, and attending formal meetings away from home. Taking care of the children may therefore strengthen an academic woman's claim for time for her career later on in her married life. Thus different choices are possible for academic women, be they married or single, with or without children. Spouses, paid child-minders, parents and other members of families such as those mentioned in the stories of five of the women, may also help with childcare. These people are critical to the lives and functioning of most academic women.

Working Conditions

The conditions under which people labour determines their work output, satisfaction and morale. In Zimbabwe, wageworkers spend at least eight hours of their time per day in the workplace. Academics have more flexible schedules, since their work is not as structured as that of other workers. Their work is built around the schedules of their students, so lectures, tutorials, and other interactions with students may be spaced out over many days, a few hours at a time. In the free spaces of a day, a lecturer may insert reading, fieldwork, seminar and conference attendance, and other activities. Domestic responsibilities also impinge on this timetable, necessitating the harmonisation of academic activities with fetching and transporting children, cooking, cleaning, and/or supervising domestic and other workers.

At some universities such as those in Nigeria, according to a Nigerian visiting professor at the University of Zimbabwe, there are childcare facilities on campuses, primary schools and support services to make the lives of academics with children easier. There are no such facilities for staff or students at the University of Zimbabwe in spite of the presence of more than three thousand adult women who are students and lecturers, secretaries and administrators, and close to seven thousand adult men who are students, lecturers, administrators, and service staff on campus. Thus, all these people have to make alternative child care arrangements for their children off campus, necessitating constant movement off campus at lunch times and in the middle of afternoons when school children leave their schools. A lot of time, fuel, and peace of mind is lost in this constant movement of people on and off campus.

It is quite common to see children of staff members loitering all afternoon on campus after leaving school at lunchtime. These children have to wait on the campus until their parents can leave at 4:30 p.m. This applies particularly to support staff who are usually not able to break up their days because of their relatively inflexible working hours.

The physical environment also presents many problems for academics. The push from the World Bank for a reduction of funding to higher education, the drive to privatise universities and institute cost recovery through higher fees and levies, has had a negative impact on various aspects of university life in Africa. Gaidzanwa (2001) documented this problem with respect to student life under structural adjustment at the University of Zimbabwe. Reduced funding to higher education has eroded the quality of the working and learning environment at the University of Zimbabwe. The deterioration of the working environment at the university is characterised by broken doors and windows, litter all over the campus, overgrown grass on quadrangles and paths, shortages of chalk, and teaching aids, lack of paper for student reading material production, lack of research funding and the general degradation of the buildings and classrooms. By February 2002, in most departments, there were no cleaning services, student or private, to sweep offices, corridors, and other spaces, presumably because of the lack of funds. Staff members had to sweep their own office if they considered them dirty.

In the humanities sector, the door of one lecture room came off its hinges in 2001. Business continued nevertheless and this door became a big joke as it reclined nonchalantly against the wall near the entrance to a pair of large commerce lecture rooms, symbolising the deterioration of the working environment and the mindset of the people in the university. For women academics, there are specific problems that arise as a result of their work in their departments. For example, the deterioration in safety and sanitary arrangements and facilities leads many women to prefer to work outside the university since many toilets have no door handles and doors cannot be locked or secured. As one woman in the old social sciences building remarked:

"You dare not work in the office in the evening. You may lock yourself in but you have to walk dark corridors, switching on lights on your way out. I am afraid to go to the toilet because the doors have no locks and you have to do your business knowing very well that the door is partially open. What would happen to you if you were attacked in the toilet and there was no-one to hear you? You often have to ensure that there are other people in the building if you want to work there in the evening. I do not work there on my own."

It is now common for lecturers to share offices, but these offices tend to be very small and were originally intended for single occupancy. It is difficult to hold meaningful consultations with students and members of the staff and the public when there is no privacy and where the environment is so degraded.

Safety on campus is also a problem because of poor lighting and security. There has been no lighting in the humanities car park since 2000, so that academics and students leaving campus after 18.30 hours after sundown have to depend on dim lighting in Mount Pleasant Drive outside the campus.

Many academic women in the humanities buildings told the project that they had stopped working in their offices after 6 p.m. every day because of poor security. In 2000, a senior academic woman was attacked and had her bag snatched during lunchtime in this car park, which is supposed to be patrolled by two security personnel. This incident terrorised many people, particularly women students and lecturers, some of whom had witnessed the incident and the lack of security on a supposedly guarded campus in the middle of the day. However, there has been no improvement in security since then and at the time this chapter was finalised, there was not even one functioning light on this campus car park. Thus, many women academics felt that they had been forced to work at home after 5 p.m. each day despite the fact that they might have preferred to complete their work in their offices and not to take any work home after 6:30 p.m. every day.

Remuneration

The remuneration of academics has declined in real terms since 1980 in Zimbabwe. This has been due to the decline in state expenditure especially in the service sector. University education used to be heavily subsidised in Zimbabwe until the mid-nineties when the Bretton Woods institutions insisted that Zimbabwe desist from this practice and recover the costs of university education from the students. Thus, there has been a net decline in subsidies to universities, necessitating the retrenchment of support and academic staff. The majority of retrenchees have been workers earning low pay. Amongst academics, the hardest hit have been contract and temporary lecturers and researchers, demonstrators, teaching assistants and technicians, amongst whom women were highly represented. Academic women have traditionally occupied these lower-level posts, usually on a temporary and contract basis, and they tend to stay longer than men in these posts.

The case of the demographer is particularly instructive in this respect. She worked as a temporary lecturer in a department for over four years but her experience was not considered relevant even though she is now a research fellow within the same university, in the same field. Another lecturer in linguistics also started as a temporary and contract lecturer and laboured to secure a permanent appointment, at one point receiving no response to her application for a post from the department in which she had been working. A female senior lecturer in education also worked as a temporary teaching assistant in a department for a couple of years before securing a permanent appointment. Another young woman research fellow also worked in the Centre for Applied Social Science as a contract researcher for six years until she found a home in the Institute for Environmental Studies, again on contract. With the current phasing out of teaching assistantships and other low ranking posts, which were heavily utilised by women, there is likely to be a decline in the numbers and proportions of women in academia.

While men too may, and do, work as contract and temporary workers; they tend to have a stronger male network and greater numbers in the male-dominant system, which helps ease them into permanent posts. In a relatively sex-segregated society such as Zimbabwe, men tend to mentor men, since post-graduate women are likely to be married or in serious relationships. Therefore it is often very difficult for women to penetrate male networks of clientage and patronage. Thus women in the university will generally earn less than men in the same cohort because of the slower career progress women make, their isolation from the centers of power, their domestic burdens and their lack of familiarity with institutional politics. For many academics, particularly women at the lower end of the scale for temporary and contract staff, the spectre of unemployment, job insecurity, and anxiety leads to workers accepting any type of task, regardless of their job descriptions. Two of the women lecturers in demography and linguistics experienced contract work with uncertain prospects and poorer remuneration than other academics and a wide range of duties that were not relevant to their work.

The economic crisis has eroded earnings, so the issues of seniority and tenure are important insofar as they facilitate access to other work outside the university. As one example, a professor displayed a cheque given in recognition of twenty years' service to the university. The cheque was for Z$2,377 (Zimbabwean dollars), an amount that is not sufficient to purchase a lollipop in contemporary Zimbabwe. She indicated that this gratuity exemplified the erosion of the reward system in the university and the implications of this erosion for women who had lower qualifications, and fewer networks in business and the donor agencies and the private sector where remunerative consultancy work could be mobilized. Thus the bunching of women in the arts and social sciences particularly in languages, religion and philosophy, teacher education, and history militates against the diversification of their income bases at a time when the reward structures in universities have collapsed.

The Criteria and Bases for Promotion

The criteria for promotion to a higher grade are stated as research, teaching, and university service. In practice, only published research is ever given priority in determining promotion. Only one lecturer, a male in the law faculty, has ever been promoted on the basis of his teaching. Since appointments and promotions boards are usually male dominated, it is very difficult for many women to understand what transpires in these boards, since the promotions often tend to be contentious. In theory, the faculty dean is the person who sits in on the promotions committee's deliberations and has to inform applicants about the fate of their applications and the reasons for promotion decisions.

The promotions committees generate conflict with deans because of the contested criteria used to assess publications from the sciences and the humanities. Thus many academic men and women would rather desist from applying for promotion than be caught up in struggles centered on contested paper quality, given the disciplinary biases and power plays that operate in promotions committees. In any case, many men and women in the university have argued that there is little incentive for academics to seek promotion since academics are badly paid and there is little real difference between the salaries of lecturers, professors, and administrators.

As indicated by academic women in the Project workshop and focus group discussions in 2000-2001, women in many departments tend to be assigned the "caring" roles such as counseling students, career guidance, and related functions. The Coordinator of the Affirmative Action Project organizes all the project activities, research, seminars and other activities in addition to a normal departmental teaching, research, and university service load and with no extra remuneration or concessions. This is in spite of the fact that the Affirmative Action Project is a university-wide project touching on gender issues affecting staff at the university. There is no formal recognition of these roles, which the women academics say they value. Most of the stories of academic women mention the satisfaction they derive from counseling and interacting with students. However, the university continues to have a promotion system that takes only the research part of university work into account, effectively undermining the priority given to teaching. Given the bureaucratisation of the university, its failure to provide teaching and learning resources, only the most daring department chair or departmental board chair will penalize staff for poor teaching. Therefore, the only activity that will be pursued by academics avidly is research, especially if it is tied to funding that can ease an academic's financial woes.

In a very sobering and extremely worrying presentation, the Director of the Human Resources and Research Centre at the university presented a paper to the National Conference on the State of Gender Issues in Institutions of Higher Learning in Zimbabwe in 2000. In her paper, on women academics at the University of Zimbabwe, she discussed the politics of knowledge and the status of women as knowledge consumers rather than creators. She indicated that the Centre has a policy giving preference to academic women in publishing material submitted by academics. In spite of this policy, only 12 women academics have ever published articles in the *Zimbabwe Journal of Educational Research*, which the Center publishes. Since 1989, women, including women who have published more than once in this journal, have contributed only 27 articles to the journal. Men have contributed 83% of the journal articles. By the time she wrote her paper in 2001, women had contributed only 9 of the 101 articles for consideration for the year 2001.

Thus, there are many problems in the promotion system as well as in the valuation of work in the university. The low value placed on work with students, and helping them with problems that have academic consequences on teaching and supervising and grading work promptly and conscientiously leaves women at the lowest end of the status and remuneration structures, stigmatizing them as non-productive. The increasingly complex problems of students with inadequate funding for books, food, clothes, and medical care in a context of high HIV infection and AIDS, has increased the workloads of those staff who have to take on the caring and nurturing roles amongst students. Predominantly, this role falls on women in many departments at the university.

Overwork and Stress Amongst Women Academics

As part of the presentation for a seminar for academic women in the Affirmative Action Project, Busari's research on women academics showed that a significant proportion of young academic women in the sciences experienced stress and burn-out. According to Moncarz (2001) burn-out is a term suggesting self-immolation and a syndrome of chronic work-related stress. This syndrome is commonly associated with workers in the caring occupations and professions where there is constant and direct contact with others in need of service. For academics, particularly women, contact with students is very frequent, desirable and enjoyable but very draining. Over twenty of the forty academic women participating in one of the Project workshops reported exhaustion, emotional frustration, and helplessness in dealing with young, mature, disabled, and other students with problems that affected their learning.

In many departments, the "people" aspects tend to be shunted to women. These tasks include counseling students, organizing their paid employment, offering students career advice and dealing with bereavement and its aftereffects amongst students and staff. In many university departments, women academics reported that it is usually at their initiative that organization of transport, and calling on bereaved students and staff occurs; purchasing of going-away presents, congratulatory flowers for births, marriages, and celebrations and other personal expressions of solidarity with students and colleagues. Together with the pressures of academic performance and "mothering" of students, many women academics tend to be overworked. This transference of maternalism into the workplace costs women highly since they may function as "wailing walls" in their departments, eroding the time they can allocate to research and publication, activities that are highly valued and rewarded in academia.

Sexual Harassment

Almost all women, regardless of their class, age, status and specialization, mentioned sexual harassment as a problem experienced in the university. In all the workshops held by the Project with administrative, academic, secretarial and other support staff and students, sexual harassment was flagged as a major problem at work. In 1999, the Gender Studies Association at the University of Zimbabwe produced a report, "Breaking the Silence" which described sexual harassment amongst students. In 2001, the Affirmative Action Project and the Gender Studies Association also produced a collection, entitled "Speaking for Ourselves" (2001), edited by Gaidzanwa. In this collection, six undergraduate students and Gaidzanwa explored aspects of masculinity and femininity amongst university students, touching on issues of sexual harassment within and outside lecture rooms. In particular, Chagonda,

Ndlovu, and Gaidzanwa described the behaviour of some male lecturers, which emphasized shows of control, discipline, and authoritarianism towards students. These shows of control may also involve hostility to female students who repel sexual advances and male students who question the sexual harassment or sexual relationships between male lecturers and female students in the teaching and learning situation.

Female academic staff experience sexual harassment in slightly different ways. Their experiences of sexual harassment are connected to their teaching, especially of graduate students, and to their interactions with male colleagues. One academic woman also described the harassment she had been subjected to by mature business students who attended part-time courses in her department. Male post-graduate students tend to be older than undergraduate students. As mid-career people, sometimes they are the same age group as their lecturers or older. The academic woman in business related how she was verbally and sexually harassed by a few male students who passed comments on her looks and one male student who phoned her at home on the pretext that he needed academic help. Another female academic reported that a male student harassed her by sitting in her office for too long, discussing non-consequential issues and generally demanding inappropriate attention from her. A female professor experienced physical sexual harassment by an older male academic on exiting the faculty tearoom. A senior lecturer in education reported harassment as having a racial, class, and age dimension, pointing out that older males tend to be the most consistent harassers of female academics. She also reported that she had had to take legal advice and action as a result of sexual harassment.

During one focus group discussion with academic women in 2001, it emerged that almost all female academics had experienced unsolicited, unwanted and unwelcome verbal comments, and inappropriate sexual jokes which many found to be in bad taste, from male colleagues. Younger female academics reported that they experience more direct sexual harassment from male students because students did not feel that there was much social and age distance between them. The more senior the women are in the university, the less harassment they experience. More senior women tend to be harassed by their peers or senior men rather than by junior males. Young and junior academic women may be harassed by students, junior, and senior men. These issues have been raised in North America in the university context in the work of Katz and Vieland (1988), Franklin (1980) and Dziech and Wiener (1984) and Osborne (1995).

Secretarial staff tends to experience sexual harassment from students and staff. The Project workshop and focus group discussions with secretarial staff in 2000 and 2001, showed that secretarial staff tend to be looked down upon by both students and teaching staff regardless of gender, to be mistreated and sexually harassed by students and academic men. Thus, sexual harassment was reported to be rampant, and a big problem at the university.

Sexual harassment tended to be very awkward to deal with amongst academics because of the gender segregation of the society. Many women confided to the Project staff during workshops, focus group discussions, and other interactions, that it was difficult to report sexual harassment because the ensuing publicity would embarrass them, especially if they were married. They were afraid that they would be accused of consenting to the men's advances or of being compliant with the harassment. As one academic woman who refuses to be named commented:

> Women are routinely harassed at this university. However, you have to handle the harassment yourself because if you squeal, people will just say, "There is no smoke without fire." They will suspect you, the victim of the harassment, of having had an affair with your harasser.

In the absence of any mechanism to handle issues of sexual harassment sensitively, individual women have to take individual action and stop the harassment without any institutional support. As one academic woman, who was a senior lecturer reported, such women may find no support, even from other women who might side with the harassers for ethnic, racial, class and other reasons. The absence of mechanisms for dealing with sexual harassment also disadvantages students as pointed out by Ndlovu (2001) and administrative women as indicated by Chingarande (forthcoming). This institutional blindness to sexual harassment encourages and empowers sexual harassers to continue harassment with impunity.

The casual official attitude to sexual harassment was a problem for both students and staff at the university. As mentioned by Ndlovu (2001) officials from the university prefer to sweep sexual harassment issues, amongst students, under the carpet. The Gender Studies Association's report "Breaking the Silence," dealing with sexual harassment amongst students was virtually ignored by all but a few university officials. It was only when the press picked up the report, after it had gone into the public domain, that the university officials reacted. They wanted to know who had released the report to the press, rather than to effect any of the recommendations of the report. As indicated by all the students in the edited collection "Speaking for Ourselves" (2001), sexual harassment continues largely unpunished at the university.

Competition and Solidarity

Given the pressures of academia and domestic responsibilities, the stories of many academic women show some tension between the need for solidarity through interaction with peers and competition for success in academia. From the stories of nearly all the women, depending on their gender politics, many academic women find it difficult to secure mentors and draw solidarities from their peers. A senior lecturer in education graphically described the tensions that she noted between gender-based loyalties amongst women and their ethnic, racial, class, and age ties with other academics, predominantly male.

Academia tends to be a very competitive field where promotion is based on individual performance through teaching, research, and publishing academic papers and books. There is very little reward for cooperative or collaborative work since credit tends to be given to the dominant individuals, be they researchers or teachers. The small proportion of tenured academic women makes it difficult for many junior women, particularly those in faculties with very few or no women, to receive help from senior academic women. In faculties such as engineering, veterinary science and to some extent science, there are very few tenured and senior women who can give academic help to young women. As one academic woman from science said:

> Between fighting your own battles to get promoted, to secure research funds and to survive the male mafias, you do not get much time to devote to young women who are just starting out as academics.

A young academic woman observed that she has always worked in departments where there were few women anyway and hardly any senior ones, so she could not share her work experiences with other women. The women she encountered were foreign and were not invested in the university in the same way that she was. She observed that battling for survival individualized many academic women, especially in a climate of austerity within and outside the university.

Apart from the individual achievement structure of academia, a particular woman's gender politics inform the ways in which she deals with issues of competition and solidarity. As observed by the academic women in the focus group discussions, many academics, particularly women, do not want to appear to be needy or desirous of anybody's help. By casting themselves in the roles of "knowers", many academics compete even in areas where they are out of their depth or do not know the terrain. In addition, many women are demoralized and are not well versed in the culture of competition amidst the supposed collegiality of academia. As observed by Cicilia Kunyadini, who interviewed many women for this study (on which this chapter is based) and organized many of the focus group discussions, many academic women are very apathetic or alternatively do not want to be associated with any meetings or initiatives that are not associated with or do not include men. This is partly because these types of women are afraid of being labelled "feminists" or of being punished by the men who might perceive them to be ganging up against them.

As one senior lecturer remarked, many academic women collaborate or cooperate with specific men on the bases of ethnicity, age, class, and race. Thus, women whose gender politics do not accommodate women-only initiatives will not be drawn necessarily to strategizing and constructing solidarities with other academic women on the basis of gender. Similarly, women will not automatically support women who are potential competitors in the system. One lecturer in business observed that when she became an academic, she encountered resistance from some colleagues in her department who did not consider other women, particularly those who started in different careers, to be acceptable as academics. The three women to whom aggressive and unacceptable questions about their names and beliefs were articulated at the Academic Appointments Board are the kinds of women whom many men's academic cabals dislike and punish. They are also the kinds of women whom less radical women will not want to be associated with. All the three women were hired on with tenure but are held out as examples of "bad" women.

As observed by a lecturer in medicine in the focus group discussions, many women may ally with men on racial, ethnic and other bases. Age may be a big factor in the deionisation of senior women who espouse feminist or radical gender politics. Since academic men are the dominant figures in academia, it is not surprising that many women are drawn to men's academic cabals because these cabals are very strong and can promise many rewards to women who join them. The complicating factor is that of gender politics, where women may find that their membership in men's cabals is construed in different ways by the men, making the women vulnerable to exploitation by cabal members. For example, many young academic women tie their fortunes to older men only to find themselves abandoned in favour of younger men when choices have to be made. As the lecturer in medicine remarked, many women in her faculty learn the hard way when their plans do not work out, or are not supported in the same way that men's agendas are. Two lecturers in business noted that in their experience, male colleagues do not necessarily mean what they say, and women academics need to be aware of these gendered issues of solidarity.

From the experiences of the women in the focus groups, young academic women are not familiar with the regulations governing promotion, publishing, seniority, and status within the university structures. Therefore, some of them tend to be gullible and can be promised goods that specific men cannot deliver. As was evident from Gaidzanwa's committee experiences, many people can make a mark in the university if they are experienced in committee procedures. However, as other women have testified, most women and men are never told what the regulations are on specific issues. The induction system in the university is a "sit by Nelly" type of induction where lecturers learn the rules as they go along. Only the ambitious lecturers learn the rules fast either because they want to make a mark quickly or because they become involved in disputes where they have to learn how to play within the rules. Competition, therefore, has to be accomplished through the committees as well as through publishing and accessing research funding.

The ambitious academic has to be an astute committee person, with all the boredom, nitpicking and time investment that committee work entails. Women academics tend to be so overburdened that they are unwilling or unable to do their apprenticeship on the boring and low-status committees until their male colleagues can trust them to represent everybody on the important and high-status committees. Thus, to be trusted by the "boys," an academic woman has to embrace an agenda which is acceptable to her male counterparts.

Issues of coalition building in the process of competition are unfamiliar or difficult for academic women because, in general, their politics tend to be personal and lie outside formal institutional structures. An ambitious academic woman necessarily has to compete primarily with men because it is the men who occupy most of the senior positions in academia. By the same token, ambitious academic women have to have some solidarity with senior men if their promotions are to be secured. It is therefore not very surprising that many junior women are initially drawn into solidarity with men, often in negative gender politics, against junior men and junior women.

Thus solidarity between women may be influenced by many issues, including the gender, racial, class, and age composition of academics in particular departments and faculties. In those departments where only one or two women constitute the staff, it may be difficult to build meaningful and effective solidarities beyond the moral and psychological solidarities between disadvantaged and disempowered people.

Solidarities are also constructed around real interests, so academic women may need to focus on issues on which agreement and real interests can be used to build meaningful solidarities. Not all issues are of interest to all women. The single and child-free women may not be too concerned about building child-care facilities, just as home-bound academic women may not be too interested in advocating the right of women academics to use the Senior Common Room in the evenings without being labeled "bad" women. Given the differences between women in life-style choices, marital status, age, class, race, and ethnicity, it is more realistic to focus on those issues that affect most women and can withstand the demands of competition between academics in general.

Having made the points above, it is important to note that, in academia, the output of an individual academic is important for her advancement. While solidarity with other academics is important, it cannot substitute for productivity in research and publishing. As was evident during the workshop for academic women that was held in 2000, academic women were timid in discussing and making strong recommendations about whether women should argue for the recognition of their teaching and counselling work, work which is considered to be "domestic" in academia.

One academic woman argued that women should strive to publish their research and make their mark in this way rather than selling shoes and other goods to their workmates. She was referring to the practices among males and females where lecturers sell vegetables, kitchenware, clothes, and other goods to supplement their meager academic incomes.

The success of academics in vending and other income-generating strategies definitely influences their commitment to academic achievement. Many women are able to generate incomes through "women's work" such as vending, and the low salaries of academics divert many women into these income-generating activities, undermining their commitment to competition and achievement in the academically approved avenues of research and publishing. Another single academic woman commented:

> Women must be willing to understand the implications of their life choices. If they get married at 23, have four children with a husband who expects to be waited on, how do they expect to be able to compete effectively as academics? Surely they do not expect other academic women who have made different choices to spend their lives trying to make those choices less damaging to married women's careers?

These are very sensitive issues for many women because they are not able to compete on the basis of the criteria presently espoused by the university. They might feel diffident about suggesting alternatives or criticizing the low value placed on work in service of students or the community, work which they excel in. However, they still feel disadvantaged by the academic competition system as presently structured, hence their appeals for solidarity, at least amongst women. At the same time, women have different interests, backgrounds, and concerns and have made different choices in life. Ironically, the single, divorced, or young and older married ambitious women are the ones who have been able to compete more successfully in the male-dominated academic system at the university. The three women in the professorial grade made very specific choices. One married professor espoused women's law, another single professor is a feminist who pioneered the teaching of women's studies at the university and the third is a science professor who is single, dedicated to her career and unapologetic about her achievements. A senior lecturer in education, who won the award of Best Teacher in the faculty of education in 1999, is divorced. Not all these women are conventional in terms of the system by any means.

This reality is very difficult to deal with because it makes the discussion of marital status and achievement in academia awkward. Young female students who might contemplate taking up academic careers should be informed informally and formally, of the link between academic success for women and age, marital status and gender politics.

Those with marriage plans early in their careers would obviously be put off by the relationship between marital status and the possibility of women making any headway in academia in the short term, especially if they desire to have children early in their careers. Conservative young women may be deterred from pursuing academic careers by the link between successful academic careers, and the deferment or avoidance of marriage, or by the prospect of deferring seniority and achievement in academia until they reach their fifties.

In addition, the current organization of the achievement and status system in academia is likely to trouble many women who may not consider academic success and marriage as mutually exclusive. Thus, the ability to compete successfully in academia is influenced by the individual women's choices, by the type of marriage relationship, the marital status, the university status and promotion system, and the academics' personal values and priorities about children, families, and work. Appeals for solidarity between women have to be contextualised and have to take into account the gender politics of individual women, the specific issues on which solidarity is possible, and the realities of competition and alliance building in specific departments and faculties.

Competition in academia is a reality, and women sometimes compete against each other, although more often they compete against the men who dominate the academic system. Solidarity is therefore required to make that competition as fair as possible and to ensure that competition does not obscure the fact that the academic status system is skewed against women as long as they perform their domestic and academic work in the social system as presently structured. Changing that system within and outside the university to make it fair to both genders then becomes the most urgent issue around which solidarities can be built between women as well as across sex lines.

Mentoring and Navigating University Politics

In many organizations, newcomers normally identify people who can ease them through the politics of a new environment, helping them make informed choices and shepherding them through difficult terrain. Since women typically constitute less than 30% of an academic community, 30% being considered by some scholars as the critical mass needed for any group to make an impact on an organization), alliance and coalition building and mentoring are critical if women are to navigate their way successfully in a male-dominated university. Mentors are important because they are usually conversant with organizational structures and politics and can help a protégé avoid some pitfalls that might not be obvious to someone new to an organization. The following example will suffice to illustrate the point.

A new female hire attended a faculty meeting where academics were assigned to committees on which they were supposed to represent the faculty. The new hire was trained in and hailed from a competitive system where academics push themselves forward to be noticed, to make an impact and to make headway. According to the culture of the faculty that had hired her, however, academics were nominated by colleagues to serve on a committee. The custom was to demur initially and then to accept the nomination gracefully. Of course, astute department members would brief their friends or colleagues about which committee they wanted to serve on so that they could be nominated for it before any other nominees could be suggested. Once a nomination was made, it was also not acceptable to nominate another person for the same committee unless and until the initial nominee had turned down the nomination for a reason such as absence on a sabbatical leave during that year.

The female hire broke many unspoken rules by volunteering herself for a high-status committee and then expecting faculty members to defer to her action. She was immediately treated as a shameless, pushy, and immodest person who was out to get what she could before she had done her time in the trenches of unpopular committees. Of course there was a bigger problem in the negative expectation that she would compound her "error" on a larger scale by behaving inappropriately on the committee where the interests of the faculty could be jeopardized by reactions to her "alien" style. Individual faculty members were not willing to embarrass her by nominating another person so she was tolerated as a representative on that committee, but she was not considered a good team player.

The sexist overtones of her case were exacerbated because she was not only female but also an "alien" in the sense that she was white and hailed from outside the continent. If she had had friends, mentors, or colleagues who could have apprised her of the culture of the organization, she would have saved herself a lot of problems and embarrassment. Her major mistake was that she behaved like what Mars (1982) termed a "hawk." According to Mars, a "hawk" is a person who usually works in an environment, occupation, or situation that emphasizes the person's autonomy and individuality, and where the control of colleagues is greater than the control of the organization over a member. In these occupations, there is individual competition in entrepreneurial flair, and returns to the successful "hawks" can be very much higher than those of their colleagues. Amongst "hawks," group solidarities are weak, and allegiances shift depending on the issues. Mars also notes that amongst "hawks" there is a climate of suspicion that is more common than a climate of trust.

It is these dilemmas that many academic women have to deal with because they operate in individually competitive systems, but with an ideology or expectation that solidarity based on kindness, gender interests, humaneness and nurturing will operate, at least amongst women. In "hawkish" occupations, mentors are special people because often, they are successful themselves and do not feel the need to compete with their protégés. In academia, mentors explain organizational cultures, and facilitate networking and the building of important connections. They introduce their protégés to successful "hawks" and procure recent literature, publishers and publications, write recommendations and references for research grants, and steer opportunities their protégé's way. Mentors also defend their protégés from the malice of other senior "hawks" who might be out to harm other "hawks" protégés. Thus, to be successful, an academic has to be astute in selecting a mentor. The choice of mentor depends on the protégé's interests in the short and long terms.

The first female dean of commerce chose her professional mentors carefully, relying on vice chancellors and pro-vice chancellors at the University of Zimbabwe and at Africa University. All her mentors at work are black men partly because there are very few or no women in the higher rungs of tertiary education bureaucracies in Zimbabwe. Given that she has focused her career on achievement in the administrative track, she needed mentors who could help her with her day-to-day work and choices. The demographer also had two black male academics as mentors because they were well versed in the area of her academic interest. The social science professor chose a senior white woman, one of the few women who had achieved professorial status in her early forties and who had high academic standing. The young research fellow in environmental studies chose as a mentor a senior white foreign female academic of professorial status because of her forthright and assertive style. She also had a white male professor who worked with her and whose views on gender she helped to shape and change. One of the lecturers in business found it difficult to secure a mentor because of her past experience as a university administrator and she felt that some academics did not welcome her in her department.

The experiences of all these women show that it is possible to make different choices in mentors in pursuit of specific goals, and mentors can be chosen for their competence and personal qualities. While solidarity and emotional support may be important for academic women, they still need some support that is related to their work. Sometimes such support may not exist or be available amongst women. Thus women may have to find mentors outside their workplaces, mentors who may help them with the more general aspects of human support. Aunts, mothers, parents, siblings, and friends have been mentioned in all the stories as sources of support and mentoring regarding attitudes to work, achievement, determination, persistence, and the will to succeed. Of course, mentors can also become friends as relationships at work change, mature, and solidify.

What is important is the realization that a mentor is important but does not necessarily have to share every interest or belief of the protégé. As one academic woman explained: "Part of the problem for many women is that they may want mentors, friends and colleagues, sometimes in one person!"

This need for an all-in-one support person is usually difficult to satisfy because friends tend to be cheerleaders and less critical and objective than colleagues. Mentors may also need to be people once removed who may be able to articulate painful issues without any risk of injuring feelings of friendship and collegiality. Colleagues may not be completely trustworthy in "hawkish" occupations; in any event, they are often suspected of being motivated by envy and competitiveness rather than genuine interest in the other person. It is also worth noting that the academic women mentioned in the previous paragraph all chose mentors once removed by race, gender, and sometimes, nationality. This is a very interesting phenomenon in that it allowed the mentors to feel comfortable with their protégés and vice versa because of the distance in terms of gender or race, facilitating some aspects of relationships and perhaps, foreclosing others. In these instances, the weight of the need probably did not become too heavy for the mentors to bear. Academic women are particularly needy at the university because of their exclusion and such "distanced" relationships may be important for their advancement because they can articulate their need to mentors who would not feel unduly threatened or burdened by them.

In some instances, excessive need may be embarrassing to the "needer" and in "hawkish" occupations, people may not feel comfortable articulating their need to people who may be frightened or burdened by the weight or intensity of the need. This may partly explain why Cicilia Kunyadini was so frustrated by her lack of success in organizing as many focus group discussions with academic women as she would have desired. It is probable that many women did not feel comfortable articulating their frustrations, needs, and desires to other women whom they felt to be competitors rather than potential mentors or "sisters in the academy." Thus, mentoring tends to be a personalized relationship that is comfortable for the mentor and safe for the protégé. The mentor can be of use to a junior person and the protégé can reveal her weakness without fear of exploitation. The women who attended the focus group discussions were usually women who knew each other and were comfortable talking about work issues. The different experiences of women in academia and in the university definitely have an impact on the comfort with which women can articulate problems that they experience within the institution.

Conclusions

The stories contributed by the academic women in this study are very revealing, broadening general understanding of the thinking, attitudes, and behaviours of academic women at the University of Zimbabwe. These academic women have raised issues pertaining to the gender spread in academic hiring, and pointed out the gender statistics, which have always been skewed against women. There has been little success registered by the Staff Development Programme in improving women's qualifications and hiring at the university. This suggests the need to revisit the Staff Development Programme as a whole and to custom-design staff development to take into account the specific gender needs of male and female academics.

Entry into academia tends to be varied, with some women entering academia accidentally and others by design. Women do not constitute a critical mass in academia in Zimbabwe. Until they reach about 30% of the academic population, it is unlikely that they will have a significant impact on the gender climate of universities. In addition, marriage tends to complicate their academic careers, necessitating the postponement of academic achievement well into middle age for most women. This negatively affects women's statuses, earnings and most likely, the attractiveness of academia to many young women who might have marriage in mind. For women, lives that most closely resemble the medieval monastic ideal seem to be the most likely route to academic achievement on a par with men. Significantly, male academics do not have to eschew marriage and children in order to perform excellently in academia.

The imperatives of childrearing also hold back academic women who are mothers, making it difficult for them to undertake training overseas or to exercise the mobility necessary in academia, especially when their children are very young. In the absence of a crèche, nursery school, and primary school at the university, academics and administrators, especially women, have to spend significant time during their working days ferrying children to and from their schools, away from the university campus.

The deteriorating working conditions at the university also create problems for all academics at the university. The decayed infrastructure, poor maintenance, and shortage of teaching aids and resources make the teaching and working environment extremely stressful, unsafe, and unhealthy. The declining remuneration and real incomes of academics continue to de-motivate many academics from excelling in academia. In particular, women are bunched at the lower end of the income scale where they constitute the bulk of the demonstrators, temporary lecturers, contract staff, and junior lecturers. As a result, they have relatively little seniority, status, and influence in the institution.

The promotion criteria tend to over-emphasize research and publication, to the detriment of teaching and service to students and the community. Women tend to spend more time with students in maternal roles in the academy, dooming them to nurturing roles that are not valued in the academic promotions system. In addition, the findings by Busari, that burn-out, overwork, and stress are prevalent amongst junior women in sciences is very disturbing and needs immediate attention.

The absence of an institutional policy on sexual harassment and a code of conduct governing gender relations present significant problems for all women at the university, be they students, academics, or administrators. There is need for official action that is effective, in curtailing and minimizing sexual harassment. This would go some way towards restoring confidence in the institution amongst students, and academic and administrative staff, some of whom perceive themselves to be disadvantaged by the vagueness of the gender policies on fraternization in the university.

The imperatives of solidarity, competition, and the navigation of institutional politics continue to present problems for many women. They are caught between the desire for emotional and professional support in a competitive work environment. The differences women experience between their personal lives and their occupational choices have to be understood. It is necessary for academic women to be made aware of the implications of their personal, occupational, and life choices, and how these choices influence each other and the outcomes they can expect from their careers. The issues involved in the choice of a mentor are quite varied, depending on what individual women expect from their mentors and what types of mentors are available within and outside the work environments.

This chapter has discussed the above issues with reference to the choices made by different academic women. These choices are in turn influenced by the women's backgrounds, their ambitions, aspirations, and desires, as well as the circumstances in their workplaces. The experiences of these women will go a long way towards illuminating the lives, circumstances, and choices of such women, linking work, family life, and achievement and furthering an understanding of the working lives of academic women at the University of Zimbabwe. Some of the general problems analyzed in this chapter are found in other African countries as well as outside of Africa. Focusing on a case study with real life stories provides the ground for a deeper understanding of the sociological context of the reproduction of gendered educational inequality.

References

Assié-Lumumba, N. T., 1995. "Gender and Education in Africa: A New Agenda for Development." Africa Notes. April.

Assié-Lumumba, N. T, 2002. "Gender, Access to Learning, and the Production of Knowledge in Africa." In *Visions of Gender Theories and Social Development in Africa: Harnessing Knowledge of Social Justice and Equality*, ed. Association of African Women for Research and Development. Dakar: AAWORD, 95-113.

Bacchi, C., 1994. "The Brick Wall: Why So Few Women Become Senior Academics." *Australian Universities Review* 36: 1, 36-39.

Barrow, J., 1997. "Black Afro-Caribbean Women in Higher Education in the United Kingdom from the 1950s to the 1990s." In *Women as Leaders and Managers in Higher Education*, ed H. Eggins., Buckingham, U.K.: Open University Press, 63-69.

Bernard, J., 1964. *Academic Women*. Pennsylvania State University Press.

Busari, E., 2000. "Gender Dimensions of Job Satisfaction and Work Burn-Out for Sustainable Development of Women Scientists and Technologists in Institutions of Higher Learning." Paper presented at the AAP/GSA National Conference, 'The State of Gender Issues in Tertiary Institutions in Zimbabwe." Harare.

Chagonda, T., 2001. "Masculinities and Resident Male Students at the University of Zimbabwe: Gender and Democracy Issues." In "Speaking for Ourselves," ed. R. Gaidzanwa. Harare: AAP/GSA/Ford Foundation.

Chivaura, I., 2001. "The Affirmative Action Policy in Student Admissions at the University of Zimbabwe." In "Speaking for Ourselves," ed. R. Gaidzanwa. Harare: AAP/GSA/Ford Foundation.

Dziech, B., and L. Wiener, 1984. . Boston: Beacon Press.

Dyanda, C., 2000. "The Role of the H.R.R.C. and Experiences with Female Academics at the University of Zimbabwe." Paper presented at the AAP/GSA Workshop for Academic Women, University of Zimbabwe.

Franklin, P., 1981. *Sexual and Gender Harassment in the Academy: A Guide for Faculty, Students and Administrators*. New York: Modern Languages Association.

Gaizadnwa, R. B., et al., 1989. "Factors Affecting Women's Academic Careers at the University of Zimbabwe." HRRC.

Gender Studies Association (GSA), 1999. " Breaking the Silence: A Survey of Sexual Harassment at the University of Zimbabwe." University of Zimbabwe,

Hansen, K., 1986., "Domestic Service in Zambia." *Journal of Southern African Studies* 13 (1).

Kajawu, N., 2001. "Producing Men and Women: Gender Stereotyping in Secondary Schooling in Zimbabwe.," In "Speaking for Ourselves," ed., R. Gaidzanwa. Harare: AAP/GSA/FORD.

Katz, M., and V. Vieland, 1988. *Get Smart: A Woman's Guide to Equality on Campus.*, New York: Feminist Press at the City University of New York.

Mars, G., 1984. *Cheats at Work*. London: Unwin Paperbacks.

Morley, L., and V. Walsh, eds., 1996. *Breaking Boundaries: Women in Higher Education*. London: Taylor & Francis.

Moncarz, E., 2001. "Overwork and Unemployment as Stress Factors, Women's Health Collection."

Ndlovu, S., 2001. "Femininities amongst Resident Female Students at the University of Students." In "Speaking for Ourselves.," ed., R. Gaidzanwa. Harare: AAP/GSA/FORD.

Osborne, R., 1995. 'The Continuum of Violence Against Women in Canadian Universities: Towards a New Understanding of the Chilly Campus Climate." *Women's Studies International Forum* 18 (5/6): 637-46.

Sall, E. ed., 2000. *Women in Academia: Academic Freedom in Africa.*Dakar: CODESRIA. Sciama, L., 1884. "Ambivalence and Dedication: Academic Wives in Cambridge University, 1870-1970." In The Incorporated Wife, ed., H. Callan and S. Ardener. London: Croon Helm.

CHAPTER 9

PHILOSOPHICAL AND INSTITUTIONAL CHALLENGES IN INTEGRATING WOMEN IN SCIENCE AND TECHNOLOGY IN AFRICA

Catherine A. Odora Hoppers

Introduction

It has been stated that the twenty-first century will be the century of knowledge, indeed the century of the mind. Innovation is the key to the production as well as the processing of knowledge. A nation's ability to convert knowledge into wealth and social good through the process of innovation will determine its future (Mashelkar 2002). It is recognized that development in the twenty-first century demands the mustering of all human, financial, institutional, and other resources towards this objective. Africa needs science and technology in order to develop and be counted in the present global world, but science and technology also need to develop the capability to embrace and accommodate both men and women as full citizens in the ranks without discrimination.

By science is meant the attainment of "objective knowledge," and science therefore characterized by a strictly cognitive attitude, while technology aims at producing concrete results (in the form of objects, commodities, tools, or procedures) and is therefore characterized by a pragmatic attitude. This distinction is crucial when we foreground the so-called "neutrality of science," especially when we draw attention to the social or moral responsibility of science.

Among feminist science scholars, as among scholars in non-Western societies, there has evolved a sense of feeling trapped in the world of science and with powerful, monolithic assumptions. These scholars have found themselves caught in the uneasy relationship between feminism and science, in the case of feminists (Wertheim 1999), and between the Western understanding of science and other ways of knowing, in the case of other civilizations (Smith 1999).

Feminist scholars in particular, have long argued that far from being value-neutral as it has been posited, science is a culture-laden activity. For this, they have been viewed with great unease by the mainstream scientific establishments almost in the manner that one views an enemy battalion. Thus, when Londa Schiebinger brought out her poignant book entitled *Has Feminism Changed Science?* she laid to rest the notion that women in and of themselves change the nature of science simply by becoming scientists.

This paper agrees with Schiebinger's conclusions and argues that the story of women in science and technology is highly complex, and that the culture of science is not rooted in the chromosomes of its practitioners. This is not to deny that feminist perspectives have made an impact on both the culture and content of science. Indeed, women's involvement in this field has opened up new lines of inquiry that have led to significant new discoveries (Wertheim 1999). Quantitatively speaking, more and more women are joining the field of science. Especially obvious is the influx into areas such as psychology, medicine, and some of the biosciences. The entry into the so-called "hard sciences" of physics, engineering and computing has been far more limited.

One of the things feminist analyses have made clear is the fact that with respect to gender, race, and a lot more, science is not value neutral. The feminist eye has uncovered bias in the culture of science itself as well as in the fundamental assumptions about how science is done. The link between the façade of value neutrality and the absence of moral responsibility on the part of scientists (Buarque 1993) over the products of their invention has also been brought out in areas such as peace and war (Hague Appeal For Peace 1999, Natural Resources Defense Council 1998), the production of "terminator technologies" (ETC Group 2002), and the theft of intellectual property rights of indigenous communities (Posey and Dutfield 1996, Laird 1994).

Lingering issues relating to the baggage of the history of science have been elaborated by scientists emerging from indigenous cultures. Some of these voices point at the link between science and colonialism and imperialism, and the subsequent silencing of other ways of knowing (Smith 1999). Others, like Weskott, have attacked the methodology of science, and especially the way scientific practices posit some groups as "objects" (Weskott 1987), denying billions of the world's population will and agency (Capra 1988). The confluence between science and patriarchal attitudes is best seen in the critique by Carolyn

Merchant who traced the genesis of the passionately vicious approach to nature to Bacon. *Nature,* Bacon said, has to be *hounded in her wanderings, bound in service, and made a slave. She* [note the pronoun], *was to be put in constraint.* [And the work of the scientist was to] *torture nature's secrets from her* (C. Merchant in Capra 1988: 226). Similar words have been commonly used during the period of colonial penetration and defilement to express what was to be done to Africa (whose virginity was to be wrested away).

Some Third World scientists have also urged that science must, in fact, be understood as a mode of cognition where violence is justified in the objective pursuit of knowledge. The socialization of the vivisectional mandate in science and its extension to humans has, in their analyses, had enduring consequences in our daily lives (Visvanathan 1997).

Such sharp and rounded appraisals of the philosophical, theoretical, ideological and applied basis of science have enabled us to question the default settings of science, and made clear that the male body has been the standard for research, resulting in the unnecessary suffering and death of women. It can thus be said that feminism has deepened sensitivity to context and brought richness to the understanding of origins, evolution, and human relations in general (Borg 2000).

What started off as voices from the marginalized has been finding its legitimacy also in international declarations. This was attempted at Budapest in 1999 when it became clear that the issues surrounding the integration of science and society on the one hand, and women in science and technology on the other, require a critical revisiting of the principles underlying science, gender, and society.

The World Conference on Science was organized by UNESCO in cooperation with the International Council for Science (ISCU) from June 26 to July 1. 1999, in Budapest, Hungary, to help strengthen the commitment of UNESCO's member states and other major stakeholders towards science education, research, and development, and to define a strategy that would ensure that science responds better to society's needs and aspirations in the twenty-first century. The conference produced a Declaration titled *Science and the Use of Scientific Knowledge*, and also the *Science Agenda: Framework for Action*, both of which stressed:

- The need for political commitment to the scientific endeavor and to the solution of problems at the interface between science and technology;

- The need to foster new partnerships in science and the use of science for sustainable human development and the environment; and

•   The need to re-orient science towards the goals of peace.

Certain implications for science education can be drawn from these position statements: there should be more science education, and research and development work, but that such work should become more responsive and more inclusive. From the perspective of communication, accountability, and participation, the injunction was for more strategic dialogue among science councils and other communities of scientists around the vision of society.

The Declaration was at pains to emphasize its vision of what science in the twenty-first century should be: a science that can appreciate interconnectedness and interdependence; a science that can decipher the meaning of words such as "responsibility" and "ethics" in the use of scientific knowledge; a science that can comprehend the fact that science is a product of culture, or cultures, and that its diverse manifestations must therefore be recognized; a science that can be seen by all to be a shared asset. The science education of the twenty-first century should include ethics as a core element, and should train children in history and philosophy, as well as in the cultural impact of science.

The Declaration was not only profound but it also called for a drastic change in the attitude, methods, and approaches that prevail in the scientific field. It also brought to fresh relief the problems of development, especially the social and human dimension. Science, the document emphasized, must transform itself; it must become inclusive, opening up to women and to other forms of knowledge in terms of its culture of admission and operation; and it must open itself to the democratic gaze and scrutiny of all citizens. Most of all, it must take a stand on issues affecting global development such as pollution, depletion of natural resources, poverty, and widening disparities in well-being.

How can science become inclusive when its gate-keeping operations are controlled by the norms of only one gender group? How can science begin to appreciate the "interconnectedness and interdependence" of things, and decipher the meaning of words such as "responsibility" and "ethics" in the use of scientific knowledge, without paying attention to the micro practices in the corridors of its institutions?

We know today that the uncritical use of science and technology has polluted lakes, poisoned rivers, made holes in the ozone, and caused acid rain to fall from the clouds. An absence of skepticism has led to wholesale adoption of Western technology, prompting disdain for African and even Asian accomplishments, handing epistemic privilege to the West on a silver platter, while graduates from this eschewed field bask in the symbolic power of titles and write eloquently about cyberspace in Western scientific journals (Volmink 1999: 61-77).

Implications for Women, Social Development and Transformation in South Africa

South Africa is held in very high esteem today, especially for the new national Constitution it adopted following the demise of apartheid. Human dignity, non-racialism and non-sexism are paramount in the Constitution, along with the achievement of equality and the advancement of human rights and freedoms. Equality includes the full and equal enjoyment of all rights and freedoms. Unfair discrimination on the basis of race, gender, sex, pregnancy, marital status, ethnic or social origin, color, sexual orientation, age, disability, religion, conscience, belief, culture, language and birth is taken as a violation of the Constitution. On the other hand, there are legacies of institutionalized discrimination and exclusion in such spheres as the academy which have yet to be brought under direct scrutiny in the post apartheid period.

Given the nature of the practice of science and what still needs to be done to transform and humanize the field, it is not surprising that women, as "objects" of science have found it extremely difficult, even in a new dispensation as is the case in South Africa, to find adequate expression or theories with which to define their intention in joining the field (Primo 1999). It is not that they have not tried. On the contrary, their voices are dispersed all over the landscape. Women have tried to grapple with the implications of this legacy, and at various points in the process, some responses have emerged.

For some, the effort is to infuse present scientific practice with new and different values. If masculinist values have over-determined the way science and technological innovation are currently organized, then the presence of women as traditional nurturers and as a life-giving force in the field may itself introduce new values and sensibilities. From this new, human-centered values may arise, and perhaps even new social organizations making for a better quality of life.

Others skip over the deeper issues and argue that the challenge lies in the utilization of the products of science. It is the products of science and technology that must be re-directed. Appropriate technology that suits rural and localized settings and responds to development needs at affordable prices would be good enough. The internal culture of the field itself is less of a concern.

For others, the worst aspect of scientific practice is the manner in which it intersects with the economy to produce technologies that deepen the marginalization of women and indigenous societies and thereby threaten survival. For still others, the issue is that there is not enough local content in science and technology. Large-scale entry and expanded access should receive priority (Primo1999: 16-25).

In South Africa, the government's Science and Technology White Paper of the Ministry of Arts, Culture, Science and Technology is prefaced by emphases from then Minister Mtshali, who urged science to serve both the goals of competitiveness and social and economic development, well-being and essential services. Former Deputy Minister Mabandla also reiterates a similar line but goes further to underline the need to reconstruct the cultural and intellectual foundations of science, urging that Science and Technology must go deep in the African context, that they must be service oriented, and that the unacceptably high race and gender disparities in the field must not be tolerated (Mtshali and Mabandla 1996).

The Science and Technology White Paper itself does outline some basic requirements of a sound science and technology policy: it should be geared toward promoting competitiveness, creating employment, enhancing the quality of life, developing human resources, working towards environmental sustainability, and promoting an information and innovation society. It is disappointing that the policy document does not contain a single reference or allusion to the fossilized problems of the scientific field or the need to transform it in specific terms.

Neither does the White Paper attempt to educate its readers as to crucial problems with the way science is presently organized and executed. It does not highlight the way the current mode of organization can end up "shooting in the foot" the very objective of science and technology that is so clearly outlined in the foreword of the White Paper, nor does it outline strategies for a change in such a direction.

As a result, a serious vacuum exists in the theorization as to how the S&T field could itself be transformed, leaving all intellectual work and policy energy grossly neglected in the direction of the most widespread of all the problems of the field: *access*. Moreover, science is narrowly interpreted as those activities that take place within the natural sciences, rather than science as a *process of knowledge production* in generic terms (Mokate 1999).

Examining the gender dimension of science and technology policy and its relevance for South African development, Mokate cryptically urges the scientific community and the policy stakeholders to begin to demystify science and open it up to people who have been intimidated and excluded from it in the past. She raises the following questions: What is the nature of South Africa's science and technology system—that is, of whom is it comprised, how does it function, and with what resources? What types of outputs does the (South African) science and technology system produce, and for whom? What is the impact of those outputs on women's social position (i.e., are they freeing, or enslaving, them)?

Citing Harding and McGregor (1996), Mokate highlights the following as issues important to consider in developing a gender-conscious framework in science and technology. *Firstly*, these fields impact men and women differently, depending on how their social activities are assigned. *Secondly*, women's and men's culturally different interests and values structure social activities and projects, including those in the realm of science and technology. *Thirdly*, women and men also have distinct interactions with nature owing to their differing biological makeup and their assigned social roles and activities.

Fourthly, the way scientific projects are organized has an impact on what we end up knowing about nature. The exclusion of women from the definition of what science and technology should concern itself with, disproportionately represents men's interests, needs and hopes. *Finally*, the exclusion of women leads to ignorance and neglect (at a systemic level) of local factors, and, in particular, of indigenous knowledge that could inform scientific inquiry (Mokate 1999).

Current Experiences of Women in Science and Technology

The inclusion of women in science and technology is felt to be simply the best practice in human resources development because women constitute 50% of the available talent. The actual complexity of the issue of gender and science and technology is best addressed in research done on women, who have accessed the field, and here, the pulse changes dramatically, from one of abstract analysis to a confrontation with frustrating experiences on a daily basis.

Thanks to a great expense of research time and energy by hundreds of academics, it has been demonstrated that women have read books; they have earned the credentials, proved their competence, and entered professions in unprecedented numbers in what they believed to be a first step towards leadership. As it happened, the problem that initially appeared to be one of access had other facets embedded in institutional culture and practice.

Thus, although attention needed to be drawn in a continual manner to the problem of unequal representation in the field as a whole, there was also a need to acknowledge that more precise techniques being applied in research in this area are gradually providing documented proof of discrimination and male nepotistic tendencies in institutions, and are revealing evidence of other "death-blows" to women's aspirations that had hitherto been brushed aside as anecdotal.

One major aspect of attention captured in research done on this issue is the stunted career progression of women in science and technology. Another is the male bias in the manner in which rewards and recognition are attributed. A study conducted by the Swedish Medical Research Council showed that in some instances women had to be roughly 2.2 times more productive than their male counterparts before similar recognition was granted (Wenneras and Wold 1997).

The problem for women in research extends at a practical level to difficulty obtaining grant approvals, poor quality of office space, and lack of access to research resources and to positions of responsibility in comparison with male counterparts. Substantial disparities in salary, rank, and tenure exist between male and female faculty, with women's salary progression more limited than men's, and women's employment on a less secure footing.

Women are rarely found in high-ranking posts or at decision-making levels. If one happens to be appointed at a senior level, that single instance is likely to be showcased to the extent that it blurs the overall picture and keeps further attention from the rest of the organization *over time*. Though women have been gaining access to academic appointments, they have been disproportionately *relegated to non-tenure tracks or even probationary positions*. Thus, controlling for rank, and category of institution and discipline, the largest salary disadvantages for academic women reflect precisely their relegation to non-remunerative appointments (Wenneras and Wold 1997, emphasis added).

This shows that gender bias is still alive and well, and indeed kicking! At the beginning of the twenty-first century, women remain a minority in the scientific disciplines. Lane concludes that there has been a wait for women to "trickle up" within the system for several decades, and we seem no closer to equality of either access and treatment, or career development for women in this field (Lane 1999).

A Critical Analysis of Gender Policy in the Context of the "Establishment" Culture

It is clear therefore that there has been a serious problem with the minimalist interpretation that is given to the notion of "equal opportunities" when otherwise progressive policies are being translated into operational strategies. In most cases, equal opportunity gets collapsed too quickly into "equal remuneration," and even then, there is no tracer facility to track down the empirical progression of women up the ladder from the original entry point.

In some instances, equal opportunity is interpreted in defensive procedural terms as gender-blind policies that then fail to take into account subtleties in the behavior of senior male scientists who are sexist enough to discriminate but too subtle to give the victim the clarity necessary to initiate a complaint. Yet, from a gender perspective, a male-dominated culture exists in the traditional epicenters of science and higher education, creating an "establishment" atmosphere, the "norm," opposition to which is posited as amounting to violating an invisible "institutional" ethos, if not the norms of science itself.

The ripple effect is felt downstream, where, several decades deep into the women's' struggle, young girls looking upwards at the scientific tree, see no role models with whom to identify, and find few female mentors to encourage them. School career advisors, themselves victims of the male culture, and who are basically inarticulate in relation to the dominant culture, are ill-prepared to extol the virtues of a career in science and technology in a manner that is pertinent for previously "intimidated or excluded groups" (Mokate 1999). Primary school teachers giving science lessons are all too frequently themselves unfamiliar with science and are therefore ill at ease in communicating its excitement to both boys and girls (Lane 1999).

Of course, some of the difficulty faced at the higher levels of the educational systems can be traced back to constraints that lie at societal level: negative traditional attitudes and social practices; gender stereotyping in the curriculum; irrelevant and rigid curriculum; gender unfriendly classroom culture; and limited prospects in the labor market (Hyde 1996). It is unfortunate that national systems appear to be devoid of policies that prevent or at least anticipate this outcome.

Institution-based authoritarianism goes beyond the "right" and "left" of the political spectrum in that it touches the *interpersonal interactions* in the multiple settings of everyday life. When violence, marginalization, oppression and suppression permeate the ethos, content, and organization of teaching, it is unlikely that the same educational system can be entrusted with changing the behaviors and leading them to make decisions that support the intellectual and social integrity of the people under its care and to whom it is accountable. It would be an educational system that has yet to move beyond the narrow and mechanical role of passing on technical knowledge and skills, and not just to a selected category of people (males) but to all.

Following a major study of gender in higher education institutions around the continent some years ago, African scientist Katherine Namuddu has written of the ignorance and injustice that compete for clout in the mind of those in charge of the curriculum at nearly all levels. She states that this blind insensitivity and cruelty is even more acute at tertiary levels, because it is there that the curriculum is most silent about the issues of social justice. Instead of taking leadership positions on key issues confronting the developing societies of Africa and the structural limitations to real progress, these institutions housing African academicians and manufacturing senior policy makers are fossilized in the identity ascribed them in and by the colonial era.

Trapped both in time and space, they lament the rarified glories of the past "like nobles marooned in their crumbling castles as feudalism declined in Europe" (C. Doyle cited in Namuddu 1992). Instead of organizing courses on gender for both males and females and making these imperative, male academics subject any female who attempts to introduce the subject of gender to a continuum of responses ranging from *outright resistance* to *direct insults* and harassment to *diversion tactics* such as changing the topic away from that concerning gender (emphasis added).

Moreover, in the efforts to address the problem of access and completion, solutions are cast in terms of marginal modifications in family behaviors and school offerings. Those efforts aimed at family behaviors consist of announcements that attempt to persuade parents to realize that their daughters' education is important, or that propose to ease the loss of domestic work foregone by girl children while attending school (through incentives such as free uniforms, scholarships for girls from poor families and flexible school hours), or that seek to reduce parents' fear for their daughters' safety (by building schools closer to home, providing more women teachers, and supplying women teachers with proper facilities in rural areas so they may serve in those areas).

The problem of access is addressed by building more schools under the assumption that both boys and girls will benefit equally. Support for girls' education via the avoidance of more transformative changes is also reflected in international documents (including the Beijing Platform for Action) that tirelessly invoke the need to "move toward parity" in schooling statistics.

Now and then, projects and policies make reference to the need to remove sexual stereotypes from school textbooks, but conservative exercises in eliminating gender stereotypes have led to a spate of robotical deletion and replacement of "men" by "men and women" and "boys" by "boys and girls" without any investment in understanding how such stereotypes found their way there in the first place. It is also not uncommon for states to go on to offer a non-sexist education, but not to go so far as instituting an anti-sexist education. A non-sexist curriculum would offer a gender-neutral curriculum, but it is an anti-sexist education that would address the various forms of gender discrimination and subordination in society and attempt to modify knowledge and attitudes about them (Stromquist 1995).

Stromquist argues that there is a difference between a "girl friendly" initiative and one that is girl or gender focused. The first does not change anything fundamental in the structure of education, while the second seeks a transformation in the balance of power between women and men. Apart from limited, "one-shot" efforts, the key purveyors of educational content, the teachers, are seldom targeted for gender-sensitive training.

Yet the mainstream curriculum is a "dominant, or hegemonic, curriculum derived historically from the educational practice of European upper-class men." The proposed handling of the curriculum is limited to instrumental knowledge rather than counter-hegemonic knowledge needed to address prevalent gender ideologies.

Shortchanged by the Thatcher Syndrome?

When women massively enter the mainstream through a shortsighted affirmative action or access strategy, they are happily absorbed into precisely the same problematic mold. The implication is that "successful" women should emerge who have praise for the luck they have had in negotiating their way through the system but are impotent in terms of gender awareness, and are totally unable to develop any gender strategies in a coherent manner. Their increased education would, then, not affect or threaten the status quo and so the basic structures of ideological and material domination are retained intact and sustained.

Under these conditions, the situation is increasingly favorable for the rise of the phenomenon of "honorary males" that Longwe so articulately deals with in the Zambian context. "Honorary males" are top professional women who are accepted on sufferance within the male system and have been schooled to believe that *women already HAVE equality* simply because they themselves are already so comfortable at the top. "I got to the top, so what is wrong with you others?" (Longwe 1997).

This "Thatcher syndrome" is also characterized by the tendency to block other women who may want to follow in her footsteps. The "honorable male" would cry "merit" while violently opposing affirmative action and kicking away at every ladder that any other woman may want to use. There is also an aversion to remembering the structural dimensions and constraints to women's empowerment or advancement. This is the consequence of what Longwe calls "schooling for individualism" and the so-called "self reliance" which is not used for women's empowerment or for a struggle for justice and equality for all (Longwe 1997).

Yet gender should be seen as a heuristic tool. It is an instrument, a lens that enables us to perceive things and details in relationships that could not be seen before. Speaking "gender" means trying to understand how society has made one what one has become, how it has shaped one's behavior, one's aspirations, and one's attitude towards oneself as well as towards society at large. Talking "gender" means talking politics, and talking action at the same time, because the realization that comes with self-understanding demands that action be taken not at some time in the future, but *now*.

The constant challenge, therefore, is to create an alternative framework for addressing the new and diverse problems, while at the same time developing a program for political action that begins with the cadres and fans outwards to all others. This entails both broadening and deepening actions, in which the process is also the output. Because records of processes are often left out of documentation in preference to neat outputs that are seen at the *end*, it is all the more important that spaces be created well in advance where this very important dimension can be recognized.

Gender is also part of a vision of development that both redresses gender inequalities and constructs a new ethical basis for continued development. This is what is meant when it is said that the end result of increasing women's participation in politics must be a different and a better politics. Delivering effective and quality development for women, for example, implies changing the current pattern of development. It means reaching out and responding to the needs of the poor, a majority of whom are women, far more effectively and consistently than political systems have shown themselves capable of doing in the past. It means bringing the experience and perceptions of women to bear on reshaping society (Ginwala 1995).

Short-Changed by Affirmative Action: Women's Survival Path in Institutions

Women who gain access to mainstream institutions face, at one point or another, the unenviable task of simultaneously maneuvering within and against dominant discourses and practices. They maneuver within them because they are part of the setting and are partly constituted by these discourses and practices. They maneuver against them in attempts to carve out a new space for women's claims (Bacchi 1996). Institutional access for women has either been "hard won" through individual effort, or a consequence of pressures for affirmative action, by which is meant some kind of initiative, taken either voluntarily or under the compulsion of law, to increase, maintain, or rearrange the number or status of certain group members within a larger group.

To begin with, affirmative action identifies recipients as the ones who need rehabilitating and reforming, and not the institution itself. Secondly, the type of conceptual categories such as "equal opportunity," "equal results," or even "excellence" within which assessment/evaluation criteria or norms are located and applied within institutions which serve to contain the success of affirmative action by delimiting the parameters of "change debate", and restricting the understanding of the issue to access. It happens very rarely, if at all, that the incorporation of women leads to fundamental debates on issues such as the meaning of integration and/or its paradigmatic implications for the institution (Bacchi 1996b). Oftentimes women find that they gain categorical recognition, but this recognition is embedded within a largely patronizing or assimilationist framework.

Most pernicious however, is the fact that by ignoring the characteristics of the receiving system, affirmative action in fact inadvertently serves to couch "in-groups" and render them invisible and safely stowed away in their fairly conservative positions of privilege, reinforcing what Bacchi refers to as "the power of the insiders." This keeps the unproblematized institutional cultures and processes as the "unmarked standard," representing the universal, while women and Blacks fumble along, constantly on the defensive, eternally the ones who need to explain themselves (Bacchi 1996c: 11).

Once inside the institution, the category (be it "woman" or "Black") sticks as a label, and is used at whim by the insiders either as proof of benevolence, or as a demonstration of congenital incapacity. Either way, there is often a negative ascription that prevents institutions from taking full advantage of the opportunity offered by women's access, and blocks the reflection that might lead to a more advanced understanding of the implications of its previous policies (see Odora Hoppers 1999).

This analysis brings to light two issues that require urgent and critical attention. On the one hand, the institutions in question have already fulfilled their legislative mandate by granting access, and should be congratulated; on the other hand, by failing to take more profoundly into account the deeper implications either of the previous policy omission or of the current practice of granting access to previously marginal perspectives, the institutions reinforce the view that the problem lies with the *victims*, and not with the *institutions themselves*. In fact, it often turns out in the end that the dominant group can avoid noticing its own discriminatory practices, as affirmative action is speedily repositioned in terms of a more bureaucratic task category: "human resource management."

Yesterday's oppressor becomes the new mentor; a reconditioned status quo is smoothly ensured. Thus what was once physical/numerical marginality becomes a *discursive marginality* in the sense that institutions are not compelled to transform in any fundamental manner the tenets of their policies and practices beyond a surface response to legislative injunctions to implement affirmative action. It is this consistent assimilationist framework that has led some to think of a possible patriarchal conspiracy to prevent the rise of a truly progressive agenda at the institutional level, and has led to calls for strategic reversals and for more work on the structural tenets of institutions.

Women also enter institutions only to find that they have to "compete" with the power holders on paradigms that are congruent with the power holders. Often, academic research is not posited as a form of political practice. Disinterested inquiry remains the approach, and the analyst's accountability is not an issue. Language, already deeply implicated in the maintenance of power relations, is taken as neutral. The problem of lexical gaps, which often leaves women without the words to describe their experiences, and the fact that women often occupy a negative semantic space within language, is not made an issue (Gill 1995: 166-169). The "discursive imperialism of mainstream institutions" (Wilkinson & Kitzinger 1995: 3) remains untouched and unaffected by the introduction of women into the institutions.

Failure to take into account incumbent institutional cultures implies that groups that have been previously marginalized and thus denied opportunities at the level of the *formation* of human capabilities (UNDP 1995), are further preempted from making use of their experiences of oppression or marginalization as springboards for institutional transformation. Thus, although at an official institutional level there is endorsement of affirmative action, faculty members and officials in scientific institutions abrogate their role in institutional policy formulation and implementation by allowing administrators to assume the major responsibility for affirmative action requirements, leaving aggrieved female staff to seek relief in court actions.

Thus, although it does serve as a useful monitoring device, the setting of goals in an affirmative action plan usually does not guarantee representation for the groups for whom the goals are set. Affirmative action officers should be appointed from the highest possible level of professionals if they are to be able to decipher the nuances of professional discrimination and thus be in a position to recommend action that is appropriate and relevant to the various contexts.

Affirmative action officers should also be better equipped and have the power of oversight over search and appointment procedures and practices for faculty and academic administrative positions. In other words, an affirmative action officer should have the authority to defer a prospective appointment pending appropriate institutional review from a gender perspective. The burden of retrenchment should neither fall inequitably on those individuals who have benefited from affirmative action themselves. In order to move forward, therefore, an examination of policies, especially those in fields such as science and technology, should be undertaken to be certain that they are scrupulously non-discriminatory both in principle and in practice. The adequacy of facilities available within institutions for addressing gender-based complaints should be carefully scrutinized A review should be undertaken of recruitment policies and procedures that, while supposedly neutral, have an adverse impact on women.

Women, Science and Technology: The Way Forward

The point of emphasis throughout this chapter is that the problems of women pose a challenge to society as a whole. The transformation of gender relations cannot be seen or undertaken in isolation, but is inextricably linked to the transformation of society and its related institutions. At the same time, a critical deconstruction and demystification of the contents and practice of science needs to be undertaken in a manner that can make the conclusions of such a critique feed into other agendas aimed at integrating women into the field.

Accordingly, the issue of *quantity* needs to be considered at certain intervention points for women in science and technology at the level of practice. Although the problem of access has been treated as an end in itself, numerical power is not only strength, but also a right for women. Next comes the issue of *content*. Focus on gender-sensitive and societal issues along with maximum use of local and indigenous scientific knowledge as a launching pad for science learning for all children, will serve to re-orient the field of science in the direction of the excluded. Teacher training and in-service training have to take into account the complexity of the issues and not avoid dealing with issues such as gender and the nature of the sciences at a structural level.

At the level of professional entry and survival in institutions however, we need to keep a careful eye on *integration strategies* and their possibilities and limitations, *career paths for professional women, gender discrimination in professional work,* and *senior professional women's relationships with junior female staff,* especially in terms of creating spaces for greater interaction and mentoring.

As for the relation between science and society, there is a need to democratize science, and make its boundaries with society porous. In this regard, *popularizing science and technology* (i.e., ridding science of its exclusiveness), embracing a new ethics of interconnectedness with nature and people, and recognizing other ways of knowing would go a long way toward establishing science as the story of all animals, not just the lion.

References

Bacchi, C.L., 1996a. "The Politics of Solidarity." In C. L. *The Politics of Affirmative Action.* London: Sage Publications.

___, 1996b. "The Politics of Misrepresentation." In C. L. Bacchi, *The Politics of Affirmative Action.* London: Sage Publications.

___, 1996c. "The Political Use of Categories." In C. L. Bacchi, *The Politics of Affirmative Action. London*: Sage Publications, 11-12.

Borg, A., 2000. Book review of *Has Feminism Changed Science?* Summer 2000, *http://www.amwa-doc.org/index.cfm?objectid=E1D922C6-D567-0B25-5F141F31BE85B8E7*

Buarque, C., 1993. *The End of Economics? Ethics and Disorder of Progress.* London: Zed Books, 5-9, 75-77.

Capra, F., 1988. *Uncommon Wisdom: Conversations with Remarkable People.* London: Flamingo, 127-39.

ETC Group, *http://www.etcgroup.org/article.asp?newsid=297*

Hague Appeal for Peace, 1999. Conference Background Documentations. *http://www.haguepeace.org/resources/HagueAgendaPeace+Justice4The21stCentury.pdf*

Hyde, K.A.L., 1996. *Girls Education in Eastern and Southern Africa: An Overview.* Prepared for the Regional Mid-Decade Review Towards Education For All Meeting. Johannesburg, South Africa.

Gill, R., 1995. "Relativism, Reflexivity and Politics: Interrogating Discourse Analysis from a Feminist Perspective." In *Feminism and Discourse: Psychological Perspectives,* ed., S. Wilkinson and C. Kitzinger. London: Sage Publications, 166-69.

Ginwala, F., 1995. "Discrimination is Not the Problem." *The Progress of Nations.* New York: UNICEF.

Laird, S., 1994. "Natural Products and the Commercialization of Traditional Knowledge" In *Intellectual Property Rights for Indigenous Peoples: A Sourcebook,* ed., T. Greaves. Oklahoma City: Society for Applied Anthropology, 145-149, cited in J. Mugabe, 1999.\

Lane, N. J., 1999. "Why Are There So Few Women in Science?" *Nature Debates* (September 9).

Longwe S. H., 1997. "Education For Women's Empowerment or Schooling for Women's Subordination," in Anonuevo C. M., *Negotiating and Creating Spaces of Power, Women's Educational Practices Amidst Crisis,* UNESCO Institute for Education, Hamburg.

Mashelkar, R., 2002, "The Role of Intellectual Property in Building Capacity for Innovation for Development: A Developing World Perspective" In Odora Hoppers, ed. *Indigenous Knowledge and the Integration of Knowledge Systems: Towards a Philosophy of Articulation*, Cape Town: NAEP.

Mokate, R., 1999. "Women in Science and Technology: A Review of Conceptual Issues." In *South Africa's Contribution to the Theme on Science and Technology for Sustainable Development*. DACST Report, The Second International Conference of Third World Organization for Women in Science February 8-11.

Mtshali, L., and B. Mabanda, 1996. In preface to "White Paper on Science and Technology: "Preparing for the 21st Century." September.

Mugabe J., 1999. "Intellectual Property Protection and Traditional Knowledge: An Exploration in International Policy Discourse." Paper presented at the WIPO/UN Commission for Human Rights Roundtable.

Namuddu, K., 1992. " Gender Perspectives in African Higher Education." Paper presented at the Senior Policy Seminar on African Higher Education, University of Zimbabwe.

Natural Resources Defense Council, n.d. *http://www.nrdc.org/nuclear/ tkstock/tssum.asp.*

Odora Hoppers, C. A., 1999. "Between 'Mainstreaming' and 'Transformation': Lessons and Challenges for Institutional Change." Paper presented at the HSRC/CSD International Workshop on International Strategies for Building Research Capacity Among Women in Higher Education, Pretoria. February.

Posey, D., and G. Dutfield, 1996, "Beyond Intellectual Property." Ottowa: International Development Research Center.

Primo, N., 1999. "Women in Science: Making a World of Difference?" In *South Africa's Contribution to the Theme on Science and Technology for Sustainable Development*. DACST Report, The Second International Conference of Third World Organization for Women in Science, February 8-11.

Schiebinger L., 1999. *Has Feminism Changed Science?* Cambridge, Mass.: Harvard University Press.

Smith, L. T., 1999. D*ecolonizing Methodologies: Research and Indigenous Peoples*. London: Zed Books.

Stromquist, N. P., 1995. "Romancing the State: Gender and Power in Education." Presidential address, Comparative and International Education Society. *Comparative Education Review* 39 (4): 423-54.

UNESCO, 1999. "Declaration on Science and the Use of Scientific Knowledge and the Science Agenda: Framework for Action." UNESCO General Conference, 30th Session, Paris, 30C/15.

United Nations Development Programme, 1995. "The State of Human Development." *Human Development Report.* New York: Oxford University Press.

Visvanathan, S., 1997. *A Carnival For Science: Essays on Science, Technology, and Development.* Delhi: Oxford University Press.

Volmink, J., 1999. "Who Shapes the Discourse on Science and Technology Education?" In *African Science and Technology Education into the New Millenium: Practice, Policy, and Priorities,* ed., P. Naidoo and M. Savage. Kenwyn, South Africa: Juta, 61-77.

Wenneras, C. and A. Wold, 1997. "Nepotism and Sexism in Peer Review." *Nature* 387: 341-43.

Wertheim, M., 1999. Review of "Has Feminism Changed Science?" June 22. *http://www.salon.com/books/feature/1999/06/22/feminismscience.*

Weskott, M., 1987. "Feminist Criticism of the Social Sciences." *Havard Educational Review* 49 (4).

Wilkinson, S., and C. Kitzinger, 1995. Introductionto *Feminism and Discourse: Psychological Perspectives,* ed., S. Wilkinson and C. Kitzinger. London: Sage Publications.

CHAPTER 10

IVORIAN WOMEN:
EDUCATION AND INTEGRATION IN THE ECONOMIC DEVELOPMENT OF CÔTE D'IVOIRE[1]

Rose Eholié

Introduction

Côte d'Ivoire, like other Third World countries, is faced with the problem of underdevelopment, and it is prepared to join these countries in implementing measures to remedy this situation. Among these measures, it is generally agreed that education occupies a special place, with Science, Technology and Vocational education being considered the most effective means.

Hence, shortly after the 1960 Independence, the Ivorian state supported the education of young Ivorian boys and girls; but as elsewhere in Africa, any lasting and appropriate development must take into account material improvement and traditional values. On this subject, it should be stressed that certain attitudes linked to the idea that men are more important than women have been prevalent in society, and the fear of scientific disciplines, that is anchored in the collective conscience of young Ivorian girls, have led to the situation where this field is practically occupied by men only.

At the end of the 20th century, with a change in mindset, it is noticeable that there is an increasing marked will of women to take their place in the economic development of the nation. However, the key question is: is there really an equal opportunity for boys and girls with regard to education, training

---

[1] The first version of this chapter is based on a paper presented at the World Bank in Washington, D.C. in May 1993.

and employment? How, then, should the contribution of the Ivorian women to the national economic development be translated?

A brief historical overview will best describe the conditions surrounding the access of girls to education in the country. In 1946, well before independence, President Félix Houphouët-Boigny decided to send young Ivorian men and women to be educated in French schools, since Côte d'Ivoire did not have secondary schools in a sufficient number. He was then engaged in the fight for justice and equality and for him education was already a priority. It was the first important step of a process that was to lead to the emerging of the Ivorian women and to their increasingly occupying important places in the post- independence Ivorian society.

Prior to 1960, the progression suffered from the low rate of girls enrolled in schools because in the new society in formation, women did not benefit from the same occupational expectations and were considered worth being relegated to domestic tasks. Shortly after independence, however, the objective of the government was to lead Côte d'Ivoire to achieve a sufficient standard of living, and to achieve this, both Ivorian men and women who were resolutely inclined to progress, and who were convinced that the fight against underdevelopment must be based on the total capabilities of the nation, were needed. It is clear that such a policy required a new state of mind and to be driven by new values and a change of attitude.

In addition, decisions were made to give equal chances to all citizens. In particular, in Côte d'Ivoire education is now legally available to all without discrimination to gender, race, or religion. However, it does not do enough to adopt a law and expect it to change lives immediately. The achievement of equality requires a strong will of the women themselves. That is why since independence, a better integration of women into the Ivorian society is noticeable.

President Houphouët-Boigny said on the occasion of the National Day of the Woman in Abidjan on May 20, 1975:

> It is thus a question of becoming aware of the place really occupied by women and which will be made for them within the family and the city, in the cultural life of the nation. In a majority of these fields, the institutions necessary for progress exist: the civil code, obligatory education for all children, boys and girls, the vocational training and higher education, the administrative entrance examinations which are opened to both genders. The way is thus delineated for a greater participation of the Ivorian woman in political responsibilities, the vital development of the country and the progress of our society.

Thus, increasingly, the Ivorian woman has the ambition to prove her intellectual and professional value, without neglecting her role as a wife and mother. As a result, there has been an increasing opening of the university and all sectors of the developing economy to girls and women.

The first part of this article is devoted to the issues related to the education of the women of Côte d'Ivoire. The second part addresses their integration into the process of economic development in Côte d'Ivoire. The third part deals with the representation and participation of the Ivorian woman in the teaching and research in the scientific disciplines. The conclusion primarily deals with recommendations.

Education of the Ivorian Woman

The schooling of young Ivorian girls has seen a slow but regular progression on all levels of education since independence. This study covers a period of eleven years, from 1981to 1992.

Primary School

Table 4 in the Annex shows the enrollment of students. Graph 1 provides the percentage of girls and that of boys out of the total enrollment. As is noticeable, there is a minimal progression in the number of girls. This weakness can be explained by social factors such as early pregnancies and the reluctance of some parents to enroll their daughters.

Although considerable efforts have been made at providing an equal opportunity for boys and girls, in actuality, the objective has not yet been achieved. A great disparity still remains between the schooling of girls by region, with the urban and affluent zones registering higher proportions of the enrollment (approximately 40%) than the poor areas especially in the North with the lowest rates of schooling (30%). In general, the enrollment rate for girls reflects the rate of schooling for the area.

Secondary School

Graphs 2 and 3 and table II in the appendix provide some indications of the state of the enrollment by gender.

Generally, the percentage of girls in secondary schools seems constant, remaining at 30%. Graph 3 shows an important decrease between the first cycle (6ème to 3ème the equivalent of the first to the 4th grades after elementary school) and the second cycle (2nd to Final Grade, or the equivalent of a three-year high school). This situation is due to the bottleneck at the end of the first cycle where there is an examination for entrance in the second cycle.

When the proportions of girls in the various courses in Graph 4 are compared, (Arts-A, 23.2%; Mathematics-C, 7.1%; Natural Sciences, 12.2%; and Business-B, 13.2%), a strong representation of girls in course A is noticeable. This is a general pattern: girls are more easily assigned in larger proportions (taking into account the important role played by orientation services) to these disciplines and consequently, are clustered in careers in the Arts, administration or legal. This choice is also reflected at the level of higher education.

Percentage of the number of students at the primary level (81-92)
(GRAPH 1)

Total Public and Private

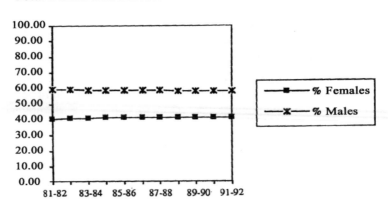

Percentage of the Number of Girls
at the Secondary Level (81-92)
(GRAPH 2)

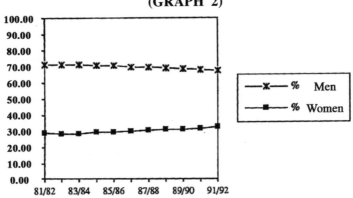

Percentage of the Number of Girls at the Secondary Level (81-92)

% by Class (GRAPH 3)

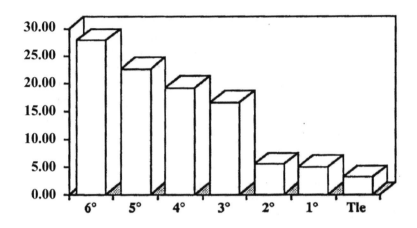

% by Course (GRAPH 4)

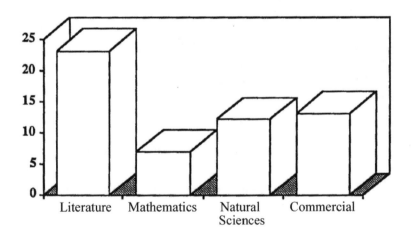

Higher Education

It is worth providing a brief historical background of higher education in Côte d'Ivoire until the creation of the National University of Côte d'Ivoire.

The University of Abidjan was created in 1964 and was composed of four (4) large schools: Sciences, Law, Humanities and Medicine. Between 1966 and 1971, these schools were transformed into the Faculties of Science and Technology (FAST), Medicine, Humanities and Social Sciences, Law, Economics and the Institute of Odontology (I.O.S.). The school of Pharmacy that was created in 1977 was transformed into a faculty in 1981. The University of Abidjan was renamed the National University of Côte d'Ivoire (UNACI) in June 1977 before it became the University of Cocody.

Four Higher Professional Schools (Grandes Écoles) constitute a specific group of higher education. These are: the Higher National Institute of Technical Education (**INSET**), the Higher National Institute of Agronomy (**ENSA**), the Higher Teacher Training School (**ENS**), the Higher National School for Public Works (**ENSTP**).

Graphs 5 to 11 (table 6 in the appendix) emphasize great disparities and especially irregularities in the growth of the students by faculties. The Faculties of Pharmacy, Medicine, and the Institute of Odontology are the most prized. A comparison of the student's population over a period of (12) twelve years records an average representation of girls of approximately 23% in Medicine, 39% in Pharmacy, and 35% in Odontology. By descending order, the Faculty of Arts (approximately 23%) is next followed by Law (19%), Economics (12%) and in last position, the Faculty of Science and Technology (10%). These trends contradict preconceived ideas and also perhaps partly the historical facts concerning the preferences of the female population for these disciplines.

Why does the medical field attract so many girls?

Like any social phenomenon, the factors which explain the tendency of the girls to lean toward the medical disciplines can be complex, even though they seem simple. However, one can advance, as the principal reason why the medical field attracts girls; the fact that these disciplines lead to definite professional careers (in Dispensary, hospitals, medical and dental practices, pharmaceutical industry). In the same way, the humanities, legal, and economic fields make it possible to direct girls toward the liberal professions (lawyer, notary) or banking careers.

On the other hand, the hard sciences repel girls, because of psychological factors. In particular, although unjustified on the basis of intellectual ability of the female population, the fear of hard science disciplines anchored in the collective conscious of the young females of Côte d'Ivoire causes them to hesitate in choosing, and even rejecting, these disciplines. Thus, the proportion of girls is 5% in Physics-Chemistry, 4% in Mathematics and 3% in the Technology.

Percentage of Student Size by Faculty

FAST (GRAPH 5)

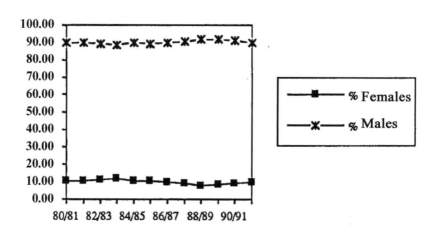

PHARMACY (GRAPH 6)   MEDICINE (GRAPH 7)

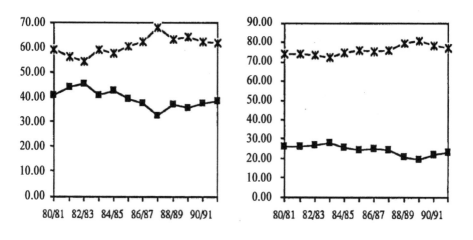

Rose Eholié

I.O.S (GRAPH 8)

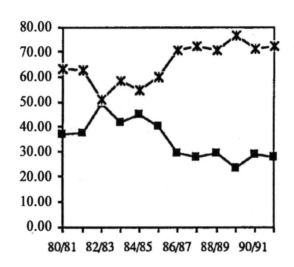

HUMANITIES (GRAPH 9)

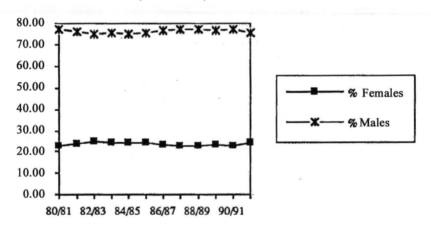

LAW (GRAPH 10)

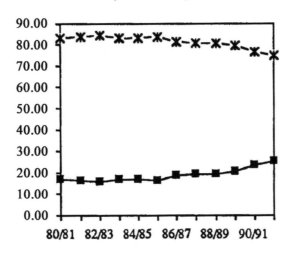

ECONOMICS (GRAPH 11)

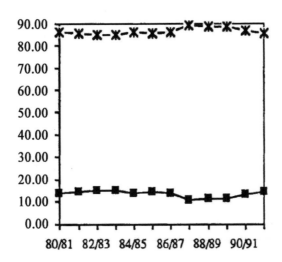

The Higher Schools

Graphs 12 to 15 indicate the percentages of girls compared to that of boys. Table 7 in the appendix provides the numbers.

The analysis of these graphs shows by field of education preferential choices of students as follows:

- National Higher Institute of Technology (**INSET**): 12%.

- National Higher Institute of Agronomy (**ENSA**): 11%.

- Higher Teacher Training School (**ENS**): 6%.

- National Higher School of Public Works (**ENSTP**): 3%.

Although the proportion of girls is low in these schools, it is necessary to note in the young Ivorian girls an awakening and the start of a tendency to exert themselves in certain types of occupation hitherto reserved to men only. Indeed, as graph 14 shows, since 1987 there has been at the INSET, for example, a more significant number of girls, especially at the Higher Institute of Computer Science (ISI). They make a practical interpretation of the job opportunities relating to the disciplines. The increasing popularity of the ISI is explained by the fact that the computing sector has become a good provider of employment.

The choice of students going into the Agronomy is explained by the fact that Côte d'Ivoire created many state-owned agro-pastoral companies shortly after its accession to national sovereignty.

However, because of the economic crisis, many of these public companies were dissolved. It then posed a problem for employment, and the girls preferred to embrace other spheres of activities.

**Percentage of the Student Population
in the Higher School ENSA (GRAPH 12)**

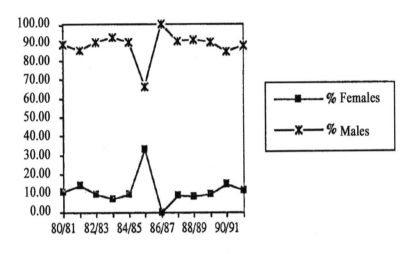

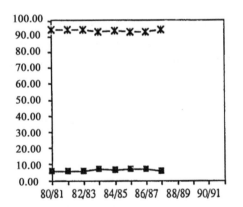

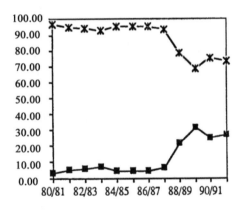

ENSTP (GRAPH 15)

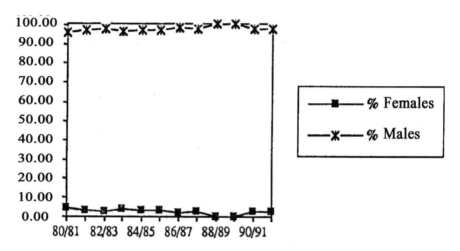

The statistics show that educated girls account for approximately 20% of the female population, while 80% constitute a great mass of illiterates. Thus, the question of the proportion of the girls educated at the higher educational level and their representation in the various disciplines must be dealt with in the global context of schooling at all levels of the educational system and the role of women in national development.

Participation of the Ivorian Woman in the Economic Development
of Côte d'Ivoire

This study does not claim to address all aspects of the question, but it tries to provide a critical perspective, based on observation, on the occupations of the educated Ivorian women, and the implication of uneducated and illiterate women in the process of national economic development.

In general, girls who could not, at the end of secondary education, pursue their studies to the higher education level tend to choose the track of vocational training (typewriting, accountancy, ancillary medical professions, seamstress, hairstyling, etc). Thus among this group, 40% were trained as office employees (typists, operators), 15% are training in accountancy, 30% in ancillary medical professions (midwife, nurses, welfare officers) and 15% work in other sectors (seam, hairstyle etc).

Ivorian Women, Education, and Development

The students who choose the humanities, legal or economic fields in higher education tend to move on to careers in banking, law or notary. The scientists form part of the technical and technological sector. Table 1 below shows that women in agricultural engineers are most numerous (47) because of the development of agro-nutritional and agro-industrial companies.

Table 1 (1988)

SECTOR OF ACTIVITY	Number of Females
Chemistry	8
Mines - Geology	1
Civil Engineering (Sc. Geographic)	15
Civil Engineering (Construction)	9
Civil Engineering (Urban Planning/Technilogy of TP)	15
Civil Engineering (Hydraulics)	12
Agronomy	47
Civil Aviation	3
Electronics	4
Textile	1
Computing	14
Statistics	6
Architecture	6
Higher Technicians	21
Physics	1

However, an analysis comparing their situation with those of their male counterparts shows that they do not occupy as interesting and satisfactory positions as men do. This situation is evidence of disreputable discrimination.

In addition, the introduction of computer science into all the branches of industry favored the effective introduction of engineers in computer science into the companies (14).

It is comforting to see women in other sectors such as construction (9), urban planning (15), hydraulics (12), and civil aviation (3) fields which, in the recent past, were completely unknown to women and reserved for men.

It is, however, important to point out that especially women engineers have a role in design; they are generally confined in the engineering offices and design departments. Rare are those who have any chance for practical experience in the field. In the various sectors of production, even with equal qualification, they are often relegated to subordinate positions because men have difficulty accepting the authority of women. Therefore, women cannot always give the full measure of their real capacity nor do they have the opportunity to take part fully in the development of the nation.

Table 2 (1988)

a) Medicine

Medecine	Men	Women	% Women
Civil Service	357	107	23
Private Sector	60	2	3

b) Pharmacy

Pharmacy	Men	Women	% Women
Civil Service	49	58	54
Private Sector	125	80	39

Ivorian Women, Education, and Development

c) Odontology (I.O.S)

IOS	No. Men	No. Women	% Women
Civil Service	51	46	47
Private Sector	70	21	23

Although their progression and access to positions of responsibility are real, this development especially remains slow in the private sector. With the change of mindsets, Ivorian men have an increasing tendency to go beyond the sexual stereotype, and to take into account the knowledge and the know-how of women.

Table 2 above provides an indication of the situation in 1988 of the female personnel in Medicine, Pharmacy, Odontology, as well as in the civil service and in the private sector. The analysis based on this table makes it possible to make some important observations:

1) That there are few women doctors in the private sector. In Côte d'Ivoire, this sector is hardly accessible to women. In general, men prefer to be medically cared for by men. There needs to be a change of mentalities here. Moreover, within the family, there are many constraints to what professions a wife can subject herself to without the consent of her husband.

2) That the Ivorian woman prefers to work in the hospitals as a civil servant.

3) That there is a significant proportion of women in Pharmacy and Odontology. This is in relation to the number of female students in the first paragraph. Thus, this profession will in the long term count a majority of women.

The situation of the Ivorian woman in the teaching and research sectors

Primary School Teaching

Graph 16 and table 8 in the appendix indicate that the body of teachers is made up of a majority of certified teachers among whom women represent only 15.45%; in contrast, women are numerous among the non-certified instructors as they account for 50% of this category of teachers.

Secondary School Teachers

As shown in graph 17 (and table 9 in the appendix) the percentage of women is constant and increases relatively little (20%) on this level of the education system.

Higher School and Higher Education Teachers

At the creation of the University in 1964, there were two (2) women out of a total of ninety (90) members of the teaching staff. These occupied the posts of Assistant Professors in the Faculty of Science. This situation is explained by the fact at that time, few young Ivorians had reached higher education. In 1975, a woman held the chair of a full professor at the Faculty of Science for first time.

With regard to the distribution of women teaching by Faculty and rank (see graphs 18 to 24; tables 10 to 13 in the appendix), it appears that there is no full woman professor at the Faculty of Medicine, the Faculty of Pharmacy or the Institute of Odontology, although the intermediate bodies and the number of students, constitute a relatively high percentage (e.g. 23% female in Medicine, 35% in Odontology and 39% in Pharmacy).

There is not one single woman professor at the Faculty of Economics; this can be explained by the small percentage of female students at the start (graph 11). In the face of this observation, it becomes necessary to raise some important questions such as the following: What factors do prevent women from attaining this rank? Why are they so few in higher education?

Percentage of the Number of Teachers in Primary Education
(GRAPH 16)

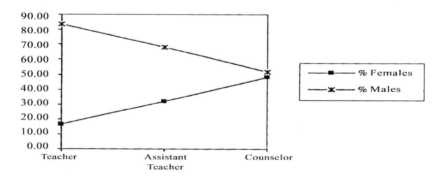

Ivorian Women, Education, and Development

Percentage of the Number of Teachers at the Secondary Level

(GRAPH 17)

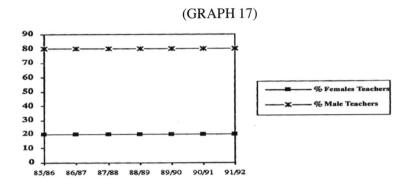

Percentage of Number of Teachers at the Higher Education Level by Faculty and by Status
FAST (GRAPH 18)

PROFESSORS

ASSOCIATE PROFESSORS

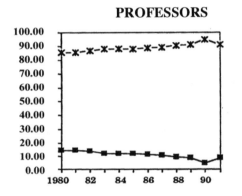
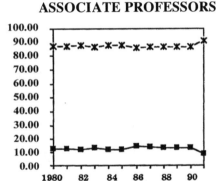

Rose Eholié

LECTURERS

ASSISTANTS

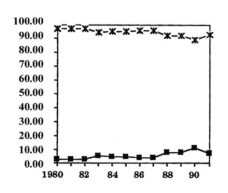

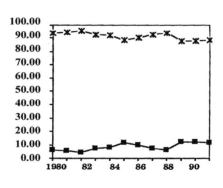

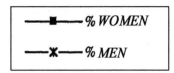

Percentage of the Number of Teachers in Higher Education by Faculty and Status

PHARMACY (GRAPH 19)

ASSOCIATE PROFESSORS

LECTURERS

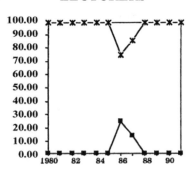

ASSISTANTS

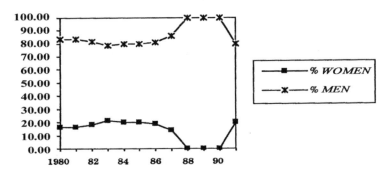

Percentage of the Number of Teachers in Higher Education by Faculty and Status

MEDICINE (GRAPH 20)

ASSOCIATE PROFESSORS   **LECTURERS**

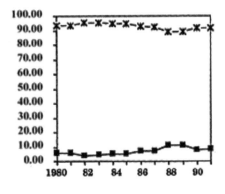
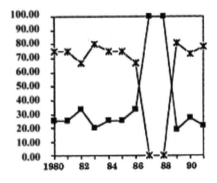

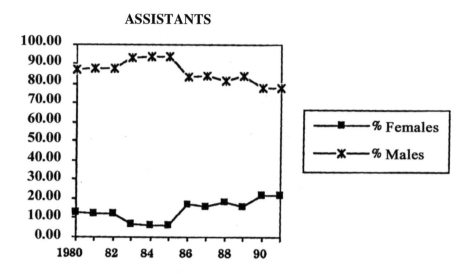

Percentage of the Number of Teachers in Higher Education by Faculty and Status

IOS (GRAPH 21)

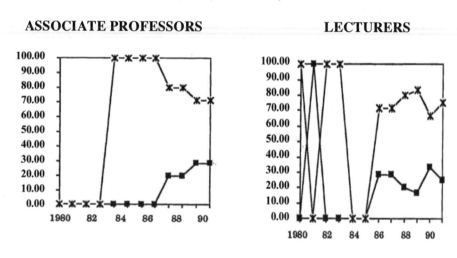

ASSISTANTS

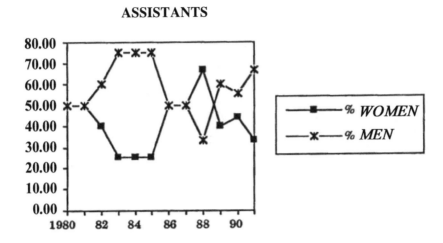

Percentage of the Number of Teachers in Higher Education by Faculty and Status

HUMANITIES (GRAPH 22)

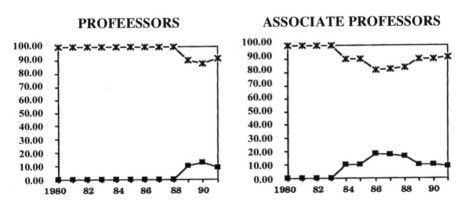

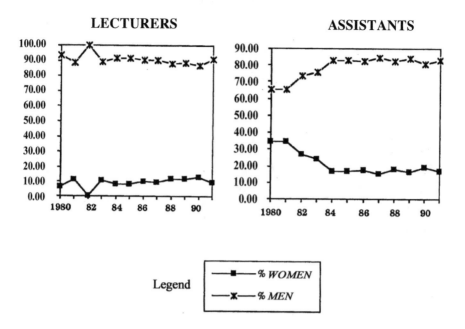

Percentage of the Number of Teachers in Higher Education by Faculty and Status
LAE (GRAPH 23)

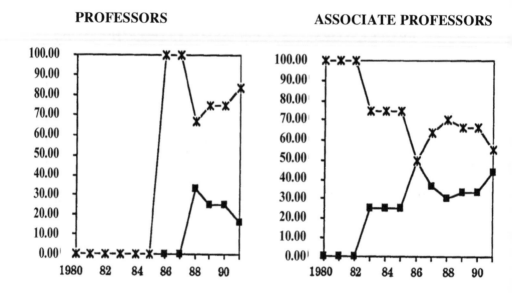

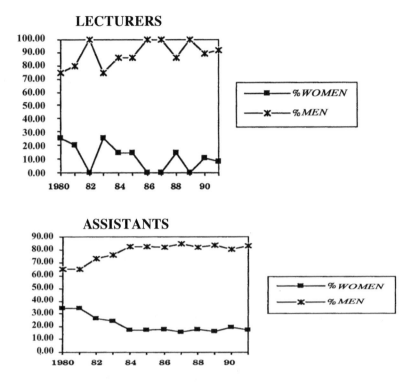

It should be recognized that higher education and university research were regarded for a long time as fields reserved for men. There is also the fact that it takes much time and self-sacrifice to reach this position. The Ivorian woman aspiring to make a family quickly sees her promotion blocked by multiple pregnancies, the education of her children, and by men encumbering women with the care of the home. Discouragement and an abandonment of the university career often follow this. For the Higher schools (Grandes Écoles) there are no statistical data available to analyze the professional career of women.

Scientific Research

The Ministry for Scientific Research that was created in 1971 has the role of initiating and promoting scientific research in all fields in Côte d'Ivoire.

Thereafter, several institutes especially aimed at agronomic research were created. These Institutes have a dynamic role to play in the economic development of the country. Their objective aims at improving plant species for higher production of cash as well as food crops.

Although agronomic research is a priority, the participation of women in this sector is negligible. (cf. table 3 below).

Table 3 (1988)

SECTOR OF ACTIVITY	Men	Women	% Women
Center of Oceanographic research	24	3	11
Research Institute for Oil and Oil Products	19	1	5
Research Institute fruits et citrus	7	2	22
Research Institute for Coffee and Cocoa	9	1	10
National center for florist	8	2	20
Ivorian center for technology research	21	4	16
Pasteur Institute	18	3	14
Institute for Mathematic research	21	4	16

How is this phenomenon explained? The explanatory factors are complex. The major and obvious causes are psycho-sociological and biological as indicated earlier (e.g. mentality of the women and also of men, missed opportunities due to pregnancies, the education of the children, domestic tasks, the lack of understanding and shared responsibilities for the home by men, etc.).

And yet, in the field of research, the woman can excel for several reasons, such as she has several features that can facilitate research

- She is more intuitive;

- She has great dexterity; and

- She is more calm and patient.

In addition to the psycho-sociological and biological factors mentioned above, it should be stressed that the low participation of women in this field is also essentially due to the weakness of the number of girls in the scientific disciplines, since there is no discrimination, and given that promotion and the nomination in the various bodies of researchers are done without any prejudice to gender, but based on a high level in scientific qualifications.

It follows from this study that the situation of the woman teaching at the University and in the Higher Schools (Grandes Écoles) could be improved and modified only at the price of personal efforts, a great perseverance and an eagerness to devote unfailing efforts to work hard. The woman must draw from deep within her the strength to assume her destiny and to claim, with equality, the same positions and the same considerations as men do.

It also follows from this that, to increase the representation of women and to achieve the gender equality in this field, it is essential to adopt a policy that will promote equal access to primary education and the conditions for success of the girls from primary to the higher education. Studies showed that, all things being equal, girls obtain school results similar to or higher than the boys do. In fact, as the pupils advance in the system, the variation in the advantage of girls is consolidated (Assié-Lumumba 1985).

In this study a particular emphasis was laid on formal education and training. The statistical data of teaching emphasize the rate of illiteracy of the women (approximately 80%). This rate varies according to the context:

- Rural environment: 86.3%;

- Urban environment (except Abidjan): 71.9%;

- Abidjan: 56.7%.

The rate of illiterate women is explained by the heavy socio-cultural constraints (the role of wife and mother reserved for the woman, attitude of the families privileging the education of boys to the detriment of girls etc.). Moreover, decision makers do not have the push and a systematic way of sufficiently taking into account the social and cultural constraints with which girls and women are faced in order to set up infrastructures and programs of sensitization which will enable girls to succeed based on their natural abilities which are at least equal to those of the male population.

It should be noted, however, that the Ivorian government carries out a fight for the elimination of illiteracy in general and of women in particular.

Information campaigns via the media (radio especially) are organized to sensitize parents to the importance of educating girls.

Child care facilities (daycare centers, nurseries, and kindergartens) were created to ensure that women were free to pursue courses in the Institutions of Female Education (IDEF). These institutions placed under the supervision of the Ministry for the Advancement of Women offer courses for the elimination of illiteracy, health education, family life and home economics. The Center for multi-purpose Education of Kaniasso in the department of Séguéla in the North of Côte d'Ivoire, for example, has been successful in training female rural counselors and extension workers in concepts of management and who in turn provide guidance to women who are peasants. What is the role of the illiterate or uneducated woman in the process of economic development in Côte d'Ivoire?

It must be acknowledged that women represent human resources (50% of the national population) without whom no appropriate development can be realized. Indeed, taking into account the economic crises, unemployment, the massive exodus of the rural young to the urban centers, women are increasingly taking charge and practically securing the household finances where the husband loses his job.

Moreover, in times when employment is rare, they have come to understand that it is advisable to think in terms of income than wages. They have become more and more aware that they can generate wealth by being self employed more in the rural area than in the urban area. Thus, they carry on gainful employment in the informal sector such as farming, rearing animals, trade, the craft industry, etc.

The illiterate women of the rural areas largely take part in the agro-pastoral activities; they contribute to 80% of food production of which more than 60% are commercialized. Moreover, they farm- and engage in fishing activities which entail- the preservation and distribution of fish. In order to achieve these they have organized themselves into Cooperatives (Groupements à Vocation Coopérative-GVC) and associations.

An example is the GVC of Assiè-Akpessé in the administrative unit (sous-préfecture) of M'Batto in the south of Côte d'Ivoire which has 22 women. Thanks to World Bank funds of CFA696, 380 or US $2,530, this GVC has been able to carry out market gardening. The sale of the produce has returned to the members a sum of two hundred million CFA francs or US $7,270 with a profit of a million and eighty CFA francs or US $3,360.

The Grand-Lahou Cooperative (Association coopérative pour le progrès des femmes de Grand-Lahou- ACOPROF) was created in September 1991. Two years later it was successful in grouping women from twelve villages to engage in marketing of fish, shellfish (crabs, shrimps, lobsters), food crops and the marketing of atiéké (steamed cassava semolina). They have received support and encouragement from the Ivorian Ministry for the Advancement of Women.

In the urban areas, in the informal sector, the illiterate women play an important role as wholesalers, distributors or retailers of manufactured goods and food stuff. They excel in this trade. In this type of activity, they operate either as individual traders (e.g. cloth, fish) or as within cooperatives (G.V.C.). These groups are very dynamic. They serve as a link between the rural and urban illiterate women, and facilitate the development of distribution networks. For example, the G.V.C of the Adjamé market (a municipality in Abidjan) brings together more than forty women for the distribution and sale of food products (aubergines, tomatoes, okra, peppers etc.).

This association benefits not only from the supervision of the Ivorian Ministry of Commerce, but equally also from the Canadian Government Aid for the construction of a storage facility and from the European Development Fund (FED) for the purchase of two vehicles.

In this informal trade sector in Abidjan, it is important to mention the trade in pork. Indeed, the women of Man (in Western Côte d'Ivoire) buy and fatten pigs and prepare and sell the meat. They have formed the National Cooperative of Pork Sellers. For this purpose, a slaughter house financed by France at the level of two hundred million CFA francs or US $727,270 was constructed and started operations on December 16, 1991. These saleswomen market more than 100 tons of pork per month.

It is notable that in this informal sector, one finds not only the illiterate women but also women who dropped out of school without qualifications in search of paid employment. In the urban areas, the latter work mainly in catering, hairdressing, and as typists. Because of the economic crisis, women operating in the informal sector should be encouraged.

Unfortunately, though the salaried women and their male counterparts can benefit from banking accounts and bank loans, women in the informal sector cannot. The latter have difficulty in accessing bank credits because the commercial banks require co-laterals. Very often, the women in the informal sector do not have the required qualifications or necessary training that will enable them to develop projects that are likely to be funded. Therefore, they self-finance with the Rural Savings and Credit Unions (Caisses Rurales d'Epargne et de Prêts-CREP), the Cooperatives (GVC), and with the"tontines" which constitutes a system of savings where the members take turns to receive the collections of a specific period.

After this brief overview of the role of the woman in the economic development process in Côte d'Ivoire, their great participation in the fight against underdevelopment and poverty must be recognized. However, it seems that they have been relegated to the background at the decision making level, and encounter considerable constraints in playing their role.

Conclusion

It is worth outlining a number of important suggestions: The author challenges the international community to encourage and support all measures aimed at the advancement of women.

On the level of educating women, the author appeals to the Non Governmental Organizations (NGO), to provide to the women's scholarships and the material means in order to prepare them for responsible positions in the national policies for education and research which will enable them to be involved in decision making on the level of management in sectors such as agriculture and the environment

On the concerns of the women who are out of school, it is necessary to reinforce and materially help the centers of vocational training and trade apprenticeship.

For the rural women, the NGOs must be encouraged and the GVC associations must be reinforced and helped to initiate operational and profitable micro-projects. They should ensure an equitable distribution of the resources with the micro-projects and the supply of technologies necessary to the rural woman who is responsible to a large extent for food security.

Finally for the woman operating in the informal sector, it would be desirable for the NGOs to provide special funds to these women for micro-projects by creating, for example, a guarantee (co-lateral) fund.

The aim of this study is to analyze the education and integration of women into the economic development process of Côte d'Ivoire.

The participation of woman in politics was intentionally not discussed. This could be the subject of another study, for instance, "Women, Democracy and Development." However, in this field, just like in the economic field, the access of the female population to education remains a determining factor.

The responsibility of the woman in the economic development process of Côte d'Ivoire keeps on widening. Ironically, with the economic crisis, certain constraints disappeared and the women discovered other spheres of operation. Of course, numerous obstacles still remain, but generally, the evolution at the beginning of the nineties was spectacular and profound.

The Ivorian woman has become aware that it depends on her to forge her own destiny, counting initially on herself, to organize and defend her rights. However, encouraging measures and various types of assistance will be of great help because there is a long way to go, even though encouraging signs exist.

Bibliography

Assié-Lumumba, N., 1985, "The Fallacy of Quota-Like Solutions to Unequal Educational Opportunity: The Case of Female Education in the Ivory Coast," Paper presented at the 29th Annual Comparative and International Education Society Conference, Stanford, California, 1993.

Assié-Lumumba, N., 1993. L'enseignement supérieur en Afrique francophone: Evaluation du potentiel des universités classiques et des alternatives pour le développement. AFTHR, Note technique n° 5, Washington: La Banque Mondiale

Ba, F. H.., 1993, Femme et éducation: une équation déterminante pour le développement humain en Afrique. *Revue Internationale de Pédagogie*, mars, 39 (1-2).

Bouya, A., 1993, Les filles face aux programmes scolaires de sciences et technologie en Afrique : étude socio-psychologique. Dakar, Sénégal: UNESCO, Bureau régional de Dakar.

Brock, C., N. Cammish, R. Aedo Richmond, A. Narayanan, and R. Njoroge, 1997, *Gender, Education and Development: A Partially Annotated and Selective Bibliography. Education Research Paper* (DFID-Ser-19).

Browne, A.and H. Barrett, 1991, Female Education in Sub-Saharan Africa: The Key to Development? *Comparative Education*, pp. 27,275-85.

Centre Interafricain pour le Développement de la Formation Professionnelle. Centre de documentation, 1982, Formation et emploi des femmes. Abidjan. Série bibliographique no 1; Variation : Série bibliographique.

Diarrassouba, V. C., 1979, L'Université ivoirienne et le développement de la nation. In *Les Nouvelles Éditions Africaines*.

Futrell, M. H., 1995, The Impact on Society of Educating Women. *Education International, 1*(4 v2 n1), pp.14-19.

King, E. M., and A. M. Hill, 1993, *Women's Education in Developing Countries: Barriers, Benefits, and Policies.* Edited by Baltimore and London: The Johns Hopkins University Press, published for the World Bank.

Kouamé, A., 1999, Éducation et emploi des femmes à Abidjan. Paris, France: L'Harmattan. 287p.

Lachaud, J. P., 1997, *Les femmes et le marché du travail urbain en Afrique subsaharienne.*

Psacharopoulos, G. and M. Woodhall, 1985, Education for Development: An Analysis of Investment Choices. New York: Oxford University Press.

PNUD, 1993, Côte d'Ivoire *Politique de Développement et Emploi en Côte d'Ivoire* [Bureau International du Travail; Organisation des Nations Unies pour le Développement Industriel; Programme des Nations Unies pour le Développement: June 1993].

Robertson, C., 1992, Gender, Education and Employment in Côte d'Ivoire (Social Dimensions of Adjustment in Sub-Saharan Africa Working Paper no. 1), eds., Simon Applegate, Paul Collier et Paul Horsnell. Chicago: *Comparative Education Review*, May ,36 (2), 253.

Stromquist, N. P., 1990, Women and Literary: The Interplay of Gender, Subordination and Poverty. *Comparative Education Review, pp.*34, 95-111.

Sudarkasa, N., 1982, Sex Roles, Education, and Development in Africa. *Anthropology and Education Quarterly,* 13 (3), pp.279-288.

Saint, W., 1992, *Universities in Africa: Strategies for Stabilization and Revitalization.* Washington, D.C.: The World Bank.

Vijverberg, Wim P. M., 1993, Educational Investments and Returns for Women and Men in Cote d'Ivoire. *Journal of Human Resources*, 28 (4). Special Issue: Symposium on Investments in Women's Human Capital and Development, Autumn, pp. 933-974.

Sources

ARCHIVES:

- de la scolarité de l'Université Nationale de Côte d'Ivoire
- du Service du Personnel de l'Université Nationale de Côte d'Ivoire
- de l'École Nationale Supérieure d'Agronomie (ENSA)
- de l'École Nationale Supérieure des Travaux Publics (ENSTP)
- de l'Institut National Supérieur de l'Enseignement Technique (INSET)
- de l'École Normale Supérieure (ENS)
- de la Faculté de Médecine.
- de l'Ordre des Médecins, Pharmaciens, Chirurgiens-Dentistes
- du Ministère de la Santé Publique et de la Population
- du Ministère de la Recherche Scientifique
- du Ministère de la Promotion de la Femme

Appendix

Ivorian Women, Education, and Development

TABLE 4: NUMBER OF STUDENTS IN PUBLIC AND PRIVATE PRIMARY SCHOOLS

SCHOOL YEAR	PUBLIC SECTOR				PRIVATE SECTOR				TOTAL			
	BOYS	GIRLS	% GIRLS	TOTAL	BOYS	GIRLS	% GIRLS	TOTAL	BOYS	GIRLS	% GIRLS	TOTAL
1980-81	529322	351647	39.92	880969	85404	58212	40.53	143616	614726	409859	40.00	1 024585
1981-82	565142	380371	40.23	945513	81615	57996	41.54	139611	646757	438367	40.40	1 085124
1982-83	595816	405831	40.52	1 001647	77154	56114	42.11	133268	672970	461945	40.70	1 134915
1983-84	609298	420330	40.82	1 029628	74356	55840	42.89	130196	683654	476170	41.06	1 159824
1984-85	618111	428679	40.95	1 046790	75470	57196	43.11	132666	693581	485875	41.19	1 179456
1985-86	635389	443027	41.08	1 078416	76450	59645	42.83	136095	711839	502672	41.39	1 214511
1986-87	653801	455144	41.04	1 108945	80025	62561	43.88	142586	733826	517705	41.37	1 251531
1987-88	683038	474895	41.01	1 157933	82948	65814	44.24	148762	765986	540709	41.38	1 306695
1988-89	712534	497702	41.12	1 210236	85629	68400	44.41	154029	798163	566102	41.50	1 364265
1989-90	732411	513444	41.21	1 245855	88398	70934	44.52	159332	820809	584378	41.59	1 405187
1990-91	747494	520921	41.07	1 268415	81099	65351	44.62	146450	828593	586272	41.44	1 414865
1991-92	768322	540735	41.31	1 309057	75971	62757	45.24	138728	844293	603492	41.68	1 447785

Rose Eholié

TABLE 5: NUMBER OF STUDENTS OF GENERAL SECONDARY EDUCATION IN PUBLIC AND PRIVATE SCHOOLS

YEAR		6°	5°	4°	3°	1° CYCLE	2°	1°	TLE	3° CYCLE	TOTAL
1981/82	Classes	1020	899	811	685	3415	259	263	158	680	4095
	Males	38576	35628	31519	24614	130337	10243	8581	3415	22239	152576
	Females	20135	15660	12048	8399	56242	2165	2061	805	5031	61273
	TOTAL	58711	51288	43567	33013	186579	12408	10642	4220	27270	213849
	Repeaters	4779	5915	6231	5726	23198	1720	3522	8171	6213	36064
1982/83	Classes	1012	942	838	778	3570	292	292	174	758	4328
	Males	37797	35532	31700	26533	131562	10671	9827	4135	24633	156195
	Females	19332	15551	12160	9407	56450	2442	2304	846	5592	62042
	TOTAL	57129	51083	43860	35940	188012	13113	12131	4981	30225	218237
	Repeaters	7325	8006	7998	7149	30478	2029	3940	1349	7318	37796
1983/84	Classes	1018	935	875	816	3644	298	328	195	821	4465
	Males	38653	35966	32896	29200	136715	11765	11277	4608	27650	164365
	Females	19388	15995	13085	10771	59239	2756	2635	877	6268	65507
	TOTAL	58041	51961	45981	39971	195954	14521	13912	5485	33918	229872
	Repeaters	6251	6746	7145	8715	28857	2100	5144	1229	8473	37330
1984/85	Classes	1008	932	882	859	3681	321	347	233	901	4582
	Males	37172	37503	33943	30564	139182	14313	12725	6649	33687	172869
	Females	20526	16629	14063	11868	63086	3901	2997	1190	8088	71174
	TOTAL	57698	54132	48006	42432	202268	18214	15722	7839	41775	244043
	Repeaters	5918	6931	8230	10049	31128	2533	5578	1844	9955	41083
1985/86	Classes	1038	942	905	907	3792	318	383	231	932	4724
	Males	41451	36990	36054	34353	148848	12695	15373	7060	35128	183976
	Females	21271	17673	15065	13726	67735	3509	3888	1222	8619	76354
	TOTAL	62722	54663	51119	48079	216583	16204	19261	8282	43747	260330
	Repeaters	6365	6958	8759	14486	36568	3682	7112	2944	13738	50306

Ivorian Women, Education, and Development

TABLE 5 (CONTINUED): NUMBER OF STUDENTS OF GENERAL SECONDARY EDUCATION IN PUBLIC AND PRIVATE SCHOOLS

YEAR		6°	5°	4°	3°	1° CYCLE	2°	1°	TLE	2° CYCLE	TOTAL
1986/87	Classes	1125	1004	952	987	4068	353	418	254	1025	5093
	Males	40672	38674	35123	32768	147237	12689	13894	6572	33155	180392
	Females	22767	17848	15183	12500	68298	3975	3902	1272	9149	77447
	TOTAL	63439	56522	50306	45268	215535	16664	17796	7844	42304	257839
	Repeaters	7271	7784	10234	13415	38704	2289	7003	2597	11889	50593
1987/88	Classes	1129	1051	989	1019	4188	370	439	286	1095	5283
	Males	43019	38440	37745	35639	154843	13100	14330	7461	34891	189734
	Females	23047	19244	16607	14241	73139	3856	4504	1678	10038	83177
	TOTAL	66066	57684	54352	49880	227982	16956	18834	9139	44929	272911
	Repeaters	6447	6685	9771	15800	38703	2877	7048	2031	11956	50659
1988/89	Classes	1192	1059	1010	1013	4274	422	461	327	1210	5484
	Males	47292	40825	38791	38793	165701	16503	17166	9791	43460	209161
	Females	27005	19738	18291	16120	81154	5429	5305	2338	13072	94226
	TOTAL	74297	60563	57082	54913	246855	21932	22471	12129	56532	303387
	Repeaters	7677	7288	10698	17105	42768	2715	9206	5001	16922	59690
1989/90	Classes	1206	1112	1025	1020	4363	450	560	306	1316	5679
	Males	50917	44952	41358	41705	178932	19180	21831	9513	50524	229456
	Females	28466	22694	18932	18036	88128	6658	7244	2223	16125	104253
	TOTAL	79383	67646	60290	59741	267060	25838	29075	11736	66649	333709
	Repeaters	9216	7543	10982	18710	46451	3594	11907	5879	21380	67831
1990/91	Classes	1225	1146	1080	1052	4503	472	494	552	1518	6021
	Males	48513	48428	44546	43627	185114	20237	18552	22297	61086	246200
	Females	28818	24713	21454	19405	94390	7692	5644	7106	20442	114832
	TOTAL	77331	73141	66000	63032	279504	27929	24196	29403	81528	361032
	Repeaters	5611	4264	6965	13935	30775	2840	3365	4732	10937	41712
991/92	Classes	1296	1160	1112	1112	4696	521	514	660	1695	6391
	Males	54609	48000	47895	46160	196664	22927	19326	28911	71164	267828
	Females	30704	26439	23705	21246	102094	9366	7297	10021	26684	128778
	TOTAL	85313	74439	71600	67406	298758	32293	26623	38932	97848	396606
	Repeaters	6259	7956	10781	18302	43298	3526	3034	17541	24101	67399

Rose Eholié

TABLE 6: NUMBER OF STUDENTS OF THE NATIONAL UNIVERSITY OF CÔTE D'IVOIRE

YEAR		SCIENCES & TECHNOLOGIES		MEDICINE		PHARMACY		I.O.S		LAW		ECONOMIC SCIENCES		LETTERS		OTHERS		TOTAL	
		Enrolled	%	Enrolled	%	Enrolled	%	Enrolled	%	Enrolled	%	Enrolled	%	Enrolled	%	Enrolled	%	Enrolled	%
1980 - 1981	Women	188	10.28	291	26.01	36	40.91	21	36.84	619	16.84	290	13.81	804	22.90	166	31.03	2415	18.70
	Men	1640		828		52		36		3057		1810		2707		369		10499	
	Total	1828		1119		88		57		3676		2100		3511		535		12914	
1981 - 1982	Women	199	10.28	323	25.96	43	43.88	22	37.29	574	15.93	279	14.13	815	23.98	203	29.17	2458	18.89
	Men	1736		921		55		37		3030		1695		2584		493		10551	
	Total	1935		1244		98		59		3604		1974		3399		696		13009	
1982 - 1983	Women	225	10.99	356	26.61	47	45.62	28	49.12	531	15.42	273	14.89	791	24.96	176	23.95	2427	19.07
	Men	1823		982		56		29		2912		1560		2378		559		10299	
	Total	2048		1338		103		57		3443		1833		3169		735		12726	
1983 - 1984	Women	265	11.67	403	27.89	48	40.68	25	41.67	537	16.69	273	14.72	771	24.47	200	26.85	2522	19.61
	Men	2005		1042		70		35		2681		1582		2380		545		10340	
	Total	2270		1445		118		60		3218		1855		3151		745		12862	
1984 - 1985	Women	234	10.42	387	25.16	62	42.47	33	45.21	460	16.59	214	13.52	869	24.75	215	24.24	2474	19.40
	Men	2012		1151		84		40		2312		1369		2640		672		10280	
	Total	2246		1538		146		73		2772		1583		3509		887		12754	
1985 - 1986	Women	235	10.68	367	23.83	62	39.24	30	40.00	400	16.09	188	14.05	880	24.35	320	26.91	2482	19.70
	Men	1965		1173		96		45		2086		1150		2734		869		10118	
	Total	2200		1540		158		75		2486		1338		3614		1189		12600	
1986 - 1987	Women	246	10.12	424	24.69	68	37.36	26	29.21	520	18.51	193	13.75	913	23.49	427	24.99	2817	19.80
	Men	2186		1293		114		63		2290		1211		2974		1282		11413	
	Total	2432		1717		182		89		2810		1404		3887		1709		14230	
1987 - 1988	Women	273	9.20	478	23.70	77	32.08	26	27.66	561	19.38	180	10.56	1084	22.98	562	24.87	3241	19.18
	Men	2693		1539		163		68		2334		1525		3634		1698		13654	
	Total	2966		2017		240		94		2895		1705		4718		2260		16895	
1988 - 1989	Women	264	8.07	480	20.46	122	36.86	30	29.13	598	19.19	183	11.06	1163	22.74	452	18.80	3292	17.95
	Men	3007		1866		209		73		2519		1471		3952		1952		15049	
	Total	3271		2346		331		103		3117		1654		5115		2404		18341	
1989 - 1990	Women	322	8.29	532	18.99	159	35.55	18	23.38	669	20.24	216	10.97	1340	23.43	526	18.46	3782	17.97
	Men	3563		2270		287		59		2637		1753		4378		2323		17270	
	Total	3885		2802		446		77		3306		1969		5718		2849		21052	
1990 - 1991	Women	366	9.14	627	21.62	208	37.55.	33	28.70	809	23.51	271	12.97	1409	22.69	446	21.85	4169	19.52
	Men	3640		2273		346		82		2632		1818		4801		1595		17187	
	Total	4006		2900		554		115		3441		2089		6210		2041		21356	
1991 - 1992	Women	462	10.14	772	22.55	298	38.21	41	27.51	771	25.31	320	14.04	1978	24.55	455	22.35	5097	20.95
	Men	4093		2651		482		108		2274		1960		6079		1581		19228	
	Total	4555		3423		780		149		3045		2280		8057		2036		24325	

Ivorian Women, Education, and Development

TABLE 7: NUMBER OF STUDENTS OF THE HIGHER SCHOOLS

YEAR		ENSA Enrolled	ENSA %	ENSTP Enrolled	ENSTP %	INSET Enrolled	INSET %	ENS Enrolled	ENS %	TOTAL Enrolled	TOTAL %
1980 - 1981	Women	9	10.84	39	4.16	7	2.81	51	5.43	106	4.80
	Men	74		898		242		888		2102	
	Total	83		937		249		939		2208	
1981 - 1982	Women	8	14.04	28	3.13	15	4.87	59	5.87	110	4.86
	Men	49		866		293		946		2154	
	Total	57		894		308		1005		2264	
1982 - 1983	Women	4	9.76	20	2.48	21	5.90	51	5.33	96	4.44
	Men	37		787		335		906		2065	
	Total	41		807		356		957		2161	
1983 - 1984	Women	2	7.14	24	3.60	26	6.75	76	6.73	128	5.79
	Men	26		643		359		1054		2082	
	Total	28		667		385		1130		2210	
1984 - 1985	Women	2	9.52	14	2.99	18	4.66	82	6.38	116	5.37
	Men	19		454		368		1204		2045	
	Total	21		468		386		1286		2161	
1985 - 1986	Women	3	33.33	10	2.89	21	4.24	96	6.71	130	5.70
	Men	6		336		474		1334		2150	
	Total	9		346		495		1430		2280	
1986 - 1987	Women	0	0.60	5	1.48	28	4.51	85	7.10	118	5.45
	Men	7		333		593		1113		2046	
	Total	7		338		621		1198		2164	
1987 - 1988	Women	1	9.09	8	2.19	42	6.16	69	5.87	120	5.37
	Men	10		357		640		1107		2114	
	Total	11		365		682		1176		2234	
1988 - 1989	Women	8	8.25	0	0.00	288	21.65			296	16.15
	Men	89		406		1042				1537	
	Total	97		406		1330				1833	
1989 - 1990	Women	11	9.32	0	0.00	425	31.55			436	23.00
	Men	107		431		922				1460	
	Total	118		431		1347				1896	
1990 - 1991	Women	35	14.77	13	2.52	353	25.09			401	18.60
	Men	202		503		1054				1759	
	Total	237		516		1407				2160	
1991 - 1992	Women	43	11.34	14	2.40	382	26.09			439	18,38
	Men	336		570		1044				1950	
	Total	379		584		1426				2389	

TABLE 8: TEACHING PERSONNEL OF THE PRIMARY LEVEL BY TYPE OF TEACHERS, QUALIFICATION AND GENDER 1991/1992

		TEACHERS			ASSISTANT TEACHERS			COUNSELORS			TOTAL		
		With Classes	W/O Classes	% Women with classes	With Classes	W/O Classes	% Women with classes	With Classes	W/O Classes	% Women with classes	With Classes	W/O Classes	% Women with classes
PUBLIC	MEN	23951	1549		2273	181		53	25		26277	1755	
	WOMEN	3982	916	14.26	818	214	26.46	5	19	8.62	4805	1149	15.46
	TOTAL	27933	2465		3091	395		58	44		31082	2904	
PRIVATE	MEN	1565	104		1279	132		74	12		2918	248	
	WOMEN	434	42	21.71	700	100	35.37	90	39	54.88	1224	181	29.55
	TOTAL	1999	146		1979	232		164	51		4142	429	
TOGETHER	MEN	25516	1653		3552	313		127	87		29195	2003	
	WOMEN	4416	958	14.75	1518	314	29.94	95	58	42.79	6029	1330	7.07
	TOTAL	29932	2611		5070	627		222	95		85224	3383	

Note: -Included in these numbers: nursery teachers

-Not featured in this table: public teachers assigned to administrative functions (IEP – DREP)

-Teachers without classes: Resigned Professors, Education Advisors, Home Tutors, Substitutes

Ivorian Women, Education, and Development

TABLE 9: NUMBER OF TEACHERS IN THE GENERAL SECONDARY LEVEL FROM 1985 TO 1992

	TOTAL	FEMALE PROFESSORS	%FEMALE PROFESSORS
1885-86	7188	1437	19.99
1886-87	7912	1582	19.99
1887-88	8708	1742	20.00
1888-89	9525	1905	20.00
1889-90	10115	2023	20.00
1890-91	10788	2158	20.00
1891-92	9263	1853	20.00

* Estimation based on a 1990 constant feminization rate

Rose Eholié

TABLE 10: NUMBER OF TEACHERS AT THE HIGHEST LEVEL: PROFESSORS

YEAR		SCIENCES & TECHNOLOGIES		MEDICINE		PHARMACY		I.O.S		LAW		ECONOMIC SCIENCES		LETTERS		TOTAL	
		Enrolled	%	Enrolled	%	Enrolled	%	Enrolled	%	Enrolled	%	Enrolled	%	Enrolled	%	Enrolled	%
1980 - 1981	Women	2	14.29	0	0.00	0	-	0	-	0	-	0	0.00	0	0.00	2	5.71
	Men	12		17		0		0		0		1		3		33	
	Total	14		17		0		0		0		1		3		35	
1981 - 1982	Women	2	14.29	0	0.00	0	-	0		0	-	0	-	0	0.00	2	5.88
	Men	12		17		0		0		0		0		3		32	
	Total	14		17		0		0		0		0		3		34	
1982 - 1983	Women	2	13.33	0	0.00	0	-	0	-	0	-	0	0.00	0	0.00	2	5.26
	Men	13		17		0		0		0		1		5		36	
	Total	15		17		0		0		0		1		5		38	
1983 - 1984	Women	2	11.76	0	0.00	0	-	0	-	0	-	0	-	0	0.00	2	4.88
	Men	15		19		0		0		0		0		5		39	
	Total	17		19		0		0		0		0		5		41	
1984 - 1985	Women	2	11.76	0	0.00	0	-	0	-	0	-	0	-	0	0.00	2	4.88
	Men	15		19		0		0		0		0		5		39	
	Total	17		19		0		0		0		0		5		41	
1985 - 1986	Women	2	11.76	0	0.00	0	-	0	-	0	-	0	-	0	0.00	2	4.88
	Men	15		19		0		0		0		0		5		39	
	Total	17		19		0		0		0		0		5		41	
1986 - 1987	Women	2	11.11	0	0.00	2	0.00	0	-	0	0.00	0	-	0	0.00	2	3.92
	Men	16		26		2		0		1		0		4		49	
	Total	18		26		2		0		1		0		4		51	
1987 - 1988	Women	2	10.53	0	0.00	2	0.00	0	-	0	0.00	1	0.00	0	0.00	2	3.70
	Men	17		25		2		0		2		1		5		52	
	Total	19		25		2		0		2		1		5		54	
1988 - 1989	Women	2	9.09	0	0.00	0	0.00	0	-	1	33.33	0	0.00	0	0.00	3	5.08
	Men	20		24		2		0		2		1		7		56	
	Total	22		24		2		0		3		1		7		59	
1989 - 1990	Women	2	8.33	0	0.00	0	0.00	0	-	1	25.00	1	10.00	1	10.00	5	6.85
	Men	22		23		2		0		3		9		9		68	
	Total	24		23		2		0		4		10		10		73	
1990 - 1991	Women	1	4.55	0	0.00	0	0.00	0	-	1	25.00	1	0.00	1	12.50	3	5.26
	Men	21		20		2		0		3		1		7		54	
	Total	22		20		2		0		4		1		8		57	
1991 - 1992	Women	2	8.70	0	0.00	0	0.00	0	-	1	16.67	0	0.00	1	9.09	4	6.15
	Men	21		21		3		0		5		1		10		61	
	Total	23		21		3		0		6		1		11		65	

Ivorian Women, Education, and Development

TABLE 11: NUMBER OF TEACHERS AT THE HIGHEST LEVEL: ASSOCIATE PROFESSSORS

YEAR		SCIENCES & TECHNOLOGIES		MEDICINE		PHARMACY		I.O.S		LAW		ECONOMIC SCIENCES		LETTERS		TOTAL	
		Enrolled	%	Enrolled	%	Enrolled	%	Enrolled	%	Enrolled	%	Enrolled	%	Enrolled	%	Enrolled	%
1980 - 1981	Women	2	12.50	1	6.25	0	0.00	0	-	0	0.00	0	0.00	0	0.00	3	6.83
	Men	14		15		3		0		2		3		4		41	
	Total	16		16		3		0		2		3		4		44	
1981 - 1982	Women	2	12.50	1	6.25	0	0.00	0	-	0	0.00	0	0.00	0	0.00	3	6.53
	Men	14		15		3		0		2		4		5		43	
	Total	16		16		3		0		2		4		5		46	
1982 - 1983	Women	2	11.76	1	4.17	0	0.00	0	-	0	0.00	0	0.00	0	0.00	3	5.77
	Men	15		23		3		0		2		3		3		49	
	Total	17		24		3		0		2		3		3		52	
1983 - 1984	Women	2	13.33	1	4.76	0	0.00	0	-	1	25.00	0	0.00	0	0.00	4	7.55
	Men	13		20		3		0		3		4		6		49	
	Total	15		21		3		0		4		4		6		53	
1984 - 1985	Women	2	11.76	2	5.41	0	0.00	0	0.00	1	25.00	0	0.00	1	10.00	6	7.79
	Men	15		35		3		2		3		4		9		71	
	Total	17		37		3		2		4		4		10		77	
1985 - 1986	Women	2	11.76	2	5.41	0	0.00	0	0.00	1	25.00	0	0.00	1	10.00	6	7.79
	Men	15		35		3		2		3		4		9		71	
	Total	17		37		3		2		4		4		10		77	
1986 - 1987	Women	3	14.29	3	6.98	0	0.00	0	0.00	3	50.00	0	0.00	2	18.18	11	11.96
	Men	18		40		1		2		3		8		9		81	
	Total	21		43		1		2		6		8		11		92	
1987 - 1988	Women	3	13.64	3	7.50	0	0.00	0	0.00	4	36.36	0	0.00	3	17.65	13	12.62
	Men	19		37		2		2		7		9		14		90	
	Total	22		40		2		2		11		9		17		103	
1988 - 1989	Women	3	13.04	6	11.11	1	14.29	1	20.00	3	30.00	0	0.00	3	16.67	17	13.49
	Men	20		48		6		4		7		9		15		109	
	Total	23		54		7		5		10		9		18		126	
1989 - 1990	Women	3	13.04	6	11.11	1	12.50	1	20.00	4	33.33	0	0.00	2	10.00	17	12.88
	Men	20		48		7		4		8		10		18		115	
	Total	23		54		8		5		12		10		20		132	
1990 - 1991	Women	3	13.04	6	8.00	1	11.11	2	28.57	4	33.33	0	0.00	2	10.53	18	11.61
	Men	20		69		8		5		8		10		17		137	
	Total	23		75		9		7		12		10		19		155	
1991 - 1992	Women	2	8.70	6	8.33	1	12.50	2	28.57	4	44.44	0	0.00	2	9.09	17	11.18
	Men	21		66		7		5		5		11		20		135	
	Total	23		72		8		7		9		11		22		152	

Rose Eholié

TABLE 12: NUMBER OF TEACHERS AT THE HIGHEST LEVEL: LECTURERS

YEAR	ASSISTANTS	SCIENCES & TECHNOLOGIES Enrolled	%	MEDICINE Enrolled	%	PHARMACY Enrolled	%	I.O.S Enrolled	%	LAW Enrolled	%	ECONOMIC SCIENCES Enrolled	%	LETTERS Enrolled	%	TOTAL Enrolled	%
1980 - 1981	Women	1	2.63	1	25.00	0	0.00	0	0.00	1	33.33	1	25.00	3	6.25	7	7.07
	Men	37		3		1		1		2		3		45		92	
	Total	38		4		1		1		3		4		48		99	
1981 - 1982	Women	1	2.63	1	25.00	0	0.00	0	0.00	1	33.33	1	20.00	6	11.32	10	9.43
	Men	37		3		1		2		2		4		47		96	
	Total	38		4		1		2		3		5		53		106	
1982 - 1983	Women	1	2.78	1	33.33	1	100.00	2	100.00	1	33.33	0	0.00	0	0.00	6	11.76
	Men	35		2		0		0		2		1		5		45	
	Total	36		3		1		2		3		1		5		51	
1983 - 1984	Women	2	5.26	1	20.00	0	0.00	0	0.00	1	50.00	1	25.00	6	10.53	11	10.09
	Men	36		4		1		2		1		3		51		98	
	Total	38		5		1		2		2		4		57		109	
1984 - 1985	Women	2	4.65	1	25.00	0	0.00	0		1	33.33	1	14.29	5	8.33	10	8.40
	Men	41		3		2		0		2		6		55		109	
	Total	43		4		2		0		3		7		60		119	
1985 - 1986	Women	2	4.65	1	25.00	0	0.00	0		1	33.33	1	14.29	5	8.33	10	8.40
	Men	41		3		2		0		2		6		55		109	
	Total	43		4		2		0		3		7		60		119	
1986 - 1987	Women	2	4.17	1	33.33	1	25.00	2	28.57	1	16.67	0	0.00	7	9.72	14	9.72
	Men	46		2		3		5		5		4		65		130	
	Total	48		3		4		7		6		4		72		144	
1987 - 1988	Women	2	3.91	2	100.00	1	14.29	2	28.57	0	0.00	0	0.00	7	9.33	14	9.21
	Men	49		0		6		5		4		6		68		138	
	Total	51		2		7		7		4		6		75		152	
1988 - 1989	Women	5	7.94	1	100.00	0	0.00	1	20.00	0	0.00	1	14.29	9	11.84	17	10.63
	Men	58		0		4		4		4		6		67		143	
	Total	63		1		4		5		4		7		76		160	
1989 - 1990	Women	6	7.89	22	19.13	0	0.00	1	16.67	0	0.00	0	0.00	9	11.54	38	12.79
	Men	70		93		5		5		9		8		69		259	
	Total	76		115		5		6		9		8		78		297	
1990 - 1991	Women	7	10.94	32	26.89	0	0.00	1	33.33	0	0.00	1	11.11	10	13.16	51	17.96
	Men	57		87		4		2		9		8		66		233	
	Total	64		119		4		3		9		9		76		284	
1991 - 1992	Women	6	7.32	28	21.54	0	0.00	1	25.00	0	0.00	1	8.33	8	9.20	44	13.25
	Men	76		102		4		3		13		11		79		288	
	Total	82		130		4		4		13		12		87		332	

TABLE 13: NUMBER OF TEACHERS AT THE HIGHEST LEVEL: ASSISTANTS

YEAR	ASSISTANTS	SCIENCES & TECHNOLOGIES		MEDICINE		PHARMACY		I.O.S		LAW		ECONOMIC SCIENCES		LETTERS		TOTAL	
		Enrolled	%	Enrolled	%	Enrolled	%	Enrolled	%	Enrolled	%	Enrolled	%	Enrolled	%	Enrolled	%
1980 - 1981	Women	1	5,88	9	12,50	1	16,67	1	50,00	11	20,37	0	0,00	9	34,62	32	15,84
	Men	16		63		5		1		43		25		17		170	
	Total	17		72		6		2		54		25		26		202	
1981 - 1982	Women	1	5,56	9	12,33	1	16,67	1	50,00	11	20,37	0	0,00	9	34,62	32	15,76
	Men	17		64		5		1		43		24		17		171	
	Total	18		73		6		2		54		24		26		203	
1982 - 1983	Women	1	4,35	8	12,12	2	18,18	2	40,00	8	14,81	0	0,00	8	26,67	29	12,95
	Men	22		58		9		3		46		35		22		195	
	Total	23		66		11		5		54		35		30		224	
1983 - 1984	Women	2	7,41	6	6,45	3	21,43	2	25,00	8	14,55	0	0,00	7	24,14	7	2,65
	Men	25		87		11		6		47		38		22		257	
	Total	27		93		14		8		55		38		29		264	
1984 - 1985	Women	2	8,00	5	6,17	3	20,00	2	25,00	7	12,96	1	2,63	6	17,14	26	10,16
	Men	23		76		12		6		47		37		29		230	
	Total	25		81		15		8		54		38		35		256	
1985 - 1986	Women	3	11,54	5	6,17	3	20,00	2	25,00	7	12,96	1	2,53	6	17,14	27	10,51
	Men	23		76		12		6		47		37		29		230	
	Total	26		81		15		8		54		38		35		257	
1986 - 1987	Women	3	10,00	15	16,67	3	18,75	1	50,00	5	8,62	1	2,04	8	17,78	36	12,41
	Men	27		75		13		1		53		48		37		254	
	Total	30		90		16		2		58		49		45		290	
1987 - 1988	Women	3	7,14	19	15,70	2	14,29	2	50,00	4	7,14	3	6,25	8	15,38	39	11,64
	Men	39		102		12		2		52		45		44		286	
	Total	42		121		14		4		56		48		52		335	
1988 - 1989	Women	2	5,88	22	18,18	0	0,00	2	66,67	3	5,26	3	5,88	9	18,00	41	12,85
	Men	32		99		3		1		54		48		41		278	
	Total	34		121		3		3		57		51		50		319	
1989 - 1990	Women	5	12,20	3	15,79	0	0,00	2	40,00	3	5,88	2	3,92	9	16,36	24	10,71
	Men	36		16		2		3		48		49		46		200	
	Total	41		19		2		5		51		51		55		224	
1990 - 1991	Women	8	12,12	5	21,74	0	0,00	4	44,44	2	3,64	3	5,56	11	19,30	33	12,36
	Men	58		18		3		5		53		51		46		234	
	Total	66		23		3		9		55		54		57		267	
1991 - 1992	Women	8	11,43	5	21,74	1	20,00	3	33,33	3	5,88	3	5,77	9	16,98	32	12,17
	Men	62		18		4		6		48		49		44		231	
	Total	70		23		5		9		51		52		53		263	

CHAPTER 11

"IN A NUTSHELL, SCIENCE AND TECHNOLOGY MUST BE FOR THE WELFARE OF THE PEOPLE": AFRICAN WOMEN SCIENTISTS AND THE PRODUCTION OF KNOWLEDGE

Josephine A. Beoku-Betts

Introduction

Let me tell you something. You know when our people were making cake in those days—common plantain cake, you know what they do? They take the ripe plantains and mash it up, mix it up with the green one and bake. What is the ripe plantain doing? They don't bother to put sugar. They mix it up like that and bake it. What do we do? We take the flour and put sugar. We put in every refined thing. They don't bother to refine anything. They used it as it is. But we don't want to learn recipes from them. We want to learn the lovely one that's imported. Advanced technology and all that. We really need to bridge the gap. Local women may not understand what they do, but we can interpret what they do into science. When we start from their point they will listen and see what they are doing is what we are doing in another way. We need to work together, because there's a lot to be learned from both ends.
(Dr. Tema, Lecturer in Biochemistry)

The above narrative is from an interview with a Nigerian biochemist regarding her perspective on the role of science and technology in her society and the framework within which that process should take place. Dr. Tema's outlook on science reflects a way of knowing that is interactive, multi-dimensional, and derived from the concrete experiences and needs of her particular social and physical environment. It is different from the western and Eurocentric scientific tradition that is viewed as more rational, objective, value free and detached from nature. Her narrative also indicates that African women have been pushed to the margins of scientific knowledge production and use, through the process of westernization as well as colonial and neo-colonial policies of formal education that have consistently marginalized African knowledge systems. The African woman challenges this process in her recognition that what is needed is a less dependent scientific tradition that is informed by the daily experiences of her community, including her validation of the traditional knowledge that women produce from the reality of their own local experiences.

The lack of scholarly literature on the perspectives and experiences of non-western women of color in the sciences has been observed by several scholars (Rosser 1999, Jordan 1999, Harding 1991 and 1998). For example, Rosser (1999), a noted feminist scholar, has acknowledged the fact that much of her own scholarship on women in science in the United States has largely overlooked the particular experiences of Third World women graduate students who encounter significant problems in U.S. universities (1999: 113). In Jordan's (1999: 113) analysis of the situation of Black women in science in the U.S. she points out that their relatively small number in any given scientific discipline makes it difficult to conduct meaningful qualitative and quantitative research on their participation. Harding (1991: 194) also comments on the difficulty of incorporating women of color and the consequences of their particular experiences into discussions on science and technology, because of the lack of systematic analyses on this area in the social studies of science.

Such concerns suggest that very little empirical or conceptual work has been done to examine the diverse experiences and perspectives among women scientists or to study the varied conditions which influence how women come to learn, practice, and perceive the role of science in society. According to Harding (1991), one of the consequences is that only partial and distorted accounts can be produced about European and American experiences, as well as the experiences of historically dominated and marginalized societies in the Third World. This knowledge gap has fundamental implications on both the theoretical and the policy levels for the development of distinctive visions for advancing sustainable scientific communities in the global system of the 21st Century.This paper is based on a qualitative study of 15 African women scientists representing various disciplines and countries, mainly from the English speaking Western Africa region. The study examines the factors that motivate women and girls to achieve high academic goals in scientific disciplines and examines the extent to which they are aware of how particular educational and employment contexts (e.g., family, teachers, self-motivation, educational and research situations) impact their lives and ability to accomplish their academic and career goals. I also explore the extent to which African women scientists are aware of how the experience of marginalization in local and global contexts, including the global scientific community, (e.g., colonialism and globalization) shapes their perspectives and understandings and situates them in the opportunity structure in scientific disciplines. For example, since the 1980s the inability to keep up with high per capita external debt payments and structural adjustment programs proposed by international financial agencies has led to high reductions in human resource development and educational initiatives for cost sharing, which have discouraged enrollment and continuation rates for women in African universities (Assié-Lumumba 2000; Beoku-Betts 1998; Subbarao et al. 1994). While these conditions do not affect women only, they have a more severe impact as they interact with other factors that specifically hinder women's educational and professional attainment in the sciences. Such conditions are likely to provide an environment for women to develop a politicized understanding of how they are positioned within this process, as they negotiate their own needs and those of their societies in the local and global systems.

The study also examines how African women scientists locate themselves in relation to science as it has been defined largely through western discourses. Given the different historical, material, political, and cultural contexts of their countries, I investigate how much this unique positioning enters into the decision of women to enter science and how, if at all, it shapes their practice of science, and leads them to involvement in wider public debates and political struggles about globalization and nation building. I aim to find out if their concerns and priorities regarding scientific practice, as Sandra Harding (1998) and other gender-related but non-feminist frameworks have suggested are context specific, with a broader social purpose designed to foster social change and development in their societies. Are their scientific practices linked to struggles against international corporations? Are they involved with international agencies, and, if so, how? Are their priorities organized around such concerns as medicine, public health, environmental violations, and technology transfer, in contrast to their western counterparts where scientific discourse in academic contexts would more likely be influenced by research and teaching concerns within the academy? In sum, how are their concerns similar to and different from those of their western counterparts, given the different material, political, and cultural contexts that influence their views of science?

The underlying argument of this paper is that the perspectives and meanings African women scientists bring to the production of scientific knowledge are shaped by their awareness of relations of subordination, which as women and as intellectuals they experience in local and state patriarchal structures and in the wider context of their societies' unequal location in global socio-political and economic relations, including in the world of science. As intellectuals, their position would not necessarily be described as neutral but rather as critical and activist, in the sense that, their academic identities are defined not solely by the dictates of their disciplines, but also from the vantage point of gender, acknowledgement of other forms of truth and knowledge, and their shared membership in a historically marginalized continent (Mama 2004).

Thus their angle of vision is context-specific and grounded in a sense of commitment to social change and social justice in their societies and in the wider region. Although some may view this approach as essentialist, this is not the intention. African women scientists are not a homogenous group, nor are all their concerns shared. They represent diverse societies with complex national histories and patriarchal trajectories. The experience of British colonization and post-colonial legacies of economic and political marginality in the global system, however, have created a particular set of experiences that allow for an interrogation of their shared marginality. This location of marginality is what potentially positions them, whether consciously or unconsciously, to engage in fundamentally broader understandings and uses of science.

In the following sections of the paper, drawing on feminist and non-feminist analyses, I shall review some of the factors that interact with gender to shape the experiences and vantage point African women scientists bring to the understanding and utilization of scientific knowledge. I will also discuss the effects of colonialism and its persistence through continuing inequalities under globalization, including the privileging of western science. This will be followed by a description of the study and method and analysis of interviews with women scientists. Data analysis will focus on recurrent themes in the study such as (1) factors influencing the decision to go into science and choice of research area (e.g., role of family, teachers, ability and self motivation, role of the state and availability of resources), (2) defining and articulating scientific practice to reflect a broader agenda for social transformation in their societies (i.e., academic research, interest in local knowledge systems).

Contextual Frameworks

The interconnected nature of colonialism and current conditions of globalization, and their impact on gender relations and on the politics of knowledge production in Africa, provide a context for understanding the epistemologies that evolve from the concerns and priorities African women scientists bring to the production and utilization of scientific knowledge. As Mama (2004) points out in explaining the generally complicated identities of Africa's postcolonial intellectuals, including those who are feminist, "their survival depends on carefully navigating these spaces . . . [and the continuous risk of] being compromised by the pragmatic terms on which they have secured marginal spaces within overwhelmingly patriarchal institutions" (2004: 5).

For example, Tamale and Oloka-Onyango (2000) note that "the academic environment is governed by patriarchal values and beliefs, and that female lecturers and students are generally considered less knowledgeable than their male colleagues, but also have to work twice as much to legitimate their positions and authority" (cited in Manuh 2002: 45).   While this may not necessarily mean that they have a particular style of practicing science, the configuration of all these experiences creates the conditions to integrate the experiential with the analytical in context specific ways.

In other words, "they are critical and activist, committed to political, social, and cultural transformation in the societies in which they are located" (Mama 2004: 5). This vantage point enables them to challenge and work to transform the prevailing knowledge base of science in their societies and "to propose which kinds of science will most advance both the growth of knowledge and the social welfare of the most vulnerable groups in their cultures" (Harding 1998: 9).

European industrial expansion in Africa through colonialism in the 19th Century destroyed and distorted the environment, natural resources, indigenous cultures, and systems of scientific knowledge in these societies. The modern/westernized science and technology that evolved from this process, sought to replace the indigenous systems by privileging western epistemologies as universal truth, and imposed this system of knowledge on other societies by means of capitalist expansion and military prowess. One example was that the dominant models of education in colonized societies until the 1980s were either European or North American. In the colonial period, particular secondary schools and colleges (e.g., Achimota in Ghana, Bo School and Fourah Bay College in Sierra Leone) were established to train the sons of chiefs for leadership positions, and African men generally, for the lower levels of the colonial civil service. The education of women was not much of a priority at this point, other than to prepare them for the supporting role as housewives for African men recruited into the colonial civil service (Assie-Lumumba 1995; Mama 2004). The use of European languages such as English for instruction and research in the arts, humanities, and sciences, also reinforced patterns of western hegemony in the educational systems imposed on African societies. One of the effects of this process was that it perpetuated "a pervasive western outlook in students, creating among them not only the impression that 'west is best' but also the feeling that everything that is of African origin is "primitive" (Mohamedbhai 1995: 1).

In the aftermath of colonialism, support for university education was continued by former colonial governments, international foundations and financial institutions, providing Africans with ample opportunity to study abroad, especially in Europe, from first degrees to doctoral degrees (Akilagba Sawyer 2002). Although these donors have continued to support the promotion and development of science and technology in these countries, the imposition of particular preconditions tends to undermine efforts to build a more relevant and self-sustaining research and training capacity. In the 1980s for example, international financial institutions such as the World Bank actually suggested that tertiary level education would not be a funding priority at that time for African educational development (Mama 2004).

As the process of neo-colonialism continues in the form of globalization and neo-liberal economic policies, funding for higher education in Africa is now geared towards the needs of the global market. This has led to an increasing decline in commitment to and funding for education, with an adverse impact on higher education. As stated by Mama (2004: 3):

> The kind of relevance now being called for speaks not of responsiveness to development or to regional and national agendas, but rather responsiveness to the labor needs of the global market. "Diversification" no longer refers to greater social inclusivity, but to privatization, and "access" no longer means access to education for marginalized groups but access to the education "market" by would-be-service providers.

Many scholars also feel that the system of training in science and technology in these regions of the world parallels the unequal divisions between countries in the global political and economic system. What is considered legitimate scientific knowledge in the world of modern/western science is only what is defined and sanctioned as scientific in Europe and North

America (Goonatilake 1993; Third World Network 1993). For example, most of the scholarly publications by African universities and research institutions are viewed by the wider scientific community as mediocre "backwood cousins" that do not meet international standards (Gaillard 1991). Mohamedbhai (1995) states that those disciplines that promote the development of subjects such as endogenous technology, rural development, and new and renewable sources of energy, tend not to be covered in the science curricula. This is because the faculty themselves have not been trained or do not have access to the relevant knowledge in these areas. Many of the research and development investments made by foreign donors are also made with the expectation that the African recipients will focus on the projects that the donors want to be studied, whether or not they are deemed as national priorities (Enos 1995).

These problems are not unique to African universities. Altbach (1985) among others has applied the concept of center and periphery to locate these societies in the community of modern/westernized science. Societies categorized as on the periphery are characterized as such because much of the quality of their work is seen as not measuring up to international standards. They are also perceived as being largely dependent on scientific developments produced in western centers.

When these conditions interact with gender bias, the implications for the education of women and girls have been adverse, especially for those who wish to pursue scientific careers. Assié-Lumumba (1995) argues that since the colonial period, there has been gender stratification of the educational system, in terms of expectations of what the future roles of men and women are expected to be. As already mentioned, in the colonial period, schools were established for the sons of chiefs, who although they would not be able to assume autonomous power, were still privileged over their female counterparts whose education was designed to reinforce European societal perceptions of women's roles in family life. These key historical factors have still remained in African societies. Some of the social values perpetuated under colonialism have even been appropriated by the local patriarchy or allowed to go unquestioned by the state patriarchy, thus reinforcing unfavorable conditions for the education of women and girls. This can be seen in the lower achievement levels for girls in school, family expectations for girls rather than boys to assist adult women in productive activities as well as daily household work, high drop-out rates as a result of pregnancies, and a tendency towards lower participation in science disciplines, especially in the physical and natural sciences (Gaidzanwa 1997; Beoku-Betts 1998). Women are also underrepresented among researchers, faculty administrators, and other high-level decision-making positions in the workplace. A research report on women and academic careers in Zimbabwe, for instance states that "women tended to be concentrated in the middle and lower ranks of the academic ladder, with only 22 percent in positions of senior lecturer and above" (Gaidzanwa 1997: 281). All these factors put women in a disadvantageous position in terms of access to available resources for training, and position them differently in terms of their own expectations to pursue scientific careers and the perspectives they bring to the production and utilization of scientific knowledge.

Study and Method

The findings reported in this chapter are selected from a larger study I conducted in the 1990s on the perspectives and experiences of African and Caribbean women in academic and administrative careers. I draw on a small sample of 15 doctoral level scientists in research and academic institutions mainly in the English speaking Sub-Saharan West Africa region, and specifically in countries that were colonized by the British. The criteria for selecting the particular group were that they must have attained their undergraduate degree in a scientific discipline in their home countries and their graduate degrees in other, preferably western countries, and they must have had experience teaching or doing research work in their own countries.

I found study participants through my own participation in a conference on women in science, as well as through key individuals. As a result of these contacts, I was able to gain access to women scientists through snowballing techniques and by processes of earning the trust and confidence of those who were willing to be interviewed. As an African researcher, I was also able to gain their trust and participation by explaining my interest in bringing the voices of African and Caribbean women to the discourse on recruiting and retaining women in scientific disciplines and careers. I conducted semi-structured interviews to give study participants the opportunity to voice their opinions and experiences on their own terms. The interview schedule allowed ample opportunity for the study participants to elaborate or to introduce issues considered relevant. Each interview was completed in 1.5 to 2 hours, although in some cases subsequent interviews were necessary. Interviews were conducted face to face or by telephone and were tape-recorded. After transcribing the taped data, I searched for general themes and sorted them for relevance and order of importance. The purpose was to provide a descriptive map to show how African women perceived the impact of particular experiences on their perspectives and thinking about the role of science in their societies. The main themes addressed are (1) factors influencing the decision to go into science and choice of research area (e.g., role of parents, teachers, ability and self-motivation), (2) defining and articulating scientific practice to reflect a broader agenda for social transformation in their societies (i.e., academic research and interest in local knowledge systems).

The data analysis strategies employed are qualitative and inductive. As described by Anselm Strauss (1990: 4-6) qualitative analysis is a form of analysis that "occurs at various levels of explicitness, abstraction and systemization." It involves extensive use of field observations, interviews and data collection techniques, and emphasizes "the necessity of grasping the actors' viewpoints for understanding interaction, process, and social change" (Strauss 1990: 4-6). Qualitative research focuses on the individual and explores in depth the lives of the study participants, thus developing a rich and comprehensive picture of their lives through their own voices. This study was not designed to provide a microcosmic representation of the full range of experiences and perspectives African women scientists bring to issues in the study. While there is a need for more context specific case studies or for larger comparative investigative studies on men and women scientists on the subject, this study provides a descriptive map that, when integrated into the body of scholarship on science, gender, and culture, has enormous potential to broaden understanding of science itself, as well as to deepen and adequately complicate the discourse regarding the significance and impact of diversity on the development of global scientific practice.

Characteristics of the Sample

Study participants ranged in age from 37 to 67 years. The fifteen women came from various countries in Sub-Saharan Africa: seven from Ghana, three from Nigeria, three from Sierra Leone, and one each from Cameroon and Zimbabwe. They included three professors, two associate professors, four senior lecturers/research fellows, four assistant professors/research fellows, one postdoctoral fellow, and one advanced level Ph.D. student. The latter two were at the time completing their studies in prominent U.S. universities. The fields of study were represented by two physicists, one chemist, one mathematician, one plant pathologist, one plant physiologist, one horticultural scientist, one pharmacologist, three biochemists, one nutritional scientist, one infectious disease specialist, and two zoologists. All but one of the study participants studied overseas for the Ph.D. Seven studied in the United States or Canada, seven studied in Europe and one studied in Ghana. Among those who studied in Europe, five were trained in the U.K. and two were trained under sandwich programs arranged between their home universities and universities in Norway and Germany respectively.

Among the 15 women, four had at least one parent who had never attended school and seven had at least one parent who had only attended primary school. In most cases, it was the mothers who had either never been to school or had attended only primary school. Five women had parents who had completed secondary school, these being mainly their fathers. Among those with university degrees, five women had fathers who had completed university and only one person had both parents who had completed university. Eight of the women were married, four women were divorced or separated and three women were single, but hoping to get married and have families while pursuing a career. Nine women had two or more children, two had one child, one was pregnant, and two had no children. The majority of the study participants (12) were also responsible for raising the children of less privileged extended family members in their homes. All names used in this paper are pseudonyms. In order to protect the anonymity of study participants, I do not mention countries in individual narratives because it would be easy to identify the small number of women within each of the different scientific fields discussed. The following section will analyze the interviews with study participants.

"If You Were Bright, You Were Put in the Sciences": The Decision to Do Science

What factors influenced the women in this study during their adolescent years to pursue science? How were their ambitions formed? Who were the people who influenced their decision to do science? While there is very little published information available on this subject for Africa, other studies suggest that children are influenced by appraisals from others and that they respond accordingly in positive or negative ways. The types of messages communicated to a child by those close to them also help to shape their self-concept. At particular points, it may be the family or significant authority figures such as teachers. At other points it may be peer group influence. These elements, individually or in combination, impact the formation of a child's aspirations in ways that foster conformity or defiance (Etzkowitz et al. 2000; Murray 2000).

The choice of a science path in high school for most of the women in this study was influenced by a combination of factors, which included tracking, self-motivation, teacher influence, and family influence.   The following statements capture typical reasons for going into science:

> I would put the total group of parents, parental influence, and teachers' influence. But I think I got into it because I was interested. I was doing well and I was pushed along, you see. But there were really crossroads where somebody came in and helped with this decision. (Dr. Turay, Associate Professor of Physics)

> Gosh [laugh]), actually, when you are growing up, you want to go to school. At that time you don't know whether it's science or arts, you just want to go to school. And in school, I was actually better in the maths and in the arts subjects. I was getting the highest scores in history, and in maths and in English. And my highest scores in the sciences were low compared to my scores in the Arts. So, if I were to go by scores, I wouldn't have picked science. But somehow, the teachers and the principal ... kept telling me "You'd be a good scientist. You analyze things the way you tell your story." It's like you are being talked into it when your ability is seen. (Dr. Tema, Lecturer in Biochemistry)

These narratives indicate that the initial decision to do science was based on parental and teacher influence, as well as ability and self-motivation. Also significant is the European-based model of education that fosters early specialization through tracking. Thus, although there were some students who naturally favored the sciences, the majority, regardless of regional differences, were streamlined into it because of their aptitude. The fact that most of the women also attended all girls' schools was of added significance, inasmuch as they were encouraged to explore their own abilities and interests and to develop self-esteem (Sara-Lafosse 1992; UNESCO 1994).

In the context of parental influence, many of the parents were not highly educated or economically privileged enough to give their children the kind of exposure that would encourage them to pursue science and to develop their scientific skills. It is clear, however, that many parents fully appreciated the value of a good education and the need to make the necessary financial sacrifices for their daughters to attain these objectives. For example, one person described the influence of her parents as follows:

> My parents were not too keen on my going beyond secondary school. They felt that my secondary education was enough for me to get a husband. My father was more supportive than my mother.   He

insisted that he was paying the fees and did not mind. I was the first girl in my village to go to university and to become an associate professor. I attributed it a lot to my father's encouragement. He only went to middle school, but he was prepared to support me. Because of that I launched a scholarship in my village to support girls' education. (Dr. Dabo, Associate Professor, Biochemistry)

Such women could succeed in their academic studies because they were raised in supportive family environments where their success would mean success for the family and community as a whole. These findings are consistent with studies of African American college educated women and men whose parents supported their education because they felt that they would have a better chance of accomplishing what they did not have the opportunity or inclination to pursue (Etter-Lewis 1993). Through her effort to establish a scholarship for girls' education in her village, Dr. Dabo (in the above narrative) also demonstrates an awareness of gender and class bias in opportunities for girls' education in her community. In cases where educational reforms such as Structural Adjustment Policies have been imposed in many African countries, the impact has been more adverse on lower income groups, especially women and girls. Against this backdrop, therefore, her vantage point is gendered and grounded in a sense of shared marginality and commitment to gender and class equality in her community.

Study participants also mentioned the influence of teachers on their early development, especially in all girls' schools, which almost all of them attended. In many ways the impact of teachers in these formative years was as significant as that of their families, in terms of motivating their interest, sustaining their academic performance and effectively engaging them in learning about the relevance of science to their local environment. According to Drs. Tema and Turay:

We had this science debating society where we discussed science topics. And you could argue for and against something as wide as UFO's, you know, to something as near as you dipping your hand in your mother's pot of soup and it going sour. We had such topics to discuss. And you were faced with the challenge of "What have you done? Why did it go sour?" and all that. Or you keep a piece of pounded yam overnight, what is happening to it? And then some of you are saying yes, it should spoil because of this, and some say no, if you had done this it shouldn't spoil, that kind of thing. So, we had such tiny groups created by one reverend sister. I will never forget. (Dr. Tema, Lecturer in Biochemistry)

[My father} was really in dire straits at that time, as well as financial constraints. So, instead of me going to sixth form, he suggested that I go to training college as a teacher. But then the headmistress of the school came in and said that she would put in some arrangement for financial help towards my sixth form. This was a British woman. So, I really think at that crossroads, she is the one who helped. She came to my father and talked to him about trying to put me through sixth form and the benefits of sixth form studies against going to training college. And she actually went out of her way to arrange some further scholarship for me. So, that really did help. (Dr. Turay, Associate Professor, Physics)

By portraying how science classes were very popular and accessible to them, these narratives show how the influence of teachers could have a positive effect on a student's academic achievement. Such findings are consistent with studies of North American college women who, when asked about the background of their science interests, mentioned important teachers who offered them new expectations and channels of communication in science classes (Etzkowitz et al. 2000: 44). In many societies, and even now in many African countries, science education is imparted in a very abstract manner that is often removed from the reality of students' lives. Thus, when science is taught in more creative and interesting ways, the outcome is more likely to lead to success. These narratives show how the influence of teachers on their students can form the desire to become a scientist in the early years. They also show how pedagogical style can make a difference in forming interest in a subject and attaining success in a discipline. In sum, the timely intervention of teachers was critical at particular junctures, where decisions taken would have altered the career paths of study participants.

For some women, the desire to study science and to succeed in this subject at school grew out of pure self-determination and individual initiative. For example, one woman talked about taking a leadership role in class to tutor other students. The fact that the vast majority of study participants attended all girls' schools was also significant in fueling their self-determination, inasmuch as there was very little commentary on such issues as fear of success or math anxiety. The study shows that those women who attended co-educational schools were also motivated by the competitive atmosphere among their peers, with some viewing this as a challenge to outperform their male colleagues. In some cases, there were study participants for whom pure interest in the subject and an understanding of the future benefits it would bring for them and their families and communities provided strong incentives to pursue science as an academic goal.

The study suggests that the path towards science is based on a complex interplay of factors, such as family and teacher influence as well as tracking, self-motivation and a women centered environment, where among their peers, young girls are more likely to accomplish high academic goals in science disciplines. This latter point is supported by studies that show that girls who are schooled in an environment that is exclusively women-oriented are more likely to have higher educational aspirations than their counterparts in co-educational schools. While there is no consensus on this issue, studies on schools in some African countries have found that girls in all-girls schools perform better than girls and boys in coeducational schools in mathematics, biology, and physics (Eshiwani 1985; Bolt 1986; Forge 1989; Obisodun 1991) Knowledge of these factors is salient for understanding the ways in which academic achievement is accomplished for many African women and how future understandings of science and its practice are influenced by their gender experiences. This latter point will be addressed in the following section.

"The Gap between the Test Tube and the Lab and the Layman Should be Closed": Scientific Practice

An underlying argument of this paper is that the perspectives and meanings African women scientists bring to scientific knowledge production are influenced by an awareness of relations of subordination, which they as women and as intellectuals experience in local and state patriarchal structures and in the wider context of their societies' unequal location in global socio-political and economic relations, including the world of science. Whether or not they are conscious of it, what they bring to the production of scientific knowledge is socially situated, in the sense of their involvement in shared concerns with others who are engaged in the same community of interest. According to Harding (1998), women scientists from Third World societies bring different resources to projects of re-examining scientific and technological change from the standpoint of their lives in global and local social relations.

The local is the object of their expertise, and this will tend to produce different questions, different priorities, and different patterns of science studies (1998: 83-85). Harding points out that, "Pure physics, chemistry, and formal biology are only rarely, if at all, the object of postcolonial feminist science studies. Sciences that study objects of mixed natural and social knowledge—

such as health sciences, agricultural, and environmental sciences — "are far more the object of southern feminist interests" (Harding 1998: 87). This viewpoint is consistent with studies on African women in science, which indicate that among women enrolled in scientific disciplines in African universities, a growing proportion is inclined towards the biological and life sciences (Makhubu 1995). Given the importance of agriculture, environment, and health as critical areas for development in Africa, women scientists in these fields are in a unique position to link their knowledge with the knowledge representing centuries of experiences with indigenous women scientists in farming, environment and medical practices.

For example, a study on women farmers in Sierra Leone found that "women could name 31 uses of trees on fallow land and in forests whereas men could only name eight" (People and the Planet.net 2004). In linking these knowledge bases systematically with the growing importance of bio-medical and environmental sciences as a frontier for research, an alliance can be established to develop research initiatives that can advance knowledge in sustainable bio-medical, environmental, and agricultural sciences. The problem lies, however, in the extent to which contemporary African states can control the appropriation of this comparative advantage by protecting their intellectual property rights in the face of globalization. The following section will examine the extent to which study participants are influenced by these concerns. I will examine some of the reasons why they chose their particular area of research and their interpretation of whether or not they bring broader meanings to the definition and practice of science, through their academic research and valuation of local knowledge systems.

Research Interests

In determining what it was that led them as professionals to a particular area of research, study participants most often framed their reasons around the subject's relevance to the development needs of their country, interest in the subject, availability of scholarships and research funding, and limited knowledge of career choices. For example:

> Some of the decisions were made for us by the government, you know. Because later, when I got back from England and applied to go to the United States, and still wanted to go back to medicine, they said "no. You are too good at biochemistry . The country is going to lose a potential biochemist." The decision was made again. So

certain issues do interfere. (Dr. Fatmatta Sago, Lecturer in Plant Pathology)

This response reflects the conditions shaping training opportunities and research practice for many African scientists, irrespective of gender. As Hountondji points out (2002: 1), "what matters most is how much the country's and societies, concerned benefit from the work of their scholars." In other words, what scientific research can provide for the greater benefit of the community is of vital importance in allocating funds and in the way individual scientists arrive at their decisions about what to do. In the case of women, there is also the problem of lower representation of women in the medical sciences in Sub-Saharan African countries. The relatively high percentage represented in statistics for the medical sciences more likely reflect those women being trained as nurses, para-medicals, and other ancillary professionals (Beoku-Betts and Logan 1993). Some of the participants in this study reflect this concern in their accounts when stating that, although they would have preferred to study medicine, they did not have that opportunity, and they decided to pursue more viable alternatives that were also relevant to the development needs of their societies.

Another issue affecting the practice of scientific research for many African scientists is the extent to which governments are willing to make political decisions that fully grasp the relevance and importance of science and technology for development. In most countries, the scientific community is not a strong critical mass that can effectively interact and influence the national agenda; accordingly, their relationship with policymakers is very poor. These conditions affect how much investment is put into scientific research by governments, in terms of funding for universities and other research centers, retention of good scientists, and the extent to which foreign donors can control the amount and type of research undertaken by scientists in these countries. For example, although Ghana has progressed from the status of a "low human development" country to a "medium human development" country (UNDP 2000) and there is a commitment to the development of science and technology in the form of a national policy, it is able to allocate only 0.3 percent of its revenue to science and technology (ibid.). Another problem is that much of the funding for scientific and technological research comes from foreign donors. Scientists are therefore constrained in their efforts to apply their talents in creative and productive ways. This is a concern that study participants are aware of and expressed in their interviews. Several of the senior scientists mentioned having to struggle to gain recognition and credibility for opening up new areas of research that they perceived to be more relevant to the needs of their countries in the 1960s and 1970s. It was a struggle because they were challenging conventional scientific practices deemed to be relevant and legitimate research, as determined by research institutions in Europe and North America. Some women said they had to sacrifice the timely advancement of their careers by being bypassed or delayed for promotion, or not being recognized as valid scientists in their particular disciplines. This is expressed in the following account:

> The nature of the research that I wanted to do was different, because at that time, people were all just isolating compounds from metal products and purifying them and making nice research. And I thought that was meaningless. I mean if you had a big pharmaceutical industry, then you could do that. I just wanted to show that we can put science into the art of healing with herbs. So, as a biochemist, how do you go about it? So the nature of the work was different. Maybe that's why I couldn't get sufficient funding, because no one was doing things like that. . . . This is what I wanted to do. At the beginning it was really rough because I had no money and I had done no work in this area. But I was really excited because it was a relatively new area in terms of the approach and I thought it was meaningful. . . . As for my other colleagues, they all ignored me as I did this African thing, but that's okay, because your colleagues don't have [to support you]. (Dr. Dogu, Professor of Biochemistry)

There were also junior scientists who were planning to return home or had recently done so, and were experiencing feelings of isolation or frustration in their attempts to fit in with conventional science in their societies. For example, some women were concerned that they could not undertake basic research because it was not viewed as a priority by governments or funding agencies.

> We are not in a position to do basic research in my country. Donor agencies are more concerned with the prevalence of a particular problem, [and] support programs on a regional basis. It's limited because [we] are not really trained to conduct basic research for [ourselves]. There is no need for sophisticated research, just primary level research. Vaccines are produced in the developed countries. Some of the problems I see are that we develop problems in a developed country setting and apply it to the Third World. There is a need for lots of commitment on the part of the government and the people. Otherwise, we'll constantly be fitting into other people's

agendas and not ours. (Ms.Bodu, Ph.D. candidate, Infectious
Diseases).

We see from these accounts that study participants struggle against two
fronts: marginalization of African knowledge systems and privileging of
western conventional science, received as a package. As such, they are aware
of the failure of conventional approaches to produce relevant and applicable
research for the benefit of their societies and the limited support provided by
foreign donors, who come with the expectation that African recipients will
focus on projects they want to be studied, whether or not they are deemed as
national priority. The ability of these women to resist and survive these
conditions is worthy of note, nonetheless. For example, several of them
mentioned that they held on to their goals and were ultimately able to prove the
significance of their work by publishing and participating in national and
international conferences. As one person stated:

> If you recognize that something is important that you want to do,
> ignore the resistance and move on. (Dr. Dogu, Professor,
> Biochemistry)

Research agendas are also shaped by the provision of logistical support
for scientific practice. Unlike the senior scientists who maintained an active
research agenda and publication record, junior level scientists expressed
concern about the lack of equipment, laboratory supplies and adequately funded
support services and resources to establish themselves professionally. They
were also disgruntled with the low salaries that made it difficult for them to
maintain a decent standard of living. Problems faced by these scientists have
increased significantly since the 1980s, as a result of economic recession and
structural adjustment programs implemented in many African countries. One
of the effects is that senior scientists who have had a longer time to establish
themselves have maintained an international and regional publication record of
three to five publications a year, whereas junior level scientists have on average
published between zero to one publication a year. In an effort to address these
concerns, several women talked about becoming involved in non-academic
activities, such as international consultancies to supplement their income and as
an alternative publication base; they have also considered relocating elsewhere
for better-paying positions. The following statements are representative of this
discussion:

Because of the facilities in my country, I couldn't do much research. I didn't have papers in chemistry. Because, if you look, most of my papers were on gender [since] you can collect [the] information. Because if there is no electricity, what can one do without electricity. So, if the facilities were there, maybe now I could have been [an] associate professor by now. Also attending conferences, getting funding support from the university. ... I think that in a lot of countries in Africa they can't afford to buy the equipment, they can't afford to fund research. (Dr. Bouya, Lecturer in Chemistry)

These statements are not unique. They are consistent with other studies on this subject in Africa (Akilagba Sawyerr 2002; Enos 1995). For example, a number of scholars have reported that science departments in African universities are seriously lacking in equipment, laboratory supplies and adequately equipped workshops and technical services to repair, maintain, and support existing resources. Libraries are also poorly stocked, and since the 1980s, many have cancelled books and journals (Gaillard 1991, Veney and Zeleza 2001) According to Gaillard, the average career of Third World scientists is now much shorter than that of their western counterparts because they are forced to take on administrative responsibilities before they even have time to establish themselves in their research. These problems are often exacerbated by the fact that in many universities there is little opportunity for communication with colleagues through such forums as department research seminars or national and regional research conferences.

From a gender perspective, African women in science face many invisible impediments owing to the limited quantity of women in the career pipeline and to the exclusionary practices in academia. Studies in African higher education systems find that women are subject to sexual harassment, exclusion from "old boy" networks and are almost never part of the hierarchy of deans and departmental administrators (Manuh 2002, Prah 2002, Gaidzanwa 1997, Imam and Mama 1994). Women are also more disadvantaged because of domestic responsibilities, which they have to juggle with their academic careers. Such responsibilities are usually taken for granted by male counterparts and are not raised in discussions on academic freedom or on the social responsibilities of intellectuals in academic institutions (Imam and Mama 1994).

In spite of these conditions, the women in this study are highly committed to the idea of using their expertise not just for personal gain but to foster new research priorities that are more applicable to their natural and social environment. In many cases research projects are driven by goals set by international funding agencies, thus confining them to a marginal role in the international division of scientific labor, e.g., classification studies (Hountondji 2002). There are many cases, too, where research programs are self-funded because the scientists believe their work will make a difference in the quality of life of their communities. As mentioned earlier, study participants seem to be aware of the growing importance of biotechnology and environmental sciences as a frontier for research. Given their high level of representation in the life sciences, they may well be aware of their potential to have an impact on this area, through the development of research practices that acknowledge the value of local knowledge systems and that are driven towards sustainable scientific practices. Some accounts indicate an awareness of this potential to shape local research priorities in these emerging directions:

> I am working on butterflies (chiromids). I am trying to catalogue different types of butterflies on which very little work has been done. They [butterflies] look like mosquitoes but don't bite. They are indicators of pollution in the environment and of forest degredation. Their immatures are in water and they are acquatic. When there is no forest or water, they cannot survive. They are also sensitive to pollution in the water. So, when there are a lot of them in the water, it means the water quality is good. We use them as indicators to know the level of pollution in the country. Some of it is funded by the Wildlife Society in my country and I do the rest on my own. (Dr. Leona, Assistant Professor, Zoology)

> I work on maize. It's the number one staple crop in my country. It is cultivated everywhere, every backyard. Farmers work hard on it but yield is very low. We have pests here. The most important are Lepidoptera. The larvae all enter the maize. Most of the insecticides used are useless. They pump the insecticide outside but the larvae are inside. That's the source. What most people use kills from the outside and is harmful to your health. Some people put it in the soil, so you are killing yourself gradually. It's like using DDT, which is harmful. So we are looking for ways to control the pests without these insecticides. How best can we enhance the performance of natural enemies that can kill the pests? (Dr. Gidwa, Senior Lecturer, Zoology)

In the following section I will examine the perspectives that study participants bring to understanding the role of science in their societies, including the gender awareness that they bring to scientific practice.

Perspectives on the Role of Science

Participation in the production of scientific knowledge involves not only research practice, but also engagement in the discourse on how to apply that knowledge for the benefit of people in any given society. How do study participants contribute to this debate and what perspectives do they bring to it? In general, issues addressed reflect an awareness of Africa's unequal position in global science and technology arrangements and the lack of political will on the part of African governments to apply creative and appropriate scientific and technological innovations to societal needs. For example:

> In Africa, I think we have to do applied research because in the western world they are doing a lot of research pertaining to what's happening in their own environment. And who should do the research pertaining to our own environment but ourselves? Who should do the research to find out what our foodstuff contains? Or whatever pollution is taking place—pollution of our water, the air, or the soil. So, that's why I think it's important. At least we should know the extent of the pollution and how it's affecting plants as well as animals. (Dr. Bouya, Lecturer Chemistry)

> In a nutshell, science and technology must be for the welfare of the people, all of the people, the society and the community. If it's going away from that then we have to be careful. If it's not of direct benefit to mankind then we are not going anywhere. That's why if you take what you have and then put science into it to make it better, it automatically satisfies that criterion. I think that in the Third World it appears as if we are always taking the science and technology from the north, but I think our contributions can come from this aspect--for the welfare of the entire society. And that is what we should try to bring to bear on science and technology for the rest of the world. (Dr. Dogu, Professor of Biochemistry)

In each of these narratives, there is concern that the type of science currently practiced is not relevant to the development needs of African societies and a consequent result is continuing dependency on western science and technology. There is a sense, also, though not explicitly stated, that African societies do not have the luxury of practicing science for the sake of science or for the benefit of international donors who come with preconditions. For example, the issue of how the products of scientific research are used and how this information is developed and commercialized for the benefit of the general public is mentioned. This suggests that without clearly developed nationally coordinated research policies and the political will to undertake projects deemed as national priorities, African scientists become more vulnerable to the demands of external interests, which are less likely to invest in projects of little interest to them.

Study participants also put a lot of emphasis on the need to acknowledge the value of indigenous scientific knowledge and to integrate these thoughts and practices into the development of science and technology in Africa. They are aware that the indigenous scientific knowledge in their societies is a unique and valuable resource, which has been marginalized, appropriated by the west, and not carefully studied and harnessed to improve the quality of life in Africa. This is stated plainly in the following accounts:

> Modern science [has] come to overshadow indigenous technology. But, there are many indigenous practices. If we were to study them, we would see their benefits to society. We should encourage this so that the two can be married. We should not sideline them because we feel that their technologies are archaic. There's something we can learn from them. Most of their technologies are environmentally friendly. (Dr. Leona, Lecturer, Zoology)

While many studies acknowledge the benefits of making more effective use of the indigenous scientific knowledge systems (Richards 1985, 1986, 1996; Brokensha et al. 1980), the issue arises as to who benefits from this use? How are those who produce this knowledge positioned in the decision-making and allocation process? Who becomes the legitimate owner of the product? Hountondji (2002) discusses this issue in the historical context of how western appropriation of African indigenous knowledge systems has benefited western science. He notes that western pharmaceutical products, for instance, are developed out of natural products based on indigenous scientific knowledge. These products are then collected and classified by western scientists (including western trained Africans), and in turn processed and developed into new products and devices for the global market. This system effectively maintains the unequal division of scientific labor in the global scientific community and African scientific capacity remains in a state of what Tema (2002) describes as "intellectual dependency." Hountondji (2002: 36) challenges these practices as unacceptable and proposes that "what is needed, is to help the people and their elite capitalize and master the existing knowledge, whether indigenous or not, and [to] develop new knowledge in a continual process of uninterrupted creativity, while applying the findings in a systematic and responsible way to improve their own quality of life."

Study participants were also asked whether they felt women brought a gendered perspective to scientific practice. While there were varied responses that cut across age and professional status, some women did not think there was any gender difference and that men and women practiced science in the same way, because they had received a standard scientific training, which meant that the universal and rational notion of science was accepted without question. Others felt there was a lack of critical mass among women scientists to make a definite determination as to the impact of their presence and perspectives on scientific practice:

> We are different people. I believe some may agree with my own perspective, others may have their own, but I wouldn't say on the basis of gender. With the gender issue, there are very few women scientists among us. [There is] not enough of a critical mass to assess. Our interaction is mostly with the men. (Dr. Kelfa, Senior Lecturer, Plant Physiology)

In other cases, women questioned the universal notion of an abstract and detached science and tried to articulate the standpoint they thought they were bringing to the sciences.

> Well, most places that I know, more women tend to do biological sciences, and the biological sciences are automatically linked to humanity, much more so than the physical sciences. Women scientists don't do the more abstract science. So, I would like to think that means that the realm itself in which they are going to operate more or less is impinging on the needs of the society. I think that females even when they think of the world at large, in their own little micro-environment, they tend to think of the effect and that's why I think women should or do bring their perspective. I firmly believe that that is what is going to save the situation. Women need to make men see that whatever they do should be for the welfare of the society. I think women are in a position to do that. (Dr. Dogu, Professor, Biochemistry)

The differences in responses reveal that while some women have a gendered understanding of scientific practice, others do not have a common understanding of their experiences and social location within the scientific community. Because they do not all share the same experiences, and because many view their experiences and concerns as shared African concerns, they bring different perspectives and understandings. These differences are a fundamental aspect of learning how ideologies of knowledge shape women's perceptions and claims to knowledge (Luttrell 1989).

In articulating their standpoint on what they might bring to science, a number of study participants envision a science that is not divorced from the lived experiences and values of a particular society and a science that places the needs of the population at the center of the analysis. There is also an element of awareness among some of the growing presence of women in the biological and life sciences. They are aware of the distinctive patterns of knowledge arising from women's lived experiences, and this awareness gives them a unique opportunity to advance a broader and more comprehensive understanding of the role of science in their society and in the global context.

Expanding the meaning of science to encompass a wider range of experiences and perspectives would seem to capture the understandings these women bring to thinking about the production and utilization of scientific knowledge. Such a perspective contextualizes science within everyday experiences and makes it less abstract and more pragmatic. For example, interviews of some of the senior women scientists show evidence of practical application of their ideas, from initiating science fairs to encouraging more school girls to take up science, launching popular television quiz shows on science for schools and the general public, and establishing foundations to train young men and women to be middle level technicians. Among the junior category of women scientists, there was also a pragmatic approach in their conceptualization of the role of the scientist in society. For example:

> Science and technology should play an important role. What about starting programs where we find ways to intervene? There are different patterns of science and technology in Europe and Africa. What makes it different? How can we solve problems right there and then? Vaccines in Europe might not work in Africa. You have to develop it right there and then. We are still too dependent on this technological transfer bandwagon. (Ms. Bodu, Ph.D. candidate, Infectious Diseases)

These narratives validate the importance of local scientific knowledge and environmental concerns, and they raise conceptual issues that go against the grain of conventional discourses on science. While they do not necessarily approach science from a gender perspective, their interests and concerns reflect what Hill Collins (2000) describes as two interrelated levels of knowledge of

Black feminist intellectuals: their everyday thoughts, experiences, and actions, and a more specialized knowledge which is more abstract. It is this sense of social responsibility and engagement between lived experiences and intellectual insight that differentiates the perspectives of African women scientists and that hold the promise of broadening understandings and uses of science in the global system.

Conclusion

As Rosser points out (1990: 54), the lack of women in science is not a question of what is wrong with women but "what is wrong with science and science teaching that fails to attract females [and keep them in the sciences]." This paper has explored how African women in academic scientific careers come to choose science and locate themselves in scientific practice. It has also analyzed the influence of marginalization in local and global contexts on their perspectives and understandings about the role of science in society. I have argued that the perspectives and meanings they bring to the production and utilization of scientific knowledge are shaped by their own awareness of relations of subordination, which they as women and as intellectuals experience in local and state patriarchal structures, including the world of science. As scientists located on the African continent and because of their historical and lived experiences, they are more likely to view science in terms of a broader social purpose designed to foster social transformation in the quality of life of their communities. These concerns are expressed in their accounts about the role of science and about what conditions would foster more relevant and sustainable scientific communities in Africa.

While recognizing the limitations of generalizing on the basis of a small sample of fifteen women scientists, representing five (mainly West African) English speaking African countries and a variety of scientific disciplines, some salient themes emerge that are relevant to feminist discourse on gender and science. Issues related to the decision to pursue science, the choice of research area, and perspectives on scientific practice situate the concerns and priorities of African women scientists and offer potential for closer examination in larger, comparative studies on this subject. While most of these women may not be aware of what intellectual perspectives they bring to their work, the understandings they bring to thinking about the issues and the ways in which these are articulated strengthen and validate arguments in favor of "situated knowledge..

The study suggests that African women who pursue scientific careers are influenced through recognition of their ability by family and teachers, and through their own interest in the subject. Their social environment, in the context of their awareness of the economic and social conditions of their societies, the availability of funding, and development priorities, is also salient, even if their subject of study is not a first preference. The narratives also reflect awareness of Africa's unequal position in the global division of scientific labor, and the lack of political will and financial inability on the part of most African governments. This peripheral position makes it difficult to apply creative and appropriate scientific and technological innovations that would benefit African people, especially those who are most marginalized.

The need to be less dependent on western science and technology and to explore alternative ways of integrating or harnessing indigenous scientific practices with modern/westernized scientific practices to improve the quality of life is of special significance. This calls for a broader and more pragmatic way of looking at science, one that encompasses a wider range of experiences, including indigenous knowledge systems. In this regard, study participants draw attention to the fact that indigenous knowledge producers know things that scientists do not know and vice versa, and that we need to foster conditions under which these different knowledge systems can promote mutually beneficial dialogue. This approach to conceptualizing and practicing science in ways that recognize and validate indigenous scientific knowledge and environmental concerns is not necessarily unique. However, it raises questions and conceptual concerns that go against the grain and seek to integrate the experiential with the analytical. While they may not recognize, affirm, or agree to characterize their perspectives and actions as feminist, the approach of these women scientists is transformational and rooted in a tradition of joining scholarship and activism and reclaiming positive African cultural legacies that create a socially significant space from which they participate in the production of science and its use.

Furthermore, these narratives help us understand why the inclusion of different perspectives and approaches can open space for more discussion on cultural diversity in the production and utilization of scientific knowledge. Given the importance of agriculture, environment and health as critical areas for development in Africa, the work of women in this study points to a key area for scientific development; the marriage of indigenous knowledge, particularly in the life sciences, with scientific knowledge in the figure of the African woman scientist.

References

Altbach, P. J., 1985. "Center and Periphery in Knowledge Distribution: An Asian Case Study." *International Social Science Journal* 37: 109-18.

Assié-Lumumba, N. T., 2000. "Educational and Economic Reforms, Gender Equity, and Access to Schooling in Africa." *International Journal of Comparative Sociology* 41 (1): 89-120.

Assié-Lumumba, N. T, 1995. "Demand, Access, and Equity Issues in African Higher Education: Policies, Current Practices, and Readiness for the 21st Century." Background Paper for the Joint Colloquium on the University in Africa in the 1990s and Beyond, Lesotho, January 16-20.

Barr, J. and L. Birke, 1998. *Common Science? Women, Science and Knowledge*. Bloomington: Indiana University Press.

Beoku-Betts, J. A., 1998. "Gender and Formal Education in Africa: An Exploration of theOpportunity Structure at the Secondary and Tertiary Levels," in *Women and Education in Sub-Saharan Africa: Power, Opportunity and Constraints*, edited by M. Bloch, J.A. Beoku-Betts, B. Robert Tabachnick, Boulder and London: Lynne Rienner Publishers, pp. 157-184.

Beoku-Betts, J. and B.I. Logan, 1993, "Developing Science and Technology in Sub-Saharan Africa: Gender Disparities in the Education and Employment Processes." In *Science in Africa: Women Leading from Strength,* ed. American Association for the Advancement of Science. Washington, D.C., 117-64.

Bolt, M. K., 1986. "The Relationship of Teacher Behavior to Student Achievement in High and Low Achievement High Schools in Nairobi, Kenya." Unpublished Ph.D. dissertation, University of Oregon. Eugene, Or.

Brokensha, D., D. M., Warren, and O. Werner, eds., 1980, *Indigenous Knowledge Systems and Development*. Washington, D.C.: University Press of America.

Enos, J. L., 1995. *In Pursuit of Science and Technology in Sub-Saharan Africa: The Impact of Structural Adjustment Programs*. New York: Routledge.

Eshiwani, G. S., 1985. "Women's Access to Higher Education in Kenya: A Study of Opportunities in Attainment in Science and Mathematics Education." *Journal of East African Research and Development* 15: 91-110.

Etter-Lewis, G., 1993. *My Soul Is My Own: Oral Narratives of African-American Women in the Professions.* New York and London: Routledge.

Etzkowitz, H., C. Kemelgor, and B. Uzzi, 2000. *Athena Unbound: The Advancement of Women in Science and Technology,* Cambridge: Cambridge University Press.

Forge, J. W., 1989. *Science and Technology in Africa.* London: Longman.

Gaidzanwa, R. B., 1997. "Gender Analysis in the Field of Education: A Zimbabwean Example." In Imam, A., Mama, A. & F. Sow (eds.) *Engendering African Social Sciences,* ed. A. Imam, A. Mama, and F. Sow. Dakar: CODESRIA Book Series, 271-95.

Gaillard, J., 1991. *Scientists in the Third World.* Lexington: The University Press of Kentucky.

Glover, J., 2000. *Women and Scientific Employment.* New York: St. Martin's Press, Inc.

Goonitalake, S., 1993. "Modern Science and the Periphery: The Characteristics of Dependent Knowledge." In *The Racial Economy of Science: Toward a Democratic Future,* ed. S. Harding. Bloomington and Indianapolis: Indiana University Press, pp. 259-267.*

Harding, S., 1998. *Is Science Multi-Cultural? Postcolonialisms, Feminisms, and Epistemologies.* Bloomington: Indiana University Press.

Harding, S., 1991. *Whose Science? Whose Knowledge?: Thinking From Women's Lives.* Ithaca, N. Y.: Cornell University Press.

Hill Collins, P., 2000. *Black Feminist Thought: Knowledge, Consciousness, and the Politics of Empowerment.* 2nd ed. New York: Routledge.

Hountondji, P. J., 2002. "Knowledge Appropriation in a Post-Colonial Context. In *Indigenous Knowledge and the Integration of Knowledge Systems: Towards a Philosophy of Articulation,* ed. C. A. Odora Hoppers. South Africa: New Africa Books, 23-38.

Imam, A., and A. Mama, 1994. "The Role of Academics in Limiting and Expanding Academic Freedom." In *Academic Freedom in Africa,* ed., M. Diouf and M Mamdani. Dakar: CODESRIA Book Series, 73-107.

Jordan, D., 1999. "Black Women in the Agronomic Sciences: Factors Influencing Career Development." *Journal of Women and Minorities in Science and Engineering* 5 (2): 113-28.

La Fosse, S. V., 1992. "Co-educational Settings and Educational and Social Outcomes in Peru." In *Women and Education in Latin America: Knowledge, Power and Change,* ed. N. Stromquist. Boulder, Colo.: Lynne Rienner Publishers, 87-105.

Luttrell, W., 1989. "Working Class Women's Ways of Knowing: Effects of Gender, Race, and Class." *Sociology of Education* 62 (1): 33-46.

Makhubu, L., 1995.   "Women in Science: The Case of Africa" In *The Gender Dimension of Science and Technology*, ed. S. Harding and E. McGregor. Paris: UNESCO, 29-33.

Mama, A., 2004. *Critical Capacities: Facing the Challenges of Intellectual Development in Africa*. Inaugural Lecture Prince Claus Chair in Development and Equity, Institute of Social Studies, April 28. *http://www.gwsafrica.org/knowledge/amina.html*.

Manuh, T., 2002. "Higher Education, Condition of Scholars and the Future of Development in Africa." *CODESRIA Bulletin* 3-4: 42-48.

Mohamedbhai, G. T. G., 1995. "The Emerging Role of African Universities in the Development of Science and Technology." Background Paper for the Joint Colloquium on the University in African the 1990s and Beyond, Lesotho, January 16-20.

Murray, M. A. M., 2000, *Women Becoming Mathematicians: Creating a Professional Identity in Post-World War II America*. Cambridge: The MIT Press.

Obisodun, B., 1991. "Women in Science and Technology Development in Nigeria." In *The Role of Women in the Development of Science and Technology in the Third World*, ed. A. M. Faruqui et al. Teaneck, N.J.: World Scientific Publishing Company.

Odora Hoppers, Catherine, A., ed., 2002. *Indigenous Knowledge and the Integration of Knowledge Systems: Towards a Philosophy of Articulation*. South Africa: New Africa Books.

People and planet.net, 2004. "Women and Environment." *People and Biodiversity*, posted May 20.

Prah, M., 2002. "Gender Issues in Ghanaian Tertiary Institutions: Women Academics and Administrators at Cape Coast." *Ghana Studies* 5: 1-20.

Richards, P., 1985. *Indigenous Agricultural Revolution: Ecology and Food Production in West Africa*. London: Hutchinson, and Boulder, Colo.: Westview Press.

Richards, P., 1986. *Coping with Hunger: Hazard and Experiment in an African Rice Farming System*. London and Boston: Allen and Unwin.

Richards, P., 1996. *Fighting the Rainforest: War, Youth and Resources in Sierra Leone*. Portsmouth: Heinemann.

Rosser, S. V., 1990. *Female Friendly Science: Applying Women's Studies Methods and Theories to Attract Students*. New York: Pergamon Press.

Rosser, S. V, 1999, "International Experiences Lead to Using Postcolonial Feminism to Transform Life Sciences Curriculum." *Women's Studies International Forum* 22 (1): 3-15.

Rosser, S. V, 2000. *Women, Science, and Society: The Crucial Union.* New York and London: Teachers College Press.

Sall, E., ed., 2000, *Women in Academia: Gender and Academic Freedom in Africa.* Dakar: CODESRIA Book Series.

Sawyerr, A, 2002. "Challenges Facing African Universities: Selected Issues." Paper presented at the 45th Annual Meeting of the African Studies Association. Washington, D.C., December 5-8.

Strauss, A., 1990. *Qualitative Analysis for Social Scientists.* Cambridge: Cambridge University Press.

Subbararao, K., L. Raney, and J. Haworth, 1994. *Women in Higher Education: Constraints and Promising Initiatives.* Washington, D.C.: World Bank.

Tamale, S., and J Oloka-Onyango, 2000. "'Bitches' at The Academy: Gender and Academic Freedom in Africa." In *Women in Academia: Gender and Academic Freedom in Africa,* ed. S. Ebrima. Dakar: CODESRIA Book Series, 1-23.

Tema, B. O., 2002. "Science Education and Africa's Rebirth." In *Indigenous Knowledge and the Integration of Knowledge Systems: Towards a Philosophy of Articulation,* ed. C. A. Odora Hoppers. South Africa: New Africa Books.

Third World Network, 1993. "Modern Science in Crisis: A Third World Response." In *The Racial Economy of Science: Toward a Democratic Future,* ed. S. Harding. Bloomington: Indiana University Press, 484-518.

United Nations Ddevelopment Programme, 2000. *Ghana Development Report: Science, Technology, and Human Development.* Accra: ISSER.

Veney, C. R., and P. T. Zeleza, eds., 2001. *Women in African Studies.* Lawrenceville, N. J.: Africa World Press, Inc.

CHAPTER 12

WOMEN AND SCIENTIFIC EDUCATION: THE CASE OF HIGHER EDUCATION IN CÔTE D'IVOIRE[1]

DENISE HOUPHOUËT-BOIGNY
FREDERICA KOBLAVI MANSILLA

Introduction

Since the attainment of independence in 1960, Côte d'Ivoire has followed an encouraging policy of education, aimed at granting to all Ivorians, without distinction to gender or social status, an equal chance to education and training. Thus for this country education is not only a priority, but the priority of the priorities.

This article aims at giving insight to science education for girls and young women at the higher education level in Côte d'Ivoire. Two similar studies were previously carried out by Mrs. Rose Eholié, Professor of Inorganic Chemistry and a member of the National Committee of Evaluation of Higher Education and Research.

The co-authors of this article took part in the development of "the Role of the Women in the Scientific and Technological Development of the Third World: the case of Côte d'Ivoire" which was the first of these two studies and which was published in 1988. The second study entitled "Woman of Côte d'Ivoire: on and Integration in the Process of Economic Eevelopment of Côte d'Ivoire" was carried out in 1993.

---

[1] This chapter is based on a paper presented at a UNESCO Conferenece in Ouagadougou, Burkina Faso, in January 1999 by the two authors and another paper presented in March 2002 at the CEPARRED Conference at Cornell University by Denise Houphouët-Boigny.

Th study uses the statistics that were provided by Mrs. Rose Eholié and which cover the period of from 1980-1981 to 1991-1992 and extends these up to 1997-1998.

The first part of this study offers a brief overview of the educational situation in Côte d'Ivoire as described by the National Development Plan of the Educational /Training Sector (PNDEF). The second section describes the higher educational system of Côte d'Ivoire. The third sections presentss briefly the statistics. The fourth section analyzes the growth in student enrollment in the scientific education structures. Finally the last part, which is flowed by the conclusion, describes the participation of women in scientific and technological development.

A Brief Overview of the Educational Situation in Côte d'Ivoire

The Geographical and Socio-demographic Situation

Located in the intertropical zone of West Africa, in the middle of the Gulf of Guinea, Côte d'Ivoire extends some 322.450 km^2 over the surface with approximately 600 km of maritime coastalline. It is borded on the North by Burkina Faso and Mali, to the South by the Gulf of Guinea, to the East by Ghana, and to the West by Guinea and Liberia.

The General Census of the Population and Habitat in 1988 recorded 10,815,000 inhabitants; an average increase of 3.8% per annum over the 1995-1998 period. This demographic dynamism which characterizes Côte d'Ivoire combines three principal elements, namely, a natural rate of increase which is among the highest in Africa, an important migratory factor and rapid urbanization.

According to projections carried out by the National Institute of Statistics (INS), in 1995, the total population of Côte d'Ivoire was considered to be 14,208,000, corresponding to an average density of 44 inhabitants per km^2; and approximately 16 million according to the census of 1998. The population of Côte d'Ivoire is marked by its extreme youth. Until the year 2000, people younger than 15 years represented more than 48% of the total population.

The organizational Structure of the System of Education

The academic curriculum is structured into three degrees:

- the first level (premier degré) comprises the pre-school and primary education cycles. Primary school lasts normally six (6) years and ends with a diploma, the Certificate of Primary Studies.

- the second level (second degré) includes General, Technical and Professional Education. General Education includes an initial cycle of four (4) years duration with a final diploma, the BEPC (Brevet d'Études du Premier Cycle) and a second cycle of three (3) years duration has a termail diploma: the Baccalaureate.

- The third level (troisième degree) constitutes higher education

The number of students

During the period of 1991-1996, the student population grew as shown in Table 1.

Table 1: the Enrollment Growth by Level

Levels	1991-92	1992-93	1993-94	1994-95	1995-96	Annual growth average
Primary education	1 447 785	1 463 963	1 553 540	1 609 929	1 662 265	3.51%
Secondary - General - Technical and professional	396 606 21 212	414 504 22 180	445 504 23 500	463 810 24 000	489 740 25 000	5.41% 4.19%
Higher	30 064	37 811	49 831	52 202	60 500	19.1%

The growth of the student population is particularly noticeable in higher education.

However, the total number of students at the higher level represents a very small proportion of the population of young people who are of higher education age. The statistics of the gross enrollment rates in table 2 give an indication of this.

Gross Enrollment Rates

The gross enrollment rates in primary education remained relatively stable over the period. The decrease observed during in 1992-1993 corresponds to the introduction of enrollment fees, one of the policies adopted following the economic crisis and the adoption of the structural and stabilization adjustment programs (SAPs) of the World Bank and the IMF.

Table 2: Growth of the Gross Enrollment Rates by Level

Levels	1991-92	1992-93	1993-94	1994-95	1995-96	Annual evolution
Primary education	71.2%	69.5%	71.3%	71.4%	71.2%	0%
Secondary General and Technical -1st Cycle - 2nd Cycle	30.1% 13.3%	30.3% 15.4%	31.5% 15.7%	28% 14%	30.5% 14.4%	0.3% 2%
Higher	2.8%	3.5%	4.4%	4.5%	4.9%	15%

The gross enrollment rates, on the other hand, are on the increase in the other levels of education. In spite of a relatively strong growth, the rates of schooling in higher education remain relatively low (4.9% in 1995-1996) compared to those of other countries of equivalent level: Morocco (10%), Turkey (13%) and Latin America (18%).

The proportion of female students

Although slightly improved, the distribution of the number of those enrolled confirms the maintenance of a total disequilibrium to the detriment of inflow and a declining proportion of female pupils and students between primary and secondary education. One notes however, a significant increase at the higher level. Between 1991-1992 and 1995-1996, the growth of the proportion of female students by level is shown in the Table 3.

Generally, the under-enrollment of school-age female population can be explained by the combination of a great number of factors, particularly in sociocultural and financial conditions. For example, in Korhogo (in the North of the country) the rate of female schooling in primary education is only 33% (a girl for two boys). Table 4 shows the number of students in the final class (at the baccalaureate level) in 1997 for the whole country.

Table 3: Proportion of female students by level

Levels	1991-92	1995-96	Annual evolution
Primary education	41.7%	42.3%	+1.4%
Secondary - 1st Cycle - 2nd Cycle	34.2% 27.3%	34% 30%	-0.6% +9.9%
Higher Level	19.5%	25.4%	+30.3%

Table 4: Numbers of Final Classes of Secondary Schools in 1997

Track	Female students	Male students	% Female students	Total
A	11 027	14 757	42.76%	25 784
C	138	1 227	10.10%	1 365
D	5 255	20 242	20.61%	25 497

Beyond this observation, in considering the ratio of students population at the entry to higher education, the ratio of approximately a female student for a male student at the literary baccalaureate (A Track), falls to a female student for four male students at the scientific baccalaureate (C and D Tracks).

The higher educational system

In 1998 the Ivorian system of higher education comprised three types of structures, namely:
- Universities;
- Public Higher Professonal Schools (Grandes Écoles);
- Private Institutions of Higher education.

In addition, some institutions offer post-baccalaureate training and, based on this fact, can be classified in the category of Higher Professional and Technical Educational institutions. They are in general specialized schools attached to technical ministries. This is the case of the School for National Administration and the National Institute of Youth and Sports, inter alia.

Universities

Côte d'Ivoire has three (3) autonomous universities. These are:
- The University of Abobo-Adjamé;
- The University of Bouaké;
- The University of Cocody.

Each university includes a Unit of Training and Research (Unité de Formation et de Recherche-UFR), Schools, and Research Centers. The Regional Units of Higher Education (URES), located in the hinterland of the country, are affiliated with the universities.

* The University of Abobo-Adjamé
This university was reorganized in August 1996 and comprises four (4) Units of Education and Research (UFR), two Schools and a Regional Unit of Higher education (URES) located in Daloa (in the Mid-west of the country).

* The University of Bouaké
This university was also reorganized in August 1996 and is composed of four (4) Units of Education and Research (UFR), a School and a Regional Unit of Higher Education (URES) located at Korhogo (in the North of the country).

* The University of Cocody
This university, which is the oldest of the Ivorian higher education institutions, was reorganized in August 1996 as well and includes thirteen (13) Units of Education and Research (UFR) and a School. With the exception of the first year's instruction for Medicine, Pharmacy and Odontology, which are provided at the University of Abobo-Adjamé, the University of Cocody offers complete university education from junior college to post-graduate education, in practically all the fields of traditional university.

The framework of Education and Research relating to each university are presented in the table located in the appendix

The Higher Schools (Grandes Écoles)

The Public Higher Schools are divided into two main categories according to their respective areas of scpecialization.

The first category includes Public Higher Schools of Vocational and Technical training. There are two of them and their mission is to train engineers and high-level technicians in their respective spheres of activities. They briefly presented below, along with the dates of their creation:

* The Higher National School of Statistics and Applied Economics (ENSEA, 1961);

* The Felix HOUPHOUËT-BOIGNY National Polytechnic Institute (INP-HB) of Yamoussoukro, which was created from the regrouping of the four (4) Higher Schools existing in Yamoussoukro in September 1996 namely:
· The Higher National School of Public works (ENSTP, 1963);
· The Higher National School of Agronomy (ENSA, 1965);
· The Higher National Institute of Technical Teaching (INSET, 1975);
· The Agricultural Institute of Bouaké (IAB, 1977).

The Félix HOUPHOUËT-BOIGNY National Polytechnic Institute (INP-HB) of Yamoussoukro is composed of six (6) schools:
- The Higher School of Agronomy (ESA);
- The Higher School of Trade and Administration of Enterprisess (ESCAE);
- The Higher School of Industry (ESI);
- The Higher School of Mines and Geology (ESMG);
- The Higher School for Public Works (ESTP);
- The School for Continuing Education and Training of high Officers (EFCPC).

The second category includes the two Higher Schools for teacher training which aim atproviding initial educating and upgrading of teachers for the secondary schools for thegeneral as well as the technical and professional cycles.
They are also briefly presented with their dates of creation:
- The Standard Higher School (ENS, 1964);
- The National Institute of Technical and Professional Teacher Training (IPNETP, 1975).

The Private Institutions of Higher Education

Since 1991, the Ivorian Government has encouraged the creation of private institutions of higher education. These institutions essentially offer education to the level of Diploma for Higher Technicians (BTS).

The principal fields of education offered by these schools are: Accounting and Business Administration, Business Finance, Secretarial, International Trade, Insurance, Industrial Maintenance, Management Information Systems, etc.

The DESS and Engineering fields are at the experimentation stage in the private schools. For the year 1998-1999 for example, sixty (60) private higher education institutions were accredited of which two were in the process of opening their doors.

The Other Post Baccalaureate Education Institutions

Generally these are public or private owned insitutions of higher technical and professional education that do not emanate from the Ministry in charge of Higher education. These are:
- The regional Academy of Maritime Sciences and Technology (ARSTM);
- The Higher National Institute of Arts and Culture (INSAAC);
- The National Institute of Youth and Sports (INJS);
- Centers of Ggidance and Teacher training (CAFOP) (Abengourou, Abidjan, Aboisso, Bouaké, Dabou, Daloa, Grand-Bassam, Katiola, Korhogo, Man, Odienné, Yamoussoukro);
- National Institute of Social Education (INFS);
- The National School of Administration (ENA);
- The Management and Commercial School (ECG);
- The National Institute of Education of Health Agents (INFAS) (Abidjan, Bouaké, Korhogo);
- The Inter-African Higher School of Electricity (ESIE);
- The African Higher Institute of the Post and Telecommunications (ISAPT);
- The Institute of Communication Sciences and Technology of (ISTC);
- The Higher Catholic Seminary of Anyama;
- The Higher Catholic Seminary of Abadjin-Kouté;
- The National Police Force School (ENP);
- The Center of Electronics and Applied Data Processing (CELIA);

- The Center of Office Automation, Communication and Management (CBCG);
- The Center of Electrical Trades (CME);
- The Higher Multinational School of Postal Services of Abidjan (EMSPA).

A Brief Presentation of Statistics

The student population of Côte d'Ivoire (all types of schools included) is experiencing a constant change. This population is essentially characterized by a heightened rhythm of increase, an unequal distribution over the national territory, a low representation of females, a concentration of schools within the universities and a rather recent propensity toward the professional fields.

The distribution of Students by Type of Institution

For the 1997-1998 academic year, 100,724 students registered at the beginning in the post-baccalaureate level. Among them, 82,173 students or 82% were registered in institutions that were controlled by the Ministry of Higher Education, Research and Technological Innovation (MESRIT), and 18,551 students or 18% were enrolled in institutions other than those of MESRIT.

Table 5: Disttribution of Students by type of Institution

Structures	Registered students	% Student
Universities	48 576	48%
Public Higher Schools	6 209	6%
Private Higher Education Institutions	27 388	27%
Institutions outside MESRIT	18 551	18%
Total	100 724	100%

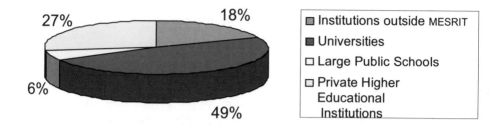

27%   18%

6%

49%

- ■ Institutions outside MESRIT
- ■ Universities
- □ Large Public Schools
- □ Private Higher Educational Institutions

The Distribution of Students by Gender

Despite the important efforts at schooling, in 1977-1998 female stduents represented only 27.1% of the total enrollment of students registered in post-baccalaureate education.

The highest proportion of girls/young women is in the private higher educational institutions, with 37.6% including 20.4% in the Universities and 17.7% in the Public Higher Schools. The proportion in the institutions excluding MESRIT is 32%.

The first figures show clearly that female students are a minority in the post-baccalaureate educational system. Their significant presence in the private insitutions of higher education (BTS primarily) is related to the short vocational training that these institutions offer. Female students prefer these short courses on completion of which they are sure to find employment. They also represent a strong proportion of the s students enrolled in institutions outside MESRIT, which offer vocational training.

The under-representation of female students in the scientific and technological fields as well as the teacher training fields is striking, as shown in table 6.

In the schools with science courses which do not depend on the Ministry of Higher Education, the distribution of female students in 1997-1998 as indicated in table 7 reveals extremely variable proportions depending on the institution.

Table 6: Representation of Female Students in the Fields (year 1997-1998)

Universities	Female students	Total	% Female students
UFR Science of the University of Cocody	472	5024	9%
University of Abobo-Adjamé + URES of Daloa	703	3945	15%
UFR Odonto-Stomatology	108	253	30%
UFR Medical Sciences	1018	345	23%
Pharmaceutical URF Sciences	390	863	29%

Higher Schools	Female students	Total	% female students
Higher school of Agronomy (INP-HB)	72	514	12%
Higher school of Industry (INP-HB)	53	677	7.8%
Higher school of Public works (INP-HB)	31	369	7.8%
Higher school of Mines and Geology (INP-HB)	25	379	6.5%
National school of Statistics and Applied Economics (ENSEA)	8	182	4.7%

Teacher Training Schools	Female students	Total	% female students
Higher teacher training school (ENS)	153	1787	8.6%
National Teaching Institute of Technical and Professional Teachers (IPNETP)	86	367	19%

Table 7: Number of Female Students in the Other Instituions in 1997-1998

Other Structures	Female Students	Total Number	Proprotion
Regional Academy of Marine Sciences and Tecnology (ARSTM) * Higher school of Navigation * Higher school of the Maritime transport	1 29	126 110	0.8% 26.4%
African Higher institute of Electricity (ESIE)	3	33	9.1%
African Higher institute of Posts and Telecommunications (ISAPT)	2	47	4.3%
Center of Electronics and Applied Data processing (CELIA)	20	260	7.7%
Center of Electricity Trades (CME)	0	20	0%

At the universities, the scientific UFR of the University of Cocody records the lowest proportion of female students (9%). It should be stressed that these UFRs offer academic scientific courses. Such low rates of representation of women in these units of the universities have important implications with regard to the limited participation of the female population in the production of knowledge in the scientific field.

On the other hand, female students are increasingly more numerous in the UFRs relating to health sciences where the education is professional

In the schools having more than one hundred (100) pupils, it is noticeable that the lowest rates of female students are concentrated at the National School of Statistics and Applied Economics (4.7%) and at the Higher School of Navigation (0.8%).

At the Regional Academy of the Marine Science, in comparison with the Higher School of Maritime Transport that counts 29% of female students, the 0.8% representation of female students at the Higher School of Navigation is undoubtedly explained by future terms of employment (training courses of long duration at sea). Elsewhere, in the other Public Higher Schools, the rate of female students is 8% on average, except for the Higher School of Agronomy where it reaches 12%.

From the statistical distributions, the weak attraction of female students for hard sciences is obvious. The ffemale students are attracted to the natural sciences and especially to the health sciences where they represent is the most significant proportion, with up to 30%.

The interest for health sciences lies in the fact that these are professional fields leading to direct employment and the liberal professions; the latter in addition are lucrative and allow women to balance family life and professional careers.

The low representation of female students is quite striking in the two Higher Schools of Teacher Training (including all institutions). These are the Higher Teacher Training School for General Teaching (8.6% female students) and the National Teaching Institute of Technical and Professional Teaching (19%). A measure is being considered to sensitize female students so that they can become interested in acquiring teaching skills at the higher level.

Table 8: Number of female students population in the private higher educational system (year 1997 - 1998)

Specialties of BTS (industrial fields)	Female students	Total	% female students
Chemistry quality control option	117	649	18%
Industrial and food chemistry	13	68	19.1%
Electronics	114	1207	9.4%
Electrical engineering	109	829	13.1%
Cold and air-conditioning	0	5	0%
Thermal genius	1	53	1.9%
Industrial data processing	7	83	8.4%
Industrial data processing and maintenance	295	2748	10.7%
Data-processing maintenance	11	210	5.2%
Maintenance of the systems of production	61	525	11.6%

The highest rate of females is observed in the chemistry field, which is remarkable. .

The Growth of Students in Scientific Educational Structures

Our study in based on an investigation covering approximately eighteen (18) years.

The Universities

Based on figure 2 and tables 10, to 13 in the appendix, it can be observed that the percentage of female students in the scientific UFR (Mathematics, Physics, Chemistry, and Biological sciences: 10% on average) has been practically constant over eighteen (18) years and remain relatively low.

In the UFR Medical Sciences the average is 21.8%, in the Pharmaceutical UFR Sciences the average is 31.7%, while in the Odontotology UFR, the average is 33%. The latter (high enough for a relatively recent field), is linked to the insufficient number of dental practices.

It should however be noted that the year 1992-1993 corresponds to an appalling decrease in the strength of female studentss in all the fields (scientific Medicine, Pharmacy, Odonto-Stomatology and Science fields). Moreover, since that year, a decreasing number of female students in Pharmacy is noticeable. As previously indicated, these were the years of economic crisis and programs of structural adjustment. These factors did not encourage schooling at the lower level because of enrollment fees. Neither did it encourage schooling at the higher level because of the limited prospects for employment after school.

The more recently created University of Abobo-Adjamé offers courses in natural sciences and has an average of 15.6% femeale students enrolled over five (5) years (figure 3).

The Public Higher Schools

Over eighteen (18) years, the enrollment of the ESA (resulting from the fusion of ENSA and IAB), which trains engineers and high-level technicians in agronomy, has an average representation of female students of 12%. The corresponding figure is 3% at the Higher School of Public works (ENSTP and current ESTP).

The Higher National Institute of Technical Teaching (INSET) has registered a significant growth since 1988-1989, reaching an average of 29.4%. But this average is not significant since it includes students in the tertiary sector programs.

The numbers of female students in the science fields at the Higher Teacher Training School do not vary much. Women who are training to teach Mathematics, Physics and Chemistry account for an average 5.8% of the student, which is three times less than at the IPNETP which trains teachers of technical courses, and where females account for 17.3% of of the enrollment.

The very low rate of women teaching sciences can be explained by an insufficient sensitization of female students at the secondary level.

At the National School of Statistics and Applied Economics, the female students account for 5.24% of the total number, which is still negligible.

The very low rates in the public works and building trades can be explained by the prejudices which are disseminated by social values and by the prejudices conveyed with regard to this sector as reserved to men. The female population internalize these values, consciously or unconsciously, and adapt their behavior to these prejudices which guide their choices. These choices are also influenced by reservation toward the working conditions of this sector.

Participation of women in the development of science and technology

Women Teaching in the Universities

The study which is the basis of this article is interested in the representation of women in teaching of exact sciences as well as the health sciences. Having reviewed the statistical representation of female stduents in the fields of science at the higher educational level, it is important to show the representation of women who are members of the teaching staff and are, strictly speaking, teachers or researchers.

As figures 6, 7, and 8 show, in many years, there were no women professors in health sciences. Tables 22, 23, and 24 in the appendix, representing the size of teachers in the Medical field, Odontology and Pharmacy show that the rate remained at 0% during 12 years. In each of these fields, the highest number of women professors does not exceed five (5). The highest proportion of women teaching in these three fields is clustered at the rank of assistants in medical sciences.

It should be added that the rate of female teachers in the scientific UFR is weak with very little increase. Over an eighteen (18) year period, the average rate of assistants (9%), lecturers (7.5%), associate professors (10%) and professors (10%) remains weak. These figures reflect the weakness of the rates of female students in these fields and also the fact that higher education and research are considered and treated as fields reserved for men. Moreover, the careers of university teachers require time, availability and a lot of self-sacrifice. These two factors are inevitably not compatible with the life of wives and mothers for the young professional women of a procreative age.

Concerning the representation of women teaching in the large schools, no statistical data is available. However, on the basis of the representation of female students in the disciplines of these higher schools, there is little risk of error to suppose that they are very few.

Women in Scientific Research

In Côte d'Ivoire, at the higher education level, in addition to the body of teachers, there is a body of researchers, which is a profession parallel with that of teaching. The teachers do research and the researchers also take part in teaching; in the professional track for researchers, research is however, the prevalent field. Table 9 shows that there are very few women in scientific research, although they often have the necessary qualities for this activity: intuitive spirit, dexterity and patience, as Professor Eholié pointed out (see chapter 10 in this volume) and as noted by the authors of this study. The low representation of women in scientific research is related to the weakness of the number of female students in the scientific disciplines.

At the time when this study was undertaken, there was no woman director of research (the highest rank) in Côte d'Ivoire, and no woman who had reached the higher rank of "maître de recherche", the research track. There were eight (8) women research lecturers and fifteen (15) women research associates (the least rank).

Conclusion

The access of women to the scientific culture and scientific careers, their participation in the production and the transmission of scientific knowledge remains weak because of prejudices and constraints which are sociocultural (ambivalent attitude of the parents with regard to the field assignment and the schooling of the females), socio-economic (attitude of parents towards investing in the family), and institutional (general lack of motivation in teachers). The political good will has not made it possible to overcome these negative factors.

Côte d'Ivoire adhered to all the world declarations on education and wishes to achieve education for all. Toward that goal, it has adhered to the Convention of 1979 on "the Elimination of all forms of discrimination with regard to women" which was ratified in 1981 at the same time as 137 other countries.

This is expressed in the National Development Plan of the Education Sector (PNDEF) which covers all levels of education and training; it constitutes an operational framework for the implementation of key reforms in this sector during the 1998–2010 period. The actions envisaged by this plan includes among others, the development of a national scientific and technological culture: the school must be able, according to this plan, to develop in each person from Côte d'Ivoire and of Côte d'Ivoire a scientific and technological culture likely to propel industrial, economic and social changes; it plans also the promotion of an environment that is favorable to the access of the female population to schooling in general and to technological and scientific education. It also plans to increase the representation and partication of the female students in the fields of science and teacher training.

Furthermore, the PNDEF plan to design and the draftg a program for sensitizing and information and the adoption of particular incentives (special scholarships reserved for female students). In the field of education, the results of a change of policy take place in a long process and are visible often only in the long term. Thus, by the combination of all these measures, the results which are inclined toward an equal representation of students in the disciplines of study and of professional women in science will be visible in the first decades of the 21st century. These results will not only be beneficial to the girls and women whose right to education will have been respected, but they will also be a salutary puff of oxygen conveyed by qualified human resources putting their knowledge and skills at the service of national development to reabsorb the economic crisis and to reposition Côte d'Ivoire as a model of development in Africa.

List of Institutes and Research Structures

- CIRT: Ivorian Center for Technology Research
- CRAU: Center for Architecture and Town Planning Research
- CRE: Center for Environmental Research
- CRO: Center for Oceanologic Research
- GERME: Study Groups and Research in Electron Microscopy
- I_2T: Ivorian Society of Tropical Technology
- IDEFOR: Forests Institute
- IDESSA: Savannah Institute
- INSP: National Institute for Public Health
- IPCI: Pasteur Institute of Côte d'Ivoire
- IREN: Institute for Research on Renewable Energy
- IRMA: Institute of Mathematical Research
- SGL LAMTO: Station of Ecology and Geophysics of Lamto
- UAA: University of Abobo-Adjamé
- UBKE: University de Bouaké
- UNC: University de Cocody

Bibliography

Ajeyalemi, D., (1990). *Science and Technology Education in Africa: Focus on Seven Sub-Saharan Countries.* Lagos: University of Lagos Press.

Assié-Lumumba, N. T., 2004. Éducation des filles et des femmes en Afrique: Analyse conceptuelle et historique de l'inégalité entre les sexes. In Ayesha Imam, Amina Mama, et Fatou Sow, eds., Sexe, genre, et société: *Engendrer les sciences sociales africaines.* Dakar: CODESR1A et Paris: Karthala.

Assié-Lumumba, N. T., 1994). Demand, Access, and Equity Issues in African Higher Education: Past Policies, Current Practices, and Readiness for the 21st Century. Association of African Universities.

Assié-Lumumba, N. T., (1993). *L'Enseignement supérieur en Afrique francophone: évaluation du potentiel des universités classiques et des alternatives pour le développement.* Washington, D.C.: World Bank.

Beoku-Betts, J. A., (2000). Living in a Large Family Does Something For You: Influence of Family on the Achievement of African and Caribbean Women in Science. *Journal of Women and Minorities in Science and Engineering.* 6 (3), 191-206.

Bloch, M. N., J. A. Beoku-Betts, & B. R. Tabachnick, (1998). *Women and Education in Sub-Saharan Africa: Power, Opportunities, and Constraints.* Boulder, CO: Rienner Publishers.

Gibbons, M., (1998) *Higher Education Relevance in the 21st Century.* Paper prepared for the World Bank as part of its contribution to the UNESCO World Conference on Higher Education. Paris, (5-9 October 1998).

Houphouët-Boigny, D., & F. K. Mansilla, (1999). *Femme et éducation scientifique: cas de l'enseignement supérieur.* Ouagadougou: UNESCO.

Jacobs, J. A., (1996). Gender Inequality and Higher Education. *Annual Review of Sociology*, 22, 153-185.

Leigh-Doyle, S., (1991). Increasing Women's Participation in Technical Fields: A Pilot Project in Africa. *International Labour Review.* 130:427-44, no 4.

Makhubu, L. P., (1998). The Right to Higher Education and Equal Opportunity Particularly for Women: The Major Challenge of Our Time, *Higher Education in Africa: Achievements, Challenges and Prospects.* Dakar: UNESCO Regional Office for Education in Africa.

Mariro, A., (1998). (Ed.) Access of Girls and Women to Scientific, Technical and Vocational Education in Africa. UNESCO. Paris.

Miller, J.V., and L. Vetter, (1996). Vocational Guidance for Equal Access and Opportunity for Girls and Women in Technical and Vocational Education. Paris: UNESCO.

Mlama, P. M., (1998). Increasing Access and Equity in Higher Education: Gender Issues, *Higher Education in Africa: Achievements, Challenges and Prospects*. Dakar: UNESCO Regional Office for Education in Africa.

Namuddu, K., (1995). Gender Perspectives in the Transformation of Africa: Challenges to the African University as a Model to Society, *Women in Higher Education in Africa* (pp. 17–57). Dakar, Senegal: UNESCO.

Nare, Z. C., (1995). Being a Woman Intellectual in Africa: The Persistence of Sexist and Cultural Stereotypes, *Women in Higher Education in Africa* (pp. 1–11). Dakar, Senegal: UNESCO

Obanya, P., (1999). Rapport sur l'état de l'éducation en Afrique, les progrès réalisés dans l'éducation des filles et des femmes. Dakar, Sénégal: UNESCO-BREDA. p. 161

Pérez, S., (1995). Les femmes enseignantes dans l'enseignement technique et professionnel au Bénin, en Côte d'Ivoire, au Mali, au Sénégal: une étude comparative. Genève: Bureau international du Travail (BIT).

Subbarao, K., & et al., (1994). *Women in Higher Education: Progress, Constraints, and Promising Initiatives.* Includes enrollment patterns in various fields, and access to faculty and administrative positions, 1970-88; Africa, Middle East, and South Asia. Washington, D.C.: The World Bank.

UNESCO, (1999). Rapport sur l'état de l'éducation en Afrique: les progrès réalisés dans l'éducation des filles et des femmes. Dakar: UNESCO-BREDA.

UNESCO, (1996). Promotion of the Equal Access of Girls and Women to Technical and Vocational Education. Paris: UNESCO.

UNESCO, (1995). *Women in Higher Education in Africa.* Dakar: UNESCO Regional Office for Education in Africa (BREDA).

Woodhouse, H., and T. M. Ndongko, (1993). Women and Science Education in Cameroon: Some Critical Reflections. Interchange; 24 (1-2), 131-58.

Zymelman, M., (1990). Science, Education, and Development in Sub-Saharan Africa. Washington, D.C.: World Bank.

Annexes

Sources of information

- Plan National de Développement du secteur Éducation/Formation (PNDEF) 1998-2010
- Scolarité de l'Université de Cocody
- Scolarité de l'Université d'Abobo Adjamé
- Scolarité de l'École Normale Supérieure (ENS)
- Scolarité de l'Institut National Polytechnique Félix HOUPHOUËT-BOIGNY (INPHB)
- Scolarité de l'École Nationale de Statistiques et d'Économie Appliquée (ENSEA)
- Scolarité de l'Institut Pédagogique National pour l'Enseignement Technique et Professionnel (IPNETP)
- Annuaires Statistiques du Ministère de l'Enseignement Supérieur et de la Recherche Scientifique.

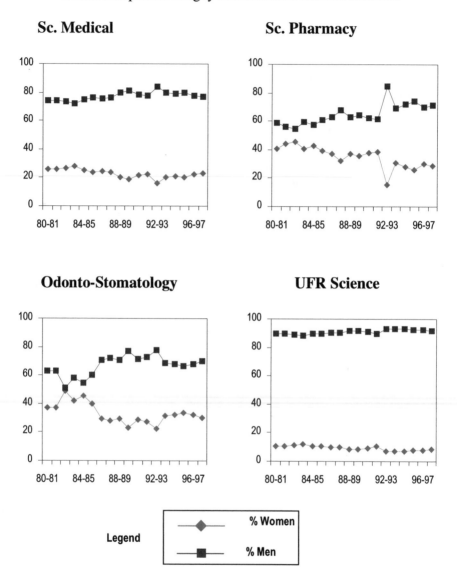

Figure 2: Size of Students by UFR

University of Abobo-Adjamé

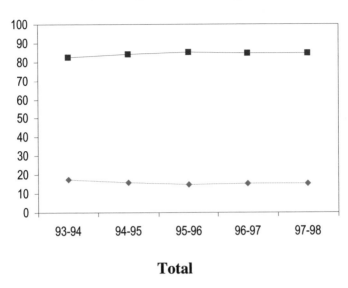

Total

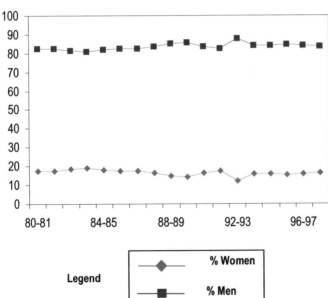

Figure 3: Size of Student Population University of Abobo-Adjamé

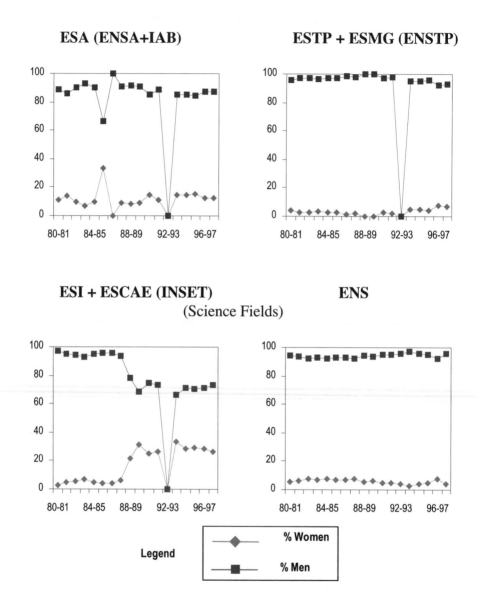

Figure 4: Size of Students Population of the Public Higher Schools

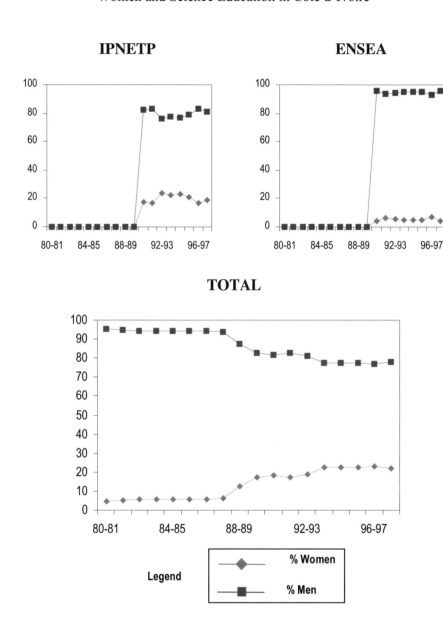

Figure 5: Size of the Students of the Public Higher Schools

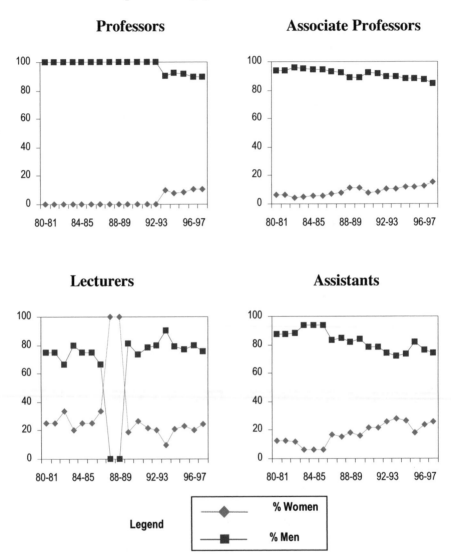

Figure 6: Size of Teachers (UFR Sc. Medical)

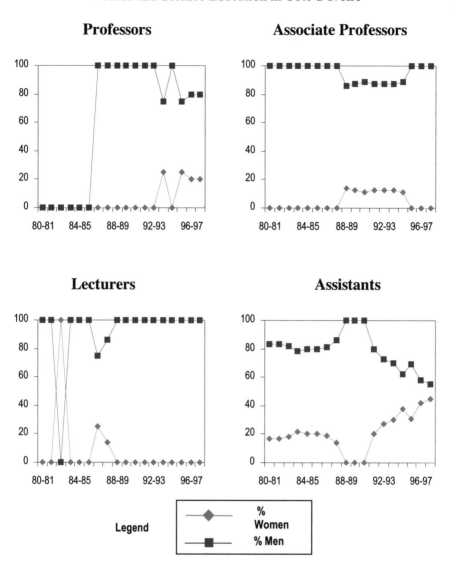

Figure 7: Size of Teachers (UFR Sc. Pharmacy)

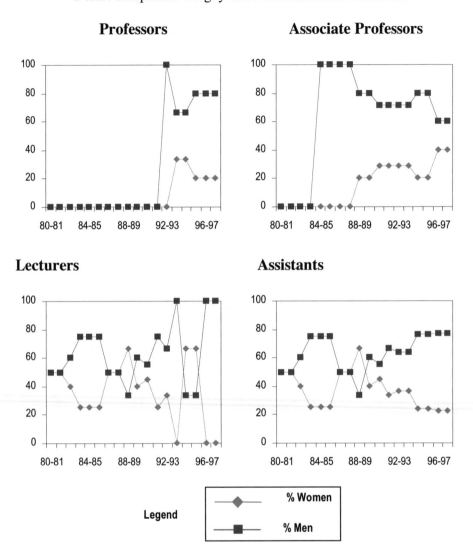

Figure 8: Size of teachers (UFR Odonto-Stomatology)

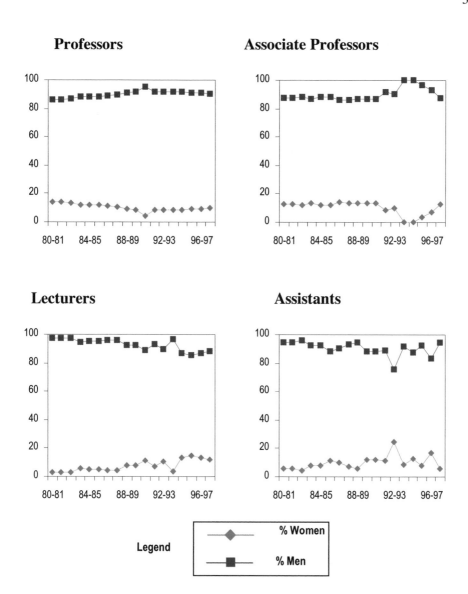

Figure 9: Size of Teachers (UFR Sciences)

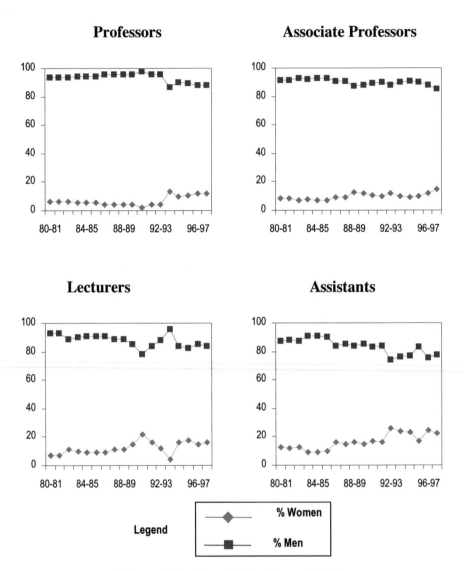

Figure 10: Size of Teachers (Total)

TABLE 9: SIZE OF RESEARCHERS BY FACILITY (YEAR 1998)

CENTER	RESEARCH DIRECTORS			RESEARCH PROFESSORS			RESEARCH LECTURERS			RESEARCH ASSOCIATES		
	W	M	%	W	M	%	W	M	%	W	M	%
CIRT					4	0		11	0	1	2	33
CRAU					1	0		6	0	2	1	67
CRE								1	0			
CRO					1	0		16	0	1	1	50
GERME										0	1	0
I2T										1	17	6
IDEFOR		3	0		4	0	2	31	6	1	17	6
IDESSA					2	0	1	27	4	5	15	25
INSP								2	0	3		100
IPCI							2	21	9			1
IREN											1	0
IRMA					1	0		5	0		2	0
LAMTO					0		2	5	29			
ORSTOM		1	0		2	0		4	0			
UAA					0		1	2	33	1		100
UBKE					1	0		3	0		1	0
UNC								1	0		7	0

TABLE 10: SIZE OF STUDENTS UFR
MEDICAL SCIENCES

YEAR	M	W	%
1980-1981	828	291	26
1981-1982	921	323	26
1982-1983	982	356	27
1983-1984	1042	403	28
1984-1985	1151	387	25
1985-1986	1173	367	24
1986-1987	1293	424	25
1987-1988	1539	478	24
1988-1989	1866	480	20
1989-1990	2270	532	19
1990-1991	2273	627	22
1991-1992	2651	772	23
1992-1993	3806	720	16
1993-1994	4336	1107	20
1994-1995	4167	1100	21
1995-1996	3641	928	20
1996-1997	3325	942	23
1997-1998	3425	1018	23

TABLE 11: SIZE OF STUDENTS UFR
PHARMACY

YEAR	M	W	%
1980-1981	52	36	41
1981-1982	55	43	44
1982-1983	56	47	46
1983-1984	70	48	41
1984-1985	84	62	42
1985-1986	96	62	39
1986-1987	114	68	37
1987-1988	163	77	32
1988-1989	209	122	37
1989-1990	287	159	36
1990-1991	346	208	38
1991-1992	482	298	38
1992-1993	1053	192	15
1993-1994	1015	445	30
1994-1995	996	384	28
1995-1996	1005	352	26
1996-1997	896	389	30
1997-1998	963	390	29

TABLE 12: SIZE OF STUDENTS UFR
ODONTO-STOMATOLOGY

YEAR	M	W	%
1980-1981	36	21	37
1981-1982	37	22	37
1982-1983	29	28	49
1983-1984	35	25	42
1984-1985	40	33	45
1985-1986	45	30	40
1986-1987	63	26	29
1987-1988	68	26	28
1988-1989	73	30	29
1989-1990	59	18	23
1990-1991	82	33	29
1991-1992	108	41	28
1992-1993	182	52	22
1993-1994	310	142	31
1994-1995	308	147	32
1995-1996	270	137	34
1996-1997	226	107	32
1997-1998	253	108	30

TABLE 13: SIZE OF STUDENTS UFR
SCIENCES

YEAR	M	W	%
1980-1981	1640	188	10
1981-1982	1736	199	10
1982-1983	1823	225	11
1983-1984	2005	265	12
1984-1985	2012	234	10
1985-1986	1965	235	11
1986-1987	2186	246	10
1987-1988	2693	293	10
1988-1989	3007	264	8
1989-1990	3563	322	8
1990-1991	3640	366	9
1991-1992	4093	462	10
1992-1993	4278	330	7
1993-1994	5764	435	7
1994-1995	5410	415	7
1995-1996	5173	424	8
1996-1997	5646	469	8
1997-1998	5024	472	9

TABLE 14: TOTAL STUDENT ENROLLEMENT IN THE UNIVERSITIES

YEAR	M	W	%
1980-1981	2556	536	17
1981-1982	2749	587	18
1982-1983	2890	656	18
1983-1984	3152	741	19
1984-1985	3287	716	18
1985-1986	3279	694	17
1986-1987	3656	764	17
1987-1988	4463	874	16
1988-1989	5155	896	15
1989-1990	6179	1031	14
1990-1991	6341	1234	16
1991-1992	7334	1573	18
1992-1993	9319	1294	12
1993-1994	15045	2887	16
1994-1995	14730	2786	16
1995-1996	13416	2427	15
1996-1997	13605	2559	16
1997-1998	13610	2691	17

TABLE 15: TOTAL STUDENT ENROLLMENT AT
UNIVERSITY OF ABOBO-ADJAMÉ (EXCEPT URES DALOA)

YEAR	M	W	%
1980-1981			
1981-1982			
1982-1983			
1983-1984			
1984-1985			
1985-1986			
1986-1987			
1987-1988			
1988-1989			
1989-1990			
1990-1991			
1991-1992			
1992-1993			
1993-1994	3620	758	17
1994-1995	3849	740	16
1995-1996	3327	586	15
1996-1997	3612	652	15
1997-1998	3945	703	15

TABLE 16: ESA STUDENT
ENROLLEMENT

YEAR	W	M	%
1980-1981	9	74	11
1981-1982	8	49	14
1982-1983	4	37	10
1983-1984	2	26	7
1984-1985	2	19	10
1985-1986	3	6	33
1986-1987	0	7	0
1987-1988	1	10	9
1988-1989	8	89	8
1989-1990	11	107	9
1990-1991	35	202	15
1991-1992	43	336	11
1992-1993			
1993-1994	86	492	15
1994-1995	69	400	15
1995-1996	80	450	15
1996-1997	73	501	13
1997-1998	72	514	12

TABLE 17: ESTP AND ESMG
STUDENT ENROLLMENT

YEAR	W	M	%
1980-1981	39	898	4
1981-1982	28	866	3
1982-1983	20	787	2
1983-1984	24	643	4
1984-1985	14	454	3
1985-1986	10	336	3
1986-1987	5	333	1
1987-1988	8	357	2
1988-1989	0	406	0
1989-1990	0	431	0
1990-1991	13	503	3
1991-1992	14	570	2
1992-1993			
1993-1994	39	721	5
1994-1995	35	723	5
1995-1996	34	770	4
1996-1997	60	714	8
1997-1998	56	748	7

TABLE 18: INSET STUDENT
ENROLLMENT

YEAR	W	M	%
1980-1981	7	242	3
1981-1982	15	293	5
1982-1983	21	335	6
1983-1984	26	359	7
1984-1985	18	368	5
1985-1986	21	474	4
1986-1987	28	593	5
1987-1988	42	640	6
1988-1989	288	1042	22
1989-1990	425	922	32
1990-1991	353	1054	25
1991-1992	382	1044	27
1992-1993			
1993-1994	468	922	34
1994-1995	409	1011	29
1995-1996	449	1076	29
1996-1997	442	1061	28
1997-1998	428	1167	27

TABLE 19: ENS STUDENT
ENROLLMENT

YEAR	W	M	%
1980-1981	44	775	5
1981-1982	64	981	6
1982-1983	74	854	8
1983-1984	77	1011	7
1984-1985	88	1107	7
1985-1986	104	1395	7
1986-1987	85	1081	7
1987-1988	89	1090	8
1988-1989	59	940	6
1989-1990	65	965	6
1990-1991	47	915	5
1991-1992	52	1056	5
1992-1993	32	782	4
1993-1994	15	499	3
1994-1995	13	290	4
1995-1996	21	410	5
1996-1997	18	206	8
1997-1998	6	132	4

Denise Houphouët-Boigny and Frederica Koblavi Mansilla

TABLE 20: IPNETP STUDENT ENROLLEMENT

YEAR	W	M	%
1980-1981			
1981-1982			
1982-1983			
1983-1984			
1984-1985			
1985-1986			
1986-1987			
1987-1988			
1988-1989			
1989-1990			
1990-1991	12	57	17
1991-1992	19	96	17
1992-1993	47	152	24
1993-1994	89	308	22
1994-1995	96	324	23
1995-1996	78	289	21
1996-1997	55	268	17
1997-1998	86	367	19

TABLE 21: ENSEA STUDENT ENROLLMENT

YEAR	W	M	%
1980-1981			
1981-1982			
1982-1983			
1983-1984			
1984-1985			
1985-1986			
1986-1987			
1987-1988			
1988-1989			
1989-1990			
1990-1991	7	150	4
1991-1992	10	150	6
1992-1993	8	139	5
1993-1994	8	150	5
1994-1995	9	168	5
1995-1996	11	203	5
1996-1997	15	207	7
1997-1998	8	182	4

TABLE 22: TOTAL STUDENT ENROLLMENT
IN ALL THE SCHOOLS

YEAR	W	M	%
1980-1981	99	1989	5
1981-1982	115	2189	5
1982-1983	119	2013	6
1983-1984	129	2039	6
1984-1985	122	1948	6
1985-1986	138	2211	6
1986-1987	118	2014	6
1987-1988	140	2097	6
1988-1989	355	2477	13
1989-1990	501	2425	17
1990-1991	610	2738	18
1991-1992	660	3112	17
1992-1993	218	942	19
1993-1994	847	2950	22
1994-1995	790	2757	22
1995-1996	865	3006	22
1996-1997	835	2765	23
1997-1998	830	2936	22

TABLE 23: TEACHING STAFF IN UFR OF MEDICAL SCIENCES

YEAR	PROFESSORS			ASSOCIATE PROFESSORS			LECTURERS			ASSISTANTS		
	W	M	%	W	M	%	W	M	%	W	M	%
1980-81	0	17	0	1	15	6	1	3	25	9	63	13
1981-82	0	17	0	1	15	6	1	3	25	9	64	12
1982-83	0	17	0	1	23	4	1	2	33	8	58	12
1983-84	0	19	0	1	20	5	1	4	20	6	87	6
1984-85	0	19	0	2	35	5	1	3	25	5	76	6
1985-86	0	19	0	2	35	5	1	3	25	5	76	6
1986-87	0	26	0	3	40	7	1	2	33	15	75	17
1987-88	0	25	0	3	37	8	2	0	100	19	102	16
1988-89	0	24	0	6	48	11	1	0	100	22	99	18
1989-90	0	23	0	6	48	11	22	93	19	3	16	16
1990-91	0	20	0	6	69	8	32	87	27	5	18	22
1991-92	0	21	0	6	66	8	28	102	22	5	18	22
1992-93	0	21	0	9	76	11	2	8	20	31	89	26
1993-94	2	19	10	9	76	11	1	9	10	36	94	28
1994-95	3	35	8	9	67	12	6	23	21	35	96	27
1995-96	3	34	8	9	67	12	9	30	23	22	101	18
1996-97	4	33	11	10	68	13	8	32	20	33	104	24
1997-98	4	33	11	10	56	15	14	44	24	30	85	26

TABLE 24: TEACHING STAFF IN UFR OF SCIENCES OF PHARMACY

YEAR	PROFESSORS			ASSOCIATE PROFESSORS			LECTURERS			ASSISTANTS		
	W	M	%	W	M	%	W	M	%	W	M	%
1980-81	0	0		0	3	0	0	1	0	1	5	17
1981-82	0	0		0	3	0	0	1	0	1	5	17
1982-83	0	0		0	3	0	1	0	100	2	9	18
1983-84	0	0		0	3	0	0	1	0	3	11	21
1984-85	0	0		0	3	0	0	2	0	3	12	20
1985-86	0	0		0	3	0	0	2	0	3	12	20
1986-87	0	2	0	0	1	0	1	3	25	3	13	19
1987-88	0	2	0	0	2	0	1	6	14	2	12	14
1988-89	0	2	0	1	6	14	0	4	0	0	3	0
1989-90	0	2	0	1	7	13	0	5	0	0	2	0
1990-91	0	2	0	1	8	11	0	4	0	0	3	0
1991-92	0	3	0	1	7	13	0	4	0	1	4	20
1992-93	0	3	0	1	7	13	0	2	0	3	8	27
1993-94	1	3	25	1	7	13	0	2	0	3	7	30
1994-95	0	5	0	1	8	11	0	2	0	6	10	38
1995-96	1	3	25	0	8	0	0	2	0	7	16	30
1996-97	1	4	20	0	8	0	0	2	0	10	14	42
1997-98	1	4	20	0	6	0	0	3	0	9	11	45

TABLE 25: TEACHING STAFF IN UFR OF ODONTO-STOMATOLOGY

YEAR	PROFESSORS			ASSOCIATE PROFESSORS			LECTURERS			ASSISTANTS		
	W	M	%	W	M	%	W	M	%	W	M	%
1980-81	0	0		0	0		1	1	50	1	1	50
1981-82	0	0		0	0		1	1	50	1	1	50
1982-83	0	0		0	0		2	3	40	2	3	40
1983-84	0	0		0	0		2	6	25	2	6	25
1984-85	0	0		0	2	0	2	6	25	2	6	25
1985-86	0	0		0	2	0	2	6	25	2	6	25
1986-87	0	0		0	2	0	1	1	50	1	1	50
1987-88	0	0		0	4	0	2	2	50	2	2	50
1988-89	0	0		1	4	20	2	1	67	2	1	67
1989-90	0	0		1	4	20	2	3	40	2	3	40
1990-91	0	0		2	5	29	4	5	44	4	5	44
1991-92	0	0		2	5	29	3	9	25	3	6	33
1992-93	0	2	0	2	5	29	1	2	33	4	7	36
1993-94	2	4	33	2	5	29	0	2	0	4	7	36
1994-95	2	4	33	1	4	20	2	1	67	4	13	24
1995-96	1	4	20	1	4	20	2	1	67	4	13	24
1996-97	1	4	20	2	3	40	0	2	0	5	17	23
1997-98	1	4	20	2	3	40	0	2	0	5	17	23

Denise Houphouët-Boigny and Frederica Koblavi Mansilla

TABLE 26: TEACHING STAFF IN UFR SCIENCES

YEAR	PROFESSORS			ASSOCIATE PROFESSORS			LECTURERS			ASSISTANTS		
	W	M	%	W	M	%	W	M	%	W	M	%
1980-81	2	12	14	2	14	13	1	37	3	1	16	6
1981-82	2	12	14	2	14	13	1	37	3	1	17	6
1982-83	2	13	13	2	15	12	1	35	3	1	22	4
1983-84	2	15	12	2	13	13	2	36	5	2	25	7
1984-85	2	15	12	2	15	12	2	41	5	2	23	8
1985-86	2	15	12	2	15	12	2	41	5	3	23	12
1986-87	2	16	11	3	18	14	2	46	4	3	27	10
1987-88	2	17	11	3	19	14	2	49	4	3	39	7
1988-89	2	20	9	3	20	13	5	58	8	2	32	6
1989-90	2	22	8	3	20	13	6	70	8	5	36	12
1990-91	1	21	5	3	20	13	7	57	11	8	58	12
1991-92	2	21	9	2	21	9	6	76	7	8	62	11
1992-93	2	21	9	2	18	10	9	76	11	12	37	24
1993-94	2	21	9	0	20	0	3	82	4	4	45	8
1994-95	2	22	8	0	32	0	14	89	14	8	55	13
1995-96	2	20	9	1	26	4	15	88	15	4	50	7
1996-97	2	20	9	2	26	7	13	83	14	8	39	17
1997-98	2	19	10	4	27	13	12	88	12	3	49	6

TABLE 27: TOTAL NUMBER OF TEACHING STAFF

YEAR	PROFESSORS			ASSOCIATE PROFESSORS			LECTURERS			ASSISTANTS		
	W	M	%	W	M	%	W	M	%	W	M	%
1980-1981	2	29	6	3	32	9	3	42	7	12	85	12
1981-1982	2	29	6	3	32	9	3	42	7	12	87	12
1982-1983	2	30	6	3	41	7	5	40	11	13	92	12
1983-1984	2	34	6	3	36	8	5	47	10	13	129	9
1984-1985	2	34	6	4	55	7	5	52	9	12	117	9
1985-1986	2	34	6	4	55	7	5	52	9	13	117	10
1986-1987	2	44	4	6	61	9	5	52	9	22	116	16
1987-1988	2	44	4	6	60	9	7	57	11	26	155	14
1988-1989	2	46	4	11	78	12	8	63	11	26	135	16
1989-1990	2	47	4	11	79	12	30	171	15	10	57	15
1990-1991	1	43	2	12	102	11	43	153	22	17	84	17
1991-1992	2	45	4	11	99	10	37	191	16	17	90	16
1992-1993	2	47	4	14	106	12	12	88	12	50	141	26
1993-1994	7	47	13	12	108	10	4	95	4	47	153	24
1994-1995	7	66	10	11	111	9	22	115	16	53	174	23
1995-1996	7	61	10	11	105	9	26	121	18	37	180	17
1996-1997	8	61	12	14	105	12	21	119	15	56	174	24
1997-1998	8	60	12	16	92	15	26	137	16	47	162	22

CHAPTER 13

LINKING BASIC EDUCATION TO HIGHER EDUCATION BY ADDRESSING GENDER, SEXUALITY AND HIV/AIDS IN EDUCATION: THE CASE OF EASTERN AND SOUTHERN AFRICA

Changu Mannathoko

Introduction

The HIV/AIDS pandemic in Eastern and Southern Africa is highlighting the vital importance of strengthening the linkages between higher education and basic education in order to address gender, sexuality and HIV/AIDS in education. Gender inequalities overlap with other cultural, social, economic and political modes of discrimination between women and men. The gender-based unequal power relations between women and men profoundly affect girls' and women's ability to protect themselves against HIV infection. In Southern Africa particularly, women face a greater risk of HIV infection than men because their lower socio-economic status and the patriarchal power relations compromise their capacity to protect themselves.

In this chapter it is argued that education is a complex system embedded in political, cultural and economic contexts. These dimensions are interdependent, influencing each other in ways that are sometimes unforeseeable. The power of a gender perspective in the analysis of HIV/AIDS in education is that it compels one to be comprehensive in analysis and go beyond education to identify the interfaces with political choices made by the state in the critical areas of health, nutrition, economic exploitation, finance, social welfare and local government. The issues of poverty reduction (or better yet, poverty eradication), gender-sensitive learning environments, life-skills education and research and development are used to illustrate how linkages between basic education and higher education in the arena of HIV/AIDS prevention and mitigation can contribute to the empowerment of girls and women.

Poverty Reduction

Countries throughout the region have poverty reduction strategy papers (P.R.S.P.s) which maintain that children's access to, and retention in, basic education may increase incomes by around 40 percent (Colclough 2003). Basic education has also been shown to have positive benefits in the following areas:

- Reduction in girls' and women's fertility rates and child mortality and morbidity
- Increase in women's and men's agricultural productivity and small enterprise development.
- Empowerment and participation of citizens and better governance.

With basic education people have a better chance of accessing social services and more opportunities to participate actively in realizing their human rights through voting and community involvement (Asian Development Bank 2003). Education is a human right because people with access to it are empowered to take more control of their lives and break the poverty cycle. Through education, disadvantaged and marginalised children and adults can break out of poverty and realise their political, economic and social rights.

In other words, the relationship between education and poverty reduction is evident because, other things being equal, educated people have higher income earning potential and have the potential to improve the quality of their lives. Governments throughout Sub-Saharan Africa acknowledge that poverty is both a cause and result of insufficient access to or completion of quality education. That is why quite a number of governments in Eastern and Southern Africa have put in place education policies that have created free basic education for all children (for example, Botswana, Kenya, Malawi, Namibia, Uganda, South Africa and Tanzania). Some of the actions that have proven fruitful in addressing access and the gender parity goal are in the areas of policy, safety and security, and community capacity development.

Box 1

Policy Changes to Increase Access and Financial Support to Primary Education

♦ **Malawi** has stopped requiring school uniforms in order to allow children from poor families to have access to schooling
♦ **Tanzania** launched free education for all in January 2002, and the number of girls and boys in school has increased. The Complementary Opportunity for Basic Education in Tanzania (COBET) and the Complementary Opportunity for Primary Education (COPE) in Uganda cater to girls out of school and over-aged children. The government of Tanzania is exploring ways to provide over-aged children with a three-year primary education programme whilst keeping the first-year primary school classrooms free for 6-8 year olds.
♦ **Uganda's** education policy allows free education for four children per family, of whom two must be girls.
♦ **Madagascar** is promoting parental involvement in schooling through the DINO project. The DINO contract between parents and schools in a community gives parents the responsibility of monitoring access and retention of children in school. This helps them to work together with the school to ensure that all children in that community attend school and those children that do not attend school are followed up. The provision and expansion of school feeding programs and take-home rations have immediate, positive impacts on enrolment and attendance. These programs can be the catalyst to define and introduce other complementary interventions (educational and infrastructure inputs, health, water and sanitation) required for ensuring the basic quality and sustainability of primary education.
♦ **Kenya** has created more access for girls by providing boarding facilities, as demonstrated by the joint UNESCO/UNICEF study on Nomadic Education in East Africa. In **Namibia** too, boarding facilities are proving to provide more access to schooling for girls from marginalized social groups.
♦ Eritrea promotes girls' education in part by involving and empowering parents and community members. PTA guidelines have been developed and many PTA committees established. Support for decentralization processes is provided through community capacity development and the strengthening of school, district, and provincial authorities in local analysis, planning, and management.

Kenya, Malawi, Tanzania and Uganda have rapidly increased access to primary education through several interventions, namely promoting policy development and implementation of basic education, targeting the most vulnerable children including orphans, girls and over-aged children, communicating and advocating effectively for girls' education and promoting community capacity development. Kenya, Madagascar and Namibia have successfully used the interventions of promoting community capacity development, focusing on adolescent girls and promoting policy development to accelerate girls' access to basic education. The following cases serve as illustrations of policy changes designed to increase access and financial support to primary education.

In Uganda and Tanzania, the success of the non-formal education programmes (COPE and COBET respectively) is evident in the large numbers of over-aged girls enrolled. That is why both governments are engaging their development partners such as the World Bank in discussions of how to scale up the initiatives.

Poverty is impacting most dramatically on the lives of children who are orphans and on families taking care of orphans. The most tragic result of HIV/AIDS is the explosion in the number of children orphaned by AIDS. In 1999, out of the 13.2 million children orphaned by AIDS globally, 12.1 million were living in Sub-Saharan Africa. The traditional African extended family system cannot cope adequately and if not supported may soon be unable to cope. Throughout the region many cities and towns are filling up with street children. These are children without shelter, food, education or clothing. Government sectors, NGOs, youth groups and community-based organisations need to be strengthened to collaborate with schools as care and support systems for orphans and other vulnerable children.

The government of Swaziland, in collaboration with UNICEF, has developed a bursary scheme for orphans in primary schools as explained below. This grant scheme is one of the few examples of programmes that address the impact of poverty on the education of girls and boys who are orphans. The scheme is a good illustration of the inter-linkages between child protection, HIV/AIDS and girls' education because it assists responsible adults to organise children's lives at home in ways that ensure that they can attend school regularly, arrive on time, and have time after school to complete their school homework assignments. Children as rights holders are made aware of their responsibilities to share the burdens of household work equally between boys and girls.

Box 2

The Swaziland E.F.A. Community Grants Scheme

The E.F.A. Community Grants scheme commenced in January 2003 and represents a direct intervention for poverty alleviation. Investments that relieve the burden of school fees on the poorest families allow those families to retain cash to use either for economically productive activities or on essential social services. Such enhanced retention of funds in a community has the potential to enhance the local economic "multiplier effects" of cash resources in that community.

UNICEF Swaziland, through the Government-UNICEF Community Action for Child Rights programme, has developed a Community Education for All Grant initiative. The purpose of the grants is to enable all primary-school-aged children, especially orphans, to go to school while still maintaining a strong sense of community responsibility to ensure the success of these children's education, and its relevance to the communities' own conditions and priorities. A central strategy of that cooperation seeks avenues to inject resources into the poorest communities, with a focus on directing those resources to the needs of children.

This example from Swaziland demonstrates that poverty is both a cause and effect of inadequate access to and completion of quality education. The majority of orphans drop out of school because of poverty, and this guarantees that they remain in the vicious circle of poverty. The income-earning potential of children is reduced, along with their capacity to improve the quality of their lives. The Swaziland programme recognises that eliminating poverty requires the provision of access to quality basic education.

That is why the benefits of access to basic education described above are in turn dependent on the quality of the basic education delivered. The components of quality basic education that have to be focused on to ensure the retention and achievement of girls and boys include curriculum content, learning processes, learning environments, teacher training and outcomes. In this context, a gender-sensitive learning environment is important for the protection, development and participation of children and adolescents, as will be seen below.

Gender-Sensitive Quality Learning Environments

The environments of the family, school, community and university can be studied to identify how they can protect learners in a gender-sensitive way.

Girls and women may find any or all of these learning environments unsafe and insecure.

Box 3

Child Abuse in and around School

Call on Men and Boys to Fight Against Child Abuse
The National Association of People Living with AIDS (Napwa) has called on all men and boys to join them in their campaign against the rape of children on World AIDS Day. (*Soweta*n, South Africa, Nov. 30, 2001)

93 Girls Shun Cut, Opt for Training
Ninety-three girls in Samburu have been trained on womanhood instead of undergoing circumcision. The girls, many of them in primary school, attended the one-week training at D.E.B. Maraial Primary. "[F]amilies have realised that female circumcision was outdated and a health hazard, especially the risk of HIV infection. Mrs. Moraa said many girls had died after undergoing circumcision." (*Daily Nation*, Kenya, August 8, 2001)

Abuse by Teachers
One girl said her primary school teacher had proposed to her when she was in Grade 6: "He told me that he loved me and I yelled at him. After that in class he tried to hit me, or send me out of the class for no apparent reason. The memory makes me cry every time I think about it." (Preliminary Investigation of the Abuse of Girls in Zimbabwe Junior Secondary Schools, DFID, Serial No.9, 2000: 65).

Research and information from the mass media, UN agencies, donors and NGOs expose the degree to which sexual abuse, rape, incest and other forms of violence are dominant in all these environments. As illustrated below, throughout the region child abuse in and around the school is a major problem.

The operational study UNICEF undertook on gender, sexuality and HIV/AIDS in education in 2001-2002 confirmed that sexual harassment was a major issue confronting girls and young women in all learning environments in the seven countries studied. It was striking how many girls (and a few boys) were keen to talk about their experiences of sexual harassment to our interviewees, sharing information that they were unable to divulge to teachers and other adults. This implies that the interviewers were developing the sort of friendly, young person-centred relations with them that enabled them to talk openly about these concerns. Pupils are much more likely to voice these concerns to teachers who are learner-centred and gender-sensitive than to those who are authoritarian and judgmental. The interviewees commonly reported incidences of sexual harassment in schools by both boys and male teachers against girls. This presumably contributed to the difficulties young people had in complaining about sexual harassment, at least in the presence of male teachers. Indeed, some of our interviewees expressed cynicism about male teachers who discouraged girls from having sexual relations with boys while they "proposed" to girls.

Examples of sexual harassment as captured in interviews include the following cases of Zambian girls in their late teens:

> Kelita: They [the male teachers] discourage us. When they do find you with a boy, they tell you to stop but they are also interested in you. Here at school some teachers propose and when you don't respond positively, they stop talking to you so even if they discourage us it is not with him. Charity: Some teachers even give exam papers [leakage] to finalists; even mock exam papers may be involved.
>
> Interviewer: What would you do if you were faced with such a situation?
>
> Catherine: Just receive the paper and run away. What is important is not to allow him to have access to your body.
>
> Interviewer: What is not good about receiving leakage papers?
>
> Namangolwa: The teachers want something and then they only give to girls. It is better to write only what you know in exams otherwise you become addicted to leakages.

However, it is important that male teachers not feel excluded from becoming HIV/AIDS life-skills educators because of the fear of not being taken seriously. For men teaching about HIV/AIDS, life-skills education can give them the opportunity to act as important role models for boys and demonstrate that it is possible for males to be responsible, caring, sensitive, approachable, non-authoritarian, non-aggressive and pupil-centred. It is important, too, not to assume that sexual desire is mainly male and that heterosexual relations inevitably entail males harassing females. Indeed, in HIV/AIDS life-skills education, what is required is greater equality in sexual relations between males and females, for girls to be able to express their sexual desires more openly. Many believe that this would make girls less vulnerable to forms of sexual abuse. Precisely because girls are not supposed to express sexual desire in the same way that boys do, they are left open to the accusation that, even if they report sexual harassment, they actually "encouraged" the advances or "sent a signal."

The following cases of girls in Botswana aged 16 and above constitute another set of examples of sexual harassment revealed in interviews:

> Girl 5: Yesterday something happened. There was this girl in class whom some boys were touching and she kept on hitting them with books and telling them to stop; and then all of a sudden she started crying, as if something, part of her had been taken away.
>
> Interviewer: Do they report it to anybody?
>
> Girl 6: Some teachers don't take it serious [sic], teachers think we encourage it; we sent a signal.
>
> Girl 2: At one time some people in my class were harassing me though not sexually; I reported it to my guidance and counselling teacher, and she told me that I thought too much of myself, and it never stopped.
>
> Girl 5: At one time a boy kissed me on the cheek and I didn't like it, it felt so wrong and painful, and I thought of reporting but I felt teachers will think that I was joking or I wanted it to happen.

It is not just fear that they may be disbelieved that can make girls reluctant to report an incident, but also fear that they may be seen as "bad" girls for speaking openly about sex in this way. Usually fondling or touching private parts is spoken of as something that boys as well as male teachers do to girls, and not vice versa. While most boys interviewed said that they enjoyed being touched by girls, others like the one in the extract below who did not, felt too embarrassed to report this to teachers or parents. This was presumably not because he would be seen as 'bad' and promiscuous like the girls who reported sexual harassment, but rather because of the assumption that, as a supposedly macho young man with a powerful heterosexual drive, he would be laughed at and ridiculed for presenting himself as the victim of sexual harassment.

> Botswana boy aged 16:
> Some girls demand to touch us. For example, at one time a girl came to me and told me that she wanted to touch me there (pointing at his private parts). I just left her, but I felt disturbed the whole day; I didn't tell anyone. However, for boys to do this they think about it before because girls will report it but boys won't.

While HIV/AIDS life-skills teachers need to take a strong stand against sexual harassment, they must do so without taking the side of girls against boys and presenting boys as the enemy. Doing this risks alienating the boys from the teacher, as well as from girls (Redman 1996) and may result in them becoming more macho as they try to re-assert themselves in relation to girls. A much better strategy would be to focus on the benefits for both boys and girls of developing more equal relations between boys and girls (sexual and non-sexual). For example, there are the benefits to boys of not always being expected to take the sexual initiative and of knowing for sure whether particular girls like them. While sexual harassment must not be tolerated in schools, it is important that the schools' response to this consists not simply in punishing boys, but in exploring with boys and girls in HIV/AIDS life-skills classes what sexual harassment is, why it takes place, whether boys and girls have similar desires, why girls get blamed and boys do not for being seen as too sexual and so on. Here the aim of HIV/AIDS life-skills education must be to empower and enable boys and girls to negotiate sexual relations with each other, whether this means resisting, delaying, or entering into sexual relations and whether sexual relations mean kissing, cuddling, being close, or having penetrative sex. It must not reinforce the stereotype of girls as weak, fragile, and passive, by having teachers present them as in need of protection from active, strong, and sexually predatory boys.

First, the school has to be accessible to girls through a safe journey of a reasonable length. The school grounds, classrooms and corridors have to be places where girls feel physically safe and psychologically at ease. There must be separate, well-maintained and equipped latrine facilities for girls. If physical education is offered there should be changing facilities that are private and clean.

Classrooms have to be places in which girls feel respected and listened to, where their voices and their opinions are heard as loudly and as often as those of boys, and where their participation in all activities is highly valued. The provision of boarding facilities may be required in order to allow girls in remote and sparsely populated areas to attend school. A hostel may provide a girl with time, space, and resources for homework, and with time to interact with friends that she might otherwise be denied. However, attention also has to be given to ensure that the facilities are safe, comfortable, and conducive to learning and have adequate food and supervision.

Year after year, situation analysis and studies of girls' education in Eastern and Southern Africa show that girls are less likely to benefit from quality basic education than boys. Many may not even enter school, but those that do are in no way guaranteed quality-learning environments (UNICEF ESARO Yearly Technical Reports for 2001 and 2002). In countries like Malawi, Zambia and Swaziland, where the HIV/AIDS prevalence rates are very high among adolescents, some girls are undernourished, physically weakened from exposure to HIV/AIDS or other diseases, and psychologically alienated by situations of violence and conflict. Learning under the above conditions is difficult at best, and even more so when uncomfortable, male-dominated classrooms, irrelevant, and outdated curricula that portray girls and women in subservient roles, and policies that unfairly discriminate against them are added to the mix. Such a situation hardly represents quality, and it undermines girls' rights in multiple domains. HIV/AIDS and rising numbers of orphans in countries impact on the quality of learning for children, particularly girls. In all learning environments, including schools, girls are confronted with responsibilities and prejudices that take them away from learning—for instance, they may be care givers, they may be abused, and they face both stigmas and gender stereotyping.

Given the impact of the HIV/AIDS pandemic in countries throughout the region, it is justifiable that the girls' education programme has a strong component dealing with gender and HIV/AIDS. This linkage focuses on gender and sexuality issues and the empowerment of girls through HIV/AIDS and life-skills education. The girls' education initiatives already give high priority to the safety and security of girls by supporting interventions that:

- protect girls from abuse as they travel to and from school daily as well as in school;

- work with social workers and counsellors to deal with cases of child abuse, rape, and violence within families, schools, and the community;

- provide scholarships for girls from poor families in order to release them from domestic labour to attend school;

- develop school-based psycho-social guidance and counselling services; and

- link basic education to income capacity development activities for widows, orphans and adolescents heading households.

The figures in the graph below on retention rates in ESAR countries demonstrate that at both the first and the final grades of primary schooling, girls drop out of school at higher rates than boys. This is the result of hindrances of various sources.

Quality basic education programmes are succeeding in those countries that have a comprehensive education system that takes into account the inter-connected rights and principles that are prerequisites for quality education.

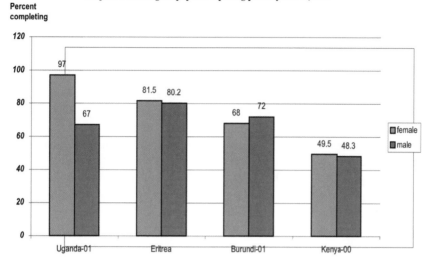

Graph 1. Percentage of pupils completing primary school, LYA

Source: ESAR YTR report, 2001

In these countries, child-friendly schools have a multi-faceted approach to education that demands macro-level policy changes from governments and education authorities, plus micro-level changes from families, schools and communities. Addressing quality in education for girls is a vehicle for promoting quality education for all and for achieving quality learning outcomes for boys and girls alike.

It is also important to recognise that this vision of quality education for girls is not limited to the formal school system: the provision of complementary schooling is a very important means of providing first and second chance opportunities to girls who would otherwise be excluded. This can enable teenage mothers and girls who need to work during regular school hours to attend school.

Under such conditions, girls are able to play and enjoy their childhood, free from sexual exploitation, harassment and violent abuse. They have supportive families and/or care givers, who believe in them and their right to education, who value learning and are involved as much as possible in the school and in decision-making processes regarding girls' education. In quality learning environments, girls feel confident and empowered to participate actively in the school, to make responsible decisions about their own future, and to play an important role in their family, community, and society throughout their life cycle.

As young girl learners grow to adolescence they have different needs at different times. Adolescent girls are particularly vulnerable and it is important that they be physically and psychologically comfortable attending school. They must have protection against the pervasive gender stereotyping and discriminatory attitudes that challenge their right to attend school, especially beyond primary school. They must have protection against exploitation by male students and/or teachers and access to information to protect themselves against early pregnancy and HIV infection.

The policy environment of a school is also significant for girls. There must be consistently implemented policies against discrimination, harassment and abuse by pupils or by members of staff. These policies should be in place to ensure that if girls do become pregnant they can continue their education without stigma, discrimination or adverse effects. Equally important is the right to education for girls and boys affected or infected by HIV/AIDS or participating in community or home-based care activities for others affected by HIV/AIDS. Comprehensive and well-implemented gender and education policies not only draw attention to discriminatory practices but also provide recourse against them.

Quality learning environments for girls depend both on the physical elements of a school and on the policies and practices that prevail within it. School must be a place in which attention is given to fulfilling all girls' rights and where girls are assured access to information, protection, and support, and in some instances to services such as meals and healthcare.

On another level, women learning in African universities are also confronted with issues of safety and security in their everyday lives as students:

- The accommodations they have to stay in are insecure; time and again women students are abused, raped and physically assaulted in these universities. Cases have been documented in some universities in Botswana, Kenya, South Africa, Tanzania and Uganda.
- The pregnancy rate among women students in some universities is very high and the majority of these pregnant women are single. A significant number are HIV positive, and the universities have to deal with the issue of preventing mother to child transmission of HIV/AIDS. Should these pregnant women be given drugs that will protect the baby from being infected? Who will pay for the drugs and the counselling that has to go with them?
- The above factors in turn impact on the quality of learning that women can get from the universities, especially because at times their academic performance is affected by gender-insensitive pedagogy and prejudices on the part of professors.

Women teachers and head teachers who are well respected and whose gender needs are well met can be inspirational role models for female students. With relevant training, support and professional recognition, women teachers can also provide information, guidance and advice for girls on subjects such as sexuality and reproductive health. They may also conduct girls-only science and mathematics classes to promote the active participation of girls in these traditionally male-dominated subjects.

At the University of Botswana the Education, Democracy and Development Initiative project is funding a programme on Women in Science and Technology. The aim of this project is to encourage girls to participate in science- based programmes at schools and universities and sensitise parents to encourage their daughters to study science subjects in schools in order to prepare for science careers.

> Recent statistics from the University of Botswana indicate an overall enrolment of 52% in favour of men. While in some faculties there are more female students than male in the Faculty of Science and the Faculty of Engineering and Technology, the female enrolments are 28% and 12% respectively. Thus there is need to address this problem from the earliest education levels. (Sisai Mpuchane, University of Botswana 2003)

Women scientists participating in this initiative are mentors for budding girl scientists. The initiative is ensuring that learning environments such as the school, the family and the university are developing into healthy, safe, protective and gender-sensitive learning forums that provide care, support, adequate resources and facilities for all children including girls. Above, this chapter has demonstrated and analysed how gender-sensitive learning environments are vital for the safety and security of children, particularly girls and orphans. At the same time, these learning environments have to be gender sensitive in order be consonant with the relevant curricula and life-skills education. The HIV/AIDS pandemic affects girls and women, boys and men at all levels of the education system. At all levels, poverty, cultural practices, gender-based violence, teenage pregnancy, orphans and life-skills education cannot be ignored. Linkages between basic education and higher education should give special focus to life skills and a relevant curriculum content in the fight against HIV/AIDS in the education sector.

Curriculum Content and Life-Skills Education

The HIV/AIDS pandemic has brought sharper focus on the urgency of linking basic education with higher education through improving the quality of curriculum content, including life skills. The curriculum development process, for both in-school and out-of-school education programmes, should be gender-responsive, rights-based and participatory. Ways must be found for involving young people and NGOs actively in the process of curriculum development. In 2001-2002 UNICEF joined forces with governments and young people from 12 countries in Eastern and Southern Africa to confront issues linked to gender, sexuality and HIV/AIDS in education. The twelve participating countries decided to undertake operational research on gender, sexuality and HIV/AIDS in education in seven of the participating countries. Regional research was undertaken in Botswana, Kenya, Rwanda, South Africa, Tanzania, Zambia and Zimbabwe. The regional study findings demonstrated that HIV/AIDS education was being taught as a series of moralistic injunctions against pre-marital sex. This manner of delivering HIV/AIDS education effectively silenced young people because they were made to feel that sex was a dirty word and they should not talk about it. Below are examples from the study of what school girls and school boys from Kenya said they learnt as part of HIV/AIDS education.

Lessons that Boys Learnt from School Teachers

- Girls can bring diseases to us (age 14)
- Not to have sex because of HIV/AIDS (age 13)
- Boys start looking for women and can be infected (anonymous)

Lessons that Boys Learnt from Parents and Grandparents

- Avoid sex with girls; it is shameful and can bring diseases (14 year-old)
- Sex is bad manners or habits; you should not have a girlfriend (15 year old)
- Do not choose girls who are sexy because they may have diseases (14 year old)

Girls said they received the following messages about girls from HIV/AIDS education in school and home

- Not to walk with the boys (age 16)
- Not to have sex because I may end up pregnant (age 15)
- My mother told me about menstruation and tells me about boys (age 16)
- Behave well and avoid evil things (age 16 , out of school)

The HIV/AIDS education these young people received was problematic because it emphasised avoiding sex without acknowledging that the majority of these young people were already sexually active. The curriculum took no cognizance of the fact that sexuality was highly significant in the lives of these young people. Throughout the study, in each of the seven countries, it was evident that sexuality was important in the way the young people were emotionally engaged when they spoke about heterosexual relationships and feelings. HIV/AIDS education was contributing to young people's worries concerning sex by representing their sexual desires, pleasures, and anxieties in a negative light. This explained why these young people were of the view that sexual desires and concerns were topics they did not wish to discuss with adults. It was evident that HIV/AIDS was not being taught within a life-skills framework that requires a learner-centered and rights-based approach.

Teachers in Botswana, Rwanda, Zimbabwe and Zambia admitted that they felt embarrassed and vulnerable in HIV/AIDS education lessons. In Botswana teachers spoke about the unease they felt as adults being addressed as sexual beings by children and adolescents in HIV/AIDS lessons.

Teacher 1 (male): They ask whether we teachers have been tested. They feel teachers are always talking about these things, while even they could be infected.

Teacher 2 (female): I remember one student wanted to know if I have ever used a female condom, and how it feels. I told them that I have never used it and that they should not become personal when we talk about these things.

Teacher 3 (male): I remember there was this child at one point when we were discussing abstinence and withdrawal who said that he knows from experience that withdrawal is impossible. And I was supposed to make a comment on that.

It is promising that the young people felt enough at ease with these teachers to ask them intimate questions related to the teachers' own experiences of sexuality. What is worrying about the above quotations is the teachers' embarrassment by the explicit talk from young people because their embarrassment may inhibit the young people from speaking openly about their sexuality, their desires, and sex in general.

Throughout the region, curriculum materials, publications and posters on HIV/AIDS, sex education, family life and life skills education have been analyzed for gender sensitivity, and the majority of the materials turn out not to be gender sensitive. These materials are silent on critical gender concerns including gender identity and power relations, gender and inter-generational issues, gender-based cultural practices, and gender, sexuality and HIV/AIDS (UNICEF 2002b).

UNICEF's experience in Eastern and Southern Africa has contributed to an emerging concept of life skills that encompasses the following four categories:

- ❑ **Inter-personal skills**, skills for learning to live with oneself and others. These include skills such as empathy, active listening, negotiation and conflict management, relationship building and community building. They require learning to recognise and respect the rights of others, and also developing an understanding of one's own rights and the way these are balanced by responsibilities. Communication skills are another important component of this category.

- ❑ **Skills for building self-awareness**. Here the focus is on skills for self-assessment, identification of personal strengths and weaknesses, values clarification, identification of rights and responsibilities and their implications for socially just action.

- ❑ **Critical and creative thinking skills**. These include analytical abilities, information-gathering skills, and skills for evaluating information. Learning how to access information and where to turn for support and intervention also falls under this head. Decision-making skills are critical thinking skills with a focus on problem solving and include skills for assessing personal risks and consequences.

- ❑ **Coping and stress management skills**. These are the skills needed for self-control, coping with peer pressure, managing time, tackling difficult situations, seeking help, and dealing with anxiety.

The life skills curriculum recognises the need to ensure that young people in schools are given a chance to develop their psycho-social life skills, and that they can translate their knowledge into practice. Life skills require a systematic curriculum that enables young people to develop the skills of self-assessment, assertiveness and negotiating capacity, that helps them cope with emotions and pressures (from peers, partners, traditions, etc.), and leads them to reflect upon difficult situations they might face, offering ways and means of confronting such situations successfully (Mabala 2003).

Successful HIV/AIDS prevention education for young people depends on at least three interlocking interventions:

❑ Increasing boys' and girls' knowledge and skills related to HIV/AIDS, ensuring that they know how to avoid infection, and changing their attitudes towards HIV/AIDS

❑ Creating environments (including physical, psychosocial and service delivery elements) in which girls and boys are allowed to exercise their knowledge, . be it in the family, the community or the school.

❑ Providing gender-sensitive support services (educational, health and social) that will support them in acquiring that knowledge and exercising choices and rights

Not only their individual values, knowledge and skills but also young people's outcomes are dependent on the environments they live in, and the social support and guidance they receive from adults in those environments as well as from their peers. Outcomes for young people are influenced as well by their access to services of adequate quality and the degree to which they are permitted to exploit that access.

Interventions for young people must therefore focus not on imposing choices on them, but rather on expanding the range of choices available to them, enhancing their capacity to make decisions, improving the orientation, depth and consistency of knowledge and skills in order to permit them to make choices that are ultimately in their own best interests. The importance of having materials that respond in approach and content to the differing needs and concerns of boys and girls has not been adequately recognised.

Research and Development of a Database

The issues described and analysed above also show how vital research is to addressing gender and HIV/AIDS in education. It is critical to link higher education concretely with basic education through strategic collaboration on HIV/AIDS issues; the examples provided below are based on social science surveys and studies:

• Undergraduate and graduate courses in universities and colleges train students to do research on gender, HIV/AIDS and basic education.
• Southern African Development Community (SADC) countries have set up regional courses on gender and development and one or two data bases on both quantitative and qualitative data.
• Universities provide technical expertise to governments, NGOs, youth organisations on HIV/AIDS-related matters including orphans, human rights, the disabled, and gender-based violence.

The cases presented below are a situation analysis of the girl child in South Africa from gender and human rights perspectives (1997-98), and they illustrate how higher education can effectively support the needs of basic education.

Box 4.
Situation Analysis of the Girl Child in South Africa: From Gender and Human Rights Perspectives (1997-98)

In 1997 the South African Ministry of Education with the support of UNICEF undertook a study of the situation of the girl child in South Africa. The provinces of Gauteng, Northwest, Free State and the North were selected for specific focus. Academics from the universities of the North, North West, Qwa Qwa and Venda were involved throughout the research project.

Throughout the study, these academics were provided with training on how to study children using a gender lens and from a gender perspective. The by-products of this study were:
• A booklet on the situation of the girl-child in South Africa. This booklet described and analysed the findings of the study.
• A booklet describing and analysing the gender methodology used throughout the study.
• A video on gender matters in the classroom, which was developed in the Northern Province. The video addressed the findings of the study, which identified school curriculum and pedagogy as gender insensitive. It identified the gender-based barriers and then demonstrated the positions and actions teachers were taking to address these barriers.

The findings of the study and the by-products that followed helped the government identify the areas that required attention in the various provinces. The study highlighted the powerful role of cultural practices, for example the way taboos linked to food impacted the basic needs of girls.

Cultural practices are an area that requires rigorous research to investigate the tension between traditional and modern practices and values. How can cultural practices such as early marriage and sexual liaisons between adult men and teenage girls be stopped? As a consequence of these cultural practices in Southern Africa, there are more HIV-positive young women than young men. The situation is further worsened by the sexual abuse and sexual harassment of girls and young women. Throughout the countries in the region, governments need to strengthen legal frameworks and policies that can effectively protect girls from sexual abuse by adult men in their families, their schools, and their communities. The University of Botswana began to address these issues in 1996 when it launched a regional course on Gender and Development in Southern Africa. The course explored ways to broaden the response to HIV/AIDS to include boys and young men, beginning with an acknowledgment that girls and young women are far more vulnerable than young boys and men to HIV/AIDS as shown below in Box 5.

One positive result of this course was the publication by UNICEF ESARO of a book of case studies written by students and academics who participated in this course (C. Mannathoko et al. 2001). The book brought home the point that the focus on HIV/AIDS and other gender and sexuality issues should be expanded to include men. It is men that drive the HIV/AIDS pandemic although women are more vulnerable to HIV.

Box 5.
Gender and Development in Southern Africa Course (1996-2002)

The University of Botswana launched the regional course on Gender and Development in 1996. The course targeted development workers, government officials, NGO leaders and academics from countries throughout Southern Africa. It was a six-week course that had five modules. The objectives of the course included introducing participants to gender and development and utilising their experiences on the ground to plan how they will mainstream and institutionalise gender in their own institutions.

A critical component of the course was the development of skills in writing case studies on gender and development rooted in the students' own experiences. The best case studies have been used in gender and development workshops throughout Eastern and Southern Africa because they tackle issues that confront women and children in everyday life. These case studies cover HIV/AIDS, cultural practices, socialisation and education, violence against girls and women, poverty, and power sharing.

In this region the HIV infection rate among teenage girls is five times the rate among teenage boys. Under no circumstances should resources be diverted from protecting young women from HIV. That is why it is strategic to look closely at how women, men, girls and boys interact in everyday life. There is a need to understand how the power relations between males and females manifest themselves in their lives in the villages, in families, between young lovers and out in the street.

However, teacher education does not adequately train teachers on issues of gender, sexuality and HIV/AIDS. At a professional level, teachers' professional challenges are linked to inadequate teacher education and training on HIV/AIDS and life-skills education. Teacher education in all the countries in the region needs to incorporate continuous high-quality gender-responsive life skills and rights-based approaches and content (especially for advocacy and action research). The personal challenges and conditions of service confronting women and men teachers, especially those related to the gender dimensions of HIV/AIDS need to be addressed. Deployment and transfers, substitute teaching, sickness, retirements and medical support are all issues that impact teachers. This also includes focusing on how gender identities influence teacher unions, codes of conduct and sexual misconduct.

Universities throughout the region can contribute productively to basic education by investigating critical questions such as the following: What are the interconnections between the family, school, community and university environments? Are these environments protective to both girls and boys? In which environments are girls exposed to violence and exploitation? How is this violence related to HIV infections among girls and women? These are the pertinent questions CEPARRED can work collaboratively with African higher education institutions to answer. Some universities are working rapidly to address some of these questions, but their work should not stop there; the universities need to go further and document and disseminate the research findings. It is also essential to document the lessons learned and to disseminate information about good practices.

Documentation and Dissemination of Lessons Learned and Good Practices

In the process of researching gender and HIV/AIDS in education it is important to focus not just on the problems but also on how the people in these communities address the problems. This is a way to accumulate information on good practices within the area of gender and HIV/AIDS.

All over Eastern and Southern Africa young people are developing exemplary organisations that focus on prevention of HIV/AIDS. Clearly, young people are the most affected by HIV/AIDS; they are also the key to defeating the pandemic. It is important to support their participation in collecting, documenting and disseminating the good practices in which they participate. This is a challenge for all governments, agencies and adults; it is important to collect information, document, and share information on good practices throughout the region.

An example of a good practice is the launching of the Girls Education Movement (GEM), which aims to promote Education for All (EFA) and link it to existing initiatives. In August (15-17 2001), President Yoweri Museveni of Uganda launched the African GEM in Kampala at a meeting of ministers of education from forty African Union (AU) member states. GEM focuses on galvanising action for the achievement of education for all in Africa.

> I am a Zambian boy aged 18 and still doing the secondary course which is Grade 11 the second highest grade in Zambia, at the school called the Kamwala high school. I feel very much concerned about ill treatment which is done to our African girls, that's why I've come to join the (GEM) to support the girls' future. I feel I can assist this girls' movement in terms of sensitizing or to be a good male adviser to the African girls. (G J.Chanda, Lusaka, Zambia, 2-11-01)

The GEM launch provided a forum to the African Ministers of Education for listening to the voices of the children of Africa in view of giving a greater push for girls' education. GEM ensures that the commitments made by the African heads of states (governments) at the U.N. Special Session on Children in New York in September 2001 reflect the aspirations and interests of the children, especially the girls, of the continent.

During its first two years the GEM agenda made strides in several countries throughout the region, especially in Botswana, Uganda, Tanzania and South Africa, where through implementation of various activities, girls participated in partnership with boys in advocating for girls' education. The examples below (Box 6) illustrate some of the GEM activities in Uganda and South Africa.

Because of its interactive nature, GEM is a non-hierarchical structure in which young people, and especially girls, take the lead in promoting quality education for girls, at community, district, national and international levels. As

---

Box 6: Progress on the Girls' Education Movement (GEM)

Uganda's GEM aims at galvanizing action for the achievement of EFA in Uganda and Africa through links with Global Movement for Children (UNGASS), UNAGEI and AGEI. Young people have used GEM as a forum for preparations of GEM launch and as a platform for sharing ideas and experiences and best practices, and taking action. A GEM desk has been set up at the Forum for African Women Educationalist (FAWE) Uganda chapter offices. In addition, a plan of action based on the GEM Agenda has been prepared and preparations are underway to set up an E-group as a way of facilitating networking in Uganda. GEM clubs and chapters have also been initiated in some schools in selected districts. A training and development programme was set in motion to enable Child Friendly Schools (CFS) to support girls' education through GEM in the Mbarara district, the Child Friendly Schools have GEM work plans as part of their own plans.

South Africa's GEM network aims at contributing to the development, participation, and protection of girls through a human rights approach. South Africa Girl Child Alliance (SAGCA) co-ordinates the activities of GEM in South Africa. After the initial launch in Africa, SAGCA launched GEM chapters in two provinces in South Africa where girls' education lags behind and HIV prevalence is much higher among girls than boys. In March 2003, the Minister for Education launched GEM-South Africa in Cape Town. GEM girls are mainly focusing on science, mathematics and technology (SMT), ICT and gender-based violence. SAGCA has done groundbreaking research on gender, sexuality, and HIV/AIDS in education in South Africa. Their focus was on provinces of KwaZulu Natal and Limpopo, where issues related to orphans, gender-based violence, HIV/AIDS, and inadequate life skills are major constraints on the education of girls.

---

a loose network, it seeks in particular to mobilise and empower girls to demand their rights to education from responsible adults, to articulate and advocate their vision for girls' education, and to be part of implementing that vision.

Box 7: The Sara Communications Initiative

The SCI materials are available in English, Swahili, French, Portuguese, and two African languages (Kinyarwanda, Kibaganda). The different story episodes of the materials produced are all based on extensive research in countries of the region.

In Kenya, Tanzania, Uganda and Zimbabwe these stories have also been serialised in national newspapers. Issues addressed include girls' access to education, discrimination in education, sexual harassment, sugar daddies, HIV/AIDS, child labour and especially domestic labour, teen pregnancy and FGM. Sara resources aim to communicate information regarding the survival, protection, and development of children, and especially adolescent girls, including specific messages on education, health, nutrition, and freedom from exploitation and abuse. They create awareness and advocate for the reduction of existing disparities in the status and treatment of girls; they also support social mobilisation processes designed to realise the potential of female children. Furthermore, the character of Sara provides a dynamic role model for active and assertive girls and, especially in her relationship with her boy friend, Juma, provides a model for improved gender relationships, beginning at an early age. Additional materials such as T-shirts, caps, and bags accompany the stories. UNICEF has promoted the use of Sara materials throughout the region, assisted by partners such as FAWE and other local organisations such as drop-in centres for adolescents, schools, and educational authorities. The Sara stories not only reach the girls and boys but also involve parents, teachers, and other responsible adults in the community in a process of reflection, analysis, and action on the issues that are raised.

Another example of innovative ways of utilising strategic communication and advocacy skills in championing the rights of the child to basic education and protection is evident in the Sara Communication Initiative (SCI), which is outlined in Box 7. The SCI is an innovative strategy developed in the ESAR using popular forms of media such as animated films, radio broadcasts and comic books to promote the children's rights and support their implementation and realisation with a special focus on adolescent female children. SCI is proving particularly effective in life skills education programmes for young people because it enables them to address and tackle the difficult issues of HIV/AIDS prevention, care, and support, and partnership building.

Conclusion

A comprehensive approach is required to strengthen the link between basic education and higher education where gender, sexuality and HIV/AIDS are concerned. No single or simple strategy will suffice. Schools, education systems, and higher education institutions need to develop relevant policies guaranteeing the right of HIV/AIDS-affected children to education, while prohibiting discrimination and harassment. Policies and programmes need to provide for life-skills education and create venues for needed health and nutrition services.

Thus all government sectors and society as a whole need to act urgently to provide support so that education systems can do both what they are supposed to do in their schools and classrooms, and what they need to do in their surrounding communities. There is a need to continue to find new ways and methods to include the voices of children and adolescents in the fight against HIV/AIDS as well as to strengthen strategies that are already in use such as GEM, Sara, peer-education and child-to-child. In all the dimensions of their educational and societal missions, higher education institutions can play a leading and supportive role towards winning the battle against HIV/AIDS, poverty and underdevelopment.

References

A Human Rights Approach to Poverty Reduction Strategies, 2002. Office of the High Commissioner for Human Rights (OHCHR).

Berge, N. E., 1998. *Fulfilment of the Convention on the Rights of the Child in Education: An Analysis and Case Study*. UNICEF.

"Call on Men and Boys to Fight Against Child Abuse," 2001. Johannesburg, South Africa: *Sowetan* November 30.

"Campaign Against Violence on Women," 2001. Gaborone, Botswana: *Mmegi Newspaper*, November 22-29.

"Child Abuse Alarms Medic," 2001. *Daily Nation Newspaper*, May 24. Nairobi, Kenya

Colclough, C., and S. Al-Sumarral 2003. *Achieving Schooling for All in Africa: Costs, Commitment and Gender.* Brighton: University of Sussex.

De Waal, A., and N. Argenti, 2002. *Young Africa: Realising the Rights of Children and Youth.*, Asmara: Africa World Press.

"Girl Child Education Problems Listed," 2001. Nairobi, Kenya: *Daily Nation Newspaper*, July 24.

"Half Females (First Year Students at UB) have Been 'Sexually Harassed.'" 2001. Botswana Gazette, Research Findings, November 21.

"How a Widow is Dealing with HIV Costs," 2001. Nairobi, Kenya: *Daily Nation*, May 17.

"ILO Wants Protection for Women, 2001." *Nairobi, Kenya: Daily Nation*, May 24.

Mabala, R., 2003. "The Inter-Linkages Between Girls' Education and HIV/AIDS in Emergencies." UNICEF Eastern and Southern South Africa Region Education Newsletter, September, 3 (1).

Mannathoko, C., B. Mazile, and M. Commeyras, eds., 2001. *Gender Tales from Africa: Voices of Children and Women against Discrimination.* Nairobi, Kenya: United Nations Children's Fund, Eastern and Southern Africa Regional Office.

Mlamlele, O., et al., 2001. "Opening Our Eyes: Addressing Gender Based Violence in South African Schools: A Module for Educators." Canada South Africa Management Programme.

"Pupil Raped By Teacher," 2001. Nairobi, Kenya: *Daily Nation*, July 23.

"Putting Things Right for Kids," 2001. Johannesburg, South Africa: *Sowetan,* November 30.

"Reaching Out, Reaching All," 2002. Proceeding of the ADEA Biennial Meeting, Association for the Development of Education in Africa.

"Save Girls From Cut," 2001. Nairobi, Kenya: *Daily Nation*, December 6.

"Teacher Arrested Over Affair With His Pupil," 2001. Nairobi, Kenya: *Sunday Nation*, July 22.

"Teacher Charged with Raping Pupil," 2001. Nairobi, Kenya: *Daily Nation*, July 4.

"2001 Law Targets Child Molesters," 2001. Nairobi, Kenya: *Daily Nation Newspaper*, July 5."U.N. Warns of AIDS Threat for Child Labourers," 2001. Nairobi, Kenya: *Daily Nation*, July 25.

UNICEF, 2000. "The Impact of HIV/AIDS on Education in Kenya and the Potential of Using Education in Widest Sense for the Prevention and

Control of HIV/AIDS." UNICEF Nairobi UNICEF Eastern and
Southern Africa Region Education Newsletter, April, 3 (1)

UNICEF, 2002a. "Gender, Sexuality and HIV/AIDS in Education." Nairobi,
Kenya: Eastern and Southern Africa Regional Synthesis Report.

UNICEF, 2002b. "Life Skills Education with a Focus on HIV/AIDS." Nairobi,
Kenya: Eastern and Southern Africa Region Education Newsletter.

"Warning Over School Safety," 2001. Nairobi, Kenya: *Daily Nation,* May 15.

"Women in Science Project," 2003. Gaborone, Botswana: Booklets and Video
on Botswana Women in Science, Education Democracy and
Development Initiative.

CHAPTER 14

WOMEN'S EMPLOYMENT AND WELL-BEING IN EAST AND SOUTH EAST ASIA: LESSONS FOR AFRICA?

Amiya Kumar Bagchi

Introduction

Women have been producers and providers for their families from time immemorial: in Sanskrit, a language whose literature goes back at least three thousand years, the word used to denote a daughter is duhita, the one who milks (the cow). In societies in which money had not become the principal medium of exchange and store of value, the special position of women as providers was often recognised even when they were subjugated to the authority of adult males. With the arrival and growth of capitalist production relations, women were subjected to a triple process of marginalization and devaluation of their labour: they lost many of their traditional occupations and were more rigidly confined to their homes; women's labour was more narrowly confined to niche occupations and those women who were compelled to sell their labour on the market found their earnings depressed for long periods; those women who were allowed to take up "men's" occupations were offered lower pay for the same work until laws against gender discrimination corrected this bias in some countries. But labour power directly and indirectly sold on the market has become the principal means of livelihood for the majority of men and women in almost all countries, and hence women's access to gainful employment and the terms of that employment have become matters of serious interest to scholars, activists and policy-makers in all continents, including Africa.

In addressing these issues, it has first to be pointed out that among developing countries, in several respects, the nations of Sub-Saharan Africa (SSA) have a better record in their treatment of women and girl children than North African lands, West Asian countries, the countries of South Asia, except Sri Lanka, and even South-East and East Asian regions except Japan. For a start, the ratios of women to men are higher in Sub-Saharan Africa than in all the other developing regions in the world (Sen 1999: 104-107). The only regions that do better in this respect are the developed market economies and some countries of the ex-Soviet bloc. It could be surmised that in the case of the former the contribution of the higher life expectancy of both women and men is the principal cause of their apparent superiority over Sub-Saharan Africa rather than any marked advantage in respect of an even-handed treatment of women in those societies. This would not be true of most of the other developing regions, including East and South East Asia (ESEA) because they enjoy better health facilities and often much higher life expectancies for both women and men than Sub-Saharan countries.

The second related aspect in which the SSA countries do better than ESEA or India is the nurturing of children. Families in India and countries or regions of East Asia such as the Republic of Korea, Taiwan, Hong Kong, and the People's Republic of China resort to female feticide on a large scale (Agnihotri 2000, Park and Cho 1995, Zeng Yi, Tu Ping and others 1993). Going by the record of those countries with no gross discrimination against the birth of girl children, it is thought normal that there should be 106 boys born for every 100 girls. This seems to be nature's protection for keeping a gender balance in view of the greater vulnerability of boys to childhood mortality. Findings, however, indicate that in Taiwan, South Korea, and China, more than 112 boys are born for every 100 girls, that the disparity increases for higher birth orders and that this disparity has increased substantially since 1980 (Park and Cho 1995).

It is suspected that births of girls are under-reported in the People's Republic of China because of the one-child family policy in a country with a long tradition of son-preference. Even after taking account of the bias generated by under-reporting, a distinct residue of sex selection which brings disadvantage to the birth of girls remains (Zeng Yi et al. 1993). There is also a positive association between the success of a country or a class in the battlefield of economic competition and the bias against the birth of girls. Agnihotri (2000) calls it the "prosperity effect." The phrase "competition effect" might be a better characterisation, in view of the revealed effect of the need to succeed in the unbridled competition of the market place. But that is a minor matter compared with the light it throws on the dark side of success in a grossly unequal world. So far, no evidence has appeared of a similar nature for SSA countries, but given the diffusion of facilities for prenatal sex selection, hopefully policy-makers in those nations are aware of the potential for their abuse.

A third area of gender relativity in which the SSA counties appear to possess an advantage over most other developing regions except ESEA is in women's participation in activities that are directly or indirectly remunerated in money (Mehra and Gammage 1999). In this respect, the ESEA countries are comparable. However, according to Mehra and Gammage (1999), the women's participation rate in SSA has been declining between 1970 and 1999, whereas in ESEA it has more or less remained constant. Measuring women's participation rate in gainful work is extremely problematic, mainly because much of women's work in producing household goods tends to be overlooked, and women workers are overwhelmingly concentrated in the informal sector (Elder and Lawrence 1999/2001, UN 2000: 122) for which few official agencies collect data on a regular basis. This tendency has been aggravated by the erosion of the formal sector under the neo-liberal policy stance of most Third World governments, beginning in the 1980s and becoming more pervasive and intrusive in the 1990s. Moreover, some of the estimated variations are mainly due to the change in the classification of women's occupations. For instance, the apparent jump in the measured involvement of women in gainful work in Bangladesh between the 1980s and 1990s is primarily due to a re-classification of women's employment, although women are getting involved in paid work outside the family in that country, as they are in most other poor lands of the world.

If the apparent decline in women's activity rate in recent years is not a statistical artefact, it can be attributed to several causes. One is the greater rate of enrolment of girls in schools and their relief from burdensome work at a younger age. Another could be the declining importance of labour-intensive agriculture, in which women were the main participants (see Boserup 1981 and Platteau 1990). Yet another reason could be that with economic distress becoming endemic, women have had to opt out of paid work outside the home and to go back to domestic production. A larger percentage of women are engaged in agriculture in SSA than in all other regions of the world (Mehra and Gammge 1999, figure 2).

A silver lining in women's involvement in agricultural production and especially food production (Platteau 1990) is that this practice does far better in preventing endemic malnutrition than its apparently low per capita income would indicate. Major countries of South Asia probably have a higher fraction of malnourished children and adults than many of the countries with lower incomes per head (Svedberg 1991, Svedberg 1999). Whether this record will survive in the face of the change in crop-mix enforced by neo-liberal regimes and the recrudescence of epidemic disease in several lands of SSA is yet to be seen.

Social and Political Bases of Economic Growth in East and South-East Asia[1]

The main lessons that African women and indeed all policy-makers interested in the future of all the people of the Third World, can learn from the experience of ESEA are related to their macroeconomic policies up to the beginning of the 1990s and to the social and political strategies that delivered record rates of economic growth and an improved standard of living in that part of the world (Bagchi 1987, Bagchi 1987a, Amsden 1989, Wade 1990, Khan 1998, G. Sen 2002).

The World Bank (1993) famously styled the growth performance of Japan, Taiwan (China), Hong Kong (China), the Republic of Korea, Indonesia, Singapore, Malaysia and Thailand as the "East Asian miracle." (The acronym ESEA will continue to be used to designate these eight countries or regions). In his introduction to *The East Asian Miracle*, Lewis Preston, President of the World Bank at the time, wrote a message intended for the ideal reader of the volume: "The authors conclude that rapid growth in each economy was primarily due to the application of a set of common, market-friendly economic policies, leading both to higher accumulation and better allocation of resources" (World Bank 1993: 91).

However, the authors of the World Bank book never asked how market-friendly economic policies are put in place and implemented. Nor did they spell out the reasons for the high rates of saving and investment that made the high rates of growth feasible. Practically all the economies in question had started out after World War II with agriculture employing a major fraction of the population, and Thailand and Indonesia continued to have the majority of their population engaged in agriculture even in 1980.

However, the section on "dynamic agricultural sectors" (World Bank 1993: 32-37) has not a word on land reform, and the index does not carry any such entry. Yet it was well known that it was land reform that had freed the peasants from feudal oppression in the People's Republic of China, South Korea and Taiwan, tapped the energy of the peasants for improving productivity and accessing markets, released manpower and other resources for non-agricultural production and led to the high rates of growth that were the focus of the World Bank study.

---

[1] This section draws on Bagchi 2002a.

The neglect of the essential requirements of social change continues to be a hallmark of the market-centred approaches to the study of developing economies. The World Bank has attempted to push the idea that a pro-peasant land redistribution can be effected purely by utilising the market without any amount of confiscation of the property of the landlords, who had almost invariably accumulated their property by using coercion and expropriating the original cultivators or forest-users. Once this concentration of property has been allowed to grow up, how can poor peasants with little collateral to offer compete with landowners who have every market: the credit market, the product market, and even the land market itself are biased in their favour (for a critique of the market-centred approach to land reform, see Bagchi 1982, chapter 6, and El-Ghonemy 2002).

Since the end of the apartheid regime in South Africa the new government, under World Bank persuasion and pressure, has been trying to implement a programme of restitution of land to the black majority that had been expropriated by the invading whites since the seventeenth century. However, the total number of beneficiaries of this restitution between 1994 and 2001 comes to 217,940 (Levin 2002: 168). When it is noted that the labour force dependent on agriculture in South Africa was nearly six million in 1990 (WDR 1996: 195), the pitiful nature of the market-centred approach to land reform becomes starkly clear.

This author would still argue, as he had in the 1980s (Bagchi 1982, chapter 6; Bagchi 1984, Bagchi 1987a, Bagchi 1987b, chapter 2. Bagchi 2002) that there are three basic requirements for any polity to emerge as a developmental entity. The first is the abolition of all non-market private power in the countryside (and by extension, in the urban areas). Non-market power can be exercised by individual landlords, landlords' lineages, upper caste groups, mine-lords, haciendas and plantation owners, politicians, military men, policemen, and bureaucrats in collusion with traditional power-holders. Communities and their leaders can also exercise non-market coercion. Non-market power is usually combined with the subjection of women to men's authority at home and outside. But in a situation in which the primary locus of non-market power is landlord control, pro-peasant land reforms accompanied by the attainment of universal literacy will go a long way towards freeing the energy of the peasants and mobilising resources, incentives and innovations for development.

It may be objected that in many developing countries, now, even without land reform, agriculture has ceased to employ the major part of the population, and landlords have often become absentees. In some cases, they do not even own the major fraction of cultivatable land. So how can the abolition of landlord domination figure in transforming such a society? It may well be that in most of these cases, landlord-peasant relations have been transformed into patron-client relations, and landlord or patron power is exercised through the state apparatus that acts in the interest of preserving that power, often by bending or violating the laws on the statute books.

The introduction of pro-peasant land reforms can not only free peasants to become subjects working for their own benefit, but it can also endow them with collateral with which they can negotiate a highly imperfect credit market. Such reforms can also improve the purchasing power of the poor and extend the domestic market and productivity at the same time.

The second social requirement for effective development, which has already been mentioned, is education, starting with the achievement of universal elementary education and then progressing towards the diffusion of secondary and tertiary education among wider and wider circles of the population. It has been suggested that "learning how to learn" should be a necessary accompaniment of education, and conventional education does not always deliver this (Bagchi 2000).

This said, it should additionally be argued that for "learning how to learn" to be a widely diffused goal, it has to be embedded in the consciousness of a people that can act as a collective—a form of consciousness very crudely and approximately captured by the word "nationalism." Learning how to learn is a particular imperative for the ruling class. In a geopolitical system in which all territories are organised in states endowed with a coercive apparatus meant for both offence and defence, it is critically important that rulers recognise the peculiar strengths of other states and their economic and social organisation and try to emulate them or surpass them through innovation.

Two of the most successful examples of such learning by rulers occurred in Europe and in Asia, in the two island nation-states of Britain and Japan. The rulers of England learned from the statecraft, economic policies and the manufacturing technologies of Italy, and in the seventeenth century they learned extensively from the military, naval, and civilian innovations of the Netherlands (Wilson 1968, Bagchi 2000). At a later stage, Japanese rulers, starting at the time of the Meiji Restoration, set in motion an extensive programme of "learning from the barbarians." Japan's rise to the position of the second industrial nation of the world in the post-1945 period is also based on learning from the USA and Europe, but of course the Japanese came up with their own innovations as they learned. The other countries of East Asia not only learned from Japan but also introduced programmes similar to the

Japanese policies of learning how to learn from foreigners, friendly or otherwise.

As in the case of learning how to learn, in other cases also a population group needs to be organised into an effective collective for absorbing new lessons and putting them into practice. "Nationalism" has been perhaps the major organising principle in all these cases.

There are at least three aspects of an effective collective, namely, collective assurance, collective insurance, and collective action that are relevant if any positive content can be projected into the idea of nationalism. As many social scientists have pointed out, in a very large number of situations individuals face some form of Prisoner's Dilemma, or what Sen (1967) styled as the Isolation Paradox. To take a particular case, if one knows that one's consuming a little less today will be matched by others in one's society or polity also consuming a little less, then one may be assured that aggregate saving will go up, and one is prepared to make the sacrifice; lacking such assurance, one may simply decide that one's consuming a little less will not matter at all, and that gluttons will take advantage of one's abstinence, and one will therefore not make the sacrifice.

The relevance of this kind of example can be seen clearly when one considers the wartime patriotism of the British, and the high rate of saving they managed to notch up during the Second World War, and contrast that with their pre-war or post-war record. There are other areas in which an agency enforcing co-operation can enhance welfare, productivity or growth, such as the control of urban congestion, the sequencing and determination of the scale of investment projects, and so on. Without co-ordination, the latter might become infructuous or unprofitable through none co-operation or strategic behaviour of the agents involved, et cetera.

The second function of an effective collective is to insure against certain common ills, namely, defence against external attack, sickness, unemployment, starvation, illiteracy, and impoverishment caused by ageing. Of course, states as collectives did not assume all the functions listed here until the coming of the welfare state or the socialist state. But it is surprising how many of these functions were performed by states or communities in the past -- although often in an incomplete or fragmentary manner. The edicts of Asoka, the Indian emperor ruling in the third century B.C.E., listed virtually all the functions mentioned. The Chinese evolved the concept of "ever normal granaries," which were supposed to ensure that, in good years and bad, prices of food-grains would remain stable and famines would be prevented. The eighteenth century Chinese imperial practice in this regard still compels our admiration (Davis 2001: 280-85). In Europe, the church and the monasteries performed many similar functions until these were taken over by the post-Reformation nation-states.

A third function of an effective collective is the ability to act in concert. This is most clearly seen in the sphere of military defence against external enemies, and—in spite of the attempt to privatise these services in the U.S.—in the function of preserving internal law and order that is entrusted to the police and the judiciary. As has been noted, this function is highly apparent in the kind of economic policy that Japan has pursued since the Meiji Restoration (for descriptions of the relevant policies, see (Morishima 1982, Johnson 1982, Yamamura and Yasuda 1987). As this author has argued elsewhere (Bagchi 2000), thorough land reforms and democratisation of Japanese society were required before Japan could really take off on a path of rapid economic growth. The political and social basis had to be laid before collective action could produce striking results in the domain of economic and human development.

In theory, any collective can perform the three functions sketched above. In practice, the nation-state has become the widest circle of "we" that is, the broadest collective of individuals that the modern world has produced so far. In view of the vast literature on the uses and abuses of nationalism, and on the idea of a collective body or community, it should be made clear that for this author an effective collective remains a voluntary association of free individuals. Although in many phases of history and many contexts governments have been able to override the interests of many individuals who have often been stereotyped into religious or ethnic groups or oppressed as the landless; in the long run, it is the willing co-operation of individuals and the abjuring of narrow self-interest in particular spheres that has made a collective body effective. The so-called ineffectiveness of democracies can be traced in many, if not most, cases to the abuse of the civil and substantive freedoms of individuals and groups. The fact that a democratic Britain was able to mobilise its resources for war far more effectively than Nazi Germany is a powerful illustration in support of this contention.

A second caveat that should be entered is that nationalism, even inclusive and egalitarian nationalism can easily turn into imperialism. But in most cases the roots of modern imperialism will be found in the self-interest of a fraction of the ruling class—financiers, industrialists, arms merchants—and politicians dependent on their patronage. These groups then can drag the whole ruling class into international conflicts and precipitate wars. In several phases of history, however, for at least some time, the ruling classes have been able to collaborate more or less as a super-imperialist cartel. Nevertheless, the very nature of inter-capitalist competition would ensure that such a cartel would eventually disintegrate. Thus the followers of both Lenin and Kautsky can claim to have some phases of history on their side. The fiscal soundness and high rates of saving in ESEA in the period of financial repression has led to some improvement in women's education and standard of living as compared to men's, but gender discrimination continues.

The social transformation in the countries of the East allowed the setting up of successful developmental states. The ruling classes of such states seek to raise the level of technology, promote economic growth, and elevate the military and political status of their country relative to other states—particularly relative to those states which they perceive as threats to their security—and they use various measures of state patronage and state intervention to advance their goals. In this sense England, Netherlands, USA, Germany, France and Japan have all been developmental states in the earlier parts of their careers as industrialised states (Bagchi 2000). In modern times, Brazil, India, Turkey and several other Third World states have sought to pursue similar developmental objectives. Without the social foundations and the effective nationalism needed to pursue those objectives, they can be regarded only as failed developmental states. In a society dominated by landlords or communities claiming powers of coercion over individuals as regard to their access to common property resources or other private and public goods, the capacity of the state is also fractured (cf. Migdal 1988).

Table 1. Current Account Balances of China (PRC), South Korea and Taiwan (US$ million)

	PRC	South Korea	Taiwan
1985	-11,417	-887	9,198
1986	-3,034	4,617	16,277
1987	300	9,854	17,999
1988	-3,802	14,161	10,177
1989	-4,317	5,056	11,384
1990	11,997	-1,745	10,769
1991	13,272	-8,291	12,015
1992	6,401	-3,939	8,154
1993	-11,609	1,016	6,714
1994	6,908	-3,855	6,154
1995	1,618	-8,250	5,006
1996	7,243	-23,061	

Source: Bagchi 1998, Table 5.

For the states to be able to act autonomously they must have control over their economic policy. This argument will be illustrated by taking the cases of the People's Republic of China (PRC), Taiwan and South Korea. The PRC followed the policy of total self-reliance as far as foreign aid or foreign loans are concerned. Even after it had decided more purposefully to engage in foreign trade and give freer play to market forces, it never allowed any large balance of payments deficits to emerge, and quickly eliminated any such deficits (Table 1).

Some of the apparent deficits of the PRC are really a statistical artefact, because some of the enterprises in the country were exporting capital and were bringing it back as foreign direct investment, because the latter received favourable treatment in respect of taxes and labour regulations. The PRC in fact built up massive foreign exchange reserves, exceeding US$ 150 billion by the middle of the 1990s. Taiwan was greatly dependent on the USA for economic and military aid in the 1950s, but after the Guomindang government realised that the US government would not back its attempt to re-conquer the mainland from the Communists, it tried to make itself independent of US aid. This was one of the chief motives driving its policy of expanding exports as much as possible. The government also intervened intensively by taking control of the banks, regulating the imports and exports by fixing tariff rates, imposing quantitative restrictions, and setting up government enterprises in areas in which the private sector was unwilling to venture or the government considered to be of strategic importance.

Table 2. Domestic Investment (I) and Saving (S) Rates of China, South Korea, and Taiwan, 1970, 1980 and 1994 (percentages of GDP)

	I	I	I	S	S	S
	1970	1980	1994	1970	1980	1994
PRC	28	35	42	29	35	44
South Korea	24	32	38	15	25	39
Taiwan	30	30	24	n. a.	33	29

Source: Khan 1998, Table 5.2.

The government also strictly controlled the inflow of foreign capital and the entry of foreign enterprises. By the end of the 1970s Taiwan had emerged as a major net investor abroad. This was, of course, made possible because its domestic rate of saving regularly exceeded its rate of domestic investment. Table 2 reproduces data on the rates of saving and investment of the PRC, South Korea, and Taiwan.

South Korea was more dependent on foreign aid or foreign loans than either Taiwan or China. But in its case also a surplus of domestic saving over investment emerged in the late 1980s. However, the current account, and more importantly, the overall balance of payments turned negative, partly because South Korea also began investing large amounts overseas and because Korean firms also began borrowing heavily abroad. South Korea became embroiled in the financial crisis of 1997 primarily because it permitted capital account convertibility from 1993, whereas neither China nor Taiwan has as yet permitted domestic firms to transfer funds abroad or foreigners to invest in the two states or lend money to their domestic firms in an unregulated fashion. Concentrating on the period up to 1997, it can be seen that as the rates of investment and saving rose in East Asia, so did rates of economic growth. This became the fastest growing region in the world.

The growth was supported not only by the expansion and upgrading of capital equipment but also by the improving standards of health and education of women, men, and children in the region. By 1997, the adult literacy rates for both women and men were above 95 per cent in both South Korea and Taiwan. For China, the adult literacy rate was 74.5 per cent for women and 90.8 per cent for men. China has obviously some way to go before attaining universal literacy, and there is a gender gap in education as in most other areas of the quality of life in that country (HDR 1999).

Taking the ratio of enrolment in third-level education for the respective age groups starting around 17-19 years and lasting for 3-4 years as an indicator of the attainment of higher education in the population, the findings indicate that in Eastern Asia, for women, this ratio rose from 11 in 1980 to 20 in 1994-1996, and for men the ratio rose over the same period from 15 to 25. By 1996, in respect to higher education, Eastern Asia, starting from a lower base had either overtaken or come near South America, but this region had a long way to go to reach the standards of Western Europe, Canada or the USA in these respects (UN 2000, chart 4.6).

The strategies promoting health and education varied from country to country and period to period. In respect of the spread of primary education, the state played the major role in all the countries. This could be said also of primary health care in the initial years of the march towards better standards of living. As income and literacy, especially women's literacy, improved, public action was supplemented by private efforts. Women's literacy made its contribution also by lowering the desired fertility levels, thereby bringing down the dependency ratio and raising the savings rate.

The downside of the East Asian achievement is, in spite of the enormous increase in per capita income and in health and educational standards; women continue to suffer enormous discrimination in labour markets and many areas of decision-making, including those relating to choices between boys and girls. The reasons for pay differentials have been classified in various ways (Gunderson 1989, Anker 1997/2001). They can be roughly divided into differences in human capital endowments, differences in access to different occupations and differences in pay for the same or very similar work. While women of East Asia have done almost as well as men (although there are significant differentials in respect to access to technical and managerial qualifications), they continue to suffer severe differentials in pay in comparison with men (Bagchi 1987, Lindauer 1997, UN 2000). The ratio of the average pay of women to that of men is low all over East Asia, and especially low in Japan and South Korea: in both countries they fall short of 60 per cent (UN 2000. Elder and Johnson 1999/2001). Furthermore, women are still not found in superior decision-making positions in administration, politics, business, or academic life in most of these countries, in spite of the high attainments in the field of education. One partly negative lesson that SSA countries can draw from the experience of ESEA is not to allow patriarchy to get a foothold in any area of decision-making in the name of tradition or in the name of the nation having to win in a highly competitive marketplace.

Lessons from the Financial Crisis of 1997 in ESEA

All the countries of ESEA except the Philippines experienced high rates of growth and improvement in their standard of living until 1997, although this author has grave doubts about the reported rates of growth and poverty reduction in Indonesia (Bagchi 1998, Bagchi 2002a). Then, beginning with Thailand in July 1997 and spreading to Malaysia, Indonesia and South Korea, most of the regions in ESEA except the PRC, Taiwan, and the Philippines were involved in a severe financial crisis. While the growth rates of the countries directly suffering from this financial crisis plummeted, the other countries of ESEA also suffered from some decline in their growth rates.

The basic reason for the financial crisis of ESEA in 1997 was financial liberalisation (Bagchi 1998, Wade 1998, Stiglitz 2001). The erroneous theory of financial repression inhibiting the growth of developing countries was put forward by McKinnon (1973) and Shaw (1973). In the same year Black and Scholes

(1973) and Merton (1973) published their theory of options pricing, which apparently provided a rigorous formula linking the prices of forward options to fundamentals. Policy advocates all over the developing world then began to preach the virtues of removing the heavy hand of government and the system of directed credit from banking and financial systems. Most governments of ESEA, especially those of the more successful lands, resisted these overtures until the late 1980s, complying with them in only a half-hearted fashion. Then Thailand relaxed many of the restrictions on the banking business, allowed new financial institutions and instruments to be created with only a lax supervision by the monetary and stock market authorities, and put its faith in anchoring the value of the baht to that of the dollar. All this encouraged domestic capital market operators and other firms to borrow heavily in international markets, and a large amount of foreign funds entered the Thai economy, and when productive investment opportunities faltered, this pushed up the values of real estate and other property to high levels and fuelled speculation. By the beginning of 1997, the dollar anchor of the baht could not be maintained any longer. On 2 July 1997 the value of the baht was floated, and that started the Asian financial crisis (Bagchi 1998, Lauridsen 1998).

The sequence and the major forces in the case of the crisis in South Korea were quite different. The South Korean government had maintained a strict control on the allocation of credit and of foreign exchange, until the middle of the 1980s. It had also restricted the entry of foreign players into the domestic stock and money markets. Then in 1993 it was pushed both from domestic borrowers and big firms and by the G7 countries and international organisations and, as a qualification for joining the OECD (only the second Asian country to do so), the South Korean government liberalised capital flows into and out of the economy (Bagchi 1998, Bagchi 1999, Bagchi 2002a).

In all these cases, the unregulated inflow of funds and borrowing by domestic firms ultimately led to the crisis. But the contagion in the financial markets and the herd behaviour of international investors played a big role in spreading the crisis across ESEA. Analysts have discounted the role of overvalued exchange rates or trade linkages among the affected countries (see, e.g., Baig and Goldfajn 1998). Financial markets are pitted with various kinds of external effects and the state has a major role to play in regulating them (Stiglitz 1993). The policies of financial liberalisation in ESEA and indeed in most other countries have ignored this elementary fact. It is instructive that the PRC and Taiwan, which had operated capital and money markets with heavy doses of regulation and barred the free entry into and exit of capital from their economies were virtually unscathed by the crisis except to the extent that their exports and economic activity were adversely affected by the recession following the crisis.

The crisis affected the fortunes of women and men differently in the spate of retrenchments that followed. In South Korea, women's employment was generally cut first (Bagchi 1999). In all the crisis–affected countries the proportion of people in poverty increased dramatically, and as women all across the developing world bear the brunt of poverty in various ways, women were affected in multiple ways by the eruption of the crisis. The lesson can be drawn that a poor country with weak manufacturing and financial sectors has no business mandating capital account convertibility and other related measures of financial liberalisation. Top regulators of the world are aware of the systemic risk posed by the financial innovations sweeping the world, but they do not have the courage to speak out and say that such innovations relate only to human organisations and can be re-arranged or reversed.

There has been a considerable amount of propaganda about cronyism in ESEA (for a more extended discussion, see Bagchi 2002a). First of all, it is difficult to find an objective definition of cronyism. One observer's cronyism is another's friendly relation between business and government. It is difficult to find a country which is entirely free of the usual characteristics of cronyism, as the cases of Enron and Arthur Andersen in the U.S. would indicate. Moreover, within ESEA two of the worst cases of cronyism occurred in the Philippines and Indonesia, and the two had completely liberalised financial regimes long before the crisis broke. Both the countries were characterised by landlord–military domination of civil society and government. As it happens, the Philippines was more like Latin America or South Asia than like the Tigers of East Asia in its economic performance. It has already been argued that there is reason to be sceptical about the touted rates of economic growth and improvement in the standard of living of the Indonesian people under the heel of the Suharto dictatorship.

To return to an earlier point, cronyism is more likely to crop up in a landlord or clan-dominated system than in a system which has been purged of non-market private coercion through appropriate agrarian transformation, the spread of education, and the growth of an effective collective will for continual expansion of human capabilities. SSA countries, like most other developing countries can draw these and many other lessons. To concentrate only on lessons of export-led growth is to be blind to the real material foundations of sustainable human development on a continuous basis. This author thinks that to try to advance the welfare of all human beings by promoting competitiveness and social

Darwinism is a disastrous path for humanity, but he has desisted from arguing that out in this paper.

References

Agnihotri, S. B., 2000. *Sex Ratio Patterns in the Indian Population: A Fresh Exploration*. New Delhi: Sage.

Amsden, A. H., 1989. *Asia's Next Giant: South Korea and Late Industrialisation*. New York: Oxford University Press.

Anker, R., 1997/2001. "Theories of Occupational Segregation by Sex: an Overview. *International Labour Review* 136, no. 3; reprinted in Loutfi 2001: 129-55).

Bagchi, A. K., 1982. *The Political Economy of Underdevelopment*. Cambridge: Cambridge University Press.

Bagchi, 1984. "The Terror and the Squalor of East Asian Capitalism. *Economic and Political Weekly* 19, no. 1 (Jan. 7): 21-22.

Bagchi, 1987a. 'East Asian Capitalism: An Introduction." *Political Economy: Studies in the Surplus Approach* 3 (2): 115-32.

Bagchi, 1987b. *Public Intervention and Industrial Restructuring in China, India and Republic of Korea*. New Delhi: ILO-ARTEP.

Bagchi, 1997. *Economic Theory and Economic Organisation, I, A Critique of the Anglo-American Theory of Firm Structure.*, Calcutta: Centre for Studies in Social Sciences, Occasional Paper no. 165, September.

Bagchi, 1998. "Growth Miracle and Its Unravelling in East and South-East Asia." *Economic and Political Weekly* 33, no. 18 (May 2): 1025-42.

Bagchi, 1999. "A Turnaround in South Korea." *Frontline* (Chennai), (July 30): 62-65.

Bagchi, 2000. "The Past and the Future of the Developmental State." *Journal of World-Systems Research* 11, no. 2 (Summer/Fall): 398-442. http://csf.colorado.edu/jwsr

Bagchi, 2002a. "Agrarian Transformation and Human Development: Instrumental and Constitutive Links." In Ramachandran and Swaminathan 2002: 153-65.

Bagchi, 2002b. "Governance in East Asia: What's New?" *European Journal of Development Research* 14, no. 1 (June): 200-18.

Baig, T., and I. Goldfain, 1998 , "Financial Market Contagion in the Asian Crisis." IMF Working Paper (WP/98/155), November.

Black, F., and M. Scholes, 1973. "The Valuation of Option Contracts and a Test of Market Efficiency. *Journal of Political Economy* 81, no. 3: 637-54.

Boserup, E., 1981. *Population and Technology*. Oxford: Blackwell.

Crockett, A., 2001. "Monetary Policy and Financial Stability." Speech given by A. Crockett, General Manager of the Bank for International Settlements, HKMA Distinguished Lecture, Hong Kong, February 13. Internet: bis.org.

Crotty, J., and K. Lee, 2001. "Economic Performance in Post-Crisis Korea: A Critical Perspective on Neoliberal Restructuring." Mimeo, University of Massachusetts, Amherst, October 31.

EIU, 2000. *Country Profile 2001: South Korea, North Korea*. London: Economist Intelligence Unit.

Elder, S., and L. J. Johnson, 1999/2001. "Sex-Specific Labour Market Indicators: What they Show." *International Labour Review* 138, no. 4 (1999), repr. in Loutfi 2001: 251-304.

El-Ghonemy, M. R., 2002. 'The Land Market approach to Rural Development." In Ramachandran and Swaminathan 2002: 230-44.

Gertler, M., 1988. "Financial Structure and Aggregate Economic Activity: An Overview." *Journal of Money, Credit and Banking* 20, no. 3: 559-88.

Gunderson, M., 1989. "Male-Female Wage Differentials and Policy Responses." *Journal of Economic Literature* 27, no. 1: 46-72.

HDR, 1999. *Human Development Report*. New York: Oxford University Press..

Jensen, M. C., and W. H. Meckling, 1976. "Theory of the Firm: Managerial Behaviour, Agency Costs and Ownership Structure." *Journal of Financial Economics* 11: 5-50.

Johnson, C., 1982. *MITI and the Japanese Miracle: The Rise of Industrial Policy, 1925-1975*. Stanford, Calif.: Stanford University Press.

Khan, A. R., 1998. "Growth and Poverty in East and Southeast Asia in the Era of Globalisation." in *Globalisation, Growth and Marginalization*, ed., A. S. Bhalla. London: Macmillan, pp. 125-48.

Lauridsen, L., 1998. "The Financial Crisis in Thailand: Causes, Conduct, and Consequences?" *World Development* 26, no. 8: 1575-91.

Levin, R., 2002. "Land and Agrarian Relations in South Africa: Contemporary Challenges and Perspectives." in Ramachandran and Swaminathan 2002: 166-78.

Lindauer, D. L., 1997. "Labour Market Outcomes: An Overview." In *The Strains of Economic Growth: Labour Unrest and Social Dissatisfaction in Korea,* ed. D. L. Lindauer, J. Kim, et al. Cambridge, Mass.: Harvard Institute for International Development, pp. 35-53.

Loutfi, M. F. ed., 2001., *Women, Gender and Work*. Geneva: International Labour Office.

McKinnon, R. I., 1973., *Money and Capital in Economic Development*. Washington, D.C.: Brookings Institution.

Mehra, R., and S. Gammage, 1999. "Trends, Countertrends, and Gaps in Women's Employment." *World Development* 27, no. 3: 533-50.

Merton, R. C., 1973. "Theory of Rational Option Pricing." *Bell Journal of Economics and Management Science* 4, no. 1: 141-83.

Migdal, J. S., 1988. *Strong Societies and Weak States: State Society Relations and State Capabilities in the Third World*. Princeton: Princeton University Press.

Morishima, M., 1982. *Why Has Japan "Succeeded?" Western Technology and the Japanese Ethos*. Cambridge: Cambridge University Press.

Park, C. B., and N.-H. Cho, 1995. "Consequence of Son Preference in a Low-Fertility Society." *Population and Development Review* 21, no. 1 (March): 59-84.

Patel, S., J. Bagchi, and K. Raj, eds., 2002. *Thinking Social Science in India: Essays in Honour of Alice Thorner*. New Delhi: Sage.

Platteau, J.-P., 1990. "The Food Crisis in Africa: A Comparative Structural Analysis." In *The Political Economy of Hunger,* ed. J. Drèze and A. Sen vol. 2, *Famine Prevention*. Oxford: Clarendon Press, pp. 279-387.

Ramachandran, V.K., and M. S. Nathan, eds., 2002. *Agrarian Studies: Essays on Agrarian Relations in Less-Developed Countries*. New Delhi: Tulika.

Robinson, R., K. Hewison, and G. Rodan, 1993. "Political Power in Industrialising Capitalist Societies: Theoretical Approaches." In *Southeast Asia in the 1990s: Authoritarianism, Democracy and Capitalism*, ed. R. Hewison and G Rodan. St. Leonards, NSW: Allen & Unwin, pp. 9-39.

Scott, K. E., 1999. "Corporate Governance and East Asia: Korea, Indonesia, Malaysia, and Thailand." In *Financial Markets and Development: The Crisis in Emerging Markets*, ed. A. Harwood, R. E. Litan, and M. Pomerleano. Washington, D.C.: Brookings Institution Press, pp. 335-66.

Searle, P., 1999. *The Riddle of Malaysian Capitalism: Rent-Seekers or Real Capitalists?* Honolulu: Allen and Unwin, and University of Hawaii Press.

Sen, A. K., 1967. "Isolation, Assurance and the Social Rate of Discount." *Quarterly Journal of Economics* 82, no. 1 (February): 112-84, reprinted in Sen 1984: 135-46.

Sen, A. K., 1984. *Resources, Values and Development*. Blackwell: Oxford.

Sen, A. K., 1999. *Development as Freedom*. New York: A.A. Knopf.

Sen, G., 2002. "Gendered Labour Markets and Globalisation in Asia." in Patel, Bagchi, and Raj 2002: 192-213.

Shaw, E. S., 1973. *Financial Deepening in Economic Development.* New York: Oxford University Press.

Singh, A., and B. A. Weisse, 1998. "Emerging Stock Markets, Portfolio Capital Flows and Long-term Economic Growth: Micro and Macroeconomic Perspectives." *World Development,* 6, no. 4: 607-622.

Stiglitz, J.E., 1993. The Role of the State in Financial Markets. Proceedings of the World Bank Development Economists' Conference. Washington, D.C.: World Bank.

Stiglitz, J. E., 2001. "From Miracle to Crisis to Recovery: Lessons from Four Decades of East Asian experience." In Stigliz and Yusuf 2001: 509-526.

Stiglitz, J. E. and S. Yusuf, eds., 2001. *Rethinking the East Asian Miracle,* Washington, D.C.: World Bank; Oxford and New York: Oxford University Press.

Svedberg, P., 1991. "Undernutrition in Sub-Saharan Africa: A Critical Assessment of the Evidence." In *The Political Economy of Hunger,* ed. J. Drèze and A. Sen, vol. 3, *Endemic Hunger.* Oxford: Clarendon Press, pp. 155-96.

Svedberg, 1999. "841 Million Undernourished?" *World Development* 27, no. 12: 2081-98.

U.N., 2000. *The World's Women.* New York: United Nations.

Wade, R., 1990. *Governing the Market: Economic Theory and the Role of the Government in East Asian Industrialisation.* New Jersey: Princeton University Press.

Wade, R., 1998. "From `Miracle' to `Cronyism': Explaining the Great Asian Slump." *Cambridge Journal of Economics* 22, no. 6 (November): 693-706.

Williamson, O., 1985. *The Economic Institutions of Capitalism.* New York: The Free Press.

Wilson, C., 1965. *England's Apprenticeship 1603-1763.* London: Longmans.

Woo, J.E., 1991. *Race to the Swift: State and Finance in Korean Industrialisation.* New York: Columbia University Press.

WDR, 1996. *World Development Report 1996: From Plan to Market.* New York: Oxford University Press.

World Bank, 1993. *The East Asian Miracle: Economic Growth and Public Policy,* Washington, D.C.: IBRD.

Yamamura, K., and Y. Yasuba, eds., 1987. *The Political Economy of Japan,* vol. 1, *The Domestic Transformation.* Stanford, Calif.: Stanford University Press.

Zeng Y., T. Ping, et al., 1993. "Causes and Implications of the Recent Increase in the Reported Sex Ratio at Birth in China. *Population and Development Review* 19, no. 2 (March): 282-302.

CAN AFRICAN WOMEN LEARN FROM EAST AND SOUTH EAST ASIA? RESPONSE TO AMIYA KUMAR BAGCHI'S PAPER

Asma Barlas

Before I respond to Professor Bagchi's paper, I just want to say how happy I am to have met him. I read some of his earlier work in graduate school where one of my concentrations was Development. Even though we had too few courses specifically about women's roles in economic production, I did learn about the paradox of women's oppression in the face of their dual productivity (as producers and reproducers), and this paradox has remained with me, more or less unresolved, over the years.

I therefore welcomed the opportunity to read a paper whose title suggests both that it is about women's well-being in East and South-East Asia and that women in Africa can learn from the experiences of women in that part of the world. On both these counts, however, I am a bit disappointed because the paper turns out not really to be about women and, perhaps as a result, I am unsure about the lessons African women can learn from it.

The paper begins promisingly, by unsettling some stereotypes of Africa. We learn that Sub-Saharan Africa has a better record of treating its women and nurturing its children, especially girls, than many other countries, including those we consider developed. For instance, it has done a better job of "preventing endemic malnutrition than its apparently low per capita income would indicate." Further, there is no evidence there of practices like female feticide that have become rampant in countries like India and China.

We learn also that not only do women outnumber men in Sub-Saharan Africa, but that a larger percentage is employed in agriculture than in any other region of the world, and—while this may be changing—more women also participate in the monetized sectors of the economy. It thus is tempting to think that the higher ratio of women to men, as well as their role in food production, must have something to do with their relatively better status. It also is tempting to think that, by now, all countries would have recognized gender equity as one of the primary indicators of successful development.

To the contrary, however, as Bagchi points out, there is a positive association between sex bias and economic success. Countries that discriminate against the birth of girls are in fact thought to be doing better in the competitive market place, revealing, as he calls it, the "dark side of success in a grossly unequal world." I feel it would have been productive in a paper about women to address these tensions between how we continue to define economic success and women's well being, but Bagchi doesn't do that.

There is then the question of why women who play approximately comparable roles in food production in different societies are so unequally recompensed. For instance, Vandana Shiva provides some astonishing statistics that show that women in most Indian villages do as much work as men and field animals *combined* but in spite of that they neither play much of a role in the monetized sectors of the economy nor are they well treated. To the contrary, as Bagchi notes, female feticide is increasing in India. What accounts for these differences between sub Saharan African societies and India? Could it be that their patriarchal structures are different? If African women are better off than their sisters in South and East Asia on this score, what lessons can they learn from the latter?

Bagchi suggests that countries in Sub-Saharan Africa should not allow "patriarchy to get a foothold in any area of decision-making in the name of tradition or in the name of the nation having to win in a highly competitive marketplace." Now, while I am completely supportive of this suggestion, I am just as completely baffled by it. How can one keep patriarchy at bay in a patriarchal society? Given that women are excluded from decision-making processes, how exactly are they supposed to ensure that patriarchy does not get a foothold in these processes? In fact, isn't patriarchy already in place everywhere? And are all traditions always or necessarily patriarchal? Bagchi doesn't say.

The second lesson he wants Sub-Saharan Africa to draw from the experiences of East and South-East Asian countries is that sustainable development requires not just economic, but also social and political reforms. Land redistribution, universal education, a sense of national belonging, all are necessary for enabling the success we associate with what used to be called the newly industrializing countries, or NICs. It seems the moral still is that the "East Asian miracle" can be replicated, albeit with some adjustments.

This, of course, leads me to wonder about all that literature that, for the better part of a quarter century, obliged us to question this assumption and taught us that the causes of underdevelopment weren't always endogenous but exogenous. That is, they had to do not only with such factors as the rates of savings or fiscal policies, but also with the role of a state in the global political economy, something over which states have little control.

Perhaps what most depressed me about reading Bagchi's paper is the realization that in the years I have been out of graduate school, there has been a permanent epistemic shift in how we think about economic development. The mantra now is free-market capitalism and neo-liberalism; there is not even a pretense that things *can* be done differently and perhaps *should* be done differently if we are to ensure people's basic rights and protect the environment from imminent destruction. Sustainable development, it seems, now is successful capitalist development, as it seems to be in Bagchi's paper.

Perhaps economists cannot be idealists and perhaps Bagchi merely is keeping abreast of the current thinking while I have fallen behind. But, to me, the most interesting point he makes is one that he never follows up: "I think that to try and advance the welfare of all human beings by promoting competitiveness and social Darwinism is a disastrous path for humanity, but I have desisted from arguing that out in this paper." More's the pity!

RESPONSE TO THE COMMENTS OF ASMA BARLAS

Amiya Kumar Bagchi

I am sorry to have disappointed Professor Barlas. While I have always believed in the necessity of struggle against an unjust social order and a global political alignment favouring the rich and the powerful, I have always believed in the necessity of a scholar to engage in description and analysis rather than to put out formulas for instant revolution.

Certainly I should have warned all women and democrats in Africa against patriarchy gaining a *new* foothold in African societies rather than incautiously phrasing my warning in such a way that readers might come away with the impression that those societies were not patriarchal. Patriarchy, like other structures of oppression, is transforming itself all the time, in African societies as elsewhere. One of the most frightening forms of patriarchy and class oppression in India today, for example, is the organisation of the Durga Vahini, in which women are being armed and trained by the Hindu communalist organisations to take part in anti-Muslim riots, as they did in Gujarat recently. Another example is the spread of the dowry system among all communities. Earlier, only upper caste Hindus had to pay dowries to get their daughters married. Now the system has spread among all classes of Hindus, Muslims and the Scheduled Tribes or Adivasis. But the spread of education among women has also meant the increase of resistance against dowries. African democrats and women can learn negative lessons from these developments as well.

Let me clarify that upholding the necessity of pro-peasant land reforms and the achievement of universal literacy do not mean upholding the capitalist order that may be built up on that foundation. After all, China until the late 1970s and Cuba until today achieved both goals without embracing capitalism. The point is that even those who want a vibrant capitalism rather than the semi-feudal, semi-patrimonial social formations that have proved so oppressive to poor peoples all over the world will have to struggle for peasants to acquire rights over their land, women to get out of the more obvious forms of patriarchal oppression, and everybody to have access to education and reasonable healthcare. The current global order is stopping those changes from occurring in most poor countries. So, paradoxically enough, even the talk of allowing markets to work freely, in the mouths of the leaders of G8 or top spokesmen of the IMF, the World Bank or the WTO, turns out to be pure humbug.

Let me clarify also that exogenous factors can overwhelm a poor country and prevent even a socialist leadership from bringing about the social transformation it desires: the cases of Nicaragua under the Sandinistas, Mozambique under the leadership of Samora Machel and his comrades or the fight of the Palestinians today to survive in freedom and dignity come easily to mind. However, in most cases the structures of oppression are both exogenous and endogenous. Imperialism could not dominate most poor countries without the willing collaboration of a dominant section of the upper classes in those countries, including the countries in Africa, especially since the time they became formally independent. This means that the struggle against imperialism also involves struggles against the ruling classes of most poor countries. Hence I could never agree with those revolutionaries whose rhetoric was directed only against the imperialists or more metaphorically, the West.

I never said that extreme discrimination against women was necessary for economic success even under capitalism. Female infanticide was being practised in parts of China, India and Japan long before Europe-led capitalism invaded those countries. In China, under the Maoist regime a sustained campaign was mounted against extreme forms of gender discrimination, including female infanticide. With policies of liberalisation and the one-child policy enforced by the Chinese government, gender discrimination has increased and female feticide seems to have become more prevalent. Similar developments have occurred in Taiwan, Hong Kong and South Korea, but interestingly enough, not in Japan, where sex ratios have conformed to what nature seems to ordain without those extreme forms of gender discrimination. This does not mean Japan has ceased to practise patriarchy in a systematic fashion, but only that patriarchy has taken other forms. I have only speculated that the virulence of gender discrimination against girl children in some countries of East Asia may have something to do with their perception that they need more boys to win in the ruthless competitive game in which they seemed to be winners until the crisis of 1997 stalled their winning spree. This hardly constitutes an endorsement of their perception or of the cut-throat competition on unequal terms in the current global order that is destroying the lives of hundreds of millions of people.

Finally, I come to the issue of Social Darwinism. The phenomenon was there long before the term was coined, and, I believe, has run like a red thread in the woof of the ideology of well-formed class societies. But as modern capitalism has done with many other forms of inegalitarian ideologies and structures of exploitation, it has given Social Darwinism a more precise and elaborate form and has used it to justify slavery, eugenic experiments against workers and people who were perceived to be genetically inferior. There is plenty of evidence that most upper-class Europeans regarded poor people in their own countries as racially or genetically inferior. The history of that ideology and its use to motivate and give killing power to the murderous competition unleashed on the world on Europe-led capitalism is coterminous with the history of capital since the sixteenth century. I have written a book covering those issues but it will take some time to edit it properly and publish it.

CHAPTER 15

HIGHER EDUCATION IN AFRICA AND LATIN AMERICA: COMPARATIVE INSIGHTS FROM GLOBALIZATION AND GENDER PERSPECTIVES

Nelly P. Stromquist

Introduction

The current surge of active and aggressive economic globalization has pushed education—particularly post-secondary and technical education—to the fore as a leading vehicle to boost the competitive edge of countries, relying on its potential to enhance not only their labor force but also the range of value-added products they can manufacture. While there is a growing shift toward the unquestionable value of education for economic purposes, many also look for education to serve social and political purposes. As Chanana (2000) remarks, regardless of point of view, there seems to be consensus on the high contemporary social importance of education, whether it serves for reproduction of existing social stratification or for social transformation. Those promoting the latter view see education as a means of righting social wrongs, as a way to help mobilize people to attain social justice and equality.

The present era will be seen historically as one of remarkable political, economic, and cultural change. The international economy is assuming increasingly complex forms of organization, some of which are being codified through global agreements such as those enacted by the World Trade Organization. These agreements include provisions for education, thus rendering this field part of the commercial exchanges protected and augmented through the General Agreement on Trade and Services (GATS).

Simultaneously, the political culture of gender issues is changing. Since 1978, about 190 countries have endorsed the Convention on the Elimination of All Forms of Discrimination Against Women (CEDAW). In Latin America all but six of the 35 member states of the Organization of

American States have ratified the Convention to Prevent, Punish, and Eradicate Violence Against Women in 1995 (popularly known as the Belem do Para Convention) (Htun 1998), a major legal breakthrough in recognizing a major form of women's oppression and seeking to eradicate it. Latin America has a significant application of affirmative action for women in the form of electoral quotas. At present, eight of the 20 Latin American countries have national laws mandating that political parties reserve 20 to 30 percent of candidacies at all levels for women (FLACSO 1995). In consequence, the number of women in political office, particularly at the community level, has been increasing. In addition, many countries now have not only laws mandating maternity leave and protection during pregnancy, but also laws modifying the rape and adultery legislation that was highly regressive for women in the past.

In the African continent, the New Partnership for African Development (NEPAD), a formal agreement in existence since 2001 that establishes the key development parameters for the African region, recognizes the importance of promoting gender equality. Unfortunately, an analysis of NEPAD conducted by Longwe (2002) amply demonstrates that activities toward that end are not present. In a region where women face seriously constraining marriage laws, customary laws in many countries and other laws inherited from European countries (where they are now obsolete) under which women are treated as legal minors and are forbidden to inherit property and even to own land (according to some traditional laws, mostly local versions of Sharia law), this represents a major disjuncture between gender policy objectives and strategic action.

Latin America and Africa, two regions perhaps at opposite ends of the development continuum in the Third World, offer grounds for useful comparisons in terms of ongoing social change, educational policy, and higher education in particular. Latin America and Africa as concepts serve as heuristic devices to enable us to reduce our complex world and thus to synopsize regions with considerable diversity. Little El Salvador is very different from giant Brazil; the ancient political culture of Egypt is not easily comparable to relatively recent nation-states that resulted from the Europeans' partition of the African continent; any of the Sub-Saharan countries, classified among the least developed countries in the world, and all former administered colonies, are different from South Africa, a settler colony with its apartheid policy dismantled only 10 years ago. Nonetheless, both Latin America and Africa present a number of commonalities fostered by the proximity of their member nations, by colonial experience, by their low levels of industrialization, and by the weak degree of solidity of their state apparatuses. Because of its closeness to the US, the center of economic globalization and the source of many features of the emerging university model, Latin America tends to experience new influences earlier than Africa; thus understanding developments in Latin America offers a window onto the future of other developing regions. I contend that important insights emerge from comparing the two regions, and I take their higher education systems as the key reference point from which to examine the implications of ongoing globalization trends, changes in gender perceptions and conditions, and the emerging positioning of each region.

Global and Regional Educational Initiatives

Since the world education conference in Jomtien in 1990, "education for all" (EFA) has been present in public policy discourse. At a meeting in Dakar in 2000 to consider the accomplishments of Jomtien, the following education objectives were reiterated: to attain universal primary education completion by 2005, to eliminate gender disparities in primary and secondary education by 2005, and to achieve gender equality at all levels of education by 2015. These objectives also recognized the need to provide education of "good quality."

Also since 2000, countries have been trying to respond to the Millennium Development Goals (MDGs), a long-term global agreement by all UN countries to achieve progress and social justice. The MDGs identify education as a key priority and refer to it in two of its eight goals (UN 2000; UN 2003). Goal 2 seeks to "ensure that, by 2015, children everywhere, boys and girls alike, will be able to complete a full course of primary schooling." It must be remarked that this objective does not specifically refer to free or public schooling. The indicators to operationalize attainment are net enrollment ratios in primary education (which would include both private and public education) and enrollment in the 5th grade of primary education.[1] This second indicator effectively reduces the definition of primary schooling to four years of education. Goal 3 of the MDGs seeks to "promote gender equality and empower women." To this end, a related goal seeks to "eliminate gender disparities in primary and secondary schooling by 2005 and at all levels by 2015." This goal takes gender parity in schooling as an indicator of women's empowerment. It can be readily seen that while education figures prominently in the MDGs, it is unlikely that equal access to tertiary education for women and men may be realized by 2015, particularly in Africa. It is of interest that

---

[1] At present, in many countries primary school comprises six years of education.

the MDGs take *access* to education (independent of content or the nature of the schooling experience) as an indicator of women's empowerment—a one-dimensional solution long questioned by feminist scholarship.

In seeking the promotion of gender equality, the NEPAD document recognizes the importance of women's access to education, and expresses an intention to work on education efforts to "close the gender gaps in school enrollments." The careful analysis of NEPAD conducted by Longwe (2002) finds, however, that no specific activities are identified to implement this strategy.

Government rhetoric on gender is frequent. Action lags considerably. Fees for schooling (which puts enrollment for girls at a disadvantage) are still charged in 26 of the 35 countries unlikely to reach the gender parity goals for primary schooling in 2005 (UNESCO 2003a). Male and female stereotypes can still be found in textbooks, in both Africa and Latin America.[2] Illiteracy, defined as the lack of literacy skills sufficient for the acquisition of even rudimentary forms of access to reading and writing, continues to affect predominantly women, who represent two-thirds of the world's illiterates. Illiteracy levels are much higher in Africa than in Latin America. However, some patterns are similar: rural populations tend to exhibit higher levels of illiteracy than urban residents; illiteracy levels are high among indigenous populations and among groups that speak minority languages. There are also sub-regional and internal differences.

In higher education, Africa and Latin America exhibit significant differences in enrollment rates, with Africa lagging substantially behind Latin America in the overall access and in the access of women and men to higher education, and Sub-Saharan Africa lagging even more (Table 1).

---

[2] A study by FLACSO (1995) of textbooks in five Latin American countries found that women appeared in only 18 percent of the titles, 23 percent of the figures, and 20 percent of the text. It further found that when women do appear in textbooks they are depicted in traditional roles, cooking or cleaning the home. These findings are similar to those detected in the mid-1980s in a number of other textbook studies in the Latin American region.

Table 1. Tertiary Education Gross Enrollment. Africa and Latin America, 1970-1997

	Africa			Sub-Saharan Africa			Latin America/Caribbean		
	Total	Male	Female	Total	Male	Female	Total	Male	Female
1970	1.6	2.4	0.7	0.8	1.3	0.3	6.3	8.1	4.5
1980	3.7	5.3	2.0	1.7	2.7	0.7	13.7	15.5	11.9
1990	5.1	6.7	3.4	3.0	4.1	1.9	16.8	17.3	16.4
1997	6.9	8.6	5.2	3.9	5.1	2.8	19.4	20.1	18.7

Source: UNESCO, 1999, pp. II.18 and II.19.[3]

The Economic Context of Latin America and Africa

Latin America and the Caribbean on one hand and Sub-Saharan Africa on the other are the two regions in the world that have experienced negative rates of growth in terms of the GDP, while the five other regions (East Asia and the Pacific, Middle East and North Africa, Europe and Central Asia, and South Asia) have reported considerable convergence in economic progress (Behrman and Sengupta 2004).[4]

While Latin America is more industrialized than Africa, the former is still heavily dependent on exports of agricultural and mineral raw materials. Both regions have seen limited international assistance and scant foreign investment. In Latin America, most of the foreign direct investment (FDI) has been for short-term financial gain (Vilas 1996). According to the UN Economic Commission for Latin America and the Caribbean, the combined external debt in 2002 (owned by both public and private sources) for the region was $800 billion, a debt that has been growing since 1988. Poverty has increased in Latin America, as the region has produced poor people at double the rate of the total population throughout the 1980s. Unlike the cases of Korea, Taiwan, Indonesia, and Thailand, the promotion of export growth in Latin America has not been complemented by protecting the domestic market,

---

[3] These rates are higher than those reported by UNESCO in 2003 (see, for instance, UNESCO, 2003c). They are cited, however, because they enable us to see trends over 30 years.

[4] This classification of the world regions, far from perfect, is the one utilized by the World Bank in the presentation of various statistics.

nor by increased public expenditure on education. A number of public policies have targeted the poorest of the poor, but these programs have been found to fragment the population and weaken ties of solidarity (Vilas 1996). Since weak internal markets lead to migration, Latin America—and Africa to a lesser extent, but still at a relatively high rate among higher education graduates— have produced an international worker migration that has registered contours of illegality, by which workers are "deprived of institutional protection in the receiving country while extra surplus value is generated for the sake of firms" (Vilas 1996: 297).[5]

For its part, Africa faces the lowest FDI investment of all regions, has the greatest external debt per capita (not in the total size of the debt) in the world, and is facing a major health catastrophe with serious consequences for the livelihood and progress of the surviving population, most of them very young children. Sub-Saharan Africa today has a per capita GPD $200 smaller than it was in 1974—a decrease of about 11 percent in 30 years.

Under the current economic and social contexts in Latin America and Africa, it is difficult for governments to act in favor of social services, including education. Yet, it must be remembered that not everybody in those regions is interested in solidarity: small and powerful economic groups do well without democracy and without social inclusion (Vilas 1996).

In this paper I focus on developments in higher education and explore a set of three interrelated questions:

- Are the globalization forces affecting African and Latin American universities similarly so that there are trends toward convergence rather than divergence?
- What forms of gender policies are present at higher education levels and how is this manifested in Africa and Latin America?
- What is the space, if any, for social critique in the increasingly globalized university?

Some Impacts of Economic Globalization on Higher Education

Globalization is a complex phenomenon characterized by the simultaneous expansion of economy and technology (as related to information,

---

[5] The migration of Latin American workers generates a very large economic contribution to their countries. In the case of Mexico, one of the largest Latin American economies, the remittances for 2002 were superior to the direct foreign investment in Mexico and amounted to 79 percent of its oil exports and its *maquiladora* exports.

communication, transportation, and the production of goods and services), both of which create enormous consequences for politics and culture (for an extended treatment, see Stromquist 2002). As globalization emphasizes one general economic model, the discourse of the market permeates specific sectors, including education. Today, many business terms have taken hold in educational systems. We speak now in education of quality control, competition, managerialism, entrepreneurship, market forces, user fees, and customer choice. These influences are felt most at the tertiary level for many innovations, and high-skilled personnel are derived and sought from those institutions. The volume of world exports was estimated in 1995 to be 10 times greater than it was in 1990. With a daily turnover in foreign exchange markets close to $2 billion by the end of 1990s, it is undeniable that the dynamics of globalization are fast, strong, and require access to information and processing technologies. This exchange is predicated on knowledgeable people who can identify markets and products on a continual basis and have the flexibility to move in search of optimal conditions the world over. In this context, higher education emerges as of utmost importance.

The current educational situation is characterized by a hegemony controlled by the North, primarily the US and European countries. This hegemony propels the *internationalization* of activities and enterprises, but not necessarily the development of *internationalism*. We define the first as the expansion of contacts with others with the purpose of selling them our services and goods. The latter refer to the creation of values of solidarity and social justice among countries. An effective conceptualization of internationalism is provided by Jones, who defines it as "common sense notions of international community, international cooperation, international community of interests, and international dimensions of the common good" (2000: 31).[6]

Carnoy (1990) and others have found that even states in transition toward a socialist agenda face political and economic constraints linked to globalization that prevent them from realizing rudimentary social policies. However, our full understanding of the impact of globalization in the developing world is fragmentary. Social science research is lagging behind the understanding of economic and political structures; few transnational teams are following current developments and their impact on education. This limited

---

[6] It should be noted that there is no consensus on the use of these terms. Welch (2002:434) refers to internationalization as the process of "developing a value system that seeks an international moral and political order predicated on respect for difference, social, justice, and mutual respect within and among nations." I would have called that internationalism.

understanding is a consequence of the fact that most researchers have access to only piecemeal evidence derived from case studies or from field reports (Galbraith 2002).

There are important signs that the US is not moving toward internationalism. And this is true not only of its current government. A telephone survey of 1,006 US citizens age 18 and older conducted in 2002 by the American Council on Education found that 80 percent of Americans believed that the US should be involved in world affairs (an increase of about 15 percent from five years previously) and 68 percent agreed that international issues and events had a direct impact on their lives. But, regardless of these feelings, ignorance prevailed, as only 72 percent of the respondents could indicate that the US borders with both Mexico and Canada and only about 25 percent could identify Vicente Fox as the present Mexican president (Hayward and Slaya 2001). Knowledge of Africa would be similarly abysmal.

Another sign of the little understanding of the Other may be gleaned from the fact that four-year colleges and universities in the US requiring a foreign language for admission have decreased from 34 percent in 1965 to slightly over 20 percent in 1995 (Hayward 2000).

A third sign is that government policies in the US have played an active role in the lack of knowledge of developing countries: federal funding for almost all postsecondary international areas (e.g., educational and cultural exchanges, language study, faculty research) has declined by almost 24 percent over the last decade (Hayward 2000).

A fourth indicator is that foreign language enrollment as a percentage of total higher education enrollment has decreased over the past 40 years in the US, from 16 percent in the 1960s to about 8 percent from the mid-70s to the present. Most of those who sign up for foreign language courses while in college are humanities or social science majors and "few reach even an elementary level of competence" (Hayward 2000: 1). Very few Americans study abroad for more than one semester and that proportion has decreased from 18 percent in 1985 to 10 percent in 2000 (Hayward 2000).

In the US, international students number over half a million, but they are still less than 4 percent of all US higher education enrollment (Koh 2002). At the more advanced levels and in certain disciplines, international students represent a high percentage. They represent, for instance, 13.1 percent of all graduate enrollments (Koh 2002). Despite the substantial presence of international students, there is little evidence to suggest that American students are gaining a better comprehension of other cultures.

It is now amply recognized that international financial agencies influence educational policy. Although the direct influence of these agencies is difficult to document, emerging commonalities in their objectives and rationale, the preferred terminology, and the types of innovations suggest that the proposals emanating from these lending institutions are very difficult to resist. In the Latin American context, it is the International Monetary Fund, the World Bank, and the Inter-American Development Bank that promote the value of and need for decentralization, privatization, and testing mechanisms to evaluate students and teachers. Economic globalization and the need to pay external debts have given unprecedented power to the ministries of finance and economy in the conduct of the educational systems in developing countries. These persons, who usually have a limited understanding of education, tend to follow prescriptions to introduce fees at the higher education level. An example of their views is reflected in a paper entitled "Social Expenditures of the Central Government, 2001-2002," authored by Brazil's Ministry of Finance, which asserts that "free higher education is the main obstacle to the attainment of social justice in the country."

Higher education all over the world is moving into greater differentiation in types of institutions: universities, technical institutions, professional institutions (offering professional degrees including those in teaching and nursing), and technical training centers (providing short-term vocational programs). The "university" as the main model of higher education is fading away. Moreover, as is the case for public schools (primary to secondary), public universities are now under government attack for being "highly bureaucratized, over-politicized, and having low academic levels and little connection with the production sphere" (Ibarra 1998a: 140-41).

While the universities remain crucial centers of knowledge production and dissemination, their monopoly on these matters is being broken. Globally, increasingly more research takes place in firms and institutes of the business enterprise sector (which account for about 69 percent of the global research and development [] effort), about 11 percent takes place in public research laboratories, and 17 percent in universities and other institutions providing higher education. Today, university research plays a modest role (about 15-20 percent) in the major economies of France, Germany, Japan, the UK, and the US (UNESCO Institute for Statistics, 2001).[7] As might be expected, R&D expenditures are unevenly distributed within the developing world. Three-

---

[7] In Mexico, however, most R&D takes place in public universities as the firms there do not invest in these areas.

quarters of the R&D expenditures in Africa take place in South Africa. Three-quarters of the R&D in Arab States are concentrated in Egypt, Kuwait, Morocco, and Saudi Arabia. Half of the R&D in Latin America is found in Brazil (UNESCO Institute for Statistics 2001).

The General Agreement on Trade and Services (GATS), a process begun in 1995, is another factor affecting higher education. GATS, which operates through binding rules, will most likely impact education tremendously for it includes educational supply as one more commodity to be traded, and thus education loses its place as a protected social good (Robertson et al. 2002). Not only will GATS (to be finalized in 2005) change the social purposes of education but it will also alter the strategic function of education in each of the respective countries. Not surprisingly, it was the US that introduced the inclusion of higher education into GATS and made it one of the 12 sectors now being negotiated. Five categories of education fall into GATS: primary education, secondary education, higher education, adult education, and "other educational services" (Robertson et al. 2002). In other words, practically all forms of education are now in the marketplace.[8]

Educational exports from industrialized countries have been increasing.[9] As English is becoming the lingua franca, English-speaking countries enjoy a strong comparative advantage in the trade of educational services. Education exports earned $14.4 million for the UK in 1997 and $3.2 million for Australia in the mid-90s (Bennell and Pearce 2003).[10] New Zealand has also earned considerable revenues from education, which is said to have

---

[8]Several proposals in higher education have been presented to GATS by the U.S., Australia, New Zealand, and Japan. Several institutions (the American Council on Education, the Association of Colleges and Universities and Canada, and the Council for Higher Education Accreditation of the U.S., and the European University Association are now raising issues with global implications about the distinction between public and private higher education institutions, institutional autonomy concerning academic matters, state and provincial authority over fiscal policy, independent accreditation, and quality assurance processes in higher education institutions (Green et al. 2001)

[9] Knowledge gained by a foreign student is considered an export. Exports comprise student enrollment (primarily in the industrialized countries, but new arrangements in the country of origin are appearing), educational publishing, equipment, and consultancies.

[10] The US accounts for 30 percent of all international students in the world (1995 data). France enrolled over 40 percent of the African students going abroad in the mid-1990s, most of whom were sponsored by the French government (Bennell and Pearce, 2003).

generated greater foreign exchange earnings than its wine industry. While more internationalization is occurring than internationalism, it is also the case that some advanced countries are making efforts to understand the other and provide them with relevant knowledge. A survey of all 38 universities in Australia found that there have been about 1,000 "international initiatives, including interdisciplinary approaches with an area or regional base, explicitly comparative curricula, subjects with an international focus and curricula that were broadened by an international component" (Welch 2002: 453).

The expansion of higher education throughout the world is making access to higher levels of knowledge more democratic than in previous generations. In many countries, it is clear that the student body of post-secondary institutions now includes more members of lower-income families. This democratization of higher education must be acknowledged with caution because the diversity of institutions at this level is being accompanied by new forms of stratification, from relatively unchallenged established elite institutions to numerous new private institutions, most of them of dubious academic quality and social recognition.

The diversification of higher education has produced its own hierarchies: community colleges, polytechnics and research institutions (Bennell and Pearce 2003). Vocationalization is a strong trend in higher education, which means that many fields are offering degrees for practical occupations. It must be remembered also that most of the expansion has occurred through private institutions. The market has enabled the incorporation of more students; at the same time, those unable to pay the required tuition are simply excluded from participating.

Globalization has been found to generate a demand for internationally recognized academic and vocational qualifications. The increasingly homogeneous regional labor markets based on free movement of labor will require a uniform system of education and training (Bennell and Pearce 2003)

In turn, the trend toward knowledge serving the market will emphasize the current trend toward technology and hard sciences rather than the humanities. As several observers have noted, technology is not just a tool but also a way to see the world.

The Impact of Economic Globalization on Higher Education in Latin America

The expansion of tertiary education has resulted in a large incorporation of students. By 1997, 9.4 million people were attending higher education institutions in Latin America and the Caribbean, an increase of 31 times over the 300,000 enrolled in 1950. Table 2 below shows the percent growth over the four decades in Latin America. This growth can certainly be taken as an indication of the democratization of tertiary education, although the expansion has not been able to shake the dominance of the previous leading universities. The latter continue to give education of high quality and to offer their graduates recognition that facilitates their incorporation into prestigious employment.

Table 2. Tertiary Enrollment in Latin America and the Caribbean, 1950 to 1997 (in millions of inhabitants)

Year	1950	1960	1970	1980	1990	1997
Enrollment	0.3	0.6	1.6	4.9	7.3	9.4

Source: UNESCO 2000, cited in Reimers 2002

Under the advice of international lending institutions, primarily the World Bank, the Inter-American Development Bank, and OECD, governments in Latin America have liberalized the provision of higher education (i.e., simplified the requirements and procedures for establishing tertiary institutions) and facilitated a rapid diversification of its offerings. Data from Chile indicates that the key characteristics of its higher educational system in the past 20 years have been: diversification (through the creation of new universities, professional institutes, and centers for technical and vocational training), deregulation (as new universities and institutions can be established with little or no regulations), and decentralization (as two of the oldest universities were subdivided into 16 new universities, including pedagogic universities) (Brunner 2004). Since GATS has declared that education is a commodity for trade and commerce like any other good and the impending Free Trade Agreement of the Americas (FTAA) will incorporate GATS definitions, one can expect the region soon to be characterized by a growth of diverse institutions with an ever larger offering of academic degrees.

The mantra for education, and particularly higher education, today is that it is the "basic instrument for social inclusion" (Cardoso 2004). This is true to some extent. But access to even the highest levels of education and social reward—as tertiary education affords—does not automatically resolve issues of social equity. Most of the recent expansion has occurred through a growth of private institutions, which are unlikely to cover the unmet demand expressed by low-income families. An analysis of university admissions in 1990 by social class in Chile found that while public universities had a similar proportion of students whose parents were technical and medium-size entrepreneurs, small proprietors and self-employed artisans, private universities enrolled a large percentage of students whose parents were managers, administrators and professionals, and a very small proportion of students whose parents were semi-skilled and unskilled manual workers (Brunner and Briones, cited in Fischman and Stromquist 2000). A more recent investigation of Chile's higher education (Brunner 2004) reveals that stratification continues. The students from higher socioeconomic levels attend better high schools and thus obtain higher scores in the national university admission exam and subsequently enter the most prestigious universities.

Since 58 percent of the student loans are given to the traditional universities and the remainder to the newer universities, loans tend to go to students in middle-income levels rather than low-income levels (Brunner 2004). As Reimers (2003) observes, private universities have largely emerged as an alternative to the more radicalized and politicized public universities, a strategy promoted by authoritarian governments (seeking a more docile university student body) and economic elites alike. These institutions, therefore, have emerged not because of motivation guided by social equity but rather because of social exclusion, namely, by elites seeking to create parallel settings less imbued with political concerns and less engaged in political activism.

Nonetheless, the concept of equity is being applied to higher education by the World Bank and endorsed by others such as the International Development Bank and USAID. In a curious way, these agencies argue that while primary education benefits the poor, higher education benefits the wealthier classes since it is they who are sending their children to university. The World Bank contends that if higher education is to be given equitably, countries should charge fees to these relatively wealthy students so that they pay for what is an expensive service.

These arguments by the international financial and development agencies have been met with a high degree of skepticism. Puiggrós (1996), a careful observer of Latin American education, maintains that the word "equity" has been distorted for it has been used to eliminate the provision of free public education beyond the primary level. Echoing this analysis, Reimers (2001) finds that reductions in the resources of education usually increase inequities in educational spending. Since urban students and urban schools are typically more vocal, better organized, and located much closer to the centers of power (i.e., the government or the ministry of education), it is easier for them to be heard than low-income, rural populations. Reimers (2001) further observes that while it has often been argued that adjustment programs would develop forms to protect the education of weaker sectors, he could find no study to support this promise (see also Reimers and Tiburcio 1993).

Zeroing in on the case of Mexico as a window to changes in higher education in Latin America may be useful. The public university in Mexico is very much a product of the Mexican revolution, as it was founded on the principles of social equality, justice, and mobility. The Mexican constitution does not permit fees and tuition charges for public education; it is debated, however, whether this provision applies to higher education (Rhoads and Mina 2001). Scholars frequently assert that the public university in Mexico has traditionally been seen first as a *social institution* and much less as a *business organization*. They denounce with sadness and often indignation the fact that the International Monetary Fund (IMF) was the key actor in demanding that the Mexican government reduce subsidies to public universities.

Under a discourse loaded with terms such as accountability and autonomy, Mexican public universities have been undergoing major change. In 1999, the largest university, Universidad Nacional Autónoma de México (UNAM), saw its budget cut by 30 percent. To sustain itself through this reduction in financial assets, UNAM was said to have been given authorization to increase—if it so desired—the tuition it charged students. Historically, this tuition has been minimal: at less than \$1 per year, it had only symbolic value. The decision to raise tuition at UNAM encountered strong student resistance. After protracted opposition by the students, university officials abandoned the idea of generating funds through student contributions.[11] After nine months of tense conflict, students returned to class. But returning to classes in a university whose budget has been severely reduced does not augur well for access to a satisfactory infrastructure in terms of classroom facilities, equipment, and libraries. With decreased state funds, public universities are likely to become second-rate options for ambitious students bent on finishing their studies and joining the labor market. In Mexico, postgraduate programs (master's and doctorates) have grown by 550 percent between 1970 and 1984. While the number of postgraduate fellowships increased linearly between 1971 and 1982, they declined drastically by 62 percent from 1982 to 1991 (Ibarra

---

[11] Fees have not increased in public universities but administrators have found other ways of securing resources, primarily through increased fees for various services that are provided internally and increased prices for textbooks.

1998a), reflecting a further disconnect from the state in the support of higher education.

Ibarra (1998b) offers a detailed case study based on the Universidad Autónoma Metropolitana (UAM), a large public university in existence since 1973. UAM faculty members have faced an increasing managerial rule and the gradual depoliticization of their activities. This is taking place through changes in governance and in the way salaries are computed. Governance has been shifting toward administrative rule as linkages between the university and industry are courted, negotiated, and put into effect. Salaries have been redefined to be calculated on a very low "base" level that is augmented by merit pay, mainly as bonuses for research activities. Thus, contracted (base) salaries that used to provide 100 percent of one's salary had been reduced by 2003, reduced to a base of only 38 percent on average (it varies depending on faculty rank), with any additional payment by the university to be received in the form of bonuses for research. Faculty must now engage in research to generate additional funds. The instrument used to evaluate academic productivity assigns a low and fixed number of points to teaching, student advisement, and departmental administration, while it permits large numbers of points and high ceilings for activities such as authoring books, articles, patents, publications in a foreign language (Ibarra 1998b: 318). Other Mexican universities, including UNAM, are undergoing a similar process of salary computation, a process that clearly generates internal earnings and status divisions among faculty.

This form of evaluation of academic performance, known sometimes as the use of "efficiency indices," is spreading throughout the region. In Argentina, a full professor with 20 years of seniority currently earns $1,500 per month. S/he can receive another $1,000 in incentives depending on how his or her work fits within the norms of efficiency (Puiggrós 1996; see also Mollis and Marginson 2002). In a number of Latin American countries, notably Brazil and Chile, public universities are competing with each other for limited public resources through regular external institutional evaluations. At least in the case of Brazil, this will contribute to the existing stratification in national university systems, as the weaker universities in the Northeast find it difficult to compete with the more established universities in the south of the country, and thus they will lose in the race to receive funds for greater research infrastructure and activities. Several observers feel that the pressure to research and to publish is not necessarily leading to higher quality programs. This is an empirical issue that needs demonstration.

While the promotion of research activities has much to be praised, an unintended consequence of the research emphasis is that it tends to create an often counter-productive competition among faculty members that decreases joint research efforts and solidarity as a group within the faculty. Returning to the Mexican case, since research funds are available for work on pre-designated areas and problems, professors in that country are losing their autonomy in selecting their research agenda. Thus research now leans toward practical problems of production and science and technology, not toward social problems. It is also observed that the new rules are bringing non-flexible rules for academic program definition (Ibarra 2003). Mexican university professors consider that "accountability" is being reduced to mean exclusively efficiency. They ask whether the universities should not also be held accountable for nation-building, for creating professionals, for stabilizing the political system. Noting the unilateral definition of accountability to mean mostly short-term performance evaluation of the university and its faculty, a pattern discernible in other countries of the world, Ordorika (2003) asserts that the universities now face a blueprint exported from other countries and transferred to cultures where it just does not fit.

The quality of teaching is being defined in terms of the capacity to answer market needs. This is reflected in criteria, indicators, and other parameters connected with the educational supply, programs of study, and academic personnel. Relevant indicators are the distribution of enrollment by field, the frequency of updating of the programs of study, the connection between study programs and the needs for technological, economic, and social development of the country, terminal efficiency (how many graduate within the expected time), and the social impact of the programs (Ibarra 1998a, citing Mexico's Secretariat for Public Education). Although research quality is defined as "advancing the social utility of the product," in reality it is operationalized by the number and monetary value of the agreements between the university and private industry, private service firms, or the government (Ibarra 1998a).

Ordorika (2003) and Ibarra (2003) contend that the university today is far from being autonomous but is rather operating under new forms of control. The state now controls the university much more than before through the reduction in base salaries and the imposition of criteria for what constitutes excellence. These scholars argue that the university has lost the autonomy to define its programs of study and to allocate research funds—two essential dimensions of academic decision-making. They see the new set of relations as moving the university away from a critical political role and much more into instrumental, practical problem-solving. They see further that administrative layers have been growing and making more decisions, particularly looking for links to the market and patents (Ordorika 2003).

In Latin America as a whole there is a strong trend toward privatization of higher education. From Chile to Guatemala, higher education has seen an explosion of numerous professional institutes, many of them offering short-term careers. The university as the center of advanced knowledge and the political conscience of the nation is losing out. As Ibarra (2003) notes, "the university as a counterbalance to the state and the economy, as a place to debate the vision of the nation" is gradually weakening. Confronted by strategies that gear their work into constantly measured performance in terms primarily of research productivity, university professors are said to be losing their capacity both to reflect and resist (Ordorika 2003).

The Impact of Economic Globalization on Higher Education in Africa

Unlike Latin America, the differential costs between secondary and tertiary education are very high in the African region: public subsidies are roughly three times higher for secondary education than for primary education and 30 times higher for tertiary education in the African region (1992-95 data based on a sample of nine countries, cited in Addison and Rahman 2001). These differentials emerge in part because the support to primary education tends to be exceedingly low. They emerge also because the investment of African governments in higher education comprises not only free tuition but also covers room, board, and the provision of books.

The differentials between primary and tertiary education in African countries have fueled the World Bank argument that since the poor seldom attend universities, it follows that higher-income families benefit disproportionately from public spending in education. It is worth noting that user fee policies derived from Structural Adjustment Programs have made it necessary for even the poorest families to pay school tuition starting from the first grade of primary school. Nevertheless, empirical data have indeed confirmed these differentials. In a sample of developing countries, predominantly African, Addison and Rhaman (2001, using 1992-98 data) found the share of tertiary education benefits to the richest income quintile (28 percent) to be roughly double that for the poorest income quintile (13 percent) across countries. While wealthier students do seem to benefit more than low-income students from access to the university, it is far from clear that establishing tuition payments at these levels will not work in unintended ways, i.e., discourage the participation of the most disadvantaged groups: students from rural students, less favored minorities, and women from low-income families. The educational systems function with high levels of selectivity in the Sub-Saharan region at all levels, even at levels that are not as costly to parents as is the case for primary and secondary schooling. As Table 3 indicates, only 2.5 percent of those who enter primary education in this part of the world are able to attend a higher education institution, a degree of exclusion unparalleled in other developing regions.

Table 3. Enrollment and Selectivity in Education in Sub-Saharan Africa, 1995

Level	Total Enrollment (in millions)	As Percentage of Preceding Level	As Percentage of Primary Enrollment
Primary	76.5	--	--
Secondary	18.8	24.6	24.6
Tertiary	1.9	10.1	2.5

Source: Adapted from UNESCO 1998, Tables 6, 7, and 8.

The African region has the lowest gross enrollment ratios in tertiary institutions in the world. Faced with serious budget cuts and national economies in crisis, the enrollment in tertiary education has stagnated or even declined in some countries in the early 1980s. At present, the region averages 2.5 percent, ranging from 0.4 percent in Guinea-Bissau to an exceptional 15.2 percent in South Africa (UNESCO 2003c).[12] South Africa (with 21 universities) and Nigeria (with 30 universities) represent one-third of the universities in the African region. Eight countries in Africa still have no university (Brock-Utne 2000).

Beyond some statistical data that permit the comparison across a number of countries in Africa, detailed knowledge about what is happening in its various universities is not available, perhaps because the economic crisis is affecting research productivity and also perhaps because differences in language uses (e.g., the use of French or Portuguese in former French and Portuguese colonies rather than the current lingua franca, English, which is

---

[12] In contrast, the average gross enrollment for Latin America (unweighted) is 25.1 percent (UNESCO, 2003b). Gross enrollment in tertiary education is defined as the total enrollment regardless of age as a percentage of the population in the five-year age group following on from the secondary school leaving age.

used in former British colonies) affect the dissemination of research ideas. Some trends can be gleaned from developments in South Africa, where research seems to be more common and its products, written in English, are more readily publishable in educational journals.

South Africa represents a case of particular interest, despite its unique history. In a way, South Africa parallels Mexico in terms of its nation-state having emerged out of a protracted social revolution (although the historical times and the struggle processes are different: Mexico had its revolution during 1910-1920; South Africa engaged in resistance during 1948-1994). Events in higher education in South Africa reveal the university's strong and uneasy tension between serving the global economy and increasing equality through social justice interventions. Much of the influence on higher education policies came from outside higher education, notably from the macro-economic arena, global and market forces, and broader ideological and discursive challenges (Fataar 2003). Immediately after the demise of apartheid as the key political organizing principle in the country, groups that had been engaged in the struggle for liberation produced the Reconstruction and Development Plan (RDP), a national plan of action seeking redress for the previously oppressed and excluded groups. Because of the need to satisfy international creditors and enter the global market, the RDP was abandoned after a few years and replaced by the Growth, Employment and Redistribution (GEAR) strategy which, despite the reference to redistribution, emphasizes economic growth over equity goals (Federici et al. 2000).

GEAR has affected the way tertiary education is provided. It moved from an emphasis on training disadvantaged individuals and engaging in equity strategies to positioning the country for economic competition. This produced several consequences: First, the provision of higher education was seen to fulfill an economic imperative, not a vision of social justice. Second, since competitiveness called for both excellence and cost reduction, the country embarked in a nationwide plan of institutional mergers. Third, disciplinary subjects more attuned to the condition of the economy received preference in the allocation of resources in higher education.

The first White Paper on Education and Training in 1995, produced by the National Commission on Higher Education, called for expanded access within financial limits, the development of a single coordinated system, and an expanded role for distance education. This was followed one year later by the Green Paper on Higher Education published by the Ministry of Education in 1996. According to Fataar (2003), the Green Paper gave a firm rhetorical commitment to the principles of equality, redress, justice, and democratization, but assigned a key role to the restructuring of higher education through mergers. A second White Paper on Higher Education, drafted in 1997, emphasized managerial efficiency, fiscal efficiency, and abandoned equality goals. The discourse of this document reportedly changed from "redressing" the conditions of underserved students to discussing the "crisis ridden" and highly inefficient higher education institutions in South Africa.

Owing to its apartheid legacy, South Africa has two main types of tertiary institutions: those labeled Historically Advantaged Institutions (HAIs) and those known as Historically Disadvantaged Institutions (HDIs). In the past, HAIs served mostly white South Africans, while HDIs served Blacks. The second White Paper on Higher Education represented a clear effort to align the country with economic needs. Subsequently a National Working Group was appointed by the government to provide advice on the restructuring of higher education. The working group recommended merging most of the HDIs. Since 1998 a discourse of efficiency has been utilized to divide institutions (Fataar 2003).

Presently, higher education institutions are being merged to reach benefits of scale. But, given the historical inequalities in the allocation of resources between HAIs and HDIs, it is likely that the merger will end up in the disappearance of many HDIs. The surviving HIDs would lose their special function of serving disadvantaged and rural communities and will likely need to decrease their staff (Federici et al. 2000; Fataar 2003). Observers acknowledge that there have been problems of management and administration in HDIs, but many consider that a fairer solution might have been to assign them more attention and resources, not to eliminate them. In the opinion of Federici and others, "The downsizing of the higher education system, and the introduction of cost-sharing schemes as demanded by structural adjustment, are guaranteed to limit the entry to the university to an elite" (2000: 101).

Further, given that Black students can now move into HAIs and receive tuition funds, HDIs may lose their place as institutions heavily aimed at erasing vestiges of apartheid. Researchers have not detected a large exodus into HAIs, but the enrollment of Black students in those institutions is steadily increasing.

While Federici et al. (2000) and Fataar (2003) document changes in national policies, a study by Soudien and Corneilse (2000) presents an account of how the struggles for fitting the university with either economic or social imperatives is played out within the university. Their account shows how curriculum change efforts at the University of Cape Town are caught between (1) preparing students for the global economy and (2) a nationally inspired questioning of a purely economic growth approach to education. From a complementary perspective, the changes in higher education move between the poles of policies of national equity and redress, and the creation of a narrow student academic market.

South Africa has some leverage to make its own decisions about appropriate policies although it has chosen the neoliberal economic model, while in most Sub-Saharan countries, the international financial institutions have taken the prerogative of defining domestic policies.

Additional understanding about the situation of African universities comes from a report by the Association of African Universities (1997) and a study by Ajayi et al. (1996). The first report revealed the universities' increasing pressures toward diversification and funding through industry, their own self-marketing, and seeing students as clients. The report also gave prominence to the topic of quality assurance. Ajayi et al. also refer to the emerging strategy of financial diversification, noting that by 1996, Anglophone governments were still spending an average of 12 percent of their tertiary education budgets on the provision of room and board for students, while the proportion by Francophone governments was even higher, at an average of 55 percent for the same items. The Ajayi et al. study also made reference to a "serious to devastating" brain drain, owing to civil wars and ethnic conflict, in addition to the deteriorating economic conditions.

Post-colonial Africa must face the challenges of Africanization, cultural heritage, pride, and unity (Brock-Utne 2000). This means that country-sensitive solutions must be explored. Yet globalization—through marketing values and strategies and economic competition—tends to impose decisions and behaviors that might not be the most suitable. In this sense, the situation in South Africa does not seem to differ by much that of other countries in the African region. Moulton et al. (2002), after analyzing educational reforms in five sub-Saharan countries, concluded that in all cases, educational reforms merely assumed economic growth to obtain expenditures for education.

Technological Globalization and Higher Education

Another set of forces, pertinent to the consideration of changes in higher education in the developing world, concerns the expanding technological globalization, which involves the use of information and communications technologies, primarily the Internet's e-mail and Websites. There are essentially two views about these innovations. The positive one readily asserts that Web-based technologies will expand education and through distance education bring together students and teachers from diverse racial and cultural backgrounds. Knowledge and expertise will flow beyond the conventional classroom, so there will be global awareness of many issues and social networks will be built without the constraints of time and space. This is the view that supports the notion of globalization from below, and the development of the "network society." The pessimistic view of these Web-based technologies contends that since most of them are based in the North, and since English is the dominant language of the Internet, the knowledge that is distributed will not consider particular needs of developing countries and will be disseminated on a for-profit basis rather than for the purposes of social understanding and solidarity.

The views of Altbach, a scholar who has been studying higher educational systems in the U.S. and abroad for many years, are pertinent. He recognizes that globalization has brought a major revolution in distance education, with a growing use of Internet for communication and for selling knowledge products, preparing the highly skilled segments of the global labor force, and making advanced training a constant procedure (Altbach 2002). But he warns us that if educational borders become open, as is the case in other markets, weaker countries and their domestic institutions will not be able to compete (2002).

Distance education today, operating through the quickly spreading "open universities," enrolls over 3 million students worldwide, the majority of these students in the developing countries. In those regions of the world, the most profitable fields offered by foreign providers are business and management studies, and information technologies. As has been observed by several writers, crucial fields such as basic sciences, which require laboratories and equipment and thus tend to produce scant immediate profits are avoided by open universities. Altbach foresees that higher education will also see "its most lucrative markets creamed off by the multinationals and [be] unable to afford to support the basic functions of the universities" (2002: 3).

In the case of Africa, the World Bank was instrumental in launching the African Virtual University (AVU), which has been operating since 1997. This distance-learning program intends to "raise the quality of teaching programs in key disciplinary areas to a competitive international level, to provide stable learning programs that are not vulnerable to the strikes and campus closures that characterized many African universities in the 1990s, and to expand access to higher education in cost-effective ways" (Saint, cited in Fishman and Stromquist 2000: 512). By 2000 AVU covered 12 Anglophone countries and was providing programs in math, physics, and nursing. Much of the sophisticated curriculum, however, has been mostly centrally designed by professors from the US and such industrial countries as Canada and Australia.

Altbach also observes that the globalization of communication has tightened international copyrights and opened national publishing to the international markets. Already many African domestic and regional publishers have gone out of business. More seriously, large multinationals in the textbook market are not interested in general publishing but only in the textbook market. Today, many African publishers cannot publish general books.

Higher Education and Gender

Worldwide, women constitute half of the postsecondary student population. Their participation has been growing steadily from 35 percent of enrolled university students in 1980, to 43 percent in 1998, and to 49 percent in 1995. As in the United States, women in many Latin American universities outnumber male students. In 2003 there were more women than men attending universities in 11 of 13 Latin American countries that list enrollment data broken down by sex (UNESCO 2003b). The exact distribution at national levels is not known because many countries still do not collect tertiary education data broken down by sex. Table 3 below shows university enrollment in terms of the gender parity index (GPI)[13] in the two regions this chapter covers, Africa and Latin America.

Several observations can be made of Table 4. First, few countries report tertiary enrollment broken down by sex. Even by the year 2000, only 28 of 45 African countries present such data, and only 13 of 20 Latin American countries do so. Second, most African countries exhibit considerable gender disparities in higher education. The exceptions gravitate around a context in which male labor is needed to work in the mines and thus women, by default,[14] emerge as available for higher education (the case of Lesotho, South Africa, and Namibia). Third, inequalities are so severe in sub-Saharan Africa that it is unlikely that the gender parity problem will be solved by 2015 as specified in the Millennium Development Goals. Fourth, the majority of Latin American countries that calculate sex breakdowns of enrollments have more women than men enrolled at the tertiary level.

---

[13]The GPI presents women's tertiary education enrollment as a proportion of men's enrollment; under total numerical equality, the GPI would reach 1.0.

[14] Although the lower number of male students in higher education contributes to a higher female enrollment, it is not necessarily an automatic consequence.

Table 4. Gender Parity in Tertiary Education (Gross Enrollment Ratios), 2000

Sub-Saharan Africa	
Congo*	0.13
Eritrea	0.15
Chad	0.17
Guinea Bissau	0.18
Central Africa Republic	0.19
Togo	0.20
Benin	0.24
Ethiopia	0.27
Niger	0.34
Burundi	0.36
Sierra Leone	0.40
Ghana	0.40
Equatorial Guinea	0.43
Zambia	0.47
Rwanda	0.50
Uganda	0.52
Zimbabwe	0.60
Angola	0.63
Comoros	0.73
Kenya	0.77
Mozambique	0.79
Madagascar	0.84
Swaziland	0.87
Botswana	0.89
South Africa	1.23
Namibia	1.24
Mauritius	1.36
Lesotho	1.76
Latin America	
Chile	0.92
Mexico	0.96
Colombia	1.09
Cuba	1.14
Costa Rica	1.21
El Salvador	1.24
Brazil	1.29
Honduras	1.31
Paraguay	1.36

Venezuela	1.46
Argentina	1.64
Panama	1.67
Uruguay	1.83

Source: UNESCO, 2000 data, adapted from UNESCO, 2003a, p. 77.
*The UNESCO data do not differentiate between Congo and the Democratic Republic of Congo.

It is this predominance of women in tertiary institutions in Latin America that has led policy makers in the region to consider that gender problems do not exist there. Since the number of years of schooling attained seems to show that women are enrolled in greater numbers than men, several observers believe that these trends will be sustained and eventually women will be in better condition than men. Former President of Brazil Fernando Henrique Cardoso endorses such views, as can be seen from a recent declaration:

In the future, women will be better equipped, culturally equipped, because of education, than men. Through education, we can get a better inclusion for women. It takes time, perhaps twenty years, but it is already occurring. Men are blind; they don't know that in the competition, women are becoming more effective than men. In the future, I hope we'll have to have specific programs to improve men (Cardoso 2004).

Such declarations, while optimistic on good grounds, do not anticipate any backlash or chronic blocks to women's education. Yet, as Table 5 below shows, in most regions of the world—both developed and developing areas— one finds a clustering of women and men in certain professions, with women more represented in education and the social sciences than in the natural sciences, engineering, and agriculture.

Nelly P. Stromquist

Table 5. Female Participation in Selected Fields of Study, Africa, Asia, and Europe, 1982 and 2000 Data

			Field of Study (Percent Female)				
Region	Year	Countries	Education	Social Science & Humanities	Natural Science & Engineering	Agriculture	Health
Africa*	1981	26	40	32	19	26	37
Africa*	2000	12	32	42	27	20	46
Asia**	1982	25	53	31	16	14	36
Asia**	2000	13	61	49	23	35	61
Oceania***	1982	2	68	49	22	25	56
Oceania***	2000	2	77	58	30	43	76
Europe****	1982	28	69	52	24	34	55
Europe****	2000	23	75	59	30	47	74

Source: UNESCO, 1982, 1985 and 2000, adopted from UNESCO 2003a: p. 81
* Data exclude Nigeria
** Data exclude Bangladesh and China. Data for 2000 also exclude India and Pakistan.
*** Data refer to Australia and New Zealand.
**** Does not include the former Soviet Union or its constituent countries.

The data in Table 5 further show that women have been moving into non-conventional fields of study, such as the natural sciences and engineering, and agriculture, in the past 20 years. On the other hand, some fields of study remain feminized and even increasingly so, as is the case of education, social sciences/humanities, and health, not only in developing regions but also in industrialized countries, such as those in Europe, Australia, and New Zealand. Further gendered clusters are created in fields such as education, for instance, where the majority of women are teachers at the lower levels of education while they represent a small proportion at higher education levels. This suggests that much remains to be done in social representations, inside and outside of schooling, to modify notions of femininity and masculinity that in turn shape expectations and desires about fields of study and occupational roles.

Women's studies and gender studies programs are increasing in number throughout the world. They constitute a significant source of knowledge about gender inequalities and the possibility of altering repressive social and cultural arrangements. Two challenges facing these programs are that they are significantly under-funded and that gender-sensitive knowledge content and courses have not been incorporated into regular requirements but rather remain separate from the rest of the university curricula.

The existence of enrollment ceilings at the university level, brought about by constraining cultural beliefs, has been detected in India, where after rapid change between 1950 and 1991 enrollment of men and women now seems to have stabilized. This can be observed in Table 6 below.

Table 6. Enrollment of Men and Women in Higher Education in India, 1950-51 to 1996-97

| Year | Men | | Women | |
	Enrollment	Percentage	Enrollment	Percentage
1950-51	353,549	89.1	43,126	10.9
1960-61	879,409	83.8	170,455	16.2
1970-71	2,345,470	78.1	655,822	21.9
1980-81	1,968,734	72.7	738,589	27.3
1991-91	3,579,960	68.9	1,685,926	32.0
1996-97	4,352,294	65.9	2,303,161	34.1

Source: Adapted from Chanana, 2000, Tables 2 and 3, p. 7

Several lessons from the Indian experience are worth examining. The slightly higher proportion of women at the research (Ph.D.) level in comparison to the undergraduate and master's levels suggests that flexible time schedules and a longer time span of six or seven years for doctoral studies can be made compatible with marriage and raising a family (Chanana 2000). India has experienced disciplinary shifts by sex, with more women entering commerce, law, engineering, and agriculture and veterinary sciences, but the number in those fields is far from parity. While a majority of women are confined to the arts and education, men dominate the sciences, commerce, engineering/technology, and law; men are also present in a much wider range of fields. In India, two-thirds of the women teaching in higher education do so in colleges linked to a university ("affiliated colleges") and one-third in university teaching departments and their constituent colleges. This distribution, heavily skewed by sex, suggests a need to work on changing gender ideologies, especially those regarding the private world, and not simply on enabling access to higher education.

During five decades, scheduled castes and scheduled tribes have progressed very slowly in education. Scheduled caste men represent 8.7 percent of the total enrollment and scheduled tribe men 3.02 percent. Minority women have registered much lower gains: scheduled caste women represent 2.4 percent and scheduled tribe women 0.9 percent of the tertiary education enrollment (Chanana c. 1999, citing data GOI data for 1998). Chanana observes that the poor representation of the scheduled castes and tribes is due to the fact that their advancement requires greater investment of resources in terms of time and money and also new forms of support and renegotiated roles at home. This suggests, again, that specific state policies aimed at breaking the ideological and material constraints of women, particularly poor women, must be enacted. The expectation that individual access to education will take care of that is simply not validated by the emerging longitudinal data from India or the cross-sectional data from other developing countries.

The presence of the enrollment ceiling phenomenon at the higher education level in a country such as India is of particular importance because since the 1960s the Indian development strategy, which has depended heavily on planning, is one of the few in the world that has explicitly identified the need to address the disparities between men and women in education. Further, the government created a Committee on the Status of Women in 1974, which since then has made extensive recommendations on women's education. The National Policy of Education for 1985 took a "broader view in underscoring the role of education in empowering women in order to overcome inequalities and disparities" (Chanana 2002). The National Perspective Plan, 1988-2000, further continued this frame. According to Chanana (2002), the expansion of women's enrollment in higher education up to the mid 1980s is best explained by the expansion of higher education in general because, despite official rhetoric, there has been a lack of specific policies and measures to enhance women's education.[15] The lessons from India for Latin America and Africa are that gender ideologies require serious attention and work in multiple arenas of society. Despite public policy pronouncements, little will be accomplished if more resources, especially compensatory mechanisms, are not in place.

---

[15] In India enrollment of women in undergraduate courses in engineering and technology increased from 0.09 percent in 1971 to 10.09 in 1991 and 11.14 in 1994. The enrollment of women in engineering and technology courses is estimated to reach 16 percent in the polytechnics.

Compensatory policies are those that seek to redress inequalities by giving additional resources or creating favorable conditions for marginalized groups. They represent the most tangible form of equity provision. The Latin American region has adopted very few compensatory policies so far. The largest in scope and complexity is PROGRESA (*Programa de Educación, Salud y Alimentación*; Education, Health and Nutrition Program), an effort being carried out in Mexico that has education, nutrition, and health components.

PROGRESA is also the only compensatory policy in the region that gives differential attention to girls, in an attempt to lower the dropout rate among secondary girls in rural areas.[16] By 1999, Mexico's compensatory programs had expanded to cover 46 percent of all public schools (Reimers 2002). Other compensatory programs in the region address only social class, focusing on poor populations but not on ethnicity or gender.

In Africa, a key principle of the African Charter (Article 18.3) seeks to "ensure the elimination of every discrimination against women." This Charter has been adopted in full by the Organization of African Unity since 1981. However, many African governments have been reducing support for higher education, and private higher education institutions are being promoted. Most of these new private institutions offer disciplines such as engineering, medicine, management, and computer science at high tuition costs.

Longwe (2002) observes that the proportion of women students has remained stagnant even in the highly subsidized public institutions. She predicts that if higher education shifts toward the private sector, women's enrollment may decrease. In the African region, even at the primary level of education it is difficult to find compensatory policies focused on girls. The few that exist either offer reduced or no fees at the primary education level or accept lower entrance scores at the secondary level. In several African countries short-term social marketing campaigns (attempting to persuade parents to send their daughters to school) have been carried out. Economic incentives to families to compensate for the loss of the domestic labor by their daughters do not seem to have been tried in Africa.

Longwe (2002), who has analyzed in detail the conditions of women in Africa, has come to the conclusion that higher education is crucial. Nonetheless, she argues that there must be a clear policy vis-à-vis the role of

---

[16] PROGRESA, called Oportunidades since 2002, has been found to facilitate the retention of girls in schooling even though it has not been able to modify the sexual division of labor within the household.

the private sector in higher education and in favor of encouraging women students in the private professional institutions through supportive measures. She also reminds us to examine not only the general access of women to institutions in higher education, but also their representation in fields of study, their participation as teachers and faculty members, and their presence as leaders.

In education, gender equality in access to higher education is a significant aspect of the struggle for women's advancement. But the struggle must go beyond access. It is essential not only to reach formal schooling but also to change its nature, specifically the content of what is learned and the experience lived in everyday school attendance. Even writers who are extremely sensitive to equity in higher education develop a blind spot when it comes to gender. For instance, the article by Fataar (2003) on South Africa, which is so concerned with social justice in higher education, refers to equity for groups previously affected by apartheid policies. This implies attention to various racial and ethnic groups, but not to gender.

Regarding gender issues, equality, not equity, should be the objective. *Equality* is the end result, when women and men enjoy equal conditions; translated to education, this would mean that women and men attain equal years of schooling and feel free to select similar fields of study. *Equity* refers to the means to attain the objective of equality; these means include the various policies in place to enable women to erase their educational, economic, cultural, and political disadvantage. I do not subscribe to the current usage of the word equity to mean reduced equality for women. Given that equity is the *means*, a fundamental question then becomes, under what conditions will the state enact and implement gender-sensitive policies that promote both redistribution and recognition simultaneously?

Conclusions

On the basis of the educational statistics presented herein, it can be said that higher education today offers greater access for all, but access that relies on the existence of highly differentiated institutions and that continues to be unequal for different groups. Economic globalization today has brought about greater choices at the higher education level but, simultaneously, it has also introduced a substantial decrease in the concern for social equality and the equity policies needed to make equality a reality.

Table 7. Summary of Higher Education Trends Characterizing African and Latin American Universities

Category	African Universities	Latin American Universities
Access to higher education	Expanded through privatization and diversification	Expanded through privatization and diversification
Role of education in human capital formation	Very high	Very high
Key external decision-making players	The World Bank	The World Bank, IDB
Governance	Increasing role of administrators	Increasing role of administrators
Faculty evaluation	Unspecified but emerging in the direction of external evaluation	Well established, with research over teaching indicators
Faculty remuneration	Unspecified	Linked to annual productivity—low basic salary
Financing of higher education	User fees and student loans	User fees and student loans
Efficiency	Mergers (South Africa)	Decentralization (Chile)
Equity through higher education	Loans for low-income students; still incipient	Loans for low-income students; under expansion
Quality of higher education	Threatened by Loss of state funding	Threatened by deregulation policies
Brain drain	High	High
Gender Issues	Absence of policies	Absence of policies

The principle of self-support (which leads universities to rely on user fees) and new rules for academic productivity abound. Competition for financial resources and prestige among universities has resulted in substantial differentiation among institutions, between public and private universities and institutions, and a stark differentiation among faculty members even within the same institution. The comparison between African and Latin American universities evinces considerable convergence involving multiple features.

The market is not only economic but also ideological and cultural. Youth today, and the new generation of elites being shaped in universities, are living a moment of depolitization and high consumption. Globalization in higher education has to do with who shall have the privilege to decide what knowledge has merit and who gets rewarded for having it. Politics, whether under globalization or in any other context, is a "struggle about competitive conceptions of justice" (Lebow 2004). In a fundamental sense, the politics of higher education have to do with justice and one of its major expressions, equity. The dominant ideologies that have shifted the university from being a public good to being a commercial service are bringing a strong utilitarian bent to the university. Although not readily evident, mechanisms are now in place that will lead to the loss of value of those disciplines that reflect upon society, and the types of professional training that are not readily practical. It is not clear at this point whether preoccupation with market needs will foster alternative programs and technologies that suit the particular needs of the developing countries. The space for social critique in the university is being increasingly reduced.

So, against early expectations that globalization might create a more interdependent and empathetic world, its economic and political manifestations are leading not towards multiculturalism and mutuality but to polarization and privatization. A ferociously aggressive climate is emerging in which one's own position has top priority and concerns for solidarity, understanding of the "other", and social justice are sharply reduced. In theory, questions of efficiency could be worked out so they are compatible with equity; in practice, this is not happening.

Neo-liberal economic ideas that accompany economic globalization have succeeded in reframing the problem of equity as one of poverty, rather than one of complete reconfiguration. Even the poverty objective is merely rhetorical because the existing social policies not only are very limited today but also focused on the poorest of the poor. Imperatives of an economic nature guide policy, including higher education policy; this is affecting even countries with a very recent politically transformative past such as South Africa or well-established equity legislation such as Mexico.

While with globalization greater attention has been drawn to education, this has not translated into support for higher education. With the privatization of higher education, the legitimation of the state as a body with rights to influence the distribution of essential goods is being weakened. The internationalization of educational credentials will affect decisions by nation states, such as human capital resource planning, the form of their national identity, the shrinking of social agendas, and the role of educational systems as institutions for social cohesion (Robertson et al. 2002). There is convergence between Latin American and African universities in that there is a visible reduction of state support, strong encouragement for the emergence of differentiated and private institutions, and an increasingly strong alignment between university research and private business needs and demands.

It is undeniably true that many areas of Latin America and Africa confront enormous backlogs in infrastructure for lower levels of education, not just higher education. However, work needs to be sustained and expanded at the level of higher education because this level represents the highest life stakes. There are gross differences between rural and urban areas, and major differences by social class. Mistakenly, however, gendered power asymmetries are being ignored and gender issues deemed superfluous in the urgent rush toward market competitiveness. A large segment of policy makers in both Latin America and Africa think that education for women at lower levels is sufficient. And when they do concede that higher levels are critical, their views focus on access, not educational content and outcomes.

The empirical world shows that, despite the acquisition of higher levels of education by women, in many countries there is no equal opportunity for them because social understandings about women's and men's roles and responsibilities, capabilities, and aspirations are not being modified through the education process. In such countries there are no policies centering on women in higher education. No comprehensive university programs could be detected that systematically seek to modify the university disciplines, or lived experience, to question the current clustering of field of study choices, many of which continue to reproduce traditional conceptions of femininity and masculinity. The simultaneous high presence of Latin American women in higher education and their low access to economic and political power is evidence that higher education is not sufficient to alter mindsets.

Southern African countries also have a high presence of women in higher education and while South Africa, for instance, has adopted progressive policies (e.g., higher representation of women in parliament), even in these countries there is no parallel or proportionate gender distribution of higher education or occupational ladders. In the context of the new economic and political dynamics, despite increasing discursive attention to gender issues, there is an absence of gender-focused policies at the higher education level — the level that produces the highest level of economic and political power. This makes the reiteration of women's needs an ineluctable agenda.

Faced with the challenges for professors to concentrate on research and publishing, to refrain from topics that do not contribute to immediate economic production, and to avoid political mobilization and compete with one another for salary bonuses, the role of the university in social critique is certainly becoming much weaker than in the past. Under these circumstances, university students — and ultimately society at large — are gaining compartmentalized knowledge rather than the ability or inclination to see how that knowledge fits into the grand scheme of things. This is knowledge without wisdom.

The impacts of globalization on higher education in Latin America and Africa need to be more systematically documented in the literature. Statistical indicators are available for a few transition points such as access to the university and distribution by field of study. There is a need to observe (carefully) connections among events and to sustain a comparative research program. Using data for the two countries that seem to have produced more research studies than other countries in their respective regions, South Africa and Mexico, I have presented a deeper picture of ongoing administrative and academic processes at the university. However, these findings may not be fully generalizable to other countries in those regions. In part due to the incomplete nature of the evidence discussed, a definitive conclusion to this chapter must await the answers to a number of questions to be considered in future research efforts:

- What are the consequences, positive and negative, of the current massification within a highly diversified higher education system?
- What are the social costs and benefits of the drive for individual and institutional prestige?
- What is the emerging faculty's role in entrepreneurial institutions of higher education? What is being done to preserve academic autonomy?
- What is the pace of growth of international higher education providers in Africa? What is the effect of this on the de-Africanization of national problems?
- What positive and negative effects can be linked to the increasing ties between industry and university?

- What are the longitudinal trends in the distribution of women and men by field of study? Has the relative presence of women and men in the differentiated institutions of higher education been accelerated by globalization?
- How is privatization of higher education affecting the participation of ethnic minorities?
- What coalitions exist in education, and for higher education in particular, to counter current economic globalization trends?
- What coalitions exist between women from the North and the South concerning higher education? And finally,
- To what extent can the research agenda of African and Latin American universities under current globalization contexts be made more sensitive to national and social needs?

Explicitly comparative research on the two regions is likely to detect intriguing similarities behind what may be found to be only superficial differences in access to higher education. The joint efforts of scholars in Africa and Latin America should be seriously considered as we move further into a heterogeneous, externally controlled, depoliticized and instrumental higher education system that embodies a contested and weakened concept of "university." It will be through dialogue backed by the evidence of empirical findings that alternative responses may be built.

References

Addison, T., and A. Rahman, 2001. "Why is So Little Spent on Educating the Poor?" Paper presented at Poverty Conference, Sida: Stockholm October 12.

Ajayi, J. F. A., L. K. H. Goma and G. A. Johnson, 1996. *The African Experience with Higher Education,* Accra: The Association of African Universities.

Altbach, P., 2002. "Knowledge and Education as International Commodities." *International Higher Education* 28 (Summer): 2-5.

Association of African Universities, 1997. Report of the 9th General Conference of the Association of African Universities. Lusaka: AAU, pp. 13-17.

Behrman, J., and P. Sengupta, 2004. *Convergence? Divergence? Or Some of Both? Major Trends in Selected Indicators among Country Groups in Recent Decades.,* Philadelphia: University of Pennsylvania, draft.

Bennell, P., and T. Pearce, 2003. "The Internationalization of Higher Education: Exporting Education to Developing and Trans-national Economies." *International Journal of Educational Development* 23, no. 2: 215-32.

Brock-Utne, B., 2000. *Whose Education For All? The Recolonization of the African Mind.* New York: Falmer Press.

Brunner, J. J., 2004. *Informe OECD sobre la Política Educacional en Chile.* Paris: OECD.

Cardoso, F. H., 2004. "Development in a Changing World: An Interview with Andrew Horesh, Kathryn Ogden, and Laura Tilghman." *The Brown Journal of World Affairs* 10, no.2.

Carnoy, M., 1990. "Education and the Transition State." In *Education and Social Transformation in the Third World*, ed., M. Carnoy and Joel Samoff. Princeton: Princeton University Press.

Chanana, K., 2000. "Treading the Hallowed Halls: Women in Higher Education in India." *Economic and Political Weekly* 35, no. 12: 1012-22.

Fataar, A., 2003. "Higher Education Policy Discourse in South Africa: A struggle for Alignment with Macro Development Policy." *South African Journal of Higher Education*, 17, no.2: 31-40.

Federici, S., G. Caffentzis, and O. Alidou, 2000, *A Thousand Flowers: Social Struggles Against Structural Adjustment in African Universities.* Trenton, N.J: Africa World Press.

Fischman, G., and N. P. Stromquist, 2000. "Globalization Impacts on the Third World University. *Higher Education: Handbook of Theory and Research* vo. 15. New York: Agathon Press, pp. 501-21.

Latin American Women, 1995. Compared Figures. Santiago: FLACSO.

Galbraith, J. K., 2002. "A Perfect Crime: Inequality in the Age of Globalization." *Daedalus* 131, no.1: 11-25.

Hayward, F., 2000. "Internationalization of U.S. Higher Education, Preliminary Status Report." Washington, D.C.: American Council on Education.

Hayward, F., and L. Slaya, 2001. "A Report on Two National Surveys about International Education. Public Experience, Attitudes and Knowledge." Washington, D.C.: American Council on Education.

Htun, M., 1998. "Women's Rights and Opportunities in Latin America: Problems and Prospects." Issue Brief, The Women's Leadership Conference of the Americas. Washington, D.C.: Inter-American Dialogue and ICRW, April.

Ibarra, E., 1998a. "Neoliberalismo, Educación Superior y Ciencia en México. Hacia la Conformación de un Nuevo Modelo." In *La Universidad Ante el Espejo de la Excelencia,* ed., E. Ibarra, 2nd ed. Mexico, D.F.: Universidad Autonoma Metropolitana, pp. 117-82.

Ibarra, E., 1998b. "La Universidad Autónoma Metropolitana y los Lìmites de la Modernización." in *La Universidad Ante el Espejo de la Excelencia,* ed. Eduardo Ibarra, 2nd ed., Mexico, D.F.: Universidad Autonoma Metropolitana, pp. 243-348.

Ibarra, E., 2003. Presentation at the Panel on The Latin American University Response to Neoliberalism, at the annual conference of the Comparative and International Education Society, New Orleans, March 12-15.

Jones, P., 2000. "Globalization and Internationalism: Democratic Prospects for World Education." In *Globalization and Education, Integration and Contestation Across Cultures,* ed., N. P. Stromquist and K. Monkman. Boulder: Rowman & Littlefield.

Koh, H.-K., 2002. Trends in International Student Flows to the United States." *International Higher Education* no. 28 (Summer): 18-20.

Lebow, R., 2004. "Order and Disorder." Presentation at Seminar on Justice and Order, Center for International Studies, University of Southern California, January 14.

Longwe, S., 2002. "NEPAD Reluctance to Address Gender Issues." Draft, October 22.

Mollis, M., and S. Marginson, 2002. "The Assessment of Universities in Argentina and Australia." *Higher Education* 43: 311-30.

Moulton, J., K. Mundy, M. Walmond, and J. Williams, 2002. *Educational Reforms in Sub-Saharan Africa.* Westport, Conn.: Greenwood Press.

Ordorika, I., 2003. Presentation at the panel on The Latin American University Response to Neoliberalism, at the annual conference of the Comparative and International Education Society, New Orleans, March 12-15.

Puiggros, A., 1996. "World Bank Education Policy: Market Liberalism Meets Ideological Conservatism." *NACLA Report on the Americas,* May/June.

Reimers, F., and L. Tiburcio, 1993. *Education, Adjustment and Reconstruction: Options for Change.* Paris: International Institute for Educational Planning.

Reimers, F., 2001. "Educational Finance and Economic Adjustment in Development Nations." *International Encyclopedia of Education,* pp. 1784-89.

Reimers, F., 2002. "La lucha por la igualdad de oportunidades educativas en América Latina como proceso politico." *Revista Lationoamericana de Estudios Educativos* 32, no. 1: 9-70.

Rhoads, R., and L. Mina, 2001. "The Student Strike at the National Autonomous University of Mexico: A Political Analysis." *Comparative Education Review* 45, no.3: 334-53.

Robertson, S., X. Bonal, and R. Dale, 2002. "GATS and the Education Service Industry: The Politics of Scale and Global Reterritorialization." *Comparative Education Review* 46, no. 4: 462-96.

Soudien, C., and C. Corneilse, 2000. "South African Higher Education in Transition: Global Discourses and National Priorities." In *Globalization and Education: Integration and Contestation Across Cultures,* ed., N. P. Stromquist and K. Monkman. Boulder: Rowman & Littlefield, pp. 299-314.

Stromquist, N. P., 2002. *Education in a Globalized World: The Connectivity of Economic Power, Technology, and Knowledge.* Lanham: Rowman and Littlefield.

UN, 2000. Millennium Summit. New York: United Nations, September 6-8.

UN, 2003. "Indicators for Monitoring the Millennium Development Goals." New York: United Nations Development Group *www.developmentgoalsorg/mdgun/MDG_metadata_08-01-03UN.htm*

UNESCO, 2003a. *Gender and Education for All: The Leap to Equality,* Paris: UNESCO.

UNESCO, 2003b. *Gender and Education for All. The Leap to Equality. Regional Overview: Latin America and the Caribbean,* Paris: UNESCO.

UNESCO, 2003c, *Gender and Education for All. The Leap to Equality.* Regional Overview. *Sub-Saharan Africa,* Paris: UNESCO.

UNESCO, 1999. *Statistical Yearbook.* Paris: UNESCO Publishing and Berman Press.

UNESCO, 1998. *World Education Report 1998.* Paris: UNESCO.

UNESCO, 2001. *The State of Science and Technology in the World, 1996-1997.* Paris: UNESCO Institute for Statistics.

Vilas, C., 1996. "Latin America and the New World Order." *Social Justice* 23, nos. 1-2.

Welch, A., 2002. "Going Global? Internationalizing Australian Universities in a Time of Global Crisis. *Comparative Education Review*, 46, pp. 433-471.

CHAPTER 16

A THEORETICAL PERSPECTIVE ON CAPITALISM AND WELFARE STATES AND THEIR RESPONSES TO INEQUALITY WITH A FOCUS ON GENDER: WHAT LESSONS FOR AFRICA?[1]

Tukumbi Lumumba-Kasongo

Introduction: Issues, Approach, and Objectives

Within the existing systems of production of the world economy, and structures of the states, and those of most contemporary societies, the gender inequality in Africa is a reflection of the basis of societal inequality in the ways women and men have been associated with the structures of the decision making and the systems of control of resources. The African conditions, from the period of the incorporation of Africa into the global system up to the present, must be examined through a holistic approach. Within this approach, all elements of a system of social relations have the capacity to influence one another at the different levels of their organization. They also support one another structurally and comprehensively. From this perspective, the unequal treatment of women, as it has taken various forms and social expressions, has profoundly contributed to the underdevelopment of Africa as a whole. This does not imply that African social systems before colonization were without internal contradictions. But more research is needed about them. In this specific article, I am mainly interested in the paradigms of, and contradictions derived from, both capitalism and liberalism (in its political and philosophical

---

[1] The first version of this paper was presented at the General Assembly and Seminar on "AAWORD's Vision for the 21st Century" organized by the Association of African Women for Research and Development (AAWORD), Dakar, Senegal, July 1999.

meaning) because of the nature of their impact in Africa at large and also because of their universalistic assumptions about social progress or development.

Obviously African women, men, girls and boys are not atomistic individual entities. As social agents, they are structurally the products of the complex sociological and historical relationship between the individual self and the collective self. Thus the explanation of the social and gender inequality in Africa, its origins, its policy and socio-political implications, and its economic impact cannot be reduced to a single causal factor or a single technical justification. Such a single-factor approach can often be philosophically "myopic." It is thus important to examine the dynamics of the dominant system of social relations of production with the intention of projecting how such a system evolved over time in Africa. It is vital within the context of this book that we build a solid theoretical framework which, though it may not be new, should be intellectually and historically credible, aimed at an understanding of specific social and gender inequality among the dysfunctional contradictions associated with the world system as projected at a given region of the world.

Thus there is a need to develop elements of political economic theory as tools for explaining why and how social inequality and gender inequality have had more devastating consequences in the struggles for social progress in contemporary Africa than in most parts of the world. Furthermore, as we search for African solutions to the problems of social and gender inequalities, learning from welfare states, which have developed different interpretations of capitalism and liberal political thought and which have formulated and implemented policies in different ways, is not a superfluous intellectual task.

Questions of gender relations as reflected in the gender division of labor and unequal distribution of resources, and also as projected in current state structures and political and economic relations must be examined within the broader social and historical context in the capitalist world and in welfare states. That is to say that gender relations are essentially power relations. They have to do with the distribution of power and its social impact in society at large. As theories of economic development are being studied in an effort to provide foundations for policies needed to articulate a vision of social progress in which gender inequality is critically analyzed and ultimately eliminated. Scholars should revisit classical discussions of the systems that have influenced and governed African people and their institutions during the past 300 years or so. To localize power relations, it is necessary to contextualize and historicize the arguments.

It should be noted that through slavery, colonialism, and recently the Structural Adjustment Programs (SAPs) of the World Bank and the so-called stability programs of the International Monetary Fund (IMF) in the postcolonial era, African states and people have been exposed and subjected to the logic and dynamics of contemporary capitalism. By 2004, almost all the African states, for better or for worse, and despite the different histories of state and societal formations, have claimed to be capitalistic in some way. They have also fully or partially adopted the SAPs that were designed to pave the way to the capitalization of Africa. Although the SAPs have failed to capitalize Africa, the values of capitalism or peripheral capitalism have defined African value systems and African social relations. The questions of social inequality (especially its gender dimension), social justice and equal distribution of resources have not been rigorously addressed within the structures of capitalism in Africa. This is why it is important to examine the dogmas of capitalism, especially in relation to the question of social justice and gender inequality in Africa. This article attempts to do so and also to examine some of the philosophical and political assumptions related to the welfare states in relation to gender relations and the question of inequality. The issue of what Africans can learn from the welfare states in relation to the policies and politics of gender inequality is another important intellectual preoccupation in the present work.

Capitalism, welfare states and the question of social inequality are interrelated subtopics. The types of welfare programs that will be discussed in this article, at least in terms of their principles and dogmas, are related to the development of a particular kind of capitalism. Historically, the welfare states have defined capitalism and capitalist relations differently. Social inequality is not an alien concept in any society. Both capitalism and welfare states have made efforts to define social inequality. In this article, social inequality is considered an important secondary variable that has to be understood in relation to capitalist and welfare states. As part of the global system, Africa has to respond or react to the challenges posed by social inequality.

In the new millennium, Africa is still regrettably far from dealing effectively, productively and philosophically with the questions of social inequality as part of the imperatives of social movements. In the past forty years or so, for instance, many states have decided to follow the logic and recommendations of international donors or foundations by dealing with gender inequality technically. This approach, despite the good will of some of its advocates, is epistemologically limited, historically damaging for Africa, and socially anti-progress.

Concerning gender inequality, which is the most important component of social inequality in African states, the international institutions are the most conservative forces *par excellence*. Gender inequality is a social issue and not a naturally determined phenomenon. As a social problem, the division of labor is a product of power relations. From the point of view of power relations, division of labor is based not necessarily on racial or biological morphologies or "natural imperatives" among human species but rather on the gain theory of power systems in a given society. Within this perspective, gender inequality is a serious problem in African social and political institutions and governance structures to the extent that they have forced women out of the conventional development processes as primary actors.

The creation of ministries of social or women's affairs in the 1970s and 1980s had some potential for dealing effectively with gender inequality in certain concrete social domains. So far, however, in general terms, no substantial or structural changes have occurred regarding the status of women or girls in relation to their access to resources or education or to their political participation. This is to say that despite some ad hoc policies and efforts made by some African states in balancing the demands of gender inequality, either through a human rights approach or a nationalistic approach, African states have not yet developed consistent and systematic policies that can address gender inequality comprehensively in the long run. The persistence of gender inequality means that African states have not yet fully mobilized their resources to deal objectively with development in terms of men's and women's relations. Hampered by built-in biases in most cases, these states have not been able to develop men's and women's relations from a progressive developmental perspective. In this article it is argued that social progress will remain an illusion in Africa until men and women's power relations are restructured and changed. African societies will not develop without women: historically and sociologically, African women have been the foundation of the African past, and they are still so in the non-state controlled areas of African life.

Why is it that in the twentieth century, within the context of the expanding global system, gender and class inequalities have been better articulated in the countries that adopted solid welfare programs and in declared welfare states than in "classical" liberal democracies like that of the United States? As organic African scholars, researchers and social movements are struggling to construct social theories on the basis of which to articulate national policies that may be culturally relevant and ideologically and politically progressive and in which gender and social inequalities can be addressed holistically, it is necessary to revive debates on theories that have shaped our existence as states, peoples, and economies over several centuries. Capitalism is one of those systems that should be revisited. Although capitalism and welfare states are not a monopoly of Europe, nor are they uniquely European in their origins and development, in their contemporary forms, these two phenomena have become more mature in many parts of Western Europe than in other parts of the world, as they have been shaped by the imperialistic motives and policies of the European state formations.

Because of the relative success of some welfare states, for instance, in the areas of income distribution and social mobility, it is important that some of their generalized principles be examined. A comparative analysis may help us draw some theoretical lessons in analyzing social inequality, especially gender and class and their interface in Africa.

Although the main focus of this article is not Europe, some aspects of European experience related to the debates on capitalism and welfare states can serve as useful empirical and theoretical references. Many European scholars have developed theories of welfare states that are based on the historical configurations of these states.   While capitalism, as an international phenomenon even from its genesis, has become the central dogma in world systems through SAPs, the concept of the contemporary welfare state, starting with Thatcherist policy in the 1970s, has been perceived as problematical despite its contribution in creating stable nations in Europe. In fact, in some milieux and among some scholars, it has been considered almost "taboo" and "irrational" to elevate the discourse on the welfare state as a way of dealing with social issues. However, one may argue that, although the popularity of the welfare state has declined, given the current objective conditions in Africa and the dynamics among the orbits of power tending to further regionalize capitalism (the process that is likely to continue to peripheralize and marginalize Africa), African development is practically and philosophically difficult to achieve without the establishment of some forms of welfare states. Furthermore, is the welfare state possible with the logic of the current capitalistic discourse in Africa? What kinds of welfare states should there be? Researchers should deal with these questions in relationship to the demands of social movements and the imperatives of globalization.

After World War I and World War II, the capitalist states in Europe, despite the strong interventionism of the United States through the Marshall plans and other programs, decided to build welfare states. They elaborated policies based on the needs of their people who were devastated by wars. Capitalism was appropriated differently from one country to another. At the end of the conventional Cold War politics with its ideological and militaristic international power struggle, the Fukuyama doctrine of the end of the history has been celebrated by the policies of the World Bank, the International Monetary Fund, and the emerging hegemonic tendencies of the United States' foreign policy. In Africa, the end of Cold War era does not mean that states are becoming less dependent on the countries in the North and that they are pursuing a consistent policy of self-sufficiency as articulated in the Lagos Plan of Action of 1980. Indeed, the logic and slogans of the "victory" of capitalism through privatization and "de-statization" have consciously or unconsciously been applauded in many parts of Africa. However, the majority of African people do not know exactly what to celebrate because their objective social conditions do not reflect a context for celebration. People have refused to celebrate poverty and social inequality despite the biased insistence of the transnational financial institutions that their conditions are likely to become better tomorrow if states disengage further from their social responsibilities.

Starting with the adjustment loans contracted by the governments of Côte d'Ivoire, Kenya and Senegal in the early 1980s, by 2000 more than 45 African states have partially or fully adopted the SAPs of the World Bank and the so-called stability programs of the IMF, although some African heads of state have resisted adopting and fully implementing the requirements of those programs as articulated in World Bank dogmas. For political reasons, capitalism has been established from the top through the state apparatuses. Even the countries in which there was potential for challenging the existing dominant paradigms of developments in proposing new options for economic policies and governance–for example, Uganda with Yoweri Museveni, Zimbabwe with Robert Mugabe, and Ghana under Jerry Rawlings—all have succumbed to Adam Smith's invisible hand ("natural law") with all its implications. It should also be noted that despite the "good will" of a few African leaders and the current World Bank's reformist tendency to adopt new policy language and to set up mechanisms for dealing faster with poverty; more than 300 million people are poor, and among these 200 million are extremely poor. In some countries, more than 70 percent of the population are under the poverty line on an African standard. Most of the poor are women.

This contribution offers a theoretical examination of the dynamics, social assumptions and philosophical foundations of capitalism as one of the major forces of the global system, and compares these with the claims of the welfare states. There will also be a comparison of the dynamics of capital and the mechanisms through which a surplus is produced and the way it is distributed in both the capitalist state and the welfare state. The work is basically theoretical, but specific illustrations will be given to clarify the arguments. The ultimate objective here is to try to set forth some theoretical elements of the welfare states through which gender inequality and social progress can be analyzed.

A combination of historical and structuralist approaches will be used to discuss the basic principles and assumptions of capitalism. These approaches have been intellectually influenced by leading scholars from developing countries—for example, Maria Mies, Andre Gunder Frank, Fernando Henrique Cardoso, Enzo Faletto, Claude Ake, and Samir Amin—who have attempted to deconstruct Karl Marx's Euro-centric methodology, and adapt and adopt into their analysis elements of class struggle or dialectical materialism in dealing with the dynamics of capitalism in the developing countries' orbits of global power. This approach emphasizes the role of social forces, such as class conflict, and it recognizes institutional development or mechanisms of decision making in historical terms, as part of the ethos and deontology of the capitalist state. With the exception of his limited work on India (Avereni 1968), Karl Marx did not expand his study to include non-European societies. But his logic and his assumptions about the way capitalism works in terms of its social relations and the causes of social injustices are still relevant.

This paper also argues that ad hoc, reformist-based solutions or approaches to gender inequality within the framework of the existing African peripheral capitalist states may in the long run work against women and men's struggles for gender equality in particular and the development of Africa more generally. There is a need to address gender and social inequalities at large within a progressive and unified philosophical context. This author intends to produce some elements of such a context.

Capitalism, Its Basic Assumptions, and Its Perspectives on Gender Relations

The main concern in this section is to discuss the basic principles of capitalism (or what can be called the capitalist utopia and its logic), to identify its assumptions in relation to the issue of production and distribution of resources, and to examine the way social and gender inequalities are articulated within the logic and the dynamics of capitalism.

There are many approaches to defining or discussing capitalism, capitalist modes of production, or the system that produces capital. The most popular in social sciences have been functional (or behaviorist), structuralist, and Marxist approaches. The structuralist approach is adopted here because it can be characterized as holistic with a strong historical dimension. It should be noted that capitalism is essentially an international phenomenon. One cannot define and understand capitalism outside of the international context. The holistic approach conceptualizes the process of the internationalization of capital as a component of the capitalist system. It includes the internationalization of capital as an inherent part of the process of the expansion of capital. As David Held indicates:

> While the diffusion of European power mainly occurred through the medium of sea-going military and commercial endeavors, Europe became connected to a global system of trade and production relations. At the center of the latter were new and expanding capitalistic economic mechanisms which had their origins in the sixteenth century, or in what is sometimes called the "long sixteenth century," running about 1450 to 1640. Capitalism was from the beginning an international affair; capital never allowed its aspirations

to be determined by national boundaries alone. Consequently, the emergence of capitalism ushered in a fundamental change in the world order: it made possible, for the first time, genuinely global interconnections among states and societies; it penetrated the distant corners of the world and brought far-reaching changes to the dynamics and nature of political rule (1993: 30).

Capitalism in its classical form, as defined by Karl Marx in the nineteenth century, is essentially an economic system. Marx believed that society could be reduced to economic relations. Material well-being and the means to gain this well-being are central in the ways society is organized and governed. This is to say that the development of society is associated with the quality and the quantity of the forces of production. Those who own the means of production and control them are the ruling classes. The rest of society is compelled to work for the owners of the means of production in order to earn subsistence wages. This economic relationship is the foundation of all other institutions in any given society. Government, culture, religion, philosophy and psychological dispositions function as a result of the dynamics of economic relations between the ruling class and the proletariat. They are shaped by economic power as it is determined by class relationships. All these institutions are created to re-enforce the values and power of the ruling class in a capitalist society; any historical analysis based on them as autonomous or variable phenomena is therefore circumstantial.

Among these institutions, Marx was concerned in particular with the tensions and contradictions between social relations within two classes: (1) the bourgeois class, the owner of capital and (2) the proletarian class, the owner of labor. This division, which was enhanced by the division of labor, reduces the laborers to a replaceable part of the production process. It should be noted that theories of exploitation and alienation are explanations of the social division of labor or the division of society. Thus the theory of labor, and not the gender division, explains the origins of the social tensions among human beings in a capitalist world.

Karl Marx believed that labor alone creates value, and the value of a commodity was created by the average socially necessary amount of labor required to produce it under "normal" circumstances. The value of a commodity represents human labor in the abstract, and this abstract labor gives a commodity exchange value. The fact that all commodities require labor for their production is universal to all systems of production; the differentiating aspect in capitalist production is that labor creates exchange value for a commodity, which is especially the result of capitalist social relations. The exchange value for a commodity allows one to exchange one commodity for another. He also recognized that a commodity also possesses the property of use value, that it provides a person with utility.

Surplus value is another additional value, or the most important value of a commodity produced by the laborer; this value is recognized by the capitalists upon the sale of a commodity. It should be noted that the capitalist's "right" to this surplus value stems from the "canonized belief" in individual property rights and the fact that he/she owns the means of production. The realization that surplus value leads to profit on the part of the capitalist is the motivational force behind the capitalist system. It is the acquisition of surplus value and the authority to allocate it that gives capitalist his/her power. It should also be emphasized that the capitalist drive to increase surplus value creates the second motivational force behind the capitalist system: accumulation. In short, accumulation of capital makes more surplus value possible and this surplus value makes more capital possible, creating an upward accumulation of capital. The laws of private property endorsed by the capitalist mode of production perpetuate this trend.

It should be noted within the context of this article that as the capitalist system develops, capital is increasingly allocated to a smaller and smaller group of people, who then have the power to decide how best to allocate the surplus of production to their own benefit. This process of centralization and concentration is inherent in the nature of the capitalist system.

Before closely examining the notion of gender inequality within human nature as perceived by the capitalist system, let us briefly conclude with the following concepts associated with Adam Smith's invisible law:

(1) Resources such as land, labor, machinery, and minerals are always considered scarce. Scarcity is defined as an objective phenomenon by the mainstream definition of capitalist theory. As Franklin states: "Whatever their absolute quantity, the resources can in fact be quite inadequate relative to the demand for them. Because people's wants are assumed to generate a demand greater than the means available to satisfy them, choice becomes necessary" (1993: 24).

(2) In every so-called "perfect market," there exists a larger number of buyers and sellers so that no one buyer or seller can influence the commodity price by his or her individual action. His or her input is an infinitesimal proportion of the total (Smith: 25-26).

(3) All social relations are commodified or marketable, that is to say they have prices as goods.

(4)   The principles of free entry and mobility stipulate that new firms be free to enter a profitable industry without incurring productive costs or encouraging obstacles from other firms or from the political arena (Smith: 26).

(5)   All commodities of a given industry or firm or class are said to be homogeneous or interchangeable in the eyes of the consumers. This is to say that all commodities are produced for sale.

(6)   Another important assumption related to capitalism is that the choices buyers and sellers make are based on complete knowledge of the market situation and of their alternatives. In other words, buyers and sellers know about products, prices, costs, and productivities.

(7)   And finally, the assumption of rational self-interest is vital to the functioning of the capitalist system. This means, basically, that producers are thought to seek maximum returns from their productive efforts and consumers are thought to seek maximum satisfaction from the use of their personal income (Smith: 27).

Whether in real human situations and under actual historical conditions any country has produced "pure" capitalism or not, it should be emphasized that the assumptions described above have shaped all types of capitalism; for example, the mixed capitalist system and peripheral capitalism. Most types of capitalist systems have shared the above assumptions. How are gender relations and inequality defined under capitalism based on the above assumptions? How are the issues of social justice and equality of freedom defined? In order to discuss the question of gender inequality in relation to the above assumptions, one needs first to define human nature within the logic of capitalism. As Benjamin Ward states:

> Hedonism or the pleasure-pain principle characterizes "man"(sic) in terms of...the satisfaction of the urgent demands of the body and mind; there is a clear corollary of natural indolence that follows fairly directly from avoidance of pain. Rationalism is means-ends orientation, the use of deliberative choice among alternatives in seeking the satisfaction of drive-reduction. Atomism is the assertion of the essential separateness and autonomy of each "man"(sic), with the consequent of stabilization of values by means of processes internal to the individual human organization organism (1972: 24-25).

From this general definition of human nature, three principles have been retained:

(1) hedonism (the pursuit of pleasure for the sake of satisfying the body and mind;
(2) rationalism (end-means to be used for self-satisfaction; and
(3) atomism. This is the principle having to do with the self-centered nature of individuals. Atomism also means individualism in a narrow capitalist sense.

Logically, on the basis of these principles, one cannot deal with the gender relations directly, because gender relations are essentially social relations, while the view of human nature described above depicts human beings as autonomous, islands unto themselves. A human being is assumed essentially to be individualistic. Men and women meet only in their struggles to pursue their own interests separately and individualistically. What can possibly unify men and women in their utilitarian efforts to fulfill their own teleological objectives? The problems of social justice and equality are part of human relations and not part of individualistic calculations based on the self-centered motives of an atomistic being. Under capitalism, human relations are defined mechanistically. They are commodified and quantified. This is to say that the notions of social justice and equality, freedom or other values associated with democracy, for instance, can only be understood from the perspective of individual freedom. As Christopher Pierson said, quoting Hayek:

The mirage of social justice which socialists pursue is, at best, a nonsense and pernicious and itself unjust. It means undermining the justice of the market, confiscating the wealth of the more successful, prolonging the dependency of the needed, entrenching the special powers of organized interests and overriding individual freedom (1993: 181).

According to mainstream capitalistic views, the discourses on gender relations should be located in social or cultural categorizations outside the realm of the market. This realm is considered "rational" and is viewed as the foundation of human actions and interactions. It should be noted that social categorizations are considered instrumentally "irrational." They are classified and advanced in the domain of the government. They belong to the areas of legislation, policy and politics. In other words, the discussion on gender relations is intellectually peripheralized, de facto, as it is mechanistically considered inferior to the domain of "rationality." What is irrational within the logic of the market? Because the approach of political economy is adopted by this writer, it will not be possible to define gender relations and the questions of the social inequality without briefly discussing the state.

The Capitalistic State and the Question of Gender Inequality

What kind of state fits the logic of capitalism that is discussed above? What has been the role of such a state in promoting social justice as the foundation of social progress? Historically and philosophically, how does this state perceive and define gender relations, gender inequality and the issues related to social justice?

Two schools of thought have dominated the discourse in the North, namely idealist and realist schools of thought. They also have influenced the structures of power relations all over the world, Africa included. At the heart of the capitalist states, the making of profit or the accumulation of surplus is the most important value in the world system. In other words, what is most important is how to exploit human and natural resources to the fullest in order to achieve this ultimate objective of making a profit.

One of the main differences between the realists and the idealists in political science and their perceptions of the world—and in this case their perception of gender relations as articulated by the state—is that realists tend to perceive and define the world mainly according to state-centric paradigms, while idealists maintain that although the state is vital in the management of the world affairs,, they also envision the establishment of some types of universal world (universal institutions) with common features. Idealists (both liberals and revolutionaries) argue that in addition to the state as an important actor, there are other actors that should equally participate in the management of the world politics with legitimacy. The non-state characteristics of the society can be considered as important as those of the states.

The realist school of thought, also known as power-politics theory, has developed within many facets of European-American scholarship. As reflected in the works of Thucydides, Thomas Hobbes, Niccolò Machiavelli, Georg Wilhelm Friedrich Hegel, E. H. Carr, Hans Morgenthau, and Henry Kissinger, for instance, this outlook is essentially state-centric. States are viewed as fundamentally self-interested and competitive political phenomena (Newman 1996: 17). As an irreducible element in international politics, the underlying condition for a state's development is conflict. In international relations, the state's expansionism is the motive for interactions among states and nations. It is in the name of national interests that states interact with one another. It is also in the name of those interests that they take up arms against one another. The so-called national interests are defined as natural and organic. Humanity is secondary to the interests and actualization of state power. In the classical

Western tradition, Aristotle fully explored the conditions that ought to be conducive to the "immortality" of the state in the *polis* (city-state). In this limited democracy, the citizens' participation in the *agora* was perceived to be the most important condition for advancing society and simultaneously promoting "the immortality" of the state, even if women, slaves, and traders were not qualified to be citizens. In this tradition, the state is perceived most of the time as a rational political animal, despite contradictions that may emerge from its actions and means. As Ann Kelleher and Laura Klein state:

> While the state primacy perspective of the world does not define the superiority of types of systems, it does privilege a specific type of political organization: The state is viewed as the most important unit for both national and international interaction. According to those who hold this perspective, the primary political identity for all groups and individuals should be as citizens of the state of their birth or adoption. The state primacy perspective does not argue for universal similarity in cultures or centralized power between states. In fact, it gives states a tremendous amount of autonomy in deciding the nature of their realms (1999: 41).

Within the context of state primacy, realists emphasize the sovereignty of the state. No matter how this state was created and whether it is located in the north or the south, as a reflection of human nature, it has to be a self-centered entity. As David Held wrote:

> Modern liberal and liberal democratic theories have constantly sought to justify the sovereignty power of the state while at the same time justifying limits on that power. The history of this attempt since Thomas Hobbes is the argument to balance might and rights, power and law, duties and rights. On the one hand, states must have a monopoly of coercive power in order to provide a secure basis on which trade, commerce, religion and family life can prosper (1993: 18).

What does that mean in a competitive world economy? To be able to discuss the way realists define and characterize some elements of the liberal democracy, it is necessary to briefly cite the classifications of the functions of the government as reflected in the structures of industrial societies that have adopted liberal democracies as their form of governance. Without examining the historical configurations and the social forces behind the creation a given government, realist scholars (known also as functionalists and neofunctionalists) have defined the role of government in a "perfect competitive society" in the following manner:

(1) to protect our freedom from the enemies outside our gates,
(2) to preserve law and order,
(3) to enforce private contracts,
(4) to foster competitive markets (Dodd 1955: 219), and
(5) to undertake those few public projects, like road construction, that clearly are of general value to the whole society and cannot be readily undertaken under private auspices (Franklin: 47).

First of all, it should be noted that the concept of "perfect competitive society" is a historical event in the United States following the Great Depression. Second of all, one should also mention the idea of government that should function as a balance wheel through appropriate monetary and fiscal policies. This idea is important for the functioning of any government in the capitalist world as it also relates to another notion that realists, especially mainstream economists, have produced, namely, government as a neutral entity and impartial institution. Government can represent the general interest of society as a whole and hence steer capitalism in the social interest (Franklin: 48). In short, the best government should be the government that does not govern or that governs the least. In the United States, for instance, the idea of "small government," or "taking the government off the people's back," has been part of the political lexicon during many election campaigns. However, despite controversies, the United States exemplifies the notion of a strong government paradigm. Contrary to the arguments related to the realists' laissez-faire principle, the United States government, for instance, intervened significantly in the mobilization of resources and sponsoring development projects, including banking systems, between 1944 and the 1970s.

What are the characteristics of a liberal democracy from a realist's perspective? How does a citizen interact with the state? How should a citizen pursue his/her interests? How should his/her interests be protected within the framework of sovereignty of the state?

Citizens in this historical context are individuals who are legally born in a given country or naturalized individuals who are part of a given society. As citizens, both men and women have obligations to society and the state in terms of respecting laws, paying taxes and maintaining the equilibrium of the society. They also have rights (or entitlements) in their countries to pursue the good life and happiness as part of the sovereignty principle of the state. From a realist perspective, these individuals are also buyers, sellers and producers and consumers. Within the logic of the self-regulated market or the invisible hand of Adam Smith, buyers and sellers are free to buy and sell whatever they have and wherever they choose. What is important is the quality of their goods, which should allow them to compete effectively with one another. Buyers and sellers, as citizens, should be able, and indeed in most cases are able, to participate freely in order to sell and buy services and labor according to their abilities.

Liberal democracy is the system of governance that, in principle, protects citizens' rights and the instruments of production (land, machinery, factory buildings, natural resources and the like) that are privately owned by many individuals. The institutions of the state should produce social equilibrium. This form of democracy is known as "procedural democracy." As Robert D. Grey states, citing Joseph Schumpeter:

> The democratic method is that institutional arrangement for arriving at decisions in which individuals acquire the power to decide by means of a competitive struggle for the people's vote (1942). Scholars who adopt this procedural, or elitist, version of democracy tend to be concerned primarily with stability of the system. Once the rules are in place, is the system able to maintain itself without experiencing outbursts of violence or becoming oligarchies? Rule of law and constitutionalism help regulate both government and citizens activity to limit abuses of power and keep the system running (Grey 1997: 83).

Do the people matter in this type of democracy? The implications of the answer to this question are complex, but cannot be explored in this article. However, in general terms, it can be affirmed that people do matter as consumers and as voters. The rituals of elections bring the political elite and the electors closer together for a short period of time. A fresh start can bring about new possibilities for the ordinary people. But the mass values are articulated through elitist filter; important issues are selected and elevated from their individualistic origins to the local or national agenda. As Grey indicates:

> Central to procedural definitions of democracy is the free and fair competition among political parties for the power to make public decisions. This regular competition for power keeps conflictual groups from engaging in violence, much like individuals in conflict might "settle it" through a coin toss or an arm-wrestling match rather than in a fist fight. Hence, in a procedural democracy, conflicts are legitimate and adverse to public interest (Grey: 87).

With its concern for reason, law, and freedom of choice that could only be upheld properly by recognizing the political equality of all mature individuals, this form of democracy limits the power of the state to a large extent (Held 1993: 18). As Beetham stated:

> Democracy I take to be a mode of decision-making about collectively binding rules and policies over which the people exercise control, and the most democratic arrangement to be that where all members of the collectivity enjoy effective equal rights to take part in such decision-making directly—one, that is to say, which realizes to the greatest conceivable degree the principles of popular control and equality in its exercise (Beetham 1993: 56).

How are men's and women's relations perceived from the above perspectives? In Thomas Hobbes' state of nature, the physical realm rather than the intellect was associated with power. In the West, following the Platonic traditions that Hobbes and other philosophers incorporated into their own works, women were considered "inferior animals" within the world of animals. The debate in the agora in the 5th century B.C.E. in Greece (which was essentially a slave society, since 90 percent of its population were either slaves or of slave origins) as to whether women were human beings or beasts is a reflection of the dominant traditions in the West that located gender relations in the logic of power. Despite their merit, their personal intelligence, and their immense contributions to the growth of the city-state, women could not become citizens. In this case, gender relations were perceived as naturally and historically fixed. These intellectual and social traditions of the European societies were strongly shaped by the hierarchy of patriarchy. Anthropological and ethnographical studies of most early European societies show that gender relations were conceived essentially within deterministic and static biological and social lenses. As compared to liberal political thought, the earlier philosophies essentially perceived and accepted social hierarchies as natural and God-given (Abramovitz 1989: 15).

From the point of view of realism, women and men are consumers and their values depend to a large degree on how much they can become a commodity. Capitalistic states do not perceive the question of inequality as a social concern. If addressed at all, it is examined as an economic issue. Within the framework of this study, only within the realm of social democracy can it be understood fully how gender relations could be appreciated and how much African societies can learn from them.

Welfare States and Gender Relations

Many countries in various periods of their development have produced forms of welfare states to deal with the need to include all their citizens and the questions related to the social distribution of resources. For instance, the formal discussion on the welfare state in India goes back to the writings of Kautilya in his theory of prince as the safeguard of the social order based on the Varna and Ashrama systems (Kohli 1995: 36). In many parts of Africa, the philosophical idea of the welfare state can be located in the notion of "harmonious" organized or divine cosmology and communal ethos. However, as stated earlier, the author is interested in what we can learn from the policies of the contemporary welfare states.

The concept of the welfare state in its most current popular usage was born out of liberal philosophy in Europe. It was in the seventeenth century that the philosophy of liberalism appeared in England and it dominated the thought in Western civilization by the late nineteenth and early twentieth centuries. While European nations were pursuing their interests in Africa and other regions through colonization, in Europe itself the debate on liberal philosophy, which is the foundation of welfare states, was emerging. As Sankhdher and Cranston state:

> In explaining the liberal concept of the welfare state in England during 1889 and 1914, we should begin by [making] a precision of its symbolic representation at the point of culmination in Lloyd George's mind. The Liberal philosophy, which had its origin in John Locke's ideas, was given a new turn by the philosophical Radicals and the Utilitarians. In practical politics, however, liberalism in this period, though rooted in individual liberty, extended the meaning of liberty to incorporate the idea of welfare state (Sankhdher and Cranston 1985: 245).

This is to say that representation as the key characteristic of liberalism has been one of the most important forces behind the welfare state. After the French revolution and the industrial revolution, the attributes of liberalism were expanded from an individual quest for freedom to a societal struggle against "undemocratic parliaments" and despotic monarchs. Of course this was not done without bourgeois power struggles and proletarian struggles as well. It should be noted that earlier, both classical liberalism and later Marxism, were mistrustful of the state. The classical state was conceived as an instrument of coercive forces and thus it was perceived as anti-individualism. In England, liberalism was articulated by such philosophers as Edmund Burke, Herbert

Spencer, T. H. Green, William Berridge, J. M. Keynes, Ludwig von Mises, etc. None of them paid sufficient attention to gender issues in the development of rights and capitalism. However, they were against the exercise of unlimited power by the state and monopolistic law of capitalism. The main characteristics of liberalism include the ideology of representative democracy, based on the rule of law, limited government and the individual's right to life, liberty and property (Sankhdher and Cranston 1985: 245). As Abramovitz said:

> Classical liberalism originated in seventeenth-century England, took root in the eighteenth century, and with the rise of industrial capitalism, became the dominant political theory of twentieth century Western societies. Reflecting new views of human nature which placed selfness, egoism, and individualistic self-interest at the center of human psyche, liberalism held that competitive pursuit of individual self-interest in a market free of government regulation would maximize personal and societal benefits (Abramovitz 1989: 14).

Struggles against the monarchic and strong states in their militaristic and personalized senses produced the welfare states in Europe. Welfare states in the twentieth century sought to limit the power of the ruling class. State intervention on behalf of individuals was promoted so as to create the conditions that would allow individuals to maximize self-interest and to secure liberty, equality and justice. Most of the welfare programs or packages that were produced in Europe include laissez-faire doctrines that restricted the responsibilities of the state without eliminating its regulatory role as protector of capital, property, and national security (Abramovitz: 15). Sankhdher and Cranston describe the welfare functions pragmatically as follows:

> The key functions of a welfare state were, in addition to police responsibilities, promotion of economic development and social welfare by providing full employment, equal opportunity, social security and insurance of a minimum standard of living for those downmost of the social ladder. Such an idea materialized largely in the Beveridge plan which prescribed, within a liberal democratic framework, provision of basic needs, as also remedies for problems of disease, ignorance, squalor, and idleness. It was the application of collectivist methods for the individualistic aims of laissez-faire (Sankhdher and Cranston 1985: 246).

Theoretically, how have the European welfare states perceived and defined gender relations and social inequality? First of all, it should be emphasized that each country has produced its own welfare programs based on its social, historical and political specificities and needs. Second of all, the formulation and implementation of the welfare programs should not be generalized. The success of each welfare state depends on the political culture of the country, the nature of its leaderships and that of the state itself. Thus, the Nordic countries in Europe (the Scandinavian countries) have produced stronger and more elaborated welfare states than the countries in continental Europe.

However, the idea that the government ought to protect minimum standards of income, nutrition, health, housing and education assured to every individual as a political right, not as charity (Abramovitz: 16), can be generalized as the universal claim of liberal political thought. Within the Marxist traditions, the welfare state is to use the state power to modify the reproduction of labor power and to shift the costs of socializing and maintaining workers from private capital to the public sphere (Abramovitz: 17).

Liberal political thought and Marxist thought do not deal specifically and directly with gender relations or sexual discrimination against women as an independent unit of analysis. They deal with both the role and place of an individual or a social class in a given society as quasi-secondary variables. In both traditions, gender inequality defines men's and women's relations within the framework of the individual citizen's role and worker relations. Men and women interact as private citizens or as workers. Abstraction of gender relations in the liberal and Marxist political thought is clearly a theoretical weakness that should be addressed within these traditions. However, there is a space to deal with social inequality regardless of their origins. It is in the civic arena and in the workplace that liberals and Marxists deal with the contradictions of social relations. On one hand, a legalistic approach is advanced in association with liberalism, and, on the other hand, a revolutionary approach is put forward to deal with gender inequality. This author is interested in the dynamics of this space.

Although liberal feminists have, in general, accepted the liberal theory, they criticize liberal thought for not going far enough to promote liberty, equality and justice for all. As Abramovitz states:

> The denial of equal rights to women and their differential treatment on the basis of sex without regard to individual wishes, interests, abilities, or merits interferes with women's free pursuit of self-interest, constraints their economic opportunities and deprives them of the benefits of full political participation. Arguing that this treatment of women violates liberalism's guarantee of liberty, equality, and justice for all, liberal feminists maintain that every individual must receive equal consideration regardless of sex, except

when sex is relevant to the ability to perform a specific task or to take
advantage of a certain opportunity. Extending the idea of state as a
guarantor of rights to include women's rights and family life, liberal
feminists call on the state to take positive steps to compensate women
in the market and at home. (Abramovitz 1989: 21)

The promotion of "gender-blind" laws in particular and women's rights
in general has been perceived as being among the most important mechanisms
in dealing with sex discrimination against women in welfare states. The
concept of justice that has been the philosophical and social engine in welfare
states can be summarized in the following statement by Rawls:

Justice is the first virtue of social institutions, as truth is of systems of
thought. A theory however elegant and economical must be rejected
or revised if it is untrue; likewise laws and institutions no matter how
efficient and well-arranged must be reformed or abolished if they are
unjust. Each person possesses inviolability founded on justice that
even the welfare of society as a whole cannot override. For this
reason justice denies that the loss of freedom for some is made right
by a greater good shared by others. It does not allow the sacrifices
imposed on a few to be outweighed by the larger sum of advantages
enjoyed by many. Therefore in a just society the liberties of equal
citizenship are taken as settled; the rights secured by justice are not
subject to political bargaining or to the calculus of social interests
(Rawls 1971: 3-4).

In addition to legalism, other related notions developed in the welfare
states are those of equal citizenship and equal participation in the political
affairs of the states.

Although, according to this "physiocratic" definition, men's and
women's relations can be described as atomistic, individualistic, mechanistic,
and economistic, it is no accident that statistically speaking women have been
better treated, relatively, in some areas such as employment, schooling, and
political participation in welfare states than in non-welfare states.

Before concluding this section, it is important to mention some
differences between the welfare states that are strongly promoted by the liberal
political thought as described above and those that developed out of socialist
traditions. The liberal theory of politics allows social changes through
legalistic reforms with the focus on individual rights. But not all legalisms can
promote social justice, as Wolfe said in the case of the United States. For
instance:

America's failure to contemplate, let alone redress, social injustice and inequality is another indication of its impasse, a backhand confession that ills are beyond the reach of human action to remedy them. For a "can do" culture, such an intimation of impotence was found relatively easy to accept (Wolfe 1989: 81).

A selective approach to welfare programs puts the case of the United States neither on the liberal crusade against injustice nor on a stand-pat preference for the status quo, especially during the New Deal era (ibid.). But the social cost in choosing this approach has been heavy, with a long-term impact that has been extremely difficult to deal with for many generations in the era of globalization. The principle of each according to her/his merit has retarded the discourse on the pursuit of social equality, including gender relations in the U.S. As was stated earlier, different states have formulated different policies at various periods to deal with the gender question.

The major distributive principle that socialists used was "each according to her/his needs." Whether or not all socialist welfare states or welfare states within social democracies actually attempted to transform gender relations, their principle of dealing with each according to her/his needs is worth pursuing. For instance, in the Netherlands, in 1974, the old method of emancipation policy focused on a rational model was criticized by both men and women in their governance system. The tendency to regard the government as the axis around which the world turns was characterized as "control centrism." Thus a new approach to dealing with women's emancipation, called an interactive approach, was adopted. As Prins states:

> In contrast to the traditional rational actor model, the interactive approach allows more actors to play an active role in the decision-making process. Contrary to the rational actor model with its strong internal policy-centered view, the interactive approach takes into account the broad social context with all the actors involved. An important gain compared to the discussions in the 1980s was the insight that societal actors should be left out of consideration. This is important because public administrators have the tendency to neglect social actors and to more or less treat social questions as a neutral subject, which leads to the assumption that problems are technical and managerial and "always resolvable" in the short term. Social-Political governance aims at more than the mere rational discussion of objectives and means and the relations between them (Prins 1993: 7).

This approach perceives and defines women's and men's relations in a dynamic manner, not a deterministic and legalistic one. Prins once again states:

> The first important characteristic [of women's emancipation] is that women's emancipation has to be defined as a question of socio-political governing and governance, since emancipation is a matter at the intersection of state and society. The question of women's emancipation is not a simple, politically neutral subject, but a deeply contested question in society, concerning power relations between men and women. This means that it is more than just a problem of emancipation of certain policies. It is understandable that this question cannot be translated easily into terms of governing and governance (Prins: 78).

This approach, like other social science approaches, is rooted in social and political policy. All the actors involved, such as policy-makers, members of the women's movement and political figures must be taken into account, as each group has its own sphere of interests and influences. This interactive model for dealing with women's emancipation implemented by the government in the Netherlands had a political objective, as the results of emancipation policy are processes taking place within the real dynamic political and social field of influence. Those who have more influence are likely to bring more impact to this process. Why is it that despite the fact that this model was preferred over others, this experiment did not totally eradicate, as projected, the total inequality between men and women in the workplace or the so-called private sphere in the Netherlands after fifteen years of operation? Where can problems be located in this model? What factors have led to the result of relative partial emancipation instead of total or absolute emancipation? These are complex questions that are beyond the objectives and scope of this paper but are still relevant to the discussion.

It should also be noted that between 1973 and 1978 in the Netherlands, political and official infrastructures were set up for the actualization of the interactive approach with the appointment of a coordinating government minister, an emancipation committee, an official coordinating agency, an interdepartmental coordinating committee, a sub-committee of the Cabinet, and the ministerial committee. This is to say that the institutionalization of emancipation with its own bureaucratic machinery started to live its own life. The content of the policy was defined within this new bureaucracy. The discussion was concerned with government programs. In this process, the women's movement started to be gradually isolated. Yet it is this movement that was intended to mobilize parts of female society to legitimize changes initiated by state actors. The insufficiency of support policy from the movement was mentioned as an important problem in the integrated policy mechanisms, as Prins stated:

> Although women's emancipation has been accepted as a political goal, adequate policy-making and implementation proves to be more problematic than often assumed. The emancipation of women, with as central element the achievement of equality and parity between men and women, is not enforceable in the short term nor can it be realized by planning in the long term. There is no short-cut towards equality and parity between men and women, neither is it simply a matter of long-term planning (Prins: 79).

For this approach to succeed fully, all the forces involved must avoid a "multi-track" strategy because this may lead to dual or multiple purposes. The intellectual tensions between society (social actors and social movements) and bureaucracy (government agencies and ministries) in terms of defining terms such as emancipation must be addressed at the level of conceptualization of the project and the policy. In conclusion to this section, the reflection should be on the relationship between access to resources and societal acceptance of change. Prins stated:

> That the idea of emancipation could be institutionalized on political and official levels is an important point for the women's movement. They obtained what they wanted: 'access.' However, getting 'access' soon proved not to be the same as 'acceptance.' Integration cannot be brought about by decree. Problems in the emancipation-integrated policy would prove to mainly concern the degree of institutionalization (Prins: 82).

What Should be Learned from the Capitalistic and Welfare States?

Statistically and socially, welfare states in Europe have done better in terms of broad income distribution among social groupings and gender relations than the capitalist states following the United States model. This article does not focus on the impact of the income distribution mechanisms within the gender relations but rather on the social philosophy base of income distribution and power relations. Societies and individuals have always learned from others, but the main question that is addressed in this paper on gender relations is the following: What kind of society should be constructed in which men and women are equally respected and in which their contributions have distinctly similar social acceptance and economic value?

First of all, it should be noted that the main task in this search for new models of social progress is to study objective conditions as they are, along with their contradictions. The conditions embodied in the histories, ideologies, and cultures of the present and the past may give much information about the directions to be taken for the future. Within a broad framework, the world deals with the dynamics of contradictory phenomena and with any level of social transformation through mechanisms associated with collective consciousness. Epistemologically, not all contradictions should always be considered as pathological. However, not all contradictions can be put on the same level of analysis. It is necessary to distinguish between primary and secondary contradictions. From this perspective, much can be learned from the contradictions of the capitalist world with regard to gender relations.

The essence of the capitalist state is to exploit labor and accumulate surplus. In this process, gender relations are reduced to the abilities of people to interact through the process of managing and controlling resources in the name of materialism. Because the capitalist state perceives gender relations basically in materialistic and physical terms, its ethical base for promoting social equality is weak and unpredictable. Apart from the utilitarian philosophy, the capitalist state does not have any consistent ethical foundation for justifying the struggle for social and gender equality. According to this logic, in order to struggle for social equality, society will have to change the quality and quantity of labor that is being "sold in the market." Within the capitalist state, everything is conceived as marketable. But to change the values associated with the current social practices, policies, and values associated with labor through which women are more exploited than men in most systems, African society will have to create new hierarchies of values. For instance, in most African societies, the colonial and neo-colonial states adopted laws, norms, and social behavior that have considered women as children in the same manner that Western powers have generally considered Africans as children. The struggle for changing gender relations must start with change in the nature of the African state. In capitalism, the second area of the struggle lies in determining the values of labor and the market. What men and women can sell or buy privately or publicly must be of equal value. The approach developed and used in the West has been legalistic and parliamentarian. It has promoted certain particular interests. But despite some successes, the parliamentarian approach in the West has been mainly technical. It rarely touches on the mentalities or cultural fabrics that support social inequality.

Scholars have recommended more equal education for boys and girls at every level in Africa, arguing that this should, in the long run, produce equal opportunities. Despite the validity of the assumptions behind this argument, the pursuit of gender equality entails more than equality of opportunities. It has to do with respect for value systems, with space for each person and with individual and collective autonomy. The most important question is the following: What kind of education is being advocated here, given the fact the African education has been, despite many reforms, at best an imitative system? The dialogic concept of education that was developed by the Brazilian philosopher Paulo Freire combined with the notion of "positive and empowering complementarity" developed by Assié-Lumumba (1996 and 1997) in many of her publications, as well as the collective metaphysics of the African societies, should be further explored.

Contemporary Europe would not have developed materially without the achievements of the welfare states. The Keynesian approach to the role of the state and that of the mixed economy contributed to massive resources re-allocated in the development of industries and infrastructures in Europe. There has been no discussion of the cost in material terms of this process of re-allocation. The intervention of the state into societal affairs in the European welfare states is not simply based on the Machiavellian teleology of the immortality of the state. It also has to do with the actualization of the Aristotelian notion of the "common good" or the "social good" without which there is no society.

In other words, in the discourses of the welfare states there is also an ethical foundation from a liberal perspective. This foundation has two dimensions, intellectual and social. The rational state, which also can be defined as a responsible state, has to realize its intellectual capacity in promoting social programs through which citizens are protected. Citizens must also be prepared to support the programs through heavy taxation and respect for laws that guarantee their well-being.

How far can the state go in relation to human rights issues in the case of Africa in promoting gender equality? In this author's view, the response is located first in the nature of the state. An enlightened state that can promote social democracy, social development, and social justice can decisively create a solid foundation for its citizens to harness the necessary capabilities to sustain ontological social progress. Most of the welfare states in Europe have developed various forms of social democracy with a broad social agenda. Despite the current regional economic development in Europe that is based on privatization and liberalization, the welfare states have a strong nationalistic base. There is a need to study further how this social democracy works.

Gender relations in Africa should be developed outside of the mainstream capitalist guidelines that have been incorporated in SAPs since the 1980s. Some forms of the welfare state combined with social democracy and a strong African nationalist agenda and humanism should help African policymakers and researchers to examine gender relations not as autonomous instruments of social progress but rather as part of a progressive development philosophy. Without women's real participation, and the genuine recognition of their social values and contributions, any efforts toward social progress in Africa will be doomed to fail.

References

Abramovitz, M., 1989. *Regulating the Lives of Women: Social Welfare Policy From Colonial Times to the Present.* Boston, Mass.: South End Press.

Assié-Lumumba, T. N., 1996. *Les Africaines dans la politique: femmes baoulé de Côte d'Ivoire.* Paris: L'Harmattan.

Assié-Lumumba, T. N., 1997. "Educating African Women and Girls." In *Engendering Social Science in Africa,* ed., A. Imam, A. Mama, and F. Sow. Dakar: Council for Development of Social Science Research in Africa (CODESRIA).

Beetham, D., 1993. "Liberal Democracy and the Limits of Democratization." In *Prospects for Democracy: North, South.East, West,* ed. D. Held. Stanford, Calif.: Stanford University.

Bowles, S., and H. Gintis, 1986. *Democracy and Capitalism: Property, Community, and the Contradictions of Modern Social Thought.* New York: Basic Books.

Palloix, C., 1975. "The Internationalization of Capital and the Circuit of Social Capital." *In International Firms and Modern Imperialism,* edited by H. Radice. Harmondsworth: Penguin.

Palloix, C., 1977. "The Self-Expansion of Capital on a World Scale." *Review of Radical Political Economics* 9:1-28.

Dankwart, A. R., 1970. "Transition to Democracy: Toward a Dynamic Model." *Comparative Politics* 2, no. 3 (April): 337-63.

Franklin, S. R., 1976. *American Capitalism: Two Visions.* New York: Random House.

Grey, D. R., 1997. *Democratic Theory and Post-Communist Change.* Upper Saddle River, N.J.: Prentice Hall.

Held, D., 1993. *Prospects for Democracy: North, South, East, and West.* Stanford, Calif.: Stanford University Press.

Kelleher, A., and L. Klein, 1999. *Global Perspectives: A Handbook for Understanding Global Issues.* Upper Saddle River, N. J.: Prentice Hall.

Kohli, R., with foreword by M. M. Sankhdher, 1995, *Kautilya's Political Theory: Yogakshema, the Concept of Welfare State. ,* New Delhi: Deep and Deep Publications.

Luxemburg, R., 1964. *The Accumulation of Capital.* New York: Monthly Review Press.

Mies, M., 1993. *Ecofeminism.* London, England: Zed Books Limited.

Mies, M., 1989. *Patriarchy and Accumulation on a World Scale: Women in the International Division of Labor.* London.

Pierson, C. 1993. "Democracy, Markets and Capital: Are There Necessary Economic Limits to Democracy?" In Held, D., *Prospects for Democracy: North, South, East, and West.* Stanford, Calif.: Stanford University Press.

Prins, M., 1993. "Women's Emancipation as a Question of Governance: Actors, Institutions and the Room for Manœuvre." In *Modern Governance: New Government-Society Interactions*, ed. J. Kooiman. London: Newbury Park, and New Delhi: Sage Publications, pp. 75-86.

Rawls, J., 1971. *A Theory of Justice.* Cambridge, Mass.: Belknap Press of Harvard University Press.

Sankhdher, M. M., and M. Cranston, 1985. *Welfare State.* New Delhi: Deep and Deep Publications.

Shlomo, A., 1968. *Karl Marx on Colonialism and Modernization: His Dispatches and Other Writings on China, Mexico, the Middle East and North Africa.* Garden City, N.Y.: Doubleday.

Steans, J., 1968. *Gender and International Relations: An Introduction.* New Brunswick, N.J.: Rutgers University Press.

Ward, B., 1972. *What's Wrong with Economics?* New York: Basic Books.

Wolfe, A., 1989. *America's Impasse.* New York: Pantheon Books.

General Conclusion

N'Dri T. Assié-Lumumba

The arguments in the contributing chapters cannot be easily synthesized. Suffice it to indicate that these contributions have addressed a number of complex issues that are central to the relevant analysis and understanding of the interface between gender, higher education, and the production of knowledge as a means for agency, reclaiming of human rights, and a source for informed participation in social processes. The contributors have explored the issues surrounding the basic fundamental right of women to higher education, and have argued the importance of women's access to higher education if African societies and countries are to break the cycle of poverty and human misery.

The legitimate call for a critical approach to the assumed validity of data is convincingly articulated. While keeping in mind these warnings as well as the problematics of epistemology and the limitations of the available data, especially in the African context, several contributors used data from various sources to substantiate their arguments concerning the systemic issue of women's under-representation in African educational systems. Several case studies of countries with different colonial experiences and legacies illustrate comparative patterns of gender inequality. Perceived and/or treated— especially in the increasingly globalized neo-liberal economy—as of high value in terms of their functional utility, science and technology have been made less accessible to women.

Located in the dynamics of self-fulfilling prophecy, the nature of the participation of women in these fields as students and professionals and the factors that determine their various contributions to the production of knowledge are ironically reproduced through the education process.

While many of the issues identified and problems analyzed are specific to African societies, other general issues and problems are also found outside of the African context. Similarly, while many of the issues are gender-specific, they may also be applicable to other social factors that constitute the ground of structural inequality in Africa. Comparisons between Africa and East and South East Asia and between Africa and Latin America lead to different conclusions. They deal with factors that, in comparative terms, have been major obstacles to gender equity in higher education in Africa. Some of the comparative assets in African societies that might be tapped to promote gender equity in the global and contemporary contexts have also been presented.

Familiar African predicaments and new challenges, of which the HIV/AIDS pandemic is one, require that policymakers envision education holistically, seeing its various levels as inter-related and mutually reinforcing. Just as synergy between the levels of education is needed, synergy between education and other sectors such as health care, as illustrated by the case of HIV/AIDS, is necessary if equitable and human-centered development programs are to flourish.

To break the status quo cycle, those African women in positions vested with power and authority, as illustrated by the FAWE mission's contribution to educational reforms, may not yet be very numerous, but they may have the duty and the privilege to shape the future. Efforts to understand and look forward for solutions require both an analysis of the African internal situation and also reflection, conceptualization and theorization in relation to the global context and the experiences of others in the world. Thus, the final chapter provides this necessary broader reflective effort based on the experiences of African women, especially in higher education, where African models today have their origins in the global socio-historical and contemporary contexts.

The contributions in this book have tackled many fundamental issues of interest to scholars, practitioners and policymakers, offering a balance of theory, literature, citations and concrete case studies. In searching for solutions to the structural gender imbalance in contemporary societies in Africa, as most strikingly evidenced by the unequal representation in higher education, it is necessary first to understand the complexity of the explanatory factors, as several contributions have indicated. The search for solutions requires that an understanding of the explanatory factors be accompanied by new theoretical articulations and reconceptualizations of the policy framework. Thus one of the main objectives of this book is to help elucidate the determinants of gender imbalance in formal education and their consequences for women in terms of their ability for self-realization as well as in terms of their contribution as agents, to the process of socio-economic development in Africa.

Historical factors explaining the global gender imbalance include the initial decision by most African families not to send their girl children to colonial schools, be they missionary schools in British and Belgian colonies or state schools in French colonies. Regardless of the colonial policies, with independence African countries inherited similar challenges: they had to deal with an alien institution implanted along with the European patriarchal values of the time that dictated an inferior social status and marginal learning and social space in the colonies as in Europe itself. A process of negative homogenization, whereby the African values that empowered women were ignored or destroyed while those that were actually or potentially less favorable found new fertile ground, led to the formation of a foundation for gender inequality. The combination of these two phenomena led to the recent but entrenched gender imbalance in the educational system, which, ironically, the educational process contributes continuously to reproduce.

In the beginning of the twenty-first century, that is, more than four decades after African countries started to acquire their nominal political independence; the number of higher education female students and graduates is still insignificant. This leads to limited representation of women in critical positions in the domains of politics, the economy, education, and knowledge production. In the current context of globalization, the information age and knowledge economy, and inadequate distribution of education constitute objective hindrances. Decision-making processes and planning will miss the concerns, viewpoints and inputs of women, which constitute an infringement on their rights to exercise their capabilities, and a loss for Africa not benefiting from their insight.

In addition to the low number of women at every level of the formal education system, particularly higher education, there is a broader philosophical and political question concerning the nature of education itself and the type of development to which those who acquire it are expected to contribute. In the rush to expand education at the beginning of nominal independence, many leaders failed to address fundamental questions concerning the kind of education and kind of development needed.

Despite early post-colonial commitments and policies adopted to increase overall enrollments and redress inequalities, the African states did not sustain the pace for closing the gender gap, especially at the higher education levels where the imbalance is the greatest. Unequal gender distribution of education in quantity and type, based on gender, is a major characteristic of most institutions. Thus, for example, women are overwhelmingly underrepresented in scientific fields and sub-fields. Disciplinary gender clusters are reproduced in the labor market and on the occupational ladder. Such contexts do not allow the space for women to reach their fullest potential and realize their capabilities. The issue is not the existence of clusters per se. These become a problem only because they contain embedded social values and, consequently, processes of simultaneous feminization and devaluation of fields, sub-fields and occupations. Involuntary and negative gender clusters, especially in systems that are built on a co-educational philosophy, constitute an indicator of marginalization.

Integrated development can be the foundation for social progress. In this conception of development, which includes political, social, and economic dimensions, all the African resources need to be valued, developed, and used to improve the quality of life for the general population. Such an approach is a critique of the conception of formal education as an imported alien institution and more specifically a critique of higher education as an ivory tower where a fortunate small elite obtains the legitimization of its economic and political privileges in developing its members' human capabilities.

The issue that must be dealt with by theoretical articulation, as well as by policy reformulation is how to integrate formal education comprehensively into the African social reality. It is irrelevant to continue to address the issue of imposed/imported formal education and African indigenous education in dichotomous and mutually exclusive terms. Higher education requires transformation to constitute a focal point, a catalyst for social progress.

Although women constitute the majority of those who are illiterate in European languages, they have acquired other forms of literacy, the ability to read the world around them to identify means and strategies of survival and to promote human dignity. Although historically there are some regional and ethnic specificities, African women have been involved in every aspect of society on a gender basis that allowed different but equally worthy participation of male and female in education and in the production and utilization of knowledge. Given that culture is a cumulative process, African women as a social category have acquired a wide range of scientific and technological knowledge, philosophy, political thought and cultural production that need space to grow further.

Higher education, which should no longer involve the university alone, but would include other valued alternative institutions, should be an efficient means to promote the inclusion of more females, not as beneficiaries of affirmative action policies, but as educational agents with various skills to offer. A formally "illiterate" woman trader, who travels to different places in Africa, Europe, North and South America and successfully carries out her business in a competitive and often hostile world, certainly has much to offer in any business and other programs at the undergraduate and graduate levels. Women who have been tilling the soil, planting and caring for various plants, harvesting different crops, witnessing changes in the human and physical ecology, and so forth, have much to offer in various programs in agriculture and geology, for example. In other key domains such as preventive and curative health care, including gynecology and obstetrics, care for the elderly, socialization and education, many women are highly qualified to offer valuable general and specific/technical insight in tertiary education. A policy of community involvement in formal education would be generated from a broader social philosophy. However, as the majority of the marginalized people are women, the focus on their inclusion would be an eloquent indicator of real effort to be forward looking in the improvement of people's lives, through an integrated development policy that allows human capabilities to be harnessed for the benefit of people and the local and global communities.

To really break the psychological and physical barriers between school in general (but especially higher education) and the community, schools as institutions must also organize activities that can contribute to the promotion of people's well-being in areas of expertise such as teaching, research and policy formulation, in which women have a lot to contribute. Higher education can fulfill its mission of promoting social progress by utilizing its primary assets in its basic areas of expertise to contribute to specific programs in specific communities and target populations. In the areas of research, for example, higher education researchers can feed policy-makers information needed in various areas. Women's perspectives and insight are needed here as well. A dynamic relationship between the higher education institutions and the community will create a fertile environment where education for development can have a concrete meaning and where women can also enhance their skills by benefiting from higher education community programs.

In Africa, gender-focused social policy requires not only recognition of past contributions and achievements by women in socio-historical processes but also a solid foundation for constructive interaction and participation of men and women in the various spheres of society that will lead to development. A critical participatory approach with a sense of direction is key in the formation and utilization of all human resources. The underlying philosophy has to be inclusive and democratic, which means that women and men have to be equally valued and involved. It must be emphasized that increased valorization of women's potential and input constitutes an invaluable gain for the progress of Africa. The rethinking and the reconceptualization needed for action require the inclusion of women's perspectives and voices; these may be few in number in this early part of the twenty-first century, but they have substantive, powerful and positive contributions to make.

For the African people to realize their aspirations and achieve a good quality of life by having their human needs satisfied with dignity, it is necessary to formulate long-run development planning founded on sustainability. To inject the seed for structural change and steer the impetus for permanent dynamism, it is necessary to re-conceptualize and formulate a new holistic socio-economic development policy for social progress that incorporates gender equity higher education. This is the basis for the permanent production of relevant knowledge that can help keep alert the innovative impulse to anticipate and respond to new challenges.

To deal effectively with the sustainability challenge it is necessary to start or to boost the investment in the generation and utilization of scientific and technical knowledge solidly grounded in critical thinking in the broader higher education learning experience. This goal can be achieved by aligning the missions of universities and other institutions of higher learning with sustainability goals. For instance, African institutions of higher learning, including the universities, are typically located in urban areas. Even institutions that, by their names and programmatic foci such as agriculture, are specifically created to solve problems related to agricultural production, are also located in urban areas, away from the social and physical environment where their knowledge could be of immediate use and become sharper and more relevant. More significant than the physical distance between the urban institutions and the rural communities is the social distance. In fact, these institutions are equally removed from the urban communities that surround them. Generally speaking, African institutions of higher learning are socially removed from the communities that officially constitute their *raison d'être,* and thus they tend not to play a significant role in helping to solve local problems.

Much can be gained by adjusting the curricula, pedagogy and management of urban universities to address challenges such as sanitation and improvement of the conditions of slum dwellers. Similarly, higher education institutions, including universities and research institutions located in rural areas, could serve as the locus for research, training and outreach on the management of natural resources and work toward sustainability. The lower representation of women (both as students and staff members) in higher education institutions, and especially in the sciences, is a reflection of the same ill-conceived development policies that lack a comprehensive appreciation of their society's resources.

It is equally important philosophically and practically, to integrate higher education, and to create dynamic links between higher education and the primary and secondary levels; such linking is necessary for a vision for the future that takes into account the entire educational systems and the trajectory of male and female members of society.

Adopting new policies for gender equity is a matter of honoring the human rights of the African girls and women while enhancing, at the same time, the capacity and authority of women to make indispensable inputs for the advancement of African societies. Indeed, policies that aim at removing self-destructive roadblocks and bottlenecks will clear the way for girls and women to excel in institutions of higher learning so that they can contribute more decisively toward a holistic and human-centered development process throughout Africa.

The primary and secondary level preparation of the students, the process of their selection for higher education, their living and learning conditions in the institutions of higher learning, and the curriculum, should be revised to attract all potential learners of both genders and to cover all learning and professional areas of interest. Whether choices are defined by social constructions of gender roles or genuinely by preference, if it can be proved that they do not contribute to creating and/or reproducing gender inequality, every effort should be made to provide the learning opportunity.

Universities and other institutions of higher learning should work more closely with the private sector; no matter how small it is, to create traditions of cooperation in sustainable development activities. A strong and caring state with the power and moral authority to facilitate the private sector's compliance with its policies of gender equity and development can facilitate the promotion of enterprise development, which can in turn effectively address the problem of poverty. Doing so will require the establishment of programs designed to promote enterprise creation and development, especially among the urban poor. Similar efforts need to be adopted in rural areas. More specifically, institutions of higher learning and other mechanisms could serve as business incubators as well as sources of ideas and support for upgrading urban and rural economic activities. Such programs require the involvement of men and women alike, both as agents with relevant knowledge and as beneficiaries.

Finally, to give concrete meaning to CEPARRED's commitment to dynamically linking intellectual discourse to the production of tools for change, a few areas for practical policy consideration are suggested below.

Policy alignment: African countries and regional integration organizations must align their policies and government structures with the need to place science and technology at the centre of development with solid social science foundations. This will require the appointment of highly qualified and enlightened science and innovation advisors to presidents and prime ministers in order to help leaders to better understand the role of innovation in development and to meet the funding needs of programs in a cost-effective manner. Many countries in emerging economies in Asia, for instance, have such models.

University infrastructure rehabilitation and development: There is a need to renew the idea of development universities and of education in general. While African countries must be cautious about considering science and technology, especially information and communications technologies, as a neutral development tool and/or a panacea, governments must support the development of communication facilities as they make renewed commitments to the general development of the higher education infrastructure, especially those of universities. This renewal can promote functional links with, and productive and substantial contributions by African experts in the Diaspora.

Dynamic and integrated institutional design: To close the historical gap between the institutions of higher learning and their social surroundings, there should be a deliberate effort to dynamically link research, teaching and community outreach together. Every field of study, from medicine to agriculture, can have its corresponding community-based location for outreach and involvement in teaching and research.

Curriculum and pedagogy reform: While there have been numerous reforms undertaken by all African countries since the 1960s, in order to meet the new objective it will be necessary to forge new curricula while phasing out the older ones. The philosophy of education and learner-centered pedagogy aim at encouraging creativity, innovative capacity, a spirit of inquiry, and entrepreneurship. These reforms should also systematically promote cooperation with the private sector and the communities in which the institutions of higher learning are located. Governments should boost their support to higher education institutions to produce knowledge as the driving force for social progress, especially the universities that have been neglected since the 1980s, and renew their confidence in their roles, for the development of African societies. Full inclusion of women is indispensable in order to produce fruitful process of change.

University management: It is important to have the caring state provide the framework and guidance ensuring a global commitment needed to implement a national, regional and continental agenda for social progress. However, institutions of higher learning, including the universities, should have a degree of autonomy in management that can enable them to adapt to fast-paced change and its local implications in the global context. The institutions in question need this power and authority to position themselves, by their activities, as the driving force for community development. This will bring back the lost legitimacy of higher education institutions—especially the universities—and of African states as caring and enabling. A renewed legitimacy requires that, through access of girls and women to education at all levels and of all types, women regain access to their social space so that they can play their full roles as central members of communities and nations and as indispensable agents and driving forces for change and beneficiaries of social progress.

Social progress is a global, integrated, and comprehensive process of continuously improving the well being of all members of society, making positive use of all resources, including the full capabilities of both male and female members of society. It is a cumulative process which makes use of past experiences, learning from past mistakes and limitations, but also building on past achievements, ideas, scientific skills, and technical know-how from a human-centered ethos. Such an ethos defines inclusive involvement of all the members of society in economic and cultural production as well as in political participation and decision-making processes at various levels of society, as necessary for the well being of all. It is not realistic for African countries to search for a successful development model that would make use of only half of all human resources. The ultimate goal of this book is to make a contribution to the theoretical articulation of the quest for relevant development paradigms and policy conceptualization to address effectively the urgent need for Africa collectively to appropriate the process of genuine progress.

Contributors

N'Dri T. Assié-Lumumba, a Fellow of the World Academy of Art and Science, is Professor in the Africana Studies and Research Center at Cornell University where she is also a member of the graduate fields of Education; International Development; International Agriculture and Rural Development; and the Cornell Institute of Public Affairs. She is an educator, sociologist and historian by training. She has served as Director of the Cornell Program on Gender and Global Change. She is also *Chercheur Associé* CRAU at the Université de Cocody, Abidjan (Côte d'Ivoire), and Research Affiliate of the Institute for Higher Education Law and Governance of the University of Houston (Houston, Texas). She is co-founder and Associate Director in charge of the gender unit of CEPARRED. She has served on numerous committees of African and United Nations agencies. Her extensive publications include authored, edited and co-edited books: *Les Africaines dans la politique: Femmes Baoulé de Côte d'Ivoire*; *African Voices in Education*; *Cyberspace, Distance Learning, and Higher Education in Developing Countries: Old and Emergent Issues of Access, Pedagogy, and Knowledge Production*, and *Higher Education in Africa: Crises, Reforms, and Transformation.*

Amiya Kumar Bagchi is an eminent and prolific world scholar in economics with a humanistic approach. He has published authoritatively and extensively on capital, labor, liberalism, the political economy of underdevelopment and equity. His most recent positions include the directorship of the Institute of Development Studies Kolkata (IDSK), which was promoted as an autonomous centre of excellence in the social sciences. He is a leading authority on global movements in the struggle to end global inequality. He is an active participant in the Social Third World Forum Conferences.

Asma Barlas is Professor of Politics and Director of the Center for the Study of Culture, Race, and Ethnicity at Ithaca College, New York. She has published three books: *Islam, Muslims, and the U.S.: Essays on Religion and Politics*; *"Believing Women" in Islam: Unreading Patriarchal Interpretations of the Qur'an*; and *Democracy, Nationalism, and Communalism: The Colonial Legacy in South Asia*, as well as several book chapters and journal articles.

Josephine Beoku-Betts is an Associate Professor of Women's Studies and Sociology at Florida Atlantic University. She is co-editor of *Women and*

Education in Sub-Saharan Africa: Power, Opportunities and Constraints. Her research focuses on the educational and employment experiences and perspectives of African and Caribbean women scientists. She was formerly co-regional editor for *Women's Studies International Forum,* and co-book review editor for *Gender and Society.* She has published in *Gender and Society, National Women's Studies Association Journal, Journal of Asian and African Studies, Africa Today,* and *Journal of Women and Minorities in Science and Engineering.* She is a Fellow of the Rockefeller Foundation Bellagio Resident Scholar Program and a finalist for the 2004 Carnegie Scholars Program. Her undergraduate and graduate courses include: Introduction to African Studies; Gender, Culture, and Social Change in Africa: A Case Study of Ghana (Study Abroad Course); Global Perspectives on Gender; Gender, Science, and Technology; Women of Color in US Society; International Human Rights; and Feminization of Poverty. She is an elected member of the Nominations Committee of Sociologists for Women in Society (SWS).

Remi Clignet is a renowned emeritus Professor of Sociology at the University of Maryland. He has taught social sciences for many years at Northwestern University and at various institutions in France. He has lectured in several African universities. He has worked in several African countries as a researcher and policymaker. Additionally he has published extensively in the areas of higher education, planning and educational policy, the sociology of education, and the family from a cross-cultural perspective. While he has constantly been exploring new theoretical and empirical frontiers, many of his publications have become classic references in the study of social institutions and processes.

Cyril Daddieh is Director of the Black World Studies Program and Professor of Political Science at Miami University of Ohio. His research interests include state-civil society relations, ethnicity and conflict, gender issues in African higher education, democratization, elections and democratic consolidation in Africa. He has written extensively on the political economies of Ghana and Côte d'Ivoire.

Rose Eholié is a retired Professor of Inorganic Chemistry at the Université de Cocody (formerly Université d'Abidjan and then Université Nationale de Côte d'Ivoire). As a woman scientist in this subfield, she has been a pioneer. She has been a role model and a mentor for girls and women who have been inspired to enter and excel in scientific fields as students and professionals. She was co-founder of *Société Ouest Africaine de Chimie* (West African Society). She held many scientific and administrative functions including her service on the board of the Association of African Universities (AAU). At the time when she presented the paper that is included in this book, she was Director of Inter-university Cooperation and International Relations at Université Nationale de Côte d'Ivoire. She is a member of *L'Académie des Sciences, des Arts, des Cultures et des Diasporas Africaines* of Côte d'Ivoire.

Rudo Gaidzanwa is a noted sociologist who teaches at the University of Zimbabwe. With her impeccable sociological inquiries, Professor Gaidzanwa has emerged as a fine scholar who uses her sharp investigative tools to make solid analyses of social phenomena. Her empirical studies and analysis always bring a refreshing contribution to our understanding of social facts, with a focus on the situation of education as a social institution, particularly higher education. The wide spectrums of the themes that she has researched include African universities, the impact of the structural adjustment programs (SAPs) and the migration of highly educated Africans.

Philip Higgs is Head of the Department of Educational Studies at the University of South Africa. He is author or co-author of several books including *Readings in Teacher Education, African voices in education, Re-thinking Our World,* and, *Re-thinking Truth* and editor of *The Relationship Between Theory and Practice and Its Meaning for the Science of Education,* Series Editor of the Heinemann *Philosophy of Education Series.* He has also published in various academic journals, among others, the *South African Journal of Philosophy,* the *South African Journal of Education,* the *South African Journal of Higher Education, Journal of Pedagogics, Acta Academica, Educare, Education and Society, Perspectives in Education, Studies in Philosophy and Education, Interchange, World Studies in Education, Indilinga: Journal for Indigenous Knowledge Systems,* and the *Journal of Comparative Education and International Relations in Africa.* He serves on the editorial committees for numerous national and international journals and is editor-in-chief of the *South African Journal of Higher Education;* he is also president of the South African Association for Research and Development in Higher Education.

Catherine A. Odora Hoppers is a scholar in Philosophy whose works have been published widely. She joined the University of Pretoria in 2001. She has served on numerous commissions and as adviser for UNESCO including her technical expertise to African ministers of education under the auspices of UNESCO (MINEDAF), and the Organization of African Unity. She is a member of the Advisory Board of the Hague Appeal For Peace (New York) and of the Executive Committee and the Governing Council of the International Peace Research Association (IPRA). In South Africa he was deputy director and later a member of the board of trustees of the Centre for Education Policy Development (CEPD, Chief Research Specialist at the Human Sciences Research Council (HSRC), where she had a corporate function as coordinator of the Project on the Indigenous Knowledge and the Integration of Knowledge Systems. She has been a technical Advisor and resource person to the Parliamentary Portfolio Committee on Arts, Culture, Science and Technology; and is a member of the Ministerial Task Team on Indigenous Knowledge Systems set up by the Minister of Arts, Culture, Science and Technology. During 2001, she was appointed to head the Task Team to draft the first national policy and to redraft legislation on the recognition, development, promotion and protection of indigenous knowledge systems. She has taught in university programs in Scandinavia and in the Southern African region. Her key areas of interest include epistemology, gender, policy and development studies, African perspectives and the integration of knowledge systems.

Denise Houphouet-Boigny is a professor of Inorganic Chemistry at Université de Cocody (Abidjan, Côte d'Ivoire). She has conducted major research projects and led research teams. She has served on the Science Council of the Faculty of Science and Techniques of Université de Cocody and as Director of Higher Education at the Ministry of Higher Education and Scientific Research. She is a Member of the Société Ouest Africaine de Chimie (West African Chemistry Society) and of the *Association des Femmes Enseignantes Chercheurs* (Association of Women of the Teaching/Research Staff) in Côte d'Ivoire. She has numerous publications in peer-review science journals. Through several studies on women in tertiary education in Côte d'Ivoire she has been an advocate for the increase of women's participation in higher education especially in the different sub-fields of science. She has received numerous recognitions. She is a member of *L'Académie des Sciences, des Arts, des Cultures et des Diasporas Africaines* of Côte d'Ivoire.

Tukumbi Lumumba-Kasongo is Professor of Political Science (the Herbert J. Charles and Florence Charles Faegre Professor of Political Science), Chair of the Division of Social Sciences and former Chair of the Department of International Studies at Wells College. He is also a Visiting Scholar in the

Department of City and Regional Planning at Cornell University; a Visiting Research Fellow at CICE, Hiroshima University Japan; Director of CEPARRED; and Research Associate at the *Institut d'Ethno-Sociologie, Université de Cocody,* in Côte d'Ivoire. He is the editor of *African and Asian Studies* (a journal) and co-editor of International Studies in Sociology and Social Anthropology, a book series published by Brill in Leiden (The Netherlands). Professor Lumumba-Kasongo is a leading, world-renowned scholar with numerous publications, including the following books: *Political Re-mapping of Africa: Transnational Ideology and the Re-definition of Africa in World Politics*; *Who and What Govern in the World of the States? A Comparative Study of Constitutions, Citizenry, Power, and Ideology in Contemporary Politics*; and *Liberal Democracy and Its Critics in Africa: Political Dysfunction and the Struggle for Social Progress.*

Changu Mannathoko has taught at the University of Botswana, where she established a solid reputation as an insightful and productive scholar. She made leading contributions to many aspects of social science scholarship prior to joining UNICEF at its Nairobi office. She now serves as UNICEF's Director for Education for Eastern and Southern Africa. She has been a scholar and practitioner actively engaged in helping to combat inequality by using information and knowledge, especially through education, as tools for empowerment and agency.

Frédérica Koblavi Mansilla is a scientist who has taught at Université de Cocody (Abidjan, Côte d'Ivoire). She has conducted several studies and published in prestigious national and international journals in her field.

Takyiwaa Manuh, is the Director of the Institute of African Studies, University of Ghana, Legon. With degrees in Law and Anthropology, she has practiced Law and is an established scholar. She has served and is currently serving on numerous national, continental, and international organizations, boards and committees such as IIEP, SEPHIS, the Scientific Committee for Africa of the UNESCO Forum on Higher Education, Research and Knowledge, the Scientific Committee of the Association of African Universities, the Africa Gender Institute, the Ghana Institute of Journalism, the Council of the University of Ghana, the Working Group on Higher Education of the Association for the Development of Education in Africa, the Regional Office for West Africa of ABANTU for Development, NETRIGHT and the Media Foundation for West Africa. She is a member of the editorial board of the

African Journal of Higher Education, Africa Development/Afrique et Développement, and co- editor of *Ghana Studies Journal*. She was elected as a Fellow of the Ghana Academy of Arts and Sciences in 2005 and has received numerous awards and fellowships. She has over 50 publications in books and journals.

Ruth Meena is a political scientist and a solid leader in the area of gender relations. She has made significant contributions to the production of critical knowledge throughout and outside the African continent. She has analyzed social issues related to public policy that manufactures poverty, especially in the context of externally driven decision-making processes that marginalize the national populations. Her interests are both theoretical and practical. Her edited book on conceptual and theoretical issues of gender in Southern Africa has become a worldwide reference. She has a strong analytical capacity with an interest in helping to promote change through a better understanding of the mechanism of the social reproduction of inequality with a focus on gender.

Penina Mlama was Professor of Theatre in Education and a playwright at the University of Dar es Salaam, where she also served for many years as the Deputy Vice Chancellor prior to joining FAWE in 1999, as its Executive Director. Professor Mlama has accumulated extensive experience in processes critical to improving girls' access, retention and performance in education. She has worked with grassroots communities, teachers, students, community leaders and other stakeholders to girls' education. Her practical experience on the ground includes advocacy, gender sensitization of communities to combat practices such as early marriage, child labor and sexual harassment. She has also actively engaged in training teachers in gender responsive pedagogy and has developed modules for the purpose, using participatory methodologies. In the year 2000, Professor Mlama founded the FAWE Centers of Excellence program, which is a demonstrative experiment on transforming a school and its surrounding community into a gender responsive institution academically, socially and physically. She has published extensively in her areas of expertise.

Teboho Moja has authored articles on higher education reform issues in areas such as the governance of higher education, policy processes and the impact of globalization on higher education. Professor Moja has held key positions at several South African universities including being appointed chair of the Board of Trustees at the largest university in South Africa, the University of South Africa. She has served on the boards international bodies such as the

UNESCO-Institute for international Education Planning and the World Education Market. She has been a policy researcher and analyst for higher education in South Africa. She was appointed the executive director and commissioner to the National Commission on Higher Education appointed by President Mandela. She holds an appointment as Professor Extraordinaire at the University of Pretoria; she served as special advisor to the Minister of Education in South Africa; she is Professor of Higher Education at New York University.

Nelly P. Stromquist specializes in issues related to international development education and gender, which she examines from a critical sociology perspective. She has considerable experience in formal and non-formal education, particularly in Latin America and West Africa. Her research interests focus on the dynamics among educational policies and practices, gender relations, and social change. Her recent books include: *Feminist Organizations and Social Transformation in Latin America* (2006); *Education in a Globalized World: The Connectivity of Economic Power, Technology, and Knowledge* (2002); and *Literacy for Citizenship: Gender and Grassroots Dynamics in Brazil* (1997). She is the editor of *The Professoriate in the Age of Globalization* (forthcoming), *La construcción del género en las políticas públicas. Perspectivas comparadas desde América Latina* (2006), and *Women in the Third World: an Encyclopedia of Contemporary Issues* (1998). She was a Fulbright New Century Scholar during 2005-06.

Annex

Conference Participants

Presenters and Papers

Keynote Speaker:

Aklilu Habte, Former President of the University of Addis Ababa, and former Minister of Culture, Sports, and Youth Affairs, Ethiopia "Gender, Capacity Development, and Higher Education in Africa"

Speakers of the Welcoming/Introductory Panel:

N'Dri T. Assié-Lumumba, (Cornell University and CEPARRED-Abidjan, Côte d'Ivoire)
Tukumbi Lumumba-Kasongo, (Cornell University, Wells College, and CEPARRED-Abidjan, Côte d'Ivoire)
Ravi Kanbur, (Cornell University)
Paul N'Da, (Ministry of Higher Education and Scientific Research/Université de Cocody Abidjan, Côte d'Ivoire)

Presenters and Papers (by order of the program):

Teboho Moja, (New York University), "Subtle Politics of Exclusion in Higher Education: the Absence of Gender Issues in the Globalization Debates"
Ravi Kanbur, (Cornell University), "New Partnership for Africa's Development (NEPAD): An Initial Commentary"
Rémi Clignet (University of Maryland and Institut de Recherche Démographique, Paris) "Mismeasuring gender disparities in university enrollments", paper read by Leslie Miller-Bernal
Anne Sidonie Zoa, (La Maison Africaine, Montréal, Canada), "Les Jeunes Filles Face à L'Enseignement Supérieur: Précarité économique et

représentation sociale en Afrique subsaharienne", paper read by Nancy Kwang Johnson

Emma Akoua Atchrimi, (Centre canadien d'étude et de coopéraiton internationale/Projet droits et citoyenneté des femmes en Afrique francophone-CECI/dcf, Bamako, Mali),"Education Universitaire et Droits des Femmes en Afrique Francophone"

Cyril Daddieh (Providence College), "Attitudes of Ghanaian Students Regarding Issues Confronting African Higher Education with a Particular Attention to Gender"

Philip Higgs, (University of South Africa, Pretoria, South Africa) "Theoretical and Policy Implications of Inequalities in South Africa", paper read by Margaret Washington,

Amiya Kumar Bagchi (Center for Studies in Social Sciences, Calcutta, India), "Women's employment and well-being in East and South-east Asia: Lessons for Africa"

Denise Houphouët-Boigny, Ministry of Higher Education and Scientific Research and Université de Cocody (Abidjan, Côte d'Ivoire) "Femme et Education Scientifique: le Cas de l'Enseignement Supérieur en Côte d'Ivoire"

Penina Mlama, (Forum for African Women Educationalists-FAWE, Nairobi, Kenya and University of Dar es Salaam) "The Significance of Higher Education in Education Reform in Africa – the FAWE Experience", paper read by Micere Mugo

Josephine Beoku-Betts, (Florida Atlantic University), "Learning Science, Doing Science: African Women Scientists and the Production of Knowledge"

Ruth Bamela Engo, (African Action on AIDS and United Nations), "Civic Competence and the Effectiveness of Academic Activities in Challenging Poverty in Africa"

Changu Mannathoko, (UNICEF, Nairobi, Kenya), "Breaking the Second Wall of Silence: Addressing Gender, Sexuality and HIV/AIDS in Education"

Final roundtable panelists: "Major Issues and Looking Forward":
Muxe G. Nkondo, Professor, Vice-Chancellor and Principal (University of Venda of Science and Technology, South Africa)
Lucila Bandeira Beato, (DEPIS/DPEIBGE Foundation, Rio de Janeiro, Brazil)
Kandree E. Hicks, Graduate Student, (Cornell University)
Marieme Lo, Graduate Student, (Cornell University)
Gatua Wa Mbugwa, Graduate Student, (Cornell University)

Chairs

Anne Adams, (Cornell University)
Locksley Edmondson, (Cornell University)
Robert Harris, Jr. (Cornell University
David Lewis, (Cornell University)
Henry Richardson, (Cornell University)
Yolande Tano, (Permanent Representation of Côte d'Ivoire to UNESCO in Paris and Université de Cocody)

Discussants

Josephine Allen, (Cornell University)
Asma Barlas, (Ithaca College)
Ayele Bekerie, (Cornell University)
Parfait Eloundou-Enyegue, (Cornell University)
Lourdes Beneria, (Cornell University)
Lydie Haenlin, (Wells College)
Nancy Kwang Johnson, (Colgate University), read the paper discussed
Leslie Miller-Bernal, (Wells College), read the paper discussed
Micere Mugo, (Syracuse University), read the paper discussed
Susan Piliero, (Cornell University)
Peyi Soyinka Airewele, (Ithaca College)
Winnie Taylor, (Cornell University)
James Turner, (Cornell University)
Margaret Washington, (Cornell University), read the paper discussed

Co-sponsors

Cornell University: Program on Inequality and Development (PID), Center for the Study of Inequality, Vice Provost for Diversity and Faculty Development, Africana Studies and Research Center, Department of Education, Program on Gender and Global Change (GGC), Cornell International Program of Food, Agriculture, and Development (CIIFAD), Cornell Institute of Public Affairs (CIPA), Institute for African Development (IAD), Mario Einaudi Center for International Studies, Institute of European Studies, Office of the Dean of the College of Architecture, Art & Planning, South East Asian Program, and International Students and Scholars Office; Office of the Dean of Wells College.

Bibliography

Abramovitz, M., 1989. *Regulating the Lives of Women: Social Welfare Policy From Colonial Times to the Present.* Boston, Mass.: South End Press.

Addae-Mensah, I., 1996. "Vice-Chancellor's Address at His Induction," University of Ghana-Legon, October 9, 2. Accessed on 2/3/99 at *http://www.ug.edu.gh/vcspeech.htm.*

Addison, T., and A. Rahman, 2001. "Why is So Little Spent on Educating the Poor?" Paper presented at Poverty Conference, Sida: Stockholm October 12.

African Development Bank, 1996. "Africa in the World Economy: Towards Policies for Long-term Growth and Development in Africa." African Development Report: Economic and Social Statistics on Africa.

African Gender Institute (AGI), 2000. *Newsletter* 6 (May). Cape Town: University of Cape Town.

Agnihotri, S. B., 2000. *Sex Ratio Patterns in the Indian Population: A Fresh Exploration.* New Delhi: Sage.

Ajayi, J. F. A., L. K. H. Goma, and G. A. Johnson, 1996. *The African Experience with Higher Education.* Accra: The Association of African Universities.

Ajeyalemi, D., 1990. *Science and Technology Education in Africa: Focus on Seven Sub-Saharan Countries.* Lagos: University of Lagos Press.

Altbach, P. J., 1985. "Center and Periphery in Knowledge Distribution: An Asian Case Study." *International Social Science Journal* 37: 109-18.

Altbach, P., 2002. "Knowledge and Education as International Commodities." *International Higher Education* 28 (Summer): 2-5.

Amsden, A. H., 1989. *Asia's Next Giant: South Korea and Late Industrialisation.* New York: Oxford University Press.

Amua-Sekyi, E. T., 1988. "Ghana: Education for Girls." Paper presented at the Women's Center at Eastern Washington University, May, 1-9.

Anker, R., 1997/2001. "Theories of Occupational Segregation by Sex: An Overview. *International Labour Review* 136, no. 3; repr. in Loutfi 2001: 129-55.

Annas, J., 1993. "Woman and the Quality of Life: Two Norms or One." In *The Quality of Life,* ed., M. Nussbaum and A. Sen, 279-96. New York: Oxford University Press.

Arpentier, R., and R. Clignet, 1998. *Du temps pour les sciences sociales.,* Paris: L'Harmattan.

Assié-Lumumba, N. T., 1993. *L'Enseignement supérieur en Afrique francophone: évaluation du potentiel des universités classiques et des alternatives pour le développement.* Washington, D.C.: World Bank.

Assié-Lumumba, N. T., 1994. "Demand, Access, and Equity Issues in African Higher Education: Past Policies, Current Practices, and Readiness for the 21st Century." Association of African Universities.

Assié-Lumumba, N. T., 1994a. "Rural Students in Urban Settings in Africa: The Experiences of Female Students in Secondary Schools." In *Education in the Urban Areas: Cross-National Dimensions*, ed. N. Stromquist. Westport, CT: Praeger.

Assié-Lumumba, N. T., 1994b. "Les politiques d'éducation des filles en Afrique: instrument de promotion ou processus de marginalisation des femmes." In *L'égalité devant soi: sexes, rapports sociaux et développement international*, ed., M.-F. Labrecque. Ottawa: International Development and Research Center.

Assié-Lumumba, N. T., 1994c. "History of Women's Education in Francophone Africa." *International Encyclopedia of Education.* 2nd ed., Oxford: Pergamon Press.

Assié-Lumumba, N. T., 1995. "Demand, Access, and Equity Issues in African Higher Education: Policies, Current Practices, and Readiness for the 21st Century." Background paper for the Joint Colloquium on the University in Africa in the 1990s and Beyond, Lesotho, January 16-20.

Assié-Lumumba, N. T., 1995. "Gender and Education in Africa: A New Agenda for Development." *Africa Notes* (April).

Assié-Lumumba, N. T., 1996. "The Future Role and Mission of African Higher Education." *South African Journal of Higher Education* 10 (2).

Assié-Lumumba, N. T., 1997. "Educating Africa's Girls and Women: A Conceptual and Historical Analysis of Gender Inequality." In *Engendering African Social Sciences*, ed., A. Imam, A. Mama, and F. Sow. Dakar: Council for Development of Social Science Research in Africa (CODESRIA).

Assié-Lumumba, N. T., 1998. "Women in West Africa: Dynamics of Issues in Education, Economy, Culture, Health and Politics." In *Women in the Third World: An Encyclopedia of Contemporary Issues,* ed. N. Stromquist. New York: Garland Publishing.

Assié-Lumumba, N. T., 2000. "Educational and Economic Reforms, Gender Equity, and Access to Schooling in Africa." *International Journal of Comparative Sociology* 41 (1): 89-120.

Assié-Lumumba, N. T., 2000. "Educational and Economic Reforms, Gender Equity, and Access to Schooling in Africa." *International Journal of Comparative Sociology* 41 (1): 89-120.

Assié-Lumumba, N. T., 2001. "Gender, Race, and Human Capital Theory: Research Trends in the United States from the 1950s to the 1990s." *Journal of Comparative Education and International Relations in Africa* 4 (1-2, 2001): 1-25

Assié-Lumumba, N. T., 2001. "Gender, Race, and Human Capital Theory: Research Trends in the United States from the 1950s to the 1990s." *Journal of Comparative Education and International Relations in Africa* 4 (1-2).

Assié-Lumumba, N. T., 2002. "Gender, Access to Learning, and the Production of Knowledge in Africa." In *Visions of Gender Theories and Social Development in Africa: Harnessing Knowledge of Social Justice and Equality.* Dakar: Association of African Women for Research and Development, AAWORD Book Series .

Assié-Lumumba, N. T., 2002. "Gender, Access to Learning, and the Production of Knowledge in Africa." In *Visions of Gender Theories and Social Development in Africa: Harnessing Knowledge of Social Justice and Equality,* ed., Association of African Women for Research and Development. Dakar: AAWORD, 95-113.

Assié-Lumumba, N. T., 2004. "Éducation des filles et des femmes en Afrique: analyse conceptuelle et historique de l'inégalité entre les sexes." In *Sexe, genre, et société: engendrer les sciences sociales africaines,* ed. A. Imam, A. Mama, and F. Sow. Dakar: CODESRIA and Paris: Karthala.

Assié-Lumumba, N. T., 2004. "Sustaining Home-Grown Innovations in Higher Education in Sub-Saharan Africa: A Critical Reflection." *Journal of International Cooperation in Education* 7 (1).

Assié-Lumumba, N., 1985. "The Fallacy of Quota-Like Solutions to Unequal Educational Opportunity: The Case of Female Education in the Ivory Coast." Paper presented at the 29th Annual Comparative and International Education Society Conference, Stanford, Calif., 1993,

Assié-Lumumba, N., 1993. "L'enseignement supérieur en Afrique francophone: Évaluation du potentiel des universités classiques et des alternatives pour le développement." AFTHR, Note technique n° 5. Washington: World Bank.

Assié-Lumumba, T. N., 1996. *Les Africaines dans la politique: femmes baoulé de Côte d'Ivoire*. Paris: L'Harmattan.

Assié-Lumumba, T. N., 1997. "Educating African Women and Girls." In *Engendering Social Science in Africa,* ed. A. Imam, A. Mama, and F. Sow. Dakar: Council for Development of Social Science Research in Africa (CODESRIA).

Association of African Universities, 1997. Report of the 9th General Conference of the Association of African Universities. Lusaka: AAU, pp. 13-17.

Atakpa, S. K., 1996, *Factors Affecting Female Participation in Education in Relation to the Northern Scholarship Scheme*. Accra: Ministry of Education, cited in Amua-Sekyi 1988, 3.

Ba, F. H., 1993. "Femme et éducation: Une équation déterminante pour le développement humain en Afrique." *Revue Internationale de Pédagogie* 39 (1-2).

Bacchi, C. L., 1996a. "The Politics of Solidarity." In C. L. Bacchi, *The Politics of Affirmative Action*. London: Sage Publications.

Bacchi, C. L., 1996c. "The Political Use of Categories." In C. L. Bacchi, *The Politics of Affirmative Action*. London: Sage Publications, 11-12.

Bacchi, C. L._, 1996b. "The Politics of Misrepresentation." In C. L. Bacchi, *The Politics of Affirmative Action*. London: Sage Publications.

Bacchi, C., 1994. "The Brick Wall: Why So Few Women Become Senior Academics." *Australian Universities Review* 36: 1, 36-39.

Bagchi, A. K., 1982. *The Political Economy of Underdevelopment*. Cambridge: Cambridge University Press.

Bagchi, A. K., 1984. "The Terror and the Squalor of East Asian Capitalism. *Economic and Political Weekly* 19, no. 1 (Jan. 7): 21-22.

Bagchi, A. K., 1987a. "East Asian Capitalism: An Introduction." *Political Economy: Studies in the Surplus Approach* 3, no. 2: 115-32.

Bagchi, A. K., 1987b. *Public Intervention and Industrial Restructuring in China, India and Republic of Korea*. New Delhi: ILO-ARTEP.

Bagchi, A. K., 1997. *Economic Theory and Economic Organisation,* vol. 1, *A Critique of the Anglo-American Theory of Firm Structure*. Calcutta: Centre for Studies in Social Sciences, Occasional Paper no. 165, September.

Bagchi, A. K., 1998. "Growth Miracle and Its Unravelling in East and South-East Asia." *Economic and Political Weekly* 33, no. 18 (May 2): 1025-42.

Bagchi, A. K., 1999. "A Turnaround in South Korea." *Frontline,* Chennai (July 30): 62-65.

Bagchi, A. K., 2000. "The Past and the Future of the Developmental State." *Journal of World-Systems Research* 11, no. 2 (Summer/Fall): 398-442. http://csf.colorado.edu/jwsr

Bagchi, A. K., 2002a. "Agrarian Transformation and Human Development: Instrumental and Constitutive Links." In Ramachandran and Swaminathan 2002: 153-65.

Bagchi, A. K., 2002b. "Governance in East Asia: What's New?" *European Journal of Development Research* 14, no. 1 (June): 200-18.

Baig, T., and I. Goldfain, 1998 , "Financial Market Contagion in the Asian Crisis." IMF Working Paper (WP/98/155), November.

Barr, J., and L. Birke, 1998. *Common Science? Women, Science and Knowledge.* Bloomington: Indiana University Press.

Barrow, J., 1997. "Black Afro-Caribbean Women in Higher Education in the United Kingdom from the 1950s to the 1990s." In *Women as Leaders and Managers in Higher Education,* ed. H. Eggins. Buckingham, U.K.: Open University Press, 63-69.

Basson, A. C., 1999. "The Regulation of Unfair Discrimination by the Employment Equity Act 55 of 1998." *South African Mercantile Law Journal* 11 (2).

Becker, G. S., 1964. *Human Capital.* New York: National Bureau of Economic Research.

Beetham, D., 1993. "Liberal Democracy and the Limits of Democratization." In *Prospects for Democracy: North, South.East, West,* ed., D. Held. Stanford, Calif.: Stanford University.

Behrman, J., and P. Sengupta, 2004. *Convergence? Divergence? Or Some of Both? Major Trends in Selected Indicators among Country Groups in Recent Decades.* Philadelphia: University of Pennsylvania, draft.

Bennell, P., and T. Pearce, 2003. "The Internationalization of Higher Education: Exporting Education to Developing and Trans-national Economies." *International Journal of Educational Development* 23, no. 2: 215-32.

Beoku-Betts, J. A., 1998. "Gender and Formal Education in Africa: An Exploration of the Opportunity Structure at the Secondary and Tertiary Levels." In *Women and Education in Sub-Saharan Africa: Power,*

Opportunity and Constraints, ed. M. Bloch, J. A. Beoku-Betts, and B. R. Tabachnick. Boulder, Colo.: Lynne Rienner Publishers, 157-184.

Beoku-Betts, J. A., 2000. "Living in a Large Family Does Something For You: Influence of Family on the Achievement of African and Caribbean Women in Science. *Journal of Women and Minorities in Science and Engineering* 6 (3): 191-206.

Beoku-Betts, J., and B. I.Logan, 1993. "Developing Science and Technology in Sub-Saharan Africa: Gender Disparities in the Education and Employment Processes." In *Science in Africa: Women Leading from Strength,* ed., American Association for the Advancement of Science. Washington, D.C., 117-64.

Berge, N. E., 1998. *Fulfilment of the Convention on the Rights of the Child in Education: An Analysis and Case Study.* UNICEF.

Bernard, J., 1964. *Academic Women.* Pennsylvania State University Press.

Bhoola, U., 1996. "Working Women: Equity and Affirmative Action." *Indicator South Africa* 13 (4).

Bhorat, H., 2001. "Wage Differences." *South African Labour Bulletin* 25 (1).

Black, F., and M. Scholes, 1973. "The Valuation of Option Contracts and a Test of Market Efficiency. *Journal of Political Economy* 81, no. 3: 637-54.

Blau, P., and R. Duncan, 1967. *The American Occupational Structure.* New York: Wiley and Sons.

Blaug, M., 1972. "The Correlation Between Education and Earnings: What Does It Signify?" *Higher Education* 1: 53-77.

Blay, K., 1990. Interview conducted at Delaware State University, May 1990.

Bloch, M. N., J. A. Beoku-Betts, and B. R. Tabachnick, 1998. *Women and Education in Sub-Saharan Africa: Power, Opportunities, and Constraints.* Boulder, Colo.: Lynne Rienner Publishers.

Boahene A., 2001. "C173b Released to 5 State Varsities," *Daily Graphic.* Accessed on 10/31/2001 at *http://www.graphic.com.gh/dgraphic/news/g26.htlm.*

Bolt, M. K., 1986. "The Relationship of Teacher Behavior to Student Achievement in High and Low Achievement High Schools in Nairobi, Kenya." Unpublished Ph.D. dissertation, University of Oregon. Eugene, Or.

Borg, A., 2000. Review of Schiebinger, *Has Feminism Changed Science?* Summer 2000, *http://www.amwa-doc.org/index.cfm?objectid=E1D922C6-D567-0B25-5F141F31BE85B8E7*

Boserup, E., 1970. *Women's Role in Economic Development.* London: George Allen and Unwin Ltd.

Boserup, E., 1981. *Population and Technology*. Oxford: Blackwell.

Bouya, A., 1993. "Les filles face aux programmes scolaires de sciences et technologie en Afrique: étude socio-psychologique." Dakar, Sénégal: UNESCO, Bureau régional de Dakar.

Bowles, S., and H. Gintis, 1975. "The Problem With Human Capital: A Marxian Critique." *American Economic Review* 6: 74-82.

Bowles, S., and H. Gintis, 1986. *Democracy and Capitalism: Property, Community, and the Contradictions of Modern Social Thought*. New York: Basic Books.

Brock, C., N. Cammish, R. Aedo-Richmond, A. Narayanan, and R. Njoroge, 1997. *Gender, Education and Development: A Partially Annotated and Selective Bibliography. Education Research Paper* (DFID-Ser-19).

Brock, D., 1993. "Quality of Life Measures in Health Care and Medical Ethics." In *The Quality of Life,* ed. M. Nussbaum and A. Sen, 95-132. New York: Oxford University Press.

Brock, R., 2002. "Two Professors Offer Advice on Making Computer Science More Open to Women." *Chronicle of Higher Education,* January 25.

Brock-Utne, B., 2000. *Whose Education For All? The Recolonization of the African Mind*. New York: Falmer Press.

Brokensha, D., D. M. Warren, and O. Werner, eds., 1980. *Indigenous Knowledge Systems and Development*. Washington, D.C.: University Press of America.

Browne, A. and H. Barrett, 1991. "Female Education in Sub-Saharan Africa: The Key to Development?" *Comparative Education* 2: 275-85.

Brunner, J. J., 2004. *Informe OECD sobre la Política Educacional en Chile*. Paris: OECD.

Buarque, C., 1993. *The End of Economics? Ethics and Disorder of Progress*. London: Zed Books, 5-9, 75-77.

Bunyi, G., 2003. *Interventions that Increase Enrolment of Women in Tertiary Institutions*. World Bank Regional Training Conference on Improving Tertiary Education in Sub Sahara Africa. Accra.

Busari, E., 2000. "Gender Dimensions of Job Satisfaction and Work Burn-Out for Sustainable Development of Women Scientists and Technologists in Institutions of Higher Learning." Paper presented at the AAP/GSA National Conference, "The State of Gender Issues in Tertiary Institutions in Zimbabwe." Harare.

Calfat, G. G., 1997. *Explaining the Expansion of Human Capabilities in Developing Countries: The Role of Economic Growth and Deprivation,* Antwerp: University of Antwerp, Centre for Development Studies.

Capra, F., 1988. *Uncommon Wisdom: Conversations with Remarkable People.* London: Flamingo, 127-39.

Cardoso, F. H., 2004. "Development in a Changing World: An Interview with Andrew Horesh, Kathryn Ogden, and Laura Tilghman." *The Brown Journal of World Affairs* 10, no.2.

Carnoy, M., 1990. "Education and the Transition State." In *Education and Social Transformation in the Third World*, ed., M. Carnoy and Joel Samoff. Princeton: Princeton University Press.

Carnoy, M., 2000. "Globalization and Higher Education." *Perspectives in Education* 18 (3).

Carter, M., and M. Carnoy, 1974. "Theories of Labor Markets and Worker Productivity." Discussion paper. Palo Alto, Calif.: Center for Economic Studies.

Centre Interafricain pour le Développement de la Formation Professionnelle, 1982. "Formation et emploi des femmes." Abidjan : Centre de documentation, série bibliographique n° 1.

Chagonda, T., 2001. "Masculinities and Resident Male Students at the University of Zimbabwe: Gender and Democracy Issues." In "Speaking for Ourselves," ed., R. Gaidzanwa. Harare: AAP/GSA/Ford Foundation.

Chambas, M. I., 2000. Interview conducted in Accra, August 31.

Chanana, K., 2000. "Treading the Hallowed Halls: Women in Higher Education in India." *Economic and Political Weekly* 35, no. 12: 1012-22.

Charmes, J., 1993. *Suivi des caractéristiques et comportements des ménages et des groupes vulnérables en situation d'ajustement structurel 1990-1992 (ELAM2).* Projet BEN/87/023: Cotonou.

Chazan, N., 1983. *Anatomy of Ghanaian Politics: Managing Political Recession, 1969-1982.,* Boulder, Colo.: Westview Press.

Chen, M., 1995. "A Matter of Survival: Women's Right to Employment in India and Bangladesh." In *Women, Culture and Development: A Study of Human Capabilities*, ed. M. Nussbaum and J. Glover, 37-60. New York: Oxford University Press.

Chivaura, I., 2001. "The Affirmative Action Policy in Student Admissions at the University of Zimbabwe." In "Speaking for Ourselves," ed. R. Gaidzanwa. Harare: AAP/GSA/Ford Foundation.

Christian, P., 1975. "The Self-Expansion of Capital on a World Scale." In Pailloix 1975.

Cloete, N., et al., eds., 2002. *Transformation in Higher Education: Global Pressures and Local Realities in South Africa.* Cape Town, South Africa: Juta & Co.

Cohen, G. A., 1993. "Equality of What? On Welfare, Goods, and Capabilities." In *The Quality of Life*, ed. M. Nussbaum and A. Sen. New York: Oxford University Press.

Colclough, C., and S. Al-SumarraI S., 2003. *Achieving Schooling for All in Africa: Costs, Commitment and Gender.* Brighton: University of Sussex.

Crockett, A., 2001. "Monetary Policy and Financial Stability." HKMA Distinguished Lecture, Hong Kong, February 13. Internet: bis-org.

Crotty, J., and K. Lee, 2001. "Economic Performance in Post-Crisis Korea: A Critical Perspective on Neoliberal Restructuring." Mimeo, University of Massachusetts, Amherst, October 31.

Daddieh, C. K., 1995. "Education Adjustment Under Severe Recessionary Pressures: The Case of Ghana." In *Beyond Economic Liberalism in Africa: Structural Adjustment and the Alternatives,* ed. Kidane Mengisteab and Ikubolajeh Logan. London: Zed Books Ltd., 23-55.

Daddieh, C. K.,1997. *Education and Democracy in Africa: Preliminary Thoughts on a Neglected Linkage.* Accra, Ghana: Institute of Economic Affairs, Occasional Papers Number 10.

Dahlman, C., and R. Nelson, R, 1995, "Social Absorption Capability, National Innovation Systems," In *Social Capability and Long-Term Economic Growth,* ed. B. H. Koo and D. H. Perkins, 82-122. New York: St. Martin's Press.

Daniel, G. F., 1997-98. "The Universities in Ghana." *The Commonwealth Universities Year Book,* vol. 1, 649-56.

Dankwart, A. R., 1970. "Transition to Democracy: Toward a Dynamic Model." *Comparative Politics* 2, no. 3 (April): 337-63.

De Koker, J Y., 1999. "Recent Legislation Affecting the Status of Women in South Africa." *The Bluestocking.*

De vos, P., 2000. "Equality for All: A Critical Analysis of the Equality Jurisprudence of the Constitutional Court." *Tydskrif vir Hedendaagse Romeins-Hollandse Reg* 63 (1).

De Waal, A., and N. Argenti, 2002. *Young Africa: Realising the Rights of Children and Youth.* Asmara: Africa World Press.

Denison, E. F., 1962. "The Sources of Economic Growth in the United States and the Alternatives Before Us." Supplementary Paper Number 13. New York: Committee for Economic Development.

Department of Education, 2001. "National Plan For Higher Education in South Africa." Department of Education, Government of South Africa, February. http://education.pwv.gov.za/DoE_Sites/Higher_Education/HE_Plan/nat ional_plan_for_higher_educati.htm (accessed 02/20/2001).

Department of Education, 2001. "National Strategy for Mathematics, Science and Technical Education in General and Further Education and Training." Department of Education: Government of South Africa, November.

Development Co-operation Directorate (DAC), 1999. "DAC Scoping Study of Donor Poverty Reduction Policies and Practices: A Synthesis Report." DAC Informal Network on Poverty, March.

Development Nations." *International Encyclopedia of Education*, pp. 1784-89. Development." In Ramachandran and Swaminathan 2002: 230-44.

Diane, H., and C. Taspcott, 1991. "Affirmative Action and Equal Opportunity for Women in Namibia." International Labour Organization, Technical Background Paper.

Diarrassouba, V. C., 1979. "L'université ivoirienne et le développement de la nation." In *Les Nouvelles Éditions Africaines*.

Dixon-Mueller, R., and R. Anker, 1988. "Assessing Women's Economic Contributions to Development." *Training in Population, Human Resources and Development Planning* 6. Geneva: International Labour Office.

Dreze, J., and A. Sen, 1989. *Hunger and Public Action*. New York: Oxford University Press.

Duru, B., M. A. Kieffer and C. Marry, 2001. "Dynamique des Scolarités." *Revue Française de Sociologie* 42 (2): 251-80.

Dyanda, C., 2000. "The Role of the H.R.R.C. and Experiences with Female Academics at the University of Zimbabwe." Paper presented at the AAP/GSA Workshop for Academic Women, University of Zimbabwe.

Dziech, B., and L. Wiener, 1984. Boston: Beacon Press.

Economic Commission for Africa (ECA), 1994b. "Women, Environment and Sustainable Development. Fifth African Conference on Women, Conference Papers on Priority Issues, vol. 2, part 5. Dakar, Senegal: ECA.

Economic Commission for Africa (ECA), 1994c. "Critical Issues of Equity and Sustainable Development with Examples from Africa." Fifth Regional Conference on Women, Women's Rights, vol.2, part 11A. Dakar, Senegal: ECA.

Economic Commission for Africa (ECA), 1999. "The Status of Women: Liberia, Zimbabwe, Burkina Faso. Congo, Swaziland, Somalia. Sierra Leone, Egypt, Zambia, Sudan, Botswana, South Africa Seychelles, Lesotho, Eritrea, Ethiopia and Nigeria." Dakar, Senegal: ECA.

Economic Commission for Africa (ECA), United Nations, 1994a. "African Platform for Action." Dakar, Senegal: ECA.

EIU, 2000. *Country Profile 2001: South Korea, North Korea.* London: Economist Intelligence Unit.

Elder, S., and L. J. Johnson, 1999/2001. "Sex-Specific Labour Market Indicators: What they Show." *International Labour Review* 138, no. 4 (1999), repr. in Loutfi 2001: 251-304.

El-Ghonemy, M. R., 2002. 'The Land Market approach to Rural

Emang Basadi Women's Association, 1999. *The Women's Manifesto: A Summary of Botswana Women's Issues and Demands.* Gabarone: Emang Basadi Women's Association.

England, P., 1993. "The Separate Self: Androcentric Bias in Neoclassical Assumptions." In *Beyond Economic Man*, ed. M. A. Ferber and J. A. Nelson. Chicago: The University of Chicago Press.

Enos, J. L., 1995. *In Pursuit of Science and Technology in Sub-Saharan Africa: The Impact of Structural Adjustment Programs.* New York: Routledge.

Erikson, R., 1993. "Descriptions of Inequality: The Swedish Approach to Welfare Research." In *The Quality of Life*, ed. M. Nussbaum and A. Sen, 67-83. New York: Oxford University Press.

Eshiwani, G .S., 1985. "Women's Access to Higher Education in Kenya: A Study of Opportunities in Attainment in Science and Mathematics Education." *Journal of East African Research and Development* 15: 91-110.

ETC Group, *http://www.etcgroup.org/article.asp?newsid=297*

Etter-Lewis, G., 1993. *My Soul Is My Own: Oral Narratives of African-American Women in the Professions.* New York and London: Routledge.

Etzkowitz, H., C. Kemelgor, and B. Uzzi, 2000. *Athena Unbound: The Advancement of Women in Science and Technology*, Cambridge: Cambridge University Press.

Fagerlind, I., 1989. *Education and Development.* New York: Pergamon Press.

Fanon, F., 1960. *Les Damnés de la terre.* Paris: Maspero

Fataar, A., 2003. "Higher Education Policy Discourse in South Africa: A Struggle for Alignment with Macro Development Policy." *South African Journal of Higher Education*, 17, no.2: 31-40.

FAWE 1994, 1995, 1996, 1997, 1998, 1999, 2000, 2001, 2002, 2003. Annual Reports. Nairobi: FAWE.

FAWE, 2001a. "Statistical Overview on Girls' Education at the University Level." Nairobi: FAWE.

FAWE, 2001b. " Promoting Girls' Education through Community Participation." FAWE Best Practices, Paper No 1.

FAWE, 2001c. "Promoting Female Access to University Education through Affirmative Action: A Case Study in Tanzania." FAWE Best Practices, Paper no 2.

FAWE, 2001d. "In Search of an Ideal School for Girls." FAWE Centers of Excellence. Nairobi: FAWE.

FAWE, 2002- 2006. "Strategic Plan." Nairobi: FAWE

FAWE, 2003. "Mainstreaming Gender into Education for All National Action Plans." Nairobi: FAWE.

Federici, S., G. Caffentzis, and O. Alidou, 2000, *A Thousand Flowers: Social Struggles Against Structural Adjustment in African Universities.* Trenton, N.J.: Africa World Press.

Fischman, G., and N. P. Stromquist, 2000. "Globalization Impacts on the Third World University. In *Higher Education: Handbook of Theory and Research,* vol. 15. New York: Agathon Press, pp. 501-21.

Flaherty, D., 1995. *Regional Inequalities in South Africa: Issues, Measurement and Policy Implications.* Halfway House: Development Bank of Southern Africa. 12, 20.

Flood, T., 1998. *Beyond Inequalities: Women in South Africa.* Oxford: African Books Collective. 27.

Forge, J. W., 1989. *Science and Technology in Africa.* London: Longman.

Franklin, P., 1981. *Sexual and Gender Harassment in the Academy: A Guide for Faculty, Students and Administrators.* New York: Modern Languages Association.

Franklin, S. R., 1976. *American Capitalism: Two Visions.* New York: Random House.
Free Press.

Futrell, M. H., 1995. "The Impact on Society of Educating Women." *Education International* 1 (4.2.1) : 14-19.

Gaidzanwa, R. B., 1997. "Gender Analysis in the Field of Education: A Zimbabwean Example." In *Engendering African Social Sciences,* ed. A. Imam, A. Mama, and F. Sow. Dakar: CODESRIA Book Series, 271-95.

Gaillard, J., 1991. *Scientists in the Third World.* Lexington: The University Press of Kentucky.

Gaizadnwa, R. B., et al., 1989. "Factors Affecting Women's Academic Careers at the University of Zimbabwe." HRRC.

Galbraith, J. K., 2002. "A Perfect Crime: Inequality in the Age of Globalization." *Daedalus* 131, no.1: 11-25.

Gender Studies Association (GSA), 1999. " Breaking the Silence: A Survey of Sexual Harassment at the University of Zimbabwe." University of Zimbabwe,

Gernholtz, L., 1999. "Gender Bias in Law." *The Sowetan* (16 March).

Gertler, M., 1988. "Financial Structure and Aggregate Economic Activity: An Overview." *Journal of Money, Credit and Banking* 20, no. 3: 559-88.

Ghanaian Chronicle, 2001. "Bottom Tree: Sexual Harassment in Our Schools: Action Needed." Accra, February 7.

Gibbons, M., 1998. "Higher Education Relevance in the 21st Century." Paper prepared for the World Bank as part of its contribution to the UNESCO World Conference on Higher Education, Paris, October 5-9.

Gibbons, M., 1998. *Higher Education in the 21st Century*. Washington: World Bank.

Gill, R., 1995. "Relativism, Reflexivity and Politics: Interrogating Discourse Analysis from a Feminist Perspective." In *Feminism and Discourse: Psychological Perspectives*, ed. S. Wilkinson and C. Kitzinger. London: Sage Publications, 166-69.

Gintis, H., 1971. "Education and the Characteristics of Worker Productivity." *American Economic Review* 61: 266-79.

Ginwala, F., 1995. "Discrimination is Not the Problem." In *The Progress of Nations*. New York: UNICEF.

Glover, J., 2000. *Women and Scientific Employment*. New York: St. Martin's Press, Inc.

Goody, E., 1982. *Parenthood and Social Reproduction: Fostering and Occupational Roles in West Africa*. Cambridge: Cambridge University Press.

Goonitalake, S., 1993. "Modern Science and the Periphery: The Characteristics of Dependent Knowledge." In *The Racial Economy of Science: Toward a Democratic Future*, ed. S. Harding. Bloomington and Indianapolis: Indiana University Press, 259-67.

Greenhalg S., 1985. "Sexual Stratification: The Other Side of Growth with Equity." *Population and Development Review* 11: 265-314.

Grey, D. R., 1997. *Democratic Theory and Post-Communist Change*. Upper Saddle River, N.J.: Prentice Hall.

Gunderson, M., 1989. "Male-Female Wage Differentials and Policy Responses." *Journal of Economic Literature* 27, no. 1: 46-72.

Haddad, W. D., et al., eds., 1990. *Education and Development: Evidence for New Priorities*, Washington, D.C.: World Bank Discussion Papers, 95.

Hague Appeal for Peace, 1999. Conference Background Documentations. *http://www.haguepeace.org/resources/HagueAgendaPeace+Justice4T he21stCentury.pdf*

Hansen, K., 1986. "Domestic Service in Zambia." *Journal of Southern African Studies* 13 (1).

Harding, S., 1991. *Whose Science? Whose Knowledge? Thinking From Women's Lives*. Ithaca, N. Y.: Cornell University Press.

Harding, S., 1998. *Is Science Multi-Cultural? Postcolonialisms, Feminisms, and Epistemologies*. Bloomington: Indiana University Press.

Hayward, F., 2000. "Internationalization of U.S. Higher Education, Preliminary Status Report." Washington, D.C.: American Council on Education.

Hayward, F., and L. Slaya, 2001. "A Report on Two National Surveys about International Education: Public Experience, Attitudes and Knowledge." Washington, D.C.: American Council on Education.

HDR, 1999. *Human Development Report*. New York: Oxford University Press.

Held, D., 1993. *Prospects for Democracy: North, South, East, and West*. Stanford, Calif.: Stanford University Press.

Hill Collins, P., 2000. *Black Feminist Thought: Knowledge, Consciousness, and the Politics of Empowerment*. 2nd ed. New York: Routledge.

Hountondji, P. J., 2002. "Knowledge Appropriation in a Post-Colonial Context. In Odora Hoppers 2002, 23-38.

Houphouët-Boigny, D., 2003. *Improving Women's Participation in Tertiary Education: The Case of the University de Cocody*. World Bank Regional Training Conference on Improving Tertiary Education in Sub-Sahara Africa. Accra.

Houphouët-Boigny, D., and F. K. Mansilla, 1999. *Femme et éducation scientifique: cas de l'enseignement supérieur*. Ouagadougou: UNESCO. *http://chronicle.com/free/2002/01/2002012501.htm* (accessed 01/20/2002). *http://education.pwv.gov.za/DoE_Sites/Maths%20and%20Science/Fina l-doc.pdf* (Accessed 01/20/2002)

Htun, M., 1998. "Women's Rights and Opportunities in Latin America: Problems and Prospects." Issue Brief, The Women's Leadership Conference of the Americas. Washington, D.C.: Inter-American Dialogue and ICRW, April.

Human Rights Watch Report, 2001. *Scared at School: Sexual Violence against Girls in South African Schools.*

Hyde, K. A. L., 1996. "Girls' Education in Eastern and Southern Africa: An Overview." Prepared for the Regional Mid-Decade Review Towards Education For All Meeting. Johannesburg, South Africa.

Ibarra, E, 1998b. "La Universidad Autónoma Metropolitana y los Lìmites de la Modernización." In *La Universidad Ante el Espejo de la Excelencia,* ed. Eduardo Ibarra, 2nd ed. Mexico, D.F.: Universidad Autonoma Metropolitana, pp. 243-348.

Ibarra, E, 2003. Presentation at the Panel on The Latin American University Response to Neoliberalism, at the annual conference of the Comparative and International Education Society, New Orleans, March 12-15.

Ibarra, E., 1998a. "Neoliberalismo, Educación Superior y Ciencia en México. Hacia la Conformación de un Nuevo Modelo." In *La Universidad Ante el Espejo de la Excelencia,* ed. E. Ibarra, 2nd ed. Mexico, D.F.: Universidad Autonoma Metropolitana, pp. 117-82.

Imam, A., and A. Mama, 1994. "The Role of Academics in Limiting and Expanding Academic Freedom." In *Academic Freedom in Africa*, ed. M. Diouf and M. Mamdani. Dakar: CODESRIA Book Series, 73-107.

Jacobs, J. A., 1996. "Gender Inequality and Higher Education." *Annual Review of Sociology* 22: 153-85.

Jensen, M. C., and W. H. Meckling, 1976. "Theory of the Firm: Managerial Behaviour, Agency Costs and Ownership Structure." *Journal of Financial Economics* 11: 5-50.

Johnson, C., 1982. *MITI and the Japanese Miracle: The Rise of Industrial Policy, 1925-1975.* Stanford, Calif.: Stanford University Press.

Jones, P., 2000. "Globalization and Internationalism: Democratic Prospects for World Education." In *Globalization and Education, Integration and Contestation Across Cultures,* ed. N. P. Stromquist and K. Monkman. Boulder: Rowman & Littlefield.

Jordan, D., 1999. "Black Women in the Agronomic Sciences: Factors Influencing Career Development." *Journal of Women and Minorities in Science and Engineering* 5 (2): 113-28.

Kadalie, R., 1995. "Women in South Africa." *Publico* 15 (4): 25.

Kajawu, N., 2001. "Producing Men and Women: Gender Stereotyping in Secondary Schooling in Zimbabwe." In "Speaking for Ourselves," ed. R. Gaidzanwa. Harare: AAP/GSA/Ford Foundation.

Karabel, J., and A. H. Halsey, eds., 1977. *Power and Ideology in Education.* New York: Oxford University Press.

Karega, R. G. M., 2001. Statistical Overview on Girls' Education at the University Level. Paper commissioned by the Forum for African Women Educationalists (FAWE).

Karega, R. M., 2001. *Statistical Overiew on Girls Education at the University Level.* Forum for African Women Educationalists.

Kasente, B., 2001. "Popularizing Gender: A Case Study of Makerere University." Paper commissioned by Forum for African Women Educationalists (FAWE) and presented at the 10th General Conference of the African Universities Association. Nairobi: FAWE.

Kasente, D., 2001, *Popularising Gender: A Case Study of Makerere University.* Forum for African Women Educationalists (FAWE).

Katz, M., and V. Vieland, 1988. *Get Smart: A Woman's Guide to Equality on Campus.*, New York: Feminist Press at the City University of New York.

Kelleher, A., and L. Klein, 1999. *Global Perspectives: A Handbook for Understanding Global Issues.* Upper Saddle River, N. J.: Prentice Hall.

Kelly, M. J., 2001. "Challenging the Challenger: Understanding and Expanding the Response of Universities in Africa to HIV/AIDS. Report commissioned by the ADEA Working Group on Higher Education, March.

Kethusegile, B. M., 2000. *Beyond Inequalities: Women in Southern Africa.* Bellville: UWC. 15.

Khan, A. R., 1998. "Growth and Poverty in East and Southeast Asia in the Era of Globalisation." In *Globalisation, Growth and Marginalization,* ed. A. S. Bhalla. London: Macmillan, pp. 125-48.

King, E. M., and A. M. Hill, 1993. *Women's Education in Developing Countries: Barriers, Benefits, and Policies.* Baltimore and London: The Johns Hopkins University Press, published for the World Bank.

Koh, H.-K., 2002. Trends in International Student Flows to the United States." *International Higher Education* no. 28 (Summer): 18-20.

Kohli, R., with foreword by M. M. Sankhdher, 1995, *Kautilya's Political Theory: Yogakshema, the Concept of Welfare State.*, New Delhi: Deep and Deep Publications.

Koo, B. H., and D. H. Perkins, eds., 1995. *Social Capability and Long-Term Economic Growth.* New York: St. Martin's Press.

Kouamé, A., 1999. *Éducation et emploi des femmes à Abidjan.* Paris: L'Harmattan.

La Fosse, S. V., 1992. "Co-educational Settings and Educational and Social Outcomes in Peru." In *Women and Education in Latin America: Knowledge, Power and Change,* ed. N. Stromquist. Boulder, Colo.: Lynne Rienner Publishers, 87-105.

Lachaud, J.-P., 1997. *Les femmes et le marché du travail urbain en Afrique subsaharienne.* Paris: L'Harmattan.

Laird, S., 1994. "Natural Products and the Commercialization of Traditional Knowledge." In *Intellectual Property Rights for Indigenous Peoples: A Sourcebook,* ed. T. Greaves. Oklahoma City: Society for Applied Anthropology, 145-149.

Lal, D., 1995. "Why Growth Rates Differ: The Political Economy of Social Capability in 21 Developing Countries." In *Social Capability and Long-Term Economic Growth,* ed. B. H. Koo and D. H. Perkins, 288-309. New York: St. Martin's Press.

Lane, N. J., 1999. "Why Are There So Few Women in Science?" *Nature Debates* (September 9).

Latin American Women, 1995. Compared Figures. Santiago: FLACSO.

Lauridsen, L., 1998. "The Financial Crisis in Thailand: Causes, Conduct, and Consequences?" *World Development* 26, no. 8: 1575-91.

Leah, N.W., 1997. *Beyond Beijing. Fourth Conference on Women: A Summary of the Global Platform and Africa Regional Platforms for Action with a Focus on Education.* Forum for African Women Educationalists.

Lebow, R., 2004. "Order and Disorder." Presentation at Seminar on Justice and Order, Center for International Studies, University of Southern California, January 14.

Leclerc, G., 1979. *L'observation de l'homme.* Paris: Le Seuil.

Leigh-Doyle, S., 1991. "Increasing Women's Participation in Technical Fields: A Pilot Project in Africa." *International Labour Review* 130 (4): 427-44.

Levin, R., 2002. "Land and Agrarian Relations in South Africa: Contemporary Challenges and Perspectives." In Ramachandran and Swaminathan 2002: 166-78.

Lévi-Strauss, C., 1958. *Anthropologie Structurale.* Paris: Plon.

Li, X., 1995. "Gender Inequality in China and Cultural Relativism." In *Women, Culture and Development: A Study of Human Capabilitie,* ed. M. Nussbaum and J. Glover, 407-26. New York: Oxford University Press.

Linares, A., 1967. "Évolution de l'école et des idéologies scolaires en Espagne." In *Éducation développement et démocratie,* ed. R. Castel and J.-C. Passeron, 151-80. Paris: Mouton.

Lindauer, D. L., 1997. "Labour Market Outcomes: An Overview." In *The Strains of Economic Growth: Labour Unrest and Social Dissatisfaction in Korea,* ed. D. L. Lindauer, J. Kim, et al. Cambridge, Mass.: Harvard Institute for International Development, pp. 35-53.

Lloyd, C. B., and B. T. Neimi, 1979. *The Economics of Sex Differentials.* New York: Columbia University Press.

Longwe, S. H., 1997. "Education For Women's Empowerment or Schooling for Women's Subordination." In *Negotiating and Creating Spaces of Power, Women's Educational Practices Amidst Crisis,* ed. C. M. Anonuevo. Hamburg: UNESCO Institute for Education..

Longwe, S., 2002. "NEPAD Reluctance to Address Gender Issues." Draft, October 22.

Loutfi, M. F. ed., 2001. *Women, Gender and Work.* Geneva: International Labour Office.

Luttrell, W., 1989. "Working Class Women's Ways of Knowing: Effects of Gender, Race, and Class." *Sociology of Education* 62 (1): 33-46.

Luxemburg, R., 1964. *The Accumulation of Capital.* New York: Monthly Review Press.

Mabala, R., 2003. "The Inter-Linkages Between Girls' Education and HIV/AIDS in Emergencies." UNICEF Eastern and Southern South Africa Region Education Newsletter, September, 3 (1).

Makhubu, L. P., 1998. "The Right to Higher Education and Equal Opportunity Particularly for Women: The Major Challenge of Our Time." In *Higher Education in Africa: Achievements, Challenges and Prospects.* Dakar: UNESCO-BREDA.

Makhubu, L., 1995. "Women in Science: The Case of Africa" In *The Gender Dimension of Science and Technology,* ed. S. Harding and E. McGregor. Paris: UNESCO, 29-33.

Mama, A., 2004. *Critical Capacities: Facing the Challenges of Intellectual Development in Africa.* Inaugural Lecture Prince Claus Chair in Development and Equity, Institute of Social Studies, April 28. *http://www.gwsafrica.org/knowledge/amina.html.*

Mannathoko, C., B. Mazile, and M. Commeyras, eds., 2001. *Gender Tales from Africa: Voices of Children and Women against Discrimination.* Nairobi, Kenya: United Nations Children's Fund, Eastern and Southern Africa Regional Office.

Manuh, T., 2002. "Higher Education, Condition of Scholars and the Future of Development in Africa." *CODESRIA Bulletin* 3-4: 42-48.

Margolis, J., and A. Fischer, 2002. *Unlocking the Clubhouse: Women in Computing*. Cambridge, Mass.: M.I.T. Press.

Mariro, A., ed., 1998. "Access of Girls and Women to Scientific, Technical and Vocational Education in Africa." Paris: UNESCO.

Mars, G., 1984. *Cheats at Work*. London: Unwin Paperbacks.

Masanja, V. G., 2001. *Structural Changes and Equal Opportunities for All: A Case Study of the University of Dar es Salaam Tanzania*. Forum for African Women Educationalists.

Masanja, V., 2001. "Structural Changes and Equal Opportunities for All: A Case Study of the University of Dar es Salaam." Paper commissioned by FAWE and presented at the 10th General Conference of the Association of African Universities. Nairobi: FAWE.

Masanja, V., et al., 2001 (February). "Female Participation in African Universities: Issues of Concern and Possible Action. Paper presented at the General Assembly of the African Association of Universities, Nairobi.

Mashelkar, R., 2002. "The Role of Intellectual Property in Building Capacity for Innovation for Development: A Developing World Perspective" In *Indigenous Knowledge and the Integration of Knowledge Systems: Towards a Philosophy of Articulation*, ed. Odora Hoppers. Cape Town: NAEP.

May, J. ed., 2000. *Poverty and Inequality in South Africa: Meeting the Challenge*. New York: Zed Books. 32.

Mckinnon, R. I., 1973. *Money and Capital in Economic Development*. Washington, D.C.: Brookings Institution Press.

Mckown, R. E., and D. J. Finlay,, 1974. "Ghana's Status Systems: Reflections on University and Society." *Journal of Asian and African Studies* 11 (July-October): 166-79.

Meena, R., 2000. *Gender Frameworks for FAWE Country Chapters*. Forum for African Women Educationalists.

Meena, R., ed., 1992. *Gender in Southern Africa: Conceptual and Theoretical Issues*. Southern Africa Political and Economic Series.

Mehra, R., and S. Gammage, 1999. "Trends, Countertrends, and Gaps in Women's Employment." *World Development* 27, no. 3: 533-50.

Merton, R. C., 1973. "Theory of Rational Option Pricing." *Bell Journal of Economics and Management Science* 4, no. 1: 141-83.

Merton, R., 1973. *Sociology of Science*. Chicago: University of Chicago Press.

Mies, M., 1989. *Patriarchy and Accumulation on a World Scale: Women in the International Division of Labor*. LondonPalloix, C., 1993. *L'internalisation du .capital*. Paris: Maspero.

Mies, M., 1993. *Ecofeminism*. London, England: Zed Books Limited.

Migdal, J. S., 1988. *Strong Societies and Weak States: State Society Relations and State Capabilities in the Third World*. Princeton: Princeton University Press.

Milazi, D., 1993. *African Women in Decision-Making Positions: Vanguard for Gender Equality?* Pretoria: Centre for Development Analysis. 4.

Miller, J. V., and L. Vetter, 1996. "Vocational Guidance for Equal Access and Opportunity for Girls and Women in Technical and Vocational Education." Paris: UNESCO.

Mlama, P. M., 1998. "Increasing Access and Equity in Higher Education: Gender Issues." In *Higher Education in Africa: Achievements, Challenges and Prospects*. Dakar: UNESCO-BREDA.

Mlama, P., 2001. "Gender Equity Programming in Higher Education." Paper presented at the Ford Foundation Policy Forum, Nairobi, October.

Mlama, P., 2001. "Gender Equity Programming in Higher Education." Higher Education Policy Forum. Nairobi.

Mlamlele, O., et al., 2001. "Opening Our Eyes: Addressing Gender Based Violence in South African Schools: A Module for Educators." Canada South Africa Management Programme.

Mohamedbhai, G. T. G., 1995. "The Emerging Role of African Universities in the Development of Science and Technology." Background Paper for the Joint Colloquium on the University in Africa—The 1990s and Beyond, Lesotho, January 16-20.

Mokate, R., 1999. "Women in Science and Technology: A Review of Conceptual Issues." In *South Africa's Contribution to the Theme on Science and Technology for Sustainable Development*. DACST Report, The Second International Conference of Third World Organization for Women in Science February 8-11.

Moll, P., 1998. *Discrimination Is Declining in South Africa but Inequality Is Not*. Cape Town: South African Network for Economic Research. 5.

Mollis, M., and S. Marginson, 2002. "The Assessment of Universities in Argentina and Australia." *Higher Education* 43: 311-30.

Moncarz, E., 2001. "Overwork and Unemployment as Stress Factors." Women's Health Collection, no. 6.

Morishima, M., 1982. *Why Has Japan "Succeeded?" Western Technology and the Japanese Ethos*. Cambridge: Cambridge University Press.

Morley, L., and V. Walsh, eds., 1996. *Breaking Boundaries: Women in Higher Education*. London: Taylor & Francis.

Morrow, R. A., and C. A. Torres, 2000. In *Globalization and Education: Critical Perspectives*, ed. N. C. Burbules and C. A. Torres. New York: Routledge.

Moulton, J., K. Mundy, M. Walmond, and J. Williams, 2002. *Educational Reforms in Sub-Saharan Africa*. Westport, Conn.: Greenwood Press.

Mtshali, L., and B. Mabanda, 1996. In preface to White Paper on Science and Technology, "Preparing for the 21st Century." September.

Mugabe, J., 1999. "Intellectual Property Protection and Traditional Knowledge: An Exploration in International Policy Discourse." Paper presented at the WIPO/UN Commission for Human Rights Roundtable.

Mukholi, D., 1995. *A Complete Guide to Uganda's Fourth Constitution: History, Politics, and the Law*. Kampala, Uganda: Fountain Publishers.

Murray, M. A. M., 2000, *Women Becoming Mathematicians: Creating a Professional Identity in Post-World War II America*. Cambridge: The M.I.T. Press.

Musisi, B. N., 2001. "A Reflection On and Taking Stock of Innovations at Makerere University." Higher Education Reform. Nairobi.

Najafizadeh, M., and L. A. Mennerick, 1992. "Professionals and Third World Public Well-Being: Social Change, Education, and Democratization." In *Development and Democratization in the Third World: Myths, Hopes and Realities,* ed. Kenneth E. Bauzon. Washington: Crane Russack, 242-48.

Namuddu, K., 1992. " Gender Perspectives in African Higher Education." Paper presented at the Senior Policy Seminar on African Higher Education, University of Zimbabwe.

Namuddu, K., 1995. "Gender Perspectives in the Transformation of Africa: Challenges to the African University as a Model to Society." In Subbarao et al. 1995, 17–57. Dakar, Senegal: UNESCO-BREDA.

Nare, Z. C., 1995. "Being a Woman Intellectual in Africa: The Persistence of Sexist and Cultural Stereotypes." In Subbarao et al. 1995, 1–11. Dakar: UNESCO.

Nation, The, 2000. "Why Violence And Rape Thrive In Schools." Nairobi: May 1.

Natural Resources Defense Council, n.d. *http://www.nrdc.org/nuclear/*

Ndlovu, S., 2001. "Femininities amongst Resident Female Students at the University of Students." In "Speaking for Ourselves.," ed. R. Gaidzanwa. Harare: AAP/GSA/FORD.

Nussbaum, M., 1995. "Human Capabilities, Female Human Beings." In *Women, Culture and Development: A Study of Human Capabilities*, ed.

M. Nussbaum and J. Glover, 61-104. New York: Oxford University Press.

Nussbaum, M., 1995. Introduction to *Women, Culture and Development: A Study of Human Capabilities*, ed M. Nussbaum and J. Glover, 1-36. New York: Oxford University Press.

Nussbaum, M., 1999. *Sex and Social Justice*. New York: Oxford University Press.

Nussbaum, M., 2000. *Women and Human Development: The Capabilities Approach*. New York: Cambridge University Press.

Nussbaum, M., and A. Sen, eds., 1993. *The Quality of Life*. New York: Oxford University Press.

Nussbaum, M., and J. Glover, eds., 1995. *Women, Culture and Development: A Study of Human Capabilities*. New York: Oxford University Press.

Nzegwu, N., 1995. "Recovering Igbo Traditions: A Case for Indigenous Women's Organizations in Development." In *Women, Culture and Development: A Study of Human Capabilities*, ed. M. Nussbaum and J. Glover, 444-67. New York: Oxford University Press.

O'Neill, O., 1993. "Justice, Gender, and International Boundaries." In *The Quality of Life*, ed. M. Nussbaum and A. Sen, 303-23. New York: Oxford University Press.

Obanya, P., 1999. "Rapport sur l'état de l'éducation en Afrique: les progrès réalisés dans l'éducation des filles et des femmes." Dakar: UNESCO-BREDA.

Obisodun, B., 1991. "Women in Science and Technology Development in Nigeria." In *The Role of Women in the Development of Science and Technology in the Third World*, ed. A. M. Faruqui et al. Teaneck, N.J.: World Scientific Publishing Company.

Odora Hoppers, C. A., 1999. "Between 'Mainstreaming' and 'Transformation': Lessons and Challenges for Institutional Change." Paper presented at the HSRC/CSD International Workshop on International Strategies for Building Research Capacity Among Women in Higher Education, Pretoria. February.

Odora Hoppers, Catherine, A., ed., 2002. *Indigenous Knowledge and the Integration of Knowledge Systems: Towards a Philosophy of Articulation*. South Africa: New Africa Books.

Olsson, B. 1998. "How to Make Universities Gender Aware: The Swedish Experience." Paper presented at the World Conference on Higher Education. Thematic Debate on Women and Higher Education: Issues and Perspectives, Paris, October.

Ordorika, I., 2003. Presentation at the panel on The Latin American University Response to Neoliberalism, at the annual conference of the Comparative and International Education Society, New Orleans, March 12-15.

Osborne, R., 1995. 'The Continuum of Violence Against Women in Canadian Universities: Towards a New Understanding of the Chilly Campus Climate." *Women's Studies International Forum* 18, nos. 5-6: 637-46.

Park, C. B., and N.-H. Cho, 1995. "Consequence of Son Preference in a Low-Fertility Society." *Population and Development Review* 21, no. 1 (March): 59-84.

Patel, S., J. Bagchi, and K. Raj, eds., 2002. *Thinking Social Science in India: Essays in Honour of Alice Thorner*. New Delhi: Sage.

Pellow, D. and N. Chazan, 1986. *Ghana: Coping with Uncertainty*. Boulder, Colo.: Westview Press.

People and planet.net, 2004. "Women and Environment." *People and Biodiversity*, posted May 20.

Pérez, S., 1995. "Les femmes enseignantes dans l'enseignement technique et professionnel au Bénin, en Côte d'Ivoire, au Mali, au Sénégal: une étude comparative." Geneva: International Labour Organization.

Pilon, M., 1996. "Les femmes chefs de ménage en Afrique: État des connaissances." In *Femmes du sud, chefs de famille*, ed. J. Bisilliat, 235-56. Paris: Karthala.

Platteau, J.-P., 1990. "The Food Crisis in Africa: A Comparative Structural Analysis." In *The Political Economy of Hunger,* ed. J. Drèze and A. Sen vol. 2, *Famine Prevention*. Oxford: Clarendon Press, pp. 279-387.

Posey, D., and G. Dutfield, 1996, "Beyond Intellectual Property." Ottowa: International Development Research Center.

Prah, M., 2002. "Gender Issues in Ghanaian Tertiary Institutions: Women Academics and Administrators at Cape Coast." *Ghana Studies* 5: 1-20.

Price, R. 1974. "Politics and Culture in Contemporary Ghana: The Big Man Small Boy Syndrome." *Journal of Modern African Studies* 1 (2, Summer): 173-204.

Primo, N., 1999,. "Women in Science: Making a World of Difference?" In *South Africa's Contribution to the Theme on Science and Technology for Sustainable Development*. DACST Report, The Second International Conference of Third World Organizations for Women in Science, February 8-11.

Prins, M., 1993. "Women's Emancipation as a Question of Governance: Actors, Institutions and the Room for Manœuvre." In *Modern*

Governance: New Government-Society Interactions, ed. J. Kooiman. London: Newbury Park, and New Delhi: Sage Publications, pp. 75-86.

Psacharopoulos, G., and M. Woodhall., 1985. Education for Development: An Analysis of Investment Choices. New York: Oxford University Press.

Puiggros, A., 1996. "World Bank Education Policy: Market Liberalism Meets Ideological Conservatism." NACLA Report on the Americas, May/June.

Ramachandran, V.K., and M. S. Nathan, eds., 2002. Agrarian Studies: Essays on Agrarian Relations in Less-Developed Countries. New Delhi: Tulika.

Rawls, J., 1971. A Theory of Justice. Cambridge, Mass.: Belknap Press of Harvard University Press.

Reimers, F., 2001. "Educational Finance and Economic Adjustment in

Reimers, F., 2002. "La lucha por la igualdad de oportunidades educativas en América Latina como proceso politico." Revista Lationoamericana de Estudios Educativos 32, no. 1: 9-70.

Reimers, F., and L. Tiburcio, 1993. Education, Adjustment and Reconstruction: Options for Change. Paris: International Institute for Educational Planning.

Republic of Ghana, 1992. Constitution of the Republic of Ghana. Accra: Government Printer, Assembly Press.

Republic of Ghana, 1999. A Decade of Educational Reforms: Preparation for the Challenges of a New Millennium. Background paper prepared for the Ministry of Education by the Forum Technical Committee. Accra: November.

Republic of Namibia, 1997. "National Gender Policy." Office of President: Department of Women's Affairs. Windhoek, Namibia.

Rhoads, R., and L. Mina, 2001. "The Student Strike at the National Autonomous University of Mexico: A Political Analysis." Comparative Education Review 45, no. 3: 334-53.

Richards, P., 1985. Indigenous Agricultural Revolution: Ecology and Food Production in West Africa. London: Hutchinson, and Boulder, Colo.: Westview Press.

Richards, P., 1986. Coping with Hunger: Hazard and Experiment in an African Rice Farming System. London and Boston: Allen and Unwin.

Richards, P., 1996. Fighting the Rainforest: War, Youth and Resources in Sierra Leone. Portsmouth: Heinemann.

Robertson, C., 1992. Review of S. Applegate, P. Collier; and P. Horsnell, Gender, Education and Employment in Côte d'Ivoire. In Comparative Education Review 36 (2): 253.

Robertson, S., X. Bonal, and R. Dale, 2002. "GATS and the Education Service Industry: The Politics of Scale and Global Reterritorialization." *Comparative Education Review* 46, no. 4: 462-96.

Robinson, R., K. Hewison, and G. Rodan, 1993. "Political Power in Industrialising Capitalist Societies: Theoretical Approaches." In *Southeast Asia in the 1990s: Authoritarianism, Democracy and Capitalism*, ed. R. Hewison and G. Rodan. St. Leonards, N.S.W.: Allen & Unwin, pp. 9-39.

Robinson, W., 1950. "Ecological correlations and the behavior of American Individuals." *American Sociological Review* 15: 145-64.

Rosser, S. V., 1990. *Female Friendly Science: Applying Women's Studies Methods and Theories to Attract Students*. New York: Pergamon Press.

Rosser, S. V., 1999. "International Experiences Lead to Using Postcolonial Feminism to Transform Life Sciences Curriculum." *Women's Studies International Forum* 22 (1): 3-15.

Rosser, S. V., 2000. *Women, Science, and Society: The Crucial Union*. New York and London: Teachers College Press.

Ryder, N., 1965. "The Concept of Cohort in the Study of Social Change." *American Sociological Review* 30: 840-61.

Saint, W., 1992. *Universities in Africa: Strategies for Stabilization and Revitalization*. Washington, D.C.: The World Bank.

Salia, A. K., n.d. "But SRC Rejects Any Such Mover, *Daily Graphic:* Accessed on 10/31/2001 at *http://www.graphic.com.gh/dgraphic /topstories/a23.htlm.*

Sall, E. ed., 2000. *Women in Academia: Academic Freedom in Africa*. Dakar: CODESRIA.

Sall, E. ed., 2000. *Women in Academia: Gender and Academic Freedom in Africa*. Dakar: CODESRIA Book Series.

Samoff, J., Metzler, J. and T. Salie, 1992. "Education and Development: Deconstructing a Myth to Construct Reality" In *Twenty-First Century Africa: Towards a New Vision of Self-Sustainable Development*, ed. Ann Seidman and Frederick Anang. Trenton, N.J.: Africa World Press, 101-147.

Sankhdher, M. M., and M. Cranston, 1985. *Welfare State*. New Delhi: Deep and Deep Publications.

Saunders, S., 2001. "Case Study." Paper presented at a conference titled "Globalisation and Higher Education: Views from the South," Cape Town, March 27-29.

Sawyerr, A, 2002. "Challenges Facing African Universities: Selected Issues." Paper presented at the 45th Annual Meeting of the African Studies Association, Washington, D.C., December 5-8.

Schiebinger, L., 1999. *Has Feminism Changed Science?* Cambridge, Mass.: Harvard University Press.

Schultz, P. T., 1991. "Differences between Returns and Investments in the Education of Women and Men." Seminar paper, Institute of Policy Reform.

Schultz, P. T., 1992. *Investment in the Schooling and Health of Women and Men: Quantities and* Returns. Washington, D.C.: World Bank.

Schultz, T. W., 1972. *Human Capital: Policy Issues and Research Opportunities.* Human Resources Colloquium, Atlanta University. New York: National Bureau of Economic Research; distributed by Columbia University Press.

Schultz, T. W., 1977. "Investment in Human Capital." In *Power and Ideology in Education*, ed. J. Karabel and A. H. Halsey, 313-24. New York: Oxford University Press.

Sciama, L., 1884. "Ambivalence and Dedication: Academic Wives in Cambridge University, 1870-1970." In *The Incorporated Wife*, ed. H. Callan and S. Ardener. London: Croon Helm.

Scott, K.E., 1999. "Corporate Governance and East Asia: Korea, Indonesia, Malaysia, and Thailand." In *Financial Markets and Development: The Crisis in Emerging Markets*, ed. A. Harwood, R> E. Litan, and M. Pomerleano. Washington, D.C.: Brookings Institution Press, pp. 335-66.

Searle, P., 1999. *The Riddle of Malaysian Capitalism: Rent-Seekers or Real Capitalists?* Honolulu: Allen & Unwin and University of Hawaii Press.

Sen, A. K., 1967. "Isolation, Assurance and the Social Rate of Discount." *Quarterly Journal of Economics* 82, no. 1 (February): 112-84, repr. in Sen 1984: 135-46.

Sen, A. K., 1984. *Resources, Values and Development.* Blackwell: Oxford.

Sen, A. K., 1999. *Development as Freedom.* New York: A.A. Knopf.

Sen, A., 1985. *Commodities and Capabilities.* New York: Elsevier Science Publishing Company Inc.

Sen, A., 1993. "Capability and Well-Being." In *The Quality of Life,* ed. M. Nussbaum and A. Sen, 30-53. New York: Oxford University Press.

Sen, A., 1999. *Development as Freedom.* New York: Alfred A. Knopf, Inc.

Sen, G., 2002. "Gendered Labour Markets and Globalisation in Asia." In Patel, Bagchi, and Raj 2002: 192-213.

Shaw, E. S., 1973. *Financial Deepening in Economic Development.* New York: Oxford University Press.

Shlomo, A., 1968. *Karl Marx on Colonialism and Modernization: His Dispatches and Other Writings on China, Mexico, the Middle East and North Africa.* Garden City, N.Y.: Doubleday.

Singh, A., and B. A. Weisse, 1998. "Emerging Stock Markets, Portfolio Capital Flows and Long-term Economic Growth: Micro and Macroeconomic Perspectives." *World Development*, 6, no. 4: 607-22.

Smith, L. T., 1999. *Decolonizing Methodologies: Research and Indigenous Peoples.* London: Zed Books.

Solloway, S., 1996. *Born to Rebel.* New York: Vintage.

Someah-Addae, K., 1988. "The Educational System in Ghana as a Source of Gender Inequality in Vocational and Technical Education. Thesis presented to the Department of Vocational and Technical Education, Faculty of Education, University of Cape Coast in partial fulfillment of the requirements for the Master of Philosophy Degree (Vocational and Technical Education).

Soudien, C., and C. Corneilse, 2000. "South African Higher Education in Transition: Global Discourses and National Priorities." In *Globalization and Education: Integration and Contestation Across Cultures,* ed. N. P. Stromquist and K. Monkman. Boulder: Rowman & Littlefield, pp. 299-314.

Southern Africa Development Community (SADC), 1999. "Gender and Development: A Declaration by the Heads of State or Government of the Southern African Development Community."

Southern Africa Research and Documentation Centre (SARDC), 1997a. "Beyond Inequalities: Women in South Africa." University of Western Cape. SARDC.

Southern Africa Research and Documentation Centre (SARDC), 1997b, "Beyond Inequalities: Women in Namibia." University of Namibia. SARDC.

Southern Africa Research and Documentation Centre (SARDC), 1997c. *Beyond Inequalities: Women in South Africa.* Ed. Bookie M. Kethusegile. Harare, Zimbabwe: SARDC

Southern Africa Research and Documentation Centre (SARDC), 1999. "SADC Gender Monitor: SARDC in Collaboration with Women in Development." Southern Africa Awareness Project, issue 1 (Feb.). SARDC.

Southern Africa Research and Documentation Centre (SARDC), 2000. "Beyond Inequalities: Women in Southern Africa." SARDC.

Steans, J., 1968. *Gender and International Relations: An Introduction.* New Brunswick, N.J.: Rutgers University Press.

Stiglitz, J. E. and S. Yusuf, eds., 2001. *Rethinking the East Asian Miracle*, Washington, D.C.: World Bank; Oxford and New York: Oxford University Press.

Stiglitz, J. E., 1993. "The Role of the State in Financial Markets." Proceedings of the World Bank Development Economists' Conference. Washington, D.C.: World Bank.

Stiglitz, J. E., 2001. "From Miracle to Crisis to Recovery: Lessons from Four Decades of East Asian Experience." In Stigliz and Yusuf 2001: 509-26.

Strauss, A., 1990. *Qualitative Analysis for Social Scientists.* Cambridge: Cambridge University Press.

Stromquist, N. P., 1990. "Women and Illiteracy: The Interplay of Gender Subordination and Poverty." *Comparative Education Review* 34 (1): 95-111.

Stromquist, N. P., 1995. "Romancing the State: Gender and Power in Education." Presidential address, Comparative and International Education Society. *Comparative Education Review* 39 (4): 423-54.

Stromquist, N. P., 2002. *Education in a Globalized World: The Connectivity of Economic Power, Technology, and Knowledge.* Lanham: Rowman and Littlefield.

Subbarao, K., et al., 1994. *Women in Higher Education: Progress, Constraints, and Promising Initiatives.* [Includes enrollment patterns in various fields, and access to faculty and administrative positions, 1970-88; Africa, Middle East, and South Asia.] Washington, D.C.: World Bank.

Subbararao, K., L. Raney, and J. Haworth, 1994. *Women in Higher Education: Constraints and Promising Initiatives.* Washington, D.C.: World Bank.

Sudarkasa, N., 1982. "Sex Roles, Education, and Development in Africa." *Anthropology and Education Quarterly* 13 (3): 279-88.

Sutherland-Addy. E., 1995. "Profils des femmes scientifiques d'Afrique." Forum for African Women Educationalists.

Svedberg, P., 1991. "Undernutrition in Sub-Saharan Africa: A Critical Assessment of the Evidence." In *The Political Economy of Hunger*, ed. J. Drèze and A. Sen, vol. 3, *Endemic Hunger*. Oxford: Clarendon Press, pp. 155-96.

Svedberg, P., 1999. "841 Million Undernourished?" *World Development* 27, no. 12: 2081-98.

Tamale, S., and J. Oloka-Onyango, 2000. "'Bitches' at The Academy: Gender and Academic Freedom in Africa." In *Women in Academia: Gender and Academic Freedom in Africa,* ed. S. Ebrima. Dakar: CODESRIA Book Series, 1-23.

Tema, B. O., 2002. "Science Education and Africa's Rebirth." In Odora Hoppers 2002.

Tembe, J., 2002. "Mozambique's Mothers Back in School." *BBC News*: Tuesday, March 19.

Third World Network, 1993. "Modern Science in Crisis: A Third World Response." In *The Racial Economy of Science: Toward a Democratic Future,* ed. S. Harding. Bloomington: Indiana University Press, 484-518.

Thurow, L. C., 1977. "Education and Economic Equality." In *Power and Ideology in Education*, ed. J. Karabel and A. H. Halsey, 325-335. New York: Oxford University Press *tkstock/tssum.asp*

Tshoaedi, M. 2000. "In the Union . . . Women Union Officials Speak Out." *South African Labour Bulletin* 22 (2): 55.

U.N., 2000. *The World's Women*. New York: United Nations.

UN, 2000. Millennium Summit. New York: United Nations, September 6-8.

UN, 2003. "Indicators for Monitoring the Millennium Development Goals." New York: United Nations Development Group *www.development goalsorg/mdgun/MDG_metadata_08-01-03UN.htm*

UNESCO, 1995. *Women in Higher Education in Africa*. Dakar: UNESCO-BREDA.

UNESCO, 1996. "Promotion of the Equal Access of Girls and Women to Technical and Vocational Education." Paris: UNESCO.

UNESCO, 1998. "Higher Education in Africa: Achievements, Challenges and Prospects." Paris and Dakar: UNESCO.

UNESCO, 1998. *World Education Report 1998*. Paris: UNESCO.

UNESCO, 1999. "Declaration on Science and the Use of Scientific Knowledge and the Science Agenda: Framework for Action." UNESCO General Conference, 30th Session, Paris, 30C/15.

UNESCO, 1999. "Rapport sur l'état de l'éducation en Afrique: les progrès réalisés dans l'éducation des filles et des femmes." Dakar: UNESCO-BREDA.

UNESCO, 1999. *Statistical Yearbook*. Paris: UNESCO and Berman Press.

UNESCO, 2000a. "Dakar Framework for Action." World Education Forum. Paris and Dakar: UNESCO.

UNESCO, 2000b. "Statistical Document." World Education Forum. Paris and Dakar: UNESCO.

UNESCO, 2001. *The State of Science and Technology in the World, 1996-1997.* Paris: UNESCO Institute for Statistics.

UNESCO, 2003/4. "Gender and Equality for All: The Leap to Equality." EFA Global Monitoring Report. Paris: UNESCO.

UNESCO, 2003a. *Gender and Education for All: The Leap to Equality,* Paris: UNESCO.

UNESCO, 2003b. *Gender and Education for All: The Leap to Equality. Regional Overview: Latin America and the Caribbean.* Paris: UNESCO.

UNESCO, 2003c, *Gender and Education for All: The Leap to Equality.* Regional Overview. *Sub-Saharan Africa.* Paris: UNESCO.

UNICEF, 2003. "The Impact of HIV/AIDS on Education in Kenya and the Potential of Using Education in Widest Sense for the Prevention and Control of HIV/AIDS." Nairobi, Kenya: UNICEF Eastern and Southern Africa Region Education Newsletter, April, 3 (1).

UNICEF, 2002a. "Gender, Sexuality and HIV/AIDS in Education." Nairobi, Kenya: Eastern and Southern Africa Regional Synthesis Report.

UNICEF, 2002b. "Life Skills Education with a Focus on HIV/AIDS." Nairobi, Kenya: Eastern and Southern Africa Region Education Newsletter.

United Nations Development Programme (UNDP), 1995. *Human Development Report.* New York: Oxford University Press.

United Nations Development Programme (UNDP), 1998. *Governance and Human Development in Southern Africa.* Ed. Ibbo Mandaza. SADC Regional Human Development Report. Harare: Sapes Books.

United Nations Development Programme (UNDP), 1999. "Human Development Report." New York: UNDP.

United Nations Development Programme (UNDP), 2000. *Human Development Report: Human Rights and Human Development.* New York: Oxford University Press.

United Nations Development Programme, 1993. *Politique de Développement et Emploi en Côte d'Ivoire,* June.

United Nations Development Programme, 1995. "The State of Human Development." *Human Development Report.* New York: Oxford University Press.

United Nations Development Programme, 2000. *Ghana Development Report: Science, Technology, and Human Development*. Accra: ISSER.

United Nations Educational Scientific and Cultural Organization (UNESCO), 1999. *Statistical Yearbook*. Paris: UNESCO Publishing & Bernan Press.

United Nations Educational Scientific and Cultural Organization (UNESCO), 1999. *Statistical Yearbook*. Paris: UNESCO Publishing & Bernan Press.

United Nations, 1989. "Statistics Indicators on Women in Africa, Department of International Economics and Social Affairs." New York: UNDP.

United Nations, 1995. *The World's Women*. New York: United Nations.

United Nations, 1995. *The World's Women*. New York: United Nations.

Valdes, M., 1995. "Inequality in Capabilities between Men and Women in Mexico." In *Women, Culture and Development: A Study of Human Capabilities,* ed. M. Nussbaum and J. Glover, 426-32. New York: Oxford University Press.

Van Reenen, T P., 1997. "Equality, Discrimination and Affirmative Action: An Analysis of Section 9 of the Constitution of the Republic of South Africa." *South African Public Law* 12 (1).

Veney, C. R., and P. T. Zeleza, eds., 2001. *Women in African Studies*. Lawrenceville, N. J.: Africa World Press, Inc.

Vijverberg, W. P. M., 1993. "Educational Investments and Returns for Women and Men in Cote d'Ivoire." *Journal of Human Resources* 28 (4): 933-94. Special Issue: Symposium on Investments in Women's Human Capital and Development.

Vilas, C., 1996. "Latin America and the New World Order." *Social Justice* 23, nos. 1-2.

Visvanathan, S., 1997. *A Carnival For Science: Essays on Science, Technology, and Development*. Delhi: Oxford University Press.

Volmink, J., 1999. "Who Shapes the Discourse on Science and Technology Education?" In *African Science and Technology Education into the New Millenium: Practice, Policy, and Priorities*, ed. P. Naidoo and M. Savage. Kenwyn, South Africa: Juta, 61-77.

Wade, R., 1990. *Governing the Market: Economic Theory and the Role of the Government in East Asian Industrialisation*. New Jersey: Princeton University Press.

Wade, R., 1998. "From `Miracle' to `Cronyism': Explaining the Great Asian Slump." *Cambridge Journal of Economics* 22, no. 6 (November): 693-706.

Ward, B., 1972. *What's Wrong with Economics?* New York: Basic Books.

WDR, 1996. *World Development Report 1996: From Plan to Market*. New York: Oxford University Press..

Welch, A., 2002. "Going Global? Internationalizing Australian Universities in a Time of Global Crisis." *Comparative Education Review* 46, pp. 433-71.

Wenneras, C. and A. Wold, 1997. "Nepotism and Sexism in Peer Review." *Nature* 387: 341-43.

Wertheim, M., 1999. Review of Schiebinger, *Has Feminism Changed Science?* June 22.
http://www.salon.com/books/feature/1999/06/22/feminismscience

Weskott, M., 1987. "Feminist Criticism of the Social Sciences." *Harvard Educational Review* 49 (4).

Whitaker, J. S., 1988. *How Can Africa Survive?* New York: Council on Foreign Relations Press (see especially chapter 6).

Wilhelm. 1998. 40.

Wilkinson, S., and C. Kitzinger, 1995. Introduction to *Feminism and Discourse: Psychological Perspectives,* ed. S. Wilkinson and C. Kitzinger. London: Sage Publications.

Williamson, O., 1985. *The Economic Institutions of Capitalism*. New York: The

Wilson, C., 1965. *England's Apprenticeship 1603-1763*. London: Longmans.

Windham, D. M., 1976. "Social Benefits and Subsidization of Higher Education: A Critique." *Higher Education* 5: 237-52.

Wolfe, A., 1989. *America's Impasse*. New York: Pantheon Books.

Woo, J.-E., 1991. *Race to the Swift: State and Finance in Korean Industrialisation*. New York: Columbia University Press.

Woodhouse, H., and T. M. Ndongko, 1993. "Women and Science Education in Cameroon: Some Critical Reflections." *Interchange* 24 (1-2): 131-58.

World Bank, 1988. *Education in Sub-Saharan Africa: Policies for Adjustment, Revitalization, and Expansion*. Washington, D.C.: World Bank.

World Bank, 1988. *Education in Sub-Saharan Africa: Policies for Adjustment, Revitalization, and Expansion*. Washington, D.C.: World Bank.

World Bank, 1988. *Education in Sub-Saharan Africa: Policies for Adjustment, Revitalization, and Expansion*. Washington, D.C.: The World Bank.

World Bank, 1993. *The East Asian Miracle: Economic Growth and Public Policy*, Washington, D.C.: IBRD.

World Bank, 1999. "Ghana: Women's Role in Improved Economic Performance." *Findings* 145 (October). Washington, D.C.: The World Bank.

World Bank, 2000. "Higher Education in Developing Countries: Peril or Promise." Washington, D. C.: World Bank Task Force on Higher Education and Society.

World Bank, 2001. "Africa Development Indicators." Washington, D.C.: World Bank.

World Bank, 2001. "Sub-Saharan Africa: HIV/AIDS on University Campuses." *Findings* 188 (August). Washington, D.C.: The World Bank..

World Bank, n.d. Document related to "Education Adjustment" under the project "Ghana-Education Sector Development," accessed on 10/21/2002, at *http://www.worldbank.org/pics/pid/gh50620.txt.*

Yamamura, K., and Y. Yasuba, eds., 1987. *The Political Economy of Japan,* vol. 1, *The Domestic Transformation.* Stanford, Calif.: Stanford University Press.

Zeng Y., T. Ping, et al., 1993. "Causes and Implications of the Recent Increase in the Reported Sex Ratio at Birth in China." *Population and Development Review* 19, no. 2 (March): 282-302.

Zymelman, M., 1990. *Science, Education, and Development in Sub-Saharan Africa.* Washington, D.C.: World Bank.

Index